Burton: Snow upon the Desert

Other books by the author

France and the Jacobite Rising of 1745
The Jacobite Army in England, 1745
The Jacobites
Invasion: From the Armada to Hitler
Crime and Punishment in Eighteenth-Century England
Charles Edward Stuart: A Tragedy in Many Acts
Stanley: The Making of an African Explorer

Burton: Snow upon the Desert

Frank McLynn

The Worldly Hope men set their Hearts upon
Turns Ashes – or it prospers; and anon,
Like Snow upon the Desert's dusty Face
Lighting a little Hour or two – is gone.

Edward FitzGerald, The Rubáiyát of Omar Khayyám

JOHN MURRAY

First published in 1990 by
John Murray (Publishers) Ltd
50 Albemarle Street, London W1X 4BD

Reprinted 1990

British Library Cataloguing in Publication Data
McLynn, F. J. (Frank J)
Burton: snow upon the desert.
1. Exploration. Burton, Sir Richard, 1821–1890
I. Title
910.92

ISBN 0–7195–4818–7

Typeset and printed in Great Britain by
Butler & Tanner Ltd, Frome and London

To Lucy

Contents

Illustrations

Between pages 240 and 241

Credits

2, National Portrait Gallery; 4, Mansell Collection; 5, Royal Geographical Society

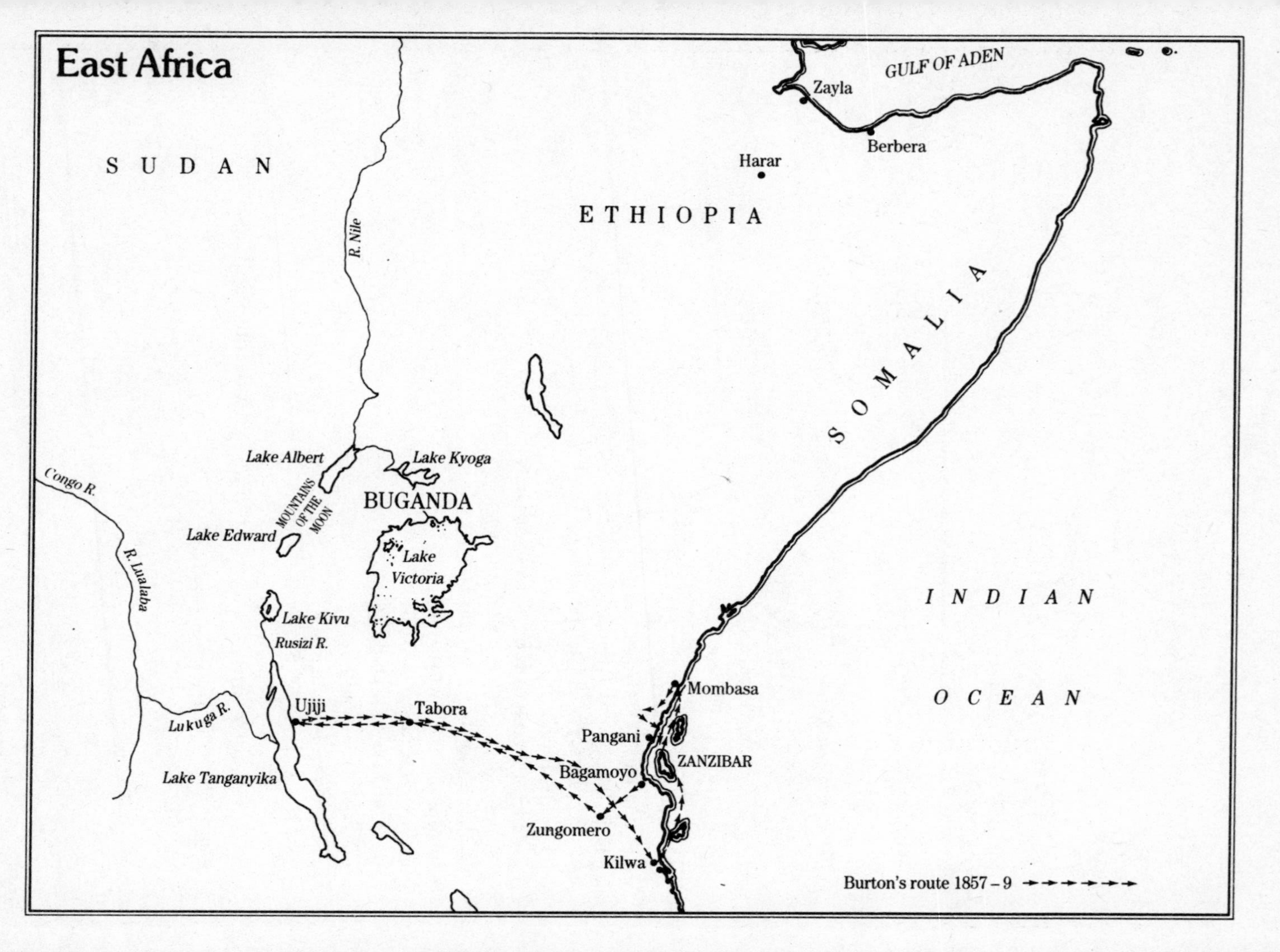
East Africa
SUDAN
ETHIOPIA
SOMALIA
GULF OF ADEN
Zayla
Berbera
Harar
R. Nile
Lake Albert
Lake Kyoga
BUGANDA
MOUNTAINS OF THE MOON
Lake Edward
Lake Victoria
Lake Kivu
Rusizi R.
Congo R.
R. Lualaba
Lukuga R.
Lake Tanganyika
Ujiji
Tabora
Bagamoyo
Zungomero
Kilwa
Pangani
ZANZIBAR
Mombasa
INDIAN
OCEAN
Burton's route 1857 – 9

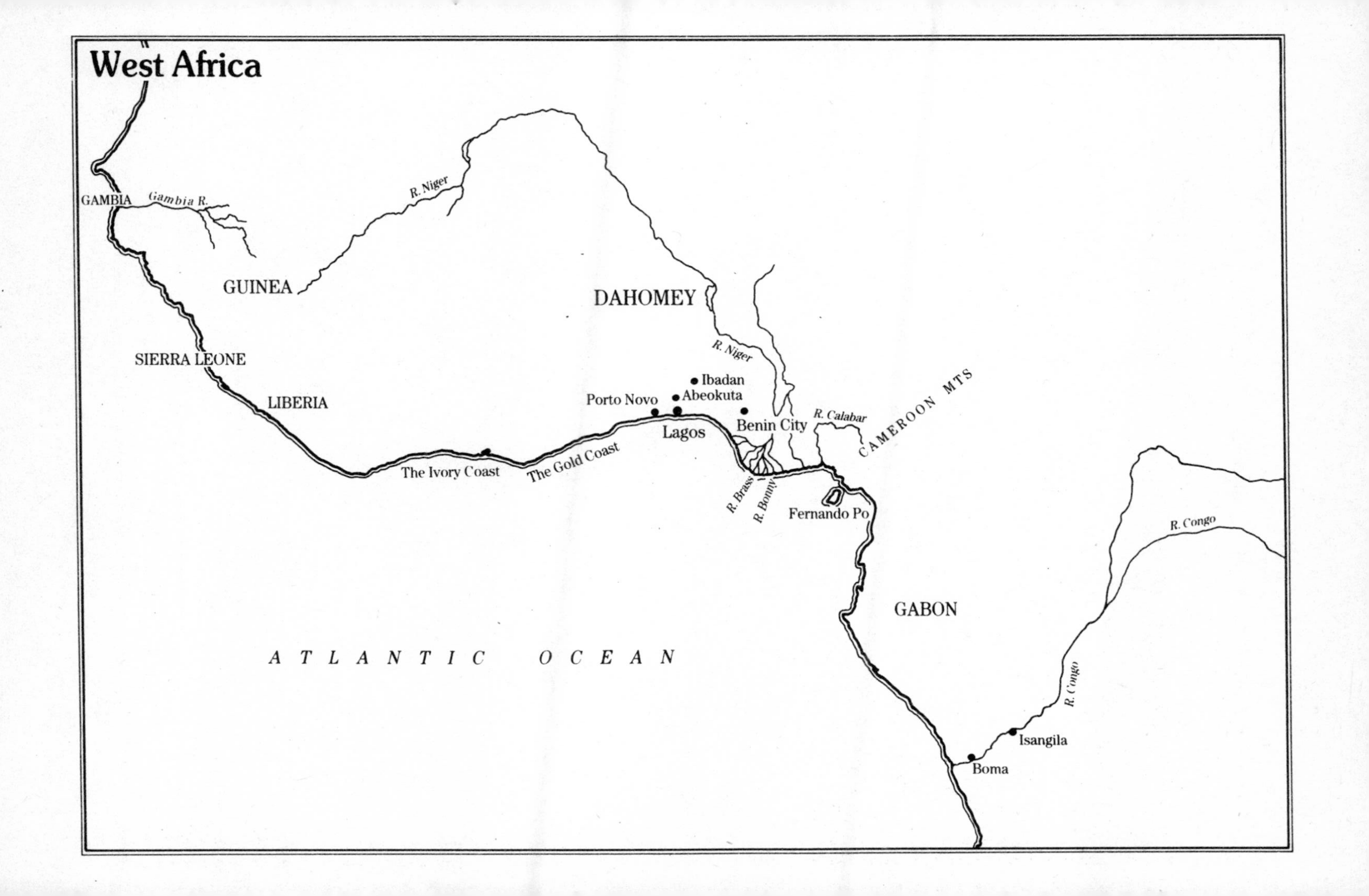
West Africa
GAMBIA
Gambia R.
R. Niger
GUINEA
SIERRA LEONE
LIBERIA
DAHOMEY
R. Niger
Ibadan
Abeokuta
Porto Novo
Lagos
Benin City
R. Calabar
CAMEROON MTS
The Ivory Coast
The Gold Coast
R. Brass
R. Bonny
Fernando Po
GABON
R. Congo
R. Congo
Isangila
Boma
ATLANTIC OCEAN

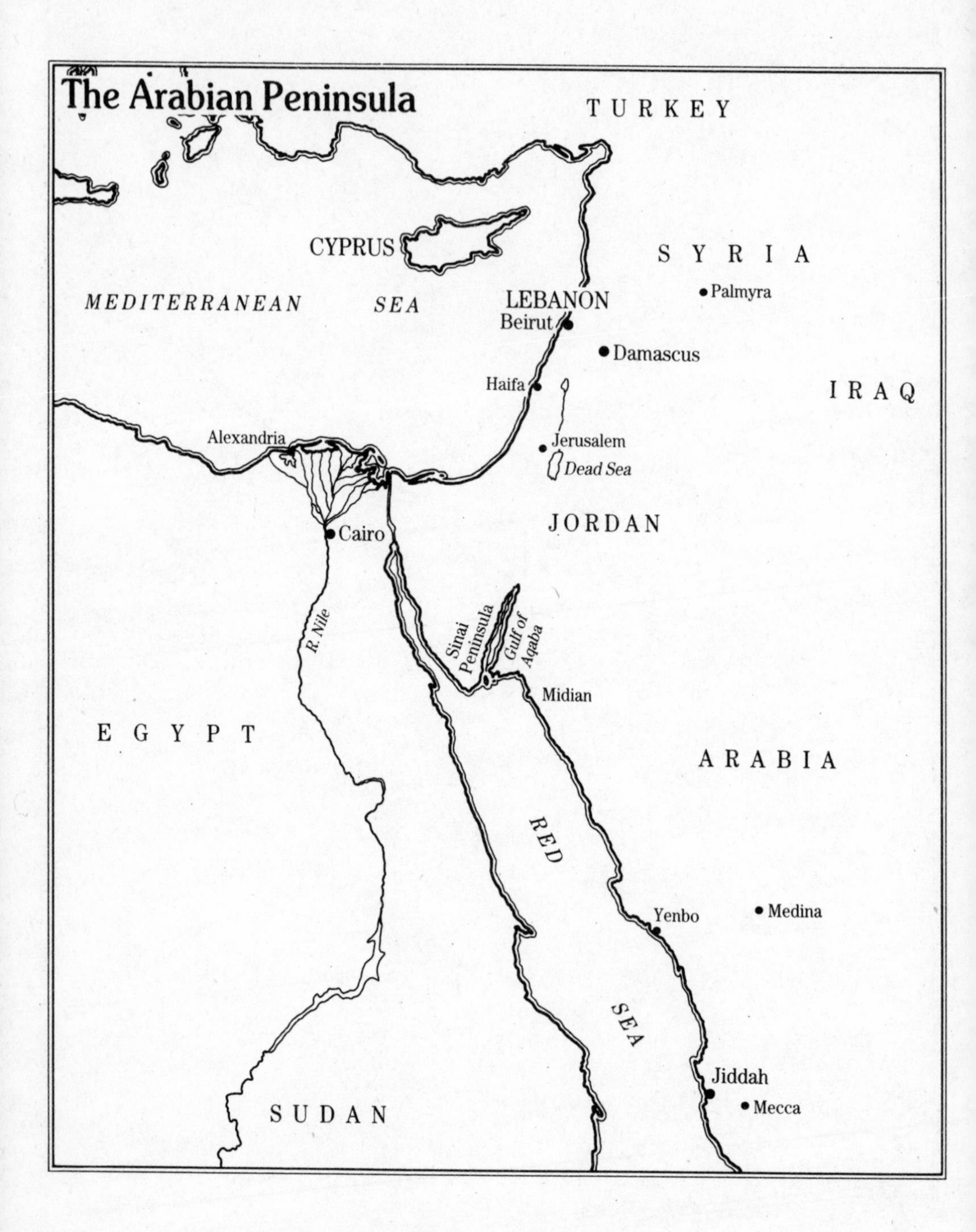
The Arabian Peninsula
TURKEY
CYPRUS
SYRIA
MEDITERRANEAN
SEA
LEBANON
Palmyra
Beirut
Damascus
Haifa
IRAQ
Alexandria
Jerusalem
Dead Sea
JORDAN
Cairo
R. Nile
Sinai Peninsula
Gulf of Aqaba
Midian
EGYPT
ARABIA
RED
Yenbo
Medina
SEA
Jiddah
Mecca
SUDAN

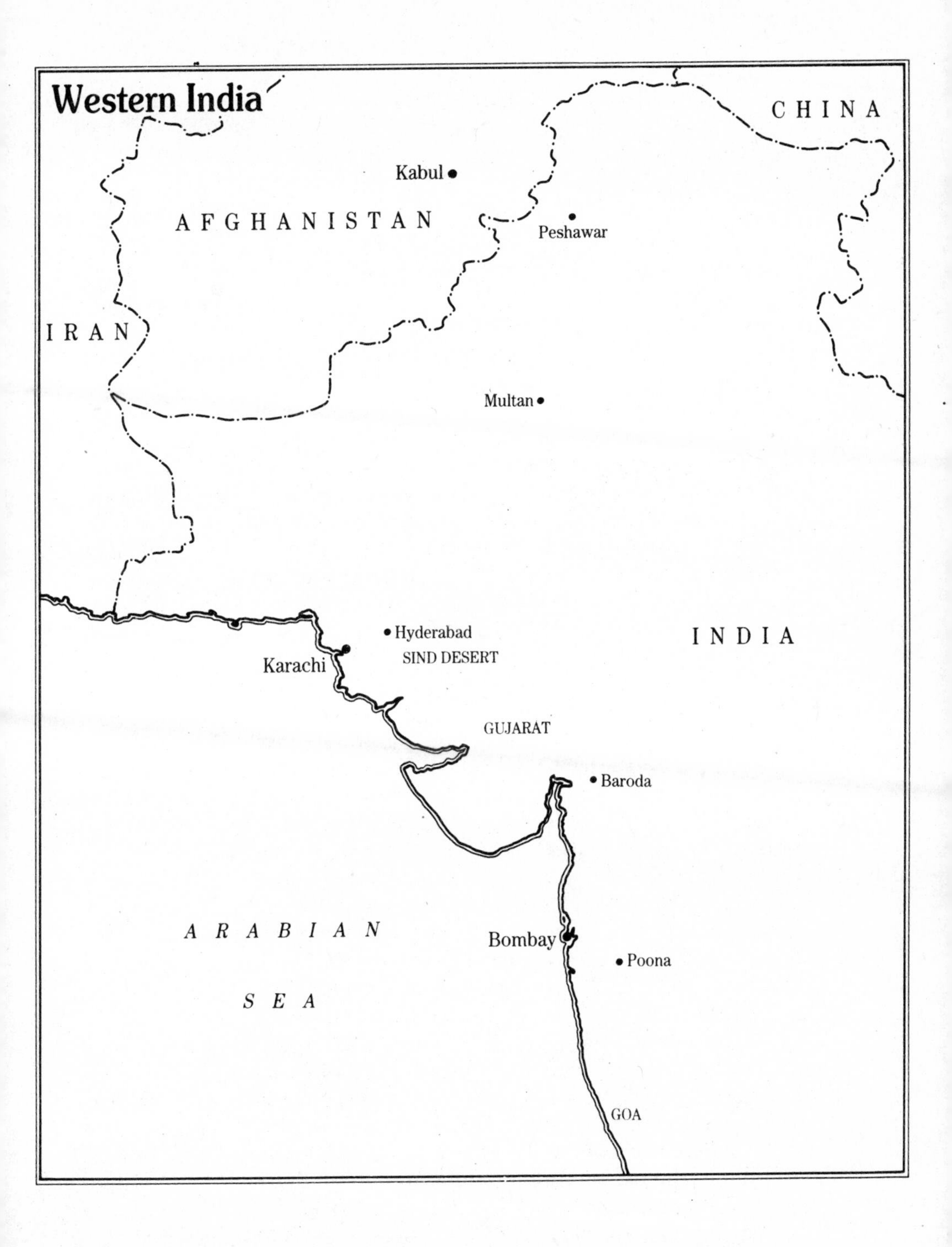
Western India
CHINA
Kabul
AFGHANISTAN
Peshawar
IRAN
Multan
Hyderabad
SIND DESERT
Karachi
INDIA
GUJARAT
Baroda
ARABIAN
SEA
Bombay
Poona
GOA

Preface

IT is often claimed that, since his wife Isabel burned his diaries and journals, there is really little more to be said about Sir Richard Burton than we already know. There is no point in pretending that the loss of these private papers is not an incomparable blow to the student of his life. But a wealth of archival material does exist, which no previous biographer has used. Foremost among this is the consular correspondence between Burton and his superiors at the Foreign Office, especially for the years 1861–71. Other hitherto unused sources are the Michell and Mackinnon Papers at the School of Oriental and African Studies, University of London, the Blackwood Papers at the National Library of Scotland, and the Royal Archives at Windsor Castle. Stanley's private papers contain a number of lengthy and penetrating observations on Burton and, since the last scholarly biography (Fawn Brodie's *The Devil Drives,* 1967) the Royal Geographical Society has acquired new holdings of relevance, notably photocopies of the correspondence between Speke and Sir George Grey from Auckland Public Library. Additionally, there are published collections of primary material which have eluded previous biographers by their obscurity. For the South American years this would include the journals of F. J. Stevens and the travel writing of William Hadfield, but the pattern also holds good for the other periods of Burton's life.

Yet scholarship does not a biography make, at least not unaided. I am fully persuaded of the validity of psychobiographical techniques, even though there are increasing signs of hostility to this methodology in English literary circles. This is not the place to rehearse the familiar arguments for and against. I can do no better than refer the interested reader to the work of that peerless historian Peter Gay. This is not the first life of Burton to approach him from the perspective of 'psychohistory', but anyone acquainted with the work of Fawn Brodie will see at once that my approach and conclusions are very different.

My list of those to whom acknowledgements are due must be headed by Her Majesty the Queen, for gracious permission to use the Royal Archives. Lady de Bellaigue, the Registrar at Windsor Castle, was her usual singularly helpful self. At the Royal Geographical Society I must single out Mrs Christine Kelly, the archivist, for special mention, not only for her professionalism but for the rarer gift of 'lateral thinking' when it comes to helping a researcher. David Ward, librarian at Royal Holloway and Bedford College, University of London, also gave valuable assistance. At John Murray, Grant McIntyre and Roger Hudson were enthusiastic and supportive throughout, as was my agent Andrew Lownie. But the most important influence on the book was my wife Pauline, with whom I conducted many a 'Socratic dialogue' on Burton's impulses and motives.

Twickenham
January 1990

1

Childhood and Youth

RICHARD BURTON was born on 19 March 1821 at Torquay. The nineteenth was also the date of the last day he spent on earth – a fact the superstitious Burton, with his fascination with numerology and cabbalistic signs, would have found significant.[1] There were many such coincidences in Burton's career which he, a Jungian *avant la lettre*, would have relished. Burton prided himself on his 'second sight', said to have been inherited from his mother, who displayed her Scottish fey presentiment by saying, when she first entered the house at Bath where she later died: 'I smell death here.'[2] Even his mother's maiden name, Baker, was destined to be a significant one in Burton's career. Apart from Burton's own use of it, it was the surname of his personal physician, as well as of one of his great rivals in the exploration of the Nile, and one of his scholarly interpreters.[3] It is hardly surprising that the adult Burton was so strongly attracted to Islam. There was so much 'synchronicity' in his life as to suggest that its pages had indeed in some occult sense already been written. 'Kismet', 'baraka' – the Western clichés about the Arab world trip easily off the tongue, but they do seem peculiarly apt for the career of Islam's greatest Western interpreter.

Burton's father, Joseph Netterville Burton, was a feckless, fainéant army officer, whose military career came to an end in the year of Richard's birth. The Burtons claimed descent on the male side from a certain Edward Burton who had been knighted by Edward IV during the Wars of the Roses. Joseph Netterville's father, the Reverend Edward Burton, Rector of Tuam in Galway, was himself the son of an English clergyman who had emigrated to Ireland and there married a girl of alleged Franco-Irish lineage. This girl, Sarah Young, was the daughter of Drelincourt Young, a boy who had been taken to Ireland as a child from France and adopted. The story of his adoption was that *his* father, always referred to as 'Louis le Jeune', was in reality a bastard son of Louis XIV, sired on the Countess Montmorency; this 'Louis le Jeune', a Huguenot, feared for his son's safety and had him spirited away to Ireland by the Jacobite Lady Primrose.

Sarah Young was certainly Richard Burton's paternal grandmother. What truth there is in the rest of the farrago of family legend is impossible to determine, but Burton always believed implicitly that he had Bourbon blood and often commented on his grandmother's portrait, which showed clearly the characteristic Bourbon pear-shaped face and head. It was once put to him that his pride in French royal lineage was misplaced, since it came from a 'dishonourable union'; surely Irish blood was a fitter subject for boasting. 'Oh no,' replied Burton, 'I would rather be the bastard of a king than the son of an honest man.'[4] Many people born into illegitimacy escape from the 'stigma' through the fantasy that they are royal changelings. Burton neatly turned this on its head by conflating bastardy with royal descent. Always the lover of paradox and originality, Burton could not even be conventional in the way he conducted his 'Family Romance'.[5]

Joseph Burton, though of mixed blood, was more Roman than anything else in appearance. Of moderate height, he was strikingly good-looking, with dark hair, high and delicately modelled nose and piercing black eyes. His sallow, olive complexion lent credence to the legend – also embraced by his son – that there was gypsy blood in the Burtons. His looks were apparently his fortune for, despite what has sometimes been alleged, the fact that he was a Lieutenant-Colonel in the 36th Foot does not necessarily argue for substantial inherited wealth.[6] The inference is strengthened by the circumstances of his marriage. It was the classic case of the dashingly handsome army officer marrying a plain-looking heiress. Joseph Burton was in need of money. This was the spur for his pursuit of Martha Baker, rather than the universal law cynically adumbrated by his son whereby good-looking men invariably marry homely women.

Some time in 1818 Joseph Burton and his younger brother Francis made the acquaintance of a crossgrained English squire named Richard Baker. Baker lived with a tough-minded Scottish wife and three daughters at Barham House in Hertfordshire. Martha Baker, the second daughter, was no beauty but she had her attractive features: luxuriant brown hair, a tall graceful figure, large grey eyes and tiny hands and feet. There was additionally in the ménage a ne'er-do-well son Richard, the only child from Baker's first marriage. In point of idleness, financial incompetence and debauchery young Richard left Joseph Burton standing, but there was apparently enough similarity between the two to appeal to Martha Baker, who was absurdly besotted with her half-brother. The interest of the Burton brothers quickened when they learned that each daughter would inherit an estate of £30,000 on her father's death. Sensing the natural attraction of the second daughter

Martha to Joseph, the younger Burton brother laid siege to Sarah, the eldest girl.

Having recently completed a tour of duty in Sicily, Joseph's regiment was gazetted for further Italian service, this time in Genoa. Joseph sensed that he was no particular favourite with Richard Baker, and still less with the prickly and jealous Richard junior. He used all his arts during a whirlwind courtship with Martha to persuade her to marry him before his departure to Genoa. It proved an inspired decision. While the regiment was in Genoa Princess Caroline of Brunswick arrived there with her retinue. Long separated from the Prince Regent, Caroline had been the butt, for more than a decade, of trumped-up charges from 'Prinny', desperate to find a pretext to divorce his detested wife. The opportunity for allegations of an 'affair', however tenuous, seemed to present itself in the form of Caroline's Italian courier. Joseph was one of those called to give evidence in the disgraceful kangaroo court in the House of Lords in 1821.[7] Outraged by the pressure being exerted on him to lie, Joseph declined to appear as a witness. The penalties for putting truth before the desires of the British power élite are well known. The Duke of Wellington immediately ordered Joseph to retire on half-pay as a punishment.

Joseph returned to England to his bride, to find that brother Francis had cemented the Burton–Baker ties by marrying the eldest daughter Sarah. Yet any hopes of retiring to a life of moneyed ease were dashed when Baker *père* announced that even on his demise her share of the family fortune would not devolve intact on Martha and Joseph. Fearing, not without reason, that his son-in-law would simply squander Martha's fortune, Baker tied the money up in such a way that it would be released in dribs and drabs over the years. Joseph, an inveterate stock-exchange gambler, lost considerable sums while attempting to play the market and like most unsuccessful gamblers, grumbled that he lost only because he ran out of capital at the crucial point. To the end of his life it was a running grievance that he had been deprived of millions simply because his skinflint father-in-law would not let him get his hands on his wife's fortune *en bloc*.

Richard Francis Burton was born a year after the marriage. His financial prospects, already diminished by Baker's suspicion of Joseph, took a further knock when Joseph's elder brother, who had not taken the precaution of marrying an heiress, and his sisters, heard of the alleged fortune and arrived in hopes of sharing in the wealth and battening on their 'rich' brother. But if the substance of the Burton household was temporarily wasted by the grasping and impecunious Burton relations, it was the Bakers who dealt young Richard's prospects the mortal blow. His maternal grandfather took a decided shine to his young grandson and decided to leave to him the £100,000 he had originally intended to bequeath to the wild scapegrace Richard Baker junior, now in disgrace and in exile. In alarm that her beloved half-brother would be cut off without a penny, Martha so neglected the interests of her own son that she fought a war of attrition to persuade her father to put off the evil day when he would finally disinherit the wild colonial boy. So successful was she in her delaying tactics that her father eventually dropped dead on the very day he was going to his lawyers to change the will in his grandson's favour. Burton never forgave his mother for her actions, which had such a devastating effect on his expectations.[8] The fate of Richard junior, with his £100,000, provides a clue to the sort of thing that might have happened had Joseph Burton been able to get his hands on his wife's lesser fortune. The hapless incompetent was swindled out of it by the notorious French confidence trickster Baron Thierry, the same who ended his days in a Pacific cannibal's cooking-pot.

Immediately after his birth in Torquay, Richard Burton was brought to the Baker home in Hertfordshire and baptised at Elstree. His first infant memory was of being taken down from bed after the family dinner to eat white currants. Later that same year (1821) Joseph Burton decided that thenceforth he and his family would reside abroad. The combination of the Caroline scandal and his marriage to a rich wife provided incentive and opportunity for quitting England. Officially he gave out the reason for his departure as the need to find a kinder climate for his asthma. But it is clear that one important motive must have been pique at Richard Baker for depriving him of the expected legacy. To separate him from his daughter and beloved grandson would be an appropriate punishment.

So began an odyssey of wandering around the Continent. It was not just in appearance that Burton father and son resembled the gypsies. Bored and discontented, Joseph progressively withdrew from the mainstream of the household, preferring to hunt, carouse and whoremonger, amusing himself by polishing up and firing off his huge collection of hand-guns. He took his family first to Tours. There in 1823 young Richard's sister Maria was born, and a year later a second son, named Edward.

Burton's memories of Tours centred around the extremes of temperature. He remembered crossing the river there on foot in winter when it was frozen, and lying on his back in a hot, broiling sun in the summer and exclaiming, 'How I love a bright burning sun!'[9] It was a love that never left him. In this provincial backwater Richard Burton's character and personality took shape. He was a rough, mischievous boy who at a very early age showed a character trait that became notorious later: his inability to take criticism. When his French next-door neighbours complained of his noisy and boisterous ways, he calmly gathered up a sackful of snails, climbed the wall between the two properties and deposited the molluscs on their prize plants.[10] At other times he would respond to being thwarted by towering fits of temper.

On the credit side, the young Richard was brave, affectionate and stoical, with an instinctive sympathy for animals and underdogs in general.[11] When he had toothache, it was known only by the obvious swelling in his face the next day. He loved throwing stones, but when one hit a girl and cut her forehead, Burton rushed up to her, flung his arms around her neck and burst into a paroxysm of sobs. Once he was found rolling around on the floor, howling with rage. When asked the matter, he said he had just realised that some women had carriages to parade around in, while his own mother had to go on foot.[12]

Burton's early education was perfunctory. Like John Stuart Mill, he was put to Latin at three and Greek at four; but there all similarity ended. Richard shone at French and drawing while loathing dancing and music.[13] Already he and his brother were beginning to show the fascination with deadly weapons that was one of the most striking things about them as young men. They became the ringleaders of a gang of Anglo-French ruffians who broke fine old church windows and shot at church monuments.

Burton's parents had little idea of how to discipline their children. The Burton boys liked nothing better than fist-fights with the local *gamins*, and would physically attack their maids if they tried to restrain them in any way. In a word, Richard and Edward were outrageously spoiled brats, as a notorious incident demonstrated. In a vain endeavour to inculcate the virtue of self-restraint, their mother pointed out a tray of apple puffs in the window of a *pâtisserie*, whetted their appetites with a mouth-watering description of the cakes, then asked them to undergo the heroism of voluntary self-sacrifice. They at once smashed through the glass of the shop window, scooped up the puffs and decamped. 'Our father and mother had not much idea of managing their children; it was like the old tale of the hen who hatched ducklings', Burton recorded scornfully.[14]

Burton's parents compounded their fecklessness in the matter of discipline by trying to sap the confidence of their offspring. Joseph Burton openly put it to them that they had inherited their mother's homeliness rather than his own good looks. Richard was informed that his nose was cocked and crooked, and that his teeth were his only decent feature, Maria that she was inelegant, and so on.[15] Since Edward, by common consent, looked like a Greek god, it might have been thought that the Burton parents would be stumped by him. Not a bit of it. When his two siblings pointed out that Edward was the handsomest boy in Tours, the reply was as predictable as it was immediate: 'Handsome is as handsome does.'

The 1830 revolution in France, which replaced Charles X with Louis-Philippe, spawned a surge of anti-British feeling in Tours. At the same time cholera was sweeping the larger French cities. Such at least was the official reason given for the uprooting of the Burton family when Richard was nine. There is, however, more than a suspicion that a row involving one of Joseph Burton's many mistresses was involved. Whatever the truth, Joseph decided it would be better if the family moved on. The trauma for the children was profound, the more so as travel in the 1830s was not something to be undertaken lightly.

They set off along the 'interminable avenues of the old French roads, lined with parallel rows of poplars, which met at a vanishing point in the far distance.' Ever afterwards Burton remembered 'the smell of those closets in the old French inns where cat used to be prepared for playing the part of jugged hare.'[16] Also, Burton's parents were travelling on a budget, which involved haggling and dickering over room and meal prices. He had a vivid memory of one massive innkeeper's wife bellowing at his parents, the mottled veins on her neck bulging in fury: 'If you are not rich enough to travel, you ought to stay home.' Once in England, 'Everything appeared so small, so prim, so mean, the little one-familied houses contrasting in such a melancholy way with the big buildings of Tours and Paris. We revolted against the coarse and half-cooked food, and, accustomed to the excellent Bordeaux of France, we found port, sherry, and beer like strong medicine; the bread, all crumb and crust, appeared to be half baked, and milk meant chalk and water.'[17] He was appalled at the routine brutality of the British – 'even the women punched their children'. At last Burton began to realise how exceptional his father was in his sparing of the rod.[18]

For reasons unclear Joseph Burton took the family to live in Richmond in Surrey, and placed Richard and Edward in a preparatory school run by the Reverend Charles Delafosse, a clergyman distinguished only by his bibulous propensities and 'no more fit to be a schoolmaster than the Grand Cham of Tartary'. The school was a regular Dotheboys Hall. 'Instead of learning anything at this school, my brother and I lost much of what we knew, especially in France, and the principal acquisitions were, a certain facility of using our fists, and a general development of ruffianism.'[19]

Burton at this time was a thin, dark little boy, with small features and large black eyes. He was extremely proud, sensitive, shy, nervous, with a melancholy, affectionate disposition. This hardly seems a recipe for survival in such a hellish school, yet Burton was from the earliest days possessed of great physical toughness and overabundant courage. He was forever in schoolboy brawls; at one point he had thirty-two 'affairs of honour' to settle. Edward, too, was involved in fistic enterprises, though not on the scale of his pugnacious brother. On one occasion Richard was beaten 'thin as a shotten herring'. The servants, when undressing him for the weekly bath on Saturday night, frequently found him black and blue. The experience at Richmond convinced Burton that mixed schools were essential as a civilising influence, at least up to a certain age; otherwise a glorification of brute strength and a contempt for women and the feminine would begin to creep in.

Burton's Dickensian experiences at the Richmond establishment were cut short by an attack of measles, which carried off a number of the boys. Joseph Burton was easily persuaded by his sister Georgina to withdraw them and abandon the attempt to give them an English education. It seems he missed the boar-hunting and shooting of the French forests and was glad of a pretext to return there. He had tried to prepare his boys for Eton; the experiment had not been a success, but he could not be blamed. Henceforth his sons would be educated by tutors.

Richard and Edward were overjoyed at their 'liberation'. 'We shrieked, we whooped, we danced for joy. We shook our fists at the white cliffs, and loudly hoped we should never see them again. We hurrah'd for France and hooted for England, "The Land on which the sun ne'er sets-nor rises", till the sailor who was hoisting the Jack looked upon us as a pair of little monsters.'[20] Having cast England into anathema, the Burton boys then turned on their tutor and governess. H. R. du Pré, son of a rector and graduate of Exeter College, Oxford, had as his main qualification for the job a desire for paid European travel and a willingness to beat his charges. The stout and red-complexioned Miss Roxton lacked even these attributes. They began testing the mettle of their overseers in Paris. Taken out for a walk there, they ran away and dodged back to the Hotel Windsor by side streets. Once with their parents, they gave out that Roxton and du Pré had been run over by an omnibus. The ordeal by madcap sons continued at Orléans and produced Miss Roxton's resignation.

The first port of call for the itinerant Burton family was Blois. Unlike Tours, the town lacked Joseph's three prerequisites: an Anglican parson, a good physician, and an organised hunting fraternity. Burton's father therefore joined his wife in hypochondria and professional invalidism, and the two became devotees of quacks and nostrums: 'nothing offended them more than to tell them that they were in strong health, and that if they had been hard-worked professionals in England, they would have been ill once a year, instead of once a month.'[21]

Richard continued his Latin and Greek, which he was held to for six or seven hours a day. At the time he regarded it as so much wasted effort, and far preferred physical disciplines such as swimming, which he mastered in this period, and fencing, for which he soon showed a marked aptitude. The Burton boys fenced without masks, and this almost ended in tragedy, when Burton one day accidentally passed his foil down Edward's throat and nearly destroyed his uvula.

The interlude in Blois came to a sudden end after a searing family row. Martha's mother told her son-in-law bluntly that his hypochondria was dragging his wife down; she then accused Joseph of having wasted his wife's legacy on a Sicilian mistress at Tours, and of wanting to return to her. Burton overheard the row and thus received a nasty initiation into the real world of adults.

Whatever the truth, the upshot of the blazing row was that the Burtons settled in Pisa, which was simply the best choice in a bad bunch. Burton recalled that the Pisan servants were savages who had to be taught the rudiments of service. Besides, 'the dulness of the place was preternatural ... there was no feeling between the Italians and English; they simply ignored one another.'[22]

An Italian master and a violin maestro were added to the ménage. Edward proved to have musical talent, but Burton's six-month struggle with the fiddle ended when he smashed his instrument over the music teacher's head. On the credit side, Burton proved an adept pupil with firearms, learned to dance, and mastered the ingenious art of playing two games of chess simultaneously while blindfolded. But greatest of all Burton's loves was fencing. He began to work out a synthesis of the best points in French and Italian technique and already showed signs of the brilliance that eventually made him a master swordsman. At the age of fifteen he pledged himself to a project which he took forty years to fulfil – a handbook on the foil and sabre, for use by infantrymen.[23]

The charms of Pisa soon palled for the restless Joseph Burton. The family spent the summer of 1832 in Siena, where most of the English expatriates were fugitives from justice of one kind or another, either criminals or political refugees. Then they moved on to Perugia, which Richard liked, and to Florence, where he became a 'walking catalogue' of the city's art treasures. The very slowness of travel which so wore down Martha was a boon to her sons, as it meant they got to know Italy thoroughly. The drawback was the restricted diet: food in Italy seemed to Burton to consist almost entirely of roast pigeon and omelettes.

Already Richard and Edward were preparing their campaign of psychological dominance over du Pré that eventually culminated when Richard threatened to thrash the thrasher. The boys had been allowed to begin regular shooting with an old single-barrelled Manton, a hard hitter that had been changed from flint to percussion. After practising in secret, they proceeded to give the tutor the fright of his life. They inveigled him into their stratagem by boasting tiresomely about what good shots they were. Du Pré took the bait: he told them he had half a mind to let them shoot at him from fifty yards' range, just to show

how bad they were. When Edward accepted the challenge with alacrity, some suspicion seems to have dawned in the tutor's mind. He quickly substituted his hat, and was appalled and dumfounded to see it at once riddled like a sieve. Du Pré took his revenge by working on their mother's fears. She forbade all shooting excursions, but the brothers got round the interdict by hoarding their own pocket-money and browbeating their sister Maria out of hers. With the proceeds they bought a brace of claw-handled pistols. At this their father finally put his foot down and ordered the weapons returned to the shop. 'The shock was severe to the *pun d'onor* of we [sic] two Don Quixotes', Burton commented ruefully.[24]

The travelling family now proceeded to Rome, and then Naples, with which Richard was enchanted, both because of its natural beauty, and because Neapolitan society was the least strict in Italy. Here he honed to perfection his fencing skills – for the Neapolitan school was the most famous in Europe – and here too occurred the final confrontation with du Pré. The tutor rashly threatened the now strapping boys with a thrashing, to which they replied with a threat in kind. Du Pré found discretion the better part of valour and admitted defeat. The Burton brothers were now effectively out of control.

To celebrate his passage of this manhood ritual Richard pushed himself to the limit in outrageous exploits. On being told it was impossible to creep over Naples' 'Natural Arch', Burton proceeded to execute the said impossible. Next he insisted on taking the dog's place in the 'Grotto di Cane' and was pulled out just in time to avoid suffocation by the poisonous gas. On another occasion, he was caught trying to descend the crater of Vesuvius. Cross-questioning by Italian officialdom revealed a wild story about being in pursuit of Satan, who, he was told, had just been seen vanishing into the mountain, bearing away the soul of a usurer.[25]

Naples at this time was gripped by a cholera epidemic, and the mortality was huge – to the extent that the ordinary people took to murdering physicians in the belief that they were poisoners, and the king had to make a public display of eating 'poisoned' food to set their minds at rest. The two madcap Burton brothers decided to take advantage of this carnival of death by going the rounds as *croquemorts* and witnessing the hideous mass burials. Then they visited the best brothel in Naples and, after being initiated into its lubricious wares, stood treat for the entire 'house'. Shortly afterwards Martha Burton intercepted a highly-charged correspondence between her sons and the whores. Pandemonium broke out in the household. Joseph and du Pré got out horsewhips for a terrible chastisement, but the scapegrace pair climbed to the chimney-tops and refused to come down until they had been granted a full pardon for their transgressions.[26]

In 1836 they moved to Pau, where Richard and Edward got in with the local smugglers and other low life, and learned to drink and smoke with the worst of them. They built their boxing skills up preparatory to the thrashing they still intended to administer to the luckless du Pré when the right moment came. Burton no longer bothered to conceal his drinking from his father. After one stupendous binge, Joseph roared out: 'the beast's in liquor!'[27] It was at Pau that Burton first evinced his unique flair for languages by quickly mastering the Béarnais dialect – a mixture of French, Spanish and Provençal.

Richard (and Edward too) met and fell in love with Caterina, daughter of a Baron de Meydell. To avoid another Naples-type scandal, Joseph Burton whisked his family away to Marseilles, thence to Livorno and Pisa, where he made another attempt to put down roots. For a while all was peaceful. Richard made progress in drawing, painting and Classics, but finally conceded defeat on the musical front – later a source of very great regret, since it meant that he was unable to record aboriginal melodies in the tribes he travelled among. But such tranquillity could not last. The brothers had got in with a crowd of opium-taking, wine-swilling medical students at the University, and their nightly carousing brought them into confrontation with the 'police'. Richard made good his escape from the mêlée, but Edward was taken and thrown in jail. As soon as Joseph had secured his release, he moved the family on to Lucca.

By now it was early 1840 and, with Richard nineteen and Edward seventeen, their father concluded that he had had enough of the uphill struggle. It was time to oversee the breakup of the family. Richard showed scant sympathy for his father's stoical endurance during the turbulent years of his teens. 'Our father, like an Irishman, was perfectly happy as long as he was the only man in the house, but the presence of younger males irritated him.'[28] The two boys were sent to England and separated, with strict instructions not to correspond with each other. Edward was placed under a country vicar while Richard was put through his paces in Homer and Virgil by Professor Scholefield; Joseph had still not abandoned his ambition that his sons should go to Oxford. Scholefield was appalled at his charge's ignorance. He was backward in Classics but, more seriously, knew next to nothing about Christianity. Richard barely knew the Lord's Prayer, broke down during the recital of the Apostles' Creed, and had never heard of the Thirty-Nine Articles. But intensive cramming followed by a further period of tutoring in Oxford itself during the Long Vacation of 1840 worked wonders. By the beginning of the Michaelmas Term in autumn 1840, Burton's tutor Dr Greenhill was able to enter his name at Trinity College as a fully matriculated student.

*

What general assessment can we make of the nineteen-year-old Burton, on the eve of his Oxford career? Some pointers are obvious enough. There was always an element of the gypsy in Burton, which was why he enjoyed Romany company so much.[29] The itinerant nature of his youth gave him a natural affinity with them. Moreover, not only did he *look* physically like one of the travelling race; his surname is one of the few authentic Romany names. Like them he was a perennial 'outsider', in but not of the English culture and ambivalent towards many of its most characteristic manifestations. Burton's early youth and upbringing made him a 'natural' as a traveller and explorer.[30] But, unlike H. M. Stanley, another great African adventurer with a rootless childhood, Burton did not revel in the fact. He recognised that it gave him advantages, but these were outweighed by the disadvantage of being a kind of 'Wandering Jew' or 'Flying Dutchman', condemned to rove forever without coming to safe anchorage. 'England is the only country where I never feel at home', he remarked ruefully.

Rootlessness and alienation fed into the general tenuous sense of identity that bedevilled Burton throughout his life. Burton regretted that he was not more strongly British, partly because it was his consciousness of belonging to the 'empire on which the sun never sets' that gave him his sense of effortless superiority.[31] In particular he condemned his father's decision not to persevere with the experiment of an English education for his boys after the Richmond débâcle. This left him with a major handicap when trying to thread his way through the labyrinth of the British Establishment.

> The conditions of society in England are so complicated, and so artificial, that those who would make their way in the world, especially in public careers, must be broken to it from their earliest days. The future soldiers and statesmen must be prepared by Eton and Cambridge. The more English they are, even to the cut of their hair, the better. In consequence of being brought up abroad, we never thoroughly understood English society, nor did society understand us. And, lastly, it is a real advantage to belong to some parish. It is a great thing when you have won a battle, or explored Central Africa, to be welcomed home by some little corner of the Great World, which takes a pride in your exploits, because you reflect honour upon itself. In the contrary condition you are a waif and a stray; you are a blaze of light without a focus.[32]

The other salient aspect of Burton's youth was his inadequate training in the norms of deference and authority necessary to one entering the hierarchical worlds of the Army, the East India Company and the Consular Service. The perfunctory and intermittent attention he received from his father produced a situation where 'the boy became a man without the most elementary notions of discipline and obedience.'[33] This would have been fine if Burton had possessed private wealth, or even if his childhood had been deprived. In the latter case, though inwardly contemptuous of authority, he would probably have been wary of it and fearful of antagonising those above him. But Burton had been brought up, in effect though not intention, to think of himself as a demigod. This stirred resentments and made his superiors feel they could not rely on him to follow their orders rather than his own views.[34]

If the legacy of Burton's parents had been confined to mere neglect and wrongheaded though well-intentioned decisions, they would have transmitted to him no more than the normal bequest of parents to children. But by their failure to provide strong 'role-models', they left Burton confused and alienated at a deeper level. By placing the emphasis wrongly, as usual, Burton's Boswell, his wife Isabel, drew attention to deficiencies that were not deficiencies and neglected the real areas where Richard had suffered as a result of his parents. Only a purblind English Catholic sensibility could point to the bigotry of Low Church Anglicanism as the Achilles' heel of Joseph and Martha Burton.[35]

Burton's references to his parents are invariably contemptuous, but no man can escape the genetic endowment transmitted by his father. Many of Burton's characteristics can be seen as chips off the paternal block. His sense of 'honour' and lamentation for the bygone days when 'gentlemen' settled disputes by the duel is a distinct echo of his father. While serving in Sicily under Sir John Moore Joseph Burton wounded an officer in a duel, nursed him back to health, and had rechallenged him within three months, when the recuperated 'brother' insulted him again. Again Joseph's accuracy stood him in good stead. Again he wounded his challenger, and once more he had to nurse him back to health. As a recent biographer has remarked: 'They surely would have found due cause to insult one another again but for Sir John Moore's decision to withdraw the regiment to England.'[36]

Burton of course tried to evade the direct martial legacy of his father by opting for the sword rather than the pistol as his favourite weapon. Where his father was a big-game hunter, Burton was an animal conservationist ahead of his time. Where his father was slothful, Burton had the maniacal industry of an elder Pliny. In these areas he was consciously going against the paternal grain. But in his own business and financial transactions he showed himself every bit as inept as his much-derided father. He also ran true to form in embracing his father's method of dealing with an overpowering actuality – escape from it by travel. Burton's habitual reaction to stress in adult life was to find a new corner of the world to explore. And the parental determinism manifested itself also in the military career. To spite his father all Richard had to do was not take Holy Orders; thereafter any career was open to him, it did not have to be the Army. But always the animus remained and it coloured many of his sour asides. 'Nothing astonishes

Hindus so much as the apparent want of affection between the European parent and child', was one of the milder animadversions.[37]

Yet if Burton despised his father, as a male prototype, his mother left him with a strong distaste for the feminine principle and triggered the misogynism that was to be so marked a feature of his adult personality. All Burton's anecdotes of his mother – and they are few enough – show her in a foolish light. Burton never forgave her for, as he saw it, losing him £100,000 by her partiality for her absurd half-brother Richard. This he perceived as unnatural and unmaternal, and by implication he frequently contrasted his mother with examples of the ideal mother he saw in the four corners of the globe.[38] When he states that an ungrateful son is rare in India because of the close relationship of mother and son, we can surely read this as a lament for the sort of mothering he never had himself. Having extolled the selfless devotion of the Hindu mother, who will never leave the side of her son night or day, be he well or sick, rich or poor, he goes on to portray the situation in the 'civilised' West.

> The parents are engrossed by other cares – the search for riches, or the pursuit of pleasure – during the infancy of their offspring. In the troublesome days of childhood the boy is consigned to the nursery, or let loose to pass his time with his fellows as he best can; then comes youth accompanied by an exile, to school and college ... there is little community of interests and opinions between parent and child – the absence of it is the want of a great tie.[39]

Burton held firmly to two opinions concerning mothers and sons. One was that the mother is *the* crucial formative influence on the development of male offspring. The other is that mothers have an irremediable tendency to spoil their sons and make excuses for them.[40] This situation might be thought to have suited Richard's scheme of things perfectly, but with his shrewd and sensitive antennae for all sexual nuances he suspected that there was somewhere a hidden price to pay. In the first place, how could he take seriously the special pleading of a woman as resolutely silly as his mother? In his remembrances Burton spared her nothing. He castigated her for being plain and he ridiculed her for her inability to manage staff properly. He always recalled her losing a good French chef by asking him to boil a gigot of lamb. '*Comment, madame, un gigot – cuit à l'eau, jamais!* Neverre!'[41]

Consequently, when relating the story of his mother's intercession with his father on the 'beast's in liquor' occasion, Burton is at pains to ridicule her well-meaning intervention. He tells how she began by bursting into a flood of tears to soften him up, then offered him a five-franc piece, and finally requested that he would read Lord Chesterfield's *Letters to his Son.* With complete lack of sentimentality Burton comments scathingly: 'It need hardly be said that the five francs soon melted away in laying in a stock of what is popularly called "a hair of the dog that bit".'[42] Burton guessed that his mother was trying to manipulate him, but could not penetrate to the depth of her game. The most likely explanation is that she was trying to distract him from the carnal appetites which she had detected in him in Naples, by converting his drunken excesses into venial sins. More broadly, as Fawn Brodie puts it: 'his mother . . . had subtly applauded his wildness and adventurousness, while at the same time disparaging and repudiating his sexuality.'[43]

Burton was also bitter about the resigned and matter-of-fact way his mother parted from him in Italy in 1840, and spoke witheringly of the 'Spartan nature of the British mother, who, after the habits of fifteen years, can so easily part with her children at the cost of a lachrymose last embrace.'[44] Yet here he surely failed to understand the true meaning of 'Spartan' and the degree of self-abnegation forced on the upper-middle-class women of the time. His mother confided to Georgiana Stisted that Richard's departure was 'just as if the sun itself had disappeared.'[45]

One of the most potent results of Burton's detachment from his parents was a certain blurring of reality and a tendency to withdraw into fantasy at moments of stress. It was often said of Burton that he delighted in telling tall tales, of murder, cannibalism and other atrocities, in which he claimed to have participated, while knowing well that he had not. This is often ascribed to the familiar wish to *épater le bourgeois*, but it may be that the propensity had deeper pathological roots. Burton relates that as a boy he was an accomplished liar and could not understand what moral turpitude was supposed to attach to a lie, unless the motive of the liar was fear of the consequences of the truth. He went on to say that he abandoned mendacity for an equally tenacious cleaving to the truth, and that it was his determination to call a spade a spade that involved him in so much trouble with authority and public opinion.[46] But in fact Burton never wholly abandoned a tendency to be 'economical with the truth' when fantasy was more colourful or more useful to him than reality. As an anthropologist Burton frequently drew attention to cultural relativism, and there is more than a dash of relativism about his own posture *vis-à-vis* the world. The 'expedient exaggeration' not only provided better 'copy' for Burton as wit and raconteur ('never let the facts interfere with a good story'); it also spirited away reality into the realm of the relative and made Burton's 'truth' the truth of Humpty-Dumpty – a classic defence mechanism for enduring the unendurable. Two of Burton's earliest books contain giveaway utterances. When analysing the folk-ways of the Sindians of northern India he says of their tendency to lie: 'Where truth is unsafe this must be expected from human nature.'[47] In the earlier book on Sind he is even more explicit. 'They deceive because they fear to trust. They boast, because they have a hope of effecting by "sayings" what there are no doings to do.'[48]

The tendency to fantasy almost certainly underlies the story Burton relates of having witnessed, with other young children in France, the execution by guillotine of a woman who had killed her small family by poisoning.[49] Now, while it is conceivable that in the 1820s a schoolmaster would have tried to warn his young charges by example of the mortal consequences of wrongdoing – taking children to executions for such 'exemplary' purposes was widespread in the eighteenth century – it is the nature of the alleged victim that alerts us to the likelihood of fantasy. It was impossible for young Richard to express openly the feelings of hatred and rage he felt towards his mother for preferring her half-brother to him in the matter of the paternal legacy. What more natural than to construct a homicidal fantasy towards his (transmogrified) mother who by her actions had 'poisoned' his future prospects?

The execution story also highlights another feature of the young Burton's psyche – and one which may explain his almost foolhardy physical courage: a morbid fascination with death. Since the classical explanation of the unconscious spring for this is a compulsion to repeat, the recurrent nightmare Burton had as a child is of considerable significance. He related that when he closed his eyes, a huge cone would form in the mind's eye, at the apex of which a demonic face would take shape and then advance grinning and with evil intent towards him, despite all his struggles to ward it off. Eventually 'its monstrous features were so close to yours, that you could feel them; then, almost suddenly, start back from you, flit away, diminish till nothing but the dark eyeballs remain in sight, and disappear presently to return with all its terrors.'[50] Taken on its own, this infantile nightmare would perhaps differ only in degree, not kind, from the night-terrors recounted by many children. But interpreted with the hindsight of Burton's many 'terrible beauty' references to death, it surely bears a stronger interpretation, with the fading and reappearance of the demonic face representing the simultaneous attraction and repulsion of a self-confessed 'dual man'.[51]

The duality in Burton's personality also extended to his sexual identity. Perhaps the most profound consequences of Burton's phantom-like parents and their failure to operate as genuine agents of formation and socialisation was that all his major ties were with Edward his brother. The feminine influence on the young Burton was notably weak. Apart from the few sour references to his mother, women appear in Burton's early memoirs as figures of fun or noises off. The solitary mention of sister Maria occurs when the brothers browbeat her into parting with her savings. For the young Richard the dominant figure was always Edward. In some such cases of brother-bonding the male can topple over completely into homosexuality. What seems to have happened to Burton is that this process was mediated by other influences, so that he rested at the half-way house of bisexuality. Many of the enigmas in Burton's life resolve themselves plausibly on this hypothesis: his marriage, his male friendships, and much else.

The prevalent theme of phallicism in Burton's writing can also be seen as a form of narcissism. Richard and Edward were united by their love of the sword. The sword represented distancing from Joseph Burton, who preferred firearms, and from the female world of tenderness. Richard co-opted Edward into a mystical worship of the phallic sabres, foils and rapiers. 'Fencing was the great solace of my life', Burton wrote. As for the sword itself, he regarded it as 'a gift of magic, one of the treasures sent down from heaven ... a creator as well as a destroyer ... the key of heaven and hell.'[52]

The ambiguous language used about the sword again hints at duality and the role of death in Burton's psychic world. His early bonding with Edward led him in later life to seek brother-substitutes in his younger male friends. A superstitious man like Burton must sometimes have wondered why the lives of all his 'brothers' ended in tragedy: Edward, Speke, Tyrrwhit-Drake, Scott, Steinhaueser, Palmer, almost as if his worship of a deadly cutting weapon had converted him into the angel of death with the terrible swift sword.

2

Oxford

BURTON never cared for Oxford, either town or gown. It had only been even vaguely tolerable to him during the high summer of the Long Vacation. 'The country around, especially after Switzerland, looked flat and monotonous in the extreme. The skies were brown-grey, and, to an Italian nose, the smell of the coal smoke was a perpetual abomination. Queer beings walked the streets, dressed in aprons that hung behind, from their shoulders, and caps consisting of a square, like that of a lancer's helmet, planted upon a semi-oval to contain the head.'[1]

The first two terms were a particular trial to Burton. It was in Oxford that he first decisively followed Montesquieu in attributing human behaviour largely to the effects of climate. He claimed that the 'detestable' climate of Oxford overwhelmed even the strongest undergraduates with nervous depression and sleeplessness, which he attributed to the effects of damp air charged with marsh gases and bacteria. The town was drained by a fetid sewer of greenish-yellow hue, containing 245 parts of sewage to every 10,000 of water. It was the climate and the lack of sanitation, in sum, which explained why Oxford had never produced a genius to set alongside Cambridge's Newton and Darwin.[2]

He complained that in autumn the Bodleian library closed at 3 p.m., since lights were not allowed. The Radcliffe Camera was even worse – damp in the wet season, stuffy during the summer and like the cave of Aeolus in windy weather.[3] And his first contact with fellow-undergraduates convinced him that he had fallen among grocers. He arrived with an impressive drooping moustache, the pilot version of the 'diabolical' whiskers that would adorn his later portraits. His peers were clean-shaven to a man. Within an hour one of them made the mistake of laughing at the hirsute newcomer. At once Burton issued a challenge to a duel – normal procedure at Bonn or Heidelberg but unheard of in the city of dreaming spires. When his insulter expressed incomprehension, Burton concluded that these callow, unsophisticated youths he was forced to associate with were also unmanly cowards.[4]

The day began with a huge breakfast, then followed two hours of wasted time at lectures: 'in my day, men were compelled to waste – notoriously to waste – an hour or two every morning, for the purpose of putting a few pounds sterling into the pocket of some droning don.'[5] The rest of the day was then free. Burton spent most of it in physical pursuits: walking, rowing, and martial arts of all kinds, especially boxing and fencing. He developed a great friendship with the Oxford fencing master Archibald MacLaren and acquired such a formidable reputation with foil and glove that, however *outré* his fellow students considered him, none dared tangle with him. In the evenings he smoked a lot and developed an interest in the new fad for hypnotism or mesmerism. There was little else that appealed to him. He despised the heavy beer which was quaffed in large quantities at drinking colleges like Brasenose, and balls or dances were unknown. In general Oxford continued to leave him cold. He detested its petty hierarchies, its college meals and the constant sound of bells, which he labelled an English fetish. Above all, what he found dispiriting was the English cult of the amateur, which meant an essential unwillingness to take the trouble to learn anything properly, whether fencing or languages.

As a consequence, Burton early took to twisting the lion's tail. He joined wholeheartedly in the practical jokes and 'fazing' of the day, aided by his singular head for liquor and his unerring aim with an airgun. On one occasion he absailed down into the Master of Balliol's garden and replaced his prize herbaceous borders with 'great staring marigolds'. Next he started on more open flouting of the rules. It was at that time forbidden to ride in tandems, or travel on Sundays. Since Abingdon was then the nearest railway station, Burton made a point of travelling there on a Sunday, and by tandem. Consorting with females of doubtful virtue was also frowned on. Predictably Burton often betook himself to Bagley Wood outside Oxford, where the pretty gypsy girl Selina bestowed her favours on 'young gentlemen'.[6]

Almost the only intellectual stimulation the young Burton received was when he went to dine with his old tutor Dr Greenhill. One evening both Dr Arnold and Dr (later Cardinal) Newman were present. Burton expected great things, but was disappointed when the two of them were content to discuss the size of the Apostles in St Peter's at Rome. Burton always retained an admiration for Newman and attended his sermons, but a similar experiment with the tedious discourses of Edward Pusey ended disastrously after Burton had been compelled to sit through an excruciating one-and-a-half hours of 'nightmarish' exquisite boredom.[7] More stimulating was an encounter with the Arabist Don Pascual de

Gayangos, whom he also met at dinner. Gayangos taught him how to copy the Arabic alphabet and how to avoid elementary errors: Burton was trying to teach himself Arabic, but had not yet realised that the language was written from right to left.

Burton's autodidacticism in the middle of what was supposed to be one of Europe's finest universities was a scandal that resulted from an early form of Catch-22 perfected by the then Regius Professor of Arabic. The professor refused to teach any *individual* who approached him, on the ground that the terms of his chair required him to teach a class. But by discouraging all individuals who showed an interest in a subject that did not form part of any recognised Honours School, he ensured that no such class could ever be formed.[8]

At the end of the first term Burton stayed with his grandmother and aunts in Cumberland Place, London. There he developed a taste for gambling clubs, and for whist, écarté and piquet. To his great joy Edward joined him in London and for a while they relived the halcyon days of their youth. All too soon the 'home of lost causes' beckoned him again, and it was from the beginning of the second term that Burton's real crisis in relations with the university began.

Burton was studying Latin and Greek on the 'Greats' course, but he soon concluded that one could learn more of the classical languages in a single year at Bonn or Heidelberg than in three at Oxford. The college teaching, for which his father paid £150 a year, was of the most worthless kind. It had no order and no system, its philology was absurd, and it did nothing to develop reasoning powers. Real disillusionment set in when he tried for, and failed to obtain, two classical scholarships, one of them at University College. Despite his by now profound knowledge of the classics, Burton was passed over in favour of a man who turned Aeschylus into a chorus of doggerel verse. His worst failing, in the eyes of the examiners, was that he insisted on speaking Latin in the Italian way and ancient Greek like modern Greek, instead of in the artificial and esoteric fashion then fashionable at Oxbridge. It was always an axiom with Burton that the ancient languages should be pronounced by accent, not quantity. When the dons corrected him, Burton made it clear that in his opinion they were ignorant fuddy-duddies. Taken aback by this bumptiousness, the tutors asked how he could be so sure in his opinion. He replied that it was already clear from his private studies of Arabic and Hebrew, where ancient Greek words were transliterated, that this was the case: a comparative analysis very quickly demonstrated that accent not quantity, was the key to pronunciation.[9] To the dons, this was an arrogant young man accusing them of philological ignorance.

Burton had right on his side. The nineteenth-century English pronunciation of Latin was a throwback to the Reformation, when an artificial mode of speaking the language was adopted to emphasise the breach with Rome. But, as his personal tutor confided, if Burton persisted in his 'errors', there was no chance of obtaining the first class honours, and hence the fellowship, that Joseph Burton had set his heart on for his son. *Aut primus aut nullus* was ever Burton's motto.[10] He at once gave up the programme of twelve hours' reading a day he had projected, and entered this bitter judgment on the whole business of the Oxbridge 'first':

> I soon ascertained the fact that men who may rely upon first classes are bred to it from their childhood, even as horses and dogs are trained. They must not waste time and memory upon foreign tongues. They must not dissipate their powers of brain upon anything like general education. They may know the -isms, but they must be utterly ignorant of the -ologies; but above all things, they must not indulge themselves with what is popularly called 'The World'. They must confine themselves to one straight line, a college curriculum, and even then they can never be certain of success. At the very moment of gaining the prize their health may break down, and compel them to give up work.[11]

He sought solace in the company of the few contemporaries who passed intellectual muster. One of them was Tom Hughes, later to win fame as the author of *Tom Brown's Schooldays*, which in Burton's view 'taught boys not to be ashamed of being called good'.[12] Hughes was at Oriel, then considered the paragon of Oxford colleges. Another close friend was Alfred Bates Richards, later poet, playwright and editor of the *Sunday Telegraph* and *Morning Advertiser*. Richards could outpoint Burton at boxing but was always several leagues his inferior in the art of the foil or broadsword. He later recorded: 'I am sure, though Burton was brilliant, rather wild, and very popular, none of us foresaw his future greatness, nor knew what a treasure we had amongst us.'[13]

Burton later summed up his Oxford days as follows:

> To be brief, my 'college career' was highly unsatisfactory. I began a reading man, worked regularly twelve hours a day, failed in everything – chiefly I flattered myself because Latin hexameters and Greek iambics had not entered into the list of my studies – threw up the classics, and returned to the old habits of fencing, boxing and single-stick, handling the 'ribbons' and sketching facetiously, though not wisely, the reverend features and figures of certain half-reformed monks calling themselves 'fellows.' My reading also ran into bad courses – Erpenius, Zadchiel, Falconry, Cornelius Agrippa.[14]

At the end of the first year Burton departed for Wiesbaden, where the family was to be reunited for the Long Vacation. Embarking at London Bridge, he was in the Scheldt the next morning, then met Edward in Antwerp for a troilistic encounter with a soubrette. They proceeded through Bruges to Cologne, where they took a Rhine steamer as far as Mainz, then drove across country to Wiesbaden, 'a kind of Teutonic Margate'. After a few weeks of concentrated fencing, the brothers departed for Heidelberg, determined to test their swordsmanship against the cream of the Neckar. The duelling scar of the Heidelberg student was already a cliché, and many terrible accidents occurred because of the hallowed custom there of fighting with broadswords without protection. The Burton brothers were determined to endure all, if they could once be admitted to the élite expatriate club. But they were just too good to be accepted. The local fencers gave them a trial. Even though Edward and Richard concealed the half of what they knew, they revealed enough to make the men of Heidelberg quake at the thought of facing such prodigies without armour and headgear. They were duly refused membership of the club.

It was at Heidelberg too that the brothers had their planned showdown with their father. In Antwerp they had taken a solemn brother-oath to seek commissions in the Army. But Joseph Burton was adamant. He had set his heart on a fellowship for Richard, followed by a living as a clergyman, so to Oxford he must return. Edward tried a tougher line, announcing that he would rather be the merest private in the British Army than a fellow at Cambridge. When his father insisted that he too return, Edward solved the problem by refusing to attend chapel at Cambridge. He was immediately asked to leave.[15]

Burton's solution was more roundabout, though with the same intention. 'As my father had refused to withdraw me from the University, I resolved to withdraw myself.' He began by provoking the college authorities to take action against him, by throwing rowdy parties and circulating insulting epigrams and caricatures dealing with the foibles of the Senior Members. When the college refused to take the bait, Burton decided to present them with a full-blooded challenge they could not ignore. A notice had been posted prohibiting all undergraduates on pain of expulsion from attending a local steeplechase meeting. Burton and his cronies hired a tandem, went to the race meeting, and made sure they were seen doing so. When haled before the disciplinary committee, Burton gave the dons no room for manoeuvre by being openly defiant and claiming he had done nothing wrong. He added a Parthian shot by stating that if he was sent down, he hoped that his father's 'caution money' – a deposit paid against loss or breakage of college property by the undergraduate – would be returned intact. The slander against the probity of the college authorities was too blatant to ignore. Burton was immediately rusticated.[16]

He decided to 'go down' in style. He hired a tandem and made his farewell to the college by having the driver steer the shaft horse straight through a bed of the finest flowers in Trinity gardens. He drove down the High Street onto the London road with a fanfare on a tin trumpet, blowing kisses to pretty shopgirls who came out of their daily prisons to view the mad cavalcade. Burton evinced his contempt for the university by recapitulating the ancient couplet:

> I leave thee, Oxford, and I loathe thee well,
> Thy saint, thy sinner, scholar, prig and swell.

Later his attitude to Oxford softened somewhat and he recalled: 'The testy old lady, Alma Mater, was easily persuaded to consign, for a time, to "country-nursing", the froward brat who showed not a whit of filial respect for her.'[17] In other words, contrary to what has sometimes been stated, Burton was merely rusticated and not expelled for good. He could easily have returned after a term or two. When it became clear that he would not be returning in the near future, if at all, the artificial bone of contention – the 'caution money' – was refunded, in April 1842.[18]

Once in London Burton made straight for his aunts' house and told them he had been given leave of absence to celebrate a 'double-first' – the very form of the lie demonstrates that at a deep level academic failure really did rankle with him. They gave a splendid dinner to celebrate the event – which added to their discomfiture when the truth leaked out.

Burton was now a failure and a wastrel, once again frequenting the London gaming clubs. In vain he pestered his father for permission to pursue a military career: to each suggestion – the Austrian service, the Swiss Guard at Naples, even the French Foreign Legion – Joseph Burton applied his veto. But one thing of permanent value had emerged from Richard's year by the Cherwell. He had laid the foundations for the Promethean linguistic achievements that were to stagger his contemporaries. In his prime he was master of twenty-five languages. With the variant dialects he could legitimately claim to speak forty different tongues. It was his initiation in Arabic at Oxford that launched him fully in this direction, though even as a youth his mastery of the Béarnais argot had marked him out as a linguist of great potential.

Burton evolved a technique for learning a language in two to three months, which he described as follows:

> I got a simple grammar and vocabulary, marked out the forms and words which I knew were absolutely necessary, and learnt them by heart by carrying them in my pocket and looking over them at spare moments during the day. I never worked for more than a quarter of an hour at a time, for after that the brain lost its freshness. After learning some three hundred words, easily done in a week, I stumbled through some easy book-work (one of the Gospels is the most come-atable), and underlined every word that I wished to recollect, in order to read over my pencillings at least once

> a day. Having finished my volume, I then carefully worked up the grammar minutiae, and I then chose some other book whose subject most interested me. The neck of the language was now broken, and progress was rapid. If I came across a new sound like the Arabic *Ghayn*, I trained my tongue to it by repeating it so many thousand times a day. When I read, I invariably read out loud, so that the ear might aid memory. I was delighted with the most difficult characters, Chinese and Cuneiform, because I felt that they impressed themselves more strongly on the eye than the eternal Roman letters. This, by-and-by, made me resolutely stand aloof from the hundred schemes for transliterating Eastern languages, such as Arabic, Sanskrit, Hebrew and Syriac, into Latin letters, and whenever I conversed with anybody in a language that I was learning, I took the trouble to repeat their words inaudibly after them, and so to learn the trick of pronunciation.[19]

For this reason, Burton was always a doughty defender of 'old-fashioned' methods of teaching, rote learning, *viva voce* chanting, and so on. He considered that these systems helped in forming pronunciation, fixed the subject in the memory and taught the elements of abstract thought. Whatever tediousness was inherent in a method of 'reading out loud' and mentally repeating whatever is said to one in a foreign language, the proof of the pudding was in the eating, for it invariably produced a mastery of the tongue within three months.[20]

One of Burton's quarrels with Oxford classics teaching was that it treated Latin and Greek entirely as a system of codes, almost as though the languages were a branch of pure mathematics. But Burton's point was that since the learning of a foreign language was an affair of pure memory, almost divorced from the exercise of other mental faculties, it should be assisted by the ear and the tongue, as well as the eyes. 'I would invariably make pupils talk during lessons, Latin and Greek, no matter how badly at first; but unfortunately I should have to begin with teaching the pedants who, as a class, are far more unwilling and unready to learn than are those they teach.'[21] Later in his career, when Consul at Trieste, Burton put this precept into practice in spectacularly disconcerting manner. While conversing with an Irish professor of Classics, he lapsed into Latin and soon had the poor academic floundering. The discomfited Irishman in effect cried mercy, by requesting with some acerbity that the conversation be continued in English.[22]

There were only two of his languages in which experts detected real weakness: German and Russian. Burton went to great lengths to avoid speaking German on the grounds that its sound was unpleasant, and its enunciation greatly irritated his brain and obscured his judgement. Where Burton would not speak, there was he self-confessedly weak as a linguist. He was both a great actor and a fine mimic, and his motivation in mastering a language was always the humanistic one of communication, not the dry academic philological one. 'Nothing goes to the heart of a man so much as to speak to him in his own patois', he wrote. The learning of languages from books rather than native speakers always excited his derision. On one occasion he was accosted on board a Thames steamer by someone who had taught himself Persian from books. When Burton did not respond to the man's babble, the stranger asked in some annoyance how it was that he, the fabled linguist Richard Burton, could not understand Persian. 'Oh, was it Persian you were speaking?' Burton replied loftily. 'I really must apologise for not recognising it as such, but the fact is I only know the language as it is written and spoken in Persia by Persians!'[23]

It will be clear, then, why the approach to Latin and Greek as 'dead languages' favoured at Oxford struck no chord with Burton. However, there are some reasons for supposing that, on other grounds, the worlds of Ancient Greece and Rome were alien territory for him. Nobody could have had greater scorn for the Greek motto *Meden Agan* ('Nothing too much') inscribed at Delphi. Moderation was never a quality of any of Burton's actions. His temperament was romantic, not classical, and of Latin and Greek authors he preferred what Robert Graves would later call the 'Muse poets' to the 'Apollonians'. Best of all he liked poets of an erotic or lubricious turn of mind, especially Catullus and Petronius. This partiality is clearly established both by the two classical authors he chose to translate, and by his many waspish asides about the sacred cows of traditional classical scholarship: dactyls and spondees are 'hateful', the great hero of the *Iliad*, Achilles, is a mere 'ruffian', and so on.[24]

The strengths and weaknesses of Burton as classicist are well illustrated in the last translation he completed in his lifetime, of Catullus's *Carmina*. Burton brilliantly matched the shameless honesty, nakedness and obscenity of Catullus, for at this level his sensibility was like that of the great Latin poet: elemental, primitive, nervous, passionate and decadent. But Burton was no poet, and it is here that his defects as classical translator show through. He was unable to follow the rhythm of the balliambic metre within which Catullus wove a polyrhythmic structure. Making a valiant attempt to overcome this flaw by a rhymed translation, Burton was forced to sacrifice the exact metre, the exact scansion and the double endings of every line. The first five lines of 'Attis', which some consider Catullus' masterpiece, emerge in Burton's translation as follows:

> O'er high deep seas in speedy ship his voyage Atys sped
> Until he trod the Phrygian grove with hurried eager tread,
> And as the gloomy tree-shorn stead, the she-god's house he sought,
> There sorely stung with fiery ire and madman's raging thought
> Share he with sharpened flint the freight wherewith his
> frame was fraught.[25]

Yet when it came to the speaking of languages, Burton was unparalleled. His zest for the spoken language was such that he was not above inventing words on the basis of euphony. On one occasion Dr Norton Shaw of the Royal Geographical Society challenged him on a new minting. 'I don't ever remember hearing that word before, Burton! Where does it come from?'

'I coined it myself of course, and who has a better right?'

'Well, it is a good word, a very good word.'

'Oh, I always coin one when I have not got one; it is the only way.'[26]

Burton would even have the audacity to correct native speakers if their articulation collided with one of his pet linguistic theories. In Argentina in 1868 he insisted on pronouncing the name of the highest peak in the Andes, Aconcagua, with the accent on the last syllable.[27] He could also upstage outstanding Arabists if he needed to, because of his unique knowledge of dialect variations. One of the leading Arabists of the second half of the nineteenth century was the Reverend Percy Badger, with whom Burton was usually on good terms. It so happened that the two had fallen out just before a state visit to England by the Sultan of Zanzibar, when Burton and Badger were to be the official interpreters. Burton got in first by addressing the Sultan, not in Arabic, but in the Zanzibari patois. Delighted by this, the Sultan began to hold forth animatedly and turned to Badger to draw him into the conversation. Badger stood frozen to the spot, speechless and thunderstruck. The sequel was all Burton had hoped. Seeing Badger unable to respond to the Sultan in this tongue that Burton spoke flawlessly, the onlookers concluded that Badger was either a charlatan, or a mere scholar with no speaking knowledge of Arabic.[28]

The peculiar mix of genetic, environmental and cultural circumstances that throws up a great linguist must forever remain elusive. In Burton's case we are dealing with linguistic talent of such a high order as, arguably, to merit that much misused word 'genius'. A strong believer in racial theories, Burton believed that a dash of Asiatic blood was necessary if one wished to have true linguistic facility.

More seriously, we might attempt to locate Burton's high linguistic talents in a cluster of psychological tendencies, among which we might include a tenuous personal identity, a consequent quest for the exotic and a love of 'the other' – that is, something different from the *donnée* of one's life. Linguistic talent is typically the product of the dreamer, the fantasist, the person who is in but not of a given milieu or culture. In Burton's case there were the additional elements of dandyism – his emphasis on spoken languages being part of an intellectual sumptuary display – and the acting ability and love of disguise. It is significant of Burton's general secretiveness that he always liked to approach a language by the back door, by mastering the language through the babel of the bazaar and the camp-fire before attempting written perfection. Burton hinted at this side of his personality when he announced 'linguists are a dangerous race'.[29]

Two other aspects of Burton as linguist should be emphasised. The first of these is what we might call the sublimatory aspect. Especially in India, when Burton began to question his own abilities as heterosexual lover, the almost manic learning of new languages seemed a form of displacement therapy, where polyglot profusion replaced the sexual promiscuity he was unwilling or unable to indulge fully. Sexual restlessness, plus the need for constant excitement and the purposive flow of fulfilling action, often blend together to take humans into the study of languages or the exploration of unknown territories; in Burton's case they took him in both directions at once. That there was a transmogrified promiscuous element in Burton's relentless language learning he himself unconsciously recognised by bestowing the title 'wife' on his favourite language, Arabic, which he described as 'a faithful wife following the mind and giving birth to its offspring'.[30]

The other aspect of linguistic studies was that it enabled Burton to stand outside societies and cultures and take a detached, Olympian standpoint. The gift of tongues was always associated in religion with the idea of being especially marked out by God, as Burton later discovered during his investigations of the Mormons. Naturally, a demigod would be able to speak in all tongues, as would a visitor from another galaxy where intellectual achievement was far in advance of that on earth. In a word, for admittance to the select coterie of Nietzschean superman, a polyglot proficiency was almost a prerequisite. Many passages in Burton's writings attest to an awareness of this aspect of power. 'A knowledge of languages and manners is all powerful in the East, and the civilised Englishman is called *Jangli* (i.e. Wild Man).'[31] Again: 'the first thing Oriental peoples, who regard the person, not his accidents, ask about you, whatever you may be, soldier, sailor, or civilian, is: "Does he speak our words?" If the answer be "No", then you are a *Kaywan*, a brute beast ... If it be a qualified, "Yes, he can but won't," then by the rule of *omne ignotum*, etc., you are a real magnifico.'[32] There was the final pragmatic point, important to the aggressive and belligerent Burton: 'If the people know or suspect you to be deep read in their language and manners, they will be chary of offending you, because they expect a return in kind.'[33]

The greatest problem Burton faced in his life was that of integrating the multitudinous aspects of his Protean personality. In this sense Oxford failed him quite disastrously, for if among the senior members of Trinity there had been just one who spotted Burton's massive intellectual and scholarly potential, his career might have been very different. He was a superb linguist, and men mentioned him in the same breath as Mezzofante. A sustained period of scholarly discipline at an early age might have made him incontestably the greatest Oriental linguist of the century. Yet Burton never had any regrets about his departure from Oxford. By great good fortune the British disaster in the Afghan war of 1838–42 made his father think again about the laurels to be earned by his son in an Indian Army career. As Burton later put it: 'As those Afghans (how I blessed their name) had cut gaps in many a regiment, my father provided me with a commission in the Indian Army and started me as quickly as feasible for the "land of the Sun". So, my friends and soldiers, I may address you in the words of the witty thief – slightly altered from Gil Blas – "Blessings on the dainty old Dame who turned me out of her houses; for had she shown clemency, I should now doubtless be a dyspeptic don." '[34]

3

India

THE Afghan disaster of 1841–42 made service in India seem both patriotic and respectable. Through friends Joseph Burton secured for £500 a commission for his elder son in the Indian Army, the military arm of the East India Company. By law the East India Directors were bound not to sell commissions, but they evaded this by inviting 'friends' to make nominations for vacant lieutenancies in return for certain 'considerations'.

Joseph Burton had had good reason for his initial reluctance to allow his son to join the Indian Army. It was despised by Regular Army officers, even though it did most of the fighting on the sub-continent. Officers in Indian infantry regiments were called 'Indians' by the snooty officers of the smart Queen's regiments. Though the 'Indians' possessed double commissions, one with the Company, one with the Crown, they were supposed at all times and places to yield social pride of place to the men of the British Army. Burton grew to detest this petty snobbery, which he contrasted unfavourably with the camaraderie in the Prussian military, and never ceased to be angry when some 'masher' in a Queen's regiment referred to him as an 'armed policeman'.

Once sworn in, Burton spent an enjoyable three months in London. He first displayed the interest in occult phenomena that he was to carry through life by having his horoscope drawn. He began learning Hindustani under the aegis of a Scottish veteran of India named Duncan Forbes, a card-sharping, chess-playing autodidact who spoke a number of Eastern languages, all of them with a broad Scots burr. Burton opted to serve in Bombay rather than in Bengal, where the Burton family had relations in the judiciary; he did not want to be overseen by his family connections or in any way bound by them. He was accordingly gazetted to the rank of ensign in the 18th Regiment of Native Infantry (Bombay).

He soon experienced further East India Company corruption; the 'friends' of the Company who sold commissions on the side also took a further cut by sending the new recruits to particular establishments for their uniforms and impedimenta: 'Dozens upon dozens of white jackets and trousers, only fit to give rheumatism – even tobacco, niggerhead and pigtail, as presents for the sailors. Even the publishers so arranged that their dictionaries and grammars of Hindostani should be forced upon the unhappy youths.'[1] Their boxes were stuffed with Wellington's *Despatches*, Army Regulations, Mill's ponderous *History of India*, and whatever the publisher chose to agree as 'necessary' with the outfitters. Because of the boredom of the long ocean voyage, and the shipboard card schools, many an officer would arrive in India having won several more uniforms after four months of seaborne gambling.

Burton left Gravesend for India in the *John Knox* on 18 June 1842. The voyage round the Cape was slow and tedious; it was not until 28 October that the ship docked in Bombay. The four months were notable for fisticuffs, horseplay and other bad behaviour by the young ensigns. Burton disliked the captain – this was to be a constant motif in his sea voyages – and took advantage of the mariner's keenness on boxing to knock him out in one of the many improvised bouts staged to keep boredom at bay. Otherwise, he worked hard at his Hindustani, worked out in the gymnasium, and taught his brother officers some of his fencing skills.

He also took an unusual but quite characteristic decision. He determined that while in tropical lands he would preserve his head from lice and other pests. He therefore shaved his hair and replaced it with a wig. This innovation added to Burton's startling appearance, for even as a young man he had the kind of face and physique that stood out in a crowd. At nearly six foot he looked shorter, because his broad chest, square shoulders and massive frame did not suggest a tall man. His hands and feet were of oriental smallness. His swarthy complexion and prominent cheekbones added to the impression of a man of the East, as did his heavy brow and drooping moustaches, which gave him the demeanour of a truculent mandarin. A pair of penetrating black eyes, a determined mouth and a short straight nose made him the ideal candidate for the 'Ruffian Dick' sobriquet later bestowed on him.

Burton's years in India almost exactly coincided with the great British military push there which secured her 'stable frontiers'. The disastrous Afghan War was meant to be a major step in this direction. A decade of much more successful campaigning converted most of India into a British colony (save for a few effectively gelded princely states). The conquest of Sind in 1843 was followed by the absorption of the Punjab in 1849, after the two bloody Sikh wars of 1845–46 and 1848–49. It was the annexation of the final territory, Oudh, in 1856 which was a root cause of the Indian Mutiny.

The Company, then, seemed to hold out the promise of almost unlimited military action – a delightful prospect for the young firebrand Richard Burton. Yet by that ill-luck which dogged him throughout his career, the decade that saw the most sustained and gruelling military actions of the century (the Indian Mutiny not excepted) left Burton after seven years of Indian service without a day's battle experience. The omens, after all, were never auspicious: 'As the Bombay pilot sprang on board, Twenty Mouths agape over the gangway, all asked one and the same question. Alas! the answer was a sad one! – The Afghans had been defeated – the avenging army had retreated! The twenty mouths all ejaculated a something unfit for ears polite'.[2]

Burton spent six weeks in Bombay on further language study. His pay – £14 or 180 rupees a month – was enough to secure for him a comfortable life-style: a horse, the rental of part of a house, a pleasant Mess, plenty of pale ale, as much shooting as he could manage and an occasional invitation to a dinner-party or a dance, where there were ten officers to every eligible young woman. He could also afford servants and a *munshi* or language teacher. While continuing to make progress with Hindustani, he hired a Parsee called Dosabhai Sohrabji to teach him the elements of Gujerati.

Although Burton's lip curled in derision at his first sight of a Sepoy – and he never lost his feelings of contempt for the Anglicised Indian soldiery – he thoroughly enjoyed Bombay, which he described as the most cosmopolitan city in the East. The time would come when characters like the Bombay governor Sir George Arthur, who used to like people to back out from his presence, would cause him more irritation than amusement, but at twenty-one Burton could afford to laugh at his antics. He noted early that India was particularly prone to drive religious bigots into a frenzy. One man got the 'call' and used to climb a tree every morning to shout out: '*Dunga Chhor-Do, Jesus Christ, Pakro*' ('Abandon the world and catch hold of the saviour'). Unsurprisingly, the man ended his days in a madhouse.[3]

At times Bombay's middle-class society seemed like a small county town in England, but with the important difference that it exhibited the familiar foreign service syndrome: ill-educated parvenus enjoying a level of affluence beyond their wildest dreams at home. English children were hideously brought up, and many of the under-fives used language that would have made a Billingsgate porter's hair stand on end. Socially Bombay was ruled by two women, nicknamed 'Old Mother Plausible' and 'Old Mother Damnable', with whom Burton had the occasional passage of arms.

At last it was time to depart to his regiment's base at Baroda in Gujerat. This meant another tedious sea voyage in an old tub or *pattymar*, which took three weeks to beat up to Baroda. After reporting to regimental headquarters and being assigned a bungalow, he introduced himself to his brother officers and impressed them by his hard-drinking abilities. There were only eight other officers on post, in addition to himself and the commanding officer, Captain James. Burton was considered unusual in that he drank port as a febrifuge. Having given sufficient proof of his toughness, he largely held himself aloof and spent up to twelve hours a day on intensive study of Hindustani. He was very quickly the best speaker of the language at HQ – not so difficult when it is remembered that a brother-officer had learned all his Hindustani from his Indian mistress and thereafter always spoke of himself in the feminine, so hugely scandalising the Sepoys.[4]

Baroda City was the domain of the Gaikwar of Baroda, who indulged a passion for cruel Roman-style animal fights. The regimental barracks was like an ante-room or porter's lodge to the princely domain. Daily life for most officers centred around 'sport', for the area teemed with game: tigers, hyenas, cheetahs, leopards, blackbuck; birds, such as cranes, partridge, peacock and quail. The favourite pastime was 'pig-sticking' – hunting wild boar with a lance. The spear used in this process was so sharp that the merest touch could cause death. The first time Burton tried out the lance, on a pariah dog, the usual experimental object, he speared the animal so hard that the point emerged at the other side of the pariah's body and buried itself in the ground, thus sending Burton flying out of the saddle. There was a grisly art in killing the boar and withdrawing the lance while at full tilt, which Burton later saw perfected on the American plains by the Sioux Indians when spearing bison. In India Burton found just one man who could master it – a certain Captain Heth of the 10th Regiment.[5]

Yet the wanton destruction of animal life always sickened Burton. 'Once a philosopher, twice a pervert' was a Voltairean motto he applied also towards the killing of beasts. He preferred to study while his brother-officers were out slaughtering the local fauna. When the assorted Nimrods returned for the heavy 'tiffin' of meat and beer at 2 p.m., Burton made do with a biscuit and a glass of port, so that he could continue studying in the afternoon instead of sleeping off the gourmandising. Burton, having been imbued in his formative years with French hypochondriacal sensibility, claimed that 'heavy grubbing' was bad for the liver; there is a certain irony in Burton's later attacks of hepatitis. Partly, too, he did not care for the meat provided. Because the cow was sacred to the Hindus and pork anathema to the Muslims, mutton and poultry were the only meats that could be safely served to the military carnivores of Gujerat. Just occasionally hams would be sent out from England, heavily disguised as 'English mutton'.

Gujerat in the rainy season was a trial even for a stoic like Burton: 'The air was full of loathsome beings, which seemed born for the occasion – flying horrors of all kinds, ants and bugs, which persisted in intruding into meat and drink. At Mess it was necessary to have the glasses carefully covered, and it was hardly safe to open one's mouth.'[6]

As a soldier Burton was distinguished by two things: contempt for the Sepoy and a determination to turn his men into expert swordsmen. He was disturbed to find that both officers and men in the Indian Army were no match for the native enemy in hand-to-hand fighting and would disgracefully extricate themselves from the consequences of their incompetence by shooting down with a revolver any tribesman who challenged them to single combat. As for the Sepoys, Burton did not know what to despise more, their lack of true martial qualities or their mangling of the English language. Parade ground square bashing provided much unintentional comedy as NCOs barked out such commands as 'Fiz bagnet', and 'Tandelees'.[7]

Burton had a higher opinion of Indian women than men. As soon as he arrived he took an Indian mistress or *bubu*, as was the universal custom of the British officer class in India. The arrangement was quickly made through one of his twelve bungalow staff. The girl was part concubine, part houseworker. It was clearly understood that the arrangement lasted only as long as the *sahib* required it, and it was her duty to take steps to avoid pregnancy. Sensing that this aspect of Burton's early career would raise a few eyebrows in late Victorian society, the egregious Isabel Burton later rewrote the episode, 'explaining' that every heterosexual officer in Baroda was 'morganatically married' to a Hindu woman.[8] This custom of the 'half-marriage' began to go out of fashion as more white women arrived and insisted that their husbands ostracise all officers who went in for this 'degrading practice'. But Burton always defended the custom stoutly because he felt that the *bubu* or 'native wife' was an important transmission belt between rulers and ruled. But adultery too throve at Gujerat. The young ensigns often managed to cuckold their superiors. It was well known that there were rooms in the native quarter of the cantonment which young bucks could rent out by the hour for a tryst with an officer's wife. Infidelity carried its risks, and Burton later told a story to illustrate how anxiety could lead to impotence. One of his friends, 'a young and vigorous officer', had seduced the wife of an English sergeant. The sergeant lurked around the bungalow in hopes of catching his wife and her lover in the act. A copper percussion cap was found under the bungalow window, from which it was inferred that the sergeant intended to shoot to kill. Nervousness on the part of the young officer led to impotence. He applied for help to the regimental surgeon, who prescribed pills and a diet, plus the surprisingly modern therapy of mutual caressing short of intercourse for ten days. Burton relates jeeringly that his young friend lasted just five days on this regimen before he was again fit enough to consummate his passion.[9]

With his *bubu* and his linguistic *munshi* comfortably ensconced in his bungalow, Burton eschewed both the fashionable 'officerly' pursuits, adultery and big-game hunting. But he did allow himself experiments with two very different kinds of animal. He collected forty monkeys of different age and species, corralled them in his bungalow and began to study their habits and language. He designated favourite animals as 'doctor', 'secretary', 'aide-de-camp', etc., and had his servants wait on them at table. If chastisement was needed, he himself administered it with a whip.[10] This menagerie was regarded by his messmates as the final proof that 'Ruffian Dick' was barking mad, but Burton's project was not so quixotic as it seemed. Twentieth-century studies of apes have in fact revealed a primitive form of language among the primates, particularly to warn of enemies. The monkeys of India – Kipling's Bandar-Log – have three distinct 'enemy' sounds, used to denote python, eagle and leopard.

The other animal experiment was much more dangerous. At Baroda he took lessons in snake-charming. This involved the difficult art of catching a cobra by the tail in the left hand when it attempted to flee, meanwhile slipping the right hand up to the snake's neck. This was a delicate and ticklish process, since to grip the cobra a few inches too far or not far enough would lead to certain death. Even as Burton agonised over whether he should continue this perilous apprenticeship, one of his messmates solved the problem for him by killing the cobra he kept caged in his bungalow. The snake-charmer was so outraged by this act of sacrilegious vandalism on the part of the *sahibs* that he refused to have any more to do with Burton.[11]

Eighteen forty-three was a great year for British arms in India. During the Afghan war the East India Company had forced the feudal rulers of Sind to allow passage of British troops across their territory. Building on this 'prescriptive right' the British then demanded that the feudal princelings declare themselves vassals of the Company. Not surprisingly, they refused. General Napier, who had assumed the command at Poona in December 1841 and was then given military powers in the as yet unconquered Sind, won two stunning victories against heavy numerical odds at Meanee and Hyderabad, and crowned his conquest with the pithy punning message to London: *Peccavi* ('I have Sind').[12] Burton rued his inability to be in the thick of the action. Typically, he combined pride in the British feat of arms with a sideswipe at his *bêtes noires*: 'the Sepoys, as usual, have behaved like curs.'

For Burton, the year of Napier's triumphs in Sind was the year when he first won his spurs as a linguist. In April 1843 he went down to Bombay to take the official examination in Hindustani. On 5 May he passed out first of twelve candidates. Returning to Baroda just before the monsoon, he applied himself to Gujerati and Sanskrit. To ease his passage in these languages Burton took to visiting the local bazaars and markets – a risky thing for a white *sahib* to do. It was this unconventionality that first won him the sobriquet 'The White Nigger' in the Mess. Burton showed his contempt for the label by ostentatiously passing up the Anglican services in favour of those given by the Roman Catholic padre. Official recognition for his labours came in June 1843 when he was appointed regimental interpreter.

On 22 August 1843 he again departed for a language examination in Bombay, this time in Gujerati. The examiner, as with the Hindustani earlier in the year, was Major-General Vars-Kennedy, an accomplished Oriental linguist. There was nothing amateur about Kennedy. He insisted that his examinees translate both from books and from specimens of demotic writing, that they write a paper in the language, and converse with a native speaker. Burton arrived in Bombay on 26 September, then honed his skills to a high pitch for the examination three weeks later. This time he was up against Lieutenant Christopher Palmer Rigby, by common consent the best military linguist in India. A year older than Burton, Rigby had already passed with flying colours in Hindustani, Somali and Amharic, and was the hot favourite to top the list in Gujerati. To his intense chagrin, he was left standing by Burton on 16 October 1843, when the 'unknown' was awarded a congratulatory first place.[13] Rigby was a brilliant 'by the book' student of languages, but his classical approach was no match for Burton's from-the-inside method, with its nuances culled from the most skilled *munshis*. Rigby never forgave Burton for this 'humiliation', and the enmity of this influential officer of the 16th Bombay Native Infantry cost Burton dear in the future.

On his return to Baroda he learned that the regiment had been ordered to Karachi. On 26 December 1843 Burton was back in Bombay and on 1 January 1844 he embarked on the *Semiramis* en route for Sind. Burton enjoyed himself on board, despite the gruelling daily routine by which officers went to bed at 11 p.m. and arose to reveille at 3 a.m.[14] The principal reason was his meeting with Captain Walter Scott of the Sind survey. Scott, nephew of the great Sir Walter, was the first of Burton's many Edward-substitutes – a brother-officer in more senses than one (Edward himself was by this time a trainee surgeon in the 36th Regiment in Ceylon). Like so many of the young men Burton was drawn to, Scott was a 'confirmed bachelor', and there is a distinct note of physical attraction in Burton's description of him: soft blue eyes, yellow hair and golden beard. Burton later remarked of their relationship: 'we never had a divergent thought, much less an unpleasant word; and when he died, at Berlin in 1875, I felt his loss as that of a near relation.'[15]

Karachi was in those days no more than a large village, containing 5000 souls, surrounded by walls pitted with embrasures, out of which oil could be poured onto besiegers. In British hands only since 1839, it was a distinctly unfriendly place, where the cliché about 'restless natives' was stark fact. The town was a mass of low hovels and mud dwellings. Everything was mud: houses, roofs, windowless walls, ventilators, parapets, platforms. In the rainy season the dwellings would dissolve 'like ice in a London ballroom'. The crashing of thunder and lightning in the monsoon season was counterpointed by the din of collapsing buildings, which sometimes buried their occupants alive. Burton's own mud hut eventually came crashing round his ears; the landslide left him with a badly damaged foot.

There were no proper streets, only narrow lanes, and the only open place was the bazaar. Ever the seeker for the esoteric and the exotic, Burton soon found what he was looking for in the shape of a great shallow artificial pond near the town, at which fakirs tended a swarm of huge, somnolent crocodiles. Burton, no zoologist at this stage in his career, insisted on calling them 'alligators.'[16] His favourite amusement was to worry the sleepy brutes with his bull terrier, then take a zigzag ride on the back of one of the saurians after muzzling its jaws by means of a fowl fastened to a hook at a rope's end. His friend Lieutenant Beresford went one better. Noticing that there were islets of rank grass throughout the pond, and that these islets and the crocodiles' backs formed a solid line across the pond, he took a run at the sacred enclosure and hopped across the reptiles' backs and the islets to the other side, jaws snapping angrily at him as he passed.[17]

It was in Karachi that Burton first came into contact with an older male he could admire and who acted as a father-surrogate. General Sir Charles Napier, a hawk-nosed Scotsman with a flowing beard like an Old Testament patriarch, was a veteran of Wellington's campaigns, a military tactician of high order, an administrator of genius, cross-grained and Rabelaisian in wit, and a natural despiser of authority. A friend and admirer of Byron, Napier was the kind of unconventional and eccentric spirit Burton had always known to exist but had never yet met in the flesh. Everything about the man appealed to Burton. He had the same ambivalent attitude to the British Establishment. In 1839 he had been given military command of the eleven northern counties of England during the Chartist agitation. Though his sympathies were with the people – like Burton he had a natural feeling for the underdog – he carried out his duties with exemplary efficiency. Napier had tweaked the collective nose of his aristocratic family by bringing back from his time as Governor of the Ionian islands two daughters born of a liaison with a Greek woman, then added to his 'eccentricity' by marrying a woman fifteen years older than himself. Now he was in India with the express purpose of raising money for his daughters' dowries.[18]

Burton admired the way Napier kept his battle casualties to a minimum by suborning sections of the enemy with secret service money – the kind of roundabout approach to a problem that would naturally appeal to Burton. With his diminutive stature, hawk's eye, eagle's beak and powerful chin, he reminded the rankers of Dickens' Fagin – *Oliver Twist* was a contemporary bestseller – and was so dubbed by them. With the junior officers he was a great favourite, as he was indeed 'amongst all who did not thwart or oppose him'.[19]

Napier and Burton always got on well, for each recognised himself in the other. Napier once tried on Burton the Duke of Wellington's old trick of asking for impossibly exact intelligence, just to wrong-foot his subordinate. He asked Burton brusquely how many bricks there were in a certain bridge. Quick as a flash Burton retorted: '229,010, Sir Charles'. On another occasion Napier asked Burton to interpret a complicated military order that took him five minutes to explain. Burton told the men, in a sentence, that they would now see how the British fought, then touched his cap to Napier. 'Have you explained all?' asked the astonished general. 'Everything, sir', replied Burton. 'Hmm. A most concentrated language that must be', said Napier gnomically before spurring his horse onward.[20]

Yet the paths of the two men did not cross very often. At the end of 1844 Napier fought against the hill tribes who were raiding into Sind. After a successful campaign, he returned to his administrative duties in March 1845. Burton, meanwhile, after a month in Karachi, was transferred with his regiment to Gharra, forty miles north. Gharra was a desert cantonment, arid, dusty and barren, where camels were the only mammals that could survive on the sparse thorn-bushes and fireplants. Burton found it 'a mild Miltonic hell, where the world shines and glistens, reeks and swelters, till the face of the earth peels and flakes, cracks and blisters.' Dead camels were allowed to fester and decay amid sun and flies just one hundred yards from the camp 'as if a little more death were really wanting'. Droves of jackals would slouch along torpidly, belly to the ground, coughing and belching with the excesses of their flesh-tearing frenzy.[21]

For nine months Burton gritted his teeth and stuck to the dreary routine as translator at courts martial. Even while he made progress in the Sindi language he diversified into Maratha or Marathi. In September 1844 he was in Bombay again for an examination in the language, this time beating six competitors out of sight.[22] His next objective was Persian, which came to be one of his favourite tongues. There was method in Burton's linguomania, for India really offered only two possibilities for the bored British officer: immersion in big-game hunting, which was the option chosen by Burton's later companion and rival John Hanning Speke; or the study of languages. There was another consideration too, which young Richard was not slow to spot: 'In India two roads lead to preferment. The direct highway is "service" – getting a flesh wound, cutting down a few of the enemy, and doing something eccentric, so that your name may creep into a despatch. The other path, study of the languages, is a rugged and tortuous one, still you have only to plod steadily along its length, and, sooner or later, you must come to a "staff appointment".'[23]

On returning to Karachi after his Marathi triumph, he was delighted to discover that as a result of his friendship with Walter Scott, he had been chosen as one of Scott's assistants in the Sind survey. Scott's task was to rebuild the Indus irrigation system – a pet project of Napier's and one of the many enlightened (but expensive) schemes for improvement that brought Napier into collision with the East India Company directors. The ostensible reason for Burton's appointment was that he could read and translate Italian works on hydrodynamics. He quickly mastered the use of the compass, theodolite and spirit level, and on 10 December 1844 set out with a surveying party and six camels to work on the Guni river and its tributary the Fulali.

Burton boasted that his surveying methods were superior to those of the Sindians, who had laid out their canals with no more scientific technique than some cotton strings and an impressionistic eye for the rise and fall of the ground. He found the work hard and exacting, but alleviated the occasional bout of depression by making anthropological jottings on the *mores* and folk-ways of Sind, especially those concerning the women. Having completed his work at Fulali, he returned to Karachi via Hyderabad, where he was surprised to find his regiment cantoned. There was plenty of good companionship in the 'Survey Mess' of six officers, headed by Scott. Full of temporary enthusiasms, Burton took up cock-fighting with gusto. This was a universally practised 'sport' in Sind, where some of the game birds were trained to such extremes of ferocity that they even attacked humans.[24] But, typically, as soon as Burton's own bird succumbed to a rival's spur, he abruptly abandoned the pastime.

In Karachi and its environs Burton also indulged a passion for involved academic hoaxes on the 'Piltdown Man' model. Burton got hold of an old Hebrew text and doctored it with 'scholiastic' interpolations, making it look as though the document related to the fabled 'Lost Ten Tribes of Israel'. He also planted a facsimile of an Etruscan pot among the rubble at the archaeological 'dig' at Sehwan, where antiquarians were trying to find traces of Alexander the Great. When both hoaxes worked, Burton gloated over the credulousness of scholars and was with difficulty dissuaded by Scott from publishing the full details of how he had hoodwinked the experts. Burton contented himself with a contemptuous aside in his first book: 'antiquarians are everywhere a simple race.'[25] It is quite clear that in this contempt for archaeology and research into ancient civilisations – which he later recanted by becoming one of the breed he had earlier derided – Burton was trying to expunge the hurt he still felt about the failure of Oxford to recognise his superlative intellectual talents.

In general Burton's life with the Sind survey was pleasant and carefree whenever he was based in Karachi, less so when 'on the road'. This was demonstrated in November 1845 when he, Scott and the other survey officers were sent north by Napier on a long reconnaissance of the northern marches of the province. Outside the immediate ambit of British military power they encountered much more overt hostility, but such was the reputation of 'the Devil's brother' (the Indian name for Napier) that aggression towards them remained purely at the verbal (or expectorative) level. Burton soon demonstrated his flawless command of Indian demotic tongues when a prostitute, whose overtures the officers had rebuffed, let fly with a stream of invective. 'Crows dressed in parrots' feathers ... corpses and eaters of corpses ... infidel Franks ... blights upon the land ... locusts', these were just some of the printable epithets applied to them by the shrieking harridan. But she must have been astounded when Burton reached down into his voluminous grab-bag of street abuse and gave her at least as good back. 'Thy locks be shaved, dame of all the dogs! May thy nose drop off, eater of the pig! ... May sweepers deposit their burdens upon thy corpse, O widow woman ... female fiend!'[26]

Burton's notorious ill-luck first manifested itself clearly in India. He and Scott departed for northern Sind in November 1845. Almost on cue, as soon as Burton was away from Karachi and Napier, the first Sikh War broke out, on 13 December 1845.

Napier himself missed the two battles of Ferozesah and Sobraon which decided the war, but this was little consolation. Burton had rushed back to rejoin his regiment; the anticlimax when the war ended without the 18th's getting in a shot was unbearable for the fire-eaters in it. On the dusty return from Rohri frayed tempers and short fuses were much in evidence. And now for the first time Burton revealed a characteristic flaw: an almost pathological desire to lock horns with authority in moments of stress. So far he had kept a low profile in India, and he had had the advantage of serving under officers he liked and respected, like Napier and Scott. But Henry Corsellis, the Regimental Colonel, and Burton were natural cat and dog. After several acrimonious instances of insubordination, their angry clash came to a head one night in the Mess. Burton was amusing his fellow officers by impromptu doggerel rhymes on their surnames. Feeling himself subtly excluded and upstaged, Corsellis rashly demanded that he too should receive the Burton treatment. 'Very well, Colonel', said Burton. 'I will write your epitaph.' At once he improvised an offensive couplet:

> Here lieth the body of Colonel Corsellis;
> The rest of the fellow, I fancy, in hell is.[27]

Corsellis was not one to forget an insult. He made a note to chastise the impudent puppy when the right moment came.

In the summer of 1846 a dreadful epidemic of cholera assailed Karachi. Seven thousand died, including 800 soldiers and Napier's favourite son John. Promotion to Lieutenant-General in November that year did nothing to staunch the outpouring of grief Napier felt at this loss. Burton narrowly escaped with his life after being stricken in September. As he emerged from the worst crisis, he had the presence of mind to apply for convalescent leave at the military sanatorium in Ootacamund near Ponnani in the Nilgiri Hills in Southern India. He was granted a two-year leave, as one who had narrowly escaped the angel of death. On 20 February 1847 he left Bombay for the south, utterly broken in health.[28]

The two-and-a-half years Burton spent in Sind were the most significant of his seven years in India and therefore merit further consideration. It was in Sind that Burton first became an anthropologist; it was here he first perfected the art of disguise that won him worldwide fame; it was here too that he experienced his one and only instance of *coup de foudre*.

As an anthropologist Burton began to elaborate two of his favourite later motifs: that climate is a crucial determinant of people's social, sexual and political behaviour, and that a ruling élite should at all times and places respect the indigenous culture and ethos. Burton was a close and perceptive observer of environment and milieu. His descriptions of Karachi at a time when the later thriving city was a mere collection of hovels, are unforgettable: the noisome foetor of dead fish, the feculent streets running with sewage, the putrefying camel corpses, fishermen naked to the waist in indigo-coloured drawers, the womenfolk of the local *canaille*, foul-mouthed and meretricious in their embroidered bodices and long coloured pantaloons. Burton as an observer was always preoccupied with 'the sex' (his invariable term for women), and as a good anthropologist he realised that the key to an understanding of a society's culture lies in its treatment of its females.[29]

He was quick, too, to learn from local folk-ways, such as pouring buckets of water over tents and table linen to achieve momentary coolness. The blinding heat was a perennial problem which Burton remembered with agonised clarity forty years later. 'In Sind we used to strip and stand in the downfall and raise faces skywards to get the full benefit of the douche.'[30] At first he was inclined to pooh-pooh some of the local lore. He was told that to sleep under a tamarind tree would bring on fever. He deliberately did so to disprove the 'superstition', and awoke with a week-long ague.[31] From then on he became convinced that the fabled wisdom of the East really was wisdom, not charlatanry. It was but a short step for a person of Burton's temperament to want to penetrate more deeply into such an intriguing culture.

It was in 1845 that Burton first took in earnest to disguise as a way of life. After passing the Marathi examination, he shifted his linguistic emphasis to Persian and engaged as *munshi* one Mirza Mohammed Hosayn of Shiraz, who became a friend and something of a mentor. Through Mirza Burton drank deeply of the Iranian and Sufic well. It occurred to him that by disguising himself as one who was half-Persian he could get round the obvious difficulty faced by a European in disguise. The Sindian would detect from subtleties in the timbre anyone, be he never so great a linguist, trying to pass himself off as a native of Sind. But a slurred accent would be perfectly acceptable in a man from the northern shore of the Persian Gulf, an area about which Burton had read a lot. Additionally, his dark eyes were an advantage in a continent where blue eyes had a bad reputation and were regarded as a badge of evil.[32]

Burton proceeded to stain his face with henna and don a false beard and flowing mane of hair. The sequel he describes. 'With hair falling upon his shoulders, a long beard, face and hands stained with a thin coat of henna, Mirza Abdullah of Bushire – your humble servant – set out upon many and many a trip. He was a Bazzaz, a vendor of fine linens, calicoes and muslins; such chapmen are sometimes admitted to display their wares, even in the sacred harems, by "fast" and fashionable dames.'[33]

It was only when absolutely necessary that 'Mirza Abdullah' displayed his stock-in-trade. Usually he merely alluded to it, boasted of the business he had done and asked a thousand questions about the trade. In the end he acquired enough confidence to be able to walk into any house without knocking. If the master considered kicking him out, he would at once flash his pack of jewellery in the mistress's direction. Burton claimed to have become quite a celebrity in Sind; he broke many a female heart and had many a marriage proposal from avaricious fathers. 'He came as a rich man and he stayed with dignity, and he departed exacting all the honours. When wending his way he usually urged a return of visit in the morning, but he was seldom to be found at the caravanserai he specified – was Mirza Abdullah the Bushiri.'[34]

Whenever Burton arrived at a strange town, dressed as a rich merchant in Oriental sumptuosity, down to the riding spear he brandished and the bulging pistols in his holsters, he would begin by overawing the locals with signs and stories of his wealth, power and influence. He would take a house near the bazaar, so as to be handy for the evening conversations. For the purposes of credibility he occasionally rented a shop and furnished it with clammy dates, viscous molasses, tobacco, ginger, rancid oil and strong-smelling sweetmeats. His shops were always crowded but did poor financial business, hardly surprisingly since Burton gave the heaviest possible weight to all the women, especially the pretty ones, to gain their favour and avert all suspicion.

Sometimes 'Mirza Abdullah' spent the evening in a mosque listening to the debates. At others he entered uninvited the first house where music and dancing suggested a party – 'a clean turban and a polite bow are the best "tickets for soup" the East knows.' His favourite observation point was the house of an elderly matron on the Fulali river, which he had first visited during the Sind survey days. She was an ageing beauty who had run away from her husband to live with a tailor. In his observation of this Indian 'Darby and Joan' couple and his conversations with them, Burton got to the very bottom of Sindian culture, 'its truly Oriental peculiarities, its regular irregularities of deduction, and its strange monotonous one-idea'dness.' Burton calculated that for four months of invaluable insights, during which he virtually lived in the couple's house, he paid a sum total of six shillings. It is not surprising that he concluded: 'When he left Hyderabad he gave a silver talisman to the dame, and a cloth coat to her protector; long may they live to wear them.'[35]

In this love of disguise there was both a conscious and an unconscious element. Consciously, it made sense for Burton to make himself invaluable to Napier by winkling out the kind of secrets the natives would never have divulged to the hated 'Frank'. Unconsciously, though, the taste for disguise does point to precisely the identity problem the rootless polyglot gypsy might be expected to suffer from. But whatever its origins, Burton's disguise yielded him a treasure trove of arcane information and laid the foundations for his unparalleled knowledge of the East. It has even been suggested that Kipling's Strickland, who was similarly a devotee of Indian disguise, was based directly on Burton.[36]

Burton's brilliance as an undercover agent led Napier to appoint him to a controversial task, whose reverberations pursued him for the rest of his life. In 1845 rumours reached the general that some of his men sought sexual gratification in three homosexual brothels in Karachi. Since Burton was the only officer with an adequate knowledge of the Sindi tongue, he was duly assigned to investigate. He accepted on condition that his report would never be forwarded to the Bombay Government. He knew that as a supporter of Napier he could expect little understanding and no mercy if the report fell into the wrong hands. Napier accepted the terms and agreed to file any memorandum among his own personal private papers.

Disguised as Mirza Abdullah, Burton made his way into the trio of lupanars or 'porneia', and came away reeling with his discoveries. Every variety of pederasty, transvestism, troilistic fellatio, etc., was practised there, and the most important clients were the Indian princes or Ameers, who were supposed to be collaborating with Napier in extirpating the bad old customs and preparing Sind for civilisation. Among many closely observed details was the nugget that young boys were preferred to eunuchs as objects of buggery since 'the scrotum of the unmutilated boy could be used as a kind of bridle for directing the movements of the animal.'[37] Napier was a bluff man of the world. He read the report, did not ask how Burton came by the information, and immediately ordered the lupanars closed. But instead of filing Burton's report with his own private papers, he placed it in the official 'India. Most Secret' file, where his successor could peruse it. There the report lay, like a time bomb ticking away, ready to explode two years later.

As ever with Burton in matters of sex, the Sindian experience shows an oscillating pattern. Juxtaposed with the Karachi brothel experience was a heterosexual encounter of a highly romantic flavour. Outside Karachi Burton espied, in a camel train, 'a charming girl with features carved in marble like a Greek's, the noble, thoughtful Italian brow, eyes deep and lustrous as an Andalusian's, and the airy, graceful, kind of figure with which Mohammed, according to our poets, peoples his man's paradise.'[38] He at once sat down and composed a letter, full of flowery and euphuistic tropes in the best *Arabian Nights* style. She replied pragmatically, revealing herself as a high-born Persian girl and asking what he knew of medicine and whether he possessed any especially efficacious European remedies. He sent her a potion of mixed gin, powdered white sugar and Eau de Cologne. The next he knew, his love was being bustled away onto a camel. She disappeared into the night and he saw her no more. Later came word that she had died suddenly of a mystery illness. According to Burton's niece Georgiana Stisted he never forgot this girl, and tears would start to his eyes whenever he thought of her. Certainly, said Georgiana Stisted, he was never the same man again.[39]

Part of this story looks like fantasy. There is no need to doubt that he saw a Persian girl and that he was smitten by her. But the 'death' looks like rationalisation on Burton's part, an inference strengthened by a poetic fragment found among Burton's papers, an extended fantasy in which a poet loves a girl, the girl is poisoned by a jealous rival, and the poet kills the murderer. All the evidence points to a courtly love-fantasy of the medieval troubadour kind, where the object of love is glimpsed once at a castle window, or a melancholic 'parallel life' fantasy of the Thomas Hardy kind, where the once-seen pretty girl becomes the definitive 'road not taken'. This squares with everything we know of Burton's romantic–melancholy sensibility.[40]

There was yet another fantasy romance in Goa in 1847. After convalescing in Ootacamund, Burton was assailed by a secondary complication in the form of ophthalmia which, typically, he ascribed to the change of climate from dry Sind to the cold and damp blue Mountains of Goa. He found it impossible to read – for Burton the omnivorous reader this was the worst torture that could have been devised. At first his condition seemed permanent: drugs, diet, dark rooms and a variety of hack medical remedies simply exacerbated his malady. Then, suddenly, his eyesight improved, though he never returned to peak fitness until he quit India. He threw himself into the study of new languages – Telugu and Toda – while honing his Arabic and Persian to a new sharpness. In six months at Goa he spent almost all his time in linguistic study, some perfunctory sightseeing apart. With his gift of tongues Burton virtually absorbed Portuguese through the pores of his skin as he visited the scenes described in the *Lusiads* of Camoens, who became one of his best-loved authors.

It was at the end of the six-month convalescence that there occurred whatever substratum of fact there is in the story of Burton and the Goan nun. Near the sanatorium where he slowly regained his strength was the convent of Santa Monaca. There one day Burton saw and fell for a young postulant who was teaching Latin prior to taking her final vows. He decided to get close to her and converse. He dealt with the sub-prioress by affecting an interest in St Augustine and making her gifts of cognac for 'medicinal purposes'. He then succeeded in making conversation with his *inamorata*. He discovered that she was unhappy with her lot and had been dragooned into monasticism by over-pious parents. Together she and Burton laid careful plans for an elopement.

The night for the elopement came. Burton and his two servants, all disguised as Moslems, opened the garden gate and the cloisters with duplicate keys. However, by some mischance they took the wrong turning and entered the bedchamber of the sub-prioress. Her sleeping form was at once raised aloft and borne off in triumph by the servants. The mistake was soon discovered. They deposited their ugly and ululating burden and decamped, leaving the pretty young postulant to her fate. Thanks to their disguises, the miscreants' identities never came to light and the nocturnal incursion was set down to simple burglary.[41]

Such, at any rate, was Burton's story. Doubtless there was a pretty young nun 'with large black eyes, a modest smile and a darling of a figure', but there in all probability the facts end; the rest is typical Burtoniana. Yet from the fact that Burton cut short his time in Goa and returned to regimental duties after just six months of a two-year leave, we may perhaps infer that there was some kind of scandal attached to his departure from the Portuguese enclave, though hardly on the level of the low comedy Burton described.

On his way through Bombay he again distinguished himself by making mincemeat of a field of thirty and passing out first *summa cum laude* in the official Persian examination. This feat, which Burton mentions almost *en passant*, took place on 15 October 1847, and was such an astounding capping of his previous linguistic exploits that even the curmudgeonly East India Company had to take notice. Burton was awarded an honorarium of 1,000 rupees from the Court of Directors – the one and only token of recognition he ever received for his seven-year Indian labours.

Back in Sind he was reassigned to the survey team but because of his weak eyes his colleagues ended up doing most of the work. He used his virtual sinecure status to work up his Sindi and perfect his Arabic, which he did by committing the Koran to heart. Now he was enthralled by the mysticism of the Sufis and steeped himself in their mental world through fasting and meditation. He lived and thought almost as a Persian.[42] But Burton was never entirely either yogi or commissar, and he proved his practical sense by passing further official examinations in Sindi and Punjabi. At the end of seven years he had a string of 'firsts' to his credit, more than enough to expunge his Oxford failures: in Hindustani, Gujerati, Persian, Marathi, Sindi, Punjabi, Arabic, Telugu, Pushtu, Turkish and Armenian.

By all normal rules of expertise and promotion he was the obvious choice to act as official interpreter to the Army during the Second Sikh War which broke out in April 1848. The 18th Regiment was ordered to advance on Multan. Burton recalled that the only way the camel corps could achieve the forced marching rate of fifty miles a day up the Indus Valley so as to catch Nao Mall by surprise was to make the camels intoxicated with *bhang* – the Indian version of hashish.[43] But even while Burton was scoring his great success in Persian, events were unfolding that were to bring his Indian career to a dead stop. Tired of his battles with the East India directors and still grief-stricken at the loss of his son in the cholera epidemic, Napier resigned the government of Sind in July 1847 and on 1 October left India for retirement in Europe.

The departure of the 'Devil's brother' and his replacement as corps commander by General Auchmuty was the signal for Burton's enemies to close in for the kill. Colonel Corsellis, who had long been casting about for a means of taking the strut out of his 'impertinent' subordinate, was tipped off that there was a damaging document written by Burton among the confidential files left behind by Napier. A search soon uncovered the two-year-old report on the Karachi brothels. Burton's reputation was irretrievably damaged. It was even proposed by

Corsellis and Auchmuty that Burton be ignominiously cashiered on grounds of moral turpitude. But the East India Company had had enough of combat with Napier. To dismiss Burton would be, by implication, to censure Napier, who had ordered the report written, and Napier was now a national hero. Dismissal was clearly not an option. But there were other ways of humiliating the contumacious Burton. He had applied for the post of official interpreter and on paper was by far the best-qualified candidate. Auchmuty informed Burton that he had been passed over and the job given to a lieutenant with a single qualification in Hindustani.

The snub had the required effect. 'This last misfortune broke my heart', wrote Burton. 'I had been seven years in India, working like a horse, volunteering for every bit of service, and qualifying myself for all contingencies. Rheumatic ophthalmia, which had almost left me when in hopes of marching northward, came on with redoubled force, and no longer had I any hope of curing it except by a change to Europe. Sick, sorry, and almost in tears of rage, I bade adieu to my friends and comrades in Sind.'[44]

Burton quit Sind on 13 May 1849. In Bombay he applied for sick-leave, easily passed the Medical Board with his impaired eyes, and suffered a severe relapse in his health that made his friends warn him that the choice was Europe or death. Burton staggered on to the teak brig *Eliza*, bound for London, increasingly convinced himself that he would not see England again. He even composed a farewell letter to his mother. But his fears were groundless. In the late summer of 1849 a thin haggard man limped ashore at London, supported by an Indian servant. The wanderer had come home to a native land he never truly recognised as such. And he had come from an adopted country that had snubbed him. As Burton later expressed it sadly in his cryptic poem *Stone-Talk*:

> A fatal land that was to me
> It wrecked my hopes eternally.[45]

4

The Impact of India

WITHOUT question the seven years Burton spent in India between the age of 21 and 28 were his crucial formative period. By 1849 most of his ideas, attitudes and values had crystallised into their mature form. Almost the first thing Burton did on arrival in England was to launch into a career as a writer, making abundant use of his Indian experiences. Anyone who would understand Burton must examine closely the multitudinous impressions of these years.

Burton always had a very keen sense of physical immediacy. His writing is suffused with a sensuousness that conveys a real impression of felt life. In India he reeled, intoxicated, through a vast landscape with a wider climatic range than Europe, varying from equinoctial Madras to the snows of the Himalayas. The racial and cultural brew, too, was as varied as all Europe put together. Here were Aryans, Jangalis, Dravidians, Christians, Jews, Afghan Rohilas, Arabs and Zanzibar Sidis, with all possible permutations and combinations through miscegenation. In addition, Burton identified three main branches of language: Semitic, Hamitic and Japhetic or Turanian.

All of this heterogeneous gallimaufry found its way into Burton's pages. On his very first days in Bombay in 1842 he conveyed chillingly the squalor of the city: where heads and limbs slid off the Hindu funeral pyre as the stench of roasting, crackling flesh wafted into his nostrils; where lizards and bandicoot rats slithered through the open sewers; where even the ancient architecture of the Portuguese seemed 'splotched and corroded as if by gangrene'.[1] The cruelty of India appalled him, particularly the treatment of women. Among the Toda in the Nilgiri hills polyandry was practised and female infants were drowned in milk or trampled to death by water buffaloes; elsewhere little girls were put down with an overdose of opium. But Burton did not see only the dark side of India. In Sind he steeled himself to endure the 120-degree heat and to appreciate the beauty of the tropical night, when the sky became the deepest, purest and most pellucid blue and the moon shed streams of silver on the desert world below.[2]

Needless to say, Burton became the leading European expert on the languages of the sub-continent. His contributions in this area were early recognised and have been hailed since.[3] Curiously, at this stage in his career Burton had something of a blind spot for animal life. Living creatures appear in his narrative if they have curiosity value, like the crocodiles of Karachi, or as pests, like the flying insects of Baroda.[4]

Burton was always far more interested in anthropology than zoology, so it is on the subject of the indigenous Indians that we should expect the sharpest observations. Here we encounter a seeming paradox. It is a staple proposition of the *bien-pensant* relativistic liberal that a distaste for non-Western cultures is purely a sign of cultural and linguistic ignorance on the part of the depreciator. No such charge can be levelled at Burton. He mastered the native languages and understood the local cultures through and through – even to the point of noting their defecatory habits (twice a day, morning and evening, as opposed to once a day among Arabs).[5] But unlike many who 'go native', Burton did not fall in uncritical love with his subject. There is a surprising acerbity to many of his observations, which cannot be set down to the blimpishness of a dyspeptic servant of the Raj.

Burton saw the Indians as a mixture of docility and refinement. He admired their acuteness in not wasting time on western-style theory and abstract thought, concerning themselves instead with hard reality. But he was contemptuous of their inability to respond to any values except those of main force, and he expressed his contempt vociferously: 'The Scindian is constitutionally a poltroon: his timidity is the double one of body and mind. An exception to the general rule of oriental resignation or Moslem fortitude, he cannot talk or think of death without betraying an abject, grovelling fear, and even his *bhang* will not give him the courage to face the bayonet with common manliness.'[6] He remarked scornfully that whereas the Indian had a greater taste for moral and didactic tales, as in the *Arabian Nights*, than the Westerner, he was just as ready to forget or disregard ethical teachings. India was above all a land of sacred cows, where mindless habit ruled supreme: 'In India it is popularly said that the Rajah [sic] can do anything with the *Ryots* provided he respects their women and their religion and not their property.'[7]

Bhang or Indian hemp, the most common Indian drug, was itself the object of many of Burton's unappreciative asides.[8] Regular drug-taking he thought a cowardly means of evading reality, which proved the essential inferiority of the Indian. 'The Indi are still, with few exceptions, a cowardly and slavish people who would raise themselves by depreciating those superior to them in the scale of creation.'[9]

Not surprisingly, then, Burton approved of British rule in India. From the contempt for the 'Franks' which 'Mirza Abdullah' had picked up in the streets and bazaars, he knew very well that Indians would always regard their own civilisation as innately superior to that of the West; this being the case, Burton felt that the issue could be settled only by military conquest.[10] Once the British had conquered India, they should rule it with an iron fist, for by the Oriental mind enlightened and liberal attitudes were always mistaken for weakness. 'The essence of Oriental discipline is personal respect based upon fear ... these people admire an iron-handed and lion-hearted despotism; they hate a timid and grinding tyranny.'[11] Were the British ever driven out of India, the result would be the return of the Dark Ages: piracy in the Cutch and the Persian Gulf would revive, as would thuggee, and detestable practices like suttee – burning widows on the funeral pyre.[12]

Burton proposed the Roman method of putting India under centralised military rule. There should be three pivots: the Himalayas, the Deccan and the Nilgiri Hills. Railways would remove the need for single stations and provide the flexibility of a mobile force.[13] The utmost severity should be visited on anyone not obeying the conqueror's laws, especially in matters of taxation, even though he knew such conduct would lead to an outcry in England. For more serious offences, Burton was fully prepared to endorse the method of blowing criminals from the mouths of cannon, as being more humane punishment than hanging or shooting.[14] Hanging should be reserved for the murder of Europeans. Speaking of the later (1858) massacre in Jeddah, Burton made the point explicit: 'These men should be hung upon the spot where the outrage was committed ... the bodies should be burned and the ashes cast into the sea ... this precaution should invariably be adopted when Moslems assassinate Infidels.'[15]

Yet Burton's point about the Roman example had a subtle implication. As with the Romans in Palestine, he believed that imperial authority should be reinforced ruthlessly, but thereafter the locals should be free to manage their own affairs; the British ought not to interfere with their customs or folk-ways. 'Let the Nigs do as they please' was Burton's crude gloss on Pilate.[16] Of the 'Young Turks' or 'Kindergarten' in India in the 1840s, only Burton and Edward Eastwick made this minority appraisal of the correct proconsular posture. They realised that the people they governed were very different from Westerners and in many ways not very admirable, but they thought attempts to change their culture were misguided and chimerical.[17]

The majority 'Young Turk' view was shared by Napier, whose statesmanship had the ulterior purpose of bringing India within the orbit of civilisation. This was the area where Burton most vehemently dissented from his mentor. He shuddered at the weakness of Napier in indulging the prejudices of the famous meeting place for the anti-slavery lobby, Exeter Hall, and other centres of English do-goodery by abolishing slavery without thinking through the implications of abolition. 'I well remember the weeping and wailing throughout Sind when an order from Sir Charles Napier set free the negroes whom British philanthropists thus doomed to endure if not to die of hunger.'[18] He roundly criticised 'the Devil's brother' for executing a man who killed his wife for adultery, then posting notices that all such wife-killers would be hanged. With typical Burton hyperbole he claimed the consequence was that the women of Sind broke free of all restraint. According to 'Mirza Abdullah', a British officer could have as many respectable women as he wanted, and the local prostitutes even threatened to petition Napier that the 'ladies' were ruining their livelihood.[19] Of course, here we are dealing with a complex 'overdetermined' Burtonian response. It was not just the interference by Napier in local folk-ways that Burton deplored; he also feared female sexuality, as he was to prove on many occasions. At an unconscious level Burton, by supporting the rights of husbands to cut down adulterous wives, was revealing his feeling that this should be the invariable punishment for *all* unfaithful women.

There were many other aspects of the British presence in India that Burton found less than satisfactory. Pre-eminent among them was the universal view that a white skin denoted superiority to a brown one, whatever the level of intellect or creativity in the respective possessors. Burton was frequently irked by the conventional wisdom of the Mess that any subaltern in Bombay was capable of governing 200 million Indians.[20] He told many stories to illustrate the boneheadedness of his fellow-countrymen. Acting Commissioner J. J. Jacob of the Sind Horse was ostracised and despised by his messmates simply because he could not play whist. One of Burton's brother-officers – called 'Tuckey' Baines from his 'trencherman' activities – dealt with the Sindi population in a fatuously ingenious way. It was his job to adjudicate in the case of petty complaints and act as a kind of local policeman. Baines would summon plaintiff and defendant, to hear their stories. The plaintiff would speak first, after which Baines would award thirty-six lashes against the defendant. When the defendant had been beaten, he was allowed to countercharge, whereat Baines promptly ordered the plaintiff to be given thirty-six lashes. Not surprisingly, the rate of complaint soon dwindled to nil, and Baines was left to enjoy the untrammelled idleness which had all along been the object of his draconian system.[21]

There seemed to Burton literally no end to the ignorance of the British in India. He noted how they earned universal contempt for boiling their rice and then discarding the nutritious starch or gluten called 'conjee' before eating the nutritionless husks.[22] He was disgusted to find that the Governor-General of India was unaware that Islamic law required a criminal to confess before guilt could be established; mere circumstantial evidence was inadmissible.[23] Most of all he detested the prejudice against the study of native languages, and the wilful undervaluation of linguistic talent, in favour of the absurd belief that a training in Latin and Greek made a man fit to administer a world empire. 'Apparently England is ever forgetting that she is at present the greatest Mohammedan empire in the world. Of late years she has systematically neglected Arabism, and, indeed, actively discouraged it in examinations for the Indian Civil Service, where it is incomparably more valuable than Greek or Latin.'[24]

So far Burton's critique of British India could be set down merely to the irritation of a Nietzschean 'superman' condemned to toil alongside morons in a great work. And it was not just the morons who irked him. In 1865 in his 'gnostic' poem *Stone-Talk* he attacked the so-called founders of the empire: Clive, Warren Hastings and Dalhousie. For the most part, though, there is in Burton's writings no condemnation of the imperial principle as such, merely of the hopeless amateurism with which the empire is ruled. But in some of his more reflective passages Burton achieves an almost Marxian perspective on the economic consequences of British rule in India. The destruction of the Indian village cotton industry by British capitalism is one of the great set-pieces of Marx's analysis. After 1813 the cotton manufacturers of Manchester and Birmingham dictated a systematic policy of the destruction of Indian industry. India was to be turned into a producer of primary products and a market for British secondary products.[25]

Burton prefigured this analysis in his writings on India. In his day the mats of Sind were still famous, but by the time he revisited India in 1876 they were a thing of the past, having been deliberately suppressed by the interests of Birmingham and Manchester.[26] Burton was convinced that India had to become a manufacturing country again to avoid starvation, and he spoke of the area on an encouraging note: 'Despite the jealousy of the manufacturing mob, which wishes to buy dirt-cheap from India, and to make her pay one hundred per cent for working her own produce, we have a conviction ... that Indian manufactures will succeed.'[27]

Burton, like Marx later, was ambivalent about the British presence in India. Both men could agree that progress was necessary to destroy such abominations as the worship of Hanuman the monkey-god, but both deplored the ruthless economic exploitation that accompanied the 'civilising' process. Yet Burton on his travels as 'Mirza Abdullah' had seen enough to convince him that a general uprising of Indians against the British was all but inevitable and would not be long delayed. In a word, he foresaw and predicted the Indian Mutiny. Yet it remained his firm conviction that if his compatriots had truly understood the Hindu mind, they could have avoided the sanguinary massacres of Delhi and Cawnpore in 1857.[28]

Yet of all the legacies of India Burton took with him into the middle years of his life possibly the most enduring was that of his wounded heterosexuality. Burton records with sorrow and regret that he failed dismally in the amatory arts when it came to satisfying his *bubu* in Gujerat. Indian males were trained from an early age in the arts of love-making, specialising in the relaxation of tension and the delay of ejaculation for as long as twenty minutes, by such methods as the taking of hashish or *bhang*, concentration on counting exercises and mantras, and the interspersal of palpitation with short breaks for the eating of sweetmeats, the chewing of betel-nuts, the drinking of sherbet and even smoking. The entire aim of the 'retaining art' was to avoid overtension of the muscles and so to delay the orgasm of the man and hasten that of the woman. Hardly surprisingly, men who had gained their early experiences in the stews of Europe could not compete with this level of expertise. Hindu women contemptuously compared European males to village-cocks. Defensively Burton countered that the vegetable diet of Indian women made them preternaturally cold and frigid, so that twenty minutes of internal vaginal stimulation was necessary to bring them to spasm.[29]

In his early days with his *bubu* Burton learned something of the astounding muscular control of these women. His mistress had made her muscles prehensile to such a point that she could catch a mosquito between her toes during the throes of intercourse. At first Burton naïvely thought that her jerking and twitching when this occurred was due to his skill as a lover.[30] He soon became a sadder and wiser man, and recorded gloomily: 'While thousands of Europeans have cohabited for years with and have had families by native women they are never loved by them – at least I never knew of a case.'[31]

The trauma caused by his abject failure as heterosexual lover explains the transition to 'romantic' love of women, as in the case of the beautiful Persian in Sind and the Goanese nun. It also sheds light on the sharp bifurcation discernible in Burton's attitude to women in his later Indian years. Increasingly, the females he discusses fall into two groups: there are the fair unattainables, who can be objects of fantasy or day-dreams; and there are the ugly crones onto whom Burton could pour out all the hatred he felt towards women.

It is significant that the sub-prioress in the Goa story was described as 'more like Gujerat ape than mortal man'.[32] This hatred was a compound of his own failure as lover and his consequent conviction that female sexuality was an unquenchable volcano, which if unbridled would subvert the very foundations of civilisation. The most rigid control of women was therefore a universal social imperative.

In disgust and disillusionment Burton turned away from the feminine principle towards the masculine. It is significant that in the seven years in India the two most important women in Burton's life were both indistinct and insubstantial, almost wraith-like in their phantom quality. But the three male influences stand out in bold relief. First there was Walter Scott. Then there was Napier. Finally came the surgeon John Steinhaeuser, whom he met in Karachi in 1845. Steinhaeuser was a devotee of Oriental languages and culture, possessed a substantial collection of Hindu documents and memorabilia, and was the one person in whom Burton could confide his linguistic ambitions. It was Steinhaeuser who first suggested the possibility of a translation of the *Arabian Nights*.[33]

Hand in hand with the greater importance of the masculine principle in the Indian years went an enhancement of the homosexual side of Burton's personality. Burton seemed to enjoy his assignment to the Karachi brothels, which the average male would have shrunk from. More seriously, it seems a reasonable inference that Burton could not have obtained his detailed knowledge of the more lubricious varieties without participating himself.

Other pointers in Burton's life tend in the same direction. Burton devotes fifty pages to homosexuality in the terminal *Arabian Nights* essay. In no way does this detailed treatment seem justified by the subject's meagre place in the stories themselves. Burton was one of those who took delight in pointing up the widespread incidence of homosexuality in history. Among his list of those who were devotees of '*le vice*' are Alexander the Great, Julius Caesar, Napoleon, Henry III and Louis XIII of France, Frederick the Great, Charles II and III of Parma, Peter the Great, William III of the Low Countries, Shakespeare, Molière, Sainte-Beuve and the great Condé.[34]

There is also a sado-masochistic element in Burton's stories and fantasies of homosexual rape. Against the hoary old chestnut that no man (or woman) can be penetrated unwillingly, Burton cites the following prescription from a Persian acquaintance (to Burton both Turks and Persians are 'born pederasts'): 'Ah! we Persians know a trick to get over that: we apply a sharpened tent-peg to the crupper-bone (*os coccygis*) and knock till he opens.'[35] One of Burton's fantasies was that he had broken into a harem and been buggered as punishment for the 'outrage'. He added to this a T. E. Lawrence-like story of having been bastinadoed by the Turks: 'the first dozen or two strokes I didn't mind too much, but at about the ninetieth the pain was too excruciating for description.'[36]

In some ways the most telling of all the evidence for the strong homosexual streak in Burton's make-up is his invariable preference for the male form over the female as an object of beauty and admiration. Burton frequently reiterates 'the artistic truth that the animal man is handsomer than woman ... the same is 'the general rule throughout creation, for instance the stallion compared with the mare, the cock with the hen.'[37]

The curious thing about the enhanced interest in homosexuality engendered by Burton's seven years in India is that by and large, unlike Persia and Arabia, such deviance was a minority interest there. Burton relates that during the nightmare nine months at Gharrain in 1843–44, where there were no camp-women, only one case of sodomy was reported. In general the Sepoys were horrified and scandalised by the practice.[38]

Burton's début as a writer was *Goa and the Blue Mountains* (1851). If this was meant to take the literary citadels by storm, it was a severe disappointment. Its 120,000 words are virtually a transcription of the diary entries he made during his six months' convalescence in the Portuguese colony in 1847. There is interesting material on the Toda mountain people and their polyandry, there are some highly idiosyncratic asides and gestures, and even some good stabs at irony. Malabar women, it seemed, wore more clothing the 'looser' they were, while 'respectable' females went naked to the waist. *Memsahibs* employing these women tried in vain to get them to change to the contrary European mode, 'but the proposal has generally been met pretty much in the same spirit which would be displayed were the converse suggested to an Englishwoman.'[39]

Yet Burton's first book is a stolid piece of unprofessional work. He was most emphatically of the school that believes in 'putting everything in'. The ingredients for a successful recipe are here, but the author is an inexpert cook. There is no editing in the modern sense, to achieve pace, rhythm or cohesion. The level of readability and the intrinsic interest of the contents is wildly uneven. In the twentieth century the script would have been returned by the publisher as a promising apprentice piece. In the much easier publishing climate of the early 1850s, when the appetite for travel books was keen, Burton's undigested diary was accepted. But the critics were on it in a trice. 'The book before us is a curious piece of patchwork, made up of the most heterogeneous materials. Here and there, the slang and persiflage are carried to an extreme which borders on the offensive; at other times, there is a succession of pages where the writer, laying aside his exaggeration and his boisterousness, permits himself to use those faculties of close and graphic observation which he certainly possesses – and these passages are the most valuable in the volume.'[40]

Scinde; or the Unhappy Valley, published later in the same year, marked an improvement, though again the refusal of the author to fashion, mould or hone his raw diary material was evident; so too was the erratic prose style. The improvement was accounted for largely by the conventional travel-writing format. A new but by no means desirable characteristic of this work was a patent disdain for the common reader: Burton at one point referred him to a dictionary if he was too ignorant to know the meaning of an obscure word.[41]

Sindh, and the Races that Inhabit the Valley of the Indus (1851), his third book, was long-term the most successful of Burton's Indian quartet. It was a brilliant, scholarly, imaginative work of ethnology – the work that first revealed Burton as a highly talented anthropologist. But once again Burton proved a poor craftsman. The notes and addenda were as lengthy as the main text and bade fair to take over, in the manner of Flann O'Brien's *Third Policeman*. This would not have been so bad, had not the main text contained the superficial trivia, and the marginalia the pure gold. Clearly the two strands should have been integrated, with the material in the notes worked into the text, but Burton wrote too fast, was bored with revisions, and never worked on more than a single draft.

Falconry in the Valley of the Indus was a technical treatise of hunting birds, relieved only by the 'Mirza Abdullah' anecdotes at the end. Yet in his notes Burton first displayed his later characteristic literary combativeness. He lashed out at all the critics of his previous books, implying that they were dishonest or incompetent ('knaves or fools' was a favourite Burton 'either – or'). He took a gleeful delight in catching out his tormentors on a point of fact, as when a scoffing reviewer had ridiculed a tale of the killing of a falcon by an eagle – a story Burton was able to prove true.[42]

Burton had many faults as a writer, few of which he ever overcame. There is little sense of progression or improvement in his massive *oeuvre* of travel-writing (forty-three volumes). The same kinds of blemishes that disfigured the early Indian quartet are still observable in late works like *The Land of Midian* or *To the Gold Coast for Gold*. He should have reduced most of his books to a quarter of their length. As it was, laid one on top of the other they made a pile eight feet high. Only the most singular adventures could sustain this weight of words. So, not surprisingly, Burton's best volumes are those describing his three most important adventures: to Mecca, to Harar, and to Central Africa. His prolixity was made worse by a pedantry in the citation of his sources and in the use of footnotes of excessive length. In defence of Burton it has to be said that he was only secondarily a writer. Unlike Kinglake and Doughty, who were amateur travellers and professional romantics and who largely followed well-worn paths in their travels, Burton was both a professional explorer *and* a genuine trail-blazer. Arguably his critics were disingenuous. Nothing succeeds like success. His later books were not essentially different from his earlier ones, but by that time Burton's worldwide fame dictated a certain caution, if not downright silence, in his reviewers. So we find lavish praise being bestowed on the selfsame methodology that had drawn the withering fire of critics of his earlier books.[43]

There is very little point in pretending that Burton's rococo prose style is not a serious strike against him, however much his hagiographers splutter.[44] Burton cannot even sustain his best mode, that of sensuous writing, without lurching into cynicism. A characteristic Burton method is to provide a lyrical description of, say, the desert, then cap it with some brutally dismissive or throwaway sardonic remark about the beauty he has just described, almost as if he despises his own positive responses to nature. But the love of paradox for its own sake is not the only problem. Burton aims for so many different targets and employs so many different styles within a single book that his prose displays oceanic troughs and peaks, plummeting from the outstanding to the atrocious within a single page. Burton never solved the problem of literary coherence. He always essayed several genres at once without ever opting for any one of them. His prose hints at irresolution and evasion, the desire not to be pinned down, always to wear a mask. The instability of attitude and 'voice' in Burton's writing is one of the clearest indications of the fragmented identity of the writer. Burton's tortured psyche often speaks straight from the printed page.[45]

5

In Limbo

BURTON arrived back in London at 2 a.m. on a September morning in 1849. He stayed for a few days with an aunt, attended to some family business, then left England to join his family in Pisa where he found his mother and father in their usual valetudinarian state. His sister Maria was with them, with her two daughters. In 1845 she had made a good match with Lieutenant-General Sir Henry William Stisted, but had opted to remain with her parents in Italy rather than face the rigours of military life in India with her husband. Her fondness for Richard was as pronounced as ever, and it was needed. Burton was suffering from severe depression.[1]

Burton and Maria eventually returned to their aunt's house in London, where his leave situation was put on a regular footing after a medical examination at East India Company Headquarters. The investigating physician found that his ophthalmia had not completely vanished. Additionally, he was suffering from the after-effects of Indian fevers, and there were traces of bronchitis and other chest infections, liver trouble and inflammation of the bladder. There was no doubt that Burton was a very ill man. He was granted indefinite sick-leave. Subject to occasional medical examinations, he was on full pay (but excluding the lucrative overseas allowances) and free to travel around Europe in search of spas and springs to help him recuperate fully.

After the scandal over the Karachi brothel report, the Bombay government was in any case in no particular hurry to have Burton back in India. He remained in the service of 'John Company' another eleven years, but never served in India again. Some men would have embraced the enforced leisure eagerly, but not Burton. Almost his first attempt at literature, even before writing *Goa and the Blue Mountains*, was to send an unsolicited report to the East India Company, full of the most trenchant criticism of the Company's administration in India. This was the first of many notable self-destructive acts.

Early 1850 saw Burton wandering aimlessly from the seaside at Dover to the spas of Leamington and Malvern in search of better health. His thoughts were now turning to a mate; his Indian experiences had convinced him of the evil consequences of celibacy.[2] He had a brief flirtation with his cousin Elizabeth, whom he found a pale epigone of the Persian girl in Sind. She was willing enough to marry, but her parents opposed the match on the grounds of Burton's status as an impecunious Bombay officer, rich in neither income nor in prospects. Love and marriage were to Burton, as to many Victorians, things apart and he would certainly have settled for her. He dedicated his first book to her with 'gratitude and affection' for her 'friendly suggestions'.

Disillusioned by the barriers to his advancement in English society, Burton showed himself a chip off the paternal block by choosing the easier option of life in an expatriate colony. He chose Boulogne for the size of its English community and easy access across the Channel. Alarmed by this eremitic lifestyle, both his sister and mother joined him there. Some men might have been touched by this evidence of feminine concern. After all, his mother was prepared to leave his father in Pisa for his sake, and Maria was willing to accept the more pinched and straitened economic circumstances of Boulogne rather than her father's house in Pisa or a position as a general's consort in India. But Burton evinced no gratitude for this homemaking. He dismissed his time with his mother and sister as 'four years' life of European effeminacy'.[3] The implication is that the two women cramped his style and denied his maleness. Clearly their presence in the same house meant he could not take the French equivalent of a *bubu* and instead would have to frequent brothels. More seriously, their fastidiousness hampered his quest for a marriage partner.

There is something frozen and impotent about Burton in the years 1849–52 that hints at profound depression and a great crisis in his life. The meek cohabitation with his mother and sister, so different from his restlessness and wanderlust of later years, coupled with his frenzied search for a marriage partner, suggest a determined attempt to solve his own true sexual identity and, in particular, to resolve in his own mind what he really felt about women.

According to Georgiana Stisted, Burton had no difficulty attracting eligible young girls and making them fall in love with him. The problem was the eagle-eyed mothers, who at once sniffed out that he was not a man of any means. In any case, his personality was all wrong for the task he set himself. He was eccentric, enigmatic, highly intelligent, a natural rebel and nonconformist. The matrons of Boulogne understood only the banal, the jejune and the ordinary, and – of course – money. To surmount this crippling financial disability, Burton's only chance of success in the Boulogne expatriate marriage market was to inveigle his way into the good books of one of the hawk-eyed matrons. This he refused to do. He would condone lack of intelligence in a pretty face, but he would never kowtow to women who had neither looks nor intelligence to commend them.

This was the root cause of his many failures at courtship in Boulogne. One of his serious flirtations was with 'a very handsome and very fast girl, who had a vulgar middle-class sort of mother'. It so happened that at this time Dr John Steinhaeuser, on leave from India, came to visit him. Burton received a note asking him to call on the girl's mother; he went to the appointment, taking Steinhaeuser as moral support. The woman did not beat about the bush. 'I sent for you, Captain Burton, because I think it my dooty to ask what your intentions are with regard to my daughter?'

Burton put on his childlike face of mock innocence and pretended puzzlement. 'Your dooty, madam?' Then, as if he had suddenly recalled something that enabled him to grasp the situation, he added. 'Alas! madam, strictly dishonourable ... I regret to say, strictly dishonourable!'[4]

A much more serious courtship was that of a young woman called Louisa, later Mrs Segrave. This was the nearest Burton came to 'true love' in Europe. Louisa was beautiful and besotted with Burton, but once again his poverty and poor prospects defeated him. In his autobiographical *Stone-Talk* Burton gives us an oblique view of the doomed relationship.

> I loved a maid; how deep that love
> The long course of a life may prove.
> What hours of happiness they were,
> Passed in that dearest presence, ere
> Harsh poverty and cursed pride
> Combined to drive me from her side
> And sent me forth to win a name,
> The trinket wealth, the bauble fame!

But in September 1850 Burton came face to face with his marital destiny, though nearly ten years stretched ahead between first meeting and eventual wedlock. Burton's favourite place to stroll in Boulogne was the city ramparts. Here he would stride out in a black, short, shaggy coat, with a sword-stick slung across his shoulder as if he were on guard. His dark hair, sallow weather-beaten skin, beetling eyebrows, enormous black moustache and determined mouth and chin made him look like Othello and the Three Musketeers rolled into one.[5] In India and aboard ship to and from England he had perfected the art of sitting at table and paralysing his companions with diabolical frownings and gruesome rollings of his eyes. This mesmeric art was not used on bumptious males alone. He liked to encounter pretty girls and stare them down with his demonic eye-rolling and mock-Satanism of physical appearance.

One day he met two unchaperoned sisters taking the air along the ramparts. One of them was a square-jawed tall young woman with blue eyes, thick brown hair and thin, warmly smiling lips. Since the girls were on their own, Burton had an exceptionally good opportunity for his basilisk-eye staring. The tall girl who met and held his gaze, Isabel Arundell, described the fierce penetrating stare as like the burning eyes of a wild beast or the unblinking, baleful glare of a venomous serpent. 'He had a fierce, proud, melancholy expression, and when he smiled, he smiled as though it hurt him, and looked with impatient contempt at things generally ... He looked at me as though he read me through and through in a moment, and started a little. I was completely magnetized, and when he had got a little distance away I turned to my sister, and whispered to her, "That man will marry me".'[6]

Next day they met again and Burton scrawled on the rampart wall with a piece of chalk. 'May I speak to you?' He laid down the chalk for Isabel to respond. She picked it up and wrote: 'No, mother will be angry.' The story is Isabel's and so far it is eminently plausible. But she at once reveals herself as a fantasist and myth-maker by adding: 'And mother found it and *was* angry and after that we were stricter prisoners than ever.'[7] Singular mother, who could find and recognise her daughter's individual hand in a chalked-up wall message!

But the paths of Isabel and Richard crossed many times in Boulogne. His great English love Louisa was a cousin of Isabel's, and in time she introduced her dashing Indian captain formally. Isabel went to extraordinary lengths to locate herself on the ramparts when Burton took his constitutional – for it seems he was as regular in the hours of his daily walks as Kant at Königsberg. She listened to his voice, treasured every word he spoke, and evolved an elaborate fantasy about Burton as the man of her life. Like many women in rebellion at the mould Victorian society insisted on fixing them in, she secretly wished to be a man. 'If I were a man, I would wish to be Richard Burton. But as I am a woman, I wish to be Richard Burton's wife.'

The meeting with Burton was for Isabel the climax of a sustained fantasy about a male beau ideal she had entertained ever since she first came to terms with her dissatisfaction and regret at being female. She detested the contemporary repressive attitude to women, but was on a tight social rein, so indulged her 'rebellion' in small ways, like smoking cigars with her sisters. Constantly she chafed at the anatomical destiny of women. 'I feel that we women simply are born, marry and die. Who misses us? Why should we not have some useful, active life? Why, with spirits, brains and energies are women to exist upon wasted work and household accounts. It makes me sick and I will not do it.'[8]

The appearance of Richard Burton on the Boulogne ramparts was the answer to Isabel's dreams in a more profound sense than that usually connoted by the cliché phrase. In the first place, the physical appearance of Burton was the exact one she had imagined for her 'dream lover'. 'My ideal is about six feet in height; he has not an ounce of fat on him; he has broad and muscular shoulders, a powerful, deep chest; he is a Hercules of manly strength. He has black hair, a brown complexion, a clever forehead, sagacious eyebrows, large black wondrous eyes ... he is a soldier and a *man*; he is accustomed to command and to be obeyed ... He is a gentleman in every sense of the word. His religion is like my own, free liberal and generous minded ... Such a man only will I wed ... But if I find such a man, and afterwards discover he is not for me, then I will never marry ... I will become a sister of charity of St Vincent de Paul.'[9]

As a matter of fact, Burton's religion was not at all like hers, since Burton fundamentally despised religion as a popular opiate, while Isabel was a scion of the old English Catholic aristocratic family, the Arundells. But Isabel was always prepared to make room in her Catholicism for outlandish superstition: phrenology, palmistry, astrology, spiritualism. At this level there was a meeting of minds between her and Burton. Isabel's superstition was especially important in her fantasy of romance with Burton. Not only did she at once perceive Burton as a man with gypsy blood; the Romany tradition was also important to her in a deeper sense, since her 'destiny' had been foretold by a gypsy woman called Hagar, whose surname was the same as Richard's. When she was a child and friendly with the 'didakoi', Hagar Burton had drawn her horoscope and made the following prediction: 'You will cross the sea, and be in the same town with your Destiny and know it not. Every obstacle will rise up against you, and such a combination of circumstances, that it will require all your courage, energy and intelligence to meet them ... You will bear the name of our tribe, and be right proud of it. You will be as we are, but far greater than we. Your life is all wandering, change and adventure. One soul in two bodies in life or death, never long apart. Show this to the man you take for your husband.'

It is easy to accuse Isabel of ex-post rationalisation and retrospective rewriting of history. She was well capable of this; like all fantasists, her future husband included, she regarded truth in the Humpty-Dumpty way – it was whatever she said it was. But there is one hard fact that gives substance to her romantic story and makes one admire the mixture of ruthlessness and monomaniac idealism with which she pursued her destiny. When she met Burton on the Boulogne ramparts she was already in danger of being consigned to the shelf as an old maid. In the early 1850s nineteen was considered perilously old for a would-be wife and mother, in a context where average female life expectancy was no longer than forty years. Most eligible girls were married by then. Those who came to Boulogne for husbands were self-confessedly the ones who had already failed in the first round of the cattle market – the 'coming-out' season in London. It took courage for Isabel to face the dismal prospect of spinsterhood and hang on into her twenties in hopes of eventually marrying Burton.

In time the Arundell family moved back to London, while Burton stayed in Boulogne. Isabel's hopes must have seemed very slender, but with her unquenchable belief in the destiny foretold by Hagar Burton she did not lose heart. For the next four years, until her next meeting with Richard, she turned aside all her parents' queries about her intended status by reference to her submission to God's will – in her own Catholic terms a near-blasphemous statement, since the only will involved was her own.

Burton, meanwhile, exhibited the dialectical course between hetero-sexuality and homosexuality that was ever to distinguish his psyche. He bounced back from his immersion in the world of the female marriage market by stressing the importance of the masculine principle in a number of different ways. First there was reinforcement of the bond with Steinhaeuser – and it is surely significant that his great friend accompanied him to the abortive and risible interview with the woman with the sense of 'dooty'. Even more significant was the thriving relationship with Foster Fitzgerald Arbuthnot, yet another of Burton's substitutes for Edward. Twelve years Burton's junior, Arbuthnot adored and idolised Burton. Burton for his part saw in the younger man sweetness and amiability combined with determination. In later years Arbuthnot was to take up Burton's mantle as interpreter of the world of Persia and the Sufis to the western world.[10]

The third main way Burton leavened the feminine world of his mother, sister and girlfriends was through the martial arts. He continued to fence under the great European masters, this time M. Constantin, who conferred on him the cherished title of *Maître d'Armes*. Burton was a fearless and formidable opponent in the ring. Preferring the sabre to the *epée*, he combined the cut and thrust technique of traditional sabering with the subtleties of rapier play.

On one occasion, he refused to don a mask and then took on the local French champion, a sergeant of hussars, disarming him on each occasion in seven subsequent bouts. The sergeant eventually became alarmed at the courage and recklessness of his opponent. He foresaw that one of them, and possibly both, might well soon take a mortal or disabling wound; he therefore withdrew from any further clashes with the 'mad Englishman' by pleading a dislocated wrist.[11]

Burton never denied that there was an erotic significance in weaponry. The phallicism of the sword was obvious, but in talking of the bow Burton claimed that its invention was the first crucial evidence of a distinction made between human weapons and bestial arms. Like the hymen of virginity, it proved a difference of degree, if not kind, between Man and the so-called lower animals.[12]

At a more practical level, Burton's obsession with killing weapons soon revealed that there was resistance to his ideas in government circles even when the ideas were at their most coldly practical. Bayonets had been invented at the end of the seventeenth century and, despite exaggerated claims for their efficacy in the battle of Culloden (1746), they were still a neglected part of the infantryman's equipment. Burton thought that with proper training the British soldier could be taught to use the bayonet in hand-to-hand fighting much as if it were an elongated sword. He produced another of his unsolicited assaults on official incompetence in the form of a thirty-six-page pamphlet, the *Complete System of Bayonet Exercise*. As with the forecast of the Indian Mutiny in his political report to the East India Company, this extremely valuable guide to killing in close combat met a cold reception in England. Burton's superiors expressed surprise at his impertinence in presuming to teach them the art of war. More astute military experts, such as the Prussians, saw the value of the pamphlet and bought it in large numbers.

Only after the fiasco of the Crimean War had revealed the ineptitude of the British infantryman did a War Office bureaucrat take the report from the shelves, dust it down and on perusal find that it contained excellent material. To cover the evidence of their previous myopia, the War Office advised the Treasury to issue a letter of thanks to Burton, together with an honorarium of a shilling for his sterling services to the Crown. This was the equivalent of 'contemptuous damages' in a lawsuit, but Burton turned the contempt back on his superiors by appearing in person at the War Office to draw his shilling. As he left, he met a beggar and handed over his 'emolument'. 'Lord love yer, sir', said the beggar. 'No, my man, I don't exactly expect Him to do *that*', Burton replied waggishly. He was not wrong. If God had Chosen Ones, Richard Francis Burton was certainly never among their number.

By the age of thirty-two Burton had a clearcut intellectual profile. His ideas, values and attitudes did not change significantly during the rest of his life. Languages were always the lodestone by which he steered. Not a day passed without time being spent reading in at least one of the two dozen or so languages he had mastered.

Burton's likes and dislikes were always very clear in all areas, ranging from the nugatory and the ephemeral to those of political theory and abstract thought. Though he had never mastered a musical instrument himself, he had the linguist's ear for music, so that a false note jarred with him as much as a wrong agreement or a misused tense. For this reason he could never abide the amateur music-making of country house weekends. His 'all or nothing' posture comes through in his gastronomic tastes: he liked either the finest cuisine or the simplest home cooking, detesting the pretentious middle-range menus preferred by so many inns and hotels. His favourite delicacy was sucking pig. He was allergic to honey. His daily alcoholic intake, except when bingeing, was three ounces of whisky and water, apart from wine to accompany meals. His favourite wine was port. Among Burton's other foibles were a pronounced distaste for the idea of cremation, and a 'bankroll under mattress' type of *naïveté* which led him to stash away the small profits of his writing in jars, until the boyfriend of one of his cooks stole £18 thus secreted and brought the distrust of banks to an end. Another characteristic Burton touch – reflecting his belief in *mens sana in corpore sano* – was forever to carry with him on his walks an iron walking stick as heavy as a gun, so that his biceps were always exercised.

Personal relations were always difficult for Burton. Here again it was all or nothing, since those who met him either loved or loathed him. He was at his most relaxed with those who presented no threat to him: servants, members of 'inferior' races, children. As with many people of autocratic temperament, he had a special affinity with animals. But with adults of his own class and race he made either staunch friends or bitter enemies – there were no half measures in anything to do with Burton. Like his hero Byron, he liked to paint himself blacker than he really was, and to affect vices as other men affected virtues. 'I'm proud to say that I have committed every sin in the Decalogue,' was a characteristic opening gambit.[13] He loved to shock and chaff, and told tall tales just to see the effect on his audience. A lover of paradox, he would toy with an audience to see how they reacted to his devil's advocacy. A favourite yarn was about how he had been shipwrecked and forced to eat a fellow human out of desperation. He would watch with satisfaction as people's eyes opened and their mouths gaped with stupefaction. Then he would bring the story to an abrupt end, 'leaving his hearers in a most unsatisfactory state of mind as to the denouement of the unfinished narrative.' He was able to play with his audience so readily because he was a master raconteur. When he chose to unfold the full array of his wit, charm and humour, he could mesmerise an audience. A dinner-party when Burton was on form was unlikely to break up before dawn.[14]

Burton's unpredictability at social occasions was notorious, and it was impossible to know whether on a given evening it would be the charming raconteur or the dour curmudgeon on display. If Burton was bored or depressed, he would openly read a book or a newspaper, whatever the company, and even walk out without a word of apology if the fancy took him. This was part of his capacity to shock; the other part lay in his blunt determination to call a spade a spade and to spare nobody's feelings. Sometimes his friends defended him from the charge of being boorish or a mere paradox-monger. Frank Harris, himself a supreme fantasist, claimed that Burton's intention was not to *épater les bourgeois*, but something more original: 'the freedom of speech he used deliberately, not to shock England but to teach England that only by absolute freedom of speech and thought could she ever come to be worthy of her heritage.'[15]

The public saw only the outrageous behaviour, the irreverent and iconoclastic wit, the prickliness and arrogance of 'Ruffian Dick'. But in private his intimates saw another side of Burton, where melancholy, tenderness and pathos were uppermost. His great friend Verney Lovett Cameron, the African explorer, said that underneath the sarcasm and cynicism was a heart as tender as a woman's. Frank Harris agreed: 'Burton's laughter had in it something of sadness.'[16] These two exaggerated aspects of Burton were part of the duality he often referred to. Some interpreted it as manic-depression; others, more plausibly, argued for a fundamental fragmentation of identity. Swinburne found Burton at once divine and demonic. Arthur Symons remarked that Burton had the jaw of a devil and the brow of a God.[17]

Even Burton's handwriting hinted at this ambiguity. It had two characteristics: illegibility and fragmentation. Swinburne once said that he had known many outstanding hands – he mentioned those of Browning, Dante Gabriel Rossetti and Matthew Arnold – but that only two counted as execrable: Burton's and Lord Houghton's (significantly, a friend of Burton's and a sharer in his passion for arcane sexology).[18] No one who has struggled to read Burton's minuscule hand would dissent from the judgement. Graphologists would have a hard time with African explorers, for their handwriting style was as various as the Continent itself. Thus Livingstone and Speke possessed somewhat childlike, though reasonably legible, hands while Stanley's writing is a model of clarity and instant readability. In Burton's case we encounter a hand so tiny and crabbed as to elicit the suspicion that even in this area Burton was being secretive, as if to lay out his thoughts clearly would give too much away. The other curious aspect of Burton's hand was the way he would split or fragment words: so 'con tradict', for example, for 'contradict'. This has sometimes been attributed to his partiality for Arabic, where such 'tmesis' occurs. Yet this is scarcely an argument that can be adduced seriously in the case of a great linguist.

More likely, the division and fragmentation in Burton's personality extended even to the realms of calligraphy.

Burton was a pessimist about his fellow-man, and this led him to embrace political stances of the most reactionary and hardline kind. He had no qualms about the ultimate penalty, and thought that all punishment should be severe: hefty fines for the rich and corporal chastisement for the poor.[19] The reactionary temper of his views is clear from a statement on policing: 'Perhaps if the police of civilised England were backed by the powers that be in the same way that the *Zaotiyeh* is protected in barbarous Turkey, we might have less of Fenians, Bradlaugh, Beales, park-rioters and other treasonable demagogues.'[20] For Burton force and power were always the triumphant principles. He was an unregenerate social Darwinist and quoted with approval the watchword of Carlyle: 'Nature herself is umpire and can do no wrong.'[21]

He detested egalitarianism and socialism and hated even more the 'humbug' of humanitarians and missionaries. He saw the contemporary 'English disease' as being the consequence of a kind of social despotism which was the checking mechanism to balance what he saw as a 'rage for equality' among people and classes born radically unequal. 'Her [England's] state is essentially empirical and transitional, she sits between two stools; the old aristocratic rule which since 1832 has been broken up, not broken down, and a young democracy whose years have not yet brought it stamina to carry the weight.'[22] In England people were constrained in artificial ways by this twin incubus, which accounted for much of the outlandish and vulgar behaviour of the expatriate British in India, when they were freed from such fetters. In England the aristocratic tradition was a function of primogeniture. A closed élite ensured that the younger scions of the aristocracy could secure places and positions. The inevitable result was a 'cult of the amateur', which set Britain at a disadvantage *vis-à-vis* France and Germany. But at least the aristocratic tradition provided a bulwark against the horrors of untrammelled equality. In the United States, 'the home of all cant', the illiterate and newly-drafted ranker thought himself every bit as good as the general who had been educated at West Point and had twenty-five years' experience behind him. For Burton 'democracy' was always synonymous with 'mediocrity'.[23]

In a word, Burton's quarrel with the British social system was not that it made obeisance to 'equality' but that its defence against it choked off all possibility of meritocracy. This meant that Burton and other Nietzschean 'supermen' were the real losers, condemned to waste their intellectual fragrance on the desert air of philistine England. 'In our day when we live under a despotism of the lower middle-class, philisters can pardon anything but superiority.' Burton detested the smugness, ignorance and arrogance of the British ruling class, its incompetence and laziness, refusal to learn foreign languages or ever to master any subject properly, even the administration of its subject peoples. He spoke with the utmost contempt of Lord Dufferin, sometime ambassador to Egypt, who actually boasted of the fact that he spoke not a single word of Arabic.[24] One of Burton's 'party turns' was to pose the riddle: why are Egyptian donkey boys so favourable to the English? Answer: because we hire more asses than any other nation. Burton was a professional, dedicated and thorough in everything he turned his hand to, whether languages, anthropology or the military arts, and it was professionalism that he admired. If only England had a military ethos like that of the Prussians, or an imperial administration like that of the French, was the burden of his lament.

Burton was a convinced imperialist in that he really did think it the function of the white races to rescue their benighted other-coloured brethren from the world of chaos and darkness. He was prepared to follow the logic of this posture even when it meant the ultimate destruction of his beloved nomad races, like the Bedouin. What he objected to was the idea that bungling amateurs from England could do this work without a high degree of training. He contrasted the 'Quaker-like peacefulness' and amateurism of England with the imperial policy of France, which sent its best men to the colonies and was prepared to show its military teeth from the outset. For this reason the French were preferred to the English as rulers in Egypt, as the indigenous inhabitants recognised France's superior diplomatic skills.[25] Only Germany, with its rash policy of Teutonisation under Bismarck, appeared to worse advantage than England as a colonial power. The sole 'plus' in the British ledger was their undoubted commitment to justice and fair play. But in general, Britain's great potential was vitiated by its amateurishness. 'Did not Voltaire think and declare that, of all the ways of Providence, nothing is so inscrutable as the littleness of the minds that control the destiny of great nations?'[26]

In his reflections on international affairs, Burton revealed himself as a worshipper of power and a despiser of the nationalistic aspirations of small nations. He was emphatically on the side of the big battalions. Despotism, he declared, was the only rule small nations and orientals understood. He accurately predicted the future hegemony of Russia in Europe and China in Asia.[27] And he showed himself sympathetic to the principles that would later be embodied in the sinister doctrine of *Lebensraum*: 'For the anthropologist, one [law] amply suffices. The body politic, like the individual, must grow to attain full development; and "earth-hunger", as it is called, characterises all young peoples in the lusty prime of life.'[28]

For the 'lesser' nations Burton had nothing but contempt. His virulence towards the declining Turkish empire is marked. 'When Turkey promises, suspect a lie; when she swears be sure of a lie. What to her are treaties, save things to be broken? Talk of a treaty between a dog and its fleas!'[29] But his particular animus is reserved for 'troublemaking' nationalism. He bracketed the Magyar with the southern Irish Catholic as two horns of a single ram, characterised by lies, treachery, 'blarney' and self-pity.[30]

Like almost all conservatives of a nostalgic, reactionary stripe, Burton sought inspiration in a mythical 'golden age' in the past. For Burton this was the Middle Ages, when the martial ethos was in full flower, when gentlemen settled disputes by the 'code of honour' and swordsmanship gave victory to the bravest and most skilled. The age of firearms was the technological equivalent of the age of liberalism, since both gave victory to the weak, the cowardly and the mediocre, in one case through guns, in the other through the voting system. Burton's writings are copiously larded with nostalgic laments for the bygone days when his beloved sword was sovereign. '... When the science of war reverted to ballistics, it practically revived the practice of the first ages, and the characteristic attack of the savage and the barbarians who, as a rule, throw their weapons ...[31]

The coming of a modern industrial society caused acute anxiety and trauma to many of the great Victorians, and they sought a return to authentic human roots in a number of different ways. Ruskin, Carlyle, Morris, Kingsley and Matthew Arnold were all in divergent ways preoccupied with the problem. For these men Burton had some respect, even if he disagreed violently with some of their panaceas. His ultimate horror and detestation was reserved for men like Cobden who seemed to personify the industrial *Zeitgeist*. But Burton's false antinomy between industrialism/democracy and chivalry/aristocracy masked all kinds of hidden premisses he had not bothered to tease out. William Morris, for example, showed how democracy, socialism and the best aspects of medieval production could all be reconciled. Here as elsewhere Burton was seriously concerned not so much to solve a pressing issue of social and political theory as to rationalise his own isolation as outsider and rebel.

Yet if Burton despised most of the political ideologies and dispensations of the nineteenth century, his onslaughts on the alleged fatuities of organised religion were even more ferocious. This is a particularly important subject to examine, since it has often been claimed that Burton was a closet Moslem; his wife also later claimed him as a secret Catholic. How wide of the mark both judgements are can readily be demonstrated. But the claims and counter-claims would not have surprised Burton. He had long been convinced that religion elicited in human beings a bubbling, bottomless well of irrationality:

'Ask the stupidest Englishman a question of politics, and he will say something clever; ask the cleverest Englishman a question of religion and he will say something stupid.'[32]

At bottom Burton shared the view, common to Feuerbach, Marx and Freud, that religion was the fantasy of Man afflicted by his own inadequacy, and its function was to enhance hopes and allay fears. Burton was irritated that his beloved Islam should have taken over the Judaic notion of a 'jealous God' – a 'horrible idea' – and he used it as an excuse for an acerbic aside on Jews. Since every race creates God in its own image and likeness, he says, the 'jealous God' alone tells us something significant about Jewry.[33]

Burton's fundamental position was agnosticism, 'An agnostic, who can have no knowledge save that which his senses bring to him, is necessarily a materialist.'[34] But he was prepared to sample and fillet every religion he encountered for *emotional* sustenance. Mysticism, esoteric mysteries and cults for initiates only particularly appealed to him. That was why within Islam it was Sufism that especially attracted him. The Sufi was to Islam what the Gnostic was to Christianity. Yet even though Burton drank deeply of the Persian well and was acknowledged as a Master Sufi, intellectually he held mysticism at arm's length, as the following quotation shows very clearly:

> In Sufistic parlance, the creature is the lover and the creator the beloved: worldly existence is disunion, parting, severance; and the life to come is Reunion. The basis of the idea is the human soul being a *divinae particula aurae,* a disjointed molecule from the Great Spirit imprisoned in a jail of flesh; and it is so far valuable as it has produced a grand and pathetic poetry; but common sense asks, where is the proof? And Reason wants to know, what does it all mean?[35]

Yet Burton was always prepared to make excuses for Eastern religions and to argue for their pragmatic utility in a way he would never do for Christianity. Indeed in his more sombre moods Burton evinced a marked distaste for Christianity. He claimed in one Shavian sally that there had been four great protesters in the history of religion: St Paul who protested against St Peter's Hebraism; Mohammed, who protested against the doctrinal perversity of Christianity; Luther, who protested against the supremacy of the Pope; and Richard Burton, who protested at the whole sorry charade.[36]

Always Burton contrasted Christianity unfavourably with Islam. In theological matters he considered that Arianism and Unitarianism (those aspects of early Christianity taken over by Mohammed) were much to be preferred on grounds of logic to the Athanasianism and Tritheism of Christianity. And he was brutally contemptuous of the deistic approach which saw all religions as confused variants of one essential truth. A visit to Oberammergau later in his life drew the following broadside: 'I found it impossible to draw any parallel between the Passion-play and my three days' pilgrimage at Meccah ... the former is performed by a company of hereditary and professional players; the latter by a moving multitude of devotees.'[37] Of course, part of the explanation for Burton's venom against Christianity can be sought in irritation at his wife's piety. Whenever he was more than normally disillusioned with her, he would draw from his intellectual quiver a barbed arrow to shoot at 'the Nazarene'. One of the things he particularly detested about Catholicism was its array of priests, monks, nuns and other contemplatives. In his view, it was infinitely to the credit of Islam that it did not utilise such hordes of 'drones'. As he once remarked sardonically: 'Moslems, like Catholics, pray for the dead; but as they do the praying themselves instead of paying a priest to do it, their prayers, of course, are of no avail.'[38]

The thinkers of the Enlightenment assumed religion would wither away as science and reason extended their sway. On the contrary, Burton argued, modern man seemed to be going backwards in his religious belief, almost as if he could jettison all his beliefs except the fetishistic part. He jeered at Protestant missionaries who so reverenced the 'cedars of Lebanon' that they sternly forbade travellers to gather cones in the area.[39]

Interestingly, though, it was precisely at the point where religion shaded into superstition that Burton found it most fascinating. His belief in palmistry, numerology, geomancy and phrenology seems bizarre in one who took such a sceptical attitude to organised religion, but again in this he was at once a typical Victorian and a true 'Renaissance Man'. In recent decades historians have come to realise that interest in subjects like astrology, magic and alchemy were not unfortunate aberrations on the fringes of the Renaissance, but central to it and to the belief that Man could master Nature. Figures like Nostradamus and the magus John Dee therefore come to have a much greater significance.

His experience of the East also led him to believe in what were commonly called 'miracles' – in reality preternatural rather than supernatural phenomena. In India, where the thaumaturge was a lesser kind of holy man, miracles were ten a penny. Here again Burton decisively dissented from Enlightenment thought.[40]

Two aspects of 'superstition' particularly interested Burton. One was the significant coincidence – what Jung would later call 'synchronicity'. Burton had many experiences of this. On 10 July 1863, while in West Africa, he read the chapter on earthquakes in the Koran. He later learned that this was the very day that an earthquake had laid waste the town and fort of Accra. On 22 February 1886 at Cannes he began translating the 504th tale, which features an earthquake, in the

Supplement to the Arabian Nights. Next morning a violent earthquake brought devastation to the entire French Riviera.[41]

Spiritualism, the great craze of Victorian England, he found even more intriguing. Into this broad river of superstition many tributaries flowed. The first was a belief in ghosts, 'that queer remnant of fetishism embedded in Christianity'. Here the anthropologist in Burton was aroused, for although Islam did not contain ghosts in its demonology – only phantasmata or jinns and other supernatural creatures – the ghost proper (a soul of a dead person), 'the embodied fear of the dead and of death', was common to most peoples.[42] Burton was for a time an enthusiastic participant in spiritualistic seances. Though the devotees of communion with 'the other side' were keen to claim him as one of their own, Burton kept his intellectual distance. He put the 'medium' on a par with priestcraft in point of charlatanry.

> Spiritualism is only Swedenborgianism systematised and carried into action among the nervous and impressionable races like the Anglo-American. In England it is the reverse; the obtuse sensitiveness of a people bred on beef and beer has made it the 'Religion of the Nineteenth Century', a manner of harmless magic, whose miracles are table-turning and ghost-seeing, whilst the prodigious rascality of its prophets (the so-called Mediums) has brought it into universal disrepute. It has been said that Catholicism must be true to coexist with the priest and it is the same with spiritualism proper, by which I understand the belief in a life beyond the grave, a mere continuation of this life; it flourishes (despite the Medium) chiefly because it has laid before Man the only possible and intelligible idea of a future state.[43]

The hallmark of Burton's personality, in intellectual matters as in everything else, was ambiguity, ambivalence and detachment. The eclecticism of his interests led him into many short-term enthusiasms, from which he always emerged with a few pearls but with many more sardonic strictures on the coterie he had just left behind. Neither Sufism nor Spiritualism could constrain him. He admired Darwin but could not follow the nineteenth century all the way in its worship of science. He was a Romantic who poked fun at most of its major figures, except Byron. He embraced the ideas of the Renaissance up to a point, but turned to Romanticism when the implications of the Renaissance seemed to lead him towards the Enlightenment and the Age of Reason. He admired the 'noble savage' so long as it was his favourite Bedouin, but not if it was an Asiatic or (especially) an African. His knowledge of primitivism did not lead him to a kind of Luddite rejection of Western technology. Far from it: like Stanley he thought that socialism meant a return to primitive conditions before the division of labour, and opposed it for that reason. He was an imperialist while despising most of the people who actually administered the Empire. He sympathised with the underdog as long as he did not commit the ultimate 'impertinence' of claiming equality. He denounced utilitarianism and 'Gradgrindery'; in the *Kasidah* he set out his credo: 'the affection, the sympathies . . . are man's highest enjoyments. Facts, the idlest of superstitions.' From this one might have expected a Sufic or mystical world-view. The exact opposite was the case, according to Frank Harris. 'A child of the mystical East, a master of that Semitic thought which had produced the greatest religions, Burton was astoundingly matter-of-fact. There was no touch of the visionary in him.'[44]

The sampling and sipping of different creeds, cultures and ideologies, as if he were a kind of intellectual wine-taster, points to a central problem about Burton: the lack of a stable identity or a real centre for the personality. In this, as in his talent for mimicry and disguise, his ability to enter into many different roles, and his powerful vocal equipment, Burton had all the natural attributes of a first-class actor. Perhaps this is why, alongside the solid and unimpeachable scholarship, a certain aura of charlatanry always seemed to hover around him. The Burton psyche was comparable to a stretch of rapids, where contradictory currents and cross-cutting eddies foamed and raged at one another in a boiling effervescent mass.

By the 1850s Burton had settled on one fixed point. He was, and remained, a dyed-in-the-wool reactionary. Already his demonology contained socialists, Americans, Turks, Hungarians and the Irish. In the ensuing decades he added blacks, Jews and women to the list. If the term 'fascist' could be used correctly as a predicate of an individual, rather than a political movement (as, indeed, it is in demotic speech), Burton would qualify for the epithet. Like many reactionaries, however, such as Henry Fielding and George Borrow, he had a soft spot for gypsies and was always prepared to put in a spot of special pleading for them.[45] Burton's description of them is remarkably self-reflexive: 'They are expert in disguises . . . remarkably intelligent, and quick, they would make capital spies in an enemy camp.'[46] Yet when the Romanies recognised him as 'one of them' and asked him to be their 'king', Burton declined. This particular Nietzschean superman did not even want a band of acolytes. Such was the degree of his alienation that he preferred to be the perpetual loner. It was no accident that Burton was drawn to desert wildernesses as his favourite habitat, for there he could truly be the Cassandra voice of his generation.

6

Pilgrimage to Mecca

IN the autumn of 1852 Burton's three-year period of hibernation and depression came to an end. It is impossible to retrieve the circumstances that enabled him to return to the world's stage invigorated and ready to do battle again. There is a possible hint in Kinglake's *Eothen* (1844) – the first great classic of Middle Eastern travel: 'I can hardly tell why it should be, but there is a longing for the East very commonly felt by proud people when goaded by sorrow.'[1] But certain it is that in late 1852, while still in Boulogne, he began to lobby strenuously for leave of absence and financial backing for an audacious project he had first dreamed about in India. This was to penetrate the holy city of Mecca in disguise.[2] In a decree in the year AD 629 Mohammed had ruled Mecca out of bounds to all infidels. There had been no relaxation of the rules, and it was still the case in the mid-nineteenth century that any unbeliever caught in the holy places could be executed. In previous centuries many interlopers had been impaled or crucified. According to the Islamic canon, death could be avoided by an offer of circumcision and conversion repeated thrice.

Burton has sometimes been accused of exaggerating the risks attaching to the clandestine pilgrimage he proposed to make, and it is true that by 1853 there was a reasonable expectation that if the *authorities* apprehended a 'Frank' in their sacred places, they would be likely to expel the intruder rather than execute him or offer him the choice of circumcision and conversion. But the expectation of 'due process' on discovery was unreasonable. Almost certainly the offender would be despatched on the spot. As Burton noted: 'The first Badawi who caught sight of the Frank's hat would not deem himself a man if he did not drive a bullet through the wearer's head.'[3]

The only feasible time for an impostor to enter Mecca was during the traditional pilgrimage season when the *hajis* (pilgrims) made their way to the holy city in their tens of thousands from all corners of the

Islamic world. There were three main caravans as well as dozens of individual shipboard voyages. The Damascus caravan, which averaged 40,000 *hajis* in the sixteenth century, started from Constantinople, swept in human tributaries as it wound through the Turkish hinterland, and collected pilgrims from Moslem Central Asia before halting at Damascus. From Damascus there was a traditional forty-day journey across the Syrian and Nafud deserts to Medina. The Cairo caravan gathered up all the contingents from North Africa before a forty-day journey across the Sinai desert and the Hejaz mountains. The Baghdad caravan catered for the huge influx of Shiites from Persia.[4]

It is important to be clear exactly what Burton's intentions were. He aimed to be the *first unconverted Englishman* to visit Mecca of his own free will, posing as a true Mohammedan pilgrim. Englishmen had been to Mecca before him but only as announced Islamic converts, or under duress. Also, Europeans of other nationalities had penetrated the holy city in disguise, most notably the Swiss Arabist Johann Ludwig Burckhardt in 1814.[5] By visiting Medina as well, Burton hoped to establish himself in the smaller group of Europeans who had visited both the holy cities.[6] To achieve his ambitions, he took the controversial decision to travel to Mecca in disguise rather than to feign a conversion to Islam. Not only would a new convert be watched closely for any signs of insincerity; the inmost secrets of Islam, such as the interior of the Kaabah were unlikely to be revealed to him. In any case, he felt that a pretended conversion was beneath his dignity.[7] Later Arabian travellers, critical or jealous of Burton, maintained that it was travelling in disguise that was the undignified course. Charles Doughty, who made it a point of honour to attest to his Christianity in the face of Arab threats, chafed at the obstacle to a visit to Mecca posed by his own 'integrity', and declared that the British Empire should be prepared to protect all Christians who wanted to visit the holy city.[8]

The journey to Mecca apart, it was Burton's ambition to establish himself as the undisputed authority on Arabia.[9] His aim was sponsorship by the Royal Geographical Society, 'for the purpose of removing that opprobrium of modern adventure, the huge white blot which in our maps still notes the Eastern and Central regions of Arabia.' He also somewhat opportunistically tried to enlist the help of the Church Missionary Society, by offering to further their aims in Arabia in 'whatever way he could'.[10] This was a dead-end. The Church Missionary Society knew better than to have proselytising aims in the heartland of Islam. Yet even with the sponsorship of the RGS he would need three years to fill in the blank map of the 'Empty Quarter' of Arabia. In bad odour as he was with the East India Company, such an extended leave of absence seemed unlikely to be granted.

Nevertheless, his powerful patrons did their best. Sir Roderick Murchison, the President of the RGS, and Burton's influential backer and friend Dr Norton Shaw, went with him to the offices of the East India Company to plead his case. But the chairman of the East India directors was the selfsame Sir James Hogg who a year before had been angered by Burton's injudicious criticisms of Company policy in India. Reluctantly he granted a mere year's leave: so Burton could not afford to dally.[11] He was compelled to cut corners in his last-minute preparations. Fortunately, anticipating permission, he had spent the winter of 1852 in Cairo and Aden with his friend John Frederick Steinhaeuser. In Cairo and Alexandria he tried out his intended disguise as a dervish; he found that his outfit brought him nothing but contempt from sophisticated Arabs, but at least they seemed to accept him for what he purported to be. Then he travelled to Aden to spend Christmas with Steinhaeuser. The two discussed a project for the complete translation of the *Arabian Nights*, with Burton tackling the verse while his friend concentrated on the prose.[12]

For such a gifted linguist, honing Arabic to the right pitch was no problem. The more difficult task was habituating himself to think, move, feel and breathe like an Arab. He began by having himself circumcised. His observations in India had convinced him that no ill effects could be expected, provided a sensible period of recuperation, some six weeks, was allowed.[13] And now Burton's minute knowledge of the East really paid dividends. A less well-prepared man might have fallen into the trap of being circumcised according to the Jewish rite. The Jewish method involved, first, the stripping off of the foreskin, then tearing and turning back the inner layer to join the outer fold. In this way the external skin did not retract far from the mucous membrane and the healed wound showed a narrow ring of cicatrice. The Islamic method was very different. Muslims did not go in for tearing, but instead sliced off the prepuce, applied styptics to the open edges, then removed the cord. When the integument freely retracted beyond the rim of the glans, they then applied a poultice.[14] Burton also grew a beard, shaved his head, and darkened his skin by staining it with walnut juice.

Having returned briefly to London to order his affairs, Burton embarked on the P. & O. steamer *Bengal* on 4 April 1853 in the guise of a Persian called Bismillah Shah ('King by the Grace of God'). He spent the two-week voyage from Southampton to Cairo thinking himself into the part of a devout Moslem.

> Look, for instance, at that Indian Moslem drinking a glass of water. With us the operation is simple enough, but his performance includes no fewer than five novelties. In the first place he clutches his tumbler as though it were the throat of a foe; secondly he ejaculates, 'In the name of Allah the

> Compassionate, the Merciful!' before wetting his lips; thirdly, he imbibes the contents, swallowing them, not sipping them as he ought to, and ending with a satisfied grunt; fourthly, before setting down the cup, he sighs forth, 'Praise be to Allah!' – of which you will understand the full meaning in the Desert; and fifthly, he replies, 'May Allah make it pleasant to thee!' in answer to his friend's polite 'Pleasurably and health!'[15]

The first test of his Islamic persona came at disembarkation in Alexandria. Most of the beggars at sight of him immediately looked the other way. One youth alone ventured a *Bakshish*, to which he received the 'shut-out' retort *Mafish* ('there is none' or 'I have left my purse at home') which convinced him 'that the sheepskin covered a real sheep'.[16] But although his disguise seemed to be holding up well, once in Egypt he discovered that there were problems about his assumed Persian identity. Persians were widely considered heretics and dissenters; such an identity would load the dice against him. He therefore returned to his old Pathan role of 'Mirza Abdullah' ('the servant of God'), portraying himself as an Afghan doctor brought up in India. For a month he perfected his new identity while staying in a small garden house in the grounds of the home of his friend John Larking, a one-time ally of Burkhardt's.[17] To Larking Burton confided the full extent of his plans.

Burton was a Method actor *avant la lettre*. He did not simply impersonate an Afghan physician; he tried to *become* the man whose identity he had assumed. He began by advertising his skills, and within a month had a flourishing practice. The deception was easy enough, for the Oriental patient was a dupe for nostrums and other quackery, and besides Burton was confident that most eastern sicknesses were variants of one basic: ague. Also, he had a secret weapon in his mastery of hypnosis. He greatly impressed one client by curing two Ethiopian slave-girls of snoring – a habit that much reduced their market value.[18]

But Burton added a further layer to his disguise by assuming the role of 'dervish' – a kind of 'chartered vagabond' recognised by Islamic culture as a suitable role for the socially and psychologically marginal. The dervish could be a disgraced nobleman, a man caught between two worlds, or the kind of psychotic we would diagnose as schizophrenic. The dervish was recognised as being an alienated being so that 'in the hour of imminent danger, he has only to become a maniac and he is safe; a madman in the East, like a notably eccentric character in the West, is allowed to say or do whatever the spirit directs.'[19] The cunning of this combined doctor/dervish persona was that it threw out an inky spoor of confusion. Any give-away slips could be rationalised as the eccentric behaviour of the dervish. On the other hand, the role of doctor would allow Burton to get as close as possible to his abiding interest: Arab women.

There was one problem, however, that he had overlooked. To leave

Egypt 'Mirza Abdullah' required a passport. This in turn meant that he had to undergo indignities when dealing with Egyptian officialdom that were unthinkable for an English officer. Treated as the lowest of the low when he waited in ante-rooms or brushed against a 'sahib' in the street, Burton endured all and consoled himself with the thought that his sufferings were a tribute to the effectiveness of his disguise. It was the payment demanded for the passport that nettled him more:

> That mighty Britain – the mistress of the seas – the ruler of one-sixth of mankind – should charge five shillings to pay for the shadow of her protecting wing. That I cannot speak my modernised '*civis Romanus sum*' without putting my hand into my pocket, in order that these officers of the Great Queen may not take too ruinously from a revenue of seventy millions. O meanness of our magnificence! O littleness of our greatness![20]

Burton remained in Cairo for a month, continuing to build up his reputation as a doctor. He became friendly with Haji Wali, a middle-aged Russian-born Moslem with a business in Alexandria. Wali was invaluable as a guide to Cairo and the Egyptian mind. With his aid Burton was able to enlist an eighteen-year-old Meccan boy to accompany him on the perilous pilgrimage. But Burton severely strained Haji Wali's patience by a roistering relationship with another extrovert 'outsider' – an Albanian army captain named Ali Agha. Agha rashly seized Burton's pistols for inspection on their very first meeting – an action which if sustained from anyone else would have led to an invitation to duel from Burton. But a few days later the Albanian again acted contumaciously, whereat Burton exhibited his skill in wrestling and threw the rambunctious Agha across the room. It took one larger-than-life spirit to recognise another, so after that there was nothing for it but that the two adventurers must carouse together.

One night the back-slapping and quaffing got seriously out of hand. They were drinking inside the compound of partitioned rooms that made up the *caravanserai* where the pilgrims were waiting until the feast of Ramadan was over and they could move on south. Ali Agha began the evening's activities by asking the 'Afghan physician' for 'a little poison that would not lie, to quiet a troublesome enemy'. Burton fobbed him off with five grains of harmless calomel. Next the two men began to match each other drink for drink on *Araki*, an Egyptian brandy. When the devout Haji Wali observed the pair breaking the strict Islamic ordinance against alcoholism, he threatened to call for the police. Ali Agha's response to this was to suggest that he and Burton go in search of some dancing girls. Burton tried to restrain him, but Ali reeled out into the open, crying out, 'O Egyptians! O ye accursed! O genus of pharaoh! O race of dogs!'[21]

Not content with this outburst, he next barged into a room where two couples were asleep, only to retreat in alarm under a barrage of insults from the women. Now baying for blood, and even threatening to make the Egyptian Pasha himself dance for his delectation, Ali Agha tripped over the night porter, whom he then began to pummel for not having looked where he (Ali) was going. Finally Burton and Agha's servant managed to get the drunken Albanian back to his quarters, but not before the entire *caravanserai* was aroused by the commotion. As Burton commented ruefully: 'No Welsh undergraduate at Oxford under similar circumstances ever gave me more trouble.'

Next morning Burton found that news of his antisocial activities had spread and that the lustre he had obtained as an Afghan healer was dimming rapidly. 'You had better start on your pilgrimage at once,' Haji Wali advised him. Burton thought this good advice and set out on the eighty-four-mile trek to Suez. The journey by camel was gruelling. Burton left Cairo at 3 p.m., hoping to be in Suez by nightfall of the following day.

> There is no time for emotion. Not a moment can be spared, even for a retrospect. I kick my dromedary, who steps out into a jog-trot. The Badawin with a loud ringing laugh attempt to give me the go-by. I resist, and we continue like children till the camels are at their speed, though we have eighty miles before us, and above us an atmosphere like a furnace blast. The road is deserted at this hour, otherwise grave Moslem travellers would have believed the police to be nearer than convenient to us.[22]

Burton found Suez a depressing and squalid town. The rooms where they lodged were clammy with dirt, the smokey rafters foul with cobwebs, the floor a battleground for a black confusion of ants, flies and cockroaches. Burton and Mohammed put their kit in order for the harrowing pilgrimage to come. Burton packed a change of clothes, a tent, a goat-skin water bag, a crude Persian rug, a pillow and blanket, a huge yellow cotton umbrella and a mosquito net. Other impedimenta included a toothpick, needle and thread, a dagger, a cache of opium, pistols, an inkstand and pen holder, worry beads, medicine chest, a pocket water purifier, plus £50 in Maria Theresa dollars and £30 in English and Turkish currency, hidden in a leather money-belt. He also took the precaution of spreading some loose change about his person and in the luggage, for if robbed by the Bedouin it was better if he did not arouse their wrath. When balked of finding money or valuables on a traveller's person or among his effects, the desert Arabs were liable to rip open his stomach in the belief that precious items had been swallowed, to be passed out later through the bowel.

During his time in Cairo Burton had practised making notes surreptitiously in a tiny, crabbed, illegible hand and had mastered the art of writing in the dark. He therefore took a supply of pencils and paper, intending to cut up any sketches he made and conceal them in empty medicine bottles. But the other part of his clandestine project faltered when Mohammed reacted so suspiciously towards his master's use of sextant and compass that Burton was obliged to discard them.[23]

On 6 July 1853 Burton sailed from the Sinai peninsula south into the Red Sea on board a two-masted fifty-ton steamer called the *Golden Wire*. Navigational techniques were not much advanced on those of the Ancient World. Without compass, log, chart or spare ropes, and carrying ninety-seven pilgrims on a ship designed to hold a maximum of sixty, the master simply hugged the coast by day and lay-to at night in the first suitable cove. Two bloody brawls took place before the ship was even clear of its moorings. Burton secured himself a desirable niche on the poop while a group of Egyptian thugs cleared it of all other inhabitants. Then a bloody scrimmage developed on the deck below between Syrians and Mahgrebi warriors from the deserts of Tripoli and Tunis. Peace had scarcely been restored when the Mahgrebis took it into their heads to charge the poop and oust the ousters. A hundred-pound earthenware jar, full of water, stood on the edge of the poop. Choosing his moment carefully, Burton toppled the jar over onto the attackers. Drenched and bruised, the Mahgrebis retreated, regrouped, consulted, decided on the better part of valour and sued for peace. Burton and his accomplices were left in triumphant possession.

The twelve-day voyage south ran the gamut of natural perils and privations. Mornings were the pleasantest time but by noon 'all colour melts away with the candescence above' and the sun beat down mercilessly until dusk when 'the enemy sinks . . . under a canopy of gigantic rainbow'. At night the tormented pilgrims would venture out to cook scratch meals of rice and onions in square clay-lined wooden boxes. But the worst hazards were the storms that plagued them all the way down the Red Sea.

Burton found the ordeal all the more testing since it was his custom to smoke opium to see himself through nerve-wracking ventures. But by an oversight his opium supply was packed in the *Golden Wire*'s hold. To make matters worse, Burton's incognito was severely tested by a well-travelled Pathan, who was suspicious of the 'Afghan doctor'.

There were frequent halts during the passage down the Red Sea and at one of these, Burton trod on a sea urchin while wading ashore. The wound became infected and Burton found he could walk only with great pain. This was a bad blow for at Yenbo, reached after twelve days, the pilgrims disembarked, ready for an eight-day, 120-mile journey by camel across the desert to Medina. Limping around the whitewashed domes and minarets of Yenbo, Burton managed to procure a camel with a *shugdug* – a large basket like a litter, normally used for carrying children and old people. Camels were also procured at three dollars a head for Burton's entourage, for by now he had acquired a second servant – an Indian Moslem called Shayhk Nur – and had many friends among the wild Egyptians with whom he had shared the poop on the *Golden Wire*.

On 18 July the column of pilgrims headed east, with the sea on their right and the mountains of Radwah on the left. The party consisted of twelve camels; they travelled in Indian file, head tied to tail with just one outrider. Setting out at dusk, they marched eight hours until 3 a.m., slept, rose at 9 a.m., then lit fires for breakfast and the inevitable communal smoke. Breakfast was biscuit, a little rice and a cup of milkless tea. Then they would sleep through the worst heat of the day until 2 p.m. when they dined. Dinner was boiled rice and butter, soft biscuit, stale bread and date-paste. They drank huge quantities of *akit* – dried sour milk dissolved in water. Occasionally Burton was able to beg a cupful of milk from a passing Bedouin woman, for Arab custom allowed all travellers to beg milk freely. The *sale* of milk was considered beneath contempt – *labban* ('milk-seller') was used in Arabic as a term of abuse.[24] Conditions in the desert were gruelling.

> On the south was a strip of bright blue sea, and all around, an iron plain producing naught but stones and grasshoppers, and bounded northward by a grisly wall of blackish rock. Here and there a shrub fit only for fuel, or a tuft of coarse grass, crisp with heat, met the eye. All was sun-parched; the furious heat from above was drying up the sap and juice of the land, as the simmering and quivering atmosphere showed; moreover the heavy dews of these regions, forming in large drops upon the plants and stones, concentrate the morning rays upon them like a system of burning-glasses. After making these few observations I followed the example of my companions and returned to sleep.[25]

On they pressed, through the villages of Al-Hamira and Bir Abbas, linking up *en route* with a larger party of two hundred camels, their riders looking like 'contrabandistas of the Pyrenees'. They trudged along under a steel-blue sky tinged with purple, the cruel sun continuing to plague them. More taxing than the burning sun and the desert winds 'like the breath of a volcano' were the bandits and marauding Bedouin who infested this route to Medina. An attempt by thieves to run off with their camels was narrowly foiled. Burton took to sleeping within his *shugduf* since it was madness to lie down to slumber on the open plain in bandit country. Fear of an attack was exacerbated by consideration of the local customs. To wound a robber, even in self-defence, involved the payment of an exorbitant sum in blood-money. To kill a marauder, even to escape one's own death, was to incur a demand for 'eye for eye'.

On the 'Pilgrimage Path' on 24 July, Burton got his first taste of bandit warfare. The Bedouin took up comfortable eyries on the rocky hills and fired down at the caravan. It was impossible to return an accurate fire, for the defenders faced into the sun and the attackers were well hidden behind crude stone breastworks. The pilgrims were further constrained by the thought that if they shot too many of their assailants, the Bedouin in the area, some 4000 in all, might swarm down on them. The Albanian pilgrims took the brunt of the murderous volleys. By the time the Bedouin broke off their attack, twelve Albanians lay dead, and a number of camels.

The pilgrims made good their escape through the pass onto the broad plain that led to Medina. They approached over a precipitous ridge of black basalt, into which previous travellers had cut steps and footholds. The sure-footed camels made their way up these steps, then continued through a valley coated in lava. Safety now seemed assured, but Burton was disconcerted by the profound silence that appeared to descend on the riders as they trooped through the defile. On the morning of 25 July he asked his servant the reason. 'Are there robbers in sight?'

'No!' replied Mohammed. 'They are walking with their eyes, they will presently see their homes.' Suddenly they arrived at the edge of a ridge and there, two miles below, was the holy city of Medina. The riders halted and all joined in the prayer of thanksgiving. 'Oh Allah! this is the Harim [sanctuary] of Thy Apostle; make it to us a Protection from Hell Fire and a Refuge from Eternal Punishment! O open the Gates of Thy Mercy, and let us pass through them to the Land of Joy!'

Burton was moved by the devoutness of his fellow pilgrims, but his interests were more secular than profane, for Medina, reached after eight days and 132 miles of gruelling trekking from Yenbo, was literally an oasis of peace and rest after the rigours of the desert. 'I now understood the full value of a phrase in the Moslem ritual, "And when his eyes shall fall upon the trees of al-Meinah let them raise their voice and bless the Apostle with the choicest of Blessings". In all the fair view before us nothing was more striking, after the desolation through which we had passed, than the gardens and orchards about the town.'[26]

Burton spent a month in Medina, touring the shrines. Mounted on a donkey to ease the pain of his still-swollen foot, he visited the Prophet's mosque, the burial place of Mohammed's daughter Fatimah (origin of an Islamic cult of parthenogenesis), and gaudy curiosity shops whose tawdry and meretricious wares drew from Burton the kind of criticism a later generation of ascetics levelled at Lourdes. In the evening he made secret notes and sketches in his room at the home of Sheikh Hamid, using a small guide wire attached to a notebook concealed inside a copy of the Koran, so that he could write in the dark. Here he recorded his impressions of a multitude of facets of Islamic culture:

circumcision, surgery, history, the martial tradition, horticulture and the Arabic language itself.[27]

While Burton was in Medina, tribal warfare erupted between the Hawazim and the Hawamid in the desert. One consequence was that the Bedouin began to levy heavy tribute on pilgrims along the normal road to Mecca. Burton therefore had the good luck to be 'forced' to accompany the huge 7000-strong Damascus caravan through the waterless Darb-al-Sharki – an arid route through the Nejd desert which no European had ever taken before. This track was famous to Burton and other Arabists as the itinerary taken by Harun-al-Rashid and the lady Zubaydah in the eighth century. Twenty Maria Theresa dollars secured him two camels and a brace of reliable drivers. He also laid in a more varied stock of provisions for the journey: apart from a plentiful supply of fresh water he took wheat-flour, rice, turmeric, onions, dates, unleavened bread, cheese, limes, tobacco, sugar, tea and coffee.

The unwieldy caravan got under way on 31 August 1853. The Damascus legion was 'the main stream that carries off all the small currents that, at this season of general movement, flow from Central Asia towards the great centre of the Islamic world.' The night before the exodus from Medina saw unbelievable scenes of confusion among the floating human population of excitable pilgrims. Tents were pulled down, camels roared and snorted as they were loaded, horses galloped in circles, women and children sat confused and lost as their lords and masters screamed and shouted at each other, every now and then loosing a pistol shot in the air. It was a great relief when the undulating Leviathan wound its way out of the holy city and halted briefly on a hill to take a last look at Medina. Repeating his 'poop strategy' of the *Golden Wire*, Burton and his party managed to find themselves a privileged position near the front of the column, away from the worst of the mêlée.

The caravan's itinerary ran south-east from Medina. After crossing the Harra lava beds, it followed the high plateau of the Nejd-Hejaz border.[28] Here was desolation on a scale not seen even on the march from Yenbo to Medina. 'Nowhere have I seen a land in which Earth's anatomy lies so barren.' The few waterholes were guarded by armed men who mulcted the pilgrims of huge sums for brackish water. Hardly surprisingly, the beasts of burden began to fall in droves. Fresh carcasses of asses, ponies and camels dotted the wayside. Some had been left to die and were being picked clean by carrion crows. Others had had their throats cut properly, according to Islamic custom, and the impoverished *takruri* pilgrims cut steaks from the carcasses.[29]

The pace the caravan leaders set was blistering. They began to march at 3 a.m. (and sometimes as early as 1 a.m.), obeying the Prophet's injunction: 'Choose early darkness for your wayfarings as the calamities of the Earth (serpents and wild beasts) appear not at night.' But the pilgrims ignored the implicit part of the advice by continuing to trek by day, halting only when the afternoon sun became unbearable. They plodded through a succession of table-top plains, separated by ridges of volcanic rock, striated with furrows and fissures. Shortage of water was always the major problem, and Burton noted the various Arab strategies for dealing with thirst. A favourite device was to carry calcified butter in a leather bottle. Burton himself found that the best remedy was not to talk, and to drink as little as possible; the more you drank, the more you needed to drink. After the first two hours, the overpowering feeling of thirst subsided and thereafter to refrain from drinking was easy.

Tempers were badly frayed. One day Burton witnessed a vehement altercation between a Turk and an Arab, whose quarrel was not helped by the fact that neither spoke the other's language. The Turk eventually ended the dispute by laying the Arab out with a heavy buffet, but his triumph was short-lived. That night his worsted opponent stole into the Turk's tent and ripped his belly open with a dagger. Still conscious, the Turk was wrapped in a shroud and left to die in a half-dug grave. This was normal practice with the ill or incapacitated, but as Burton recorded: 'It is impossible to contemplate such a fate without horror: the torturing thirst of a wound, the burning sun heating the brain to madness, and – worst of all, for they do not wait till death – the attacks of the jackal, the vulture, and the raven of the wild.'[30]

Halfway between Medina and Mecca, at Sufaynah, they crossed the point where the Medina and Baghdad roads converged, and ran into the Baghdad caravan itself, two thousand strong and, to Burton's eye, pullulating with belligerent Wahhabis, Shiites, Kurds and Persians. 'I never saw a more pugnacious assembly; one look sufficed for a quarrel.' Burton's pipe-smoking attracted the aggressive intentions of one particular Wahhabi cut-throat who unsheathed his knife for business, only to beat a hasty retreat when Burton's Egyptian friends drew their flintlock pistols. Bad blood between the two caravans reached such a pitch that the 'pilgrimage' degenerated into a race between them for Mecca.

They rode south-east, sometimes ahead of the Baghdad caravan, sometimes toiling in the rear. Laboriously they ascended a sheer ridge onto a broad gravel tableland, 'a desert peopled only by echoes'. In the night the plain broke up into a confusion of jet-black volcanic rocks. The topographical confusion was echoed in the caravan. Camels stumbled and fell after misperceiving gigantic shadows thrown against the rocks by the light of a thousand flambeaux. The confusion of the senses was compounded by the smell of incense from the thuribles swung by slaves to 'cleanse' the path of their masters. In the fuliginous chaos

Burton became separated from the Egyptians and found himself in the midst of a party of hostile Syrians. He drew his sword to slash at them, but his Egyptian friends caught up with him just in time and reined in his ardour.

Two marches later they were at el-Zaribah on the frontier of the holy lands. The pilgrims washed, shaved and donned the ritual garment – the *ihram.* Sheikh Abdullah, a forty-year-old mullah whom Burton in his capacity as physician had helped in an hour of need by giving him a pipe of opium, instructed his companions in their sacred duties.

> Then Sheik Abdullah, who acted as our director of consciences, bade us be good pilgrims, avoiding quarrels, immorality, bad language and light conversation. We must so reverence life that we should avoid killing game, causing an animal to fly, or even pointing it out for destruction, nor should we scratch ourselves, save with the open palm, lest vermin be destroyed, or a hair uprooted by the nail. We were to respect the sanctuary by sparing the trees, and not to pluck a single blade of grass. As regards personal considerations, we were to abstain from oils, perfumes and unguents; from washing the head with mallow or with lote leaves; from dyeing, shaving, cutting or vellicating a single pile or hair; and though we might take advantage of shade, and even form it with upraised hands, we must by no means cover our sconces. For each infraction of these ordinances we must sacrifice a sheep.[31]

Racing out of el-Zaribah neck-and-neck and making good time until shortly before dusk, the two caravans came under fire from Bedouin bandits in the 'Pass of Death' – a notorious place of ambush. 'A small curl of smoke, like a lady's ringlet, on the summit of the right-hand precipice, caught my eye; and simultaneously with the echoing crack of a matchlock, a high-trotting dromedary in front of me rolled over upon the sands – a bullet had split its heart – throwing the rider a goodly somersault of five or six yards.'[32]

Chaos followed, with every individual in the pass trying to escape either forward or backward and becoming hopelessly clogged. The official troops guarding the caravan seemed to have no idea how to respond to the attack, though it was obvious to Burton that the heights had to be scaled and the enemy cleared. Then it was that the Wahhabis redeemed themselves in his eyes by swarming up the hill under covering fire from their comrades. Once on the heights they cleared out the Bedouin in short order.[33]

The two caravans marched on. Their escort tried to clear the path of further snipers by firing asclepias bushes to provide an artificial light. But the tactic rebounded, since the camels became half-blinded by the flames and started to slip and slide on the 'livid red' embers that formed a carpet on the sand. Still, by morning they were just a day's ride from Mecca. At 4 p.m. they came to the final pass, the gateway to Mecca.

After nine hours hard driving through the rocky defile, the outline of the sacred city was visible and the cries of 'Mecca, Mecca!', 'The Sanctuary, O the Sanctuary', went up.[34]

At the servant Mohammed's house Burton managed to offend his mother and her Turkish guests by demanding that the store-room be set aside for his personal use, pending which he claimed sleeping quarters in the best part of the communal living room. Burton was impervious to black looks and insouciantly calculated (rightly) that he could win over the Turkish pilgrims later by charm.[35]

In the morning he hurried to the great Mosque and sacred Kaabah, 'the navel of the world'. Understandably Burton was in high excitement at his first view of Mecca in the daylight.

> There at last it lay, the bourn of my long and weary pilgrimage, realising the plans and hopes of many and many a year. The mirage medium of Fancy invested the huge catafalque and its gloomy pall with peculiar charms. There were no giant fragments of hoar antiquity as in Egypt, no remains of graceful and harmonious beauty as in Greece and Italy; yet the view was strange, unique – and how few have looked upon the celebrated shrine! I may truly say that, of all the worshippers who clung weeping to the curtain, or who pressed their beating hearts to the stone, none felt for the moment a deeper emotion than did the Haji from the far-north. It was as if the poetical legends of the Arab spoke truth, and that the wavering wings of angels, not the sweet breeze of morning, were agitating and swelling the black covering of the shrine. But, to confess humbling truth, theirs was the high feeling of religious enthusiasm, mine was the ecstasy of gratified pride.[36]

At the Kaabah Burton began by marching round the stone cube seven times with Mohammed, chanting the appropriate prayers. Then he and the Egyptians used the same main force that had secured them the poop deck on the Red Sea steamer to cut a swathe through the crowd and come close to the sacred Black Stone, which Abraham was said to have received from the Angel Gabriel. For ten minutes Burton and his party held pride of place by the monolith and he made what he thought an important discovery. 'Whilst kissing it and rubbing hands and forehead upon it I narrowly observed it, and came away persuaded that it is an aerolite.'[37]

On a second visit he waited until 2 a.m., when all the crowds had gone or were asleep, then took measurements with a piece of tape. He also drank from the sacred well Zemzem and filled a bottle with its allegedly curative waters. Next he undertook the six-hour journey to Mount Arafat, where Gabriel was said to have instructed Adam in prayer. This was a *via dolorosa* in more senses than one, for the stench of fifty thousand sweating pilgrims in the parching sun nearly turned his stomach. Five men dropped dead of exhaustion on the roadside.

'Each man suddenly staggered, fell as if shot, and after a brief convulsion lay still as marble.'

Next day he arrived at the summit of Mount Arafat to listen to the traditional sermon. But his attention was distracted by a vision of feminine beauty: an eighteen-year-old Meccan girl with citron-coloured skin and a voluptuous figure. His eyes met hers and she sensed his interest. Flirtatiously she drew back an inch or two of her *yashmak* to reveal a dimpled mouth and rounded chin. Burton raised his hand to his forehead. She smiled almost imperceptibly and turned away. 'The pilgrim was in ecstasy.'[38]

When the sermon ended, he lost sight of 'Flirtilla' (as he had nick-named the girl) in the pushing and shoving of the crowd. To compensate for his loss, once on the plain and in the safety of the *shugduf*, Burton threw caution to the winds and began openly sketching the sacred mountain. The normal prejudice against pencil and paper was heightened in his Arab comrades by the feeling that what he was attempting was sacrilege. Ali bin Ya Sin, a Meccan guide and religious official with whom Burton had clashed on the journey to Medina, called on him to desist. 'Effendi, sit quiet; there is danger here.' When Burton persisted, Ali cried out again: 'Effendi! What art thou doing? Thou wilt be the death of us.' 'Wallah!' Burton replied, 'it is all thy fault. Put thy beard out of the other opening and Allah will make it easy for us.' Having thus overcome Ali's religious scruples and browbeaten him to turn away, Burton completed his sketch of the 'Mountain of Mercy'.

Next day Burton went to Muna for the ritual of hurling seven stones against the Devil Monument. Burton's donkey became snarled up and threw its rider. Burton was pitched under the feet of a rearing, bucking dromedary and had to gouge at its underbelly with a knife to force the beast to move its hoofs out of range. The ritual slaughter of sacrificial animals followed the stone-throwing. 'Literally the land stank. Five or six thousand animals had been slain and cut up in this Devil's Punch-bowl. I leave the reader to imagine the rest.'

Only one task now remained. Burton had set himself the goal of penetrating to the interior of the Kaabah, and had Mohammed on permanent lookout to alert him when the Grand Mosque was relatively empty. Shortly after their return to Mecca from Muna, the chance came. Mohammed rushed into his house breathlessly to inform his master that the Kaabah was temporarily empty. The sequel is described thus by Burton:

> A crowd had gathered round the Ka'abah, and I had no wish to stand bareheaded and barefooted in the midday September sun. At the cry of 'Open a path for the Haji who would enter the House', the gazers made way. Two stout Meccans, who stood below the door, raised me in their arms, whilst a third drew me from above into the building. At the entrance

> I was accosted by several officials, dark-looking Meccans [who] . . . officially inquired my name, nation and other particulars. The replies were satisfactory, and the boy Mohammed was authoritatively ordered to conduct me round the building, and to recite the prayers. I will not deny that, looking at the windowless walls, the officials at the door, and the crowd of excited fanatics below –
>
> 'And the place death, considering who I was'
>
> – my feelings were of the trapped-rat description.[39]

With amazing audacity and presence of mind, even though the sweat was trickling from him in large drops, Burton managed to sketch a rough floor plan with his pencil on his white *ihram*, even as he mumbled the customary prayers. The exploit was a fitting climax to an already extraordinary adventure.

Once back in the safety of Mohammed's house, he laid his plans for departure. He broached the possibility of proceeding eastward, across the Empty Quarter, but his trusted Arab advisers soon dissuaded him. 'Wallah! Effendi. Thou art surely mad.' Reluctantly he took the road to Jeddah, where he stayed for ten days, awaiting passage to Suez. Even though the great powers had consulates here, they provided no protection against Arab fanaticism, as the massacre of 1858 showed. Burton could still not reveal his true identity, but he wanted to establish proof of his exploit as soon as possible. He therefore went to the house of Vice-Consul Cole and sent in his credentials as 'Sheikh Abdullah'. 'Let the nigger wait', was the not unexpected reply. After hours of sweltering in the sun, Burton was at last ushered into Cole's presence. At once he handed him a piece of paper which looked like a money-order. On the paper were written the words 'Don't recognise me; I am Dick Burton but I am not safe yet. Give me some money, which will be returned from London, and don't take any notice of me.'[40] Cole did as he was instructed, and took a note of his address. After nightfall he sent for Burton, took him into his private room and there entertained him royally.

Before boarding the *Dwarka* for Suez, Burton somehow betrayed his real identity to his servant Mohammed. Coldly Mohammed asked for his wages, bought enough grain to see him through a long desert journey and departed, after telling his associate Sheikh Nur: 'Now I understand. Your master is a sahib from India. He hath laughed in our beards.'[41]

At Cairo Burton resumed his identity as an English officer. According to his own account, he put on his disguise just once more, to test its impact on his brother–lieutenants at Shepheard's Hotel. A group of them sat smoking and drinking on the verandah. Burton approached and deliberately flapped the folds of his burnous against a man he knew. 'Damn that nigger's impudence! If he does that again I'll kick him', the officer expostulated. 'Well, damn it, Hawkins,' Burton replied, 'that's a nice way to welcome a fellow after two years' absence.' 'By God, it's Ruffian Dick,' cried Hawkins.[42]

The incident sounds like one of Burton's after-dinner stories, since in his private correspondence he claimed that he remained in disguise in Cairo. But it probably gave the idea for a similar gesture to T. E. Lawrence.[43]

7

The Impact of Arabia and Islam

IN his journey to Mecca Burton scored the greatest triumph of his life as an adventurer. None of his other exploits was to be so free from minor flaws and blemishes. In his assumption of the identity of the East, he put himself among a tiny handful of travellers who penetrated to the heart of an alien culture: Marco Polo, Charles Doughty, T. E. Lawrence and – Burton's only nineteenth-century rival as combined linguist and interpreter of Islam – the Hungarian Arminius Vámbéry, who travelled through Muslim Central Asia in 1862–64 in the selfsame disguise of dervish.[1]

Inevitably the completeness of Burton's success has incited his critics to attempt to pick holes in his achievement. It is variously alleged that his disguise was or 'must have been' penetrated; that he exaggerated the difficulties facing a would-be alien pilgrim; and that he was excessively ruthless and unscrupulous in his methods.

A recent critical view of Burton alleges that his disguise was penetrated on at least three occasions: when a fellow-pilgrim, Amm Jamal, spoke of the tax on foreigners; when he was trying to sketch the lovely 'Flirtilla'; and during his interrogation in a coffee shop after leaving Mecca.[2] But a close examination of these incidents reveals a different story. To avoid paying the *Jizyat*, or alien tax, Burton changed into Arab dress from his *Afghan* attire. It was Mount Arafat, not Flirtilla, that Burton was trying to sketch, so that the 'Effendi, sit quiet!' hissed at him was to do with the offence against normal religious scruple, not the blasphemy of being an infidel. The incident in the coffee shop was a suspicion as to what Burton's nationality actually was, whether Afghan or Persian, not a suspicion that he was a 'Frank'.[3]

Burton once gave signal proof of the efficacy of his disguise by joining in a dervish 'howl-in' while under the observation of Europeans. To the dancing berserkers he proved his credentials as a master dervish, which gave him the right to initiate disciples.[4] Yet it was in a way poetic justice that his real achievements were queried, for Burton was ungenerous and petty-minded in his own reaction to similar travellers. A meeting with Arminius Vámbéry at Lord Houghton's house in 1861 incited jealousy in Burton of the great Hungarian traveller. First he tried to cap Vámbéry's recitation of Hungarian folk tales by declaiming portions of the newly published version of *Omar Khayyám* by Edward Fitzgerald. Later he sneered at Vámbéry's Jewishness. Then, after Vámbéry's great journey in disguise as a dervish from the deserts of Oxus to Khiva and Samarkand in 1862–64, Burton ungenerously claimed that the Hungarian's disguise had been penetrated, that he had been dogged at every step by Russian spies, and that he had not in fact visited most of the places he described.[5]

The allegation that Burton exaggerated the dangers facing a European pilgrim derives wholly from the curious journey made to Mecca in early 1862 by an undistinguished person from Norwood called Herman Bicknell. According to Bicknell, he simply took a steamer to Jeddah, announced his wish to visit the holy places at Mecca, and was granted full facilities by the Arabs.[6] There is something unsatisfactory about this story, as should be clear when the experiences of Vámbéry and of Heinrich von Maltzam, after Burton the most famous disguised Meccan pilgrim, are recalled. If taken at face value, Bicknell's story also makes nonsense of Doughty's plea two decades later that the British empire should use force to guarantee the safety of all Christians who wished to travel to Mecca.[7] But it *is* true, as Burton himself recognised, that he made the *Haj* in the last days of the traditional caravan route. By the late 1870s the number of *Hajis* taking the overland trail had declined from tens of thousands to a mere eight hundred. Most pilgrims preferred to travel to Mecca in the comfort of 'infidel' steamers.[8]

The canard most easily disposed of is that Burton was detected as an impostor during the pilgrimage by a young Arab whom he was then obliged to kill. The occasion was said to have been when Burton urinated standing up, instead of crouching according to Moslem custom. It always irritated Burton whenever anyone took this tall story seriously, as it implied a woeful ignorance on his part of Islamic mores. Moslems never urinated in a standing position, since a single spray of urine would make their clothes ritually impure, as Burton knew very well; besides, the mistake 'is hardly possible in Moslem dress'. On the other hand, Burton had only himself to blame for the spread of the rumour, since he delighted in presenting himself as a demonic figure. 'Well, they do say the man died', was one of his ripostes to a questioner whom he despised. To Bram Stoker, the author of *Dracula*, Burton laid it on even more thickly. 'The desert has its own laws, and there – supremely of all the East – to kill is a small offence. In any case what could I do? It had to be his life or mine.'[9]

Since he was dealing with his great love – the Arab world – Burton in the *Personal Narrative* drops his guard more than in any other book. What is revealed is a fascinating amalgam of conscious and unconscious attitudes, as well as the basis of what might be termed Burton's metaphysic and his social and political theories.

Perhaps the most obvious and banal conclusion from the 1853 pilgrimage is that Burton all his life waged a one-man war against the crushing burden of money. Demands for payment always elicited from him exaggerated responses. His reaction to the passport fee in Cairo has already been noted, but it is merely the first of a number of animadversions on financial matters. He was revolted by the constant demands for *baksheesh*, especially when the demand came from the desert Arabs.[10]

For the person feeling cripplingly oppressed by money worries, and who like Burton feels his (or her) talents stifled by Mammon, there are two main responses. One is to integrate the feelings into a general political theory. The other is to retreat into financial irresponsibility, like Dickens' Harold Skimpole. For Burton the socialist strategy was ruled out by his own Nietzschean hypertrophied individualism; he therefore approached dangerously close to the Skimpole 'solution', and the feeling of hatred towards money as a destructive force was to embroil him in a long-running series of disputes with disbursing authorities.

The other obvious conclusion from the *Personal Narrative* is that Burton is a Freudian subject in more ways than one. This tendency later became obvious when Burton turned to sexology as a major interest, but it is already clearly there in 1853. It is not just in the use of hypnosis that Burton prefigures the early days of the father of psychoanalysis. Burton drew attention to the overt phallicism of the mosques in Cairo, linked it with the triangular temple architecture of India and called it 'an unconscious revival of the forms used from the earliest ages to denote by symbolism the worship of the generative and the creative gods.'[11] His explanation of his own motives for the journey also chimes with the findings of psychoanalysis. 'Man wants to wander and he must do so or he shall die.' 'Voyaging is victory.' 'Discovery is mostly my mania.' This harmonises with the Freudian notion of exploration as a metaphor for the proper preparation for life.[12] It need hardly be added that the principal motive for discovery and exploration is an examination of the self, in the sense of a quest for identity or a 'bracketing' of one's own reality; it is a hoary cliché that on worldwide travels one meets everyone but oneself. This helps to explain why Burton never established himself as one of the very greatest technical explorers, like Stanley, or Shackleton, or Amundsen. The end result was relatively unimportant. The clue perhaps lies in a revealing remark by another traveller smitten with the mystique of Arabia, Wilfred

Thesiger: 'I set myself a goal on these journeys and, although the goal itself was unimportant, its attainment had to be worth every effort and sacrifice.'[13]

The sentimental romanticisation of the East in Victorian England was a familiar ploy to escape from the ephemeral realities of the 'tight little, right little island'. More tough-minded escapism traditionally involved one of two routes: travel and exploration in the external world, or a punishing schedule of study and scholarship. Not the least extraordinary aspect of Richard Burton is the way he managed to combine all three elements of his worship of Islam and the Arab way of life. His multiple talents allowed him to enter its world at many different levels, contrasting with the one-dimensionality of other Arabian travellers, like Palgrave, Doughty or Wilfrid Scawen Blunt.

Many of his analyses of the Oriental mind sound like self-descriptions. Burton regarded as the main difference between Oriental culture and classical Greece the respective ignorance and embrace of the golden mean, and spoke of the Arabs' 'nervous, excitable, hysterical temperament'.[14] This is undoubtedly the deep reason why Burton at Oxford did not feel at ease with the Classics and hankered after the languages of the East. Later Isabel Burton was to cite Gautier, to the effect that many men have a spiritual home different from their notional nationality: thus Hugo's was Spain, Ingres's was Italy, while Lamartine, de Musset and de Vigny felt more at home in England than in their native land. In such a scheme, Burton was a natural Arab.[15]

Burton's *oeuvre* provides plenty of evidence of this. Wherever in the world he wandered, his heart always yearned to hear again the tinkle of the camel-bell. This feeling never died, as a quotation from his later career, when he was in his late fifties, shows:

> Again I am to enjoy a glimpse of the 'Glorious Desert', to inhale the sweet, pure breath of translucent skies that show the red stars burning upon the very edge and verge of the horizontal; and so strengthen myself by a short visit to the Wild Man and his old home ... This dear old Cairo! Once more I illustrate the saying of her sons anent drinking of the Nile. And what water it is! sweet, light and flavoured; differing in kind, not only in degree, from that of any other river. No wonder that the Hebrews grumbled when they lost it.[16]

Burton's love of the desert is a function of his general Nietzscheanism – precisely the quality that many of his contemporaries and later critics found so offensive. From the vantage point of the desert, the hero, dedicated to the morality of strenuousness, sees the meanness and littleness of 'civilised' life. Burton shared Nietzsche's horror of industrial capitalism and its corollary, the machine age. He also shared the

Victorian taste for primitivism as an antidote to the *Angst* and *nausée* of modern existence.[17]

Hardly surprisingly, Burton embraced the Arab as the quintessential 'noble savage' and thought it vital that the Bedouin qualities should not atrophy, despite pressure from the West.[18] He considered that the general European criticism of the Arab came from superficial travellers who had seen only the corrupted species in cities and towns: 'a few debased Syrians and Sinaites'. The wild, uncorrupted product of the desert was very different. 'The manners of the Bedawi are free and simple: vulgarity and affectation, awkwardness and embarrassment, are weeds of civilised growth, unknown to the people of the desert.'[19] This estimate did not change in the more than thirty years in which Burton had contact with the Arab world. 'The unsettled Arabs plunder and slay; the settled Arabs slander and cheat ... the Bedawi, who becomes fawning and abject when corrupted by contact with the town, is still a gentleman in his native wilds', was his judgement at the end of the 1870s.[20]

But Burton, with his worship of the martial ethos, had no great admiration for the Arab as warrior. 'The valour of the Bedawi is fitful and uncertain ... their romances, full of foolhardy feats and impossible exploits, might charm for a time but would not become the standard works of a really fighting people. Nor would a truly valorous race admire the freebooters who safely fire down upon caravans from their eyries.'[21] As in the case of India, this lack of a true martial tradition meant that strong central government was needed. Echoing Hume, Burton described all Oriental history as a record of despotism tempered with assassination. Despotism was essential in order to tax the wretched peasant or *fellah*, for whom Burton had the utmost contempt: 'the Fellah must either tyrannise or be tyrannised over; he is never happier than under a strong-handed despotism and he has never been more miserable than under British rule or rather misrule. Our attempts to constitutionalise him have made us the laughing-stock of Europe.'[22]

Here we encounter one of many confusions in Burton's thought. Both the 'golden age' of paladin warriors and the raiding nomadism of the Bedouin collided with his belief in British imperialism and the desirability of new technology like the railways, which would make the white man's burden easier to bear. And even if the Bedouin had his covetous and nihilistic side, was it really open to Burton, the supreme individualist, to object to that? In his later days as consul in Damascus he hoped for a fusion of the best of the Arab old (the Bedouin) with the best of the new technology (especially railways).[23] A moment's consideration should have shown him that the two were mutually exclusive. Faced with an ineluctable choice, what would Burton choose? There is some force to Blunt's conjecture that Burton was never a truly committed friend to the Arabs, and would have sacrificed their interests if ever they clashed with those of British imperialism, or even with his own.[24]

Another aspect of Arab sensibility to impress Burton deeply was the quasi-Gnostic contempt for matter and the material world that informed the poetry of the Sufis and the deliberations of the Bedouin sheikhs – a feeling of the ultimate worthlessness of the quotidian world later underlined by T. E. Lawrence as one of the keys to Arab culture.[25] An idea associated with this was *kayf* – a difficult concept, which Burton elucidates as follows:

> This is the Arab's *kayf*. The savouring of animal existence; the passive enjoyment of mere sense; the pleasant languor, the dreamy tranquillity, the airy castle-building, which in Asia stands in lieu of the vigorous, intensive, passionate life of Europe. It is the result of a lively, impressible, excitable nature, and exquisite sensibility of nerve; it argues a facility for voluptuousness unknown to northern regions, where happiness is placed in the exertion of mental and physical powers; where *ernst ist das leben*; where niggard earth commands ceaseless sweat of face, and damp chill air demands perpetual excitement, exercise or change, or adventure, or dissipation, for want of something better.[26]

Burton's love of things Arabian raises the obvious question: why did he not embrace Islam in totality? Or did he? It has sometimes been explicitly stated that Burton was a Muslim, and it is certain that, modern claims notwithstanding, Moslems did not hold the clandestine pilgrimage against him. Instead, whenever 'Haji Abdullah' appeared in an Islamic community, the faithful greeted him as one of their own.[27] The more likely truth is expressed by an early Burton biographer, who described him as a mixture of agnostic, deist and oriental mystic.[28] Burton's commitment to Islam was primarily emotional, not intellectual; he was far too sceptical in cast of mind to accept the Koran in its entirety. But he unquestionably had far greater sympathy for Islam than for its rival world-religion, Christianity. Like that other great nineteenth-century pioneering anthropologist, Sir James Frazer, Burton's real scorn and antipathy were reserved for the religion of the Nicene Creed.

Burton's writings on Arab literature and culture are peppered with remarks disparaging Christianity.[29] He particularly detested what he considered Christianity's attempt to 'do the dirt' on mankind, through the doctrine of original sin and the hatred of the flesh. Since the fourth century AD theologians had systematically demeaned Man: angels were ranked above humans in the scale of things, a clerisy of priests was placed between the individual and God, and the punishment of eternal Hell-fire was threatened. Islam was both more logical and more humane: the jinns and demons were considered species lower than men, the so-called 'lower animals' were admitted into Heaven (unlike in Christianity), and there was no debate on whether women had souls.[30] At his most compromising towards the faith of 'the Nazarene', Burton was prepared to make two backhanded 'concessions'. One was that Islam was closer to the original teachings of Jesus than Christianity, which had undergone Pauline and Athanasian transmogrifications. The other was to concede that Islam did not occupy the highest place in the moral scale of organised religions. The truly moral approach of 'virtue as its own reward' was found only with the Greeks, Lao-tse and the Buddhists. Christianity, with its injunction to do good merely so as to avoid punishment, ranked in the lowest scale, with Islam somewhere in the middle.[31]

In Burton's view, wherever Islam could be faulted, Christianity was even more vulnerable. It was true that euthanasia was unknown among the Arabs and that they preferred to see a man expire in agony rather than relieve him by means of soporifics and other drugs. But the same sort of superstition led to the typical Christian bromide: 'he kept his senses to the last' when the subject was suffering an excruciating wasting disease – 'this barbarity ... the same which a generation ago made the silly accoucheur refuse to give ether because of the divine(?) saying, "In sorrow shall thou bring forth children".'[32]

Burton had the kind of sensibility that, while not blind to the shortcomings of Islam, was prepared to give the religion the benefit of the doubt in a way never accorded to Christianity. In this he recalls Lamartine.[33] But it must be remembered that some of this was natural reaction. Until the nineteenth century it was the received opinion in England that Islam was intrinsically hostile to the West and all its works, that Mohammed was a lying hypocrite, that Islam was a camouflage for unbridled sensualism, that the art and thought of the Arab world was inferior.[34] The fervour of Burton's rebuttal emerges in his posthumous work *The Jew, the Gypsy and El-Islam*:

> Can we call that faith sensual which forbids a man to look upon a statue or a picture? Which condemns even the most moderate use of inebriants and indeed is not certain upon the subject of coffee and tobacco? Which will not allow even the most harmless games of chance or skill? Which vigorously prohibits music, dancing and even poetry and works of fiction upon any but strictly religious subjects? Above all things, which debars a man from the charms of a female society, making sinful a glance at a strange woman's unveiled face? A religion whose votaries must pray five times a day ... whose yearly fast often becomes one of the severest trials to which the human frame can be exposed? To whom distant pilgrimage with its trials and hardships is obligatory at least once in life? Whose prophet exclaimed with the Founder of Christianity 'Poverty is my Bride' and who

taught his followers that two things ruin men: 'much wealth and many words'.[35]

It was (and is) a staple criticism of Islam that it reduces women to second-class status; the nineteenth-century criticism gained added power from the endorsement of men whose credentials as Arabian travellers could not easily be shrugged off, men like Charles Doughty.[36] For Burton true misogynism was to be found in St Paul and the early Christian fathers, not in Islam. The Mohammedan religion's fault, if fault it was, was to insist on a kind of sexual apartheid: 'Al-Islam seems purposely to have loosened the ties between the sexes in order to strengthen the bonds which connect man and man', as Burton put it.[37] Thereafter, Arab women enjoyed many privileges not open to their Western sisters. In marriage there was no distinction, as in the West, between a man's marrying and a woman's *being married*. The total direction of the household and its inhabitants was in a wife's hands; she had the right to absent herself from her home for a month without consulting her husband; she was a legal sharer in marital property – a right not established in England until the 1882 Married Woman's Property Act. She could own her own property and will it away without her husband's consent. All this contrasted with the sickness of Western sexual mores, a sickness most clearly evinced in barbarities like the British husband's right to will property away from his wife and children, and the detestable legal category of actions for 'breach of promise'. In the treacherous Arab world of *homo lupus homini*, female advice was the only sort a man of power could trust. Most of all – and this was a theme Burton constantly reverted to – the training in sexual techniques and the art of love given to both sexes made for general social happiness and harmony.[38]

Burton was a believer in the 'semi-seclusion' of women, as practised in Ancient Greece; this allowed something between the overstrictness of Islam and the 'licence' of Anglo-American attitudes to its females. Keeping the sexes apart, he thought, allowed the freest mingling between males of different classes – one reason why in Middle Eastern countries (according to Burton) there was no equivalent of the lower-class urban *canaille* of European cities. Sexual apartheid also abolished illicit liaisons, ballroom flirtations, cicisbeism and other Western 'evils' 'for the same reason it enables women to enjoy the fullest intimacy and friendship with one another, and we know that the best of both sexes are those who prefer the society of their own as opposed to "quite the lady's man" and "quite the gentleman's woman".'[39]

Burton argued that there was no conception in Islam of women as a force of evil. On the other hand, he argued, Christianity positively bristled with such references. But it was not just Christianity itself that perverted relations between the sexes. For Burton there was a kind of double-dyed humbug about the Western approach to sexual mores. Islam kept women close, defended them from all forms of temptation, then, if they strayed from the path of virtue, killed them – beheading being the usual penalty for adultery. In the West, by contrast, civilisation placed women on a pedestal while laying them open to every conceivable kind of danger and temptation. Then, if a woman fell from grace, society's wrath was visited on the 'seducer'.[40]

Yet even Burton was forced to acknowledge the instances where Islamic culture does betray an unmistakable misogynistic flavour. Three traditional Arab apothegms make the point with clarity. The first maintains that women have three uses: the prostitute for pleasure, the concubine for service and the wife for breeding. They also have four distinct ages: 'a mischief-making brat, a demon maid, a whorish woman and a pimping crone.'[41] The second is in the form of a quatrain:

> Marriage is a joy for a month and sorrow for life
> They said 'marry'. I replied 'far be it from me to take to my bosom a sackful of snakes'.
> I am free – why then become a slave?
> May Allah never bless womankind!

The third, again a verse, runs as follows:

> From ten unto twenty,
> A Repose to the eyes of beholders.
> From twenty to thirty,
> Still fair and full of flesh.
> From thirty unto forty,
> A mother of many boys and girls.
> From forty unto fifty,
> An old woman of the deceitful.
> From fifty unto sixty,
> Slay them with a knife.
> From sixty unto seventy,
> The curse of Allah upon them, one and all.[42]

Burton always maintained that the view of women promoted in the *Arabian Nights* was at worst ambivalent, but many have seen its entire machinery as born in sexual distrust of women.[43] A telling example is the story of the man granted three wishes who wasted them because of the lechery of his wife.[44] And indeed there are many instances where Burton reveals the same kind of mistrust and where he can be said to share the mental world of his beloved Arab sheikhs.[45] There are Burton asides on women which would reduce a modern feminist to apoplexy. He believed that rape was impossible without the threat of a knife or other weapon, that women frequently 'asked for it', that therefore much 'rape' was really disguised seduction. He thought that women were completely without honour or scruple and were pathological liars. Most of all, Burton feared female sexuality and what he saw as a predilection for the most debauched specimens of the male sex, 'these skunks of the human race'.[46] Wearily he concluded: 'polyandry is the only state of society in which jealousy and quarrels about the sex [sic] are the exception and not the rule of life.'[47]

Burton's almost total acceptance of the Islamic view of women is an important clue to the inner man. Its significance will deepen when we come to examine his own private life. In the nineteenth and early twentieth century, though, it was not his embrace of the Arab view of the female that most excited debate and controversy. Rather, attention was focused on Burton's claim to be *the* definitive Arabist, as against the claims of other Britons: Blunt, Doughty, Palgrave. The *Personal Narrative* was admired, envied and detested, in roughly equal measure. Always a polemicist and controversialist, Burton gave the criticism of his peers short shrift while preserving a balanced view of their qualities as Arabian travellers.

The contrast between Wilfrid Scawen Blunt and Burton is too severe to make any comparison meaningful. Like Bishop Butler's fishwives, they argued from different premisses. Blunt was a supporter of Arab nationalism, espoused the cause of Arabi Pasha, thought of Kitchener's Omdurman triumph as a gratuitous massacre, and accused Lord Cromer of atrocities and war crimes during his twenty-five years as 'viceroy' of Egypt. Burton, for all his love of the Arabs, was always a British imperialist. When we add to Blunt's predicates a Thaddeus Stevens-like love of the black man and a prison sentence for activity in the Irish Land League, we at once perceive the chasm that separates him from Burton.[48] Blunt was one of those who sneered at the 'achievement' of Burton's Meccan pilgrimage and accused the *'Haji'* of deliberately exaggerating the dangers. Yet Blunt's most recent biographer points out that he might have saved himself from a number of errors if he had read the *Personal Narrative* more carefully.[49]

The most relevant comparisons are between Burton and those travellers who shared certain assumptions and values but disagreed as to means. Both William Gifford Palgrave and Charles Doughty were, in different ways, representatives of the British imperialist mentality, but both took grave exception to Burton's project of travelling to Mecca in disguise. Clearly there was an element of jealousy here from Arabists debarred by their own principles from visiting the Holy Places, to say nothing of Burton's vast linguistic superiority. But their arguments are worth examining further, for they shed important light on the general clash between the Burton world-view and that of the establishment

Christian standpoint; this was undoubtedly a factor which weighed against Burton's chances of worldly success.

Burton was once asked to dinner by Sir Valentine Chirol to meet a fellow Arabian traveller. The mystery guest turned out to be Palgrave. Predictably, he and Burton did not get on; Burton described him as a charlatan pure and simple. Burton was a man of many identities, but the basic core of his beliefs never really altered. After a similar background in the Indian Army, Palgrave converted to Catholicism and became a Jesuit. Later he renounced Jesuitry for a consular career.[50] His unreliable *Narrative of a Year's Journey through Central and Eastern Arabia* described a journey made in 1862–63. This work is suffused with a hatred of Islam and the Bedouin; in Palgrave's view there was no future for Arabic culture until the Koran had vanished into oblivion. So vehement was his detestation of Mohammedanism that he was taken to task for bigotry even by normally staid British reviewers.[51]

Palgrave also took a hefty swipe at Burton. He began by an implicit criticism of 'half-romantic and always overcoloured scenes of wild Beduins painted up into a sort of chivalresque knight-errants and representatives of an unthralled freedom.' If there was any doubt who was in his sights, he later made his criticism explicit:

> Passing oneself off as a wandering Darwaysh, as some European travellers have attempted to do in the East, is for more reasons than one a very bad plan ... to feign a religion which the adventurer himself does not believe, to perform with scandalous exactitude as of the highest and holiest import practices which he inwardly ridicules ... not to mention other dark touches – all this seems hardly compatible with the character of a European gentleman, let alone that of a Christian ... *c'est pis qu'un crime, c'est une bêtise*.[52]

Burton was not the sort of man to take this lying down. He replied with a dithyrambic attack, full of typical, savage indignation.

> This comes admirably à propos from a traveller who, born a Protestant of Jewish descent, placed himself 'in connection with', in plain words took the vows of, 'the order of the Jesuits' ... a popular preacher who declaimed openly at Bayrut and elsewhere against his own narration ... a gentleman who by return to Protestantism violated his vows ... It is the principle of *vieille coquette, nouvelle dévote*: it is Satan preaching against sin.[53]

Privately, Burton spread the rumour that Palgrave's anti-Arabism derived from an unsavoury incident when he was sodomised by Hasan Ali, the Agha Khan, whom he had infuriated by his Jesuitic mania for proselytising.[54]

But of all Arabian travellers it was Charles Doughty who was most consistently set up as the model of what the British voyager in Arabian sands should be. Arabists have always sharply divided into admirers of Burton and Doughty, respectively. Doughty made a point of travelling without an incognito, fearlessly, almost self-destructively proclaiming his status as a Christian. Needless to say, he received buffets, snubs, humiliation and degradation for his pains. To Burton this sort of thing was mindless masochism, like the action of the early Christians under the Roman empire who refused to make a nod of meaningless obeisance to the official gods. He praised Doughty's achievements ('two volumes to which ... the geographer, epigraphist and the student of Arabia will attach the highest importance'), while puzzling over the archaic English prose (a throwback to Chaucer and Spenser) and dissenting from his methods.

> To conclude, Mr Doughty's work suggests two lessons. The first is not to travel in a semi-barbarous land unless the people be sympathetic to the traveller, and the second is the need of a certain pliancy in opinions religious and political. I cannot for the life of me see how the honoured name of an Englishman is enhanced who at all times and in all places is compelled to stand the buffet from knaves that smell of sweat.[55]

This is the crux of the matter. Burton's defenders point out that he was the one and only European to achieve true empathy with the Arab. Doughty's particular brand of narrow, intolerant Protestant Christianity prevented him from getting to the roots of an alien religion and culture.[56] Doughty's champions turn this argument on its head and assert that Burton's uncritical love of the Arab led him unjustifiably to abuse Christianity and his own country.[57] T.E. Lawrence was undoubtedly in the Doughty camp. When pressed by Burton's admirer Norman Penzer, Lawrence conceded as follows: 'The *Pilgrimage* is a most remarkable work of the highest value to a geographer or to a student of the East.'[58] But in his introduction to the 1921 edition of Doughty's book Lawrence clearly aligned himself with Doughty against Burton, though by implication only. He distinguished between the integrity of the English travellers in Arabia who made no compromise and those who liked the native peoples and tried to live like them. 'However, they cannot avoid the consequences of imitation, a hollow and worthless thing ... the other class of Englishmen is the larger class ... they assert their aloofness, their immunity, the more vividly for their loneliness and weakness ... Doughty is a great member of the second, cleaner class.'[59]

Lawrence's distaste for Burton comes as no surprise. Lawrence had absolutely no interest in the Arab women and their customs about which Burton writes in such detail. Burton's fascination with the Arab world was primarily that of a great scholar, a detached observer, a linguist and anthropologist of genius. He was comparatively uninterested in Arabs at a personal level, the level that most exercised Lawrence. There are no Prince Feisals or Audas in Burton's writings.

He was not taken in by the humbug of the West, as Lawrence was, with catastrophic personal results, nor was he given to the famous Lawrentian bouts of agonised introspection. And the masochistic motif of redemption through suffering in Doughty that so repelled Burton was received enthusiastically by Lawrence – not surprisingly, in the light of all that is now known about him. Lawrence also felt overshadowed intellectually by Burton. His own translation of the *Odyssey* is not the work of genius that Burton's *Plain and Literal Translation of the Arabian Nights* is. Doughty, on the other hand, provided no challenge. A lover of Thomas Hardy and Herman Melville, Lawrence shared Blunt's opinion that as a writer of prose Burton was a second-rater. He told Robert Graves that he found Burton's attitudes pretentious and vulgar and his English unreadable.[60]

But Burton's genius as an Arabist, first revealed in the *Personal Narrative*, can survive such criticisms. His geographical and ethnological accuracy and his anthropological flair were all given unstinted praise by the greatest of the early twentieth-century Arabian travellers, Bertram Thomas and Harry St John Philby.[61] Apart from providing Victorian England with its most complete image of the Arab world *from the inside*, Burton fashioned a poetic myth of the perfect civilisation which sustained him through the many tribulations to come.

8

First Footsteps in Africa

'I WAS quite a nigger at Cairo and saw no English', Burton reported to Norton Shaw, secretary of the Royal Geographical Society.[1] But he did see many Europeans. Among the first was Freiherr von Maltzam, a German Arabist who seven years later emulated Burton by travelling to Mecca in disguise. Baron von Maltzam found Burton's first-hand knowledge of Meccan conditions invaluable.[2] But there was no meeting of souls between the two men. More to Burton's taste was the Italian revolutionary Galeazzo Visconti, whom Burton met at Shepheard's Hotel. Together with a young roué called Sankey, who had been travelling in the Mahgreb, they rented a house which quickly became a byword for hell-raising: 'a scene of depravity, showing what Cairo can do at a pinch, and beating the Arabian Nights all to chalk – that, too, when the Pasha has positively forbidden fornication.'[3]

One result was an attack of syphilis which had reached the secondary stage the following year in Aden.[4] Contraction of venereal disease was not, however, the only sign of Burton's self-destructive behaviour on his return from Mecca. His exploits had made him famous and had he returned to England at once, he would certainly have been lionised by the Royal Geographical Society. It is not beyond the bounds of possibility that he might have been knighted. True, he was only thirty-two and his greatest expedition lay ahead of him, but Shackleton was just thirty-five and at a similar stage in his career when he received the royal accolade in 1909. Yet it is entirely consistent with Burton's personality that he should have preferred the stews of Egypt to the baubles of Victorian fame.

Another of Burton's European contacts was with the Mombasa missionary Dr J. L. Krapf, who had just arrived from Zanzibar after a year's travelling in Abyssinia.[5] Krapf's travellers' tales enthralled Burton 'with discoveries about sources of the White Nile, Kilimanjaro, and Mts of the Moon which remind one of a de Lunatico.' The meeting with Krapf was the genesis of all Burton's African ambitions. It came to him in a flash that he could win immortality as the first man to discover the sources of the White Nile – the enigma, first raised by Herodotus, which continued to baffle Europeans. As time went on, Burton's ambitions vaulted to the point where he proposed to be the first white man to cross Africa from coast to coast; in his mind he saw himself starting from Zanzibar and emerging at the Atlantic.[6] As in so many spheres, Burton was ahead of his time. Not until three years later did Livingstone accomplish the first crossing of the continent by a European, and it was 1875 before Burton's friend Verney Cameron notched up the second Scottish 'first' (for the east-west traverse) by starting at Zanzibar and ending his journey at Benguela on the Atlantic.

Burton knew that since 1849 the Royal Geographical Society had been trying to persuade the East India Company to release its officers for the exploration of unknown Somalia. The only man to show any interest to date had been a Dr Carter, but he wanted to chart the coast from the safety of a brig since, as Burton put it in his inimitable way, 'Carter, not relishing the chance of losing his cods – that misguided people are in the habit of cutting them off and hanging them as ornaments round their arms – refused to explore the interior.'[7] Burton therefore whetted the Society's appetite by promising to explore the Somali lands *en route* to Zanzibar, from where he would launch his trans-Africa expedition.

Having finally thrown off the last of the dysentery attacks which were the ostensible reason he had tarried so long in Cairo, Burton set off for India at the beginning of 1854. On the steamer for Bombay Burton wore the loose-fitting robe and green turban of the accredited *Haji*. On board also was James Grant Lumsden, senior member of the Bombay Council, who happened to say in Burton's hearing, 'What a clever, intellectual face that Arab has!' His vanity tickled, Burton thereupon introduced himself and the two became fast friends. At Lumsden's house in Bombay Burton rattled through the remaining pages of his two-volume Mecca book.

Meanwhile he used Lumsden's influence and that of Lord Elphinstone, Governor of Bombay (whom Burton had taken the precaution of showing round the Pyramids when he passed through Cairo on his way to take up the post) to make sure that the Bombay government would support his application for another bout of exploration leave, and not insist on a return to regimental duties. Without revealing to anyone in India the full scope of his African ambitions, he asked permission to penetrate Somalia as far as the closed city of Harar, prior to travelling south-east to Zanzibar. As his companions he requested on secondment Lieutenant G. E. Herne of the Bombay Fusiliers, for his skill in surveying and photography, and Assistant Surgeon J. Ellerton

Stocks, an old acquaintance from the Sind survey. Although his friends in Bombay warned him that the financing for the project would have to come from the RGS, they were prepared to release him with immediate effect, pending a letter of approval from the Court of Directors of the East India Company in London.

Assuming that the reply would be favourable as there was no request for funds, the Bombay government granted Burton free passage to Aden and six months' study leave there, until the final authorisation from the Court of Directors came in, 'to enable him to perfect himself in the Somali language and obtain such preliminary information relative to the country he proposes to explore as the merchants of that place may be able to afford.'[8] Lieutenant Stocks died of apoplexy shortly before he was due to embark in England. Burton substituted another old Sind friend, Lieutenant William Stroyan, in Stocks' place, and departed for Aden.

Aden, 'the coal-hole of the East' as Burton was later to dub it, had been in British possession only fifteen years when he arrived for his lengthy sojourn. Originally captured from the Sultan of Lahej by a British force from India to serve as a coaling station, Aden was widely considered to be the most unpleasant garrison posting in all the East India Company's far-flung possessions. Under constant attack from Arab tribes, all European personnel were forbidden to leave the town and were left to chafe in boredom and inactivity under 'fort arrest'.

It was of a piece with his usual bad luck that Burton arrived to find Brigadier Clarke, a military martinet of the old school, in post as Acting Political Resident. Clarke would not lift a finger for Burton until he had official word from the Court of Directors. Even worse was the announcement of the new permanent political agent: none other than Napier's old opponent, Colonel James Outram. Outram had a twofold motive for thwarting Burton's plans. Not only was Burton a Napier man, but earlier in his career Outram had toyed with the selfsame Somali expedition Burton was now preparing. Not surprisingly then, Outram opposed Burton at all points, saying that the enterprise had no conceivable scientific justification, was simply a wild aventure, and was certain to end in loss of life.[9] He denied Burton permission to explore a wide area of Somaliland, limited the expedition to a visit to the 'forbidden' city of Harar, and continued to make difficulties, great and small.

Burton could live with physical discomfort; it was the contemptible behaviour of Aden's human denizens, especially Outram, that irked him. In Aden, he said, there was nothing but a 'dull routine of meaningless parades and tiresome courts martial ... where the business of life is comprised in ignoble squabbles ... where, briefly, the march of mind is at a dead halt, and the march of matter is in double-quick time to the hospital or sick quarters.'[10]

Burton spent the long wait in Aden mastering the elements of the Somali language, in which he was helped by an outline grammar written by his linguistic rival from India, Lieutenant C. P. Rigby. Burton also amassed a mine of information on Somalia from contacts in bazaars, and from local prostitutes. Meanwhile, to assuage Outram's implacable hostility to the enterprise Burton made an important, though ultimately fatal, concession. He suggested that the main Zanzibar expedition be postponed until after the dissolution of the annual Berbera fair in April 1855. He would use the time in making a dash for Harar.

In October the official reply from London finally arrived. Burton was given permission for the journey to Somaliland and thence south-east to Zanzibar; but the project for the crossing of Africa was to be put on ice until the results of the Somali expedition could be evaluated.[11] Outram now seemed outflanked, but after a close reading of the letter from the Court of Directors, he pounced on the passage where it stated that Lieutenant Burton was not to proceed if there was a likelihood that his own life or that of his companions would be endangered. This was an absurd proviso, for venture into the unknown must carry with it the risk of death. But to the triumphant pettifoggery of Outram Burton had no ready answer. He therefore again tried to placate his enemy by suggesting that, before the main Zanzibar expedition, three reconnaissance trips should be essayed: his own, to Harar; another under Lieutenant Herne to Berbera, where he would meet up with Lieutenant Stroyan; and a third party which would land at Bunder Garay and trace the watershed of the Wadi Nogal. This third party was to be under the command of a newcomer, Lieutenant John Hanning Speke.

A month before formal permission from the Court of Directors reached Burton, a twenty-seven-year-old lieutenant in the 46th Regiment, Bengal Light Infantry, arrived from Bombay in a P. & O. vessel, having completed his initial ten-year tour of military duty in India. Born in 1827 in Devon into a gentry family that could trace its origins to one William Espec who came from Normandy with the Conqueror in 1066, Speke was the second son in a family of seven, including four males, three of whom died at an early age.[12] After an interview with Wellington in 1844, Speke went to India to join his regiment. He served with distinction in the Sikh Wars and developed a taste for big-game hunting. He spent his long leaves in the hills and mountains of Tibet and the Himalayas, where he endeavoured to add an individual of every animal species to the trophies he sent home to the ancestral hall at Jordans in Somerset. For Speke the lonely hunting expeditions in the Himalayas were a golden age to which he often returned in his memories; not even the fame he later achieved in Africa could overtop them.[13]

Speke arrived in Aden with a three-year army furlough stretching ahead, which he intended to use travelling and big-game hunting in unexplored Africa. When he presented his credentials to Outram and unveiled his plans, the Resident made plain his violent opposition to the scheme. Many people would have caught the next steamer to England, but Speke now revealed obstinacy fully the match of that of the 'Bayard of India'. Eventually an exasperated Outram decided to divert this troublesome gadfly onto Burton's flank, hoping that the two pests would cancel each other out.

On the face of it, all that Speke had to offer was overweening ambition and a hypertrophied taste for slaughtering wild life. He had no scientific training, spoke neither Arabic, Somali nor any other African tongue, and had a philistine attitude to books and learning. He was slow, ponderous, lacked a sense of humour and was devoid of any obvious intellectual gifts. As Burton scathingly remarked: 'He was ignorant of the native races in Africa, he had brought with him almost £400 worth of cheap and useless guns and revolvers ... which the Africans would have rejected with disdain. He did not know any of the manners and customs of the East.'[14]

Yet Burton decided to enlist him, on condition that he meet his own expenses. This was an important proviso, for a quarter of the £1000 grant paid to the expedition by the Government of India had already been used up, and its administrators wisely decided to issue the subvention in discrete tranches. The arrangement arrived at was that Speke's furlough would be suspended and his officer's pay restored so that he could pay for his expenses as a member of the expedition on active service. Burton assigned Speke the initial task of exploring the Wadi Nogal in north-eastern Somaliland, there to collect geological samples in case the rumours of gold were true.

Why did Burton take this momentous decision, so fraught with future consequences to himself? It has been suggested that he had lately failed to secure the services of another officer for the Wadi Nogal trip, but this hardly seems convincing. It is likely that deeper motives were afoot, of which Burton was unconscious. For beneath the superficial dissimilarity, there were common elements that bound Burton and Speke together in a fatal embrace. Despite himself, Burton found something attractive about the gauche newcomer. Speke was physically tough, courageous to the point of folly and had 'an uncommonly acute "eye for country", by no means a usual accomplishment even with the professional surveyor.'[15]

That Burton found Speke physically impressive is clear from his glowing description: 'of lithe, spare form, about six feet tall, "blue-eyed, tawny-maned; the old Scandinavian type, full of energy and life," with a highly nervous temperament, a token of endurance, and long, wiry but not muscular limbs, that could cover ground at a swinging pace'.[16] There were other bonds between the two men. Although Speke hated academic learning and had been a rebellious and refractory schoolboy, the very lack of discipline in his early days, when he had preferred bird-nesting to his books and had not been brought to heel by his father, made his youth seem a pale copy of Burton's. Speke also shared Burton's view that the naked male form was infinitely superior to the female.[17]

Most important of all, both men had fraught relationships with their mothers. Burton's produced a fundamentally bisexual personality. With Speke, because of a childhood in which his father was a distant, unauthoritarian and non-interventionist figure and his mother encouraged an excessively emotional reaction to the world, the adult personality was that of a repressed homosexual; Speke seemed to have no heterosexual side to him at all.[18] In addition, Speke's intense relationship with his mother appears to have led to a profound if unconscious jealousy of his siblings. For there was surely something pathological about an aspect of Speke's behaviour when out hunting, which Burton noticed with distaste, naturally without being able to guess at its origin. To the horror of his African bearers, who felt it was some sort of blow struck at fertility and childbearing in general, Speke evinced a taste for eating the embryos of the pregnant female animals he killed.[19] The unconscious impulse for this strange behaviour is likely to have been 'revenge' against his siblings for being rivals for his mother's affection.

Yet the unconscious homosexual attraction initially drawing Speke and Burton together was not their only shared drive. Both men were self-destructive in the extreme. Speke's passion for battle and dangerous big-game hunting and his insensate slaughter of all species he came in contact with, under the guise of collecting rare specimens, was a projection of a death wish he explicitly acknowledged. He told Burton 'he had come to be killed in Africa.' Burton himself was not immune to such feelings and he too sometimes admitted that his actions were self-destructive. He could never account satisfactorily for his initial engagement of Speke and the problems he thereby brought on himself. 'Why should I have cared? I do not know.'[20]

Burton insisted that all members of his Somali reconnaissance parties should go disguised as Arabs. Outram argued that the expedition would lose caste in the eyes of the Somalis, who respected only the British uniform; Burton replied that that was the one thing they manifestly did not respect. Speke's objections to dressing as an Arab were more specific. Tall and fair, he looked like a freak in his desert costume.

Besides, the bulky and uncomfortable tent-like apparel made him sweat profusely under the Aden sun. 'It was anything but pleasant to feel. I had a huge hot turban, a long close-fitting gown, baggy loose drawers, drawn in at the ankles, sandals on my naked feet, and a silk girdle decorated with pistol and dirk.'[21] But despite Speke's protests, Burton remained adamant. On 18 October, dressed in his Arab garments, Speke set sail in an Arab dhow for the Somali coast.

Eleven days later Burton himself took ship for Zayla (modern Zeila). In this seaport on the Somali coast Burton spent a month in preparation for the journey to Harar. Again and again he received the most dire warnings of the fate that awaited him if he was foolhardy enough to set foot there. Arguably the journey to Harar would prove to be more perilous even than the one to Mecca. Not only was Harar the centre of the East African slave trade and the centre for training Islamic missionaries; even more ominously, there existed a prophecy that on the day a 'Frank' first set foot in the holy city, the Amirate of Harar was doomed. There was said to be a standing ordinance prescribing beheading for any infidel reckless enough to enter the sacred portals. But Burton was determined on 'breaking the guardian spell', as he put it. To those in Zayla who reiterated that 'the human head once struck off does not regrow like the rose' Burton replied that Harar was no different from any other African fortress, since all the continent's cities were prisons 'into which you enter by your own will and leave by another's'.[22]

The British-backed governor of Zayla, a sixty-year-old warrior called Sharmakay, endorsed the warnings about Harar with a plethora of his own: the road there was swarming with brigands, his son had recently been murdered by the Eesa tribe, smallpox was rampant, etc. Burton dismissed the objections; 'one death to a man is a serious thing: a dozen neutralise one another.' But though Burton was deaf to his entreaties on the score of Harar, he and Sharmakay established a close rapport during the month Burton spent in the town while he made his final preparations. Housed in Sharmakay's 'palace', Burton was daily treated to as much mutton, maize cakes, curds and coffee as he could eat. He had the pick of the governor's female Eesa slaves at night, and during the day sat smoking and taking notes while Sharmakay held court.

Burton very quickly amazed the inhabitants of Zayla by his grasp of Islamic lore. He was accepted as a genuine *Haj*, established himself as an expert in the Koran in daily conversations with the cosmopolitan population of Arabs, Somalis, Persians and Indians, acquired the reputation of being superior in his scholarship on the Prophet to the local mullahs, and even led prayers in the mosque.[23] His investigation into Somali sexuality was wide and deep. He reported on the universal customs of clitoridectomy and infibulation, the prevalence of casual adultery and corresponding absence of prostitution, and drew attention to the invariable Somali position for lovemaking, where both parties lay on their sides, the woman on the left, the man on the right.[24]

Burton also impressed on the locals his credentials as a man of power. His guns elicited a mixture of fear and contempt, for the Somalis held that firearms were the weapons of a coward, 'with which the poltroon can slay the bravest'. But their admiration increased when he demonstrated how easy it was to dodge a spear thrown in the daytime. Though deadly at night when the missile could not be perceived, the spear was, Burton asserted, 'a puerile weapon during the day when a steady man can easily avoid it.' His expert sword-play soon won for him the reputation of being the strongest man in Zayla: 'This is perhaps the easiest way of winning respect from a barbarous people, who honour body and degrade mind to mere cunning.'[25]

For light relief Burton drew horoscopes, read palms and narrated stories from the *Arabian Nights* which kept his audience enthralled. As Burton later recalled: 'Nor was it only in Arabia that the immortal Nights did me such notable service; I found the wildlings of Somaliland equally amenable to its discipline; no one was deaf to the charms and the two woman cooks of my caravan, on its way to Harar, were incontinently dubbed by my men 'Shahrazad' and 'Dinazad.'[26]

On 27 November 1854 Burton's mules and caravans conveyed a party of nine (including the two women) on the road to Harar. At first they travelled along the coast towards Berbera so as to avoid the hostile Eesa tribe, then turned inland into the mountains on a straight course for Harar. Burton's *abban* or chief guide was a former policeman in Aden, a Moslem whom Burton nicknamed 'End of Time'. The *abban* amused Burton by his vast store of Islamic proverbial lore, and for this reason the explorer connived at the man's 'prodigious rascality ... infinite intrigue, cowardice and cupidity'. 'End of Time' was also a very good translator of the Somali dialect of Arabic, which had significant variations from the tongue of the Hejaz.

In the light of his later savage animadversions on Africa's indigenous population, it is interesting to find Burton in Somalia remarkably indulgent towards the foibles of the people, even though the code of honour of their warriors embraced the killing of pregnant women; the dubious argument was that the slaying of a putative male embryo entitled one to wear the traditional emblem of destruction of an enemy – the ostrich plume. Normally Burton would have been down on this signal instance of cowardice, but he was seduced by the 'soft, merry and affectionate' demeanour of his hosts, and their cosmopolitanism. They were highly interested in the Crimean War and learned of its battles remarkably quickly after their occurrence. 'Many speak with fluency three or four languages and are perfectly acquainted with

English customs and manners.'[27] But Burton's indulgence did not extend to the Danakil tribe whose lands lay adjacent to the line of march, and who were notorious for their castration of all strangers. 'Wild as orang-outangs and the women fit only to flog cattle', was Burton's scathing assessment.[28]

As Burton's caravan threaded slowly into the mountains, his men were continually heckled by Bedouin nomads. After hearing the ominous word *Faranj* (Frank) imprecated after him a dozen times, Burton felt the time had come to impress his tormentors with his firepower. He shot two vultures in quick succession, bringing down the second on the wing with a lucky volley. Suitably impressed by this awesome marksmanship, the Bedouin left him in peace for a while. In a second test of his mettle some days later, they boasted of their skill with spear and shield. When Burton riposted that a good fencer would have no difficulty disposing of a warrior so armed, they challenged him to make good his words. Burton armed himself with a long stick and provided the best man among the nomads with a similar weapon. Challenging the man to run him through, Burton laid on a bravura display of thrusting and parrying. When the Bedouin 'expert' had repeatedly failed to get anywhere near his opponent, Burton put him out of his misery by several resounding blows on his backside, at which the nomadic champion retired in humiliated confusion.[29]

They trekked on past thousands of conical white-ant hills, at an altitude of 3500 feet, and passed briefly through the border of the much feared Eesa who, however, gave them no trouble. They descended into the greener country of the Harar prairie – a terrain which Burton likened to southern Italy or Provence. Hitherto there had been few traces of the fabled African fauna, but now they saw frequent signs of lions, elephants, jackals and lynxes. The caravan had one close call with a large lion at night, which Burton put to flight with his elephant gun.

As they ascended into the mountains again for the last stretch to Harar, Burton became concerned at the universal conviction among the villagers with whom they stayed that he was a Turk; Turks, it transpired, had a reputation for cruelty and treachery. It was his white skin that incurred the Turkish charge, and Burton began to regret that he had not stained his skin with walnut-juice, as on the Mecca journey. 'They will spoil that white skin of thine at Harar', one of the villagers commented lugubriously. At the last village before Harar – Sagharrah – Burton called for volunteers to accompany him into the holy city. Only two men, Al-Hammal and Mad Sa'id, were prepared to join him. Taken aback by the genuine fear of the villagers and his own Somalis, Burton made a decision that may have saved his life in Harar. Instead of proceeding disguised and with an unsealed Arabic letter of introduction,

Burton resolved to appear openly in the citadel as an Englishman. He forged a letter of introduction as if from the Political Agent at Aden to the Amir of Harar, proposing the establishment of friendly relations between the British and the 'great power' in the mountains.[30]

Leaving a letter for Herne with 'End of Time', in case the gloomiest prognostications came to pass, Burton and his two companions made their way to the outskirts of Harar on the afternoon of 3 January 1855. 'Nothing conspicuous appeared but two grey minarets of rude shape; many would have grudged exposing three lives to win so paltry a prize.' But the thought that no 'Frank' had ever before entered 'that pile of stones' excited him sufficiently to spur his mule forward towards the gates.

At the gate Mad Sa'id accosted the warder, who carried a long wand to denote his office, and informed him that an emissary from the British requested an audience. The warder sped off to deliver the message, leaving the alien trio at the gate. Half an hour later he returned with word that the strangers should enter the threshold. Once inside the courtyard the warder ordered them to dismount and follow him on the double. Burton and his men got off their mules but refused indignantly to break into a trot. Leading their animals in a leisurely gait, they came to an inner courtyard. Here followed a further half-hour wait, at the end of which the warder returned with the order that they doff their shoes. Grudgingly Burton instructed his men to obey, but he drew the line at giving up his weapons. Still bearing his revolver and daggers, he was finally ushered into the presence of the Amir.

The Amir turned out to be a thin-bearded young man of twenty-five, with yellow complexion, wrinkled brows and protruding eyes. He was dressed in a flowing robe of crimson cloth, edged with snowy fur, and wore a narrow white turban twisted round a tall conical cap of red velvet. It was at once apparent that the Amir was an invalid – Burton suspected consumption – for though he sat on a simple bench he rested his elbow on a pillow, from which there peeped out the hilt of a scimitar. Although the courtiers spoke in Harari, Burton with his genius for languages picked up enough to learn that his hunch at Sagharrah had been correct: to have entered as a Turk would have been fatal. Evidently the Amir had been warned that a Turk was on his way, which accounted for the ferocious look originally discernible on the young ruler's face.[31]

It was time for bold action. With consummate aplomb, in his clearest Arabic, Burton said 'Peace be unto you', and at once presented his credentials. The Amir smiled graciously in reply. 'The smile I must own, dear Lumsden, was a relief', Burton recorded later. At a second interview the ruler accepted Burton's gift of a revolver. But first he insisted that Burton divulge the details of his mission to the Wazir, or Chancellor, of Harar. To Burton's talk of friendly relations and commercial dealings the Wazir returned a bland: 'it is well if Allah please!'

Burton found himself lodged in a clean but uncomfortable room. He lay down to sleep that night exhausted yet 'profoundly impressed with the *poésie* of our position. I was under the roof of a bigoted prince whose least word was death; amongst a people who detest foreigners; the only European that had ever passed over their inhospitable threshold, and the fated instrument of their future downfall.'[32]

For ten days Burton remained in Harar, compiling his usual copious notes on the history and ethnology of the city. Despite its eminence as a centre of Arab learning – which was helpful to Burton since its dozens of experts on the works of the Prophet filled in gaps in his researches – the town itself was a glorified slum, just one-and-a-half square miles of narrow streets piled high with refuse, notable for a laxity of morals excessive even by Somali standards. Even a Burton could not write up a town like this into a very interesting anthropological specimen, and he also soon tired of the monotonous diet of boiled beef, peppered holcus cakes soaked in sour milk, and plantains. But divided counsels among the Amir's advisers delayed permission to depart. Some were interested in exporting coffee to the British, others feared that contact would bring them under the imperial sway of the 'Frank'. Burton finally won the day by using his 'skills' as a physician to minister to the Wazir's hacking cough. He promised to send back medicaments from Aden that could cure it. On Saturday 13 January the gates were opened, and he and his men sped out into the wilderness.

The sequel clearly shows the sharp mood-swings to which Burton was prone:

> Suddenly my weakness and sickness left me – so potent a drug is joy – and, as we passed the gates loudly salaaming to the warders, who were crouching over the fire inside, a weight of care and anxiety fell from me like a cloak of lead. Yet, dear L, I had time, on the top of my mule, for musing upon how melancholy a thing is success. While failure inspirits a man, attainment reads the sad prosy lesson that all our glories 'are shadows, not substantial things'. Truly said the sayer, 'disappointment is the salt of life' – a salutary bitter which strengthens the mind for fresh exertion, and gives a double value to the prize.[33]

Twenty-four hours took them to the village of Wilensi, where Burton's followers were now ensconced. Burton was in rare good humour, as the following passage attests: 'As we approached it [Wilensi] all the wayfarers and villagers inquired Hibernically if we were the party that had been put to death by the Amir of Harar. Loud congratulations and shouts of joy awaited our arrival. The Kalendar was in a paroxysm of delight; both Shehrazade and Deenazarde were affected with giggling and what. We reviewed our property and found that the One-eyed had been a faithful steward, so faithful indeed, that he had well nigh starved the two women.'[34]

Burton's party remained a week at Wilensi to fatten up themselves and the mules, and lay in stocks for the long desert march to Berbera that lay ahead. He himself spent the time working on a dictionary of the Harari tongue. He collected together a thousand of the most important words, and concluded from his researches that the dialect was closer to the Amharic of Ethiopia than to the pure Arabic of the Arabian peninsula. Then, on 22 January, the caravan set out for the return journey to the coast. They crossed the Harar prairie in icy rain and thick mists. By now Burton was ten days behind the schedule he had set himself, and he feared that Stroyan and Herne would be growing anxious at Berbera. He therefore split his party, leaving the women, camels and baggage in his steward's care, to be delivered at Zayla after a leisurely progress. He himself took a handpicked party on a 'short cut' – a gruelling march across an unyielding desert to Berbera.

The wells proved far fewer and sparser than his guides had promised. At night they were assailed by biting winds and thick mists which deepened into drizzle. Far from quenching their thirst, this dampness merely drenched the saddle cloths, their only bedding. In the day they could look forward to a horizon dotted only with withered aloes, and to stony ground crisscrossed by thorns. But worst of all was the lack of water. 'The demon of thirst rode like Care behind us. For twenty-four hours we did not taste water, the sun parched our brains, the mirage mocked us at every turn, and the effect was a species of monomania. As I jogged along with eyes closed against the fiery air, no image unconnected with the want suggested itself. Water ever lay before me – water lying deep in the shady well – water in streams bubbling icy from the rock – water in pellucid lakes inviting me to plunge and revel in their treasures.'[35]

Burton later confessed that he would never have ventured into this dreadful desert had the true dimensions of the water shortage there been known to him. His party survived by pure luck. On one occasion the mules found a rock spring. On another, he was guided to water by the *kata* or sand-grouse. Burton recorded his gratitude: 'I have never since shot a *kata*.'[36] Once they hit the sea-shore they found that the previously brackish waterholes had been partially purified by the recent rains. Finally, in the small hours of 31 January, the exhausted caravan limped into Berbera.

Stroyan and Herne greeted them with relief. The Berberans heard the story of the crossing of the desert with incredulity at such madness. After Burton's usual topographical investigation of any strange town he came to, he bade farewell to his brother officers, who were to continue with preparations for the main Zanzibar expedition, and boarded a leaky Arab ship for Aden on 5 February. Burton was seldom lucky with sea voyages, and this one was no exception. The ship was caught in a ferocious storm, the waves broke over them, and captain and crew abandoned all pretence at seamanship, commending their souls to Allah instead. Somehow the craft survived, and on 9 February 1855 Burton arrived back in Aden.

Burton felt justifiably pleased with his achievements. He had capped his Meccan exploit with another successful venture where no European had trodden before, and was understandably euphoric.[37] He told Shaw he felt certain the East India Company directors could not now refuse him the second year of leave he needed for the Zanzibar venture. All appeared to be going according to plan.[38] His knowledge of African customs had been considerably widened: in Abyssinia he had been reproved for eating without champing, for it was considered that good breeding required noisy masticating: 'thou feedest like a beggar who muncheth silently in his corner', the Ethiopian nomads told him.[39] Then, too, there was the invaluable addition he had made to his growing thesaurus of sexology. In Somalia he had measured an unerect penis of 6 inches; he recorded that the gigantic member did not increase proportionately when erect, so that the woman's pleasure was much increased, since she was freed from the uncertainty of the usual cycle of tumescence and detumescence.[40]

In his official report to the East India Company Burton urged the establishment of a British consulate at Berbera and the suppression of slavery in Somalia – not on humanitarian grounds, but simply because it was a barrier to commerce. Burton argued that the absorption of the Horn of Africa into an imperial scheme was inevitable, and if it was not the British one, then it would be the Turkish. Far better to build a British sphere of influence from Suez to Zanzibar, with consuls at Suez, Jeddah and Zanzibar, a missionary settlement at Mombasa and an agency at Berbera forming the links in the chain. As for his own immediate plans, he asked for a period of leave long enough to complete the Zanzibar expedition and settle the issue of the source of the Nile. He concluded by requesting the brevet rank of major while in East Africa.[41]

At this juncture the East India Company had no good grounds for rejecting him. His anthropological analysis of northern Somalia was acknowledged, then and since, as masterly.[42] He had demystified Harar, but in such a way that his name would ever afterwards be linked with the city.[43] And he had 'talked up' the success of the three separate expeditionary probes in Somali country to the point where it would be churlish to refuse endorsement for the larger expedition to Zanzibar.

Yet Burton's brave talk masked the fact that one of the subsidiary expeditions had been an embarrassing flop. Speke's venture into the Wadi Nogal ended ingloriously with the prosecution in Aden of his chief guide or *abban*, a man named Sumunter. A notorious debtor and no-good, Sumunter systematically humiliated Speke by refusing to obey orders, selling off expedition *matériel* to defray his debts, and appealing over Speke's head to the bearers. Since Speke spoke no languages, he was powerless. He worked off his rage by the usual slaughter of wildlife. Snakes, birds, antelope, hyraxes, partridges, hyenas, ostriches, gazelles – all fell to the gun of this modern Nimrod. He regretted that the local rhino had been wiped out by indigenous hunters, envied the Somalis their method of killing elephants by hamstringing, and valued the terrain only for the 'bags' it could provide him with: 'we were visited by a very singular-looking canine animal, which unfortunately I could not get a shot at', is a typical Speke journal entry.[44] Speke's only regret was that he could not visit the same fate on Sumunter; 'he seemed to me only as an animal in satanical disguise; to have shot him would have given me great relief, for I fairly despaired of ever producing a good effect upon his mind.'[45]

When Speke arrived in Aden, almost two weeks after Burton, the tale of his humiliation by the *abban* produced in Burton the contempt he always felt for those who could not master a given situation. He began to see Speke in a new light; if he had been truly rational, he would have jettisoned him then and there. Yet British credibility demanded that Sumunter be punished. Reluctantly Speke agreed to prosecute the *abban* in the Aden Police Court. Sumunter's insolence had been so egregious that it was not difficult, on the testimony of Speke's servants, to prove him guilty of serious crimes. He was sentenced to two months' imprisonment and fined two hundred rupees (with the alternative of a consecutive term of six months at hard labour if he failed to pay the fine) and banished for life from the colony, with his family.

Unknowingly, Burton gave great offence to the chieftains of northern Somalia by this punishment of Sumunter, and he compounded his sins in their eyes by announcing publicly that Sumunter had disgraced the entire system of *abban*-ship which should thenceforth be abandoned. But this was not Burton's only error of judgement. Irritated by Speke's bungling incompetence and convinced that it was the younger man's shaky grasp of Hindustani that lay at the root of the problem, Burton struck back at him by using Speke's diary as an appendage to his own *First Footsteps*. He severely pruned the diary, mangled what was left, and interpolated a series of patronising comments which deeply wounded Speke when he read them. This left a legacy of profound unexpunged hostility and antagonism that was to have disastrous later consequences. The flavour of the remarks can be briefly conveyed:

> It is evident from the perusal of these pages that though the traveller suffered from the system of blackmail to which the inhospitable Somal of Makhar subject all strangers, though he was delayed, persecuted by his 'protector', and threatened with war, danger, and destruction, his life was never in real peril. Some allowance must also be made for the people of the country. Lt. Speke was, of course, recognised as a servant of Government; and savages cannot believe that a man wastes his rice and cloth to collect dead beasts and to ascertain the direction of streams. He was known to be a Christian; he is ignorant of the Moslem faith; and, most fatal to his enterprise, he was limited in time. Not knowing either the Arabic or the Somali tongue, he was forced to communicate with the people through the medium of his dishonest interpreter and Abban.[46]

Speke departed in semi-disgrace on 20 March for the Somali coast to collect camels for the Zanzibar expedition. He landed at Kurrum, then made his way along the coast to Berbera. He detected ominous signs of unwonted hostility there towards himself and Stroyan and Herne, whom Burton had left behind to prepare an adequate supply of drinking water. The presence of the British provoked rumours that the British government intended to annex Somalia, or that they were about to suppress the slave trade, or that at the very least they were going to occupy Berbera and hand it over to their friend Sharmakay of Zayla.

Why did Burton take no notice of these reports of increasing hostility? Why did he brush them aside as typical Somali gossiping bravado? Almost certainly the answer is that in the crucial month of March 1855 the idea of discovering the fabled Mountains of the Moon and the source of the Nile became an obsession that blotted out all other considerations. In his obsession Burton indulged in a contempt for his fellow workers in the vineyard of Africa that was a common feature of the minds of the great African explorers and disfigured the work of all of them: Burton, Speke, Stanley, even the saintly Livingstone. The great figure in Nile exploration to date was the Scotsman James Bruce, who in 1770 had travelled to the fabled sources of the Blue Nile. Almost predictably, Burton felt it necessary to sneer at his precursor. 'His pompous and inflated style, his uncommon arrogance, and overweening vanity, his affectation of pedantry, his many errors and misrepresentations, aroused against him a spirit which embittered the last years of his life. It is now the fashion to laud Bruce and to pity his misfortunes. I cannot but think that he deserved them.'[47]

But why the obsession with the Nile in March 1855 rather than during the long sojourn in Aden in 1854? Fawn Brodie has ingeniously suggested that the trigger was the death of Burton's mother, news of which reached him in February. Both Bruce and Livingstone were galvanised into Nile quests, she points out, immediately after sustaining tragic family losses.[48]

Whatever the reasons, when Burton crossed from Aden on the schooner *Mahi* on 7 April, he was insufficiently prepared mentally for the changed circumstances in Somalia and nearly plunged headlong into tragedy. Superficially everything seemed set fair for the great African adventure. Stroyan, Speke and Herne had assembled a force of forty-two men, well equipped with camels and fully supplied. The personnel was a mixture of Egyptians, Nubians and Arabs. But Burton made an initial error by failing to set out with the heavily armed caravan which was then leaving for Ogaden; he preferred instead to wait for the scientific instruments he was expecting from London.

By 18 April Burton and his men were encamped a mile outside Berbera. They were situated on a rocky ridge overlooking the Red Sea from where the *Mahi* could provide covering fire onto the beach. Burton had heard the rumours of bad blood towards his expedition, but discounted them. No Englishman had been attacked in Berbera for thirty years, they had a naval escort, and besides, to fortify the camp too strongly might give the Somalis the impression the British officers were afraid.

Having deprived himself of overland protection by not departing with the Ogaden caravan, Burton was next deprived of the *Mahi*'s big guns when the ship was recalled to Aden for blockading duties. The expedition was thus peculiarly vulnerable. The first signs of trouble came at sunset on the 19th when three foragers were driven off by musketry from the camp perimeter. Such a probe was the invariable prelude to attack in this part of the world, but the Eesa scouts – for such they proved to be – concocted a story of such plausibility to account for their presence that even Burton's giant black *abban* Balyuz was taken in. Burton therefore posted no more than the usual two sentries.[49]

At about two o'clock on the morning of the 19th Burton was aroused by the panic-stricken voice of Balyuz, who yelled that the enemy were upon them. There was a rush of men like a stormy wind as some 350 marauders swept into the camp. Burton seized his sabre and ordered Herne to make for the main danger point at the rear of the camp. Finding the enemy in great force and the guard nowhere, Herne began to beat a speedy retreat but in the darkness tripped over a guy-rope and was almost clubbed where he lay before he managed to fell his assailant with a shot from his Colt. Burton meanwhile aroused Stroyan and Speke who were sleeping in the extreme right and left tents. Speke was slow to respond, thinking it to be the usual false alarm. He staggered blearily over to the primitive laager that Burton and Herne had formed at the threshold of their giant 'Rowtie' tent. Stroyan was never seen alive again.

The extreme peril was soon apparent. Outnumbered by impossible odds, the three officers quickly used up their revolver ammunition in blazing away through the embrasure formed by the tent opening. When the enemy tried to cut down the tent from behind so as to ensnare them in its folds, Burton gave the order to run for it. Then there occurred an incident that has always been controversial. As they stepped outside, Speke was hit by a volley of stones and staggered back inside the collapsing canvas. His story was that his ophthalmia produced temporary night blindness.[50] Burton, however, interpreted the momentary retreat as cowardice and yelled at him, 'Don't step back or they'll think we are retiring.'

Once outside, the three became separated. In the inky darkness Burton slashed with his sabre at anything that moved. He was just about to cut a man down when a well-known voice alerted him that his intended victim was Balyuz. Burton's fractional hesitation after this near-miss almost proved fatal. Seeing his opportunity, an Eesa spearman hurled a javelin at Burton. It lanced into his cheek, shivered four back teeth and part of his palate, then shot out again through the opposite cheek. Almost fainting from pain and loss of blood, Burton somehow kept going beyond the thick of the fighting. On the shore, supported on the arms of his bearers, he managed to signal to a ship at anchor in the harbour whose captain Burton had dined with the night before. The friendly captain Yusuf lowered a boat and brought Burton off. On board he extracted the javelin and staunched the haemorrhage.

In the morning Yusuf landed a boat party to look for survivors. Herne had miraculously survived with no more than a few blows from a war-club, even though he was at one time surrounded by a dozen Eesa, and managed to join Balyuz on the shore. Later amid the bodies of five Somali dead they came on the corpse of Stroyan. His head had been disfigured with gashes and his chest and abdomen were stippled with spear jabs.

But the most amazing survival story was that of Speke. Taken captive early in the fighting, Speke had his hands bound in front of him, was thrown to the ground and then forced to watch a war dance through the night. When one of his captors frisked him for a weapon and fumbled with his genitals, Speke thought they intended to castrate him before killing him. Numerous threats of death were offered to him, especially when he refused to abjure Christianity. Finally, one of the Eesa drove a spear through his thigh as casually as if he were putting a needle through sackcloth. 'Smelling death', Speke managed to bring his bound hands down on his attacker in a two-fisted smash. As the man staggered, Speke made off over the shingly beach towards the surf.

Bobbing and ducking he ran in a zigzag pattern towards the sea, dodging the spears hurled at him. 'I was almost naked and quite bare upon the feet', he recalled. Though bleeding from eleven spear wounds, he managed to outrun his pursuers and gnaw his way through his bonds. At first light the landing party found him.[51]

It was clear that complete disaster had overtaken the intended expedition to Zanzibar. Because of rapid decomposition of his body, Stroyan had to be buried immediately, at sea, instead of in Aden. Two days later the seriously wounded arrived back in Aden. Burton's wound was exacerbated by secondary syphilis, and the examining surgeon (his friend Steinhaeuser) told him he would not survive unless repatriated at once to England. Speke meanwhile hovered near death for days. His legs contracted painfully, he tossed deliriously with a high fever and temporarily went blind. After a long period of unconsciousness, in which he cried out frequently in pain and saturated his bed sheets with sweat, the immensely tough Speke passed the crisis. His fever subsided and the spasms in his legs departed. Three of the four British officers had survived the ordeal, but it is likely the consequences of that dreadful night in Berbera haunted Burton for the rest of his life.

9

Crimean Débâcle

THE post-mortem on the Berbera disaster was the first stage in a trail of official minutes and documents with an explosive force which ultimately blew Burton's career as an explorer sky-high. 'If I had "let well alone", I should have done well', he later concluded ruefully.[1] The most basic criticism levelled at Burton was that he had exercised insufficient care there, and in particular that he had failed to post enough guards on the fatal night. Even Speke, with no reason to support Burton, found that hard to stomach. He pointed out that their men were such cowards, it would not have mattered how many guards they had set. Burton's defence to the charge was characteristically robust. He held to his stated position that the coast of Somalia was generally considered as safe as Bombay itself. It was in any case a mere fluke that his party was still there to be attacked. If the mail from Aden had arrived in time, they would have left with the Ogaden caravan. And if the *Mahi* had not been withdrawn, the expedition would have been invulnerable on the beach; once inland, the Bedouin would not have dared to try conclusions with the superior British firepower. In a word, the disaster was all Aden's fault.[2]

Brigadier Coghlan, the new Resident at Aden, would have none of this. He replied that the military defences of the camp had been inept and that the attackers were not simply motivated by plunder, as Burton alleged. They feared that Burton intended to establish Sharmakay in Berbera. Also, Burton had made a disastrous mistake in announcing that thenceforth the British would no longer use the system of *abban*-ship. As another of Burton's critics pointed out, 'A traveller who hopes for success in exploring a new country must accept the institutions he finds in existence; he can hardly hope by his simple *fiat*, to revolutionise the time-honoured and *most profitable* institutions of a people, amongst whom precedent is a law as unchangeable as that of the Medes and Persians.'[3] The fear of the possible abolition of slavery, and the treatment meted out to Sumunter, also rankled with the Somalis.

Lord Elphinstone, Governor and President of the Council at Bombay, agreed with Coghlan that Burton had been remiss. Even stronger condemnation of Burton was voiced by the Governor-General of India Lord Dalhousie, who thought that he had failed to exercise elementary prudence. Coghlan had fined the Somalis 15,000 rupees (about £1,380) as compensation for the losses sustained by the expedition, and threatened a blockade of Berbera if they did not pay; Dalhousie thought this was an over-reaction in view of the fact that the first cause of the débâcle was Burton's carelessness. But Coghlan did institute the blockade. It hurt the Somalis and forced them to reveal the name of Stroyan's killer.

Lieutenant Lambert Playfair, acting Resident in Aden during Coghlan's absence on a tour of inspection, castigated Burton for imprudence in remaining in Berbera after the break-up of the annual fair. A deputation of Somalis then came to Aden to ask for the lifting of the blockade, and convinced Playfair that the entire fiasco was Burton's fault. Coghlan and Playfair reported to Bombay to this effect, and it would have gone hard with Burton if he had not had a resolute supporter there in the shape of his friend Lumsden. Lambert Playfair was another Rigby, and was to traduce Burton wildly in his *A History of Arabia Felix*.[4] Even though later investigations completely vindicated Burton, the Aden authorities were prepared to blacken him with any and every canard, provided they attracted no blame themselves.

Burton struck back in his usual style. In a letter to the Royal Geographical Society in December 1856 he criticised the lack of protection given to trade and to British protégés in Red Sea ports as a result of the inadequacy of the naval force at Aden.[5] Earlier that year in the Preface to *First Footsteps in East Africa* Burton vigorously attacked the official policy of the East India Company and argued for a thoroughgoing imperialism in Somalia. This angered the Court of Directors, for in asking for permission to go to Harar Burton had promised he would not include any political comments or allusions in any resulting book. The Company view was that it did not want to have to defend a toehold in Africa 1600 miles away from its main resources. Ironically, Coghlan eventually took Burton's view that it was essential to occupy Berbera, at any rate during the annual fair, to pre-empt the French or Turks.

The verbal campaign was by no means one-sided. In August 1855 the Court of Directors wrote to Burton: 'The disaster to the Somali expedition renders it in our opinion inexpedient to entertain any application for its further prosecution.' Even worse, in November 1856 he was informed that the claim for compensation by expedition members had been refused. Burton protested vociferously (but vainly) when the blockade was raised without the fine's having been paid.

Angered by the criticisms in his book, the overt contempt in his letter to the Royal Geographical Society and his failure to take the lack of compensation lying down, the Government of Bombay at last sent Burton an official reprimand in July 1857.

The East India Company was not alone in being alienated by the 'unembarrassed mind' of its most troublesome employee. Speke too was nursing a grudge. He had lost cash and property worth £510, for which he received no compensation. He had, as he saw it, been unjustly rebuked by Burton for cowardice. And when *First Footsteps* appeared, he saw that Burton had belittled and ridiculed his contribution to the expedition.[6] The seeds of the sensational rift with Burton had already been sown in 1855; the events of the later African expedition simply germinated them. Burton first got an inkling of how deeply resentful Speke was about his 1854–55 experiences when Speke in a feverish delirium in East Africa poured out a torrent of grievances against him, concentrating especially on the treatment of his diary in *First Footsteps*.[7]

Burton left Aden for London in May 1855. He visited his father in Bath, and his sister Maria in Boulogne. Edward was there, on leave from Ceylon, full of the kind of tales of big-game hunting derring-do Burton had already had his fill of from Speke. For the first time the two brothers failed to catch fire in each other's presence. The truth was that Burton was both depressed and physically exhausted. It had taken all his superlative constitutional strength to get over the after-effects of the wound through jaw and palate. General Napier had suffered agonies after a similar wound. Burton was never happy about the ugly scar left on his face. No amount of dental work or prosthetic surgery could serve to remove the sinister look he bore thereafter, much as if he really had duelled at Heidelberg and seriously overdone it.[8]

There was no chance of firing the public imagination by the Harar exploit in 1855, as England was then in the throes of the Crimean War. Burton, ever eager to see front-line action, at once volunteered for active service. He travelled down to Marseilles and embarked for Constantinople.

Burton's zest for action did not mean that he approved of the war. On the contrary, he felt that England had been manoeuvred into an unnecessary conflict by the wiles of Louis Napoleon: 'Our grand national blunder, the great artillery duel in the corner of the Black Sea, which history will call the "Crimean War".'[9]

The winter of 1854–55 in the Crimea had provided ample ammunition for the war's critics. Cholera, dysentery and malaria decimated the British and French armies. Russia's perennial secret weapon, 'General Winter', had cut further swathes through the ragged and starving armies. For want of five miles of railway at Balaclava – a lack attributable purely to incompetence – thousands were added to the casualty lists. The fatuous brainlessness of the British commander-in-chief Lord Raglan, and the even more egregious idiocy of Lord Cardigan, the man who led the infamous 'Charge of the Light Brigade', demonstrated for all time the bankruptcy of the hallowed British custom of purchasing the best commissions in the Army with a sackful of money.[10]

Burton could not even see the *raison d'état* for Britain's belligerency. Two reasons were most commonly adduced; the 'balance of power' in Europe, and the need to protect India from Russian expansionism. Both arguments, to Burton, were absurd. Turkish possession of Constantinople, and that alone, would force Russia repeatedly into war. The solution was obvious. Turkey's European possessions should be wrested from her. Constantinople itself should become a principality of Byzantium, under the protection of the Great Powers.[11] As for Russia, Burton had, it is true, once shared the general fear of 'the Bear's' expansion towards India.[12] But mature reflection convinced him that Russia had never entertained serious designs on India; in fact it was spontaneous and unwarranted British Russophobia that had led to the débâcle in Afghanistan in 1839–41. Thirty years after the Crimea Burton reiterated his conviction; 'Whatever alarmists told the world, Russia has hitherto meddled mighty little with our Eastern empire [India].'[13]

Burton did not enjoy the sea voyage from Marseilles to Constantinople. The ship was full of French soldiers, whom he found obnoxious, with the single exception of General MacMahon.[14] On arrival in Constantinople Burton lodged in a hotel on the Golden Horn, then took a steamer over the Euxine in company with a new friend named Fred Wingfield. After three days they saw the Tauric Chersonese, and landed at Balaclava to find that the incompetent Lord Raglan had just died. After the earlier disasters Raglan confided to friends that he would be stoned to death if he returned to England, but the thought did not prevent him from compounding his errors by sending thousands of his countrymen to their death in a futile frontal assault on the fortress of Sebastopol in June 1855.[15] Morale among British officers plummeted at the rumour that Lord Cardigan was returning to lead them, but in the event the command devolved on General James Simpson, a second-rater with some experience in India under Napier (who thought him useless).

Raglan's death seemed on paper to open the way to Burton's seeing active service at last. Under Raglan this would have been next to impossible, for he had a violent prejudice against officers from 'John Company' and actually tried to forbid them from volunteering for the Crimea. Not the least of the absurdities of Raglan was this aristocratic contempt for the only officers in Britain who had recent battle experience. Burton presented himself at headquarters to General Simpson, under whom he had served briefly in Sind. Simpson kept him hanging around Balaclava for a week. With Wingfield and friends Burton made almost daily excursions to the monastery of St George, where in the myth Agamemnon's daughter was supposed to have been saved from sacrifice. At the end of the week Simpson informed Burton there was nothing for him. Burton then applied to be taken on as one of the irregulars commanded by General W. F. Beatson. Beatson had been given a commission to raise a regiment of 4000 'Bashi-Bazouks'. He needed a chief-of-staff who spoke Turkish and had experience with Sepoys – for the Bashi-Bazouk experiment was really an attempt to reproduce India and get Asiatics to fight under British officers. Burton accepted the post with alacrity.

But euphoria soon turned to disillusionment. Although Beatson recommended Burton for a lieutenant-colonelcy, the prejudice against East India Company officers was still vigorous in Constantinople. He was against refused even the brevet rank of Major. Liaison with the Turks was difficult since their commander Osman Pasha accused the Allies of sacrificing his men as cannon fodder. As for the body he had joined, 'the fellows are wild men from Syria and Albania, fierce enough ... and caring little for life.' There were 1700 of them camped near Dardanelles village and Burton confided that if they had been in any part of the Turkish world they would have committed a dozen murders a day. As it was, their daily quota of rapes had to be kept out of the English newspapers to spare the blushes of well-bred ladies.[16]

Burton's first assignment was to return to Constantinople to lobby the top brass on Beatson's behalf. Resplendent in a gorgeous Bashi-Bazouk uniform blazed in gold, Burton tried to take the embassy by storm with an excess of volubility and charm. Yet almost without exception Burton found both the officers and the diplomats based in Constantinople negligible in intellect and understanding and despicable in morality. He had an especially low opinion of the British ambassador Lord Stratford de Redcliffe. Two men alone provided an oasis in this moral and intellectual desert. One was the short-sighted and valetudinarian Percy Smythe, later Lord Strangford, whom Burton rated as the second-best linguist he ever encountered (after Professor Palmer). He could speak Persian like a Shirazi or adopt the hideous drawl of a Hindustani. The other was a Mr Alison, later Minister to Persia, who knew Romaic and Turkish and had a smattering of Persian and Arabic. He affected an absent-minded eccentricity, but Burton particularly admired the way he stood up to the tyrannical Lord Stratford. One overheard conversation with 'HE' went like this:

'Damn your eyes, Mr Alison, why was not that despatch sent?'

'Damn your Excellency's eyes, it went this morning.'[17]

In Constantinople Burton was able to see something of the social evils war always brings to the great cities in its orbit. In the East it was customary for women to make the first overtures in any sexual relationship. The fair sex in Constantinople found their allurements taken up with such gusto by the visiting soldiery that they were obliged to change their habits. The messes and bar-rooms rang with ribald stories of easy conquests of Turkish women. Burton, sure that the Islamic ordinance forbidding women to appear on the streets would not be waived in this way, came away convinced that the 'conquests' were all of Greeks, Wallachians, Armenians and Jewesses.[18] This was an interesting example of Burton as ideologue of Islam. It was a constant refrain with him that women, unless guarded zealously, would revert to a 'state of nature' of promiscuous unchastity. But when the normal social ties were loosened by wartime, Burton refused to accept the evidence of his senses and claimed that the Islamic code 'must' have prevailed.

Burton returned to the Dardanelles and his duties as Beatson's secretary. The old general was so fiery that he peppered his official despatches with insulting language and even on one occasion challenged Lord Stratford to a duel. Nobody liked a wrangle with authority more than Burton, but this was going too far even for him. He excised the more intemperate outbursts when making up a fair copy, much to Beatson's disgust; 'My General did not thank me for it', was Burton's laconic comment. Stratford retaliated by sending down to the Dardanelles as his 'eyes and ears' British consul Skene. Realising that he was a spy, Beatson picked a violent quarrel with him so that Skene had to be withdrawn. But it was a case of the hydra's head; Stratford replaced Skene with another of his spies, Brigadier T. G. Neill.[19]

Meanwhile there was the rather more pressing problem of the Bashi-Bazouks themselves to attend to. Irregular cavalry was a tradition in Turkish military annals – the horsemen engaged themselves for a fixed term, looted and plundered all they could, then returned home in the winter. But these men were the dregs of humanity, culled from the slums and stews of Islamic cities from Damascus to Constantinople. They spent most of their time gambling, duelling and fighting, or being insubordinate to their officers. They despised and hated the Russians and considered their women as legitimate spoils of war, since they lacked any initial modesty.[20] Their indiscipline would have been bad enough, but Burton noticed a plethora of other problems feeding into their turbulence. First there was the fact that the local Greeks and Jews hated the English and wanted the Russians to win. There was Franco–British factionalism. The commercial work of the British consuls was at odds with the war effort. On the other hand, militarily the Bashi-Bazouks were caught between two fires of jealousy and resentment.

Turkish Pashas were not pleased to see an 'empire within an empire' and did their best to foment trouble between the Turkish regulars and these British-led irregulars. The British high command on the other hand distrusted the whole idea of irregulars.[21]

Burton secured Beatson's permission to institute daily drills and parades, hitherto unknown. He tried to inspire the men with his own enthusiasm for swordplay, and claimed in a very short time to have licked into shape a fine body of sabremen. Quite how successful Burton really was is another matter, for in unguarded asides in his *oeuvre*, when he is not portraying himself as God's gift to the Crimean war, a rather different picture emerges.[22] But he clearly achieved *some* success in civilising his unruly charges, for five years later he recalled: 'The Bashi-Buzuk [sic] left to himself roasted the unhappy Russian; in the British service he brought his prisoner alive into camp with a view to a present or a promotion.'[23]

Burton had still not seen a day's front-line service in any war. Aching for combat experience, he secured Beatson's approval of another trip to Constantinople, this time to ask Stratford's permission to march to the relief of Kars with '2640 sabres in perfect readiness'. Kars was an ancient fortress in Armenia, defended by 15,000 Turks under British and French officers. For months it had been under siege by the Russians, food was short, and its fall was imminent unless it was relieved. This seemed a heaven-sent opportunity for the irregulars to get into the thick of fighting. But Burton was soon to learn how naïve he had been to view the war purely from a military vantage point.[24]

Unknown to Burton, secret diplomacy had already concluded a deal whereby the Russians were to be allowed to win a victory at Kars to save face after the loss of half of Sebastopol. This was why General Williams and the Hungarian general Metz, the defenders of Kars, sent more than eighty official despatches to Lord Stratford without getting a reply.[25]

Burton pressed Stratford hard to be allowed to lead his irregulars across the steppes to Kars. Stratford, unable to tell him the full story, vainly tried to put him off. When Burton refused to take no for an answer, the despotic Stratford drew himself up to his full height and yelled at him: 'You are the most impudent man in the Bombay Army, sir!' Then almost without breaking stride he added, implying that Kars was not a suitable subject to detain a 'gentleman' long, 'Of course you'll dine with us today?' It was only later that Burton realised the extent of his ingenuous folly. 'A captain of Bashi-Bazouks (myself) had madly attempted to arrest the course of *haute politique*.'[26]

Stratford tried to divert Burton by proposing a mission to seek an aliance with Schamyl, the most famous bandit chief of the Caucasus. It soon became clear that Stratford's scheme was a diversion tactic pure and simple, designed to get rid of the contumacious and meddlesome captain of Bashi-Bazouks. Burton turned down the proposal and went back to the Dardanelles. There he found problems of a different hue. On 26 September the Bashi-Bazouks themselves came under siege from Turkish regulars. Civil war within the Allied ranks was only narrowly averted, thanks to Beatson's iron discipline. Instead of responding to Turkish provocation, he kept his men in camp and the Turkish Pasha was eventually shamed into retiring. But the incident was used as a pretext by the many senior generals whom Beatson had called out or insulted. Lieutenant-General Vivian relieved him of command on 28 September. Major-General Richard Smith was announced as the new commander.

Burton headed a delegation to Smith to persuade him that all the rumours about Bashi-Bazouk indiscipline – the original pretext for the encirclement by Turkish troops – were false. The delegation asked for a temporary commander until Vivian clarified his original order. When Smith turned this proposal down, all the officers in the delegation tendered their resignations. The consequence was that Burton was later accused of having been a ringleader in the fomenting of mutiny. On 18 October Beatson returned to England in company with Burton.[27]

Once at home Beatson instituted civil proceedings against his enemies and issued a writ for libel against Skene, the first of Stratford's spies. Skene had alleged that Beatson tried to dissuade regimental colonels from serving under General Smith, his successor. He further claimed that Burton had organised a round robin, in which each officer pledged himself to serve under none but Beatson.[28]

When the case eventually came to trial, Burton was in his element. Not only was he in the full glare of publicity, but in the witness box he had ample scope for his histrionic gifts and intellectual powers. Burton positively throve on locking horns with learned counsel. He played with the chief barrister for the defence, treating the exchanges like a fencing match and drawing counsel into a morass of military technicalities where Burton would have the advantage. Defence counsel Mr Bovill, later Lord Chief Justice, tried to browbeat Burton but found himself flummoxed by the 'plain soldier's' dialectical skills. A typical exchange was the following.

Bovill: 'In what regiment did you serve under the plaintiff?'

Burton: 'Eh?'

Bovill: 'In what regiment, I say?'

Burton: 'In no regiment.'

After toying with the baffled Bovill for a while, Burton revealed that technically the Bashi-Bazouks did not constitute a regiment, but a corps.[29]

It was established that Skene had indeed defamed Burton and

Beatson, but his defence was that he did so in a privileged communication, and therefore a charge of libel could not be found. The jury acquitted him on this technicality but added a rider expressing disgust that Skene had not seen fit to retract the charges when he learned how baseless they were. Though Skene's acquittal was confirmed on appeal, the universal consensus was that Burton and Beatson had won a moral victory.

The Crimean experience deeply affected Burton, even though he spent just four months at the theatre of war. It brought his cynicism about high politics and diplomacy to a new pitch. At a personal level, he felt much sadness at the deaths in battle of individuals he had known well.[30] And he attracted more criticism, both then and later, for his 'unsoundness'. Stanley Lane-Poole, an Arabist who always hated Burton, claimed that the story of Burton's proposing a march to the relief of Kars with the Bashi-Bazouks was a fiction. He had not made the proposal; therefore Lord Stratford de Redcliffe could not have turned it down. Burton lashed back furiously at Lane-Poole, who muddied the waters by riposting that it was the Foreign Office, not Stratford, that had vetoed the relief of Kars. This was true, as Burton conceded, but irrelevant to the point under discussion, which was *Burton*'s reputation and veracity.[31]

This also took a knock from another direction. One of his friends in the Bashi-Bazouk corps was an officer who really was a villain. He robbed the post office at Alexandria, then attempted to seduce an heiress with a view to marrying, 'asset-stripping' and then divorcing her. When detected in his chicanery he claimed that Burton was a co-plotter in these nefarious enterprises. Luckily Burton had a staunch ally in Percy Smythe who protested, 'No, that won't do. X is a real scamp, but Burton is only wild.'[32]

Perhaps the most curious aspect of Burton's Crimean experiences was that he left no harrowing descriptions of the dreadful, revolting and heartrending sufferings of the dying and hospitalised that are so vivid in the writings of Tolstoy, Florence Nightingale and W. H. Russell. The unkind criticism would be to say that Burton's romantic sensibility and overgrown egotism allowed him to sail above all this, to concentrate solely on personalities and episodes which impinged on himself. But the absence of any book on his experiences, so unlike his normal habit, hints at another interpretation. There are some experiences, which cannot be encompassed in the Burtonian universe of discourse, where cynicism and detachment rule. Faced with the carnage of Sebastopol, Burton's reaction was dumb horror.

10

The Dark Continent

ON his return from the Crimea, Burton began to lobby the Royal Geographical Society for support for a further African expedition. The interlude provided by the war made it plausible to imagine that the controversy over Berbera would have subsided by now, and that the trans-Africa project might be revived. Burton spent most of 1856 promoting this scheme. But first came a significant development in his private life.

Isabel Arundell still nursed her private fantasy of becoming Burton's wife. She had followed his exploits proudly, but had not dared to approach him after the Mecca and Harar triumphs. She even tried to be near the object of her besottedness by applying to Florence Nightingale to be taken on as a nurse in the Crimea. When this application failed, she took up social work in the London slums and came to form a compassionate view of the wretched prostitutes whom she saw as, like herself, tethered to the ineluctable imperatives of woman's lot. Then in June 1856 she went to the races at Ascot. As her carriage was slowly threading its way among a throng of racegoers, a gypsy woman pushed through the crowd and opened the carriage door. It was Hagar Burton, the fortune teller from her youth, who had predicted the meeting with Burton in Boulogne.

'Are you Daisy Burton yet?' she asked.

'Would to God I were,' answered Isabel.

'Patience, it is just coming,' Hagar told her. She melted away into the crowd and was never seen again.[1]

Two months later the gypsy's prediction was fulfilled. Isabel and her sister used to spend the hours between 11 a.m. and 1 p.m. in the Royal Botanical Gardens at Kew. One hot noonday in August they rounded a corner of herbaceous shrubbery and virtually collided with Burton, his newly-married cousin Louisa (his old flame) on his arm. The four of them got to talking of bygone days in Boulogne. Noticing a book under Isabel's arm, Burton asked what it was. It was Disraeli's *Tancred.* 'It is the book of my heart,' Isabel confessed. This was an artful answer, well calculated to quicken Burton's interest, for *Tancred* was a second *Eothen* and Benjamin Disraeli was a man after Burton's heart. He too had sat in Bedouin tents with coffee and dates and felt the lure of the camel's tinkling bell. Isabel asked if Burton would care to meet her in Kew Gardens on subsequent days and 'explain' the text to her. The appeal to his vanity was more than he could resist. To the evident disgust of the worldly Louisa, who could see right through Isabel, Burton readily took the bait.

For a fortnight the curious literary trysts continued. Burton had never known such devotion, such subservience, such wide-eyed admiration. At the end of two weeks, he made a proposition. Exactly what it was must remain disputed. Here is Isabel's version.

> At the end of a fortnight he stole his arm around my waist, and laid his cheek against mine and asked me, 'Could you do anything so sickly as to give up civilisation? And if I can get the Consulate of Damascus, will you marry me and go and live there? Do not give me an answer now, because it will mean a very serious step for you – no less than giving up your people and all that you are used to, and living the sort of life that Lady Hester Stanhope led.'[2]

We may infer that this speech was actually made, all bar the words 'marry me and'. All indirect evidence (including the fact that Isabel burnt Richard's account of the courtship) suggests that Burton was testing her out to see if she was a truly 'emancipated' woman as she claimed to be; in other words, if he resigned from 'John Company' and obtained a Consular berth, would she accompany him there as a mistress? But Burton had misjudged his quarry. In reply to his tentative overture, she poured out the story of her six-year silent love, her slavish devotion, her romantic monomania. She either genuinely interpreted his proposition as a proposal of marriage or, more likely, chose to understand it that way. Burton was swept away in a tidal wave of hitherto pent-up emotion. At first she was too choked by excitement to reply. 'It was just as if the moon had tumbled down and said, "You have cried for me so long that I have come".'

Taken aback by her silence, Burton said (and the form of words itself does not suggest a proposal of marriage), 'Forgive me, I ought not to have asked so much.' Then came the *tsunami.* Isabel confided that she had thought of nothing else but marriage to Richard Burton for six years, ever since she first saw him. She told him she had prayed for him twice daily and followed every detail of his career with fanatical interest. 'I would rather have a crust and a tent with you than be queen of all the world; and so I say, now, Yes! Yes! Yes!'[3]

Burton was well and truly snared. Out of boredom and the pleasure in being flattered, he had encouraged Isabel to think of herself as a partner, and now he reaped the whirlwind. Now, as later, Burton proved himself a man of insufficient moral strength to stand up to her. Beneath the superficial deference was a will of iron and a steely determination to get what she wanted. Burton's frozen, indecisive aspect – a paradoxical attribute in a man of action but deriving ultimately from deep depression – provided no defence against such ruthlessness. Compounding his vulnerability was the half-attraction he felt for Isabel: he had never in his life been loved like this. Isabel moved in for the *coup de grâce.* She insisted that he present himself at the Arundell household as her suitor.

Here he found an unexpected ally. On the one hand, most of the Arundell family were bowled over by the wit, charm and charisma of the famous traveller. Isabel's father told her: 'I do not know what it is about that man, but I cannot get him out of my head; I dream about him every night.' But on the other hand Mrs Arundell, the hard-headed Victorian matron, saw at once that he was not a suitable match for her daughter. He was a half-pay officer, he had no money and no aristocratic credentials, and he was not a Catholic. Mrs Arundell pronounced her predictable verdict. 'He is the only man I will never consent to your marrying; I would rather see you in your coffin . . . if you marry that man, you will have sold your birthright not for a mess of pottage, but for Burton ale.'

So it was left that Isabel was 'engaged' to Richard in her own mind, but the announcement could not be made public because of her mother's opposition. She deluged her 'fiancé' with the long tale of her stoical suffering on his behalf, a six-year odyssey of passion which had sustained her night and day. Now too, she divulged the full story of Hagar Burton, which made a deep impression on Burton, drawn as he was both to the Romanies and to horoscopes and other pananormal phenomena. She introduced him to Cardinal Wiseman, who gave him a 'passport' to all Catholic missions in Africa, describing him as a Catholic officer. There was method in this introduction, too. Not only would it make it harder for Burton to evade wedlock, if he knew that the intended officiating cleric was the Catholic primate of England; it would also strengthen her claim that Burton was 'really' a Catholic, despite his outer agnostic bravado.

Yet Burton was determined to escape from marriage. He did not keep Isabel informed of the progress of his negotiations with the RGS for the African expedition. One night they arranged to meet at the opera. Isabel was left to sit alone through the three acts. Richard did not appear, nor did he send any apology or word of explanation. That night in some agitation Isabel dreamed that Burton told her he was going away and would not be returning for three years. Next morning a letter arrived for her sister Blanche. It was from Burton, asking Blanche gently to break the news of his departure for Africa. He also enclosed a letter for Isabel, whose contents she never divulged. Even more curiously, he sent her a second-rate poem, one of his own compositions, on the subject of fame.[4] The gist of it was that he had to serve a higher goddess than Isabel: the urge to Do. The first and last lines sum up his true feelings for Isabel eloquently:

> I wear thine image, Fame,
> Within a heart well fit to be thy shrine!

and

> Mine ear will hear no other sound,
> No other thought my heart will know.
> Is this a sin? O, pardon, Lord!
> Thou mad'st me so!

In other words, the drum Burton marched to was not that of Love. And if Isabel had any illusion about the 'special' confidence Richard had shown her by being so honest about his true ambitions, Burton had found a way to disabuse her. He sent the identical poem to his lost love, Louisa Segrave.[5]

Burton dated his decision to return to the Dark Continent as 19 April 1856, following a correspondence with the German explorer Heinrich Barth, who had just returned from a 12,000-mile epic journey from Tripoli across the Sahara to Timbuktu. Barth replied encouragingly to Burton's enquiries about the sources of the Nile, but was insistent that no sane man would attempt to discover them.[6] Certainly a week earlier the Royal Geographical Society had approved the Burton expedition project and approached the Foreign Office and the East India Company for their support.[7]

What was the genesis of this expedition, which was to catapult Burton into the premier position among African explorers? The proximate cause was the map of Africa drawn by three German missionaries working for the British Church Missionary Society at Mombasa. Their map, the fruit of much inland travel, showed the snowcapped peaks of Mount Kenya and Mount Kilimanjaro and contained a slug-shaped sketch of a great inland lake, the size of the Caspian, which they called the Sea of Ujiji or the Sea of Tanganyika; its existence was predicated entirely on travellers' tales from Arab merchants at Zanzibar.[8]

The quest for this unknown lake was a sufficient spur for the RGS. But behind the idea of putting a new African lake on the map was the exciting notion that the great stretch of water might prove to be the

'Fountains of the Nile' issuing from the 'Mountains of the Moon', as adumbrated in the works of the Classical geographer Ptolemy. The sources of the Nile had acted as a magnet to the Ancient World. Cyrus, Cambyses, Alexander the Great, Julius Caesar and Nero had all sent expeditions to discover them, but one and all these became bogged down in the morasses of the Sudd, or failed to ascend the formidable barrier of the Nile cataracts. In 1768–70 the Scottish traveller James Bruce had traced the origin of the Blue Nile, which joins the White Nile at Khartoum, but the farthest south reached by any party before Burton's was a venture sent out by Muhammed Ali, the ruler of Egypt, in 1839, which got to Gondokoro.[9]

The composition of the Royal Geographical Society's Expedition Committee did not bode well for Burton. Admiral Sir George Back, famous for his Arctic journey to the Fish River, was a fervent Burton supporter, as was Monkton Milnes (later Lord Houghton). Francis Galton, John Arrowsmith and Rear Admiral Beechey were neutral, as far as Burton personally was concerned. But Sir Roderick Murchison, the President of the RGS, never took to Burton.[10] Even worse, Colonel Sykes, Chairman of the Court of Directors of the East India Company, was on the committee. Sykes was still smarting over Burton's criticisms (made openly to the Society) on the Company's Red Sea policy.

An open attack on its recalcitrant subordinate would smack too obviously of bad faith, pique and petty resentment, so the East India Company gave its full approval, in principle, to the Burton expedition, and when the Foreign Office put up an initial £1000 towards the cost of the venture, the East India Company was expected to match the sum. But all it offered was the release of Burton on two years' leave with full pay and allowances. This left the project seriously short of funds at a critical moment in its gestation. Next the East India Company refused to release Speke, whom Burton had requested together with Steinhaeuser and Corporal Church of the Sappers. When in September it became clear that Church too was not available, a serious question mark hung over the expedition.[11] Yet Burton persevered. He interviewed Speke and persuaded him to put up some of his own money towards the cost of the expedition, and then accompanied Speke to Bombay to plead his cause before Lord Elphinstone.[12]

Sykes countered by persuading friends in the War Department that Burton was a vital witness in the impending court martial of Colonel A. Shirley. The East India Company therefore requested that he return at once, taking the first direct steamer from Alexandria to Southampton. The letter caught up with Burton at Cairo. He confided to friends that he had no intention of heeding a mere 'request'. To the East India Company he explained that the letter reached him on the very afternoon of the day when the fortnightly Alexandria steamer left for England. The next ship would not get him back in time to testify at the court martial, so he intended to proceed to Aden without delay. From Aden he wrote to his superiors justifying his actions in three ways; he had not been subpoenaed to appear at the Shirley court martial while in England, even though there had been ample time for the writ to be served if he really was a crucial witness; had he waited in Egypt a fortnight, the expedition would have been delayed a whole year; meanwhile, he had responsibilities to the RGS and could not just abandon all their stores and equipment.[13]

Burton proceeded to Bombay and persuaded Elphinstone to release Speke for the Expedition. Sykes meanwhile tried to put pressure, through the Foreign Office, on the RGS to appoint someone other than Burton as head of the expedition, on the grounds that Burton would be attending the court martial. But the RGS had already learned that Burton intended to ignore the War Office summons, so brushed the suggestion aside. Infuriated by the way Burton was outwitting him, Sykes tried a further delaying tactic. He advised the RGS that Elphinstone needed surveying and meteorological instruments sent out from England, as Bombay could not supply the expedition's wants. But Burton had very speedily acquired what he needed in India and had taken the precaution of apprising the RGS. Once again the Society ignored a Sykes overture.[14]

It was typical of Burton's self-destructive tendencies that, having routed his enemies in the East India Company, he could not leave well alone. Aboard ship, he composed a long and furious denunciation of the East India Company's lifting of the blockade on the Somali coast – which meant that he and Speke would never be compensated for the treacherous attack on them at Berbera. After pointing out ways in which Britain could easily dominate the Red Sea, he drew attention to the danger facing British nationals in Jeddah. Burton proved a good prophet. On 30 June 1858 twenty-five Christians, including the British and French consuls, were massacred in an orgy of religious rioting.[15]

The reaction of Sykes and the East India Company to this latest piece of 'impertinence' was to see it as insult added to injury. In a cold and withering reply the Company all but put Burton on notice that his days with them were numbered. 'Your want of discretion, and due respect for the authorities to whom you are subordinate, has been regarded with displeasure by the Government.'[16]

But Burton had taken the precaution of ensuring that any answer to his philippic could not arrive until he was well launched on the inland trek. On 2 December he left Bombay on the Indian Navy sloop *Elphinstone*, which he had persuaded her namesake to send to Zanzibar to impress the Sultan that the journey to the inland sea had the sanction of the British government. After an eighteen-day voyage the ship came in sight of Zanzibar. Burton chafed at the boredom of the crossing: 'Of course we had no adventures. We saw neither pirate nor slaver.' He actually lamented the absence of storms and stated, erroneously, that the great oceanic cyclones rarely extended to Zanzibar.[17]

On the island they learned that Sultan Majid had recently succeeded his father. The Omani Arabs had been the dominant force on the East African coast ever since they expelled the Portuguese at the end of the seventeenth century. Majid's father Seyyid Said had left Muscat, the Omani capital, to make his principal base on Zanzibar. Under his energetic direction Zanzibar, originally the world centre for cloves, acquired a more sinister reputation as the chief slave market in the Indian Ocean. By 1856 the Arab traders of Zanzibar had established footholds one thousand miles into the interior, principally at Kazeh (Tabora) in Unyamwezi.[18]

The British were represented on the island by their Consul, Lieutenant-Colonel Atkins Hamerton, who had lived in Zanzibar for fifteen years. No more than fifty, Hamerton looked twenty years older. Sickness and *ennui* had taken their toll; his features lacked all colour and his hair was pure white. Hamerton pined for his native Ireland, but lacked the willpower and drive to pack up and leave, even though death now stared him in the face. He was interested in the letters Burton brought from Elphinstone and his co-religionist Cardinal Wiseman, but scornfully laid aside the messages from the RGS, on the ground that they did nothing but hound him for African 'copy'.[19] Hamerton did all in his power to help the expedition, interceding with the Sultan (who treated him virtually as a prime minister) for official backing. Yet his flagging mental powers were evinced in a failure to make the porters' contracts watertight and unambiguous – a failure that had dire consequences later.

Burton began his exploration of the island, collecting notes on every subject from the sharks in the bay to the life of the brothels. His resulting two-volume, thousand-page *Zanzibar* is an invaluable source for the island in the mid-1850s. Carefully he sketched in the sights, sounds and smells of Zanzibar: the odour of cloves and tropical spices, the slow pulse of the oily blue sea beating on the white coral beaches, the vivid greenness of the jungle that began at the water's edge. Nothing escaped Burton's attention: his topographical descriptions were as exhaustive as his meteorological data – always a key part of the spirit of place for one who believed, as he did, in the importance of climate for interpreting human behaviour. Of one hundred thousand people on the island, most lived in the town. The narrow, crooked streets contained a human flotsam of blacks, Arabs, Indians, Persians and the *petits Arabes* or *wangwana* who traditionally served as escorts for any inland expedition. Donkeys, cattle and camels mingled with the human farrago. The deep soporific heat produced a stifling airlessness made even more intolerable by the ubiquitous stench of copra and decaying fish.

On top of this was the worst sanitation Burton had ever seen. The shore-line was a cesspool; bloated corpses floated through the harbour on the tide, the ocean swell would at times invade the more wretched ghettoes, 'a filthy labyrinth, a capricious arabesque of disorderly lanes, and alleys, and impasses, here broad, there narrow; now heaped with offal, then choked with ruins.' Entropy and decay were the hallmarks on all sides. Cowries lay heaped on the shore so that the molluscs could wither away, and the stench from these mounds did olfactory battle with the 'nausea-breeding odour' of the shivered copra. Only an annual rainfall of between 85 and 120 inches prevented the local death-toll from disease being higher. As it was, dysentery, malaria, yellow fever and hepatitis were endemic, while venereal disease affected seventy-five per cent of the population. Worst of all was elephantiasis, which produced veritable human monsters, some with scrotums that reached the knees.[20]

Overlaying all this natural human horror was the man-made 'peculiar institution' of slavery. Zanzibar received up to forty thousand slaves each year, imported in Arab dhows where they were crammed together in conditions of unbelievable squalor and degradation. A third regularly died of disease or malnutrition but this 'inventory shrinkage' was shrugged off as an acceptable loss by slavers who could make a minimum one thousand per cent profit by exporting slaves to Arabia, Egypt, Turkey and Persia. The policing operations of the Royal Navy, so effective in the Atlantic, had not yet begun to 'bite' in the Indian Ocean.[21]

Sensing Burton's depression, Hamerton told him the story of the young French explorer Maizan who had been taken prisoner by an inland tribe, tortured, then beheaded. One of the sights of Zanzibar was the man who had beat the drum as the hamfisted decapitation was carried out. The only one of the culprits the Sultan had been able to apprehend, the wretched man now languished at the end of a chain attached to a cannon; he was tethered in such a way that he could neither stand up properly nor lie down. This was only the most dramatic of the horror stories Hamerton dinned into him. But he did not realise the ticklish situation Burton was in with the East India Company. 'Briefly the gist of the whole was that I had better return to Bombay, but rather than return to Bombay I would have gone to Hades.'[22]

After a fortnight of frustration and despondency Burton informed Speke that the expedition would make a preliminary reconnaissance further up the coast before attempting to strike inland. In the light of the shortage of funds and time imposed on him by the East India Company, this appears a curious decision, but it seems that three factors weighed with Burton. He did not want to strike inland during the *Masika* or rainy season; he wanted to acquire some experience in the managing of East African caravans; and, most of all, he wanted to consult with Johann Rebmann, the only surviving member of the trio of Germans who had started the entire 'inland sea' hunt.

Before starting up the coast, Burton converted a giant lifeboat into a river craft. Anticipating Stanley and the *Lady Alice* in 1874–77, he had the boat – which he christened *Louisa* – cut into seven sections weighing forty pounds each. This allowed it to be carried, then reassembled if and when the great inland lake was found. He took the *Louisa* with him when he set out by Arab dhow for Mombasa on 4 January 1857.[23] The visit to Rebmann's mission nearby was not a success. First, Rebmann refused to accompany the expedition, mainly because Burton had given his word to the Sultan that he would not try to convert his inland subjects to Christianity; to Rebmann this made a journey with Burton pointless. Even worse, Burton allowed Rebmann to convince him of the especial ferocity of the Masai tribe. This meant that the direct route across the Masai plains, which would have taken the explorers straight to (the as yet unknown) Lake Victoria, was ruled out. The legend of the Masai as unremittingly hostile to the white man continued for twenty-five years, until Joseph Thomson exposed it as a myth in his crossing in December 1883.[24]

At the end of January the dhow sailed south from Mombasa, touched at Wasin Island (opposite the present Tanzania–Kenya border), then anchored at the settlement of Tanga. After a day spent looking round the famous Tangata ruins, which Burton found disappointing, the expedition reached the Pangani river on 3 February. Here Burton decided to pay off the Arab dhow and send the Sultan's men home. On the pretext of a shooting trip, they set off up the Pangani, which was infested with crocodiles in its waters and leopards on the banks. Burton had not yet learned 'jungle-wisdom' and on his first day of relaxation he sat on a rock with his legs dangling in the water until the *wangwana* rushed up and carried him to the safety of the shore.[25]

Burton's aim was to visit Fuga, seat of the Sambaa tribe, to learn for himself what the risks of an inland journey in Africa really were. He reached Fuga on 15 February, but there was little to detain him there. Shortly after, both Burton and Speke went down with severe attacks of fever. When the boat sent by Hamerton arrived on 5 March, Speke was barely able to stagger on board, while Burton, to his irritation, had to be carried in a litter.[26] Back in Zanzibar they were both laid up for a week. There was no doctor on the island, so Hamerton put them on a massive course of quinine (twenty grains a day, reducing to two). Burton, left to his own devices, was always cautious about quinine, believing that an overdose could induce apoplexy. He preferred the then fashionable 'Warburg's drops', a compound of aloes, quinine and opium.[27]

Little had been achieved by the two-month trip to the north, but there were two developments of great significance for the future. Burton recruited a Yao freedman named Sidi Mubarak Bombay, who was to become the most famous 'dark companion' of the great African explorers. He won Speke's heart at once by making a thirty-mile detour to retrieve his surveying compass. He spoke some English, and regaled Speke, starved of conversation except with Burton, with tales of his early life and of the animals and birds they encountered. He seemed indefatigable, as fresh and lighthearted at the end of a long march as at the beginning.[28] Bombay managed to impress Burton, too, with his fluent Hindustani. Burton called him the 'gem of the party' and contrasted him with the usual contemptible 'jungly nigger'.[29] Bombay went on to accompany Burton and Speke to Lake Tanganyika, was with Speke on his great expedition from 1860–63, and later served with Cameron, Stanley and Livingstone (who did not have such a high opinion of him as Burton and Speke, possibly because he was past his best by the 1870s).[30]

The second development was more serious and far-reaching. For the first time Burton began to appreciate that he might have made a terrible mistake in inviting Speke to come with him on a second African journey. Speke disagreed vehemently with his leader's decision to avoid the Masai: he thought it would be easy enough to 'walk round' them, and attributed Burton's decision to a failure of nerve brought on by the trauma of Berbera.[31] The incompatibility between the two men soon became even more evident. Burton relished the prospect (though not so much the disappointing actuality) of examining traces of Vasco da Gama at the mouth of the Pangani and conning the enigmatic Persian inscriptions at Tangata. Few African explorers were less intellectual than Speke, who chafed at the boredom of the stopover. Burton, by contrast, would not slacken the pace of his progress to allow Speke to shoot game, his invariable panacea for stress, tedium and irritation.

It is an interesting fact that the more intelligent and creatively gifted the African explorer, the less interest he had in big-game hunting. Burton, Stanley and Livingstone were at one in regarding the 'sport' with contempt; Speke and Baker could scarcely survive a day without getting off a shot at some living creature. Allied to this was Speke's mania for novelty and for being first in the field. Nothing enthralled him so much as the prospect of being able to 'bag' some species he had not yet killed. As it later transpired, his desire to be the first man to discover the sources of the Nile was pathological. Burton cared little for being *first*, so long as he was the *best*. Geographical and anthropological accuracy meant more to him than the vulgar desire to be 'first'. When the two explorers fell ill after the Pangani, Burton was disappointed that he would not be able to visit Mount Kilimanjaro; Speke, however, was relieved, for had not the German missionaries already been there? In that case, what was the point?

Why, then, had Burton invited a man to accompany him, about whom he must already have had serious doubts after Berbera? 'For his wounds', he later explained, meaning that he was attempting to make reparation to Speke because of his sufferings and near-death at Berbera in 1855, and because the government would grant Speke no redress for his financial losses.[32] There is something about this explanation that rings only half true. More revealing is the phrase 'like a brother' which Burton often uses to describe his early relations with the younger man.[33] We have already seen that the bisexual element in Burton's nature may have had one of its origins in over-close bonding with his brother Edward. The association of ideas between Speke and Edward was strong, for Edward too was an army officer, about to undergo a baptism of fire in the Indian Mutiny. The conflation Edward–Speke seems all the more uncannily apt in the light of a bad beating the younger Burton took in Ceylon from the locals, who were outraged by his wanton Speke-like slaughter of game.[34]

A repressed homosexual himself, Speke seemed to sense that the unconscious bond between himself and Burton was sexual. In a masterpiece of projection he later claimed that Burton had made advances to him during the expedition.[35] He forgot that his earlier fulminations against Burton for his 'immoral' liaisons with black women in Ugogo and elsewhere made this a contradictory tale.

There is a clear element of self-destruction in Burton's decision to persevere with Speke on the main expedition to the interior, for as early as the Pangani Speke revealed something of the deep rage he entertained towards his 'patron' for the use to which Burton had put Speke's Somalia diary and specimens.[36]

Burton was undoubtedly shaken by the change in his protégé. This was not the man he had known in Somalia. He at once noticed that his former alacrity was gone. Habitually discontented, Speke left the administrative chores to Burton but felt free to complain that he had not been consulted if anything went wrong. Unused to sickness, he could not accept it in himself or others. He openly stated that he could take no interest in an expedition that he did not command. Moreover, he enjoyed saying unpleasant things – Burton claimed this was a typical Anglo-Indian trait.[37] Even worse from Burton's point of view was Speke's disingenuousness.

> My companion had a peculiarity more rarely noticed in Englishmen than in the Hibernian or in the Teuton – a habit of secreting thoughts and

> reminiscences till brought to light by a sudden impulse. He would brood, perhaps for years, over a chance word, which a single outspoken sentence of explanation could have satisfactorily settled. The inevitable result was the exaggeration of fact into fiction, the distortion of the true to the false. Let any man, after long musing about, or frequent repetition of, a story or an adventure, consult his original notes upon the matter, and if they do not startle him, I shall hold him to be an exception.[38]

Burton was coming to appreciate that Speke was a very dangerous man indeed, and pointed to his abandonment of Edmund Smyth (whom he had promised to accompany on a hunting trip to the Himalayas, then thrown over when Burton invited him to Africa) as evidence of his ruthlessness.[39] (There were to be further signs of Speke's single-minded egomaniac glory-hunting in 1860–63, when he abandoned a sick James Grant for a long stretch, simply because the Scot was slowing down his progress.) Back in Zanzibar, Steinhaeuser warned Burton that he was nursing a viper in his bosom, that Speke still nurtured his fourfold grievance: the treatment of his diary; the fact that he had made no money from its publication; Burton's despatch of his collection to the Calcutta Museum; and the attribution of cowardice during the Berbera attack. But still Burton made no move to rid himself of his turbulent companion.

He later confessed that he had ascribed Speke's erratic behaviour to a kind of big-game hunter 'burn-out'. The Englishman had been a crack shot in his youth, but his skill had declined by the time of the Berbera adventure. Two years later Burton opined that Speke had seriously overtaxed his nervous system through being permanently on maximum alert. In Burton's view the best big-game hunters had long lay-offs to preserve their skills.[40] Speke afterwards conceded some truth to this analysis: 'I experienced a nervous sensibility I never knew before, of being startled at any sudden accident. A pen dropping from the table even would make me jump.'[41]

At this stage Burton underrated the almost bottomless well of self-esteem in Speke's conscious personality, which led him to feel that no man could perform any task better than he. He was fooled by the quiet and modest manner and the apparent childlike simplicity. Later he realised Speke had had his own way for so long that he found it very hard to take orders. Instead of having to fit in to the strict hierarchy of the Indian Army, Speke had been indulged and cosseted by his commanding officer. His frequent requests for leave to go big-game hunting in the Himalayas had invariably been granted, with the result that he now found it almost impossible to take no for an answer.[42]

Speke did not smoke and was virtually teetotal, and spent his time vainly trying to harden his feet so that he could travel barefoot like the *wangwana*. So far he might have appeared just another of the legion of

British Victorian eccentrics. But Burton should have inferred something from Speke's complete lack of interest in women. In the telltale, cliché phrase, a 'confirmed bachelor'. Speke never had any close relationships with women, yet repressed the sexuality which would have made him an open deviant. It might have been possible to maintain that Speke was merely monkish, asexual, functionally neuter, but for the clear understanding he himself provided of the role of libido. On his 1860–63 journey he advised the Queen Mother of Buganda that her insomnia and bad dreams 'was a common widow's complaint, caused by deprivation of her husband's company at night'.[43]

Speke also realised that it was important to feign a 'normal' interest in women. For this reason his writings tend to be full of forced and artificial references to the opposite sex. From Madeira in 1860 he wrote: 'I was dancing away with the belle dames of this place until I nearly melted. There are some wondrous girls here, chummy, sweet and good natured – Don't you envy me.'[44] And his desire to project an image of normal heterosexuality backfired badly on him with the publication of his book on the 1860–63 expedition. Speaking cavalierly of 'flirting and coqueting' with African women, he got the tone wrong, as no genuine heterosexual would have done, and managed to scandalise Victorian society with his loose behaviour.[45] Yet when the prospect of a real sexual encounter presented itself, Speke shrank back in horror, as when in 1862 the Queen Mother of Buganda offered him her two daughters as concubines.[46]

What makes Speke such a fascinating psychological study is that alongside the homosexuality and the mother-fixation noted earlier was a pronounced death drive. During the very first expedition, in Somalia, he told Burton that he had come to Africa to be killed.[47] The classic sign of death drive is an excessive aggression directed towards the external world. Speke's slaughter of wildlife provides an almost textbook illustration. There is something very disturbing about the hippo hunting scene on the Pagani after the visit to Fuga, where Burton shows Speke in his element. The lust for slaughter is excessive even by Victorian 'sporting' standards and the killing is gratuitous, for Burton makes it clear that the carcasses could not be retrieved for meat. On one day Speke killed six hippo and mortally wounded a dozen others.

> Whenever a head appears an inch above water, a heavy bullet 'puds' into or near it; crimson patches marble the stream; some die and disappear, others plunge in crippled state; while others, disabled from diving by holes drilled through their snouts, splash and scurry about with curious snorts, caused by the breath passing through wounds. A baby hippo, with the naïveté natural to his age, uprears his crest, doubtless despite the maternal warning; off flies the crown of the little kid's head. The bereaved mother

rises for an instant, viciously regards the infanticide, who is quietly loading, snorts a parent's curse, and dives as the cap is being adjusted.[48]

Many similar passages can be extracted from Speke's own work. One of the reasons he got on so well with James Grant on the 1860–63 expedition was that Grant shared his enthusiasm for shooting and was prepared to indulge his murderous frenzies more readily than Burton.[49] Speke's rapport with Mutesa of Buganda was at least partly explained by their common lust for blood, though in Mutesa's case it was the human variety. And on the same expedition Bombay, whom Speke had so lauded, once questioned an order, only to have his front teeth smashed out by three vicious blows from Speke.[50]

Numerous incidents attest to a feeling in Speke that all purposeful activity must be crowned by death. His biographer describes thus the moment of his discovery of Lake Victoria in 1858:

Having attained the southern extremity of the lake, Speke celebrated the event in his customary fashion. As he trotted along, his '... trusty Blissett made a florikan pay the penalty of death for his temerity in attempting a flight across the track'. It is as if the brooding spirit with whom Speke held intensely private communion demanded a sacrifice of blood in return for its favours, if not to compensate some transgression. In this and other similar killing there is evidence of a primitive submission to ritual, for their pattern is constant and clearly-defined.[51]

Yet the most compelling evidence for Speke's death drive comes from the record of his feverish dreams, so unlike those of Burton in the same plight. Burton had a sensation of divided identity – of being two distinct people who opposed each other. In his delirium he felt he had wings and could fly.[52] Speke dreamt of 'tigers, leopards, and other beasts harnessed with a network of iron hooks, dragging him like the rush of a whirlwind, over the ground'. The animals he had killed so wantonly were now returning for their revenge.[53] The flight symbolism of Burton's dreams spoke of sexuality and creative endeavour hampered by an unintegrated personality. It was anxiety mixed with hope. If Burton's dreams spoke of Eros, those of Speke pointed to Thanatos.[54] At the most profound level these were incompatible personalities, the superficial differences serving only to mask an unbridgeable psychic chasm. The later mortal clash was already present in unconscious form. It is clear that the quarrel over the sources of the Nile was the occasion rather than the cause of a legendary hatred.

11

To Lake Tanganyika

ONCE recovered from his fever, Burton pressed on with preparations for the expedition proper. Early in May 1857 he made a brief visit to Sadani on the coast to investigate the commercial potential of further gum copal exports, which might lead to a reduction in the price of coach varnish. The visit was unsuccessful. Until the caravan was ready, there was little of any purpose he could do. While Speke sniped at him behind his back, Burton found himself increasingly irritated by the Jeremiahs who prophesied disaster once he left the safety of the mainland coast.

> The principal Chomwi assured them [the porters] that the chiefs of the Wazaramo tribe had sent six several letters to the officials of the coast, forbidding the white man to enter their country. Divers dangers of the way were incidentally thrown in: I learned for the first time that the Kargadau or rhinoceros kills two hundred men, that armies of elephants attack camps by night, and that the craven hyena does more damage than the Bengal tiger. In vain I objected that guns with men behind them are better than cannon backed by curs, that mortals can die but once, that the Wazaramo are unable to write, that rations might be carried where not purchaseable, and that powder and ball have been known to conquer rhinoceroses, elephants and hyenas.[1]

Burton spent the limbo period in Zanzibar acquiring a working knowledge of Swahili: 'my principle being never to travel where the language is unknown to me. I was careful to study it at once on arriving in Zanzibar.'[2] Here he encountered serendipity. It turned out that the Sidi language, the vocabulary of which he had published as an appendix to *Sindh and the Races* was Kiswahili itself. Quickly Burton compiled a serviceable grammar, though he achieved mastery of the language only later at Kazeh, when he languished there in illness while Speke made his dash to Lake Victoria.[3] One amusing linguistic joust was with the

Sultan's Polish medical adviser, who had anglicised his name from Gregorio to Dr Gregory. Gregory was another of those accomplished polyglots in the Vámbéry class. When he and Burton compared notes, it turned out that both could converse in twenty-odd languages and dialects, and that each knew a language the other did not.[4]

At the beginning of June Burton sent Said bin Salim to Bagamoyo to recruit 170 porters for the indispensable loads of local trade goods: cotton cloth, beads and brass wire. Salim was the *wangwana* guide provided by the Sultan, who had also recommended a Hindu customs clerk called Ramji for the expedition's administration. Additionally Burton recruited two Goanese servants called Valentine Rodriguez and Caetano Andrade.[5] Also in the party which Burton, Speke and Hamerton took over to the mainland on 16 June were seven Baluchi mercenaries from the Sultan's corps of bodyguards, later to be supplemented by a further five from the Kaole garrison.

At Kaole, near Bagamoyo, Burton received his first rude shock. Bombay and another notable 'dark companion', Mabruki, were there, ready to serve as gunbearers and general servants, but Said bin Salim and Ramji had collected only thirty-six men.[6] This meant that Burton had to take donkeys instead, and had to leave behind a good part of the trade goods, most of the ammunition, and the sectional boat *Louisa*. He struck a deal with the local Hindu traders to find more porters and send these effects after them (Burton received them eleven months later), then hired thirty donkeys with drivers. Ramji provided ten of his own slaves as additional porters; these so-called 'sons of Ramji' were later to be the source of considerable personal trouble for Burton. With his unfailing methodical accuracy, Burton made inventory of what he was taking with him into the Dark Continent: the equipment included a Rowtie tent, mosquito netting, beds, chairs, portable tables, cooking pots, books, carpenters' tools, fishing rods and nets, provisions, books, journals, chronometers, two prismatic compasses, three thermometers, sundial, rain-gauge, sextants, barometer, pedometer and elephant guns. To lighten the loads, they took just the clothes they stood up in; these later became so torn and ragged that new apparel had to be improvised from blankets.[7]

On 26 June the expedition bade goodbye to Hamerton, now seriously ill. While the consul departed to Zanzibar and the death that claimed him a few days later, Burton steered his reluctant column inland, towards the Kingani river. After many inspired ideas for blazing new trails to the inland 'sea', Burton had accepted that they would have to feel their way inland on the old caravan route pioneered by the Arabs.[8] But he was unprepared for the recalcitrance of his men. The line of march quickly became a snarling chaos; the Baluchi were reluctant to proceed inland, while the *wangwana* grew anxious and tried to sabotage progress once they left the coastline behind. In the first week the expedition covered two miles one day, and lurched chaotically for a mere hour and a half the next. 'It was like driving a herd of wild cattle', Burton recorded. On 1 July the first desertions took place. With a column just ninety men strong, Burton could not afford a single loss. His anger erupted in the first of many tirades against the worthlessness of the African.

> Supersubtle and systematic liars, they deceive when duller men would tell the truth. The lie direct is no insult, and the offensive word *muongo*! (liar) enters largely into every dialogue. They lie . . . objectlessly, needlessly, when sure of speedy detection, when fact would be more profitable than falsehood; they have not discovered with the civilised knave, that 'honesty is the best policy'; they lie till their fiction becomes subjectively fact. With them the lie is no mental exertion, no exercise of ingenuity, no concealment, nor mere perversion of truth: it is apparently a local instinctive peculiarity in the complicated madness of poor human nature. The most solemn and religious oaths are with them empty words; they breathe an atmosphere of falsehood, manoeuvre and contrivance, wasting about the mere nothings of life – upon a pound of grain or a yard of cloth – ingenuity of iniquity enough to win and keep a crown. And they are as treacherous as false; with them the salt has no signification, and gratitude is unknown even by name.[9]

The expedition crossed the fifty-yard wide Kingani river, full of crocodiles and hippos. Here Burton and Speke both sustained another attack of fever. Burton was ill for twenty days. Speke's attack was even more violent. He suffered from fainting fits, like those in sunstroke, that seemed to attack his brain. They relied on doses of quinine and mosquito netting for protection against disease. The net curtains were effective against mosquitoes but not against the ticks that carried relapsing fever. The village huts where they stayed were infested with these ticks, which lived in the mud walls and roofs and emerged at night to feed on man. It is not possible to decide in the individual cases recorded by Speke and Burton which fevers were caused by malaria and which by the relapsing fever, but it is likely that the ticks did most of the damage.[10]

On the far side of the Kingani they encountered both natural and human enemies. An African wolf killed three of their donkeys. Then Hembe, son of Marungera, the chief who had killed the young Frenchman Maizan, prepared to receive them with poisoned arrows. But once the caravan's peaceful intentions were plain, Hembe let it pass without more ado.

Even the fearsome reputation of the Doe tribe seemed overrated. Known as the cannibals of East Africa, they did not trouble the caravan.[11] Burton had more trouble with his own men. One of them dropped his double-barrelled elephant gun into the Mgeta river; despite sturdy diving by the Goans, it could not be recovered. A typical daily journal entry by Burton reads: 'At length by ejecting skulkers from their huts, by dint of promises and threats, of gentleness and violence, of soft words and harsh words, occasionally combined with a smart application of the *bakur* – the local 'cat' – by sitting in the sun, in fact by incessant worry and fidget from 6 a.m. to 3 p.m., the sluggish unwieldy body acquired some momentum.'[12]

After eighteen days and 118 miles' progress, Burton paid off the Baluchi escort from Kaole and sent it back to the coast, retaining the Baluchis from the Sultan's personal bodyguard. Though constantly wracked with fever, Burton had kept meticulous notes on the customs and folk-ways of the tribes they had encountered, the fauna and flora, the topography, and his companions' behaviour. On 25 July, at Zungomero, the chief caravan centre for the eastern inland region, Burton took stock and found that they had lost nine donkeys and were short of porters. It was also abundantly clear that Said bin Salim was dishonest and an embezzler, and that the Baluchi escort and the 'sons of Ramji' had been pilfering freely. In addition, Ramji's slaves were beginning to act in an overweening and contumacious manner, refusing to carry loads and claiming that they had the same status as the Baluchi and should bear arms instead. Burton was too sick to oversee every item of the expedition's administration and running; Speke, even when well, had no head for detail, so the only way Burton kept the undermanned and underfinanced column on its snail-like way was by sheer willpower and personal magnetism.

After two weeks halt at Zungomero, they set out again. Burton and Speke were so weak that they could hardly sit on their donkeys. The one bright spot was the arrival of thirty-six Nyamwezi porters who had been recruited at Kaole and rushed to join them at Zungomero.[13] Leaving behind them the rain and the river valley which had made such inroads on their health, they struck north-west through hilly country towards modern Kilosa, and emerged on the northern end of the Makata plain. Here they met a returning caravan that had lost fifty of its men through smallpox. In the next few days they came on the dead and dying lying by the roadside; fortunately for Burton, the disease did not spread among his own men.

News had now come through of Hamerton's death. The Baluchis, fearing they would not be paid – as their contract was with the consul – refused to go farther. Burton called their bluff and left them behind. Later they caught up with the caravan and asked for assurances that they would be paid if they continued. Burton cynically spoke of bonuses, assuring Speke that an Arab promise meant nothing. This was typical of Burton; always, his worst side was revealed when anyone asked him for money. Speke did not care for the 'ungentlemanly' and cavalier attitude Burton took towards the payment of his men and offered to return to the coast for more money to avoid future wrangles and embarrassments, as it was clear the expedition's finances would not stretch to making good Hamerton's pledges.[14]

The argument was resolved by another attack of fever on both men. They lolled hopelessly as the caravan, reduced now to nineteen donkeys, trekked across the Makata plain, short of provisions since slavers had recently picked the area clean. The irony was that the plain teemed with buffalo and other game, so that Speke should have been in his element; but he was too weak to go after it and obtain a fresh meat supply. Speke's amazing physique, which had enabled him to survive an experience at Berbera that would have killed most other men, saw him through again. Burton marvelled at how, after a day's gruelling march on the burning plain, Speke could sit shivering in the chilly evening dew, practising lunars and timing chronometers.[15]

Only when they entered Usagara did food again become plentiful. At Inenge, on 4 September, the expedition enjoyed its first milk, butter and honey since leaving the coast. Before ascending into the Usagara uplands Burton also had the good fortune to meet an Arab caravan who helped him with porters and donkeys and took mail down to the coast. The one thing Burton could always do was charm any Arab whose path crossed his.[16]

On 10 September they began to climb the Rubeho pass into the Usagara mountains. It took them six hours to reach the head of the pass. Speke was almost in a coma and became delirious. Burton's experiences were similar. 'Trembling with ague, with swimming heads, ears deafened by weakness and limbs that would hardly support us, we contemplated with a dogged despair the apparently perpendicular path ... My companion was so weak he required the aid of two or three supporters; I, much less unnerved, managed with one.' They halted at the top of the pass. This was the occasion when Speke became so violent in fever that Burton had to remove his weapons. Even after a two-day halt, Speke had to be carried onwards in a hammock.

As if the agonising debility and delirium from fever was not enough, Burton and Speke fought a running battle with insects. Burton was among the first African exporers to point up the deadly menace from the tsetse fly. Not only did it decimate the pack animals, but it could attack a man through the thickness of a canvas hammock. Soldier ants could gnaw their way through beds and chairs, destroying all in their path. Even worse than these white ants was their cousin the pismire, fully an inch long, capable of inflicting a mortal wound on a lizard or a rat. Burton described the bite from a pismire ant as being like a shot from a red-hot needle.[17]

It was a miracle that the caravan preserved any semblance of order, but gradually the iron grip exerted by Burton, even from his sick-bed or travelling hammock, began to pay dividends. The marching day began at 4 a.m. An hour later a scratch breakfast of rice-milk, whey-cakes, porridge and coffee would be eaten round a roaring fire. Then the guide would unfurl Zanzibar's red flag and, to the beat of a tambour, the reluctant expedition would get under way. Two hours of marching were followed by a halt for drinking, smoking and a chat. Then the march would resume until the heat of the day compelled a longer rest. By late afternoon on a good day they might have covered ten miles, but the daily average was only six. At night they would camp in a village. If the locals were pleased with their trade, they would move out of their huts to accommodate the travellers. If not, camp was pitched in the open or in one of the walled kraals. The night's stopover was determined by the established custom of the caravan route; every night the guide would agree with Burton the next day's itinerary and length of march.[18]

Descending from the triple mountain range of Usagara, they began to cross the plains of Ugogo. For the first time Burton felt fully fit, so he began by inspecting the porters' loads. He found that in three months they had used up six months' worth of trade goods. Apart from pilfering opened loads, porters would often jettison their packs intact on the line of march or 'forget' to take them up when leaving camp in the morning. This was particularly serious, for everyone knew that in the land of the Gogo tribe the level of *hongo* or tribute was especially high.

By 26 September they were on an open stubbly plain teeming with game, particularly elephants, giraffe and zebra. The giraffes 'stood for a moment with long outstretched necks to gaze, and presently broke away at a rapid, striding camel's trot, their heads shaking as if they would jerk off, their limbs loose and their joints apparently dislocated. 'Speke, at last on his feet, managed to shoot pallah and other antelope, guinea-fowl, florikan and partridge, but he did not have the strength to attack the vast herds of elephant in the valley that separated the tableland of Ugogo from the blue hills of Wahumba to the north. Burton noted that East Africa lacked the abundant wildlife of southern Africa. Of the myriad species of deer and antelope he saw only oryx, hartebeeste, steinbok, saltiana and pallah, plus the diminutive suiya antelope. He noticed that the local lions were smaller than in southern or northern Africa. Ugogo was far from being the best area for game; later Burton would award that palm to Usukuma and Ujiji, where in a single area one could encounter lions, leopards, elephants, rhino, wild cattle, giraffe, gnus, zebra, quaggas and ostrich; but even then they were only in vast numbers in dangerous country where the 'sportsman' could not linger for more than a day.[19]

Knowing of the Gogo's reputation for rapacity, Burton had chosen the central route through their land, reckoning thus that he would have to pay *hongo* to no more than four chiefs. The Gogo, though politically divided into independent 'kingdoms', exploited to the full their strategic position between the warlike Hehe and Masai to levy tribute on the caravans. They also controlled the scarce water supply in the region and insisted that their permission be obtained before travellers drew water from the wells.[20] Fortunately Burton possessed a skilled negotiator in Kidogo. In return for two *doti* of cloth and some beads to a chief, he was able to coax the Gogo people to trade their bullocks, sheep and poultry; also water-melons, pumpkins, honey, buttermilk, whey, curded milk, holcus and calabash-flour.

At first Burton fulminated about the novel system of paying a tax to tread the earth, even when the traveller made no inroads on property, and attributed the excessive mulcting by the Gogo to greed and envy. But once he had come to terms with his own anger about being asked to pay, he took a more reasoned view of his hosts. After all, the work required to provision caravans merited *some* recompense. Grudgingly he accepted that the Gogo were clever brinksmen who pushed their demands to the limit but no farther; consequently, there were fewer fights and massacres in Ugogo than elsewhere in Africa. And indeed how could Burton, with his admiration for the Bedouin, deny the Gogo the selfsame 'law of the water-wells' practised in the desert?[21] Instead Burton started to get inside the idiom of *hongo* and *doti*; he wrote learnedly about *barsati* cloth and *sami-sami* beads – the much prized coral bead of scarlet enamelled on a white ground.[22] He managed to recruit a further fifteen Nyamwezi porters. The one thing he found hard to take about the Gogo was their habit of staring at him: 'they have certainly no idea of manners; they flock into a stranger's tent, squat before him, staring till their curiosity is satisfied, and unmercifully quizzing his peculiarities.'[23]

At Ziwa in Ugogo, while the expedition rested and bought food, a large Arab caravan came in, travelling in the same direction. The sheikh leading the caravan presented Burton with a stolen load, taken away by one of the expedition's deserters. Inside the box were Burton's survey books, including the Nautical Almanack for 1858 and various writing materials. Delighted with this, Burton was lavish in his thanks, with the result that the sheikh suggested joining forces for the onward march. This should have ensured low *hongo* demands in the rest of Ugogo; once across the border into Unyanyembe there was the added bonus that the sheikh's brother was married to the daughter of the principal chief there.

The joint party set out together on 1 October, but the hope of lower *hongo* soon proved false. After one particular frustrating four-day spell haggling over *doti*, the Arabs insisted on night marches to avoid further mulcting, but even so, the caravan spent its final five days in Ugogo dickering over the amount of tribute to be paid. Again the Baluchi threatened to desert, the last of the donkeys finally expired and, worst of all, the fifteen Nyamwezi porters recruited just weeks before absconded. However, 'the men seemed to behave best whenever things were palpably at their worst.' On 17 October the expedition set out again, the porters shouldering the extra loads.

Eight days later they had traversed the sparsely populated country between Ugogo and Unyanyembe and were at Mgongo Tembo. Speke was again ill, four boxes of ammunition and bullet moulds had been lost on the way, but now only the Kigwe forest stood between the expedition and its first objective at Kazeh (Tabora). Burton rested his party for the last lap, but the Arabs, chafing at the many delays, insisted on proceeding without him. Burton gave them his blessing. Yet a week later he overtook them on the road, where they were stranded for lack of porters.[24]

By easy stages Burton coaxed his men through Tura and Rubuga.[25] One last danger remained: the Kigwe forest, whose 'sultan', Manwa, had an evil reputation as a highway robber. Burton took the expedition through his territory at night. On 7 November they entered the Arab trading centre at Kazeh. Both white men were tattered and gaunt, weak from fever and stricken with trachoma, which badly impaired their eyesight. They had come nearly 600 miles in 134 days – an average of four miles a day (Stanley covered the same journey in 84 days in 1871), but as European explorers they were pioneering all the way.

Burton's heart lifted at the sight of the Arab settlement, then about five years old. There were twenty-five Arabs in residence, there were clean mud buildings, spacious courtyards and pleasant vegetable gardens. With his three letters of introduction from the Sultan, Burton did not find it hard to secure a friendly welcome. Musa Mzuri, doyen of the Arabs and the earliest explorer, was away on a trading journey but his deputy and long-time colleague Snay bin Amir gave Burton and Speke every assistance. The two white travellers were at once conducted to a comfortable and well-furnished *tembe* or mud hut. At once Snay slaughtered two goats and two bullocks for a feast of thanksgiving and welcome. Next morning all the Arabs in the settlement 'waited on' them – almost literally, for in addition to the normal guest-token of a goat and rice the Arabs sent in onions, plantains, limes, tamarind-cakes and coffee.

Burton was in his element in Kazeh. The Arabs were both bemused and excited by this 'Frank' who spoke their language, had visited Mecca and had the proof to show, could fence like a master and recite the *Arabian Nights* with gusto. Soon Burton had the tall, gaunt Snay bin Amir bewitched. Educated and sensitive, with a twinkle in his sunken eye, he was almost a simulacrum of Burton in his perceptiveness, powers of retention and linguistic talent. It was a genuine meeting of minds.

In the euphoria of finding such a friend, Burton overlooked or discounted the fact that Snay's considerable fortune was built on ivory and slaves. For this tunnel vision he has been much criticised.[26] One of the people to make capital later out of this blind spot was Speke. He never felt his inadequacy more completely than at Kazeh. Burton could converse easily with these Arabs, but Speke needed an interpreter for the simplest request. Even when he questioned Snay on the 'Sea of Ujiji' and elicited the intelligence that there was not one great lake, but three, he had to use Burton as interpreter and intermediary.[27] For a man of Speke's gigantic self-esteem, this must have fuelled his hatred for Burton.

For a month the expedition rested and recuperated. The manpower of the party changed almost wholly in this period, for most of the porters took their pay at Kazeh and returned to the coast. Fortunately, with Snay's help Burton was able to recruit virtually a new expedition. The Arab advised them to strike north towards the lake he called the 'Sea of Ukerewe' and Speke endorsed this, but Burton insisted on fulfilling the terms of their original mission and pressing on to Lake Tanganyika. This, incidentally, makes nonsense of Speke's later claim that Burton did not want to move from the comfort of Kazeh and agreed to trek on only when Speke had made all the arrangements for the onward journey.[28]

Unfortunately Burton succumbed to another bout of fever during his five-week stay with Snay bin Amir, so that when the caravan moved out he had to be carried in a *machela* or hammock. To the complaints of the fresh porters from Kazeh, who had never before seen any caravan proceed at such a snail's pace, the expedition limped as far as Msene by the end of December. The effort of mounting a donkey on Christmas Day had caused a relapse in Burton, so at Msene there was another twelve-day halt. Here the porters gave themselves up to 'dancing, pombe-drinking and related pleasures'. Even in such relaxed surroundings the 'sons of Ramji' overstepped the mark, in mistaken belief that Burton was dying. Tired of their pilfering and general insolence, Burton at last dismissed them and sent a letter back to Snay to speed them on their way to the coast.

In mid-January 1858 the column moved forward reluctantly once more. The fleshpots of Msene exerted a powerful counter-pull; as Speke recorded archly, 'even Bombay became so *lovesick* we could hardly tear him away'. But worse was to come. At Kajjanjeri on 18 January Burton was laid low by a dreadful attack of malaria which paralysed his legs, so that for the remainder of the year he had to be carried everywhere over long distances by eight strong bearers in the *machela*: for the first few days he was so ill that 'I saw yawning to receive me those dark gates across the wild that no man knows.'[29] Speke too was suffering badly. He was assailed by anaemia, trachoma and chronic ophthalmia, aggravated by recurrent fevers. Speke reported that he went everywhere in a brilliant fog, his eyes sore and inflamed, seemingly filled with particles of hot, sandy grit, and so near to complete blindness that his mule had to be escorted by one of the porters.

Beset by illness and constant porterage problems, they staggered through the districts of Msenga, Uganza and Ukunda to the banks of the formidable Malagarazi river. Here, on 1 to 3 February, they were subjected to a massive *hongo* by chief Nzogera, who controlled the fords and ferries across the crocodile-infested flood.[30] Crocodiles were much in evidence too during the crossing of the Rusugi river four days later, but the splashing of large numbers of men kept them at a distance. These fearsome reptiles were a constant fact of life in the Lake Regions. For fear of them none of the people along the shore of Lake Tanganyika ever threw offal into the water when canoeing.[31]

On the last stretch to the lake it was difficult to buy food because of the devastation wrought by recent tribal wars. The long marches to reach better victualled regions triggered a fresh spate of desertions. But at last on 13 February they climbed a steep hill to find stretching below them the limpid waters of the Tanganyika Lake: 'an expanse of the lightest and softest blue, in breadth varying from thirty to thirty-five miles ... the background in front is a high and broken wall of steel-coloured mountains ... truly it was a revel for soul and sight! Forgetting toils, dangers, and the doubtfulness of return, I felt willing to endure double what I had endured; and all the party seemed to join with me in joy', wrote Burton. He was lucky: Speke could not see the lake. To him every object was 'enclouded as by a misty veil'. But Speke uncannily managed to combine the moment of triumph with death, even though he was nearly blind. On the way to the hilltop his mule dropped dead under him. As his biographer concludes: 'Again (with the mysterious regularity that persisted throughout his life), the death of an animal had been timed to expiate disappointment, just as it marked success or celebrated victory.'[32]

They dropped down to a lakeside village in Ukaranga and next morning were rowed in Arab boats to Ujiji. Expecting from the descriptions at Kazeh to find a town and harbour the size of Zanzibar, Burton was mortified to find no more than a hole in the reeds leading to a flat landing-place on a shingle beach, and the 'town' simply 'a few scattered hovels of miserable construction, surrounded by fields of sorghum and sugar-cane'. At this juncture Ujiji was a cluster of scattered villages under the jurisdiction of Mwami Rusimbi, chief of the Ha, whose headquarters were at Kalinzi and who was the last Ha chief to rule

Ujiji. His headman or *umutware munini* was a former slave, drunken, dishonest and belligerent: 'a very ill-disposed chief ... tyrannical, and, as such savages invariably are, utterly unreasonable', as Speke put it.[33] But Burton did not help matters by taking an instant, visceral dislike to the pug-nosed and greedy headman. On his first appearance Kannena was garbed in silk turban and broadcloth coat. When this failed to impress, he reverted to his normal apparel, was not recognised, and was ignominiously turfed out of the Burton encampment. Moreover, Burton made the bad mistake of revealing to Kannena that he was no trader. This removed any motive in Kannena's mind for treating the newcomers well. Burton might have shown more discretion had he been aware that he was dealing with an agent of a powerful tribe later acknowledged to be the 'Spartans' or 'Comanches' of East Africa, a tribe that caused Stanley more anxiety than any other he met in modern Tanzania.[34]

For a fortnight Burton lay in an Arab *tembe* by the lakeshore, too blind to read or write and too ill to converse. Speke, suffering from painful ophthalmia, was at first in little better shape, but he recovered faster than his older companion, so that a balanced diet of fowl and fresh fruit and vegetables from Ujiji market soon enabled him to stroll about the lakeside mart 'protected by an umbrella and fortified with stained-glass spectacles ... beads in hand to purchase fresh supplies.'[35] He and Burton were sustained through their illness by the exciting intelligence that there was a large river called the Rusizi which flowed out of the northern end of Lake Tanganyika. Perhaps this was the true source of the Nile. Burton wanted to find out for himself but was too ill to make a move. Speke nagged away at him, using the same method of attrition that had worn out commanding officers in India. Eventually the prostrate invalid gave in. With dwindling stocks of trade goods, time was against them. He therefore gave Speke permission to cross the lake to Kasenge Island, where there was said to live an Arab trader with a dhow sturdy enough to breast the storms and pyramidal waves of Tanganyika.

Speke set out in company with Bombay, Gaetano, two of the Baluchis and a complement of Kannena's savage sailors. He was away for a month, on a forlorn quest. Sheikh Hamid bin Sulayyman, his target, refused to lend the dhow except in three month's time and at a fee of five hundred dollars, but confirmed that there was a river at the north of Lake Tanganyika.[36] Disappointment at having to face Burton with yet another commission unachieved must have been galling, but before Speke had time to brood he was stricken by a freak misadventure that for a time substituted deafness for blindness as his principal malady.

On the island of Kivera on 8 March 1858 a storm bade fair to blow down Speke's tent. In the night, when the storm abated, he lit a candle to rearrange his kit which had been jostled round the tent. Immediately his quarters were invaded by a plague of black beetles. There were too many of them to expel, so Speke tried to ignore them and dropped off to sleep. He awoke just too late to prevent one of the insects entering his ear. The horrific sequel was described by Speke:

> He began with exceeding vigour, like a rabbit at a hole, to dig violently away at my tympanum ... what to do I knew not. Neither tobacco, oil, nor salt could be found: I therefore tried melted butter; that failing, I applied the point of a penknife to his back, which did more harm than good; for though a few thrusts kept him quiet, the point also wounded my ear so badly, that inflammation set in, severe suppuration took place, and all the facial glands extending from that point down to the point of the shoulder became contorted and drawn aside, and a string of bubos decorated the whole length of that region ... I could not open my mouth for several days ... For many months the tumour made me almost deaf, and ate a hole between that orifice and the nose so that when I blew it, my ear whistled so audibly that those who heard it laughed.[37]

Burton had meanwhile lain in his cot slowly improving, listening to the pelting of the *Masika* and 'dreaming of things past, visioning things present', dilating on Ujiji as an 'African Eden', not because of its intrinsic character but from its position on such a beautiful lake. The recalcitrant Said bin Salim refused to negotiate with Kannena and declared that as far as he was concerned he had fulfilled his contract, and this was journey's end. Then, 'on the twenty-ninth of March the rattling of matchlocks announced my companion's return.'[38] Though he complained that his companion had achieved 'absolutely nothing' the news about the Rusizi galvanised Burton. After difficult negotiations with Kannena, during which the headman first flatly refused to accompany them on the lake but later relented, Burton secured the hire of two large canoes and their crews. On 10 April Burton and Speke set off with this motley company, leaving Said bin Salim and the 'troublemakers' in Ujiji. Their intention was to settle once and for all whether the Rusizi flowed into or out of Lake Tanganyika, and thus determine whether it was a candidate as a true source of the Nile.

They coasted up the eastern shore to Wafanya, crossed the lake to the peninsula of Ubwari, then continued up the western shore to Uvira. There the locals were unanimous that the Rusizi was influent, not effluent. This was a terrible disappointment to the explorers. Nature contributed by hurling a succession of dreadful storms at them, and Burton added to the litany of ailments with an ulcerated tongue that made speech almost impossible. A final incident filled the cup to overflowing. The false rumour of the approach of enemy tribesmen led Kannena's rowers to panic. In the ensuing chaos the Goanese Valentine lost his head and fired Burton's Colt. He seriously wounded one of

Kannena's men (who later died). With great difficulty Burton dissuaded Kannena from slaughtering the Goanese on the spot. Yet the Ha had their revenge. 'As the crew had ever an eye on the "main chance", food, they at once confiscated three goats, our store for the return voyage, cut their throats, and spitted the meat upon their spears – thus the lamb died and the wolf dined, and the innocent suffered and the plunderer was joyed, the strong showed his strength and the weak his weakness, according to the usual formula of this sublunary world.'[39]

After an arduous thirty-three-day journey in almost continuous rain, in the uncongenial company of the scowling Kannena but amazingly revived in health, Speke and Burton arrived back at Ujiji on 13 May. It was evident that Lake Tanganyika did not possess the key to the sources of the Nile; it was actually a dead end as far as all the great river systems were concerned, as one needed to cross to the western shore and penetrate into the Manyema country before touching on the headwaters of the Congo. Not until December 1871 did Livingstone and Stanley prove conclusively that the Rusizi flowed into rather than out of the lake, but Burton had learned enough in 1858 not to be in any doubt on this score.

The return to Ujiji produced a rude shock. Said bin Salim had taken it into his head that the explorers would certainly perish on the lake, and had therefore consumed their supplies at an alarming rate during their month's absence. The spectre of starvation was beginning to loom when, on 22 May, a fusillade of shots at last announced the long-expected but virtually despaired-of relief caravan which Burton had organised with the Hindus at Kaole. Along with the supplies was a sheaf of mail from Europe, including news of the outbreak of the Indian Mutiny – the insurrection Burton had predicted and for whose prediction he had been marked down in the East India Company's eyes as 'unsound', 'insubordinate' and a 'trouble-maker'. But when Burton unpacked his boxes he found that the ammunition was of the wrong calibre and there were just enough trade goods to secure them passage back to the coast. With bitter reluctance he decided to abandon his original plan for exploring the southern two-thirds of Lake Tanganyika, as well as the scheme for returning to Zanzibar by a more southerly route via lake Nyasa.

On 26 May the expedition departed for Kazeh. Burton, who for all its beauty, had long contrasted the lake shore unfavourably with the desert, allowed himself a backward glance, as though he realised that he was not to see again this great stretch of water he had put on European maps.

> Masses of brown-purple clouds covered the quarter of the heavens where the sun was about to rise. Presently the mists, ruffled like ocean billows, and

> luminously fringed with Tyrian purple, were cut by filmy rays, whilst, from behind their core, the internal living fire shot forth its broad beams, like the sparks of a huge aerial wheel, rolling a flood of gold over the blue waters of the lake. At last Dan Sol, who at first contented himself with glimmering through the cloud-mass, disclosed himself in his glory, and dispersed with a glance the obstacles of the vaporous earth: breaking into long strata and little pearly flakes, they soared high in the empyrean, whilst the all-powerful luminary assumed undisputed possession of earth, and a soft breeze, the breath of the moon, as it is called in the East, awoke the waters into life.[40]

The return march to Unyanyembe was uneventful. After crossing the swollen Malagarazi, they trekked on at their best pace yet. When they entered Kazeh on 20 June they had marched 265 miles in just twenty-six days. Speke was intermittently blind and deaf – it was another six months before the body and detached wings of the beetle came out in the wax – but had started to nag Burton about the desirability of a diversion north to find the 'Ukerewe lake'.[41]

Back at Kazeh, tension between the two men mounted. Speke wrote in great bitterness to Norton Shaw:

> Burton has always been ill; he won't sit out in the dew, and has a decided objection to the sun ... This is a shocking country for sport, there appears to be literally nothing but Elephants, and they from constant hunting are driven clean away from the highways; all I have succeeded in shooting have been a few antelopes and guinea fowl besides hippopotamus near the coast ... There is literally nothing to write about in this uninteresting country. Nothing could surpass these tracts, jungles, plains for dull sameness, the people are the same everywhere, in fact the country is one vast senseless map of sameness.[42]

Burton meanwhile recorded laconically of Speke: 'his presence at Kazeh was no means desirable.'[43] Speke insulted the Arabs routinely and embroiled them as 'enemies' in his disputes with Burton. Nowhere on this expedition did his utter ignorance of Eastern manners and customs show up more clearly. His linguistic incompetence, 'a few words of debased Anglo-Indian jargon', which had earlier induced in Burton no more than amused contempt, now began to irritate him in earnest. To Burton Speke was precisely the type of arrogant British army officer that had engendered so much trouble in India – there seemed almost a sense in which the Spekes of this world had 'caused' the Mutiny.

Since Speke's northward journey to Lake Victoria led directly to the overt rift between the two men, it is worth probing at some length into Burton's motives for allowing his subordinate to make the journey, and thus ultimately snatch the laurel as discoverer of the Nile sources. Burton's decision was 'overdetermined' and contained both rational and irrational elements. Rationally, it was known that the lake lay within reasonable striking distance of Kazeh, and someone ought to reconnoitre it. Speke's health was better than Burton's, who was still recovering from paralysis of his legs. Moreover, one of them had to remain at Kazeh to make all preparations for the homeward journey. Speke, with his impatience for detail, was a hopeless administrator, so even at this level it made sense for Burton to be the one to remain behind. If Speke remained at Kazeh, Burton might return to a fiasco, with 'Jack' having alienated Snay bin Amir and the other Arabs.[44]

For Burton, ethnology and exploration had equal value; for Speke there was exploration, and only exploration. But Burton had seen enough of Speke by now to know that it was dangerous to underrate his persistence and his fanatical desire to be 'first'. At some level he must have sensed the risk to his own position in allowing the younger man free rein on such a potentially sensational endeavour. To give a complete account of Burton's state of mind when he sent Speke north, we have to admit an admixture of the irrational, self-destructive urges that were never far from the surface.

The two key elements here were probably depression, and a growing hatred of things African. Speke claimed that Burton told him roughly that they had done enough and he did not want to see any more lakes.[45] By contrast, in Kazeh Burton could enjoy the company of Snay bin Amir and the other Arabs and banish the immediacy of Africa by thoughts of the beloved deserts of the Islamic world which they represented. When Burton later read Speke's book treating of this episode, he scrawled in the margin of his copy 'To get rid of him!' To be rid of Speke relieved Burton of his nagging and left him free to enjoy the company of the Arabs without having a brooding, jealous and reproachful presence at his elbow at all hours.

Jettisoning the stress that Speke represented was particularly important at this juncture. Just two days before he entered Kazeh, another party from Zanzibar arrived with a fresh delivery of letters. For the first time Burton learned of the death of his father the previous September.[46] It is even conceivable that guilt he felt at the derision he used to express for his father made Burton unconsciously punish himself by sending out Speke to garner the prize. Burton was in no way obliged either to send Speke to Lake Victoria or to go himself. His doing so was at least in part a self-destructive action.

Speke set off northwards with twenty porters and ten Baluchis. After twenty-five days he came to a vast body of water which he named Victoria Nyanza 'after our gracious sovereign'. Immediately he guessed that this lake, not Tanganyika, was the true source of the Nile. Pausing only three days to take observations and readings, he then sped back towards Kazeh with the news of the greatest exploration scoop of the century.[47]

Burton meanwhile lay for long hours in the *tembe*, recuperating and putting the final touches to his mastery of Swahili.[48] His studies were interrupted on the morning of 25 August by gunshots and a babel of voices. This uproar was followed swiftly by the arrival of a wildly excited Speke. Over breakfast he blurted out his claim to have discovered the true sources of the White Nile. Burton at once dismissed his pretensions out of hand; the flavour of the exchange, with Burton at his most cold and withering, is well conveyed in Burton's own sardonic account. 'The fortunate discoverer's conviction was strong; his reasons were weak – were of the category alluded to by the damsel Lucetta when justifying her penchant in favour of the lovely gentleman Sir Proteus:

> I have no other but a woman's reason.
> I think him so because I think him so.'[49]

All the pent-up resentment and hostility in Speke came gushing out at Burton's refusal to take his great discovery seriously; at best he regarded it as a lucky *trouvaille*. Things reached the pitch where by mutual consent the entire subject of the Nile was avoided. Speke saw Burton as an envious and jealous rival, unwilling to accept facts that stared him in the face. Burton despised the lack of intellectual content in Speke's claims. Had he studied meteorology, he insisted, the palpable falsity of his 'find' would not survive a moment's reflection. If the *Masika* came to the lake Regions in October and lasted until June, how could Victoria Nyanza be the feeder of the Nile, when everyone knew from the long-standing observations at Gondokoro that the Nile fell until the end of January and did not begin to rise until March – clearly an altogether different cycle from the lacustrine one? Surely the very most a prudent man would concede was that the Victoria lake might be one of many contributory reservoirs to 'father Nile'.[50]

When Speke exhorted Burton to return with him to the Nyanza to settle the issue once and for all, Burton replied that they no longer had the resources. He suggested that they go home, recover their health, get financing for a second expedition and return to complete the great project.[51] At once Speke began to suspect that Burton intended to co-opt the Victoria Nyanza for himself and edge his comrade out of the limelight. He became determined to get to England first so that Burton could not steal his thunder. It was therefore in an atmosphere of cold politeness and mutual distrust that the two explorers brought a party of 132 porters (and a handful of Arabs) onto the homeward caravan trail on 26 September 1858.

The return march took four months and was in some ways even more of a nightmare than the outward journey. Speke soon fell seriously ill with pleurisy and pneumonia. It was at this stage, during a delirium, that he unleashed his tidal wave of bitterness against Burton; every single grievance since Berbera seemed to have been magnified a hundredfold. Burton, who was still being carried in a *machela* himself, nursed him through a crisis so terrifying that the watchers frequently gave up the patient for lost. After three violent spasms of the 'little irons' – an agonising pain in the right breast and spleen – Speke drafted an incoherent farewell letter to his family. For two weeks he wrestled with death, sleeping in a half-sitting position, propped up by a pillow; he could not lie on his side. At last the pain eased sufficiently for Speke to say enigmatically: 'Dick, the knives are sheathed', meaning either that the pain had ceased, or that in that moment he felt so grateful for Burton's ministrations that his hatred had faded.[52]

By the end of October Speke had recovered. By the time they reached Ugogo Speke 'had strength enough to carry a heavy rifle, and to do damage amongst the antelopes and the guinea fowl.'[53] There followed the expected difficult crossing of this territory. Contrary to normal custom, the Gogo levied *hongo* on the return journey as well. After a three-week slog over the plains (14 November to 5 December 1858) they began the ascent into Usagara. Learning that the former route through the mountains was closed, they struck south in a wide detour through Kisanga. Although the Nyamwezi chief Kiringawana was friendly, Burton could not secure permission to pass through his territory to Kilwa, site of the legendary port city of Quiloa and its ruins of three hundred mosques, as described in the Portuguese poet Camoens' epic on Vasco da Gama. The expedition continued through the southern end of the Makata plains to Zungomero. Here Burton insisted on striking diagonally down to Kilwa, no farther than Bagamoyo from where they then were. The response was mass desertion of his porters.

For three weeks the caravan was detained at Zungomero while Burton negotiated for replacement porters, finally hired from a caravan bound for the interior. Abandoning the attempt to reach Kilwa overland, Burton made for Kunduchi on the coast. 'On 30th January our natives of Zanzibar screamed with delight at the sight of the mango-tree, and pointed out to one another, as they appeared in succession, the old familiar fruits, jacks and pineapples, limes and coccoes.'[54] Three days later they were on the coast. It might have been expected that Burton would sail for Zanzibar at the earliest opportunity, but Kilwa had become something of an obsession with him. He rationalised his behaviour as punctilious observance of the promises he had made to the RGS, but it is more likely that he was clutching at any excuse to defer the day when he had to return to London and do battle with Speke.

On 10 February they embarked on the dhow that had been sent over by the new Consul in Zanzibar. They touched at Mafia Island and the Rufiji delta and came at last to Kilwa.[55] Instead of the romance of

Camoens, Burton experienced the most frightful cholera epidemic of his life, far surpassing anything he had seen in India.

> Soil and air seemed saturated with poison, and the blood appeared predisposed to receive the influence, and the people died like flies ... There were hideous sights about Kilwa at that time. Corpses lay in ravines, and a dead negro rested against the walls of the Customs House. The poorer victims were dragged by the leg along the sand, to be thrown into the ebbing waters of the bay; those better off were sewn up in matting, and were carried down like hammocks to the same general depot. The smooth oily water was dotted with remnants and fragments of humanity, black and brown when freshly thrown in, patched, mottled and parti-coloured when in a state of half pickle, and ghastly white, like scalded pig, when the pigmentum nigrum had become thoroughly macerated. The males lay prone upon the surface, diving as it were, head downwards, when the retiring swell left them in the hollow water; the women floated prostrate with puffed and swollen breasts.[56]

At last the expedition set sail for Zanzibar, where it arrived on 4 March 1859, but here too there was turmoil. The Sultan's elder brother at Muscat was preparing a fleet to invade Zanzibar, taking advantage of the huge recent mortality from smallpox on the island. The alarums and excursions kept Burton there until 22 March, when he embarked on the clipper-built barque the *Dragon of Salem*, bound for Aden.[57] In those eighteen days he began to perceive how truly formidable the challenge from Speke was going to be. But first he had more pressing problems to deal with. He had forgotten the East India Company, but it had not forgotten him. Even worse, in place of Hamerton as Zanzibar consul was his old enemy and linguistic rival, Captain Christopher Rigby.

12

The Slough of Despond

BY his journey through what is now Tanzania, and his discovery of Lake Tanganyika, Burton placed himself at once in the premier league of European explorers of Africa. Of all the great nineteenth-century travellers in the 'Dark Continent' only Stanley, Livingstone, Speke and Baker were to accumulate superior credentials as technicians of exploration. As an anthropologist, and in his superior intellectual range and depth, Burton surpassed them all.

As a surveyor and mapmaker Burton was accurate enough to survive the most searching examinations by later explorers. The great nineteenth-century expert on Tanganyika, Edward Coode Hore, said of his predecessor's work in the Lake Regions: 'Burton has opened out the mysteries of Central Africa, and his records and descriptions are yet unsurpassed.'[1] The greatest of all African explorers, Henry M. Stanley, began by scoffing at Burton's description of East Africa as 'an immense swamp, curtained about with the fever'. But once Stanley was convinced that he had surpassed Burton's achievements in African exploration, he relaxed and conceded the true value of Burton's work. He acknowledged the accuracy of his findings, was pleased to be able to complete Burton's work on Lake Tanganyika, and even named a segment of the lake 'Burton Gulf' in his honour. Though he took Speke's side in the dispute over the sources of the Nile, Stanley contrasted Burton favourably with Verney Lovett Cameron, his friend who crossed Africa from East to West in 1875, and grudgingly admitted the immense advantage Burton enjoyed over all travellers in Arab Tabora through his knowledge of Arabic.[2]

Later assessments of Burton concur, especially as regards his phenomenal abilities as an anthropologist. While dotting the i's and crossing the t's of some of Burton's chronology, as for example of the Kimbu–Ngoni wars, leading modern scholars point to Burton's work as the single most important source for East African history in the years between 1830–55.[3]

Any one of Burton's three major expeditions so far – to Medina and Mecca, to Harar, and to the Lake Regions of East Africa – should have established his fame. But the upshot in each case was notoriety rather than glory. Three distinct factors can be seen at work in the immediate aftermath of the East African expedition, all contributing to Burton's ultimate downfall. The man who had headed the most successful African expedition to date was fated to be denied any further opportunity there. The three factors were the pre-existing enmity and jealousy of Speke, the bad luck inherent in Rigby's advent, and Burton's perennial Achilles' heel – money.

It is true that the expedition had been under-financed and that both Burton and Speke had had to dig into their own pockets to keep it going. But this alone does not explain the almost pathological distaste evinced by Burton at the prospect of spending money. Even when engaged in tough negotiations with African chiefs, Burton's abiding obsession was money, and it lends a sour note to some of the proceedings.[4] Here there is an interesting contrast with Stanley. Stanley took a hardline attitude towards paying *hongo* because he felt it diminished his prestige, not because it diminished his coffers. For this reason he was sometimes prepared to blast passage through hostile country. Burton, on the other hand, admitted that it was more sensible to pay tribute than to fight – for one thing he did not possess Stanley's much greater military resources – but always cavilled at the amount involved.[5]

But Burton's perennially uneasy relationship with money only became an acute problem when he returned to Zanzibar. His understanding – or rather what he claimed was his understanding – of the financing of his porters and soldiers was that it was entirely the affair of the late Consul, Hamerton, who had promised to pay the *pagazis* out of public funds provided they performed efficiently. As far as he was concerned, none of the party deserved payment. His men had mutinied on hearing of Hamerton's death, had refused to follow him to Lake Tanganyika, and had had to be bribed to accompany Speke to Lake Victoria. Worst offender of all was Said bin Salim, who Burton thought deserved a horsewhipping rather than severance pay. Burton therefore washed his hands of the entire affair and quit Zanzibar without any attempt to tie up loose ends.

This was a very serious error of judgement, on two counts. In the first place, Burton was once again in bad odour with his superiors in the East India Company. Their letter of censure for his indiscreet criticisms of Somali policy to the RGS caught up with him at Kazeh on his return in 1858. Burton was forced to reply lamely that the offending letter had never been intended for publication.[6] The fact that his predictions had been fulfilled by the massacre of Christians at Jeddah in June 1858 simply infuriated the Court of Directors further; they were also maddened by the fact that Burton's warnings of trouble in India had been amply vindicated by the Indian Mutiny. In such a context it was supremely unwise of Burton to provide his vindictive superiors with the slightest pretext for a counterstrike.

In the second place, the pay question gave valuable ammunition to the new Consul Rigby, his old rival from India. It has been speculated that Rigby and Burton failed to get on at Zanzibar merely because Rigby was an implacable opponent of the slave trade, while Burton thought its horrors overrated.[7] But this is naïve. All available circumstantial evidence suggests that Rigby still nursed a grudge from the time in India a decade earlier, when Burton outdistanced him in the Gujerati examination. Rigby, who had been Military Commandant in Bushire and spoke fluent Persian, had been heard to jibe that the redoutable 'Mirza Abdullah of Bushire' had never been within a hundred miles of the place.[8]

To his great delight, Rigby soon discovered that Speke hated Burton even more than he did. He swallowed whole Speke's version of events on the expedition and encouraged him in his rancour and resentment. A Rigby diary entry from this period is significant:

> Speke is a right, good, jolly, resolute fellow. Burton is not fit to hold a candle to him and has done nothing in comparison with what Speke has, but Speke is a modest, unassuming man, not very ready with his pen. Burton will blow his trumpet very loud and get all the credit of the discoveries. Speke works. Burton lies on his back all day and picks other people's brains . . . Dr Roscher returned two days ago from the interior of Africa . . . Burton was very jealous of him.[9]

Burton wanted to wait for fresh funds and a further leave of absence that would permit a second expedition but, sick and exhausted, he was eventually ground down by Speke's nervous impatience to return to England and Rigby's 'evident anxiety' to be rid of him. Reluctantly, when HMS *Furious* docked at Aden (where the two explorers had travelled together on the *Dragon of Salem*), he agreed that 'Jack' should go ahead to England while he himself finished his convalescence. Speke was already plotting to get the leadership of a second expedition for himself, but his parting words to Burton could hardly have been more reassuring: 'Goodbye, old fellow; you may be quite sure I shall not go up to the Royal Geographical Society until you come to the fore and we appear together. Make your mind quite easy about that.'[10] These were the last words he ever spoke to Burton.

On board *Furious*, returning to England from China as Lord Elgin's secretary, was a 29-year-old travel writer called Laurence Oliphant, already with a certain name for his works on Russian travel. Masochistic and homosexual, Oliphant at once discerned the latent tendencies in Speke, who was two years senior. Oliphant listened to Speke's embittered account of his turbulent relationship with Burton, and persuaded the older man that Burton's actions were evidence of a desire for a sexual relationship with him. Jealous of the motives he attributed to Burton by transference – for it was Oliphant who *consciously* wanted such a liaison with Speke – he turned the screw of Speke's Burton-mania a notch tighter.[11] By the time he got to England, Speke was fully convinced that he had the moral right to break his word to Burton.

Once arrived in England, on 9 May 1859, Speke went straight to the Royal Geographical Society and proclaimed that he had found the sources of the Nile. Speke was as lucky on this occasion as Burton was unlucky. The quest for the Nile at once caught the popular imagination in the same way as the race for the South Pole or the conquest of Everest were later to do. Within days of his first lecture at Burlington House Speke had been nominated as the commander of a new RGS-sponsored expedition to East Africa. An interview with Sir Roderick Murchison in which Speke 'talked up' his 'discovery' of the Nile sources (for as yet he had not one shred of proof) ended in triumph when Murchison enthusiastically announced: 'Speke, we must send you there again.'[12]

Not suspecting the true scope of Speke's ambition, Burton had written to the RGS to recommend Speke's diversionary expedition for consideration. He little dreamed that it would be taken up so sensationally. When he arrived in England on 21 May, Burton found the ground cut from under his feet. 'Everything had been done for, or rather against me. My companion now stood forth in his true colours, an angry rival.'[13] Two days later Burton was presented at the RGS with the Society's Gold Medal, but then had to listen for nearly two hours to Murchison's encomium on Speke. With great self-control Burton made a gracious speech of acceptance, even throwing in a nod to Speke's 'exact topography' and astronomical observations.[14]

It was not long before the expected blow fell. Despite Burton's plea that he should not be penalised merely through having been ill in Aden, and that the Society should at the very least send out two expeditions to East Africa, Murchison backed Speke all the way against his rival. Ruefully Burton recorded: 'These were the days when the Society in question could not afford to lack its annual lion, whose roar was chiefly to please the ladies and to push the institution.'[15] The result was that Speke was confirmed as commander of the expedition to trace the sources of the White Nile; as a sop, it was announced that Burton would head a second expedition to explore the Horn of Africa. Even this consolation prize turned out to be a chimera. On the grounds that the Speke expedition was urgent, and Burton's was not, the RGS voted an immediate sum of £2500 to Speke; Burton's finances, it was blandly announced, could await the recovery of his health. Moreover, Murchison persuaded his Council members that it was not advisable to approach the government for two separate grants: Speke's £2500 was to be applied for immediately, while the notional Burton grant of £2000 would be sought later.[16] It did not require a man of Burton's intellect to see that he was being given the polite brush-off.

In private Speke, urged on by Oliphant, produced excess after excess in his denigration of Burton. In letters to Norton Shaw he taunted Burton with overrating the perils of Ugogo and with falsely stating that the road to Kilimanjaro was barred by the Masai. He overlooked the fact that the alleged 'perils of Ugogo' were inconsistent with another version of events there which he presented to the same correspondent, wherein Burton sat in his tent reading while he, Speke, did all the real work.[17] Meanwhile throughout the summer of 1859 he toiled away at an edition of his diaries which the publisher John Blackwood had agreed to bring out in advance of Burton's book. *Blackwoods Magazine* had published Burton before, but saw no problem about doublecrossing him this time with Speke. Utilising the Scottish connection, Blackwood introduced Speke to his future collaborator James Grant while their new author was in the Highlands, interspersing editing work on his clumsy diary entries with the inevitable 'sport'; this time among the stags of the Ross-shire hills.[18] In an extraordinary reference to Burton's foreign upbringing and 'unEnglishness' Speke finally descended into outright hyperbole: 'I would rather die a hundred deaths than have a foreigner take from Britain the honour of discovery.'[19]

Absurdly, he then claimed to have taught Burton surveying and observation, oblivious or ignorant of the Sind survey experience. 'I am sure everybody at Zanzibar knows it, that I was the leader and Burton the second of the Expedition. Had I not been with him, he never could have undergone the journey', was a typical outburst in a letter to Rigby.[20] Taking his cue from Oliphant, he hinted strongly that Burton was a homosexual, as was 'proved' by his experiences in the Karachi brothels. Even Speke's staunchest supporters drew back at this point. After the two books he did with Speke, Blackwood consistently refused to publish a 'tail' which mixed accusations of incompetence and cowardice with stronger charges of professional malice and jealousy and frustrated homosexual desire. Given Speke's own propensities, this ranked as a classic example of projection. Speke had to get the 'tail' printed privately for his family.[21]

Burton's reaction to all this was surprisingly mild. There is a weary, melancholic resignation about his responses that hints at severe depression. When Burton recalled how he had introduced the uneducated Speke to Euclid and Shakespeare and taught him to write readable prose, he quoted sadly an old Arab couplet:

> I taught him archery day by day.
> When his arm waxed strong, 'twas me he shot.[22]

And Isabel Burton's assertion that her husband had a Cassandra-like gift of helpless foresight is borne out by the lines he wrote after his first expedition with Speke, almost as though he suspected what lay in store in the future: 'the explorer too frequently must rest satisfied with descrying from his Pisgah the Promised Land or knowledge, which another more fortunate is destined to conquer.'[23] In Burton's references to Speke, the brotherly tone gives way to the voice of the father disappointed and betrayed by a beloved son: 'Except his shooting and his rags of Anglo-Hindustani, I have taught him everything he knows.'[24]

Clearly Burton could no longer think in a brotherly way about a man who had just betrayed him. But at another level Burton was forced to take on the role of the embattled father. His own father had died the year before; now his beloved brother Edward was for all purposes a vegetable. He survived the Indian Mutiny, but was never the same man after a terrible beating he took from the Sinhalese. His convalescence was further impeded by an attack of sunstroke. Soon he was shipped home with incurable mental illness.[25] For forty years he remained locked in catatonic silence. It is related that he emerged from the shadows of utter silence just once, shortly before his death in 1895, to protest to his cousin that he owed him no money. As Fawn Brodie remarks: 'It was a curious echo of the payment–non-payment theme that plagued his illustrious brother.'[26]

Those who, as Burton did, believe in 'synchronicity' and significant coincidences might care to ponder the following: his father died at Bath in September, the month and location of Speke's own death; Speke, too, had a beloved brother Edward, also killed while Speke was in Africa. This brother's death in the Indian Mutiny occurred on exactly the same day as that of Speke six years later.[27]

Only at the beginning of 1860 are there signs of a recovery and the re-emergence of the old, confident, arrogant, supercilious Burton.[28] For the moment he contented himself with amused contempt at Speke's expense: such was Speke's total lack of linguistic ability that he had virtually forgotten his native tongue while failing to acquire a new one; he astonished people in London 'by speaking in a manner of broken English, as if he had forgotten his vernacular in the presence of strange tongues'.[29]

As if the decline of his brother and the treachery of Speke were not enough, Burton was simultaneously assailed on his most vulnerable flank – money. Waiting until Burton was safely on the high seas, Said bin Salim came to Rigby with a rare tale of pecuniary woe. He claimed he had been promised a thousand dollars by Hamerton for guiding the expedition to Lake Tanganyika, but that Burton had refused to pay this or indeed any money at all to any of the porters on the expedition. The Sultan had been obliged to pay them all off at a total of $2300 to avoid major embarrassment. Rigby was delighted by the chance to score off his old enemy. He reported the facts to Bombay, adding that if some restitution was not made, the cause of future British travellers in East Africa would be fatally compromised. In a private letter to Bombay he severely censured Burton for non-payment and cited Speke as witness for the essential correctness of the Zanzibaris' story.[30]

The Bombay authorities decided that Rigby's version of events was true and referred the file to the Court of Directors in London. The Court wrote to Speke to get confirmation of the story and asked Burton to explain his non-payment.[31] On 11 November 1859 Burton wrote a long screed of self-justification. The so-called 'porters' he described as slaves, for whose services he had paid the Banyan Ranji, head clerk of the Zanzibar Customs House. The other financial arrangements were entirely Hamerton's concern, and were anyway contingent on the efficient performance by Said bin Salim and the others which had not been forthcoming. He expressed astonishment at Rigby's actions, since it was common knowledge that 'Orientals' always submitted bogus claims against an employer who had just left the area. Finally, if money was the subject, what about the fact that he had spent £1400 of his own money over and above the £1000 grant from the RGS?[32] By now, too, he knew that the government intended to provide Speke with £2500 for his new African expedition; he contrasted this liberality with the parsimony in 1856, which now left him and Speke with a balance of £1500 to pay off.[33]

On 14 January 1860 the India Office in London sent a formal letter of censure to Burton over his non-payment of the porters' money. They referred the issue of repayment to Bombay, with the clear threat that Burton would have to foot the bill himself. Burton replied in his usual robust vein. The basis for the adverse judgement was said to be Speke's evidence and Rigby's advice that the matter should have been referred to a Consular court in Zanzibar. These two arguments did not stand up, said Burton. Since he had not seen Speke's evidence, he had had no opportunity to comment on it. And if Rigby thought a Consular court was called for, why had he not mentioned this to Burton before he left Zanzibar? 'In conclusion, I venture to express my surprise that all my labours and long services in the cause of African exploration should have won me no other reward than being mulcted in a pecuniary liability incurred by my late lamented friend, Lt-Col Hamerton, and settled without reference to me by his successor, Captain Rigby.'[34]

Speke's underhand support for Rigby added a further twist in the spiral of his treachery. But his financial chicanery did not end there. He had promised to refund Burton £600 out of the £1400 the older man had contributed to the expedition from his personal funds. Now he attempted to palm the debt off on the India Office, and counterclaimed compensation for his losses on the Somali expedition against the royalties from *First Footsteps*. This was disingenuous on two counts. In the first place, Burton had asked the RGS to use its influence with the Foreign Office to recoup the extra £1400 (actually £1496), but the Society had refused.[35] Secondly, Burton had made no money out of *First Footsteps*: there were no royalties. Speke, on the other hand, came from a wealthy family and had private resources. A letter of 1 February expresses Burton's anger at Speke's attitude: 'The debt was contracted unconditionally by you in Africa ... had I known you then as well as I do now I should have required receipts for what was left a debt of honour. I must be content to pay the penalty of ignorance.'[36]

Letters sent from Burton to Speke descended from 'Dear Jack' through 'Dear Speke' to 'Sir'. In the end it was arranged that they would correspond through Norton Shaw at the RGS. But Burton received no financial satisfaction until Speke had left the country for Africa in the spring of 1860. Speke steadfastly denied that he had a debt of honour to Burton: 'I accepted Captain Burton's invitation to go to Africa with him under the proviso I should not be called upon to pay any money whatever, not even my passage out or I said I would not go with him.'[37] A whispering campaign from Burton's friends on this issue began to make noticeable dents in Speke's reputation. Then his mother, fearful of the effect on her son's honour that this financial scandal was having, arranged to pay the debt through Speke's brother Benjamin. In April 1860, just before departing, Speke wrote directly to Burton, beginning the letter in a half-regretful fashion: 'My dear Burton, I cannot leave England addressing you so coldly as you have hitherto been corresponding.' Burton, now fast recovering from the depths of his depression, wanted none of it. 'Sir ... I cannot ... accept your offer concerning me corresponding less coldly – any other tone would be extremely distasteful to me.'[38]

The breach between the two was irreparable. Isabel Arundell later tried to patch things up, but Speke rebuffed her with the following regretful words: 'I'm so sorry, and I don't know how it all came about. Dick was so kind to me; nursed me like a woman, taught me such a lot, and I used to be so fond of him; but it would be too difficult for me to go back now.'[39]

Both men left England in April 1860, Speke *en route* for East Africa, Burton to North America. But their differences followed them over the oceans. Speke's main anxiety as he departed was that he had not had sight of his erstwhile comrade's promised work on the Lake Regions.[40]

Burton's chief concern was the threat of civil proceedings against him in the Zanzibar courts for the recovery of the money 'owing' to the porters and Said bin Salim.[41]

In July Burton's two-volume *Lake Regions of Central Africa* appeared, to general critical acclaim. The *Athenaeum* hailed it thus: 'the picture of life in these extraordinary regions is admirable. Captain Burton observes and describes everything. His instincts are those of a traveller. He has in a twofold sense the capacity of an artist.'[42]

Speke's friends and supporters did not view the book at all in that light. Burton's references to Speke were offhand or derisory. He did not even deign to mention his name, but spoke of 'my companion'. In his journal for 4 November Rigby spoke of this 'vile, lying book'. Twelve days later in a letter to Norton Shaw he protested against the many 'calumnies' against Speke in the work, and the 'lies of brevet-captain Burton'. The letter reached Shaw in January 1861 and he showed it to Burton, now back from nine months in North America. The response this elicited from Burton shows him at his most wrathful, imperious and witheringly contemptuous.[43]

Quite apart from the money factor and his support for Speke, Rigby had by now fallen foul of Burton in yet another way. The manuscript for a two-volume work on Zanzibar, which he had completed before plunging into the interior of Africa in 1857, had got lost between Zanzibar and London. Burton had addressed it to Norton Shaw on the understanding that it would be forwarded in the diplomatic pouch. Because of Hamerton's death it was not sent. When his successor Rigby read it, he caused delay by sending it on to Bombay for clearance. After perusing the strong criticisms of official policy it contained, the mandarins of Bombay buried the manuscript in a strong-box of the Bombay section of the Royal Asiatic Society. There it lay until February 1865, when it was discovered by a curious bureaucrat and then sent on to London.[44]

Although there was more incompetence than malice in this episode, Burton was quite justified in attributing the manuscript's miscarriage to Rigby. Rigby struck back at Burton by sending selected extracts of *Lake Regions* to Speke, who was making his way towards Lake Victoria. Speke's reaction was predictably splenetic: 'It's about the most blackguard and scandalous production I ever read and must end in his entire defeat ... full of the most indignant abuse of everybody who assisted him in the late expedition and it contains many deliberate falsehoods ... [Burton is] deserving of no better end than hanging; just the end I would have recommended for him long ago.'[45]

The Speke–Burton conflict already had tragic dimensions, but before the final act could be played out, Speke would rise to new heights of glory and Burton would plumb the depths of banality.

13

Marriage with Isabel

SPEKE was not Burton's only problem in 1859. He also had to resolve his future with Isabel Arundell. With both parents dead and Edward a hopeless invalid, it was surely loneliness which made Burton contact her again. His record as a 'fiancé' had not been good. In nearly three years he wrote to her just four times, when he was sick. She for her part continued to write long, gossipy letters every fortnight, while enduring the taunts of her mother, who sneered that Burton must have lost his writing arm to the jackals.[1] All overtures were rejected in favour of the abiding dream of marriage with Richard Burton, who requited her maniacal fidelity by not writing at all in the final twenty months of his East African odyssey. When, on a lonely whim, he sent her another of his doggerel verses, hinting that her face, voice and eyes had been ever before him during his African ordeal, she came running with spaniel-like devotion.[2]

Burton's Arabic look by now seemed pronounced, with the prominent cheek bones thrown into extra relief by the disfiguring scars from the lance at Berbera. His thick, dark hair grew low on his forehead. But after twenty-one fever attacks and ophthalmia, he limped and his sight was fuzzy. He was cadaverous, and his yellow-brown skin was baggy and pendulous. His eyes protruded and his lips were drawn away from his teeth as if in some hideous rictus. This, combined with the long drooping moustaches, gave his mouth a singularly cruel look. Only a truly besotted woman could have found him attractive, but such was Isabel. Thus does she write of the joyful reunion: 'We rushed into each other's arms. I cannot attempt to describe the joy of that moment. He had landed the day before, and come to London, and had called here to know where I was living, where to find me . . . We went downstairs, and Richard called a cab, and he put me in and told the man to drive about – anywhere. He put his arm around my waist, and I put my head on his shoulder. I felt quite stunned.'[3]

This time Burton's prospects as a husband did not seem so negligible. His father's death had left him £16,000, enough to provide a small annual income. He talked sanguinely about entering the Consular Service and becoming the representative at Damascus. And he agreed to be married in the Catholic Church and to bring up any children as Catholics. But still Isabel's mother adamantly opposed the match. She used every weapon at her disposal to poison the relationship, including interception of Burton's letters. She pointed out that no Catholic prelate would ever officiate at a marriage between a daughter of the English Catholic aristocracy and a man who was a notorious atheist and profligate. Besides, he had no money.[4] She would have a wealthy marriage, like that of her daughter Blanche, or nothing. Her eldest daughter Isabel, on the other hand, would have the impecunious Richard Burton or no one. It was a case of irresistible force and immovable object.

Faced with unremitting opposition from Mrs Arundell, Burton suggested to Isabel that they elope. At this Isabel drew back in fear. Despite her romantic protestations and claim to be a free spirit, she was at heart too in thrall to the conventions of the day to be able to contemplate such a drastic step. When she counselled patience, Burton became irritated with her. There was a cooling in the relationship, and Burton sought solace in male company of the more *outré* variety.

By this time Burton had made the acquaintance of Monkton Milnes (later Lord Houghton). Milnes's 'country weekends' at his seat at Fryston were famous. In August 1859 the guests, apart from Burton, were Mansfield Parkyns of Abyssinia, John Petherick of Khartoum, Sir Charles McCarthy, James Spedding, G. S. Venables and W. E. Forster.[5] Milnes shared Burton's interest in erotica and sexology. Hearing that he was about to depart for the Continent, Milnes put him onto his friend Fred Hankey, who lived in Paris. Hankey was a sadist in a double sense, in that he derived sexual pleasure from the infliction of pain, and was also a disciple of the Marquis de Sade and shared his fascination for sexual deviancy: flagellation, scoptophilia, coprophagy, bestialism, and much else. Hankey was the spiritual ancestor of the modern purveyors of the ultimate pornographic abomination, the 'snuff' movie. His favourite pastime was to hire a room overlooking a public hanging, so that he could witness the grisly last moments even as he disported himself with a couple of courtesans.[6] Hankey had an informal harem of Swiss prostitutes in Paris, whom he hired out for the manufacture of pornographic postcards. The fact that he actually thought it worthwhile to visit Hankey in Paris shows that Burton's contemporary diabolical reputation had some foundation. It also demonstrates the zigzagging between heterosexuality and deviant forms that was so marked a feature of Burton's psyche.

In Autumn 1859 Burton joined his sister Maria and invalid brother Edward in Paris. He paid flying visits to various parts of the Continent, and spent some weeks taking the waters at Vichy to arrest a tendency to gout.[7] But he found it difficult to work either in Paris or in London. To complete his two-volume *Lake Regions*, Burton returned to the scene of his early literary apprenticeship, Boulogne, and there made rapid progress.[8]

The winter of 1859–60 saw Burton commuting between Boulogne and London, where he saw Isabel either at her own home, where the atmosphere was chilly with Mrs Arundell's disapproval, or at the houses of the few friends who actually approved of the match.[9] Increasingly, Burton became irritated with Isabel's determination to have her cake and eat it: to marry the man of her choice *and* to win her mother's approval. In pique at Isabel's irresolution he decided to teach her a stinging lesson. In Boulogne he made secret plans for his American tour, to be conducted in company with John Steinhaeuser. His emaciated and fever-ridden physique on return from Africa was enough to win him an indefinite period of sick-leave from the East India Company, subject only to the proviso that he send in occasional medical certificates. The Company would raise no objection, Burton was led to believe, wherever he spent his convalescence. The choice of Steinhaeuser as comrade again illustrates the oscillating *yin* and *yang* of feminine and masculine principles in Burton. His steadfastness was particularly important to Burton during the dark days of Speke's treachery: 'No unkind thought, much less unfriendly word, ever broke our fair companionship ... He was one of the very few who, through evil as well as through good report, disdained to abate an iota of his friendship, and whose regard was never warmer than when all the little world looked its coldest.'[10]

When the two men left for Canada in April the realisation that she had almost lost her ideal mate because of her deference to her mother precipitated Isabel into breakdown. For a long time she was in bed, hysterical and delirious with grief. When she recovered, she vowed that she would make herself a worthy wife if and whenever Burton returned to her. She spent the summer of 1860 at a farmhouse, learning to cook, clean and housekeep, to tend chickens, ride horses and milk cows, so that being the wife of a poor man would be no hardship. She asked her friend Dr George Bird to teach her fencing so that she could be the perfect mate for Richard if ever they were attacked in the wilderness. In every way she tried to make herself a paragon of wifeliness, to make up to Richard for her weakness in having failed to face her mother down.[11]

Meanwhile Burton and Steinhaeuser landed in Newfoundland, travelled through Lower Canada, then crossed the border into the USA and methodically visited every state in the Union. In the deep South the friends parted company, for Steinhaeuser's leave expired. Burton found a succession of quacks and hick doctors to certify his continuing unfitness for active duties. In August 1860 he reached St Joseph, Missouri, and set off through Sioux territory for Salt Lake City, home of the Mormons since 1847. The Mormons were the religious phenomenon of the nineteenth century: 'Their religion is singular and their wives plural', as Mark Twain remarked. Under their leader Brigham Young, the 'Latter Day Saints' were peculiarly calculated to intrigue Burton. Their position outside the pale of the United States proper, their religious syncretism and, above all, their practice of polygamy, all made them a natural subject for Burton the anthropologist.

After a month's intensive study of the Mormons at Salt Lake City, which included a couple of private interviews with Brigham Young, Burton pressed on westward to Nevada and into the California Gold Country. He then spent an enjoyable week in San Francisco before embarking for Acapulco. Proceeding to the isthmus of Panama, he crossed to the Caribbean side in December and made his way to the West Indies, from where he took the first available steamer to Southampton.[12]

As soon as Isabel heard that Burton was back in England, she left Yorkshire where she had been spending Christmas and sped to London. She ran her quarry to earth on New Year's Day 1861. Burton reacted to being cornered by giving her an ultimatum. '"Now, you must make up your mind to choose between your mother and me. If you choose me, we marry, and I stay; if not, I go back to India, and on other explorations, and I return no more. Is your answer ready?" I said, "Quite. I marry you this day three weeks, let who will say nay."'[13]

Isabel realised she could not cope with the hysterical outpourings and emotional blackmail that would be levied if she gave advance warning of the marriage. She therefore opted for a secret ceremony, which took place on 22 January 1861 at the Bavarian Catholic Church in Warwick Street. Burton was waiting outside, dressed in a rough shooting coat, puffing ostentatiously on a large cigar to hide his nervousness. As he went in, Burton made obeisance to the Catholic faith by taking holy water and making a large sign of the cross. Burton's sister Maria and her husband together with Isabel's friend Dr George Bird and his sister were present at the ceremony.

At the wedding breakfast afterwards the subject of the fight at Berbera came up and Dr Bird gauchely tried to chaff Richard. 'Now, Burton, tell me, how do you feel when you have killed a man?' 'Oh, quite jolly, doctor! How do you?' came the predictable reply. It is morally certain that Burton never did kill anyone. Despite his thirst for action and his notional service in the Crimea and in Indian wars, the desperate midnight scrimmage on the shores of the Red Sea was the only fighting Burton ever took part in, and it is doubtful whether he got in any mortal blows or shots during that confused mêlée.

That very day Burton wrote a winning letter to Isabel's father who was away from home.

> My dear Father,
>
> I have committed a highway robbery by marrying your daughter Isabel at Warwick St Chapel and before the registrar – the details she is writing to her mother.
>
> It only remains for me to say that I have no ties nor liaisons of any kind, that the marriage was perfectly legal and 'respectable'. I want no money with Isabel; I can work, and it will be my care that Time shall bring you nothing to regret.
>
> Yours sincerely,
> Richard F. Burton[14]

Isabel had hoped to keep her mother in the dark for a 'decent interval' but this was not to be. Burton had hired a two-roomed furnished flat in a block given over to 'bachelor's lodgings'. When Isabel failed to appear for a pretended sojourn with friends, her mother put some aunts on her track. They saw her entering the flat and feared that her reputation was irreparably tarnished. They reported back to Mrs Arundell, who wrote in agitation to her husband. Henry Arundell, tired of the charade, cabled back snappishly: 'She is married to Dick Burton and thank God for it.'

Mrs Arundell could not bear the thought that she had been outwitted. She never forgave Isabel for the deception and relations were strained until her death in 1872.[15] Isabel dealt with this setback by putting on a bold face to the world and lying vigorously. She concocted the incredible story that Mrs Arundell came to see the error of her ways and begged God's forgiveness for trying to impede His divine plan![16]

Monkton Milnes gave a sumptuous party for the Burtons, where Lord Palmerston was guest of honour. Palmerston was charm itself, took Isabel on his arm, introduced Richard to all the right people, and generally provided the couple with the entrée into high society. The Palmerston connection led to invitations from the Russells and others. In social terms the marriage was a glittering success. The crown of glory was provided by Isabel's introduction to Queen Victoria. This was arranged at an afternoon-tea party at Lady Russell's. The Queen had a strict rule that she would not be seen at any social gathering in the company of women with a question-mark against their sexual morality; this included elopers or those whose marriages had been contracted against society's conventions. The fact that she consented to be present with Isabel indicated that not a soupçon of blame was held to attach to the Burtons for their *fait accompli* marriage.

But at a deeper level the marriage masked myriad contradictions, and from the very first was viewed by the connections of both partners as a disastrous mistake. Mrs Arundell's snobbish distaste for Richard's penurious atheism was echoed by the Stisteds' contempt for Isabel's vanity and bigotry, her ultramontane Catholicism, and her essential silliness. 'Fatal want of tact and judgment', 'flimsy conventual education', 'very excitable brain', and 'deficiency in reasoning faculties' were merely the politest descriptions circulated. The most disastrous aspect of the marriage is that there was no money to bolster it. Within a year Burton's legacy had dwindled from £16,000 to £4000, leaving the couple an income of just £200 per annum to survive on. This would not have been so bad if Isabel had been a good financial manager. But this was precisely the area in which she was a disaster. Despite her good resolutions and her 'training' on the farm to make her a suitable wife for a poor man, frugality was beyond her. She was notoriously extravagant, especially at the dressmaker's, and would become indignant when reminded of the need to provide for rainy days. Her defenders have attempted to portray her as a model of thrift and austerity, but the facts speak for themselves. In 1886 Burton made £12,000 from his famous translation of the *Arabian Nights*. By the time of his death four years later, only a few shillings of this fortune remained.[17]

The remarkable decline in Burton's finances between 1860 and 1861 raises interesting queries, on which the record is silent. What had happened to the other £12,000? It is possible that Burton had been forced to pay his debts in East Africa, despite his furious protests; naturally, to save face, he would have concealed the fact. But even if this were the case, those debts amounted to at most £1300. The nine-month trip to the USA must hold the key. We know that Burton was interested in gambling and this was the great era of the Mississippi river-boat gamblers. Is it too far-fetched to speculate that Burton found a new focus for his bravado but was systematically outpointed by professional cardsharps? This would explain the silence, for Burton always hated to admit that he had come off second best in any encounter.

Isabel was one of those early 'emancipated' women who was not at ease with the facts of her own sexuality and biology. Fundamentally she despised her own sex and the female principle. She railed against the 'vocation of my sex ... breeding fools and chronicling small beer.' Her young fantasies were male: she wanted to be 'a great general or statesman, to have travelled everywhere, to have seen and learnt everything, done everything: in fine to be the Man of the Day.' She found a way to come to terms with her own self-assigned female inadequacy by fashioning a fantasy male: 'As God took a rib out of

Adam and made a woman of it, so do I, out of a wild chaos of thought, form a man unto myself.'[18] The meeting with Burton in Boulogne in 1850 gave her the sensation of finding her own fantasies made flesh and blood. Thereafter her project was to find meaning for herself by entering into the spirit of Burton, virtually becoming him. The lines in the marriage service about 'becoming one flesh' would have had an almost literal meaning for Isabel.

To this end, when the marriage was imminent, she drew up a seventeen-point code of conduct for herself, which amounted to a denial or negation of her femininity and her individuality as a woman. She was to be a careful nurse, to keep his home snug, to be prepared to follow him at a moment's notice, to act as clerk and amanuensis in his publishing and other worldly projects, never to confide in female friends, to hide his faults from everyone, to conceal her own ill-health so as not to annoy him, not to open his letters, not to interfere between him and his family. 'Keep pace with the times, that he may not weary of you ... never answer when he finds fault, and never reproach him when he is in the wrong ... never ask him *not* to do anything ... Do not bother him with religious talk ... let him find in the wife what he and many other men fancy is only to be found in a mistress.'[19]

This is virtually a male chauvinist's charter, well calculated to appeal to a man who admired the mores of Islam. The most interesting part of this testament of self-abnegation and female-annihilation is the absence of a mention of children. Her early diaries denote a marked lack of interest in the role of woman as child-bearer.[20] At the time of her engagement to Burton, she expressed a wish for a single male child, and later commented on her eventual childlessness with relief. Psychologically, we can see three different streams feeding into this posture.

Ouida, always unreliable about Burton – for she announced with unwarranted aplomb that he really did love his wife ('in the eyes of women he had the unpardonable fault: he loved his wife') – had this to say about the Burtons' childlessness: 'He regretted it; men always do; I do not think she did so; children would have been impedimenta in the varying life which she so keenly enjoyed in the changes from Belgravia to Syria.'[21] She was almost certainly right about Isabel, but there is much evidence that Burton had no particular taste for paternity and would have disliked the responsibilities and constraints that parenthood would have imposed on him. In India he mentioned with approval the *bubus*' invariable and effective system of contraception while cohabiting with *sahibs*. At best he was prepared to go along with Isabel's one male child, but in general he was a neo-Malthusian.[22] He advocated birth control for the poor and thought that people with severe physical defects should not be allowed to reproduce. Even among the healthy and 'eugenic' he considered that no one should bring children into the world which could not be given every creature comfort. He wrote with approval of the old Scandinavian custom of gelding sturdy vagrants, so that they might not beget bastards, and endorsed the system of Lycurgus in Sparta, where children could be brought up only with the approval of the State.[23] In financial terms, he and Isabel easily fitted into the category of people who had no right to propagate.

The fact that Isabel was prepared to abase herself at all points before him and would not demand children made marriage to her appear to have its compensations, though he did not love her, and she was Catholic and dowerless. But there were other factors in his decision, which so surprised friends and relatives. He was depressed after the double blow of the loss of Edward and Speke, so that having a safe anchorage to windward appealed to him. And he took a delight in putting Mrs Arundell's nose out of joint; he spoke with great vehemence of the 'abominable egotism and cruelty' of English matrons who were prepared to keep their daughters as spinsters simply to have them at home for their own use and comfort.[24]

Beyond this, Burton chose a plain, simple, virginal woman as a wife so that he would not be challenged in his maleness. The trauma of his failure with the women of India still rankled. The feeling that women were potentially lustful volcanoes had blossomed in the intervening years to a fully-fledged misogynism. But for Burton, the dual man, things could never be simple. His response to heterosexuality was divided. On the one hand he feared unbridled female sexuality and sublimated his own feelings of inadequacy by turning sex into an academic and anthropological subject, something to be studied and discussed rather than practised or participated in. On the other, he despised the puritanism, ignorance and Mrs Grundyism of Victorian society. He poured scorn on the devastating sexual ignorance of the well-brought-up English maiden, even as he secretly feared the likely consequences if all sexual inhibitions and dampeners were removed.

Burton's assaults on Grundyism always found him at his most eloquent.

> Let us see what the modern English woman and her Anglo-American sister have become under the working of a mock-modesty which too often acts cloak to real *dévergondage* and how Respectability unmakes what Nature made. She has feet but no toes; ankles but no calves, knees but no thighs, stomach but no belly nor bowels, a heart but no bladder nor groin, a liver and no kidneys, hips and no haunches, a bust and no backside nor buttocks; in fact she is a monstrum, a figure fit only to frighten crows.[25]

Burton often told hair-raising stories about the sexual education (or rather lack of it) of young English women. One was told that the breaking of the hymen was as painful as having a tooth pulled.[26] Another was so frightened and disgusted by the thought of the physical act that on her honeymoon night she chloroformed herself and left a note on the pillow for her husband: 'Mama says you are to do what you like.'[27] One wonders if Isabel was in his mind when he recalled some general impressions of virginal ignorance: 'I have heard of brides over thirty years old who had not the slightest suspicion concerning what complaisance was expected of them; out of *mauvaise honte*, the besetting sin of the respectable classes, neither father nor mother would venture to enlighten the elderly innocents.'[28] Even the European male was stymied by the Christian association of sex with guilt. Burton told a story of a man who was able to prolong the sex act by thinking of his mother; the thought induced such guilt that he was unable to ejaculate until he banished the subject from his mind![29]

Yet although the excesses of Grundyism were both ludicrous and harmful, Burton feared the consequences of unbridled sexuality. He agreed with the ancient Greek seer Tiresias:

> If the parts of sex pleasure be counted as ten
> Nine parts have women, one only have men.

It was an item of faith with Burton that no woman, no matter how modest and strongminded, could resist a man once he had stimulated her genitally. Most women, moreover, would yield to rape, provided they were not disgusted by the assailant.[30] The lustfulness of women was particularly a problem in the tropics. With his obsession for the alleged effects of climate on human behaviour, Burton elaborated a theory that hot, damp climates produced greater lechery in women than in men, and vice versa in cold dry habitats. 'In these hot-damp climates the venereal requirements and reproductive powers of the female greatly exceed those of the male; and hence the dissoluteness of morals would be phenomenal, were it not obviated by seclusion, the sabre and the revolver.'[31]

Here again Burton anticipates Nietzsche, recalling his notorious remark in *Also Sprach Zarathustra*: 'Thou goest to woman? Do not forget thy whip.' He often cited with approval primitive examples of the Petruchio method for taming the shrew, and deplored that civilisation had thrown out 'the good old remedy' for keeping women in line – the sword.[32]

Burton's writing on the East are suffused with a simultaneous curiosity about and dread of female sexuality. Here he is on the subject of the Egyptians and Assyrians. 'They make use of the constrictor vaginal muscles. The "*Kabbahzah*" (holder) as she is called can sit astraddle upon a man and can provoke the venereal orgasm, not by wriggling and moving, but by tightening and loosing the male member with the muscles of her privities, milking it as it were. Consequently the *casse-noisette* costs treble the money of other concubines.'[33]

Burton thought that women were devoid of any moral code, that they regarded all talk of honour and scruple as a male absurdity, were pathological liars, and systematically used their wiles to deceive gullible men.[34] They had even persuaded the male to overlook elementary facts of biology: '*Prima venus debet esse cruenta* say the Easterns with much truth, and they have no faith in our complaisant need which allows the hymen-membrane to disappear by any but one accident.'[35] And in general his *oeuvre* is potholed with peevish, petulant, hostile and derisory remarks about women.[36]

A powerful unconscious motive, then, in Burton's marriage with Isabel might have been a desire to rationalise his own misogynism, to 'prove' his case by marriage to a woman who was vulnerable to all his most facile criticisms. This self-fulfilling prophecy element, clearly self-destructive, would appear preposterous if predicated of anyone but Burton. Yet it gains further support from the tacking between heterosexuality and homosexuality evident in Burton's career in the immediate aftermath of his marriage.

During the first seven months of his marriage – the period of 'uninterrupted bliss' according to Isabel's account[37] – Burton spent much time drinking with his journalist cronies at the Garrick, Beefsteak and (appropriately) the Arundel Club. Even more time was spent at Fryston, for Burton and Monkton Milnes were now fast friends. He dedicated his volume on the Mormons, *The City of the Saints,* to Milnes, who then reviewed it glowingly in the *Edinburgh Review*. Burton quickly became one of the inner circle at Fryston, along with Carlyle, Thackeray, Coventry Patmore, Buckle, Kingsley and Froude. Milnes's speciality was dinner parties at which unlikely guests would be juxtaposed: a freethinker and a Church of England divine, a classical scholar and a yachtsman, an inventor and an African explorer, and so on. Because of this interpenetration of polar opposites, Carlyle dubbed Milnes the 'Perpetual President of the Heaven and Hell Amalgamation Society'.

Monkton Milnes was a very odd fish indeed. Superficially a happily married aristocrat, he was in fact a depressive, much given to visitations from the 'black dog' and obsessed with a Baudelairean sense of evil. He had a vast library of erotica at Fryston, including the complete works of the Marquis de Sade and much of his memorabilia. It was at Monkton Milnes's table that Burton first met the notorious Fred Hankey. He was particularly fascinated by Hankey as an exemplar of pure evil, without any conventional redeeming features – for Hankey was undoubtedly the nineteenth century's Aleister Crowley. For Burton, the experience was like that of Dr Jekyll observing Mr Hyde:

Hankey was what Burton would be like if he stifled all his ambivalence and ambiguity, drained all the goodness out of himself and left himself as a hard core of evil.[38]

Hankey represented Burton as he would have been had he given his sadism and misogynism full rein. Burton's lifelong obsession with mutilation, castration, circumcision, infibulation and clitoridectomy had a sadistic side to it. That he was actually prepared to inflict pain is clear from his singular relationship with the poet Swinburne. Burton first met the poet at one of Milnes's stag breakfasts on 5 June 1861. One witness remembered seeing Burton escorting Swinburne downstairs on his arm at a function.[39] Aged 24, and not yet a famous name (*Atalanta in Calydon* appeared four years later, in 1865), Swinburne was bowled over by Burton's magnetism, his knowledge of Eastern religions, and his general erudition. Burton, for his part, saw the young poet's genius and was prepared to indulge him in his flagellation sessions. Swinburne was a homosexual, a masochist and, later, a notorious alcoholic. Burton was often blamed for having introduced Swinburne to the 'nasty bottle' and thus almost ruining his career, yet this particular charge cannot legitimately be laid at Richard's door. But he *did* consent to thrash Swinburne, as the following extract from a Swinburne letter to Monkton Milnes in 1865, after Burton's departure for Brazil, makes clear.

> As my tempter and favourite audience has gone to Santos I may hope to be a good boy again, after such a 'jolly good swishing' as Rodin alone can administer. The Rugby purists (I am told) tax Eaton generally with Maenadism during June and July, so perhaps some old school habits return upon us unawares – to be fitly expiated by old school punishment. That once I remember and admit. The Captain was too many for me; and I may have shaken the thyrsus in your face. But after this half I mean to be no end good.[40]

Isabel may have suspected that Swinburne was in some vague sense a rival for Richard's affections, for in the same year she complained to Monkton Milnes that Swinburne was leading *Burton* astray, by tempting him into massive alcoholic binges. Swinburne's reply reveals a contempt for her ingenuousness.

> As to anything you may have fished (how I say not) out of Mrs Burton to the discredit of my 'temperance, soberness and chastity' as the Catechism puts it – how can she who believes in the excellence of 'Richard' fail to disbelieve in the virtues of any other man? *En moi vous voyez les Malheurs de la Vertu: en lui les Prosperités du Vice.* In effect it is not given to all his juniors to *tenir tête à* Burton – but I deny that his hospitality ever succeeded in upsetting me – as he himself on the morrow of a latish seance admitted with approbation, allowing that he had thought to get me off my legs, but my

native virtue and circumspection were too much for him.[41]

Burton's rebounding here from heterosexuality to homosexuality also compounds misogynism with sadism. He later related with glee the characteristic distaste of women for being buggered by their husbands. The Persians, natural sodomites according to Burton, used this knowledge of the dislike of wives for anal intercourse to force them to petition for divorce, thus forfeiting their claim to a return of dowry. Unlike in English law, buggery of wife by husband was not an offence, since the Koran said: 'Your wives are your tillage; go in therefore into your tillage in what manner soever ye will.'[42]

Burton's homosexual streak emerges clearly in his belief that anal intercourse was 'natural' and that the male nude was superior to the female. In support of the first proposition he quoted an ancient quatrain:

> The penis smooth and round was made
> with anus best to match it.
> Had it been made for cunnus' sake,
> it had been formed like a hatchet![43]

And just a year after the so-called 'seven months of uninterrupted bliss', in West Africa, Burton recorded the following verdict:

> The male figure here, as all the world over, is notably superior, as amongst the lower animals, to that of the female. The latter is a system of soft, curved and rounded lines, graceful, but meaningless and monotonous. The former far excels it in variety of form and in sinew. In these lands, where all figures are semi-nude, the exceeding difference between the sexes strikes the eye at once. There will be a score of fine male figures to one female, and there she is, as everywhere else, as inferior as is the Venus de Medici to the Apollo Belvedere.[44]

If Isabel had a homosexual proclivity in Richard to contend with (probably unknowingly), he had an even more powerful internal enemy to struggle against in her, and one he could not but be aware of: Catholicism. No more ludicrous suggestion has ever been proffered than Isabel's assertion that Richard was a closet Catholic. He may have disliked the Church of Rome marginally less than the blinkered Low Church Anglicanism of his parents, but that was as far as his affection extended. Interestingly – for as a political reactionary he ought to have embraced the tenet eagerly – he referred scathingly to 'the degrading doctrine of original sin'.[45]

Georgiana Stisted, Burton's niece, painted a poignant picture: 'He often looked, oh! so sad and weary when hearing for the twentieth time how a leaden image had tumbled out of her pocket during a long ride, and then miraculously returned to its despairing owner ... Nor were his friends spared this style of talk; and some clever men, on hearing themselves mourned over as infidels, etc., were not so forbearing.'[46]

Sometimes the sadness turned to anger, as in the 'joking but serious' episode described by the traveller Stevenson in Brazil in 1868. Burton was angered by his wife's defence of the servants' pilfering on the grounds that, still and all, they were good Catholics. 'He worked himself up into a most unseemly fury, threatening to throw the effigy of the Blessed Virgin Mary that his wife had in her oratory at Santos out of the window if she continued to interfere with his "damned little niggers". She took it all very quietly, merely saying, "Now, Richard, behave yourself and don't make yourself ridiculous. Mr Stevenson must take you for a perfect brute." '[47]

'My wife is fretting herself into a fever, which greatly increases the pleasure of my departure', he told Monkton Milnes just before leaving for West Africa in 1861.[48] These are hardly the words of a man who had just enjoyed 'a large oasis of seven months' (Isabel's words). Faced with the financial burdens of marriage, Burton had decided to apply for a Consular post in the British Foreign Office. Discreet strings were pulled, and Lord John Russell, then Foreign Secretary, was lobbied on Richard's behalf. He told the Burton supporters that the idea of going straight to a £700 per annum Consular post was fantasy; this could only be occupied by a man with some years of experience. However, he was prepared to start Burton off on the bottom rung, to be exact, in Fernando Po, a Spanish island twenty miles off the West African coast. Grudgingly Burton accepted the position, describing it as a 'governmental crumb' which might some day grow into a loaf.[49]

Burton took the posting on the understanding that he would still retain his Army half-pay. But the precedents he cited were not relevant, since the officers concerned had all asked permission of the Admiralty or War Office *before* applying to fill a position as Consul; needless to say, Burton had neglected to do so. Secondly, in his preoccupation with exploration, he had lost sight of military realities in India. Following the suppression of the Indian Mutiny, in 1858 the East India Company was dissolved, and the Company regiments were merged with those of the Regular Army. The War Office took the opportunity to weed out half-pay drones. If Burton hoped to be an exception, he had to make out a strong case for himself to the War Office. But what could he say? That he had not served in India for twelve years? That his career had been an endless series of sick-leaves and special exploration furloughs? That his only contact with the East India Company since 1849, leave applications and medicals apart, had been in the form of public and unauthorised criticism of his superiors in the hierarchy?

When the news came through that the India Office had taken advantage of his Consulship to strike him off the Indian list, Burton was aghast at the 'treachery' and 'injustice' of it all. He was left with not a penny of pension to supplement his meagre Consular stipend.[50] The cynic would say that, on the contrary, Burton had done very well out of his Army years, and could have done better, if he had only learned to curb his pen.

The transition from Army officer to Consular official was not so abrupt as the paper situation suggests. The promotion of British trade and the compilation of trade statistics, the main duties, would come easily to a man who had already, in his published work, evinced considerable talent in this direction.[51] Moreover, a posting to a back-water like Fernando Po offered the chance for further exploration and thus a return to the arena in which Burton had won his greatest laurels to date. His restlessness, his desire to explore new worlds, and the wish to keep his wife at arm's length would all be served. It was just the posting itself that stuck in the Burton craw. Fernando Po, 'the Foreign Office grave', was a standing joke.

But at least the post offered Africa, and the prospect of some exploration. In some ways the most significant story Isabel tells of her first seven months with Burton concerns the time he overslept in the last train one evening and missed his station. Burton asked the way to his destination, set his pocket compass and then set off on a cross-country trek. The picture of an anxious Isabel at home, waiting tearfully for her beloved, while an insouciant Burton strode alone across deserted heaths and open countryside, could well be taken as an epitome of their separate lives to come.[52]

14

Consul in Fernando Po

ON 24 August 1861 Burton left England with no regrets, as he openly confessed, Isabel notwithstanding. 'If Britannia chills with tears and sighs the hearts of her sons' home-returning, at any rate, with the same tenderness she consoles them under departure. Whoever landed at Southampton in other but the worst of weather? Who ever left Dover on a fine clear morning?'[1]

On 7 September his ship anchored at Bathurst in the Gambia. Burton's first glimpse of West Africa found him in sour mood. He thought Bathurst 'an aged fogy', the sharks in the roadstead the only thing vivacious about the town. 'To those who would retain the Gambia, I wish nothing worse than a year's residence, or, rather, confinement there.'[2] At Cape Palmas Burton visited the European settlement and American mission, and made a point of excoriating the Krumen, West Africa's professional labour supply. For most whites the 'Kruboys' represented the African at his most biddable, inured to the dictates of labour-time and work-discipline. But Burton, with his savage hatred of all blacks, was determined to debunk the African, by confronting him at his supposedly most 'civilised point'. The Krumen, he announced, were cowards and thieves. Not only were they liable to panic at the least threat, but even minor corporal punishment made them scream like women. Their poltroonery was so open that they actually boasted of it. They were specialists in small-scale theft: knives, scissors, pen-knives. Like starlings they acted collectively: all expected to share the proceeds of a robbery by any one of them. Masters of chicanery, they had ways of strangling goats to make it look as though the animals had been bitten by snakes; later, when Burton learned their tricks, he would order all such 'poisoned' goats to be flung into the sea, since the Krumen would exhume and eat any corpse buried on land. Worst of all Kruman faults for Burton was their tendency to be 'uppity', to put on European airs and to aspire to a life of ease. Burton decided he needed to deploy all the resources of his invective to 'take them down a peg or two'.

> Their appearance struck me as grotesque. Conceive the head of a Socrates upon the body of the Antinous or Apollo Belvidere. A more magnificent development of muscle, such perfect symmetry in the balance of grace and strength, my eyes had never yet looked upon. But the faces! except when lighted up by smiles and good humour – expression to an African face is all in all – nothing could be more unprepossessing. The flat nose, the high cheek-bones, the yellow eyes, the chalky-white teeth pointed like the shark's, the muzzle projecting as that of a dog-monkey, combine to form an unusual amount of ugliness. To this somewhat adds the tribe mark, a blue line of cuts half-an-inch broad, from the forehead-scalp to the nose-tip ... The marks are made with a knife, little cuts into which the oily smoke of a gum is rubbed. The bodies are similarly ornamented with stars, European emblems, as anchors, etc., especially with broad double lines down the breast and other parts.[3]

On 18 September Burton reached the Gold Coast, where he showed the first symptoms of the gold fever that was to plague him for the rest of his life. He waxed eloquent about 'the precious metal, in a continent which, when opened up, will supply us with half-a-dozen Californias.'[4] In the roads of Lagos Burton noted that the sea was infested with sharks. Animals dangerous to man always caused him a frisson. He set down his impressions of the shark, a more formidable assailant than the crocodile – which also abounded in the Lagos area – since it could not be beaten off by gouging. 'Few men survive a shark bite, and when seized, they usually lose their hands by snatching mechanically at the limb first hurt.'[5] The sojourn in Lagos lifted Burton's spirits, for its population contained 800 Moslems, and for the first time since Zanzibar Burton could converse in Arabic.

A few mornings later, Burton trained his eyes on the beautiful peak of Fernando Po which loomed out of the dawn mist. On his first night there he felt genuinely suicidal: 'arriving in these outer places is the very abomination of desolation'. The Consulate was located in the lower part of Santa Isabel, close to the harbour and to a military hospital built of wood with a corrugated iron roof. The hospital exhaled all kinds of noxious odours through its glassless windows. 'Breakfast and dinner were frequently enlivened by the spectacle of a something covered with a blanket being carried in, after due time a something in a dead box being borne out on four ghastly men's shoulders. And strangers fled the place like a pestilence – sailors even from the monotonous "sotuh coast" felt the ennui of Fernando Po to be deadly – gravelike.'[6]

Burton found the consular house in any case barely habitable and at once requested the Foreign Office for funds to repair and refurbish it.[7]

An epidemic of yellow fever decided him not to attempt to camp out in the husk of a building. The Spanish governor had found a spot on the heights, away from the fever-ridden hospital, to build his new barracks. It was to this location that Burton migrated for the few weeks he actually spent on the island. He rented a frame-house, constructed by a Spanish official, perched 800 feet above sea level, and in this eyrie he made his base.

On his first full day on the island Burton found little to change his opinion that he had been consigned into the outer darkness. He regarded the native inhabitants of Fernando Po, the 'Bubis', as a new low in benighted African barbarism. Even their language was uninteresting, since it depended so much on gesture that they were said to be unable to talk to each other in the dark![8] Inevitably, too, one of the locals adopted an over-familiar tone with Burton, with predictably explosive results. Greeting him with a yip-yipping laugh, 'How do, Consul? Come to shake hands, how do?', the man held out 'his black paw as if he were condescending royalty', Burton recalled disdainfully. He called for his despised Krumen and got them to pitch out the unfortunate visitor neck and crop. There were no more social calls by blacks after that.[9]

The area of Burton's consular jurisdiction covered five hundred miles of navigable river, on twenty-five different streams. He saw at once that he would need a gunboat to keep a regular oversight on his domains. In Lagos he had been told none was available. He therefore wrote to the Foreign Office to request a gunboat to be on permanent station in the Bight of Biafra. Meanwhile he asked for permission to purchase a 'zig'. In the Bonny river there was a small steamer, which, with its complement of master engineer, twenty-five Krumen and five guns, could be bought for five or six thousand pounds.[10] Meanwhile, there was another welcome development. His *Exequatur* or consular credentials has not yet been forwarded. He set out for a quick visit to the Old Calabar and Cameroons river on 29 September and returned on 2 October.[10]

The key to Burton's consular assignment was the palm-oil trade. In the 1860s British trade with the ports of the Niger Delta amounted to £1 million in exported palm-oil alone – the equivalent, in other words, of the total value of British trade with all her official West African trading posts combined (those at the Gambia, Sierra Leone, the Gold Coast and Lagos). Burton at once saw that there were boundless opportunities for the expansion of this trade, but at the same time there were formidable obstacles: lack of legal and financial institutions, inefficiency and petty rivalries. There was a clash of interests between the three types of European operating in the Delta – Royal Navy personnel, merchants and missionaries. There was also opposition to the official consular promotion of commerce, from African middlemen and Liverpool traders (the so-called 'supercargoes') in the Delta. In a word, the administration and organisation of the trade did not keep pace with its value and growth.

Burton had one of the indispensable weapons in the administrator's armoury – the ability to knife through to the essentials of a problem very quickly. It did not take him long to see where the real problems lay. His particular animus was directed at the 'supercargoes'. He derided the commercial management of the Delta markets as incompetent and outmoded. Except for New Calabar, the ports were mere brokerages. He criticised the system of paying commission agents 5 per cent, instead of a fixed salary, on all purchases of palm oil; the wide variety of unconvertible currencies; and the local practice of inflating the price of the oil by withholding supplies at times of low demand. The 'supercargoes' themselves were a lawless breed, wanting to remain outside the orbit of British control while retaining the 'right' to call in the Consul and the Royal Navy warships when it suited them.[11]

But Burton lacked the qualities of patience and attention to detail that denote the great administrator. Also, his temperament was wrong for the task of wheedling and persuading as opposed to forcing. Burton was the kind of man who believed in issuing an edict, then, if it was not obeyed, following up with the police or army. Diplomacy, in a word, was never his strong suit.[12] But the Fernando Po Consul was in an impossible situation. Burton's predecessor Consul Hutchinson had taken the line of least resistance by backing the Europeans to the hilt and imposing fines on the Africans. But the locals took their revenge by charging him with defalcation. Hutchinson was eventually recalled to London in disgrace to answer allegations that he had profiteered from the sale of goods from a wrecked vessel.[13]

Burton was out of sympathy with the European traders after the examples of piracy and murder he had seen during his journey along the West African coast. He began by trying to bring them to heel. He attempted a reform of the equity courts which heard grievances between Africans and Europeans. And he made a valiant effort to bring ships' captains under the aegis of commercial discipline. The merchants of the Delta petitioned him to oblige captains to remain in port for at least eighteen hours, instead of weighing anchor and decamping at once, so that the merchants might have time to answer their incoming correspondence and send out their replies. When the ships' masters proved recalcitrant, Burton threatened to ask the Spanish governor for use of his cannon, to blow the vessels out of the water if they left within eighteen hours. Predictably, this led to complaints from shipowners that the Consul at Fernando Po was exceeding his powers and behaving in a dictatorial fashion.[14]

Once he realised how limited were his powers, and that therefore his initiatives were a waste of time, Burton very sensibly decided to exploit the Consulate for his own ends. He left most of his official duties to Vice-Consul Laughland and spent as much time as possible on travel and exploration. He spent just one week (2 to 9 October 1861) at Fernando Po before begging a lift to Lagos from the Commodore of the West African squadron.

Next morning saw Burton far out in the Bight of Biafra: 'Fernando Po still haunted us with its presence next morning, though we had run upwards of one hundred miles.'[15] The squadron deposited him at Lagos where, after a week in the company of acting Governor McCoskry, Burton inveigled his way onto a mission to the king of Abeokuta, headed by Commander Bedingfield. This involved a four-day ascent of the Ogun river, at an average of twenty-six miles' rowing every eight-hour day. Sweat poured off Burton as he took copious notes on the bird life in the forests around them. Amid the profusion he noted parrots, toucans, ibises, cuckoos, kingfishers, blackbirds, finches, orioles, guinea-fowl, turkey and buzzards. On 1 November they entered the Yoruba fortress of Abeokuta, four miles long and two wide, the whole circumvallated by an eighteen-mile defensive wall, like the one Wellington had constructed at Torres Vedras.

The visitors were entertained by Dr and Mrs Harrison of the Church Missionary Society. Burton at once boned up on the many battles between the Abeokuta people and their great enemies in Dahomey. Within a few days Bedingfield and the other Britons had been presented to the Alake at court. The Alake was in surly mood after a number of recent reprimands from HMG. He saved face by pretending to doze through the interminable and boring speeches of welcome and response. Burton kept his end up in the carousal that followed, but was sober enough to tour the state prison next day and to begin taking his usual meticulous anthropological notes. He filled many pages with the Abeokuta beliefs in demonology and witchcraft, and with detailed observations on their women. In general Burton found the Yoruba annoyingly bumptious: 'these people can be respectful until spoiled by the Europeans, after which they are insufferable.'[16]

On a second visit to the Alake, Burton made his mark by being able to converse in Arabic with some of the royal officials. Bedingfield had to listen to a long list of complaints against the British, which he answered by repeating over and over again that Her Majesty's Government had no other interest than cotton. The Alake wagged his finger at his guests and warned that their admonitions would not deter him from his planned campaign against Ibadan. He softened his intransigence the next day by making a return visit to the embassy at the mission house.

After a week in Abeokuta, Bedingfield signed an anodyne treaty with the Alake, which opened up the Ogun river to British commerce in cotton (after palm-oil the most important West African product) and contained clauses abolishing human sacrifice and the export of slaves. The truth was that the British had no power to compel the Yoruba to desist from these practices. But the Alake did not demur at the clauses, for he was aware of commercial realities. In the 1860s, as the British and French consolidated their imperial interests at Lagos, Dahomey and the Delta, the slave trade was already in relative decline, being supplanted by the export of palm oil.[17] The foundation of the African Steamship Company in 1852 and the introduction of quinine as a remedy against tropical diseases were part of the technological breakthrough that allowed this economic shift from slaves to commerce in tropical staples.[18]

Burton returned to Lagos with the Abeokuta mission, then after a visit to the Brass and Bonny rivers he set out (21 November 1861) on HMS *Bloodhound* for an exploration of the Cameroon mountains. He came in sight of them on 10 December.

> For a distance of ten miles a huge blue silhouette stood before us, the upper heights gilt by the yet unrisen sun, and the lower expanse still blue-black with lingering night. The dorsal swell was everywhere so regular that it gave to the whole the appearance of one vast mountain rising from a single base. Every quarter of an hour, however, brought a change in the magnificent spectacle. Presently the south-western profile was broken by serrations; the highest is the uppermost of a group, to which we afterwards gave the name of the Three Sisters; below it was an extinct Vesuvius, the little Camaroons of old sailors, surging apparently impracticable and perpendicular from a rolling sea of vegetation; lower still was Botoki cone, a small but independent feature, clearly seen from Fernando Po; and in the maritime region hummocky hills and dromedary's backs here formed headlands, heaving out in accumulative grandeur from the Atlantic, whose mighty swell, slow and measured, broke at their feet, and there sank blended with the winding, waving shore, that dipped below the misty horizon.[19]

On the 18th the *Bloodhound* landed Burton at Ambas Bay. Leaving the Navy to return to Lagos, Burton set out on a trek inland with the missionaries. Accompanying him was a Spanish judge, Calvo Iturburu, likewise based on Fernando Po and as bored with it as Burton.[20]

There was much reluctance and desertion by the party's porters, so that it was 22 December 1861 before the expedition well and truly got under way. Its objective was the conquest of the highest peaks in the Cameroons range. There were some little local difficulties after a drunken chief took exception to Burton's refusal of his offer of his twelve-year-old daughter as 'wife'. Warpaint was donned before Burton managed to pacify the headman. Judge Calvo also made the mistake of becoming too-familiar with the locals, but learned the error of his ways when some overzealous horse-play led to his beard being pulled. Burton warned the missionaries that they were not instilling enough respect for the white man, with their over-affability and also their decision to camp in the villages rather than bivouacking outside, as Burton used to do in East Africa. But he consoled himself with his great success in being able to communicate with the tribesmen in sign-language.[21]

They decided to begin with an ascent of Pico Grande in the little Cameroons. The initial stages were achieved easily enough, apart from an attack by a swarm of bees. Christmas Day saw them slogging through the foothills. Two separate entries show Burton oscillating between euphoria and depression during the festivities.

> We did our best to honour Christmas Day. Kind Mrs Saker [a missionary wife] had given us a plum pudding, which fared badly in the encounter, and we had beef, but a trifle salt. A forest of Yule logs lay around us – I wished it had been my property within easy carriage of Paris – and a giant fire lighted the camp. We spent a merry evening, telling old tales around our hearth, and, cognac being deficient, we roughed it on a bottle of anisado.

This is a different mood-register from the following:

> Christmas Day was something sad to those who could not prevent 'The busy goste, aye flick'ring to and fro' winging her way to far-off regions which the heavy clay cannot reach. In such wild scenes, with wilder work before them, men are too apt to think regretfully of merry gatherings round the Yule log, the *leche de almandras*, and the Christmas tree, forgetting the inevitable worries of 'home' and the pains and penalties of civilisation, so terrible to endure after the life of liberty in the desert; besides if we lose the revelry at night, do we not also escape the headache next morning?[22]

On 27 December the expedition began the assault on Pico Grande, which was crowned with success at the turning of the year. But Burton reaped his inevitable reward for enduring cold, wet and over-exertion in Africa: he went down with swollen feet and fever. Unable to walk for a month, he had to grit his teeth through the frustration of thus wasting thirty of his forty-six days in the Cameroons.[23] He had to sit idly by while his companions made various other ascents of Cameroons peaks, until the coming of the rainy season on 19 January and universal illness and food shortage brought the entire party to the verge of utter exhaustion. Fortunately for Burton the change of climate with the coming of the rains worked wonders for his constitution. He was soon back on his feet and able to take protein nourishment, after a spartan invalid diet of iron-rust in brandy and rum, and cold arrowroot tempered with chalk. On 27 January Burton set out for a final ascent of Pico Grande. He continued mountaineering until 4 February 1862, when he regretfully bade farewell to the blue mountains of the Cameroons. But he had seen enough to inspire a report to the Foreign Office, recommending the Cameroons as the place for a second Liberia – a new colony of liberated Africans.[24]

On his return to Fernando Po, Burton found despatches from the Foreign Office awaiting him. There was welcome news in the decision to station a gunboat permanently in the Bight of Biafra, to enable him to visit all the far-flung areas where his presence might be required. The Admiralty had been issued with standing instructions to assist him in visiting all the rivers under his jurisdiction. But as to the request for a brig, the Foreign Office wanted first to know what had happened to the boat Hutchinson used to have there. Another tiresome chore was the investigation of the alleged murder of British subject Thomas Bland Lee. While protesting that he was still without his *Exequatur*, and therefore had no official status, Burton was able to clear up this case by a little amateur sleuthing. Lee, it transpired, had not been murdered; he had merely drowned after a drunken spree.[25]

In his report on the visit to the Egba capital of Abeokuta, Burton recommended that the British should become involved in Yoruba cotton on a large scale – especially now that the American Civil War had cut off the principal source of supply. To this end it would be necessary to intervene massively in the interior.[26] High politics and stirring action: these were ever the ideas that inspired Burton. He was in his element at the end of February 1862. Complaints had come in from mainland missionaries that they were being maltreated by a chieftain nicknamed 'Dick Merchant'. With the aid of Commander Perry and the *Griffon*, Burton left Fernando Po on the 27th, crossed to the mainland, and summoned the chief for a palaver. Burton refused to shake 'Dick Merchant's' hand, thoroughly browbeat him with the full panoply of rolling eyes and basilisk stare, and forced him to sign a treaty of obeisance to the British government.[27]

Two weeks later the restless Burton hit on another ingenious pretext for an exploring venture. The *Griffon* was ordered south to deliver mail along the Gabon coast, in French territory. With Perry he visited the mouth of the Gabon river and toured the coastal towns. They landed at Le Plateau, which Burton found very French, with an excellent *table d'hôte*. Again Burton's ethnological interest was much to the fore, and he wrote a long analysis of the Mponge peoples. All the typical Burton themes are present in his account of the journey: the perennial irritation with tropical insects, especially sand flies and mosquitoes: the fear of snakes.[28]

After visiting the coastal areas Burton arranged a rendezvous with Perry, then proceeded alone up the Gabon river. His first objective was to track down the allegedly cannibalistic Fan. As a good anthropologist,

Burton had a nuanced attitude towards anthropophagy.

> Cannibalism is an interesting, though somewhat morbid subject. Once, all anthropophagous tales were greedily swallowed; they are now fastidiously rejected. The pages of many African travellers show so much hearsay and little eye-sight, they supply, moreover, such ridiculous details, that the public is justified in doubting anything but personal evidence. But to deny, as some very silly philanthropists of the Ethnological Society have denied, its existence in West Africa, is to maintain, like the old African, the impossibility of water becoming hard because he had never seen it so.[29]

He spent a delightful day with the Fan, thoroughly researched the cannibal stories, then set out on 14 April with his hosts for a trip to the interior and the Londo river. The exhausting foray first made him aware of the difficulties of travel in West Africa – much more problematical than in East Africa because local society here was more brittle, and a single blood feud could close the only jungle path from village A to village B for a month or more.[30]

Next it was time to turn to Burton's most important objective on the trip up the Gabon. Gorillas had fascinated him ever since his friend Paul du Chaillu reported his amazing discovery of these simians to incredulous audiences in London in July 1861. Burton was present at Chaillu's lecture at the Ethnological Society when a member of the audience questioned his veracity as though he were a criminal on trial. The quick-tempered du Chaillu flashed back that in his country such ungentlemanly behaviour was resolved by the duel – a sentiment well calculated to appeal to Burton. After a few more ill-mannered exchanges, du Chaillu leaped over the benches to where his tormentor, one T. A. Malone, stood, and spat in his face. The meeting dissolved into chaos, with Malone appealing to the chairman, and du Chaillu bawling 'Coward! Coward!' at him.[31] Burton entered the epistolary lists on du Chaillu's behalf before he left England, and followed up with a further testimony written from Fernando Po.[32]

He was determined to do something to vindicate his friend, but the expedition up the Gabon river proved one of his most unsuccessful. He saw no gorillas in the wild, but merely one captured by local hunters. He was nearly drowned while on his way up the river, he was knocked down on another day by a bolt of lightning and during the final march he had a narrow escape from the fall of a giant branch, which grazed his hammock. Burton compensated by poking fun at accounts of the gorilla that had appeared in London publications. 'The wild huntsmen almost cried with laughter when they saw the sketches in the "Gorilla Book", the mighty pugilist standing stiff and upright as the late Mr Benjamin Caunt, "beating the breast with huge fists till it sounded like an immense brass drum" and preparing to deal a buffet worthy of Friar

Tuck. They asked me if I thought mortal men would ever attempt to face such a thing as that?'[33]

On 22 April Burton re-embarked on the *Griffon*, homeward-bound after five weeks on the Gabon river. Two days later at noon he landed at Fernando Po. It now remained to throw a cloak of official justification around a trip which had been pure exploration and sightseeing. The ingenious Burton was never at a loss for plausible pretexts. He claimed to have set out for the Gabon to investigate a complaint that British vessels could not carry their colours inland beyond the Gabon estuary; only the tricolor was to be displayed. But everyone knew this was already the case, so it was a moot point why it needed to be 'investigated' by Burton. He then proceeded to trail a red herring, suggesting an exchange between Britain and France of Gabon and the Gambia. Gambia, he argued, was a liability for the British. It was a pestilential hole and would always be in the shadow of the large French settlements at Goree and St Louis de Senegal. The trade of Gabon, on the other hand, was almost wholly English, and the climate was comparatively salubrious. Burton rounded off by suggesting that the Fernando Po Consulate be given an *Exequatur* from the French authorities, enabling the Consul to extend his duties to Gabon.[34] He scarcely seems to have noticed that this did not square with his previous protestations that the ambit of Consular jurisdiction was too large, which was why he needed a brig.

But Burton's main concern was the audience in England still avid for gorilla stories. He had to tread carefully to avoid offending Victorian sensibilities. To his disgust, du Chaillu's first stuffed specimens exhibited in London were mutilated and imperfect; all 'offending' organs, such as the penis, had been removed. The iconoclastic Burton decided that his best strategy was to debunk the entire craze. He set to work to deflate the expectations of sensation-crazed readers in Europe.

> The Gorilla is a poor devil ape, not a 'hellish dream-creature, half man, half beast'. He is not king of the African forest; he fears the *njego* or leopard and, as lions will not live in these wet, wooded and gameless lands, he can hardly have expelled King Leo. He does not choose the 'darkest, gloomiest forests' but prefers the thin woods, where he finds wild fruits for himself and family. His tremendous roar does not shake the jungle: it is a hollow apish cry, a loudish huhh! huhh! huhh! explosive like the puff of a steam engine, which in a rage becomes a sharp and snappish bark – any hunter can imitate it ... The eye is not a 'light grey' but the brown common to all the tribe. The gorilla cannot stand straight upon his rear quarter when attacking or otherwise engaged without holding on to a trunk; he does not 'run on his hind legs'; he is essentially a tree ape, as every stuffed specimen will prove. He never gives a tremendous blow with his immense open paw ... nor does he attack with his arms. However old and male he may be, he

> runs away with peculiar alacrity; though powerfully weaponed with tigerish teeth, with 'bunches of muscular fibre', and with the limbs of Goliath, the gorilla, on the seaboard at least, is essentially a coward ... Finally, whilst a hen will defend her chicks, Mrs Gorilla will fly, leaving son or daughter in the hunter's hands.[35]

Back in Fernando Po Burton found Foreign Office instructions to proceed at once to the Bonny river and conciliate Britain's old enemy King Pepple, who was now trying to levy charges on the African Steamship Company.[36] Burton was delighted to use this to promote his request for a personal ocean-going vessel. Quite apart from the yellow fever epidemic in the Bonny river, he pointed out that there was no Royal Navy cruiser available for the operation.

While Burton sat on his hands, waiting for a naval cruiser to put in to the island, word reached him of an assault on a Liverpool trader by a black on the Old Calabar river.[37] When the *Griffon* put in to Santa Isabel on 1 May, Burton commandeered her for an urgent punitive expedition. It was a dangerous mission, even in terms of seamanship. The vessel was nearly wrecked off Tom Shortt's point before coming to anchor off Duke Town on 4 May. Burton immediately convened a meeting of white traders, who regaled him with lurid tales of murder and torture. He announced that the local chieftain 'King' Archibong would be subpoenaed to appear at a Court of Equity, whose findings would be binding. Archibong refused to attend the Duke Town palaver, pleading ill-health. Burton countered by sending naval doctors to his village, who declared him to be in perfect health. Finally Burton bearded Archibong in his kraal, but the chief refused 'insolently and tauntingly' to append his signature to a document committing him to a Court of Equity.[38]

Burton was now in a quandary. The Commodore had given Commander Perry just five days to conclude the business on the Old Calabar. Archibong's stalling tactics threatened to leave Burton beached, without the military means to make his writ run. Burton decided on main force. He threatened to burn down the village if Archibong did not sign the articles by next day. Archibong refused, and revealed that he had an ally – one of the local missionaries – the Reverend Mr Anderson, who presented a memorandum to Burton protesting at the Consul's high-handed attitude.[39]

Burton detested missionaries at the best of times, but to have one cutting across his jurisdiction was much more than he could stomach. Mastering his anger, he rallied the other missionaries to his side, then repeated his ultimatum to Archibong. After much blustering, the chief grudgingly signed. The Court of Equity then met to consider the assault on Mr Lawton, the Liverpool merchant by Archibong's henchman

Yellow Duke. Predictably, Yellow Duke was found guilty as charged. To secure his freedom, Archibong was compelled to sign a treaty opening up the river to British trade and missionaries.

But this was not the end of the story. On 9 May the Navy was opposed at Ittoo, forty miles upstream from Duke Town, by sixty of Archibong's musketeers, who ordered them to retire. One of the missionaries landed to 'talk sense' into the locals. They promptly took him hostage and released him only when the cruiser turned and began to go downstream. Burton returned to Duke Town and ordered Archibong to surrender the culprits. The answer was an evacuation of Duke Town by its inhabitants. Archibong made a show of strength with armed men and declared defiantly that he would rather have all his villages burnt down than submit to the white man. A face-saving Court of Equity decided to move all trade and shipping to Parrot Island as 'punishment'; Burton meanwhile resolved that next season he would return in force and prise open the Calabar river. Middlemen like Archibong could not be permitted to interrupt the flow of trade between Benin City and the Cameroons.

On 14 May Burton left Calabar for the Cameroons. He made an ascent of the Elephant Mountain before returning to Fernando Po.[40] Every time he went back to base, he found a fresh incident to investigate. This time it was a plea for help from a Dr Henry, a merchant on the Benin river, whose factory had been plundered. Burton had to wait until 31 July for the arrival of *Bloodhound.* On 4 August he was off up the Benin river, but chief Akabwa who had committed the depredation refused to go on board for talks. The whites then responded with a trade embargo. Most consuls, seeing there was little more to be done, would have returned home at once, but not Burton. He persuaded Dr Henry, Lieutenant-Commander Stokes RN and Captain White of the Marines to accompany him on a foray into the interior.

On 8 August the party set out for the ruined city of Wari, which they reached after nineteen hours' rowing.[41] Burton sent some half-hearted messages overland to Lagos asking for 'further instructions', but when, predictably, no reply was received within ten days, the party again struck out into the wilderness. This time the destination was Benin City. First they rowed seventeen hours to Gwato. Next day (18 August) they trekked from 9 a.m. to 6 p.m. and slept in the bush. On the 19th, after an early morning two-hour march, they entered Benin City.

This inland city proved a veritable Golgotha. In front of the king's palace the ground was strewn pebble-fashion with human skulls and bones. The body of a young woman was fastened to the top of a tree as a fetish for rain. Even Burton, no friend to missionaries, was forced to concede that their presence prevented similar atrocities in Abeokuta. His gorge rose at some of the atrocities he witnessed.

> One of the first objects that met our sight was a negro freshly crucified after the African fashion, sitting on a stool with extended arms, lashed to a framework of poles. I fear it was in honour of our arrival ... During the night I heard the voice of 'Spirit Oro', and next morning we found close to our doors the corpse of a man with broken shinbones, and a gashed throat. Walking to the market we remarked a pool of blood where another victim had been slaughtered.[42]

Burton could not fathom the intentions of the Beninese. The men in the street seemed to share the contempt of their brothers on the river for the European, and were confident of their impregnability in their creeks and bayous. Burton could see no solution to the conflicts with European traders, short of the removal of all foreign factories. On the other hand, the king of Benin was affability itself, and promised to send a messenger to the Benin river, threatening interdiction of provisions if Akabwa did not surrender himself to answer for the sack of Dr Henry's premises.

On 21 August the European party left Benin City for the river, only to learn that the official despatch boat had capsized, taking the 'further instructions' with it to the bottom of the sea. Since they could not detain *Bloodhound* any longer without definite orders, Burton decided he would have to visit Lagos to find out what his orders were. On the 28th he reached Lagos and reported directly to the governor. He stayed on at his invitation until 4 September then, after a flying visit to base at Fernando Po, departed on a visit to the Batanga river.

As autumn approached, and the nature of his Consulate took shape in his mind, Burton became increasingly depressed, especially as he came to realise what a hard taskmaster he had in the Foreign Office. On Fernando Po itself he felt like 'a caged hawk, a Prometheus with the Demon Despair gnawing at my heart.'[43] Yet to stir from his headquarters was to provoke a stream of queries from London: was his business strictly official, was it necessary Consular work rather than private exploration, in a word, were his journeys necessary?

Taking stock of his relations with the Foreign Office after just one year in post, Burton could point to a number of bones of contention. In the first place, there was the cost of repairing the official Consulate. Burton spent an alleged £500 before London told him it was not prepared to defray the expense, that he should sell the house and claim a housing allowance instead. Burton then had to spill a mountain of ink to recoup his expenses – not finally achieved until 1867.[44] Another issue was the brig. The Foreign Office grudgingly granted him one, but attached such tight conditions that it was virtually useless for Burton's purposes. Moreover, they made no proper provision for the payment of the crew. Every time Burton used a vessel of the African Steamship Company, there was a wrangle over the refund of his expenses. If he asked for a cruiser to accompany him on his Consular rounds, he was accused of diverting Royal Navy ships from their lawful purposes. He could call for naval assistance only if it could be demonstrated that the life or property of a British subject was in imminent danger.[45]

What had he achieved betimes? He had chastised a few recalcitrant chiefs, had collected a few debts from King Pepple of Bonny, had secured compensation from the Bimbia chiefs on behalf of the Baptist Mission, and had kept an eye on the labour traffic between the mainland and the Spanish plantations on Fernando Po – for the Spanish could not be entirely trusted to obey the anti-slavery tenets of the Royal Navy. The Foreign Office had approved the establishment of the Courts of Equity he had set up in the Cameroons and Old Calabar rivers, but refused to grant him magisterial powers to deal with serious cases involving locals and British subjects, unless such a power had been expressly granted by a local treaty. All in all, Burton felt that his employers were asking him to promote British trade while denying him the necessary tools for the job.[46]

Even worse was their attitude to his explorations. By the end of 1862 Burton's accounts of the Abeokuta visit, the ascent of the Cameroons peaks and the gorilla hunt were beginning to appear in print in England.[47] Instead of praising the energy and enterprise of their Consul, the Foreign Office seemed more concerned with matters of protocol and the 'proper channels'.[48]

London often reminded him that it was a Consul's duty to be in post every quarter. He responded by evolving a system whereby he could be present on the first day of a quarter and then return on the last day of the next quarter, so as to fulfil the letter of the law.

Burton's most serious, and most successful, battle was over leave. In January 1862 he had requested three months' 'local leave' in Tenerife, on alleged grounds of equity with the Consul at Lagos and for reasons of mental and physical health. 'There is now not a single white woman upon the island of Fernando Po and I regret to state the fact that there is not a single coloured woman (of the servant class) whose character would justify her being kept in the house.'[49] Burton's request and its grounds evidently nettled the Foreign Office, for on 21 May a strong refusal was despatched to Fernando Po, including a brusque rebuttal of the alleged leave entitlement of the Lagos Consul. But something happened in the next twenty-four hours to make the Foreign Office change its collective mind. On 22 May leave in Tenerife was granted, though the period was shaved down from three to two months. The formal notification, in July, showed Foreign Office suspicion that it had a slippery customer to deal with, for in confirming the two months' leave it added the formal proviso that Burton had to arrange for a suitable replacement and report the exact dates of his departure and return.[50]

On 28 November he set out for his leave in the Canaries.[51] Now Fate took a hand. At Santa Cruz de Tenerife there was an epidemic of yellow fever, and no passengers were allowed to disembark. It was reported that the yellow flag was also flying at Madeira. Burton at once saw a great opportunity of getting some UK leave. He persuaded Captain Lowry of SS *Athenian*, Liverpool-bound, to take him on board on the pretext of disembarkation at Madeira. When landing permission was refused at Madeira – as Burton knew it would be – the heartbroken Consul found himself 'compelled' to steam on to Liverpool. On landing at Liverpool on 17 December, Burton reported his 'mishap' to the Foreign Office. He then asked permission to spend the Christmas season with his wife in England, instead of taking the next steamer back to the Canaries on 24 December.[52] The permission was granted. Burton, disingenuously, claimed to be hurt by people who saw through his subterfuge. 'The cold is awful, rain and frost, no snow yet', he wrote to Frank Wilson, his Vice-Consul at Fernando Po. 'At the F.O. they had the impudence to congratulate me upon my return home – speechless I pointed at the window, through which appeared a peasoup fog defiling the face of earth and heaven and when voice returned I faintly asked what they *could* mean. To make matters more pleasant I shall be dragged to "midnight mass" the day after tomorrow.'[53] Not for the first or last time, the word 'humbug' rises to the lips of the dispassionate Burton student.

15

A Mission to Dahomey

BURTON'S long absence from his new bride was not punctuated by any special expressions of regret at the separation. In fact, his indirect allusions to Isabel during the first Fernando Po period of 1861–62 seem to hint at darker feelings. 'There is no place where a wife is so much wanted as in the tropics', he reflected, but then comes the rub – how to keep the wife alive.'[1] So far this might be any man worried about his wife's survival prospects. But later remarks suggest an unconscious wish under the anxiety. 'I am surprised at the combined folly and brutality of civilized husbands, who, anxious to be widowers, poison, cut the throats, or smash the skulls of their better halves. The thing can be as neatly and quietly, safely and respectably effected by a few months of African air at Zanzibar or Fernando Po.'[2]

It might be objected, if Burton wished for the death of his wife, why did he not then invite her to Fernando Po, where 78 soldiers out of a garrison of 250 died in a yellow fever epidemic in March 1862? But the wish was unconscious, and in any case it was a feature of Burton to be immobilised by contradictory impulses. But there is no reason to dissent from the judgement of an earlier Burton biographer: 'The length and uncompromising nature of the first separation are suspicious. They suggest that the "uninterrupted bliss" of the first seven months of marriage was something of a fiction for him as for her. They may well have uncovered sexual failure, and to have roused, in Burton at least, fantasies of separation and death.'[3]

The omens for a joyful reunion were, then, scarcely propitious when Isabel met her husband at the Liverpool dockside in December 1862. She could not be faulted in her commitment. During the sixteen months of separation, she had endured the undignified life of a 'Foreign Service widow' in her parents' house. The letters she received from Richard contained no commiserations, but were replete with fulminations about the 'shocking hole' in which he had to endure exile. She spent most of her time lobbying individuals and institutions on his behalf, now collaring MPs to get support for the boat Richard wanted in the Bight of Biafra, now deluging Sir Charles Wood with petitions for her husband to be promoted to Major. No chore was too minor for her attention. She apologised to people for Richard's short temper and made sure his arrears in RGS and Athenaeum subscriptions were paid.[4]

Burton's response was ungallant. During his three weeks in England he spent most of his leisure time with Monkton Milnes and his cronies. When he was not deluging the Foreign Office with West African lore and politics, he was busy founding the Anthropological Society with James Hunt. Unkind critics said his motive was merely to find an outlet for his prolix and increasingly arcane anthropological papers. But the Consular Service came to Isabel's aid, albeit indirectly. When requesting compassionate leave for Christmas on arrival in Liverpool, Burton had pledged himself to be out of the country on 9 January 1863. With much surly backward-looking regret, Burton departed with his wife early in the New Year for the two months' 'local leave' in Madeira and Tenerife that should have commenced in mid-December.

They were three days out from Liverpool when a force twelve hurricane struck them. Their vessel shipped an enormous sea which smashed in the door of the main cabin and saloon, shivered all windows on deck, washed the quartermaster overboard and filled the hold with water to a depth of seven feet. The saloon was a chaos of floating debris, pets and animal cages. Isabel beat a hasty retreat to the captain's cabin, which the master had generously made over to 'the great explorer' and his lady until landfall at Madeira. But all the normal conventions had gone overboard with the quartermaster. One of the officers, who had taken to the bottle to blunt his terror at the sixty-foot waves outside, burst in on her as she was seasick, and collapsed on the floor. Burton, returning from a shift on the bilge pumps, heaved the comatose officer out, but not before telling his tearful wife, 'The captain says we can't live more than two hours in such a sea as this.' Isabel was past the point of fear. 'Oh thank God it will be over so soon', she moaned. It took three days for the storm to blow itself out.[5]

But the idyll on Madeira proved worth waiting for from Isabel's point of view. Ever afterwards she recalled the wondrous six weeks of 'true honeymoon' on an enchanted isle where £200 a year was the wealth of Croesus. Burton was more cynical. As he wrote to Monkton Milnes: 'My wife is too frantic with running about the churches and chapels and other places of idolatrous abominations to do anything else ... her only danger was of being burned for a saint.'[6]

After Madeira they moved on in March to Tenerife, which was still recovering from the epidemic of yellow fever that had carried off 3000 people in three weeks. To avoid possible contagion they at once walked from Santa Cruz to Oratava on the other side of the island. Light sleepers though they were, they awoke in the morning at a crude half-way house to find that their best knife had been stolen. In Oratava, less comfortable but infinitely more healthy than Santa Cruz, they rented rooms in a private house, and shared the outdoor life. After climbing the 12,000 foot peak of Tenerife, Isabel was elated enough to suggest that she might work their holiday up into a book. Burton vetoed the idea, pointing out that she would need to spend much more time reading and studying before she could realistically attempt authorship. She continued to wander enthusiastically around churches and shrines. Burton relaxed sufficiently to call Tenerife 'delightful' in a letter to Milnes but then, doubtless thinking he was not striking the right 'hellfire' image, burbled on absurdly about plans to hold midnight orgies on sanctified ground.[7] Burton, it seemed, did not have just 'sex in the head' (to use D. H. Lawrence's phrase). Even his 'diabolism' was a purely cerebral and abstract affair.

Despite Isabel's frenzied pleadings, Richard refused to take her with him to Fernando Po when his leave expired. She was forced to voyage back to England through more storms, while Burton bent his course southward to the Bight of Biafra. *En route* he pondered the rejection of the many proposals he had made to the Foreign Office during his leave. A fresh brainwave, for establishing a penal colony in Ambrizes Bay, at the foot of the Cameroons Mountains – a site Burton had originally proposed for a sanatorium – was turned down brusquely by the Foreign Office, even though (or perhaps because) their Consul tried to force their hand by appealing to the public above the heads of officialdom.[8] The contemptuous rejection of her beloved's proposal drew this tigerish assessment from Isabel. 'The British government was too tender over their darling human brutes, the cruel, ferocious and murderous criminals, though the climate was considered quite good enough for Richard and other honourable and active British citizens.'[9]

But much more bruising was Foreign Office refusal of his request for the brevet rank of Lieutenant-Colonel in West Africa. He wanted it to compensate him for the humiliation of seeing his name in the official Army Gazette under the heading 'East India Company Officers. Struck Off'. For the one and only time before 1871 Burton allowed his wounded pride to show. After rehearsing his career and achievements, he 'strengthened' his petition by mentioning as a precedent the brevet colonelcy granted to his old enemy Rigby, consul in Zanzibar.[10] It was almost conditioned reflex at the Foreign Office to turn down any request that argued on the 'impertinent' ground of precedent. It was scant consolation for Burton that his actual policy recommendations in West Africa had been largely heeded. The Foreign Office endorsed the six-month exemplary blockade on the Benin river – Burton had argued that a longer embargo would play into the hands of Britain's competitors – and, taking the point that to supply a boat without a crew was of little use, allowed him £95 a year to crew the brig they had granted him in 1862.[11]

He arrived back on post at the beginning of April 1863. The rainy season enabled him to see the island in a new light and he actually went so far as to entitle the chapter of his fourth book on West Africa 'I Fall in Love with Fernando Po.'[12] The *volte-face* is not perhaps so surprising. At its best Fernando Po could enchant the visitor, as a later traveller testified: 'Seen from the sea, or from the continent it looks like an immense single mountain that has floated out to sea . . . and anything more perfect than Fernando Po when you sight it, as you occasionally do from Bonny Bar, in the sunset, floating like a fairy island made of gold or amethyst, I cannot conceive . . . Its moods of beauty are infinite; for the most part gentle and gorgeous, but I have seen it silhouetted hard against tornado-clouds, and grandly grim . . . And as for Fernando Po in full moonlight – well there! you had better go and see it yourself.'[13]

But bewitched by the island's beauty or not, the restless Burton was almost at once on the move, this time touring the Niger delta in his fully-crewed brig. Anchoring at Lagos on 21 April, he accompanied the Royal Navy Commodore Wilmot to Epe, scene of a recent affray. The visit gave him further scope for his contempt for the black man. 'What wonderful fellows these negroes are! If it had been in Arabia there would have been a blood feud for two hundred years. Here in Africa we were received with the greatest possible civility and even gratitude for having killed their people and burnt their villages a month ago!'

Burton asked Wilmot for a cruiser to accompany him on a tour of the Oil Rivers. When the Commodore replied that none was available, Burton retaliated by refusing to accompany him and the Lagos Governor on another trip to Abeokuta. Burton's withering scorn for officialdom is again in evidence in his pen-portrait of the Governor. 'He is a talking man with negroes, knowing them well enough but not too well, has thoroughly sensible . . . ideas and the missionaries will be in his favour . . . Every trader but me who was in the River when I visited it is dead but their successors will of course keep up the old dodge. Really in this part of the world climate makes the white man a more desperate thing than the nigger.'[14]

In May Burton made a private and unofficial visit to the kingdom of Dahomey, the arch-enemies of Abeokuta. Contemporary legend made the land of the Fon tribe out to be a kind of sacrificial abattoir or charnel-house, where the bones of thousands of massacred slaves bleached in the sun on the death of a king, and the blood of the dead provided a lake of gore for the new chief to bathe in. Dahomey was a byword for the kind of benighted barbarism Victorians habitually imagined whenever they thought of the 'Dark Continent'. The vortex of darkness Burton expected to find there at once fascinated and repelled him. Also, Dahomey offered Burton the chance of making good one of his diabolic boasts to the satanic Fred Hankey. Hankey had a gruesome custom of binding the books in his library with specially prepared skin; he once told Burton he would like the skin stripped from a living female to adorn one of his volumes, and Burton had jokingly offered to provide him with such a pelt in the course of his African journeys. To Burton's discomfiture Hankey had taken him seriously, and often wrote to Monkton Milnes to remind him of their mutual friend's promise. If half the stories he had heard about Dahomey were true, Burton might actually be able to make good on his foolish boast and therefore prove himself one of Hankey's select company, for whom 'do what thou wilt shall be the whole of the law'.

Burton travelled via Whydah to Kana, where king Gelele held his summer court. The well-known French lion-hunter Jules Gerard was also there (he was afterwards murdered elsewhere on his West African travels), and the two white men were warmly greeted by Gelele, who made Burton captain of the Fanti or Alligator regiment in his army.[15] In the light of later developments, it is important to underline the fact that Consul and monarch got on well together. 'The king was most friendly, shook hands like an ancient Briton and accompanied me outside the Palace Gate.' Burton's main public aim in making this unauthorised sortie into Dahomey was to get a glimpse of Gelele's famous brigade of female warriors. They really did exist: Burton counted 2038 of them, but he was not impressed by their martial qualities. 'The Amazons are bosh. I looked forward to seeing 5000 African virgins with the liveliest curiosity, having never in my life seen a negress in such a predicament. Imagine my disappointment at finding them to be chiefly wives taken in adultery and given to the king for soldiering instead of being killed. They are mostly old and all fearfully ugly, the officers are apparently chosen for the bigness of their bums.' Burton's derisory estimates extended to the male soldiery. 'The soldiers are a rabble. These men will never take Abeokuta.'[16]

In general Burton found all Dahomey tamer than he had expected. 'I have been here and am generally disappointed', he wrote to Monkton Milnes. 'Not a man killed, or a fellow tortured. The canoe floating in blood is a myth of myths. Poor Hankey must still wait for his *peau de femme* ... The victims are between 100 and 200 a year instead of thousands. At Benin ... they crucified a fellow in honour of my coming – here nothing! And this is the blood-stained land of Dahome!'[17]

Burton was at Kana from 18 May to 19 June. Then he returned to Lagos and thence once more on his devious-circling Consular rounds back to Fernando Po. He did not tarry long on the Bonny river, for yellow fever was again cutting a swathe through the territory and had carried off 33 persons out of 200 in the first village Burton visited. After a brusque warning to King Pepple that he was in breach of the 1848 treaty with England, Burton set the brig's course for his island headquarters.[18]

Once there he succumbed to lethargy and depression. But his pulse quickened at the news that HMS *Griffon* was about to pay a visit to the Congo river. This was the sort of adventure Burton always yearned for. He cajoled passage on HMS *Torch* when it arrived at Fernando Po, transferred to *Zebra* at Loango Bay on 4 August, and on the 19th finally got himself aboard the southward-bound *Griffon* at St Paul de Loanda. This particular escapade showed Burton at his most cavalier in his disregard for Foreign Office protocol. His voyage to the Congo was completely unauthorised, nor could it be justified retrospectively since the Congo mouth lay far to the south of his area of jurisdiction. Burton 'vindicated' what was patently a personal journey of exploration by claiming that he had to get out of Fernando Po to preserve his health. But he tangled the web by trying to charge the cost of his subsistence on board the three Royal Navy vessels to the public purse, claiming that the commercial possibilities he had uncovered in the Congo made his journey chargeable to official funds![19]

On 22 August *Griffon* was off Banana Point at the mouth of the Congo, where the green of the ocean turned to a muddy brown. In the 1860s the Congo was unknown beyond 'Tuckey's Rapids' at Isangila, for the mighty cataracts on the lower river barred the passage to all; this barrier was not surmounted until Stanley's epic voyage down the river in 1877. The explorer in Burton was excited by the prospect of perhaps adding to geographical knowledge – something that had been denied him since 1859. He persuaded a handful of 'sailors' and some blacks to accompany him up the river. They stopped at Porto Dalenha, the Portuguese factory twenty-one miles from the sea, then pressed on to Boma, fifty-two miles from the Congo mouth. At first Burton found the Congo disappointing and unprepossessing after the Gambia and the Gabon, but soon he warmed to the monumental quality of the left bank of the mighty river. 'Rhine-like . . . here and there rugged uprocks passably simulated ruined castles.' The river pullulated with the crocodiles Burton so detested, but also with an amazing variety of bird-life: divers, rollers, halcyons, kingfishers, swallows, hornbills, wild pigeons, herons, kites, crows and eagles.[20]

Hearing that the local chief Nsalla would not give permission for an onward journey, Burton tracked him down and secured an audience, after offering him a box of presents containing a spangled coat, a piece of chintz and a case of ship's rum. Nsalla, a grizzled old man, cut a comic figure. He wore a crown like a nightcap and a beadle's coat of scarlet cloth. But he was suitably charmed by the gifts. In return he lent guides and a couple of his canoes for the onward journey to the cataracts.

On 12 September they were at Banza Nokki, 97 miles from the sea. The impossibility of shooting the rapids forced the party out of the canoes. They began to trek towards the Yellala cataracts, 117 miles from the sea, accompanied by the local chiefs Sudikil and Gidi Mavonga. On 16 September, from a hill one hundred feet above the river, Burton was able to view the Yellala rapids, a wild waste of churning waves. Naturally, Burton now wanted to press on as far as Captain Tuckey's 'farthest east' at Isangila, but their guides refused to take them. Appeals to Gidi Mavonga were vain. With no food and shelter, and with three marches to the nearest staging-post, Burton reluctantly abandoned his quest, but not before he had salved his anger by taking out his six-barrelled Colt and aiming it meaningfully in Gidi Mavonga's direction.[21]

The down march began on 16 September. They got back to the canoes, reached Boma on the 24th and were off Banana Point on the 27th, ready for re-embarkation on *Griffon*. Burton was convinced the Congo would not long remain a blank on the map, and his later intuition that Dr Livingstone's Lualaba river was a feeder for the Congo rather than for the Nile was triumphantly vindicated by Stanley's great epic of Congo charting in 1877.

A sympathetic Foreign Office official later shrewdly minuted against Burton's confidential report on the Congo trip (and the transparent pretext that the Congo highlands had provided a kind of sanatorium): 'I believe, however, that as long as there is a river unexplored or a mountain unascended within Captain Burton's reach, his health will always be impaired until he has accomplished both the one and the other, though it may be to the detriment of his consular duties.'[22] The official recommended that Burton's £43 expenses incurred on the Congo trip should be met, but the head of the Foreign Office minuted a curt refusal of the proposed reimbursement.

Burton arrived back in Fernando Po to find an important message awaiting him from Lord Russell. The Foreign Office had decided to make Burton its Political Officer in a formal embassy to King Gelele of Dahomey. His instructions were to make trade treaties with Gelele and to order him to make an end of slave trading and human sacrifice. Enclosed was a list of presents the British proposed making to Gelele, and Commodore Wilmot's report on his last official visit to Dahomey in December to January 1862–63. Burton thanked Russell effusively for the signal honour, but was sceptical of success; the very most he could hope for was that Gelele might agree to substitute animal for human sacrifice.[23]

Burton's mission to the Fon capital was only the latest in a long series of attempts to improve European relations with Dahomey. The weakening and collapse of the Oyo empire in the 1820s freed Dahomey from an ancient bondage and left a power vacuum in the Yoruba interior. The wars between the Egba at Abeokuta and the Fon in Dahomey were part of a continuing struggle for dominance in the search for slaves and free access to European imports on the coast. The British, on the other hand, wanted an end to the slave trade at minimum cost, since West Africa swallowed up lives and money. But they wished for no Yoruba wars; these would interrupt the trade of Lagos, while a Fon victory over the Egba would destroy a decade of missionary work.

On paper the British seemed faced with a simple choice: attack Dahomey or strengthen Abeokuta. But this simple 'either–or' was muddied by three complications. The Yoruba at Abeokuta were suspicious of the British, as Burton had seen for himself; the French were jealous of British hegemony in the area and had established a rival protectorate at Porto Novo; and, most importantly, the Admiralty and Foreign Office were well aware of the costs and logistical difficulties of mounting naval and military action inland from the Bights.

The Burton mission was basically a compromise between the view of Lord Russell, who favoured decisive military action, and that of the Admiralty, which was unwilling to overstretch its resources on the coast. Russell reluctantly agreed to try diplomacy first, and he opted for Burton on the strength of an earlier Consular despatch from Fernando Po in which Burton had argued that the destruction of Porto would have impressed Gelele sufficiently to make him want to come to terms.[24]

On 29 November 1863 Burton boarded HMS *Antelope*, and landed at Lagos three days later. Because of delays to *Antelope*, he arrived after Commodore Wilmot, who was to accompany him to Dahomey, had left. Burton was in sour and cross-grained mood as he wandered through a Lagos that had just been devastated by three fires which had swept through the thatch roofs and calabar mats in an inferno. Burton always had to find a focus for his grumpiness, and this time it was the Lagos policemen: 'I confess to holding that British Praetorian, the policeman, to be like the beefsteak, and Professor Holloway's pills – a bore, a worldwide nuisance: the meteor flag of England never seems to set upon him.'[25]

Burton took off after Wilmot and caught up with him at Wydah in Dahomey, after landing in a surf boat on 8 December. The British mission entered Wydah in state and drank ceremonial healths with their Fon escort. Burton, ever the skinflint with money, counselled

Wilmot against making lavish presents: 'the African, like the Jew to whom you have paid only twice too much, is miserable if he fancies that you escape from him with a fortune.' Wilmot replied that the level of gifts had already been decided in London.

From Wydah Burton and party pressed on to Allada 'where the purest Fon is spoken'. The embassy consisted of Burton himself, a Royal Navy surgeon John Cruikshank, a black Wesleyan missionary the Reverend Peter Bernasko, and a large body of British-trained local levies from the Gold Coast. On 16 December they were on the road from Allada to Agrime, and next day they began to cross the dreaded Agrime swamp. It took them three hours to cross the plashy marsh, swollen to an extent of seven miles at this time of the year. On arrival at Agrime, the British were greeted by an escort sent by Gelele. They moved on to Kana, the king's country quarters; the British were borne aloft in hammocks, their guides firing muskets into the air as they marched.

At Kana each side held a ceremonial review, toasts were drunk, acquaintance renewed with the 'Amazons', then Gelele came forward to greet the ambassadors. He remembered Burton from the visit six months earlier. Burton had presented him then with three coloured prints of naked women, at which Gelele noticeably perked up and asked if such items could be procured for him live. Burton's reply had been characteristic. 'I told (Heaven forgive me) a fearful fib and said that in my country the women are of a farouche chastity.'[26]

The king was about 43 years old, more than six feet tall, broad-shouldered and in every way 'a very fine looking man'. He had a very pleasant demeanour when he chose to show that side of himself, but his eyes were bloodshot, which Burton set down to lack of proper sleep. He was a great smoker but did not indulge much in the bottle. His skin was much lighter than that of most of his people, and resembled the copper colouring of the North American Sioux Burton had encountered in 1860. He was very active, fond of dancing and singing and 'much addicted to the fair sex, of whom he possesses as many as he likes'.[27]

This time Gelele displayed the cruelty that had made Dahomey a byword. No fewer than 150 of the Amazons, having been found to be pregnant, were being brought to summary trial along with their paramours. Exemplary executions followed, the women being despatched by their own sex. Burton could not resist a dig at England. 'Dahomey is therefore in one point more civilised than Great Britain, where they still, wondrous to relate, "hang away", even women, and in public.'[28]

On 20 December the embassy left Kana and travelled seven miles along the royal road between the two capitals, to Agbome, where Burton found himself unpleasantly domiciled for the best part of two months. It had become clear very early that he was in for a long haul. On 27 December Gelele inspected the presents sent him by the British. There was a forty-foot circular crimson tent, a silver pipe, two belts, a coat of chain mail and many other items, mainly silk, cloth, handkerchiefs and glass tumblers. But what the king wanted most was not there. In December 1862 he had told Wilmot that it was his heart's desire to possess a ceremonial coach and horses. He had expected the British to pick up the hint, and was now grievously disappointed. He remained poker-faced at the display of gifts and expressed not a single syllable of gratitude. To show his displeasure he did not supply his visitors with fresh water, as was his usual custom; Burton had to hire his own watercarriers, but at least he had not taken his wife's advice. Isabel had concocted a fantastic scheme for converting Gelele by showing him lantern slides of New Testament scenes – which was supposed to terrify the king into abandoning human sacrifice and embracing Catholicism. Those who knew Dahomey pointed out gently to Isabel that the king would regard the proposed lantern show as 'bad fetish', and that the English wizard or warlock might well find himself joining the list of those to be sacrificed.

After the violent storms and tornadoes of the Christmas period, life at Agbome settled into a daily routine of boring public audiences with the king, when formulaic courtesies were exchanged. Gelele was clearly determined to stall on the mission's main demands and to hold Burton at arm's length as long as possible. All the Englishman's ingenuity was needed to keep boredom at bay; his principal solution was to learn the Fon language. 'My study of the language advances well despite daily seances from 12 to 6 p.m. in a sun that would cook a steak. I make myself at home – smoke when the king lights his pipe and punish his liquor, and this combined with writing down all I see passes the time.'[29]

From late December to early January a pageant of mime and dance prefigured the actual executions, which took place on *Zan Nyanyana* ('the Evil Night'), when Gelele would renew the glorious memory of his father Gezo, and the forty-year reign that had made Dahomey a warrior state, by performing human sacrifice with his own hand. Two things about the 'customs' Burton found encouraging. One was that it was the only period of official blood-letting. A maximum of forty victims were put to death during at least two 'Evil Nights' and a similar number of Amazons was despatched in private by members of their own sex. The king decapitated the first victim only, then left his assistants to do the rest. During his visit Burton worked out that there had been about twenty-three sacrificial victims. There were twelve severed heads in front of the palace, and on the approach road Burton also saw the corpses of other men who had been gibbeted or beaten to death. But this was a long way from what he had been led to expect. There were also clear signs that Gelele was bending over backwards to meet the British demands on human sacrifice. Half of the intended victims of the 'customs' were brought before him on all fours and pardoned ostentatiously. And besides: 'During the last reign, the victims, gagged and carrying rum and cowries for the people, were marched about, led with cords, and the visitors were compelled to witness the executions. In 1862–63, the wretches were put to death within hearing, if not within sight, of the white visitors. In 1863–64, the king so far regarded the explicit instructions which I had received, that no life was publicly taken during daytime. This is, let us hope, the small end of the wedge.'[30]

After 'Evil Night' over the New Year there was a military review and further pageantry and dancing. Burton took copious notes on every aspect of Fon society. He estimated Dahomey's population at 150,000 – a little on the low side, as it turned out, but a remarkably shrewd conjecture. He found the Amazons more cruel than the male warriors, but otherwise thought the military power of Dahomey vastly overrated. The total military force of both sexes comprised no more than 9000 warriors – not enough to capture Abeokuta, which was Gelele's abiding fantasy. The problem was that Gezo had already squandered the flower of the Amazons in a futile frontal attack on the Egba's walled city. Burton also noted that game was scarce in Dahomey: elephants had been wiped out, and lions were known only by name.

On 8 January Gelele requested that Burton join in the dancing. 'Holding my wrist, Gelele led me out, and we danced opposite each other amidst tempestuous applause. On this occasion the king expects strangers not to refuse him. I therefore had the honour of executing a very notable decapitating movement.'[31] But as January wore on, there was still no sign of a private interview with the king. Wearily the visitors endured the compulsory attendance for the last of the 'customs'. By 6 February, when the festivities finally ground to a halt, the mission had been in Agbome six weeks without having been able to deliver in person to Gelele the important communications from Her Majesty's Government.

On 8 February a message arrived from Commodore Wilmot to say that a cruiser was waiting to convey the Consul back to the Bight of Biafra. Burton pressed the palace officials for a final resolution of the matter of his embassy, but there was no signs that Gelele was prepared to let them depart, still less grant a private audience. Then somewhere along the line the king changed his mind. On 13 February Burton finally managed to deliver the British demands, even though he did not relish the task. When actually in the daily milieu of Dahomean life, the full absurdity of talk of abolishing slavery and human sacrifice impinged on one: 'I felt a sense of hopelessness . . . it was like talking to the winds.'[32]

When the demands were read out to him, Gelele replied that all the things the British objected to were ancient customs of his people; he slew only criminals and war captives, and if he did not sell his slaves he would have to kill them, which the British would like even less. Burton made a forceful – too forceful – rejoinder. He stated flatly that until human sacrifice was abolished, he would advise all Englishmen to avoid Dahomey at the time of the 'customs'. Gelele was visibly disconcerted at this blunt manner of speaking: it was clear that no ambassador before had ever dared to speak so plainly.[33]

Following this unsatisfactory non-meeting of minds, the king was glad to be rid of his troublesome guests. On 15 February the embassy began the return journey. They found Wydah gutted from a recent fire, so stayed in the English fort, which had escaped, until 23 February. On 26 February Burton said a regretful farewell to his companion Cruickshank and boarded HMS *Jaseur*, Commander Grubbe, for the return to Lagos and Fernando Po.

During his time in Dahomey Burton has amassed enough material to produce an anthropological masterpiece, but at the diplomatic level his visit was a resounding failure. As if to prove the point, shortly after his departure the Dahomeans launched a catastrophic campaign against Abeokuta. Seven thousand of their warriors died outside the gates of the Egba capital – a mortal blow to the Fon military capacity, from which they never recovered. Burton was a man of force and power, not a diplomat. He lacked the secret of timing, the art of finesse, the gift of compromise. He made the mistake of handing over the store of presents too soon, and made no move to cover the gap left by Gelele's disappointment over the non-appearance of a horse and carriage. Burton did not believe in 'speak softly and carry a big stick'. At the very time he was self-confessedly stickless, he spoke at the top of his voice. The Methodist missionary Peter Bernasko was horrified by Burton's blunt speaking at the interview on 13 February – an undiplomatic act exacerbated by the fact that Burton delivered his threats in fluent and idiomatic Fon, so that there could be no confusion over his meaning. Stern-faced, angry, impatient and imperious, Burton so alienated Gelele that he told Bernasko afterwards that if Britain ever again sent him such a commissioner, all commerce between the two nations would be broken off.[34]

But Gelele was not the only man to be angry. In Burton's official report to Lord Russell, he advised against sending a consular agent to Wydah and advocated a firm blockade at the coast. If other diplomatic missions were sent to Dahomey, it should be made a point of principle that they did not go there during the 'customs'. Moreover, furious at his delayed departure, Burton recommended that in future a high-ranking Fon official should be held hostage aboard a warship at Wydah to ensure speedier proceedings. As for requesting a formal treaty, the French example in West Africa showed only too clearly that this was a waste of time.[35] The advice was just as well, for when a Fon embassy visited Commodore Wilmot near Wydah in August 1864, the ambassadors conveyed a message from Gelele that the king would never make a treaty with England as long as it employed Burton as one of its servants.[36]

The upshot was that nobody – neither Gelele nor the Foreign Office, and least of all Burton himself – was satisfied with the results of the Dahomey embassy. It always irked Burton that he never received any official thanks from London for the performance of this duty, even though Lord Russell later told him privately he had performed to his entire satisfaction. Burton had justifiable grounds for his peevishness, for in a very real sense he had been sent on a 'mission impossible'. During the private interview with Gelele, the king spoke with unusual frankness and admitted that, whereas he might be able to stop slavery if Queen Victoria could grant him an annual subsidy of £50,000, if he attempted to stop the practice of human sacrifice, his own people would kill him. As Burton shrewdly summed up: 'It is evident that to abolish human sacrifice here is to abolish Dahome.' Burton's friend, Winwood Reade, reviewing *A Mission to Gelele* later, drew attention to the limited power of the king within his own system.[37]

Whatever the rights and wrongs of it, the failure of Burton's mission gave Lord Russell pause, especially as he was under severe pressure from Isabel to grant her husband home leave. When Burton joined in with an official request for furlough on the grounds of 'broken health', Russell reflected that a decent interval would give him time to consider what to do with his brilliant but unruly subordinate.[38] Wherever he looked, Russell seemed to see the Burton Consulate bringing nothing but trouble. King Pepple was as contumacious as ever on the Bonny river, now denying shipping entry unless they paid a heavy tax. Burton was locked into a series of financial wrangles with the Foreign Office over payment for his housing in Fernando Po and his entertainment and subsistence on board Royal Navy ships, and with the Sierra Leone black lawyer William Rainy over alleged defalcation in the sale of the brig *Harriet*. In addition, local British traders were complaining to the Foreign Office that Burton was never available at the Consulate, forever absent on some exploring jaunt, and that he was worse than useless in the furthering of their interests when he *was* there.[39] All things considered, Russell decided to order a four-month period of leave while he pondered his next step.[40]

With great joy Burton learned that he was to be given a breathing-space from his 'time on the cross'.[41] He prepared to depart, but first he wrote a *tour d'horizon* of his work as Consul in Fernando Po, which is brilliant and comprehensive and the product of awesome erudition. Anyone who doubts Burton's intellectual credentials should read the report and be converted. It is difficult to know which to be more impressed by: the iron grip on detail of every kind – prices of brass, guns, cotton, palm-oil – and the effortless lucidity with which he takes the reader through the West African ethnological maze; or the highly original and idiosyncratic flair with which Burton posits theories about societies which later research confirms in detail. He shows in convincing minutiae how African rulers fought each other for monopoly and middleman positions. He analyses the wildly fluctuating price of palm oil, and warns the Foreign Office of the coming competition from petroleum and cheap tallow, and the changed situation imminent in the world economy when the American Civil War comes to an end. Naturally, as in every Burton report, there is oddity and idiosyncracy mixed in with hard analysis. In particular, Burton indulges his dislike of missionaries and the facile *bien-pensant* analysis of slavery and the slave trade indulged in by Exeter Hall liberals.[42]

Burton quit Fernando Po for ever on 7 May 1864 and made a leisurely progress to Tenerife, where he was supposed to spend his four months' leave, and where he lolled disconsolately for a fortnight.[43] When he arrived in the Canaries, he had received news which he now interpreted as an 'order' from Lord Russell to return to England.[44] It was in vain that an angry Foreign Office Under-Secretary wrote that he had *not* been ordered back, nor could any reasonable person conceivably have interpreted his instructions in that way. By this time Burton was already in England. The Foreign Office was now very angry about Burton's behaviour and warned him in no uncertain terms that he must be back on post by 7 September 1864. With stunning predictability, Burton riposted by requesting a further month's leave.[45] The angry rejection would not have been long in arriving, but at this very moment Lord Russell intervened: he notified him of a transfer to the Consulate in Santos, Brazil. The Consular Service's most ingenious escapologist had done it again.

16

The Impact of Africa

BURTON'S three years in West Africa, relatively neglected by his biographers to date, were an important episode in the formation of his attitudes and opinions. He revealed himself conclusively as an anthropologist of the first order. His previous dislike of blacks hardened into outright hatred. And for the first time, especially in his correspondence with the Monkton Milnes circle, he openly underlined his sexual oddity and psychological turmoil.

Like his friend Frank Harris, Burton had an astonishing capacity to shift gear from the realms of the intellect to the mundane world of 'fumbling in a greasy till'. Superficially, the most noticeable impact of West Africa on Burton was to quicken his gold fever. Following the German explorer and scientist Humboldt – and many of his more acidulous critics were to complain in the future that he always followed Humboldt too closely, sometimes to the point of outright plagiarism – Burton proselytised for the view that the African continent was bulging with gold.[1] His obsession with the precious metal in the years to come bade fair to make him almost a character out of his own *Arabian Nights*. Deep psychological forces may have been at work here. In his discussion of ophiolatry on Africa's west coast, Burton acknowledged his own profound, even excessive, fear of snakes. Now, in the *Arabian Nights*, the *Hawi* or juggler who plays tricks with snakes is usually a gypsy, and his recompense is supposed to be the golden treasure which the snake guards.[2] Remembering Burton's fascination with gypsies and his identification with them, his attempts to master his fear of the reptiles by trying to learn snake-charming in India, and his abiding gold fever, it is surely not too far-fetched to seek profound unconscious forces at work beneath this psychological cluster of conscious attitudes.

The mission to Gelele produced Burton's first undisputed anthropological classic. It is a necessary condition of a great field anthropologist to be a first-class observer and to miss nothing. Burton had an unrivalled eye for physical detail, for gradations of scenery, differences in habitat and fauna (he noticed, for example, the relative absence of the hippopotamus in West Africa)[3] and the small differences between tribal cultures. Never afraid of heady speculation, he also had an outstanding instinct for the 'structural' meaning of the many customs, mores and folk-ways he observed. This is a much rarer talent, and is what distinguishes the great anthropologist.

Burton had the good fortune to observe the kingdom of Dahomey before its traditional structure disappeared with the exile of the last reigning *Akhosu* or king in 1894. It was one of the many paradoxes of Burton that he was most penetrating where most he hated. His detestation of blacks did not prevent him from singularly shrewd assessments of African social structures. And his fundamental misogynism did not blind him to the truth that the way into the heart of any society is through its treatment of women. So Burton at once found the key to the Dahomey of Gelele, which was that women doubled every important office but that of the *Akhosu* himself. 'At the Dahoman Court, curious to say in Africa, women take precedence of men; yet with truly Hamitic contradictiousness, the warrioresses say, "We are no longer females but males", and a soldier disgracing himself is called, in insult, a woman. It is clear, therefore, that they owe their dignity to the fiction of being royal wives. Wherever a she-soldier is, celibacy must be one of its rules, or the troops will be in a state of chronic functional disorder between the ages of 15 and 35.'[4]

The 'Amazons' were more important sociologically than militarily. 'The origin of this exceptional organisation is, I believe, the masculine physique of the women, enabling them to compete with the men in bodily strength, nerve and endurance.'[5] But in military terms the Amazons were a farce: 'The officers were decidedly chosen for the size of their bottoms ... they manoeuvre with the precision of a flock of sheep, and they are too light to stand a charge of the poorest troops in Europe ... an equal number of British charwomen, armed with the British broomstick would ... clear them off in a very few hours.'[6]

All Burton's West African writings show a pronounced taste for the mysterious, the unusual, the strange custom and, above all, for sexuality. Burton as Freudian emerges clearly in the following passage, where he sees both bloodlust and the nursing of the dying as a form of sublimated sexuality. 'All passions are sisters. I believe that bloodshed causes these women to remember, not to forget, LOVE; at the same time that it qualifies the less barbarous, but, with barbarians, equally animal feeling. Seeing the host of women who find a morbid pleasure in attending the maimed and the dying, I must think that it is a tribute paid to sexuality by those who object to the ordinary means.'[7]

Burton's accuracy as an observer of West Africa in general and

Dahomey in particular was attested to by all who had travelled in the region, notably Winwood Reade and the lion-hunter Jules Gerard.[8] Both the pioneering French anthropologist Le Hérisse, who arrived after the collapse of the society Burton wrote about, and Melville Herskovits, who wrote the definitive anthropological treatise on Dahomey in the 1930s, paid tribute to Burton's high talents. A modern authority has endorsed their praise: 'altogether it was an outstanding collection of information from one who thought the African "at the rude dawn of faith".'[9]

The difference between Burton as student of primitive society and as racial theorist was as wide and profound as that between the dispassionate scholar and the saloon-bar bore. To put it another way, in Burton the Victorian confusion between race and culture is raised virtually to the power of infinity. Here was yet another contradiction in the 'dual man'. Burton mistrusted and (except for Islam) despised all organised religions, yet was capable of getting inside the idiom of any religious system he cared to study. He defended the idea of forced labour on theoretical grounds as a means of ending poverty, but denounced the slave trade, which he had seen at first hand. Even there his attitude was ambivalent, for though he felt qualified to talk of the evils of slavery, he did not feel that missionaries, and their armchair supporters at Exeter Hall, possessed the necessary expertise to be able to pronounce on the matter.

So it was that one of the most brilliant students of Africa despised and hated the African, and pitched into the black man with a virulence that would not have disgraced a Gobineau or a Houston Chamberlain. East Africa had left Burton with a marked distaste for 'the Hamitic race'. He was contemptuous of their religion of fetishism, their inability to think of mortality except in terms of material possessions – which led them to kill slaves on the death of a king – their inability to imagine the idea of the immortality of the soul, and their general thraldom to demonology and witchcraft.[10] But in East Africa Burton despised and derided the black man for his ignorance and idleness; full-blooded hatred had not yet made its mark.[11]

Surprisingly, in the light of later developments, Burton expected better things, as both explorer and anthropologist, from West Africa than East, which he thought after the Speke and Livingstone expeditions to be 'waxing trite and stale'.[12] East Africa, he felt, possessed 'few traditions, no annals, and no ruins, the hoary splendour so dear to the traveller and the reader of travels ... It wants even the scenes of barbaric pomp and savage grandeur with which the student of Occidental Africa is familiar.'[13]

But when Burton reached West Africa, he found it even more uncongenial than the Lake Regions had been. Burton often claimed in defence of his negrophobia that the cruelties he witnessed in Dahomey had been enough to turn the brain of any normal man. 'The modern Dahomans ... are a mongrel breed, and a bad. They are Cretan liars, *crétins* at learning, cowardly and therefore cruel and bloodthirsty; gamblers and consequently cheaters; brutal, noisy, unvenerative, and disobedient.[14] The notion of a man driven mad by Africa's 'heart of darkness', like Conrad's Kurtz, is plausible enough in the case of a sensitive soul, but it hardly squares with Burton's other self-image, assiduously promoted to Monkton Milnes, Swinburne and Fred Hankey, of the 'wickedest man alive'. Burton boasted to Milnes that Dahomey was disappointing because there was no lake of gore; but the merest trickle of blood, according to another version of himself by himself, was enough to launch him into undying hatred of the black man. Chronology is also against Burton: his most vicious outpourings of racial bile occurred, arguably, as a result of the long voyage along the West African coast to Fernando Po in August-September 1861, before he visited Dahomey.

What seems to have thrown Burton seriously off balance was the sight of black men aping their white 'betters' and aspiring to the same sort of life-style. Burton could tolerate in his derisory way the 'noble savage' of East Africa. But the besuited and top-hatted black lawyers of Sierra Leone elicited feelings of anger and rage. He was not the only African explorer to feel this way. Joseph Thomson, who idolised the East African Masai as the noblest of noble savages, felt that the West African 'nigger' was unbearably 'uppity'.[15] As for the moral influence of gentleness on the benighted African savage, Burton quoted approvingly the words of his friend MacGregor Laird, that moral influence in West Africa meant a 68-pounder worked by British seamen.[16]

Burton's hatred of the black man was compounded of three main overt elements. Blacks, he contended, were moral and mental imbeciles, but even worse were the missionaries and 'negrophils' who aided and abetted them in their vain quest to escape the biological imperatives of nature. Burton accepted uncritically the dominant racial theories of his time. 'I hold as a tenet of faith the doctrine of great ethnic centres, and their comparative gradation. I believe the European to be the brains, the Asiatic the heart, the American and African the arms and the Australians the feet of the man-figure ... [the black] is prognathous and dolicho-cephalic with retreating forehead, more scalp than face; calfless, cucumber skinned, lark-heeled with large broad feet; his smell is rank, his hair crisp and curly.'[17] Burton regarded the Sierra Leone black intellectual's refusal to admit his own biological inferiority as in itself evidence of his mental crassness, 'as if there could be brotherhood between crown and clown'.[18] Burton's *oeuvre* is studded with references to the unregenerate stupidity and mental incorrigibility of the 'moronic' black man: 'study, or indeed any tension of the mind, seems to make these weak-brained races semi-idiotic'; after all, is not the white man universally portrayed in African legend as a God?[19] On one notable occasion Burton brings down two of his unfavourite birds with one stone. 'To the question, *Quid muliere levius*? [Is there anything sillier than a woman?] the scandalous Latin writer suggests *Nihil*, [Nothing] for which I would suggest *Niger* [a Black].'[20]

Even worse than the African's stupidity, for Burton, was his crazed, insensate cruelty. Only the sentimentalist could take seriously the idea of the 'noble savage'; slaves were just as brutal and cruel as their masters. In West Africa Burton witnessed the loathsome spectacle of unfaithful wives being floated down the Bonny river to the sea, bound to bamboo sticks and mats, to be eaten piecemeal by sharks; the same fate was meted out to the slaves of a great man when he died.[21] This drew from Burton an agonised cry of hatred for the black races.

> There is apparently in this people a physical delight in cruelty to beast as well as to man. The sight of suffering seems to bring them an enjoyment without which the world is tame; probably the wholesale murderers and torturers of history, from Phalaris and Nero downwards, took an animal and sensual pleasure – all passions are sisters – in the look of blood and in the inspection of mortal agonies. I can see no other explanation of the phenomena which meet my eye in Africa. In almost all the towns in the Oil Rivers, you see dead or dying animals fastened in some agonising position.[22]

People often asked Burton why the criminals and sacrificial victims of Africa made no attempt to escape the horrible fate that awaited them. He attributed their apathy to the capricious uncertainty of their fate – itself a form of refined cruelty – which could be either death or a royal pardon.[23]

But at least the New Testament precept 'Father forgive them for they know not what they do' could be urged in defence of the benighted savages. What conceivable defence could be mounted for the missionaries and assorted 'do-gooders' in England, who singularly mixed humbug with ignorance in their support of the black man? Burton considered that the anti-slavery humanitarians were riddled with cant and hypocrisy. They talked of the 'sin and crime' of slavery, but overlooked the many areas where traditional Christianity was ambivalent on slavery, notably the New Testament occasion when the centurion's slave is converted into a 'servant' to appease the consciences of the 'unco' guid' (in flat and absurd defiance of the fact that the Greek word used – *doulos* – always signifies a slave). They ignored the poor and needy in the slums of England, who were in many cases worse off than the slaves. They failed to condemn economic imperialism, such as British action in the Opium Wars, which made the indigenous population much more effectively slaves than anything devised by the Arab traders in Africa. And, most tellingly of all, the British did not return to their native habitat the slaves recovered from slaving vessels by the Royal Navy; instead they shipped them off to the West Indies.[24] Besides, the naval interception of slave ships immediately placed at risk the ostensible objects of the mission: the slaves themselves. 'The buccaneers quite as humane made their useless prisoners walk the plank. The slave-ships, when chased and hard-driven, simply tossed the poor devil niggers overboard; the latter must often have died, damning the tender mercies of the philanthrope which had doomed them to untimely deaths instead of a comfortable middle passage from Blackland to Whiteland.'[25]

In any case the humbug humanitarians and the missionary societies knew nothing of slavery as it actually obtained in Africa. Throughout the East the slave's condition was superior to that of the poor free man.[26] This was to say nothing of the myopia involved in overlooking the more serious 'slavery' of the tens of thousands of poor white women in London who were in thrall to the lusts of rich males. The African reality was very different from that imagined by the emancipationists. 'Justice requires the confession that the horrors of slave-driving rarely meet the eye in Africa ... the fat lazy slave is often seen stretched at ease in the shade, whilst the master toils in the sun and wind ... the porter belonging to none but himself is left without hesitation to starve upon the road-side.'[27]

Burton categorically denied that the abolition of the slave trade and of slavery would benefit the African. He thought that 'Free Emigration' schemes were a snare and a delusion, and argued for a form of export of surplus labour similar to the slave trade, in particular a primary-producing colony in the Cameroons, consisting of 45,000 former slaves.[28] He also detested the only available contemporary alternative model, the colony of free blacks at Sierra Leone. He hated seeing Africans in European dress, was outraged to find them holding posts in local government and the judiciary, and was stupefied to find white men condemned by all-black juries. Sierra Leone to Burton was a modern Sodom and Gomorrah. Its men were thieves, gamblers, drunkards and rogues, and its women harlots. Miscegenation resulted in half-castes, mulattos, quadroons and octaroons, each racial thinning producing degeneracy. Things could only improve, he argued, when there was complete apartheid between black and white, with separate courts and separate institutions of all kinds.[29]

Most detested of all species of 'improvers' for Burton were the missionaries. They encouraged miscegenation and mindless manumission without thought of the consequences, and fomented the absurd fantasy of the intrinsic equality of blacks and whites. He poked fun at the missionaries' ignorance of native languages, their prudish insistence on clothing the naked aboriginals, their destruction of indigenous polygamy, their attempt to frighten the tribesmen with fire-and-brimstone tales of the punishments of Hell – or with actual corporal punishment, in the case of the Jesuits, if the mind control did not work.[30]

Burton considered that the only way forward for the black man in Africa was through emigration or the embrace of Islam. It was an item of faith for him that any black who had achieved anything in history, like Toussaint L'Ouverture and the other black emperors in Haiti, must have had Semitic blood, like the Hausa. Since 'improvement' via Islam was the sole realistic way forward for the African, it particularly infuriated Burton that the missionaries directed so many of their broadsides about 'diabolical heresies' at Islam. He noted ironically that missionaries always had a good word for the religions that were no threat to them, like Buddhism, Hinduism and Confucianism, but never one for the faith of Mohammed. 'Dr Livingstone, for one instance of many, evidently preferred the Fetichist, whom he could convert, to the Unitarian Faithful whom he could not.'[31] But, after all, Livingstone's position was merely the obverse of Burton's, who could see nothing good on the African continent except Moslems and who went out of his way to contrast devotees of Islam favourably, even in physical appearance, with the native inhabitants.[32]

Burton's attitude to the African, then, was one of unrelieved hostility and derision, with two exceptions. One was when Burton wished to poke fun at the shortcomings of his own compatriots. The visit to Gelele provided many opportunities for reflections on England's 'Bloody Code' in criminal law enforcement. And Burton liked to contrast the matter-of-fact attitude to women with the absurd mixture of reverence and tight control of the female sex in Britain. 'The Africans have in one point progressed beyond Europeans: there are as many women physicians as men.'[33]

The other exception came when Burton switched modes from virulent racialist to scholarly anthropologist. It is astonishing that a man with such a low opinion of the black man and his potentialities should have produced a book entitled *Wit and Wisdom from West Africa*. Even more amazing is the way Burton pays tribute to the sober good sense contained in the sayings, proverbs, mottoes and apothegms that he assembled, from the most diverse cultural and linguistic sources: Yoruba, Egba, Fan, Efik, Isubu, Dualla, Ga, Ashanti, Wolof and Kanuri. There is nothing cretinous or moronic about the insights gathered together here. 'Running about gives no scholars.' 'The child hates him who gives it all it wants.' 'Frowning and fierceness prove not manliness.' 'When the mouth stumbles, it is worse than the foot.' '"I have forgotten thy name" is better than "I know thee not".'

The empathy that Burton was capable of achieving when investigating aboriginal African societies alerts us to the possibility that there may be what is called in modern jargon a 'hidden agenda' in his unbridled racialism. Some of this submerged motivation is obvious. Sexual fear and envy played a part. After his own sexual failure in India, Burton took a morbid interest both in other men's genitals and in their reputed performance. In all seriousness he noted down comparative sizes of the *membrum virile* and sexual gossip from bazaar and seraglio. He concluded two things. One was that the average size of the African's penis was 6–7½ inches, as compared with 6 inches in Europe and 5 inches among the Arabs. The other was that, being of phlegmatic temperament, the black man took longer to ejaculate than the nervous and excitable Arab. Given Burton's pre-existing mistrust of women as lascivious and devious beings, his hatred of blacks is not hard to understand.[34]

So far the sexual basis of Burton's racialism does not differ significantly from that of many men in many eras, obsessed with the 'threat' from the black man. But in Burton's case we must swim in deeper waters yet. Burton's quest for gorillas had a pathological element to it. The early 1860s saw England reeling from the double shock of Darwin's theories and du Chaillu's discovery of the gorilla. The notion of an evolutionary link between humans and the most man-like of the apes seriously disturbed many with a fragmented psyche or fragile ego. In the case of the devout, a possible reaction was via sadism. R. M. Ballantyne, the well-known Victorian children's writer, produced in 1862 a fantasy inspired by du Chaillu's discoveries, called *The Gorilla Hunters*. The book – which if produced for children in the 1980s would be condemned as obscene and depraved – consists of a number of tableaux where the young heroes slaughter gorillas on sight and take a lustful pleasure in the creatures' death agonies. Ballantyne's sadism has two main roots: aggression resulting from deeply repressed sexuality, and an unconscious desire to wipe out the creature whose existence allowed Darwin to challenge the tenets of fundamentalist Christianity.

With Burton, the admirer of Darwin, we should expect the reaction to be different, and it was. Burton evinced a distaste for simians on the ground that they were like his two most hated types of human being: blacks and old women. He jeered that the African would never eat the flesh of apes because of the likeness of the animal to himself; such a repast would smack of cannibalism.[35] Burton was quite prepared to countenance genetic engineering of the most grotesque and distasteful kind. 'A traveller well known to me [i.e. himself] once proposed to breed pithecoid men who might be useful as hewers of wood and drawers of water; his idea was to put the highest races of apes to the lowest of humanity.'[36]

Burton's detestation of old women was notorious. In all societies, he thought, they were the most vindictive of their sex. Completely without honour, and pathological liars, old women would even cheat at cards if not supervised.[37] 'It is only civilisation that can save the aged woman from resembling the gorilla', was a typical remark.[38] He also disliked modern sculptors because, in their nude female studies, they fined off the frame to make them appear more simian than human.[39] Burton's legendary aversion to 'the crone' led to a famous incident once with Disraeli's wife, when she was in her seventies. Seating herself next to a low mirror, the old and homely Mrs Disraeli pointed to her reflection and said to Burton, 'There must be an ape in the glass. Do you not see it?' Burton spotted the trap and quickly retrieved himself from a delicate situation. 'Yes, madame, I see myself,' he answered quickly.[40]

Burton, then, used the primates as a focus for his detestation of blacks and old women, on the grounds of their alleged similarity. But behind the hostility to apes lurked something else – something that can only be described as lustful fascination. The key is provided by his close friend, the poet Swinburne. Swinburne revealed that Burton had confided to him that the most powerful sexual passion he had ever experienced was for a female monkey in 'Central Africa'.[41] This might be dismissed as Swinburnian 'diabolical' fantasy, if there were not support from other sources, as well as powerful circumstantial evidence in Burton's own writings. It will be remembered that when Burton kept monkeys in Gujerat, he had been attracted to the female of the species then and called one of them 'his wife'. Also, the entire point of a Frank Harris anecdote is lost if we do not give credence to Swinburne.[42]

To rationalise his 'unnatural' lusts, Burton in a classic of transference then set out to prove that it was the ape that lusted after humans, not vice versa. He quoted stories from India, Arabia and Africa to show that male primates harboured libidinous designs against human females. His favourite was a case of attempted rape in Cairo in 1853, which he claimed to have witnessed, only prevented when a sentry bayoneted the lecherous marauder. On another occasion he took a party of English girls to the zoo at Florence to see the mandrills 'when the priapism was such that the girls turned back and fled in fright'. He was fascinated by the old Portuguese story about a woman who was transported to an island of monkeys and there successfully mated with them and produced progeny. It was a recurrent motif in Burton that he would like to see 'civilisation' advance to the point where experiments could be carried out to see whether miscegenation between apes and humans would produce offspring.[43]

It has now become a cliché of popular zoology that the typical display of the rear end by the ape relates to an era of sexuality when the buttocks, not the breasts, were the principal trigger for male response.

Chaucer's Wife of Bath warns women not to dress so as to show the 'buttokkes behinde, as it were the hinder part of a she ape in the ful of the mone'. Interestingly, Gelele's 'Amazons' made an impact on Burton only through their 'bums' and 'bottoms'. Burton dwells at length on the necessity to make women always appear as unlike apes as possible, which is his principal objection both to modern sculpture and to old women. But it may be that in uttering this prescription he is unconsciously revealing at once his own distaste for women and his attraction towards the simians. In more senses than one, the modern term 'pansexualist' seems the only one to do justice to Burton's tortured libido.

17

An English Tragedy

BURTON was reunited with Isabel at Liverpool and in August 1864 they went together to choose their burial place in Mortlake Cemetery. The news of the transfer to Santos gave them some breathing space. But now there was another problem. While Burton had languished in West Africa, his great rival Speke had vaulted over him to occupy a place second only to Livingstone among African explorers.

Burton and Speke had both left England in April 1860, the former bound for the USA and Salt Lake City, the latter for East Africa. With him Speke took a Scots hero of the Indian Mutiny, James Augustus Grant. This time Speke was determined to be top dog. He knew he could expect little trouble from Grant, who was dour, dutiful, quiet, patient, self-effacing and stoical. After a long voyage via Rio, the Cape of Good Hope and Zanzibar, it was 25 September before Speke and Grant crossed the straits of Bagamoyo to begin their expedition. Speke's instructions from the Royal Geographical Society were to circumnavigate Lake Victoria, locate the source of the Nile, then proceed north to the mission-post at Gondokoro in the Sudan, where British Vice-Consul Petherick would have left them boats and supplies. Petherick, a Welsh mining engineer, had turned to ivory trading early in his career and had explored a wide area of the Bahr-el-Ghazal, on the west bank of the Upper Nile. Petherick was now employed by the RGS to ascend the river from Khartoum, trading ivory as he went. After depositing supplies at Gondokoro, he was to proceed south and try to identify the source of the Nile at the head of Victoria Nyanza.

But funding for Petherick's southern probe proved an unexpected headache. The RGS wrongly assumed the Treasury would pick up the bill. Even after a vociferous fund-raising campaign led by Sir Roderick Murchison, the subscription for Petherick's expedition stood at a mere £1200, eight hundred pounds less than the Vice-Consul's rock-bottom minimum estimate. Meanwhile the situation was immensely complicated by the announcement that Sir Samuel Baker, wealthy big-game hunter and eccentric, would be leading his own privately financed expedition to discover the sources of the Nile. At one stage Baker even threatened to add a further wheel to the waggon of confusion by taking Burton with him, after his return from the USA.[1]

None of these ramifications was known to Speke. He and Grant set out for Tabora, eager to make the December 1861 rendezvous with Petherick at Gondokoro. From Tabora they swung north-west to Usui and entered the kingdom of Karagwe, to the south-west of Lake Victoria. King Rumanika of Karagwe, who had never seen white men before, insisted on detaining the 'wizards', treating them to lavish hospitality. It was January 1862 before Rumanika permitted Speke to depart for the powerful kingdom of Buganda, on the north-west bank of Lake Victoria. Even so, he detained Grant in his palace as a virtual hostage, using the Scotsman's ulcerated leg as an excuse. Rumanika was afraid that Speke would take his 'magic' to his rival Mutesa.

Grant had already made an anchor-like contribution to the success of the expedition. His steadiness saw them through the dark days on the trek up to Usui, when both suffered fearfully from fever. While Speke the glory-hunter slaughtered all the big game he could draw a bead on, Grant quietly collected botanical specimens and made zoological notes. On one occasion he was marooned uncomplainingly for 109 days while the restless Speke darted hither and yon. Speke's egotistical journey to the north, while his comrade lay sick in Karagwe, was an uncanny replay of his dash to Lake Victoria in 1858 while Burton lay sick at Tabora. The probable motive for Speke's irrational haste on this occasion was fear that Petherick would reach the source of the Nile before him, which consolidates the moral case against him for the abandonment of Grant.

After some bumpy patches, Speke struck up a good working rapport with Mutesa, *kabaka* of Buganda. In point of brutality and murderous self-esteem Mutesa was another Gelele, but his homicidal excesses did not unduly bother Speke; doubtless they would have done had he realised that he was himself at one time considered a possible candidate for the executioner's block.[2] It was five months before a limping Grant finally staggered into Mutesa's capital to be reunited with his 'chief'. He found clear evidence of Speke's amateurism as an explorer. His lack of understanding of his *pagazis* had allowed a full-scale feud to develop between his two headmen, Bombay and Baraka, as a result of which mass desertion of porters occurred.[3] All conversation between Speke and Mutesa had to be through interpreters. The volatile and short-tempered king became so impatient with this that he would frequently get up and walk off before Speke's answer had been translated.

Mutesa was as reluctant to let them proceed with their journey as Rumanika had been. Eventually on 7 July 1862 the two explorers set out northwards. Eleven days later, as they bore in a north-easterly direction towards the headwaters of Victoria Nyanza, Speke suddenly ordered Grant on a diversionary expedition, so that he would not be present when Speke came on the 'fountains of the Nile'. While the self-effacing Grant later defended his 'boss' against the imputation of egotistical glory-hunting, he conceded that he had 'yielded reluctantly to the necessity of our parting', and there are hints in his journal entries for 18–19 July that he had had to suppress murderous impulses towards Speke arising from this signal injustice.[4] He also had his favourite goat-boy lashed twenty times for a trivial offence; this behaviour was so out of character for the normally gentle Grant that it suggests the need to find a physical outlet for the volcanic rage bottled within.[5]

On 21 July Speke came in sight of the White Nile at Urondogani. Crocodiles and hippopotami basked in the sun. Speke celebrated his discovery by shooting an antelope and several birds. Then he spent a week hacking through long grass and jungle, following the trail suggested to him by Mutesa, until he came to the place where Lake Victoria emptied into the Nile. Waterfalls twelve feet high and 600 to 700 yards wide made the scene a spectacular one. 'The expedition had now performed its functions', he concluded. '. . . I saw that old Father Nile without any doubt rises in the Victoria Nyanza, and, as I had foretold, that lake is the great source of the holy river which cradled the first expounder of our religious belief.'[6]

After naming the cataracts Ripon Falls after Lord Ripon, President of the RGS, Speke rejoined Grant at the court of Mutesa's neighbour Kamrasi, king of Bunyoro, the great rival of Buganda in the struggle for power in the lacustrine area of Central Africa. Kamrasi told them of another lake ten days' march to the west, called Luta Nzige (later to be named Lake Albert), into and out of which a mighty river poured. If this river was the Nile, and if, in turn, the river then flowed from Lake Albert to Lake Tanganyika, Burton's theory on the source of the Nile might be correct after all. But Speke chose not to make the side journey necessary to verify the situation; unlike his previous two solitary dashes, this excursion might provide him with the kind of intelligence he did not want to hear. For Speke this omission was a fatal error, as it opened the door to the counter-theories of Burton, Livingstone, Baker and all critics of the Victoria-as-source-of-Nile theory.

After building up the expedition's supplies the two explorers and their newly recruited porters set off down-river by canoe on 9 November 1862, through floating islands of papyrus that screened slithering schools of crocodiles and shoals of hippopotami. On 15 February 1863, thirteen months after the original rendezvous, Speke and Grant arrived at

Gondokoro to find, not Petherick, but the rival expedition headed by Sir Samuel Baker.[7]

The two sets of explorers spent a few days together. Baker listened spellbound to the tale of the Luta Nzige, which he interpreted as meaning that the race for the Nile sources was still open, and that he might yet cover himself in glory. Speke's concern was with the absence of Petherick. Where was he, and why had he not made good his pledge to the RGS? Baker pointed out that Petherick had performed manfully, and had deposited four boats and abundant supplies at Gondokoro before departing to trade ivory at N'yambara, seventy miles to the west. But Speke at once took it into his head that Petherick had betrayed and abandoned him. Another giant-size grievance had taken root in Speke's mind and would fester there until its full efflorescence in England.

Petherick came in on 18 February and was surprised and disconcerted by Speke's glacial reception of him. Patiently he explained how, though he had sent supplies up-river as agreed, shipwreck and the intermittent navigability of the Nile had delayed his own arrival at Gondokoro until a few weeks before. Finding the supply dumps intact, but with no word from Speke and Grant even though they were a year overdue, he assumed they had either perished or returned to Zanzibar. Moreover, his instructions from the RGS released him from all obligations after June 1862. To any normal man this would all have seemed reasonable enough, but Speke made it clear that in his opinion Petherick had been delinquent in duty and moral responsibility. Petherick later recalled a strained dinner-table conversation. 'During dinner I endeavoured to prevail on Speke to accept our aid, but he drawlingly replied, "I do not wish to recognise the succour-dodge." Mrs Petherick commented angrily, "Never mind, his heartlessness will recoil upon him yet".'[8]

Pointedly Speke turned down the offer of Petherick's boats and drew all his onward supplies from Baker, except for ninety-five yards of cloth from the Vice-Consul's store which, to show his contempt, he offered to pay for. He also gathered up malicious gossip disseminated by a rival ivory trader, Kurshid Aga, that Petherick had been involved in the slave trade. In reality this whispering campaign of black propaganda began precisely because Petherick had tried to suppress the slave trade. But in his monstrous self-regard Speke cared nothing for the truth.

Speke proved as treacherous on this expedition as he had been with Burton in 1859. From Khartoum he wrote a letter to Petherick, full of soothing reassurances, and remarkably similar in tone and content to the friendly and emollient remark he had made to Burton at Aden four years earlier.[9] Now, as then, he was aiming to lull his intended victim before driving in the knife to the hilt. Once in London he pursued his vendetta relentlessly against Petherick. In public he accused him of profiteering from the slave trade. In private he accused him of peculation and defalcation in the disposal of stores paid for out of subscription money. Since Speke on his triumphant return to London was regarded as a hero, his every word was taken as gospel. When Petherick arrived shortly afterwards, it was to find himself in Burton's 1859 situation. His Consulship was revoked and he was the object of universal pillorying. He at once instituted libel proceedings against his detractor.[10]

Instead of resting content with his triumph, in the summer of 1863 Speke continued to traduce Burton, to claim that all the real achievements on the 1857–59 expedition had been his, not Burton's, and to insinuate that the older man was an arrant coward.[11] When, almost exactly a year after Speke's triumphant return, Burton arrived comparatively unnoticed at Liverpool, he might have feared that Speke had already swept the board on the debate over the Nile sources. But he had not. Speke's own self-destructive impulses had seriously weakened both his own case and his standing with British geographers.

During 1863–64 Speke's star dimmed for a number of very different reasons, all of them traceable to his own pathology. Four principal factors stand out: Speke's obvious resentment of collaborators; his treatment of Petherick; the way he alienated the RGS; and the way his presentation of the case for Victoria Nyanza as the source of the Nile played into the hands of the coterie of geographers who favoured Burton's theory.

Speke's ungenerous treatment of Grant during this expedition did not go unnoticed. Pro-Burton personalities in the RGS concluded that his ungrateful behaviour towards Burton in 1859 had been no mere 'one-off', caused by the clash of two diametrically opposed personalities; Speke had now shown that he thought nothing of meting out such treatment to a man he professed to like and admire.[12] Grant was in France when Speke's book *Journal of the Discovery of the Source of the Nile* was published in December 1863. Speke displayed childish petulance and peevishness over his friend's absence at a time when he should have been in England to promote the book.[13]

Speke's abuse of Petherick raised even more eyebrows. Even while the RGS was making a close study of Speke's allegations against Petherick, Speke offended against protocol and good manners by launching a vitriolic public attack against the Vice-Consul, repeating the charge of profiteering from slavery. This intemperate outburst, while the case was still *sub judice*, seriously alienated the RGS. Only the pleas of Blackwood and Grant prevented Speke from consolidating the libel against Petherick in his *Journal*.[14] Even so, when Speke's book appeared, many reviewers took issue with him on this point.

When Petherick's report was read to the RGS council in April 1864, the Council moved quickly to clear the Consul of any taint of suspicion of being involved in slavery. Speke's calumnies were thereby rebutted, with further damage to his reputation. But meanwhile Petherick had been dismissed from his Consulship, and neither the RGS nor the Treasury would reimburse him for the expenses he had incurred, thinking he was the agent of both bodies, from his own pocket. He was ruined both professionally and financially because of Speke's charges. It was lucky for him that the Egyptian government, indignant at the way one of its 'faithful servants' had been treated, came to his aid and paid his expenses.[15]

Even more serious for his own prospects was Speke's alienation of the RGS. It had been a condition of the Society's support that Speke would publish his findings in their journal. But, despite many promptings from the RGS for a scientific paper on his return from the Nile quest, Speke kept all his cards up his sleeve until Blackwood published the *Journal*. While he was still on speaking terms with Petherick, he had already made his position plain privately. 'The Royal Geographical Society have not the means of spreading anything about, whereas Blackwood has a larger circulation than anybody else. Again the Royal Geographical Society is slothful to the last degree, but Blackwood does not want a week to produce a map, a paper, or anything else.'[16] It was not so much desire for gain – for Speke was a rich man in his own right – as a neurotic desire for speed that made Speke act this way. When Speke did eventually submit his 'scholarly' paper, he made clear his fundamental contempt for the Society by writing a brief, journalistic memoir of his travels, devoid of hard scientific information, tenuous in the extreme in content, and containing no footnotes or references.[17]

Murchison took Speke's behaviour as an insult. Burton's original charge that Speke had ignored the RGS remit in 1858 – which was to inquire into the geography of the 'Sea of Ujiji' – in favour of racing off north to make an illusory discovery of the Nile sources, came to have renewed force. Whereas Murchison had somewhat foolishly gone out on a limb in 1859 and claimed Speke on slender evidence as the discoverer of the Nile sources – a belief he reiterated on Speke's return in June 1863 – by 1864 he had changed his mind. Taking the advice of his friend Dr Livingstone, he was now thinking of sending out the other 'Zambezi doctor', John Kirk, to clear up the mystery.[18] By the time of Burton's arrival from Fernando Po in summer 1864, the rift between Speke and the RGS had become a crevasse.

The fourth element in Speke's vulnerability by the time his original patron landed was the effectiveness of the geographical counter-attack against the claim that Lake Victoria was the origin of the Nile. Supported by Petherick, the theoretical geographer A. G. Findlay and, most importantly, by Livingstone himself, Burton's case that Lake Tanganyika was the ultimate feeder of the Nile made more and more converts as 1864 progressed. Burton's thesis was in two parts; a negative argument showing why Speke's theory could not be correct; and his own detailed explication of the Nile fountains.[19]

Burton's critique of Speke's methodology had a powerful *ad hoc* force. He began by pointing out that Speke, at an altitude of 250 feet above Lake Victoria, could see for no more than 20 miles, yet claimed the breadth of the Nyasa was 80 to 100 miles. On his second journey Speke simply took it for granted that he was marching round the western perimeter of the lake, making no attempt to verify the hypothesis. At Rumanika's Speke evinced singular laziness, never once visiting the lake. Speke followed the shore of his 'vast lake' for just fifty miles, yet was adamant that the stretch of water was one vast lake and not two or more, as Burton claimed.[20] Most carelessly of all, after sighting Ripon Falls, Speke simply assumed that its waters descended into the Nile. He followed the river north just fifty miles to Kamrasi's capital. When he regained the banks of the Nile from Bunyoro, he had missed nearly ninety miles of its course. After tracing its course for another fifty miles, he again left it to strike across country. After a detour of 150 miles, he came on a river which he described as 'like a fine Highland stream' and which he simply assumed to be the one that began at Ripon Falls.[21]

The crux of Burton's positive argument was that nobody had followed up his own work on Lake Tanganyika and tested *his* hypothesis. This was, in essence, that Lake Tanganyika was the western source of a lake he called *Baharingo*, allegedly the eastern source of the Nile. It was an essential part of this argument that the river Rusizi flowed *out* of Tanganyika; according to Burton it did, to Lake Albert, west of Bunyoro. Lake Tanganyika was thus a feeder of the Nile; Burton asserted that it could not be *the* source, as no lake could be the origin of a river. The eastern source of the Nile, Lake Baharingo, he hypothesised, received its waters from the fabled 'Mountains of the Moon'. Speke's Lake Victoria was thus irrelevant to the entire question of the fountains of the Nile.[22]

Thus far the debate had been conducted with full scientific detachment, even though the *parti pris* on Burton's side was obvious. But in his book *The Nile Basin*, published in 1864, Burton employed a collaborator, James MacQueen, another of the 'armchair geographers' in which England at that time abounded. MacQueen's interest in geography began when he was manager of a West Indian sugar plantation. He acquired a reputation in the RGS as an expert on African geography without ever having been to the continent. The collaboration with Burton on the Nile book involved a detached theoretical first part written by Burton and a fiery philippic in Part Two composed by MacQueen. MacQueen pitched into Speke mercilessly at a personal level. It was a minor masterpiece of specious and scurrilous *ad hominem* argumentation. He smeared Speke as a sexual libertine, thus turning the tables on him in a double sense (for Burton, the true libertine, had been accused of '*le vice anglais*' in 1859 by Speke, himself a more authentic homosexual personality). MacQueen taunted Speke with having been more interested in naked girls in Buganda than in travelling to the nearby lake. He poured scorn on the lubriciousness of Speke's measurement of one of Rumanika's wives and derided his discovery of the 'lost land' of Mutesa where 'licentiousness and profligacy prevail to an unlimited extent'.[23]

Next MacQueen neatly eviscerated all Speke's charges against Petherick, working from the few references in *Journal of the Discovery* that Speke had insisted on retaining against Blackwood's advice.[24] He underlined all the occasions when Speke had sold Grant short in his maniacal glory-hunting. He used Speke's figures to prove that, according to the 'intrepid explorer', the Nile ran *uphill* for ninety miles – exactly the error Blackwood had cautioned the arrogant and cavalier Speke against including in his book.[25]

Speke made another bad mistake by alienating David Livingstone. Temperamentally, Livingstone far preferred the dour Speke to the flamboyant Burton, but he did not care for Speke's overconfident assertion that he had solved the riddle of the Nile sources. Livingstone was convinced that *he* held the key to that particular mystery; to the end of his days he remained firm in his belief that the Lualaba river was the great tributary that fed into the White Nile.[26] Moreover, Speke had foolishly tried to dispose of Burton's Tanganyika theory by claiming that the only effluent rivers on Lake Tanganyika flowed *southwards*, to Lake Nyasa.[27] Here he was entering Livingstone's domain in a double sense: not only did Livingstone feel possessive about the Nile sources in general, but in particular he knew very well from his own travels that Speke's theory was absurd, and that no large river entered Lake Nyasa from the Tanganyika basin.

Livingstone returned to England from a traumatic six-year expedition to the Zambezi, during which he had lost his wife and fallen out violently with his white missionary co-workers, in July 1864, the very month of Burton's arrival from Fernando Po. This meant that for the first time the three greatest African explorers were all in London together. The prospect of an intellectual bear-fight seemed too good to miss. The flames of controversy over the Nile were whipped up by leader-writers and amateur geographers alike.[28] In the *Saturday Review* Viscount Strangford contributed a vitriolic piece entitled 'Dishonour est a Nilo', whose theme was 'a plague on both your houses'. While supporting Burton's case intellectually, he deplored the way he had chosen to present it. 'Burton and Speke are so blind with rage and bitterness that they fight like untrained street boys. Had Burton acquired a continental tact and self control rather than a curious infelicity in the manner of displaying and misplacing his cleverness . . . the world might have rung with his name . . . So far as it is possible to see the points at issue through the haze of sneer and wrath with which they are encompassed, we believe him to be mainly in the right.'[29]

Normally a prickly and combative soul, Burton did not particularly relish dredging over the old controversy on his return to England. While still in Fernando Po, after Speke's book had appeared, he sent messages through intermediaries hinting at a reconciliation, but Speke ignored them. Instead he responded with a boastful speech in December 1863, full of withering scorn for Burton (whom he referred to as 'Mr Bigg'). He asserted that 'in 1857 he [Speke] had hit the Nile on the head, but that now [1863] he had driven it into the Med.' Burton was content to let the *Journal* speak for itself and damage Speke's reputation unaided (as it did). He contented himself with an aside on Speke's hypocrisy. On the first expedition Speke had told Burton he did not give a fig for God's providence, that Man made his own destiny. But his book was spattered with biblical quotations, expressly inserted to indulge the prejudices of the 'unco' guid.'[30]

When Burton returned to England, it was suggested that he might like to debate the origins of the Nile with Speke at the annual meeting of the British Association for the Advancement of Science, to be held in Bath in September 1864. The idea was that Dr Livingstone would act as a kind of moderator and adjudicator. Burton at first dismissed the idea, but changed his mind after hearing from Laurence Oliphant, ever a fisher in troubled water, that Speke had threatened to kick Burton off the platform if he showed his face in Bath. This was not the sort of challenge to which Burton could turn the other cheek. 'Well *that* settles it! By God, he *shall* kick me!' he spluttered.[31]

In one sense Livingstone was the perfect choice as referee of the impending bout at Bath. His private attitude was also 'a plague on both your houses'. In the first place he was annoyed to find himself no longer the undisputed king of African exploration, as on his 1856 England visit, but only first among equals. The focus of attention had shifted from the Zambezi to the Nile. Livingstone was peeved that the Speke–Burton conflict would absorb all the attention at Bath, so that his own speech denouncing the Portuguese slave trade would probably fall flat. Besides, he had more particular reasons for disliking both the combatants.

Livingstone's animus towards Speke arose not just because the Englishman's Nile theories directly conflicted with his own. The good doctor also harboured a grudge towards Speke for having suggested that he (Livingstone) had not sufficiently acknowledged the pioneering work of Portuguese explorers on the Zambezi. Like his friend Stanley after him, and like Speke, Livingstone had a pathological need to be acknowledged as first in the field in any exploration he took in hand.[32]

But if Livingstone despised Speke, he positively detested Burton. Burton, with his aristocratic hauteur, his drawled 'Yaas' (his inevitable version of 'yes'), his intellectual snobbery and 'effortless superiority', was exactly the kind of Englishman the dour Lowland Scot had taken against since his early days as a missionary. Additionally, Livingstone hated Burton for his alleged moral turpitude and rumoured dalliances with dusky beauties, his championing of Islam and consequent denigration of Christianity, his widely-trumpeted view that the black man was an incorrigible savage, and his many polemics against missionary endeavour in Africa. When, early in 1865, Burton gave evidence on conditions in West Africa before the Parliamentary Select Committee and recommended that Britain pull out of the area, leaving the benighted savages to their fate, Livingstone's anger boiled over. 'Burton seems to be a moral idiot. His conduct in Africa was so bad that it cannot be spoken of without disgust – systematically wicked, impure and untruthful.'[33]

Yet even with the prospect of a genuinely neutral umpire in the chair at the Bath meeting, Speke cannot have relished the thought of a public debate with Burton. For all his absurd fulminations against Burton's 'ignorance' and his even more risible claims to have taught the older man all he knew, Speke was aware that in dialectical terms his rival held all the aces. He spoke two dozen languages where Speke spoke none; he was supremely erudite and well-read with a stock of historical allusions, classical tags and literary references at his command, whereas Speke had barely managed to struggle through the Bible and Shakespeare; above all, Burton had a deep, fruity, *basso profundo* voice and possessed the actor's knack of voice projection, while Speke spoke haltingly in a thin, reedy tone, was deaf in one ear and suffered from faulty eyesight. Moreover, Speke knew he would face a far from friendly audience. MacQueen, Beke, Petherick, Findlay and Clements Markham were all adherents of Burton; in return he could summon as allies only Francis Galton and, possibly, Sir Roderick Murchison. Even Grant, the ever-faithful, had declined to attend the debate. Also, failure against Burton might lead Louis Napoleon to withdraw his offer of funding for a further African expedition in 1865. Great issues were at stake at Bath. As the day for the confrontation approached, Speke grew more and more nervous.

On the morning of Thursday 15 September 1864, the day before the debate, the participants met for a preliminary session at the Mineral Water Hospital in Bath. Burton entered with Isabel on his arm. He at once came face to face with Speke, whom he had not met since 1859. 'I passed my quondam companion as he sat on the President's right hand, and I could not but remark the immense change of feature, of expression, and of general appearance which his severe labours, complicated perhaps by deafness and dimness of sight, had wrought in him. We looked at each other of course without signs of recognition.'[34]

Speke seemed nervous, depressed and ill at ease throughout the morning. At one point he looked Burton straight in the eye, and his face seemed full of sorrow, yearning and perplexity. Then he turned to stone again. At about 1.30 p.m. someone seemed to beckon to him from the back of the hall, possibly by a prearranged signal. Speke's fidgeting got worse, and he finally arose and exclaimed aloud, 'Oh, I can't stand this any longer.' He shifted his chair so as to depart. The man nearest to him said, 'Shall you want your chair again, sir? May I have it? Shall you come back?' 'I hope not,' Speke answered gloomily, then flounced out of the hall.[35]

Next morning when Burton arrived for the debate proper, he noticed a knot of RGS dignitaries in the 'robing room' adjacent to the platform. There seemed to be something odd about their behaviour, and the men he knew tried to avoid meeting his eye. After a delay of some twenty-five minutes, while Burton stood alone with his notes on the platform, Livingstone, Murchison and the rest trooped silently into the hall. Murchison then announced that Speke had accidentally shot himself at about 4.30 p.m. the afternoon before, while going after partridges on his cousin's estate. Burton at once slumped into a chair with the shock. Clements Markham, who was an eyewitness, left this account: 'Everyone looked at Burton. He expressed a few words of regret and at once left the room. No one could have behaved better or more naturally.'[36]

Controlling terrible emotion, Burton returned shortly and read a paper on Dahomean ethnology which Murchison, presciently, had asked him to have to hand in case Speke did not appear for the debate. Burton rushed through the paper at great speed, speaking falteringly and with a trembling voice. Then he went home and wept long and bitterly for his departed comrade. Isabel recalled that she spent days trying to comfort him.[37]

Afterwards Burton was convinced that Speke had committed suicide rather than endure the merciless dissection of his amateurism which was promised for the Bath meeting. But his early remarks on Speke's death are cryptic and enigmatic. Five days after the tragedy Burton wrote to his Vice-Consul in Fernando Po: 'Captain Speke came to a bad end, but no one knows anything about it.' In a later letter, when it became clear that he was in some obscure way being blamed for his erstwhile companion's death, he added: 'Nothing is known of Speke's death. I saw him at 1.30 p.m. and at 4 p.m. he was dead. The charitable say that he shot himself, the uncharitable say that I shot him.'[38]

What had happened on that September afternoon on the estate of Speke's cousins the Fullers, Neston Park, near Corsham, Wiltshire? At about 2.30 p.m. he set out with his cousin George Fuller and a game-keeper named Daniel Davis for an afternoon's shooting. He fired both barrels in the course of the afternoon. At about 4 p.m. Davis was marking birds for the two guns, who were about sixty yards apart. Speke was seen to get up on a two-foot high stone wall. A few seconds later there was a report. When Fuller rushed up he found Speke bleeding to death in the field behind the wall; alongside him was his double-barrelled Lancaster breech-loader. The right barrel was at half-cock; only the left barrel was discharged. 'Don't move me', Speke said feebly to Fuller. They were his last words. He survived only fifteen minutes. When Thomas Snow, a surgeon from Box, arrived twenty minutes later, Speke was already dead.[39]

That evening a jury assembled for the Coroner's Inquest and passed a verdict of accidental death. Their hypothesis was that Speke placed his Lancaster on the rubble wall while he attempted to climb over it but that, handicapped by a paralysed arm, he gripped the muzzle end of the weapon and dragged it towards himself as he balanced on the rubble. Either the pressure on the gun caused its hair-trigger to pull, or some stone, disturbed as Speke clambered over, hit the hammer and caused the gun to go off. Snow's medical testimony was as follows: 'There was a wound on the left side, such as would be made by a cartridge if the muzzle of the gun was close to the body. There was no other wound. It led in a direction upwards towards the spine, passing through the lungs and dividing all the large vessels near the heart, but not touching the heart itself.'[40]

Speke's dramatic death has always divided commentators into those who accept the verdict of accidental death and those who think that either suicide or unconscious 'death wish' was at work. It has to be conceded that the weight of authority is very much on the side of the 'accidental death' lobby. Few at the time queried the jury's verdict. It was Burton who started the rumour that Speke's death was probably suicide, though his contemporaries had little time for the theory; Livingstone, for one, was adamant that the fatality was an accident pure and simple.[41]

But it does seem that those who would rebuke Burton as an idle scandal-mongerer have skated too facilely over the objections to the official verdict. Why this particular accident at this exact time and with this kind of weapon? Of course freak accidents can happen to anyone at any time, but that is exactly the point. Such a shooting mishap could have happened at any time during Speke's twenty-year career as a hunter of game. Why did it happen the afternoon before he was due to fight for his professional life in a debate he was likely to lose, and at a time when, according to all reliable testimony, he was seriously depressed? The argument that he was using a different kind of gun from his usual African firearms would be more convincing if the fatal weapon had ever actually been produced in evidence. One of the great mysteries of Speke's death, which the 'accidental death' faction has never addressed, is what happened to the (alleged) Lancaster.

The disappearance of the gun is not the only prima facie disturbing aspect of the Speke affair. The entire case for accidental death rests on the testimony of the two men who accompanied him on the shoot: his cousin George Fuller and the gamekeeper Daniel Davis, neither of whom, on their own admission, actually saw what happened before the fatal shot was fired. If Speke really had committed suicide, it would clearly be in the interest of his extended family and its reputation to cover up the fact. Davis, as a local retainer, could easily be browbeaten into giving the 'correct' story. And there is clearly something very unsatisfactory about the evidence of both men. Davis's testimony leads to the conclusion that the Lancaster was fired from a near-vertical position, but this is in direct conflict with the surgeon's findings. Fuller's evidence, both that given in 1864 and his later additions, is as full of holes as a sieve. He claimed, in the teeth of incontrovertible evidence, that Burton had not seen Speke on the day of his death, that the fatal shot had been fired at 1 p.m. not 4 p.m., that the killing weapon was not a Lancaster breech-loader but a muzzle loader, that the date of Speke's death was 1 September 1864, not 15 September. Instead of being on top of the wall without his gun, as in the official report, Speke was, according to Fuller, on the top of the wall, holding the gun with its muzzle end, with the right hammer at full cock, ready for firing, not at half-cock as in the Coroner's report.[42]

Speke's state of mind on the afternoon of 15 September 1864 does not permit a definitive statement that he did not commit suicide. The notion that his vanity and pride precluded his taking his own life is psychologically naïve. Pride and haughtiness often coexist with, as a defence mechanism for, intense self-loathing. In any case, the 'accidental death' lobby betrays a lack of imagination in its positing of a one-dimensional 'either–or', of act-of-God versus deliberate and premeditated suicide. The angle of entry of the shot is taken to be definitive evidence against suicide. The shot entered Speke's body under the armpit, traversing the chest at an angle and shredding the blood vessels over the heart. To deliver the shot at such an angle, it is alleged, it would be virtually impossible for Speke to pull the trigger, even if he had been standing in open ground, and not on the loose stones of a broken country dyke, where foothold was precarious. But no one has thought of postulating a loss of footing during an actual suicide attempt. Speke could have slipped while the gun was deliberately pointed at his chest, and the gun could have gone off as he fell, thus producing all the symptoms of an 'impossible angle'.

Fuller's evidence, as we might expect, loads the dice in favour of accidental death. We have already seen that he was an exceptionally unreliable witness and had motive enough to cover up a suicide. But let us assume that he was speaking the plain truth at all points. What, then, are we to make of this statement? 'I do not think that Hanning for many years before that day had shot with anything but a rifle. He did not seem to have acquired the usual precautions exercised by sportsmen accustomed to the use of muzzle-loading double-barrelled guns. My gamekeeper, who was with us, and I, both noticed this carelessness in the use of the gun by Hanning. We therefore avoided being very close to him when walking the fields, and in crossing the wall where the accident happened both the gamekeeper and I were at some distance from Hanning.'[43] Contrast this with Burton's evidence on Speke's usual circumspection with guns. 'He was ever remarkable for the caution with which he handled his weapon. I ever make a point of ascertaining a fellow-traveller's habit in that matter, and I observed that even when our canoe was shaken and upthrown by the hippopotamus he never allowed his gun to look at him or others.'[44] In other words, at the very least Speke's behaviour that afternoon was abnormal and betrayed the signs of a man under intense stress.

It is likely, therefore, that the true explanation for Speke's death is via a mixed category of verdict: 'death through misadventure while the balance of the mind was disturbed'. 'In other words, the controls which normally monitored Speke's powerful 'death drive', for whose existence there is plenty of evidence, went into abeyance. It would be of a piece with Speke's notoriously transmogrified and other-directed aggression that in such a context the gun which had slaughtered so many animals in moments of triumph should be turned on himself.

It has been necessary to deal at length with the proposition that Speke might have willed his own death, in order to dispose of the facile criticism that Burton acted like a 'bounder' in enunciating a theory (suicide) for which there was absolutely no evidence.[45] There is no reason to doubt that Burton was genuinely stunned by Speke's tragic death, and he might well have ceased to utter on the subject if his critics had left the subject well alone. But Burton was increasingly irritated by the way Speke's death caused a backlash in his favour, so that the arguments for the source of the Nile were filtered through sentiment instead of being dealt with on their own merits. The abdication from reason was seen most clearly when Grant's book *A Walk Across Africa* appeared. There is reason to believe that Grant's original intention had been to present Speke in all his ambiguity. But shock over the Bath tragedy paralysed Grant, and he hastened to turn his book into a hagiographical homage to his lost leader. After beginning jejunely (and falsely) 'the first dark cloud connected with our African expedition had suddenly appeared' (after news of Speke's death), Grant continued in guilt-laden manner about his failure to attend the proceedings at Bath: 'had I gone thither and been with my friend, this calamity might have been averted . . . I reproached myself with having silently borne all the taunts and doubts thrown upon his great discovery.'[46]

Even worse was the deliberately provocative nature of *The Times* obituary on Speke. 'Captain Speke and Captain Burton can no longer be pitted against each other for the gladiatorial exhibition. It must be very hard for Captain Burton, who has won so many laurels, to reflect that he was once slumbering under the shadow of the very highest prize of all while another, and less experienced hand reached over and plucked the fruit . . . In fact, poor Burton was ill and Speke was well. Speke was shooting Egyptian geese and catching perch in the lake while Burton lay in his hammock. Moreover, Speke had the happy sagacity to guess the vast importance of the discovery on which he had lighted. Burton was very near gaining the blue riband of the Geographers, but did not gain it. He may well be content, however, with his other achievements. In all future time Captain Speke, whose loss we deplore, must be remembered, as the discoverer of the Source of the Nile.'[47]

In his reply, Burton grumpily though civilly implied that this was sentimental pap; the tragic loss of Speke was a matter quite independent of the worth of his findings in Africa.[48] At the end of the year he made the point with greater force by printing in *The Nile Quest* the demolition job on Speke's geography he had originally intended to unfurl at Bath. Burton was widely accused of lack of taste and sensitivity, and his defence seemed unconvincing. 'I do not stand forth as an enemy of the departed; that no man can better appreciate the noble qualities of energy, courage, and perseverance which he so eminently possessed than I do, who knew him for so many years, and who travelled with him as a brother, until the unfortunate rivalry respecting the Nile sources arose like the ghost of discord between us, and was fanned to a flame by the enmity and ambitions of "friends".'[48]

Speke's death marked a watershed in Burton's life, almost as though something was extinguished also in the survivor. This is no mere biographer's hyperbole. After 1864 Burton never again undertook a voyage of exploration where he was a genuine trail-blazer. Even his consular duties henceforth did not permit illicit expeditions to the unknown; there was no equivalent of the trip up the Congo, the quest for gorillas, or the treks to Benin City or Dahomey. For better or worse, until near the very end of his life Burton's reputation was inextricably linked with the Nile quest. This explains his reluctance to give up the ghost even as the new evidence from Africa slowly but surely moved the debate in Speke's favour.

Samuel Baker's return to England in 1865, after exploring Lake Albert, added a fresh twist to the Nile plot by suggesting that Lake Tanganyika might after all be the ultimate source, with the river flowing on through the Albert Nyasa, then looping round to cut into the White Nile somewhere north of Ripon Falls.[50] Burton continued to pin his hopes on a final resolution of the problem through Livingstone's third (and last) expedition.[51] But in late 1871 Livingstone and Stanley dealt a crushing blow to the theory that Tanganyika was the ultimate feeder. Their exploration of the Rusizi river proved conclusively that this river flowed into, not out of, Lake Tanganyika. Burton's one remaining hope was that the Lualaba might, after all, prove to be the source of the Nile, as Livingstone always believed and asserted. This would provide a roundabout vindication of Burton's thesis, for Verney Lovett Cameron, the first man to cross Africa east to west (1873–75), discovered that in the wet season Tanganyika overflowed into the Lukuga, which in turn flowed into the Lualaba. There is a bated-breath quality about Burton's frequent lucubrations in the early 1870s on the work of Cameron, Stanley and Serpa Pinto, respectively the second, third and fourth European traversers of Africa after Livingstone.[52] Burton, though, always suspected that the Lualaba would turn out to be a mighty tributary of the Congo, as Stanley in his epic journey of 1876–77 finally proved it to be.[53] Stanley's great 999-day trek across Africa in 1874–77 also drove the final nail into the coffin of Burton's hypothesis that the Victoria Nyanza was not one lake but several. On 29 November 1875 Burton was forced to bow to the inevitable; in a speech before the RGS he graciously admitted his error.[54]

It was not, however, until the early 1880s, when the issue was no longer in doubt, and when Burton had switched from exploration to literature, that he finally recanted and admitted that Speke had been right all along about the sources of the Nile.[55] But Burton was never one to give in without a fight. He continued to insist that he had been right to be wrong, and he paraded his lack of repentance for the non-payment of his porters in 1859 – the issue that had first earned him Livingstone's condemnation and that of the English public. At the end of his journey down the São Francisco river in Brazil in 1867, he again refused to pay his porters on the grounds of their incompetence and failure to fulfil contractual obligations. Taking his stand on 'Let justice be done, though the heavens fall', Burton defied his critics to find fault with him. 'Mere calumny will never deter me from what I there and then did. Travellers will never be well treated as long as predecessors act upon the principle – or rather non-principle – of forgive and forget at journey's end, because it is journey's end.'[56]

18

Brazilian Interlude

BURTON, it will be remembered, was originally to have returned to Fernando Po by 7 September 1864. The notification of transfer to Santos in Brazil brought him a further extension of leave. It was Isabel, by her ceaseless importuning at the Foreign Office, who had obtained an accompanied posting for her husband. The need to gather together the effects for a family home was the official reason why the Burtons spent the winter of 1864–65 in the British Isles. The real reason was the 'pull' the Arundells had with Lord Stanley.

The Burtons began their long holiday with a two month tour of Ireland. In mild weather and amid constantly stimulating scenes they spent a delightful early winter. They were entertained by the great names of Anglo-Irish Dublin: the Bellews, the Gormanstons, Lord Drogheda. They took a jaunting-car to visit the ancestral home of the Burtons at Tuam and to Armagh to investigate his French ancestors. During the tour they acquired an Irish maid, who accompanied them to Brazil.[1]

Back in London Isabel made a point of being seen everywhere on the social round, doubtless with thoughts of the loneliness and desolation to come at Santos. Isabel's dizzy progress took her from her uncle Gerard at Garswood to the homes of Lord Stanley of Alderley, Lord Fitzwilliam, Lady Egerton of Tatton and Lady Margaret Beaumont. Richard found socialising purely for contacts a bore and preferred the literary parties he and Isabel went to together, mainly at the residences of Dr Bird and George du Maurier, where they met painters and poets: Swinburne, James Whistler, Dante Gabriel Rossetti. Burton also developed a close friendship with fellow-Africanist Winwood Reade, a young traveller and writer on the Dark Continent, and later a prominent defender of H. M. Stanley.

Two things mainly absorbed Burton's intellectual energies in this winter. One was the Anthropological Society which he had founded, and of which he was the Vice-President. He combined his interests there with his continuing membership of the Monkton Milnes coterie by organising an inner circle within the Society, called the Cannibal Club, to which only close friends were invited. Sir Edward Brabrooke, Thomas Bendyshe, translator of the Hindu classic *Mahabharata*, and Charles Bradlaugh were among the initiates. The Cannibal Club was another 'Hell Fire' excuse for alcoholic binges. The idea was that the members would meet for dinner at Bartolini's; official business would then be transacted in front of a mace shaped like a black man gnawing a thigh-bone. Burton always had a serious interest in cannibalism, which he tried to disguise by levity. He affected a humorous defence of anthropophagy: 'without cannibalism how could the New Zealander have preserved his fine development? Certainly not by eating his bat and his rat.' Burton's favourite sport was to twit his *bêtes noires*, the missionaries, on the subject. A missionary once told the Anthropological Society that he had witnessed a cannibal feast. Burton at once jumped in.

'Didn't they offer you any?'

'They did, but of course I refused.'

'What a fool you were', said Burton witheringly, 'to miss such an opportunity.'[2]

The most important recruit to the Cannibal Club, for Burton, was Swinburne. He dubbed the mace 'Ecce Homo', devised a cannibal Catechism, and gleefully recalled that he shared with Burton the distinction of having been sent down from Oxford. Burton had always been a drinker, but in his cups with Swinburne he reached new heights. Isabel and other members of polite society were deceived about what Burton and Swinburne got up to, since they usually met at Dr Bird's, and his household was generally regarded as a model of propriety. Burton's punishing schedule of drinking with Swinburne took him to the verge of alcoholism. Friends of the poet later blamed the explorer for leading the younger man astray; defenders of the explorer felt that Burton was sucked into these drinking contests because the poet implicitly taunted him with being already middle-aged and 'past it'. There is a suspicion that both men were victims of their own 'diabolical' personae, unable to lose face by admitting that the intake of alcohol was pushing each of them to the limit. Although Swinburne innocently claimed to Monkton Milnes that he and Burton traded more opinions than glasses, there is an ambivalence, part regret, part relief, about the words with which he describes Burton's absence: 'My tempter and favourite audience has gone to Santos.'[3]

Burton's other main intellectual activity in 1864–65 was directly influenced by Swinburne. It was in 1865 that Swinburne's *Atalanta in Calydon* took the British public by storm. Between bottles Swinburne

1 Burton in Arab Dress, 1848

2 General Sir Charles Napier

3 The prescribed dress for Pilgrims on the Haj to Mecca

4 Speke's Escape from the Somali

5 Speke in 1864

6 The Emir of Harar

7 & 8 Isabel and Richard Burton at the time of their marriage

9 'Explorers in East Africa':
an austere illustration from Burton's own book, *The Lake Regions*

THE IVORY PORTER, CLOTH PORTER AND A WOMAN

LADIES' SMOKING PARTY

MEMBERS OF THE WAZARAMO TRIBE

AFRICAN HOUSE BUILDING

10 Four illustrations from *The Lake Regions*

11 The Victims of King Gelele of Dahomey

12 An 'Amazon' from Dahomey

13 King Gelele (left) and King Gezo (right), 1856

14 (Right)
Burton
the Swordsman

15 (Below)
Isabel and
Richard Burton
in old age

16 (Right) The Mystical Diagram at the start of Burton's translation of the *Arabian Nights*

17 (Below) Burton's Tomb in the churchyard of St Mary Magdalene, Mortlake

read Burton excerpts from his proof copy. Stimulated by the brilliance of his young friend, Burton made his first excursion into verse. He produced a 121-page satirical poem entitled *Stone-Talk*. Uncertain of his poetic abilities, he brought it out under the pseudonym Frank Baker (Frank the shortened form of his second name, and Baker the maiden name of his mother). When Isabel later discovered that he was the author of a satire whose mordant humour she had appreciated at arm's length, she was genuinely appalled.

As literature, *Stone-Talk* was a curiosity. Purporting to be a dialogue between a (significantly) drunken scholar, Dr Polyglot, and a paving-stone in a London street, it was a thinly disguised autobiography in which the two aspects of the 'dual man' struggle with each other. The scholar is warm, witty, charming, iconoclastic and compassionate; the stone is cold, sardonic, bitter and depressed. Integration is achieved only in the passages dealing with the Crimean War and India, where the great imperial heroes – Clive, Hastings, Dalhousie and even Napier – are described as the rapers and pillagers of an earthly Eden. As for the Crimea,

> A hundred thousand souls had died –
> To gratify two despots' pride.

But elsewhere there is serious divergence between the two debaters. The enthusiasm for Darwin contrasts with the hatred for Christianity, the Bible, and the doctrine of original sin. It was typical of Burton to take the myth of Eve being fashioned from Adam's rib and then call Adam 'an hermaphrodite'. Most serious of all the bifurcations, though, is that between Burton's idealised love for the lost Louisa, and the bitter disillusionment he expresses about Isabel, 'the corseted woman'. Commenting with scabrous disgust on her plumpness, he says he frankly prefers 'a camel-load of flesh'.

When Isabel realised that her beloved Richard was the author of this farrago of gall and spleen, she set about dealing with it in a way that gave a hint of things to come. Instead of admitting that she was mortified by the strictures on herself, she used supreme cunning. She made a point of seeking out the one man most likely to have encouraged Richard in his misogynism: Monkton Milnes. She then made a pretence of asking his advice, on the grounds that suspicions about the true authorship of *Stone-Talk* were beginning to surface which, if confirmed, could seriously damage Richard's prospects at the Foreign Office. Milnes, a true friend, took fright at this and advised Isabel to buy up all the copies and burn them. This was exactly the advice she wanted to hear, though for very different reasons. The funeral pyre was constructed accordingly.

Many women would have sought some form of separation at this revelation of the truth of the marriage. It would have been easy enough, for Burton's long absences in 'difficult posts' would have permitted the fiction that it was too dangerous for his wife to accompany him. Isabel's fanaticism about *l'homme de ma vie* led her to a different solution. She would *make* her husband love her, she would redeem herself and Richard through suffering. In July 1865, after Burton had departed for Brazil, she spent a week in retreat at the Convent of the Assumption in London and recorded her own 'agony in the garden', 'I am to bear *all* joyfully, as an atonement to save Richard ... I have bought bitter experiences, but much has, I hope, been forgiven me.'[4]

But the period just before Burton departed for Brazil was a tense one for the marriage, more especially because of the dislocation involved for Richard in rebounding from the debauched milieu of Swinburne and Monkton Milnes to the Catholic pieties of his wife. Burton revived his interest in mesmerism and started to hypnotise Isabel, doubtless to probe the unconscious secrets of her libido – for this was always Burton's prime interest in women. He also resented that a Catholic woman would tell secrets to her priest in the confessional that she would not divulge to her husband.

How many secrets Burton winkled out of Isabel through hypnotism is uncertain, but her acquiescence was a signal demonstration of his power. He was determined to destroy the inner citadel where she might be able to hold out against him: 'it is the only way to get a woman to tell you the truth', was his justification of the hypnotic practices. But the long-term effect of this unilateralism – for he never taught Isabel how to hypnotise *him* – was almost certainly to heap up coals of suppressed and repressed rage in his wife. For Burton, the mesmerism seems to have been a form of unconscious revenge for the fact that he had ended up married to a woman he did not love. In Argentina in 1868 he boasted to Wilfred Blunt about the power he had over his wife. 'I have heard him say that at the distance of many hundred miles he could will her to do anything he chose as completely as if he were with her in the same room.'[5]

The conflict over hypnotism came to a head when the couple visited Lord and Lady Amberley early in 1865. The Amberleys were disconcerted by Burton's 'fierce scowling eye and repulsive hard face' but bowled over by his cleverness and brilliance in conversation. Isabel took the opportunity of an audience to complain that Richard's hypnotic sessions tired her out. Burton riposted by lifting a corner on what he had learned from his wife while she was in a trance. It seemed that he often consulted her on what was to happen in the future, and her predictions were fulfilled with uncanny accuracy. Burton confided to Lady Amberley Isabel's doubts about whether the 'white magic' of hypnotism was compatible with her devout Catholicism. On the Saturday evening there were some undignified scenes, described thus by Lord Amberley in his journal:

> Saturday. Blanche [Stanley, Lady Amberley's sister] was very anxious indeed to be mesmerised ... After dinner we had the mummers, and then Blanche was actually mesmerised, Maude [another sister] and Airlie [Dowager Lady Airlie] being present. Mrs Burton was in a state of rage (as was natural) because she was not admitted and would not allow it to be done alone with Maude, as Johnny [her brother] wished. I came into disagreeable collision with Johnny on account of his violent behaviour. There was a frightful row; Lord Stanley furious with Johnnie. Poor Jowett [Master of Balliol, Oxford], who had come in the afternoon, took no part, of course, but must have thought it a queer evening. I felt a kind and degree of anger such as I never remember on any other occasion, for I had been much provoked; and though I do not enter into the details, they made an impression which will long remain.
>
> Sunday. We heard this morning that there had been an awful row after we had gone to bed between Burton and his wife, because she was so angry at his mesmerising without her. She said he would now be doing it with women who were not so nice. He was angry at this and affected to think it folly, that he had himself said that if any man mesmerised her he would kill the man and her too, a threat that I dare say he is quite capable of executing.[6]

But at last even the Burtons' protracted leave had to come to an end. After a farewell dinner given for Richard by the Anthropological Society on 4 April, the Burtons departed for Portugal, where they spent a further two months. By now the Foreign Office was beside itself at the length of time it was taking their Santos Consul to get himself 'on the ground'. Reluctantly Burton took ship for Brazil. On Isabel he enjoined his invariable formula: 'Pay, pack and follow.'

The triple order is of great significance in an understanding of Burton. 'Follow': Burton made it a rule never to be accompanied by his wife on long sea journeys. All his major voyages were made solo. Burton so contrived it that he and Isabel travelled out to Brazil separately, then back to England separately, with the same arrangement obtaining to and from the subsequent posting in Damascus. 'Pack': it was essential that all household administration and the removal of effects be left to Isabel, so that Burton could sustain his self-image as a perennial rover, a world-Bedouin, a man apart. 'Pay': it was not just that having to pay bills sent Richard into a towering rage, so that by asking Isabel to deal with pecuniary matters he was protecting himself. On this particular occasion, the financial mess Burton had left behind in Fernando Po (especially concerning the irregular purchase of the brig *Harriet*) was so complex and labyrinthine that he needed Isabel in London to explain away his unsatisfactory conduct to Lord Stanley and other protectors at the Foreign Office. As it was, the imbroglio led the Foreign Office to suspend his salary for two years while he was in Brazil, pending solution of the intricate tangle.[7]

Burton's ship touched first at Bahia, where he disembarked and thus presented the Foreign Office with the first of many Brazilian *faits accomplis*. He requested permission to travel in the state of Bahia until his wife arrived to join him.[8] Since Isabel would be in Rio before the Foreign Office could return a written veto, once again the wandering Consul got away with his idiosyncratic notion of duty.

Imperial Brazil under Pedro II was at the crossroads when Burton arrived there. The history of the empire in Brazil, from independence to 1889, can be roughly divided into four periods. In the first period, until Pedro I's abdication in 1831, came the birth pangs of the new country, when for a long time its very survival seemed uncertain. The second period ended with the virtual abolition of the Brazilian slave trade in 1850, when Royal Navy ships entered imperial ports.[9] The third period was one of foreign expansion. A collision with Argentina over the buffer state of Uruguay was converted by machiavellian Argentine diplomacy into a Triple Alliance of Brazil, Argentina and Uruguay ranged against the isolationist power of Paraguay. The horrendous Paraguayan War of 1864–70 was the result. In the last stage of the empire, from 1870 to 1889, Pedro II's power finally weakened in face of a fourfold defection by the landowning aristocracy, the clergy, the professional classes and the army. Final abolition of slavery in 1888 was followed by republican revolution the year after.[10] Burton arrived when the empire was domestically stable, but engaged in a costly and sanguinary adventure on the battlefields of Paraguay.

Richard and Isabel met in Rio in late 1865 and set off to reconnoitre the consular post. Santos, some 230 miles to the south-west of Rio and one of the twentieth century's great coffee ports, was then a mere village surrounded by mangrove swamps, insect-ridden and as full of fever as Fernando Po. In order that his strictures on service wives might not become a self-fulfilling prophecy, Burton decided to leave Santos itself in charge of a Vice-Consul. He and Isabel would base themselves inland and upcountry in São Paulo. The 'two-centre' strategy suited Burton's purposes. If he became tired of Isabel, he could plead urgent business at Santos and decamp there. If he felt like a bit of exploration, he could mount his horse and ride off into the wilderness. Should any urgent Foreign Office despatches arrive in the meantime, he could explain his delay in replying by the necessity to commute between the two bases. Ruined roads and broken causeways were eminently plausible excuses in Latin America.

São Paulo, fifty miles inland and at an altitude of 2500 feet, had a healthier climate and was relatively free from malaria. The greatest megalopolis of the late twentieth century was then a sleepy little town of 25,000 inhabitants. Isabel made their first married home in a converted convent. Yet Burton was there but rarely and Isabel comforted herself by turning to the outdoor life. She could already shoot and fence. Now she became an expert rider. With her dwarfish servant Chico she ranged on horseback far into the São Paulo outback.[11]

Consular duties at Santos were virtually nil. Almost all Burton's official correspondence with London related to the financial mess he had left behind in Fernando Po. Otherwise he was largely free to travel and study. It was now that he began serious work on his massive project for the translation of the *Arabian Nights*. As he later recorded: 'during my long years of official banishment to the dull and dreary half-clearings of South America, it proved itself a charm, a talisman against ennui and despondency.'[12] Occasionally there were leaves at Rio, where the Burtons enjoyed the diplomatic social round. Burton was lionised by Pedro II, himself an amateur scientist, and shown special favours, much to the fury of his superiors in the diplomatic hierarchy.

For two years Burton was in limbo – a fact he found at first restful and enjoyable but gradually more and more burdensome. Nothing he did, or failed to do, was calculated to advance his career in the Foreign Office. There was no equivalent of the West African trips. In flat defiance of Consular regulations, Burton formed a Brazilian mining company, manœuvred for personal advantage through Emperor Pedro, and even floated shares in his mining company on the London Stock Exchange. Sir Edward Thornton, Minister in Rio, issued rebukes that would have wrecked the career of anyone less protected than Burton.[13] Fortunately for him, he enjoyed through the Arundells, the powerful patronage of the Foreign Secretary, Lord Stanley.

At last, after nearly two years of twilight, in the summer of 1867 Burton obtained an extensive local leave, which enabled him to explore the mines of Minas Gerais province and then travel down the São Francisco river to its mouth in Bahia province. Isabel accompanied him, first to Rio, then on some hard riding in the highlands of Brazil as far as Ouro Prêto, where she sprained an ankle and had to return to the capital.[14] Burton then continued north to Pirapora where he joined the São Francisco and floated down by raft along its length as far as the great cataract of Paulo Afonso, one of the mightiest waterfalls in the world. Abandoning the raft, Burton made his way to the lip of the falls. On a table of protruding rock, and clinging to a tree trunk for support, he peered in wonderment at the inferno of boiling and churning waters below.

> And the marvellous disorder is a well-directed anarchy: the course and sway, the wrestling and writhing, all tend to set free the prisoner from the

> prison of the walls ... The general effect ... is the 'realized' idea of power, of power tremendous, inexorable, irresistible. The eye is spellbound by the contrast of this impetuous motion, this wrathful, maddened haste to escape, with the frail steadfastness of the bits of rainbow hovering above ... The fancy is electrified by the aspect of this Durga of Nature, this evil working good, this life-in-death, this creation and construction by destruction ... I sat over the 'Quebrada' till convinced it was not possible to become 'one with the waters': what at first seemed grand and sublime at last had a feeling of awe too intense to be in any way enjoyable, and I left the place that the confusion and emotion might pass away.[15]

Depressed and disgruntled, Burton returned to his consular duties at Santos – 'alias the Wapping of the Far West', as he termed it.[16] There he spent much of his time despondently hitting the bottle. In April 1868, he fell violently ill and for a time hovered near death. Isabel called his illness 'hepatitis', but it was almost certainly alcohol-related. The symptoms she describes – yellowing of features, excessive thinness, congestion – suggest cirrhosis. Complications set in with inflammation of the lung. Doctors were summoned from Rio and closer home to the convent at São Paulo. Isabel permutated their advice and decided on a regimen of thirty-six glasses of calomel a day, castor oil and a purgative. The Rio physician put twelve leeches on the patient, cupped him on the right breast and lanced him in thirty-eight places, and placed a powerful blister on the whole of that side. Burton's agony was fearful. He lost a great deal of black, clotted blood, and could neither move hand or foot nor speak, swallow or breathe without a paroxysm of pain.

Isabel asked Burton's permission to try one of her remedies, since all the efforts of orthodox medicine had failed. In agony Burton signalled acquiescence. 'He seemed to be dying and I knew not what to do ... I put some holy water on his head, and knelt down and said some prayers, and put on the blessed scapulars ... He was quite still for about an hour, and then he said in a whisper, "Zoo, I think I'm a little better"... He has never had a *bad* paroxysm since.'[17]

Even as Burton slowly recovered, he told Isabel he had come to the end of his tether in Santos and could not continue. He intended to resign, come what might. He asked her to go at once to England and lobby the Foreign Office for a more suitable post, while he convalesced by making a trip to the River Plate. Dutiful as ever, she packed and embarked, on 24 July 1868.

Burton meanwhile set out for the River Plate and then immediately headed for the theatre of war, now approaching its fourth year of blood-letting. Francisco Solano Lopez, the Paraguayan dictator, had an army dedicated to him. Man for man they were far superior to the Allied troops, they fought with fanatical courage, and all that valour could do, they had done. But the advantage in numbers, weaponry and technology was overwhelmingly with the Triple Alliance. Brazil and Argentina could blockade the Paraná, they had armoured gunboats and Spencer and Enfield rifles, and, most important, they had almost unlimited access to the Banks of London. Paraguay fought with dugouts and flintlock muskets; her only ally was the USA, hostile to Brazil because the Empire retained the slavery the Union had expunged in the Civil War, but unable to enforce the Monroe doctrine against Argentina's backers, the British, so far south of the equator.[18]

Burton's rebellious nature had one great merit. He could never be a mere 'Foreign Office man'. So, although the British openly sided with the Allies, in the interests of free trade against Lopez's protectionism, he quickly perceived that the real villain of the piece was Argentina.[19]

Burton spent three weeks on his first visit to the battlefields (15 August to 5 September 1868). Back in Buenos Aires, haggard, gaunt, with just one suit of clothes, but still drinking heavily, he spent many roistering evenings with Wilfrid Blunt, then a young diplomat, and the 'Tichborne claimant', a man at the centre of one of Victorian England's most sensational cases. Originally a butcher in New South Wales, the 'claimant' to the estates of a pre-Conquest Catholic aristocratic family in Hampshire pretended to be the heir to the baronetcy, generally believed lost at sea off the American coast. Later revealed as an impostor, the claimant was eventually sentenced to fourteen years' hard labour (of which he served ten). His case came to trial in 1872, and Burton was called as one of the witnesses. At this stage (1868) the claimant's story seemed feasible, though Burton was later to turn on him. In Buenos Aires he was exactly the kind of larger-than-life character who could be guaranteed to attract Burton.[20]

From Buenos Aires Burton set out westwards to cross the Andes. Early talk of scaling Aconcagua was soon abandoned. This part of Burton's life is obscure, but according to his own accounts he spent Christmas Day in a running battle with hostile Araucanian Indians. He pressed on to Santiago, then up the coast to Arica, just inside the Chilean border, where he inspected the damage caused by a recent earthquake and tidal wave. He proceeded to Lima, where he was sitting in a café when dramatic news reached him. Isabel's lobbying had been successful, and he was transferred forthwith to a plum posting for an Arabist: Her Majesty's Consul in Damascus.[21]

He returned at once to Buenos Aires via the Straits of Magellan. Isabel had told him to travel to England with all speed, as his appointment had provoked much jealousy and sniping among more senior career consular officials. But Burton would never allow anyone to press him. Instead of shipping out immediately from the River Plate, he made a second trip to the theatre of war (4 to 18 April 1869). By this time the Paraguayan capital Asunción had fallen to the Allies. Burton wandered round the war-stricken town, making careful notes. Then he proceeded to interview the most important Argentine political personalities of the day.[22]

Burton arrived in Southampton on the first day of June, 1869. He was ill, haggard, unkept and in his old clothes. After having him clipped and spruced, Isabel took him to the Foreign Office to meet the new chief, Lord Clarendon, who had taken over in 1868 after Gladstone's great electoral victory. Despite much anti-Burton activity in smoke-filled rooms, Clarendon had confirmed his predecessor Stanley's appointment. But in return for his £700 and the prestige of the Damascus posting, Burton was supposed to exercise unusual prudence. Under-Secretary Murray warned that because of opposition to the appointment, Clarendon might have to recall him later; Burton cited his experience in Zanzibar to show that Moslems did not hold the Meccan *Haj* against him, and attributed the opposition to 'designing people'.[23] Assuring his chief that he would act responsibly, Burton then capped the assurance with a request for a further six weeks' sick-leave, on the grounds of his hepatitis, which was granted.

Burton soon crossed to France with Isabel, hoping to link up with Swinburne. Boulogne he found to have degenerated, and after a short stay he set out to meet Swinburne at Vichy, where they both planned to take the waters; Vichy was a favourite spot for Victorian would-be reformed alcoholics. Isabel, meanwhile, was to return to England to 'pay, pack and follow'.[24]

But when Burton left, Isabel had second thoughts. Part of her rebelled against being Richard's pack animal. The other part suspected that the 'cure' might take the form of massive doses of 'hair of the dog'. At Vichy she found Burton comfortably ensconced in the company of Swinburne, the painter Sir Frederick Leighton, the opera singer Adelaide Kemble Sartoris, and an old friend from Brazil, J. J. Aubertin. Actually, her fears of heavy drinking were groundless, as Swinburne's letters show. His correspondence with Whistler and others deals in walks and hikes rather than magnums and flagons. 'Even Captain Burton, who was born of iron, avowed himself tired and sleepy at the end of the day.'[25]

Burton and Swinburne reached the acme of male companionship when they scaled the puy de Dôme together. For the first time, it seemed, since his boyhood days with Edward, Burton had found a younger male who would not betray him, like Speke, or die suddenly, as Steinhaeuser had done while he was in Brazil. Their triumphant return to Vichy was, however, marred by the sudden appearance of Isabel, as Swinburne confessed to a female confidante. 'You cannot think how kind and careful of me he was. I feel now as if I knew for the first time what it was to have an elder brother . . . I rather grudge Mrs Burton's arrival here on Monday, though we are excellent friends, and I dare say I shall see none the less of him.'[26]

The Burtons and Swinburne went to Lyons after Vichy. There Swinburne left them and they proceeded to Turin. Burton entrained for Brindisi and thence went by ship to Beirut and Damascus; Isabel returned to Paris and London for the chores she had postponed. On the way out to join Richard she lost two of her nine boxes, in one of which was £300 in notes.[27] But by the time she had completed her journey via Marseilles and Alexandria to Beirut, she found that her husband the Consul had more serious matters on his hands than mere financial loss – and that, given his attitude to money, was saying something.

19

Damascus

BURTON arrived in Damascus with high hopes. For the first time he had a consular appointment worthy of his talents: no other nineteenth-century British Consul had his knowledge of Arabic language and culture. But there were two factors that worked against his ultimate success from the very start. One was his lack of diplomatic skills. Consular success in a post in the Turkish empire called for qualities of empathy with the overlords, rather than sympathy with the desert Arabs. Moreover, as a notorious melting-pot, Syria was a trap for the politically unwary. The country contained four schools of Sunni Muslims (Hanifi, Shafi, Hanbeli, Maliki); the Shi'ites and a breakaway faction of Shi'ites called Nusayri; dervishes and Sufis (Shadilis and Shazlis); Persians, Chaldeans, Wahhabis and Bedouin. In the mountains were two sects of the Druze (Akkal and Juhhal); in the cities there were Sephardim, Ashkenazim, Samaritan and Karaite Jews. In addition, Syria boasted no fewer than fourteen Christian sects. This labyrinth of dogma and theological susceptibility was hardly suited to a man who found all religion, with the possible exception of Islam and spiritualism, mere fanatical mumbo-jumbo. In addition, both the Turkish authorities and Burton's immediate superiors in the diplomatic hierarchy had grave reservations about his suitability for the post. Sir Henry Elliott, British ambassador in Constantinople, summed them up in a communication to Lord Clarendon as soon as the appointment was announced. 'Damascus is probably the most fanatical town in the empire, and the presence there ... of a person who had penetrated to the Prophet's shrine, is regarded as certain to cause exhibitions against him that may be productive of very undesirable consequences. By the Mussulman population Captain Burton is regarded either as having insulted their religion by taking part as an unbeliever in their sacred rites, or else, as having, at that time, been a Mohammedan and having become a renegade.'[1] The unspoken part of Elliott's objection was that both he and S. Jackson Eldridge, Consul-General at Beirut and Burton's immediate superior, were uneasy and resentful at the presence of such a talented Arabist – and one who was moreover a household name – in their midst.

After pausing a few days at Suez in September 1869 to view the preparations for the opening of de Lesseps' Canal, which was formally inaugurated by the Khedive two months later, Burton continued to Damascus, where he arrived in post in early October.[2] There was a delay of a few days until his credentials in the form of the *berat* arrived, then the new Consul plunged eagerly into his duties. He was expected to look after the welfare of permanent British residents (the number varied during his incumbency from thirty to forty-eight), to afford the protection of the Crown to British tourists, to promote trade, and to report politically on internal Damascus affairs to Elliott, with despatches routed through Eldridge in Beirut. Determined to make such a name for himself that he would soon be on the short-list for the Morocco or even the Constantinople embassy, Burton looked around for an incident to propel himself into the headlines. It must be conceded that to some extent he was trailing his coat.

He soon found the opportunity he was looking for. A young English woman called Miss Hamilton, who was travelling out to do missionary work at the Irish Presbyterian church in Damascus, complained that she had been indecently assaulted at knife-point in a carriage by a man purporting to be the Persian Consul-General for Egypt. Burton pursued the matter with gusto, 'knowing that the Persians are capable of any excess'. But the authorities refused to take any action unless Burton came to the Turkish Consulate-General with Miss Hamilton. The Turks, who were sympathetic to their Islamic brothers, immediately tried to discredit Burton by claiming that he was never in Damascus, but forever away on some archaeological dig or antiquarian exploration. This was to be a constant motif over the next eighteen months. When Miss Hamilton refused to appear for interrogation, even with Burton at her side, on the understandable grounds that she did not wish to relive the ordeal, the Persians counter-attacked by declaring that 'Mohammed Effendi' would sue for libel.[3]

Burton's official despatches are a lucid dissection of the evasions, prevarications and delaying tactics used by the authorities. The Persian Consulate-General eventually formed a trumpery court of 'respectable individuals' who found the said Mohammed innocent because there were no witnesses to the incident and the alleged weapon could not be found. At this Burton exploded. There were no witnesses because Miss Hamilton was too terrified to testify and the coach driver's silence had been bought with a few piastres. As to the knife, the young lady had already deposed that she threw it out of the window. Burton limbered up for a confrontation with the authorities, especially confident because Eldridge, who hated him, was absent on leave. But the chargé d'affaires at Beirut crushed Burton's hopes with a brusquely worded note, ordering him to let the entire affair drop.[4] This rebuke angered and humiliated Burton. He announced to his intimates that, having failed to obtain official redress, he would kill the offender himself. Whether he put out an assassination contract on the Persian – a very easy thing to do in the nineteenth-century Turkish empire – is uncertain, but Burton later cryptically noted that the man 'met his fate at other hands'.[5]

In the autumn of 1869 the restless Burton managed just two trips away from Damascus – one ten-day visit to a village called Dhumayer, and the first of two ascents of Mount Hermon he accomplished during his consulship.[6] He had just three months on his own before Isabel arrived on 31 December 1869 with a mountain of luggage that would not have disgraced a twentieth-century film star, full of romantic illusions about what she would find in Damascus. Instead of 'my Pearl, the Garden of Eden, the Promised Land, my beautiful white city with her swelling domes and tapering minarets, her glittering golden crescents set in green of every shade', she found an unprepossessing city, dirty, feculent and ugly, full of strays and maltreated animals, and with a population so tense and fearful that they locked the thirteen gates of the walled city and huddled nervously within at night.

She found Burton so ill from neuralgia that at first she did not recognise him. It did not take her long to conclude that the stress of Damascus was responsible for her husband's broken health. She and Burton soon agreed that to be shut up every night in this hole was an affront to everything they stood for. The first step was to find a proper home. A quarter of an hour's ride from Damascus, reached through fields and orchards, was the village of Salihiyyah, nestling under the Camomile mountains. Here the Burtons leased a spacious house, with a garden full of apricot, lemon and orange trees.[7]

The Salihiyyah house looked out front and back onto extensive gardens. Across the narrow road, among apricot orchards, Burton built a stable for twelve horses, with a room for their grooms. The visitor to the main Burton household would be ushered into a square courtyard painted in stripes of red, white and blue, planted with orange, lemon and jessamine trees, complete with a fountain in the middle. Onto this courtyard opened a three-sided room, spread with rugs and divans; niches in the wall were full of potted plants. Upstairs were six rooms, occupying two sides of the courtyard. On the third side was a terrace which made a delightful sun-lounge on warm evenings. The beflowered and becarpeted terrace (the 'upper room' of Biblical parlance) provided an uninterrupted view of Jebel Kaysun, the tall yellow mountain which formed the backdrop of the village. Here the delicious, pure desert air could be inhaled. Burton's bedroom above was on the same level as the minaret of a nearby mosque, so that he could join the muezzin in the call to prayer.[8]

At Salihiyyah Isabel, whose fondness for animals was a clear substitute for the children she either did not want or could not conceive, built up a veritable menagerie. She had brought out five dogs from England – a St Bernard, two brindled bull-terriers and two Yarboroughs. To these she added a local mongrel, a camel, a white donkey, three goats, a lamb, a Persian cat, and fowl in abundance: chicken, turkeys, geese, ducks, guinea fowl, pigeons. In addition, there were twelve horses, with which Isabel (an early Dr Dolittle) claimed to be able to communicate directly. But the pride of her collection was a young panther cub, which had been caught in the desert and given them as a present. The cub slept nightly by their bedside. As it grew bigger, it began to alarm the servants. When it killed the pet lamb and then began stalking further afield, the locals struck back by giving it poisoned meat. The death of her beloved big cat caused Isabel paroxysms of genuine grief. Whatever one's strictures on her, there can be no doubting her real feeling for animals.[9]

Burton rose at daybreak, walked, exercised and studied until 11 a.m., then took a big breakfast as the first of his two meals of the day. He was at the Consulate from noon to 5 p.m., then returned home to dine at dusk.[10] As always, Burton grumbled about money problems: 'the hardest trial of all was to feel that every soul had a deep design upon my purse, from the little lad who stole my kitten for a *khamsah* (five farthings) to the gray-headed dragoman who wore two medals presented to him by Her Majesty's Government, and who would rather mulct me in a piastre (2½d) than not mulct me at all'.[11]

At home the Burtons broke with precedent by holding receptions to which people of all races, creeds and tongues were invited. Here on hot days Isabel would serve coffee, sherbets, lemonade, cigarettes and *narghilehs*. The sole taboo they had to adhere to was segregation of the sexes. But on her frequent rides into the outlying country Isabel managed to dent even that barrier. She would insist on barging into harems, dressed in her full mannish riding costume, and thus initially causing consternation with the eunuchs, who took her for a man. When the situation was explained, she would chat to the women of the seraglio, but more often than not this led to mutual incomprehension. 'Pray, Mrs Burton, do not teach our women things they don't know and never saw', one defensive Arab told her.[12] The Arab women responded to Isabel with contempt or wry bemusement, depending on their age. Seeing her dressed *à la Amazone*, the older women would cry out in horror: 'This is neither man nor woman, nor anything else. Allah preserve us from this manner of pestilence!' The interest of the younger women focused on her childlessness. 'Thou hast never had a child, O lady! Let us hope that Allah may be merciful and remove thy reproach ... And does not the Sidi Beg want to put thee away, and take a second wife? Dost thou not, Ya Sitti, feel insecure of thy place?' Isabel replied, 'The English husband would not put his wife away for anything. I feel quite secure of my place. The Sidi Beg may marry another after my death, but not before.'[13]

Isabel's infatuation with Richard led her to emulate him in all things. Burton brought with him to Syria a faithful Afghan servant or *hawwas* named Mohammed, whom he had first known in India. There was nothing for it but that Isabel must find a female equivalent. She discovered a maid called Khamoor, and began Europeanising her. As one student of Burtoniana has remarked waspishly: 'Mrs Burton was nothing if not a woman with a mission, and henceforward two cardinal aims swayed her, first to inveigle the heathen into stays, and secondly, to inveigle them to turn Catholics.'[14]

The mirroring was even more bizarre when it came to the choice of close friends. Burton's most treasured social companion was Abd-el-Kadir, the famed Algerian nationalist. Kadir had caught the imagination of the world by his struggle for Algerian autonomy, his capture and imprisonment by the French (1847 to 1852), and his subsequent release by Louis Napoleon at the intercession of Lord Londonderry. The French had pensioned him off into retirement at Damascus, where he lived in exile with five hundred Algerian followers. Sharing with Burton the distinction of being a master Sufi, Kadir always dressed in snow-white robes, with turban and burnous.[15]

Abd-el-Kadir was a frequent visitor to Salihiyyah, where he and the Burtons would spend many glorious evenings on the terrace, smoking *narghilehs*. A fourth person frequently present on these occasions was the notorious 'liberated woman', Jane Digby. In a sensational life she had been the wife of Lord Ellenborough, Prince Schwartzenberg, and some half-dozen others. She finally married a Bedouin Sheikh named el-Mezrab. At 61, tall, regal and still beautiful, with fluent Arabic and a command of eight other languages, Jane Digby spent half the year in Damascus and the other half in a Bedouin tent.

This was the woman Isabel regarded as her equivalent of Abd-el-Kadir. Although there was a wealth of malicious gossip (and much truth) bruited round Damascus about Jane Digby, Isabel dismissed all criticism as envy or spite. Burton was not so sure. From the very beginning he disliked and mistrusted her, and his opinion seemed borne out when the prospect of a trip to the ruins of Palmyra loomed. The location of the two wells on the way to Palmyra was a secret closely guarded by the Bedu whose 'queen' Jane Digby was, and they charged all travellers £250 for the privilege of steering them to the waterholes.

Burton asked her point-blank for the information, which she refused. Alarmed by the Burtons' determination to go it alone anyway, Jane Digby provided a guide whose secret instructions were to lead the Burtons into an ambush; they would then be held to ransom for a princely sum. But Burton read her mind, and on the first day out promptly took the guide himself hostage. He then found the wells on his own and made a successful journey to Palmyra. When they returned to Damascus, having thwarted Jane Digby's plans, she and Isabel took up their friendship again as if nothing had happened.[16] It was circumstance and not sentiment that eventually parted them.

Isabel did not lack physical courage. One evening she was returning from a Catholic church when a soldier caught hold of her in a dark street, insulted her and cursed the Cross. Refusing to run, Isabel ordered her servants to seize the man. She then struck a match, inspected his face to warn him that she would know him again, and released him. Her campaign against animal cruelty in Syria often led her to take the whip to donkey-drivers and other offenders against her humane code.[17]

On another occasion she rode out to meet Burton, and they got lost in the mountains, and had to wait until the moon rose to find their way home. There was nothing of the 'helpless female' about Isabel. Nor was her fearlessness confined only to human aggressors. Once she heard a sound of screeching outside her back door and found a large snake trying to dispossess her cat of a bowl of milk. She at once took a cudgel and expertly broke the serpent's back. She was equal to any emergency. Once when she and Richard were camping out in the desert, a scorpion stung her husband. Isabel rubbed smelling salts into the wound, then made him drink a bottle of *raki* to keep the poison from the heart. Next morning he was completely recovered.[18]

Isabel would defy anyone or anything, man or beast, but to Richard she displayed only the most respectful deference. Burton did not even have to endure the inconvenience of giving her a direct order. He would merely leave a bookmark in a volume, on which would be written a few words indicating his wishes. In this way he achieved a despot's results without having to act tyrannically. In return he tried to shape Isabel into the perfect 'she-mate'. He taught her to swim, using legs only, then arms only, but never both together, so that when she was perfect in both modes, the two combined made her a powerful swimmer. He also tried, with less success, to make her a competent linguist.[19]

Isabel's daily life in Syria was her most enjoyable experience to date of married life. Things were especially idyllic at the Burtons' summer retreat at Bludan in the 'Anti-Lebanon', twenty-seven miles from Damascus. The stifling heat of Damascus, where temperatures could reach 125 degrees in the shade and 175 degrees in the sun, made a summer residence essential. At Bludan they lived in an 'eagle's nest' at an altitude of 5000 feet, with an unrivalled view of the mountains. They had a large stone house, whose centre was a barn-like limestone hall with a deep covered verandah. A wild waste of garden extended all round the house; through this 'paradise' rushed a beautiful stream, complete with two waterfalls. Behind was a bare ridge of hillside, which gave way to five successive ranges of mountains, one backing the other, the last of which overlooked the Hauran. Conditions were perfect. The air was wonderfully fresh, the only heat experienced was for an hour or two after 3 p.m., and blankets were needed at night. There was stabling for eight horses. The house had no windows, but only shutters, closed at night.[20]

At Bludan the Burtons used to get up very early and take long walks over the hills with the dogs. Burton took his rifle, but more out of conditioned reflex than a wish to shoot. Unlike Speke, he had always detested pheasant and grouse shooting, and would go after game only if it was a threat to life, or for the pot. The hills around Bludan were alive with gazelle, wolves and wild boar; there were also a few bear. The Burtons would have liked to eat boar, but this was impossible in an Islamic country.[21]

The hot part of a summer's day would be spent reading, writing and (for Isabel) learning Arabic. Whatever the shortage of reading matter, Burton could always return to his trio of indispensables: the Bible, Shakespeare and Euclid. In the late afternoon they would entertain visitors or casual tourists, especially with an improvised shooting-range in the garden. Before dinner the Burtons would drink a glass or two of *raki*, eat dinner on the rooftop, then sit smoking while the moon lit up Mount Hermon. Every fortnight Burton would ride into Damascus to check that his Vice-Consul had everything in hand and to read the incoming mail from Beirut. Though there was only one direct shipping line between England and Beirut, the port was served by daily steamships from Alexandria and was the target for all westbound mail from Arabia.[22]

The establishment of his two households, the necessity to get on top of consular business and the need to acquaint himself personally with all nationals under his jurisdiction, meant that it was April 1870 before Burton was able to set off on the first of his major Syrian explorations. This was to Palmyra or Tadmor – the occasion of Jane Digby's chicanery. Setting out on 5 April with seventeen camels laden with water, the Burtons rode east across trackless deserts to the famous stronghold which Zenobia had defended against the Romans. For a week they prowled among the ruins of the temple allegedly built by Solomon. Burton the amateur archaeologist was in his element.[23]

After leaving Palmyra on Easter Monday, 18 April 1870, Burton returned to Damascus where he made the acquaintance of two other

English orientalists, who soon became fast friends. One was Edward H. Palmer, later to hold the chair of Arabic at Cambridge. Palmer shared Burton's leanings towards occultism, and was the epitome of the lovable absent-minded scholar. He had a favourite expression which became his catch-phrase and which people expected of him: 'I wonder what will happen', denoting an open-eyed curiosity about the world. Palmer also shared Burton's dislike of the Turkish *wali* or governor of Syria, Mohammed Rashid Pasha. He told of a gruesome encounter which summed up the *wali* perfectly. Palmer's first experience of an Arab guide came when a sheikh called Salameh led him into a trackless wilderness and threatened to abandon him there unless he was given £25. On returning to Jerusalem, Palmer complained to Rashid. 'I know the man, he is a scoundrel, and you shall see an example of the strength and equity of the Sultan's rule', replied the *wali*. On returning to Damascus Palmer and his companions were interviewed by Rashid. 'Do you think you would know your friend again?' he asked with reference to Salameh. Palmer nodded. Rashid then clapped his hands. A soldier brought in a sack and emptied it on the floor. Out rolled four human heads, one of which was Salameh's. 'Are you satisfied?' the *wali* asked with a cruel smile.[24]

The other orientalist made even more of an impression on Burton. Charles Tyrwhitt-Drake was a young archaeologist sent out to Syria by the Palestine Exploration Fund. Aged 24, a tall attractive redhead, Drake became another in Burton's long line of surrogate brothers. But as with all such, he was destined for a tragic end. He died of fever four years later; Palmer was murdered by Arabs during the Arabi Pasha rising in 1882.[25]

With Drake and Palmer Burton planned a systematic sweep through the antiquities of Syria. All three men were delighted to find that most previous travellers had kept to the beaten track, so much of Syria still remained for them to explore. They went first to Ba'albak, to some eyes a rival attraction to Palmyra, even more beautiful but much more accessible. Here, one memorable night, Drake and Isabel lit up the ruins with magnesium flares.[26] Then the party proceeded to Bludan, where shortage of accommodation meant Palmer and Drake had to sleep in a tent in the garden.

Next the trio of explorers set out into the mountains of the Anti-Lebanon. They gathered inscriptions and fixed the sites of some fifty ruins previously unexplored by Europeans. They thought nothing of riding forty or fifty miles a day.[27] The highlight of the trip was supposed to be the Cedars of Lebanon, which they reached on 29 July, but Burton was grievously disappointed: 'Those exaggerated Christmas trees ... so mean and so ragged that an English country gentleman would refuse them admittance into his park ... for the reasonable enjoyment of life, please place me upon Highgate Hill's grassy steps rather than upon Lebanon.'[28]

On completion of the Anti-Lebanon tour, the friends went their separate ways. Drake and Palmer returned to England, but with a firm promise to return early next year for further forays into unexplored Syria.[29] On 26 August a messenger arrived at Bludan with news of an impending massacre of Christians in Damascus. Catholics trying to collect debts from Moslems had been beaten, and when the offenders were imprisoned, Moslems threatened riots to release them. The uneasy situation escalated when two young Arab servants of the Jewish Donemberg brothers were caught scratching the sign of the cross on a mosque wall. Whether or not the boys were *agents provocateurs*, the incident was considered blasphemy in both Moslem and Christian communities, and added a fresh layer of religious tension to an already tense scene. Burton thought that the Jews were fomenting trouble between the two major religions. After all, he pointed out, not a single Jew lost his life in the July 1860 massacre, when Moslems slew 3000 Christians in a single day, and some Jews made large fortunes from the plundered houses.[30]

A rumour swept the city that the July 1860 massacres, triggered by a similar incident, were about to be repeated. August 27 was supposed to be the date of the outbreak of this mini-*Jihad*. Christians were packing and leaving the city in a panic. Burton ordered his horses saddled and his guns cleaned. He gave Isabel detailed instructions on the defence of Bludan, should marauders from the city come out to the Anti-Lebanon in search of blood. She prepared for a spirited defence of their mountain fortress. She locked up her pretty maid, distributed weapons to the male servants and placed the two most trusted men on the roof with her husband's elephant guns. She herself took up station on the terrace, armed with vast numbers of a primitive version of the Molotov cocktail. She invited all Christians in the neighbourhood to join her in the fastness.

Burton meanwhile galloped to Damascus and informed the city elders that a massacre was imminent. He browbeat the council members. 'Which of you is to be hanged if this is not prevented?' he demanded. 'It will cost you Syria, and unless you take measures at once, I shall telegraph to Constantinople.'

'What would you have us do?' came the answer.

'Post a guard in every street; order a patrol all night. I will go the rounds with Holo Pasha. Let the soldiers be harangued in the barracks . . . Issue an order that no Jew or Christian shall leave the house till all is quiet.'[31]

The council elders acquiesced. All was done as Burton suggested. Tempers cooled, and after a quiet but tense three days, Christians began to drift back into the city. The prompt action of Holo Pasha undoubtedly prevented trouble, but Rashid Ali was furious that Burton had apparently exceeded his authority and given orders to the city council as if he were an imperial proconsul. He at once had Burton's friend Holo transferred to duties at St John d'Acre.[32]

Isabel took the opportunity to express in her journal her pent-up wrath at the fainéant Eldridge, a man with an interest in nothing but comfort and alcohol. 'Mr Eldridge, who had lived for ten years safely on the coast, and had never ventured up to Damascus in his life, a civilian whose dislike to the smell of powder was notorious, wrote me a pleasantly chaffing letter, hoping I had recovered my fever and fright and giving Richard instructions how to behave in time of danger.'[33]

That scare over, Burton was free to resume his nomadic existence. After 'gypsying' with the very Bedouin who were accustomed to raid right up to the gates of Damascus itself, Burton ascended Mount Hermon for the second time. His subsequent journey across the Anti-Lebanon took him to the Druze country at Muktaran. He was full of admiration for the proud and martial Druze: 'fine, tall, strong and manly . . . honest and plain spoken, and do not know intriguing, lying, stealing or spying.' At Muktaran Burton was received in great style by Sitt Jumblatt, the Druze princess. She complained that the British, her putative allies, neglected her interests in Beirut. Burton explained that he could do little, since he was subordinate to Consul-General Eldridge who 'does nothing and is very proud of what he does. Consular office awfully careless; sick of dyspepsia; nothing to do mind and body.'[34] Burton parted from Sitt Jumblatt on the best of terms, and with a promise to return. He had captivated his hosts with a pyrotechnic display of recital by heart from the *Arabian Nights*: some of the stories had his audience rolling on the ground in mirth.[35]

The year 1871 opened with a visit from a Foreign Office inspector named Kennedy, who gave the Burtons full clearance. There was one difficult moment, after the inspector complained that a party gate at the Salihiyyah property had been creaking during the night and kept him awake. Isabel at once had it removed and a new one installed, without reference to her neighbour. Kennedy queried whether this was not perhaps an example of Isabel's high-handed behaviour, which was being rumoured in London. Isabel had him meet her Arab neighbour, who called down the blessings of Allah on her for having removed the nuisance of the creaking gate.[36]

As soon as Kennedy had departed, Burton took off alone on another journey into the wilderness. There was famine in Syria in the winter of 1870–71 and the weather was unusually severe. This time Burton 'gypsied' in a literal sense. While accompanying the Damascus pilgrim caravan in the Hauran, he lit on some gypsy encampments and spent time with the Romanies. He returned to Damascus on 10 March after a seventeen-day journey in the northern desert, the worse for wear from frostbite.[37]

But Burton could not bear to remain in post for long. Tyrwhitt-Drake arrived in Damascus from England on 25 March and at once he and Burton set out overland for a tour of the Holy Land, justified under the rubric of 'local leave'. Isabel went by sea from Beirut to Haifa and joined them in Palestine. 'Captain Burton and I loved him like a younger brother', Isabel recorded of Drake.[38] The trio of travellers began their tour in Jerusalem, where they spent Holy Week of 1871. Some tension was immediately evident, for Burton and Drake, already cynical about Christianity, fell in with the passionate French sceptic and orientalist Clermont-Ganneau. Their attitude to the sacred places of Jerusalem was that of detached, sardonic archaeologists and scholars. Isabel's was devotional piety itself. The tour sustained a nasty jolt in Nazareth in early May, following an ugly incident when a Copt tried to enter Isabel's tent. Burton wound up the trip earlier than he had intended. After visits to Lake Tiberias, El Huleh and Lake Phiala, the trio returned to Damascus.[39]

Burton was back in Damascus on 19 May. After a hectic five days answering accumulated consular correspondence, he again departed for the wilderness with Drake, this time on a return visit to the Druze country, in accordance with his promise to Sitt Jumblatt. On this expedition Burton and Drake combed through the Jebel Duruz Hauran more thoroughly. Archaeologically their task was more difficult than elsewhere in Syria, for the frequent attempts by the Turks to extend their sway into the Druze mountains had led to the ruins being broken up by the defenders to form barricades.[40] Burton and Drake then returned to the summer residence at Bludan, prior to departing on an eight-day expedition (31 July to 7 August 1871) along the backbone of the mountains from Jebel-el-Shakif to the northern end.[41] The two men were planning further forays into the wilderness when the sudden news of Burton's recall from Damascus came in.

Burton's restless and peripatetic Consulate, which got him into so much trouble with his superiors in London, produced a wealth of archaeological investigation in sites never previously visited by Europeans. If Burton was no longer an explorer, he was at least a traveller in the true sense, and he did scientific work of abiding value.[42] Isabel also thought this the happiest period in Burton's life, and in her life with him.

> I can never forget some of those lovely nights in the desert ... mules, donkeys, camels, horses, and mares picketed about, screaming, kicking and holloaing; the stacked loads, the big fires, the black tents, the Turkish soldiers, the picturesque figures in every garb, and the wild and fierce-

> looking men in wonderful costumes lying here and there, singing and dancing barbarous dances ... Richard reciting the Arabian Nights, or poor Palmer chanting Arab poetry, or Charley Drake practising magic to astonish the Mogharibehs ... I have seen the gravest and most reverend Shayks rolling on the ground and screaming with delight, in spite of their oriental gravity, and they seemed as if they could never let my husband go again.[43]

In the Syrian period Isabel is far our best source for the inner Burton. Richard's own productions at this time are dry, scholarly and almost curmudgeonly in their refusal to provide human interest stories for the reader. And it is from Isabel that we get the most significant pointers to the psychic dramas of herself and her husband.

Burton generally detested missionaries. According to an (unnamed) English missionary in Damascus who confided in Isabel, this was purely because in Africa he had encountered 'job lot' specimens of the genus, the *canaille* of a noble calling. His denunciations of these slipshod evangelists incurred him the charge of being anti-missionary, so that by and large missionaries in Syria responded in kind, thus giving more impetus to the vicious circle. But Isabel's friend saw another side of the Consul. One day Burton came to call at the missionary's house. From his study, which adjoined the drawing room into which Burton was shown, the missionary could observe his every movement and gesture. He heard Burton order the servants in a harsh peremptory tone to fetch the master. The servant, not knowing the missionary was in the study, went to look for him elsewhere. In noiseless carpet-slippers the host crept to the drawing-room door and peeped through a crack.

> I came upon a scene never to be forgotten. At one side of the room stood my curly-headed, rosy-cheeked little boy of five, on the other side stood Burton. The two were staring at each other. Neither was aware of my presence. Burton had twisted his face into the most fiendish-like aspect. His eyes rolled, exposing the whites in an alarming manner. The features were drawn to one side, so as to make the gashes on his jaw and brow appear more ghastly. The two cheeks were blown out, and Burton, raising a pocket-handkerchief to his left cheek, struck his right with the flat of his right hand, thus producing an explosion, and making the pocket-handkerchief fly to the left as if he had shot it through his two cheeks.
>
> The explosion was followed by a suppressed howl, something between the bark of a hyena and a jackal. All the time Burton glared on the little fellow with the fiery eyes of a basilisk, and the child stood riveted to the floor as if spell-bound and fascinated, like a creature about to be devoured. Suddenly a very wonderful thing happened. The little boy, with a wild shout of delight, sprang into the monster's arms, and the black beard was instantly mingled with the fair curls, and Burton was planting kisses all over the flaxen pate. The whole pantomime was gone through as quick as lightning, and Burton, disentangling himself, caught sight of my Arab

> returning without me, and instead of waiting for an explanation, hurled at him a volley of exasperated epithets, culled from the rich stores of spicy and stinging words which garnish Arabic literature. Burton had revealed himself to me fully before he saw me. The child's clear keen instinct did not mislead it. The big rough monster had a big child's heart behind the hideous grimaces. The child's unerring instinct was drawn by affinity to the child's heart in man.[44]

The incident suggests that Ouida was right, that Burton would have liked a child, provided always that it was no encumbrance to him and did not impede his roving. Isabel's attitude was dead set against reproduction by this time: 'Yes, I have twelve nephews and nieces ... quite enough. Thank God we have none.' With her the maternal instinct was transferred into the ceaseless campaign against cruelty to animals and in the selfless nursing of the terminally sick and dying, which Burton in his Dahomey days had identified as a form of sublimation. But childlessness added to obvious lack of sexual fulfilment must have been a heavy burden to bear. Apart from Burton's own fairly explicit hints in *Stone-Talk* and elsewhere, his perennial desire to spend large amounts of time away from her speaks volumes. He had married her in the first place because she would not be sexually demanding and challenging and thus expose his own inadequacies as a lover, and because she promised utter obedience and deference. Besides, Burton's preferred mode of human intercourse was that of brother to sister or, even better, brother to brother. In this connection his parting words to Isabel during the threatened massacre of August 1870 are highly significant. 'I shall take half the men, and I shall leave you half. You shall go down into the plain with me tonight, and we shall shake hands *like two brothers* [italics mine] and part.'[45]

Such a marriage, particularly where Burton would not permit his wife any overt expression of anger, was likely to have built up a residue of fury at her impotence. We have direct evidence for this from the best possible source: Isabel's own record of a dream which came to her when she fell asleep in a cave on Mount Bezetha outside Jerusalem, during the 1871 tour of the Holy Land. To the astonishment of her Victorian readers, who shied away from intimate personal revelations, Isabel filled fifty pages of her *The Inner Life of Syria* with a detailed account of her dream, which is a classic of 'dream as suppressed wish', in her case the wish for power.

The dream began with Isabel standing before the throne of God, being interviewed by an incandescent Jesus Christ. After blessing her, Christ told her that, instead of sending her to Purgatory, he was putting her to work with the guardian angels to redress the wrongs of the world. Isabel's question to her guardian angel was one which many of her readers must have asked as they ploughed on through the perfervid ramblings of her unconscious: 'How can I, a poor, ignorant and half-educated woman, reform the world?'

She then took off on wings for a guided tour of the world with the guardian angels. Hatred and rage are very much to the fore during this trip round the cosmos. For Burton's co-workers there is nothing but contempt. 'The most pitiable and the most foolish thing that I saw was the condition of men of science . . . they appeared like small objects – midges – studying a little section, a little particle of this huge mosaic, Creation and very ill comprehending that.' She hanged three of her enemies for high treason, flogged all guilty of cruelty towards women, children and animals and banished Burton's enemies the 'Mrs Grundys' to Pitcairn Island, having first married them to 'a certain class of feminine men who seem to have sprung up more thickly of late'.

Next she moved on to the commanding heights of world power. She began by converting the Jews to Christianity. She abolished all republican sentiment, tidied up the 'woman question' and finished with a flight over the battlefields of the Franco–Prussian war, where 'Lucifer and his court' were commanding the French forces. She went to see the Pope and persuaded him to come and live in a gorgeous palace she had built in Jerusalem. Then it was back to England for an interview with Queen Victoria, where she petitioned for favours for Richard: the restoration of his military rank with promotion, the ambassadorship to the Porte or some other oriental court, and a knighthood. 'I shall cry like an angel for justice till it comes', she told the presumably bemused monarch. 'I shall cry for it, Madam, till I die.'[46]

Isabel records that by her watch she had slept in the cave for two hours, and woke from a profound slumber to the urgent tuggings of a goatherd who at first had thought her dead. The dream indicates Isabel's essential psychological instability – which was already clear from her short-sighted, fanatical obsession with Burton, who so ill requited her.

The megalomania and religious fervour hint at a volcanic rage at her own impotence to influence events in either the microcosm or the macrocosm. The obsession with Richard's knighthood was, it is true, eventually to bear fruit, but this public avowal of her wish must have retarded rather than accelerated her cause. The ardently desired meeting with the Pope was never to happen; all she got from her trip to the Eternal City in April 1873 was a dose of Roman fever. Burton, while doubtless relishing the flattering references to himself, must have been appalled at the cavernous frustration and longing so ineptly put on public view by his wife.

But by the time the book was published, Burton had problems of a more serious nature than Isabel's neurosis to deal with. The two years in Syria which saw Burton the Arabist at his apogee, with real power at last, and in the milieu where he most thrived, were to end in disgrace and débâcle from which he never truly recovered.

20

Disgrace and Recall

BURTON'S dramatic recall in August 1871 was an event at the end of a long causal chain. Five separate streams flowed into the river of Foreign Office discontent that finally led them to summon home their man in Damascus after nearly two years of controversy and tension. The first three would not perhaps have been enough alone to constitute 'the case of Captain Burton', but the last two turned the flow into an unstoppable flood. The five factors were, in ascending order of importance, Burton's quarrels with the local Christian community, his war of attrition with the Syrian Jews, his 'bare knuckles' slugging match with the *wali* Rashid Ali, his impossibly poor relations with his Foreign Office superiors, and his role in the 'Shazli' affair, a religious *cause célèbre*.

It was fortunate indeed that Burton was in love with the Arab world, for expatriate social life revolved almost entirely round missionaries. The Anglo-American community took in the Irish and Presbyterian missionaries and the British school, based at Beirut but with an outpost in Damascus. The various 'Reverend Misters' and their wives and children gave Burton no end of trouble. They objected to his flamboyant life-style and his sympathy for Islam; he objected to their blinkered zealotry. Burton fought a running battle with Mentor Montt, superintendent of the British school, and his wife. The Montts tried to distribute Christian tracts, urging Moslems to apostatise, and were keen to proselytise in Damascus, especially during prison visits. The religious temperature rose accordingly, and Moslems talked of burning the tracts, and the Bible too, in a public bonfire.[1] Burton flatly forbade the distribution of tracts, on the quite reasonable grounds that religious tensions in an already simmering cauldron of fanaticism would be still further exacerbated. 'I venture to suggest that missionaries, especially Protestant missionaries in Syria, be invited carefully and conscientiously to consider whether they are justified in exposing a Moslem convert to the imminent risk of losing his life.'[2]

Burton issued an official reprimand to the Montts. Stung by this rebuke, the missionaries tried to go over the Consul's head to Consul-General Eldridge. Eldridge, who hated Burton, took the Montts' side in correspondence with Ambassador Elliott, but had no power to order Burton to revoke the ban on tracts. He and the Montts continued their sniping campaign through 1870–1, and the Montts surreptitiously circulated their material on the frequent occasions when Burton was away on exploration trips. When rumours began to circulate that Burton might be recalled, Mary Montt boasted, absurdly, that the Foreign Office had ordered the Consul either to apologise to her forthwith or leave the Consulate. Another female missionary actually went so far as to get hold of one of Burton's private letters. She then changed the word 'mining' to 'missionary' by a little clever forging, so as to create the impression that Burton was violently anti-missionary, then forwarded the doctored missive to the Foreign Office.[3]

The fanatical zeal of the Montts led to the closure of one Protestant school and to the threatened massacre of Christians in August 1870. Burton expressed incredulity that no one could see how serious and damaging the behaviour of the Montts was; exasperated by the lack of official response, he broke Consular Regulations and published a newspaper article on the whole affair.[4] Nor were the Montts the only source of trouble from the Christian side. A schoolmaster at the Maydan college (one of the British schools in Syria), a former Catholic who had converted to Protestantism, beat up a Catholic boy at the school. The police were involved, and once again Burton had to keep the peace between warring Christian factions. Reporting the incident to Elliott, Burton added: 'The Maydan is one of the most dangerous places in Damascus, and converts are not unusually found ready to offend the faith which they have left. It would be very advisable if a European missionary were to take charge of the Maydan school ... a sensible man, who is not mixed up in the petty quarrels and jealousies of the place.'[5]

In his dealings with the Christian community, and especially the Protestant missionaries, Burton was firm but scrupulously fair. Despite his love of the Druze, he risked alienating them after two Druze brigands robbed two teachers at the British school at gunpoint. Burton demanded reparations from the Druze chiefs themselves. They in turn stormed down to Beirut in dudgeon, intending to play Eldridge off against him. But Burton stymied them by applying for justice to the *wali* – the one step the Druze imagined Burton would not take.[6] Reluctantly they arrested the malefactors and paid full compensation to the injured parties. In the long run Burton did not suffer in Druze estimation for this display of toughness. Ironically, too, Burton himself used the affair as propaganda ammunition against Rashid Pasha, who was on leave when the case broke: 'the chief if not the sole cause of delay has been the protracted absence of H. E. Rashid Pasha, the Wali of Syria.'[7] Given how often Burton himself was absent from his post, this statement was pharisaical in the extreme.

Burton's furious tussle with the Jews began in the wake of the August 1870 massacre scare, which he accused the Russian brothers Donemberg of fomenting.[8] The resulting furore convinced Burton that the true trouble makers in Damascus were not the Arabs but the Jews. Though only 4000 strong as against 13,000 Christians and 70,000 Moslems, they had an influence far beyond their numbers through their connections with international Jewry.

A less indomitable personality than Burton would have thought twice about crossing swords with the Damascus Jews; the predictable result, that he came off second-best, eventually pitched him into outright anti-Semitism. A whispering campaign was set on foot against the Burtons. It was alleged that Burton had had the Donemberg servants tortured, and that Isabel had ripped the diamonds out of the tiara of a Jewish woman at a party and stamped on them, exclaiming that they had been bought with the blood of the poor.[9] But it must be conceded that the Burtons did not exactly help their own cause. The genesis of the diamonds story was an encounter on the occasion of a reception for the *wali*'s daughter in November 1870. The wife of one of the Jewish financiers tried to talk business to Isabel, whereat Mrs Burton turned her back and stormed off imperiously.[10] The Burtons' version was that the overture had been in the form of an attempted bribe, but that Richard refused to be corrupted by Jews, when he had steadfastly turned down Arab bribes.[11]

The other bone of contention was Burton's refusal to help Jewish moneylenders recover their debts, as had been the custom of previous Consuls. Three of Syria's leading Jews were technically under the protection of the British Consul, who was supposed to assist creditors in consigning debtors to jail if they could not pay the monies owed; this was a legal right, which the Jews felt entitled to call on. But Burton adamantly refused to lift a finger in this regard. When one moneylender, who, said Burton, 'had ruined and sucked dry forty-one villages', asked for his aid in collecting £60,000 in debts, Burton sent the man packing. He posted a notice on the door of the Consulate that he would not assist in dunning for debts. He made a point of visiting prisons to see if Jewish financiers had gaoled any Christians or Moslems for debt; if he found any such prisoners he released them. Burton then gave an official account of his actions, with reasons, to his superiors.[12]

The affair built to climax when another of the moneylenders came to the Consulate and threatened him. The man claimed to know a member of the Royal family and boasted that he could have any Consular official recalled at a moment's notice. This was the wrong tone to use with Burton. He replied coldly that the sons of Israel knew little of English Royalty if they thought it would protect such traffic as theirs. The moneylenders then got together and indited letters to London, accusing Burton and his wife of anti-Semitism. Sir Moses Montefiore, the eminent and influential Jewish philanthropist, protested to the Foreign Office, as did Francis Goldsmid, Chief Rabbi of London. Burton wrote a vigorous defence. He distinguished between the bulk of hardworking, industrious Jews and a hard-core of usurers, and declared: 'I am ready to defend their lives, liberty and property, but I *will not* assist them in ruining villages, and imprisoning destitute debtors on trumped-up charges.'[13]

Later, when he had been recalled and the dust had settled, Burton returned to the affair and provided a longer account of his struggle with the usurers. He denounced the system whereby the British government in effect sanctioned those who, for a small outlay of money, acquired entire villages from illiterate peasants, giving them no receipt and adding compound interest at will. He adduced his admiration for Disraeli and his *Tancred* as proof that he had nothing against Jews, only against Jewish usurers, and then unfolded a sorry tale dating back to the very beginning of his Consulship.

> When I arrived in 1869, Shylock No. 1 came to me, patted me patronisingly on the back, told me he had 300 cases for me, relative to collecting £60,000 of debts. I replied, 'I think, sir, you had better hire and pay a consul for yourself alone; I was not sent here as a bailiff to tap the peasant on the shoulder in such cases as yours.' He then threatened me with the British government. I replied, 'It is by far the best thing you can do; I have no power to alter a plain line of duty.' Shylock then tried my wife's influence, but she replied that she was never allowed to interfere in business matters. Then Sir Francis Goldsmid, to our great surprise, wrote to HQ – a rather unusual measure – as follows: 'I hear that the lady to whom Captain Burton is married is believed to be a bigoted Roman Catholic, and to be likely to influence him against the Jews.' In spite of 'woman's rights' she was not allowed the privilege of answering Sir Francis Goldsmid officially.[14]

What particularly infuriated Burton was that those outside the magic circle of international influence, who were not usurers, and had genuine debts to collect, could expect no help whatever from the Turkish authorities. Burton was friendly with two men who had formed a trading company in St John d'Acre, Abraham Finzi, a Briton, and Nicolas Barbour, a Belgian. Since the local governor disliked them he refused to help them recover their genuine debts. They appealed over his head to Constantinople, but the Porte simply referred the case back to the governor, thus making them especially marked men in his eyes, and still with no prospect of getting their money.[15]

Burton survived the storm with the Jews thanks to the support of other religious leaders in Damascus, but he had identified himself in Foreign Office eyes as a 'troublemaker', and his enemies Eldridge and Elliott were not slow to turn this to their advantage. Eldridge told Elliott that Burton was a self-regarding prima donna, who expected laws that had been exercised time out of mind to go into abeyance just to avoid wounding his peculiar susceptibilities; dunning for debts via the Consul 'had always been a part of the Turkish system of government'.[16] Even before receiving this damning report, Elliott had jumped the gun by writing to London about Burton's 'unsoundness' and lack of circumspection. 'He shows as strong a bias against that denomination [the Jews] as against philanthropists of every creed, the missionaries and the educationalists.'[17]

But far more serious than his clash with the Jews was Burton's two-year combat with the *wali*. Rashid Pasha's period as governor of Syria was notorious for corruption, maladministration and venality. Born in 1830, Rashid had risen high and fast in the service of the Porte, but was destined to end his career disastrously, first recalled to Constantinople in chains in 1872, then assassinated in 1876.[18] When Burton arrived in Damascus in 1869, Rashid was still riding high. From the very beginning he was deeply suspicious of this foreigner who knew Islam almost better than he did himself and, as a master of Arabic and disguise, could be Britain's master-spy in the area and penetrate all his (Rashid's) dark designs. Even before Burton arrived, Rashid had made clear to Eldridge his 'deep anxiety' about the appointment. Protocol demanded that Eldridge stonewall such an overture with diplomatic politeness, but Eldridge, who hated and feared Burton as much as Rashid, gratuitously informed the governor that Lord Clarendon had warned the new Consul to be 'extremely careful to avoid doing anything calculated to give offence'.[19]

The first year of the Consulship passed without major incident. Burton was disgusted by what he saw of Rashid's performance, the way he had packed every court and tribunal with his cronies and placemen, and his petty persecution of foreigners whom he did not like. One example was a British subject who had worked as a surgeon in Damascus for four years. Suddenly Rashid's underlings ordered him to give up either his job or his nationality. Until now Burton had contented himself with sardonic remarks about Rashid, but this time he laid on the irony with a trowel: 'I need hardly remark that this unusual proceeding on the part of the government of Syria can hardly be known to H. E. Rashid Pasha, the Wali . . . who has ever proved himself a lover of justice and not unfriendly to the English nation.'[20]

But the gradually increasing tension between Burton and Rashid found overt expression shortly after the reception for the *wali*'s daughter in November 1870, when the Burtons set out to spend Christmas at Beirut. On their way through the passes in the Anti-Lebanon Burton's party was attacked by forty Ghiya skirmishers in Rashid's pay. The Ghiyas peppered the party with bullets, but the defenders formed a screen behind their camels and did not return fire, waiting for the Ghiyas to close the range. Baulked of an easy killing, and without the stomach for serious fighting, the attackers sheered off.[21]

Rashid reverted to diplomatic methods to get rid of this thorn in his side. On 11 January the Turkish authorities presented a *note verbale*, requesting Burton's removal from the Consulate. They complained of his long and frequent absences from his post, his hunting expeditions, and the fact that his wife accompanied him wherever he went. They claimed that Bludan, several hours' journey from Damascus, was his normal residence (it was not) and, absurdly, that Burton entertained an unnatural hatred for Islam. They particularly objected to Burton's 'meddling' in internal affairs, his hawking of stories about imminent massacres of Christians and, above all, his almost weekly column in the *Levant Herald*, where he poured out his bile about the Turkish administration of Syria.[22]

It must have been clear that, the *Levant Herald* misdemeanour aside, there was little substance to these charges. But Ambassador Elliott in his despatch to London chose to endorse the Turkish view of the situation, and boasted that Burton's initial good reception was entirely due to his (Elliott's) efforts. Lord Granville dealt with the matter by sending back a copy of Turkish complaints to Burton and asking for his comments.

Burton made a vigorous reply. He began by asking Granville to disregard the propaganda campaign against him since 'six millions of piastres are at the bottom of the whole affair'. He rehearsed all the problems British officials had had with Rashid, going right back to cases dealt with by Consul Rogers in 1866. He instanced the *wali*'s point-blank refusal to settle the claims of British subjects, his many blatant lies, and ended by turning the tables neatly on Rashid by involving him in the Jewish problems, where Burton was said to be the protagonist. He made great play of the fact that Rashid had sold to the Greek Bishop of Nazareth a graveyard and synagogue at Lake Tiberias which had belonged to the Jews for the last four hundred years.[23] Developing this ingenious theme – which switched attention from himself to Rashid as the true anti-Semite – Burton adroitly linked it with British 'Great Game' considerations. He accused the *wali* of intriguing with the Greek Orthodox Church, and through it with Russia. As for the hoary old accusation about being permanently absent from his post, Burton calmly explained that he had to make frequent visits in a country where every single rumour had to be substantiated. He assured Lord Granville that all his travelling was in the line of duty: 'The dispatches which will presently reach you may serve to prove that in travelling I do not waste my time and that I have acquired in twenty months a knowledge of the country which others do not possess after as many years of residence.'[24] The jibe at Eldridge was transparent.

Elliott again showed his unregenerate hostility towards Burton by describing his list of charges and complaints against Rashid as 'trivial'.[25] Next Eldridge colluded with Rashid in tempting Burton into a situation where he was bound to appear clearly in the wrong. Sitt Jumblatt and the Druze had invited Burton, on his first visit in 1870, to return to the Hauran to explore the volcanoes and copy Greek inscriptions. After their trip to the Holy Land, Burton and Drake set out with alacrity on this new challenge. Burton felt that he had cleared his trip through official channels, since he had actually discussed his plans with Eldridge, who not only gave him the 'all clear' but even hinted he might join the party. When Burton actually asked Eldridge to join them in late May 1871, as he and Drake were on the point of setting out, Eldridge declined to answer.

In addition to his explorations, Burton had an important message to convey to the Druze leaders. The Turks had never subdued these mountain people, and now Rashid was attempting to pick a fight with them so as to have the pretext for another campaign of 'pacification'. Burton counselled stoical patience and moderation in face of Rashid's provocations.[26] When Rashid saw that his schemes had been thwarted yet again, he sent a three-hundred-strong assassination squad into the foothills to ambush Burton as he emerged from the Druze country. But he had aroused Isabel's suspicions by asking pointedly what date the Consul was due back. Ever since the Ghiya ambuscade of December 1870, she and Burton had corresponded in code while he was away. After giving Rashid the wrong date, Isabel sent her servants into the mountains to warn her husband; her ciphered message was attached to a cork in a water bottle. Burton and Drake, forewarned, altered course on the homeward journey, then watched from a rocky eyrie as three hundred riders scoured the plains below, in evident and urgent search of someone. They lit on Burton's dragoman, whom the Consul had sent in a different direction as a red herring, and questioned him. When he refused to divulge his master's whereabouts, the *wali*'s men at first threatened to kill him, but finally contented themselves with burning down his village. Burton recorded the sequel triumphantly. 'So we rode into Damascus, escaping by peculiar good fortune a hundred horsemen and two hundred dromedary riders, sent on purpose to murder *me*. I was never more flattered in my life, than to think that it would take three hundred men to kill *me*. The felon act, however, failed.'

When the Consul returned safely, and blithely attended an official reception that night, Rashid was seen to turn white with shock and rage.[27]

But the *wali* still had a few shots left in his locker. He tried both direct and indirect assault. First he instituted a campaign of persecution against Burton's dragoman Hanna Azar and other personnel at the Consulate who could not be bribed or suborned.[28] Then he complained in the strongest possible terms about Burton's meddling in internal affairs and accused him of going to the Druze country expressly to foment revolt. This time he wrote directly to Burton, as well as to his superiors. The very night after Burton's surprise return and appearance at the Damascus reception, a shaken *wali* sat down to wrong-foot the Consul in the eyes of his superiors. After expressing extreme displeasure at Burton's recent incursion into the Jebel el Hauran, he stressed how important it was for the Druze not to receive any encouragement from agents of foreign powers; it was English sympathy for the Druze that had led them to rebel in 1860. Whatever Burton claimed his intentions were in making the visit, it was clear that the Druze would construe it as endorsement for their frequent rebellions against Turkey. Why had Burton not observed normal protocol, informed the authorities of his proposed visit, and taken a government official with him into the mountains?[29]

Burton replied blandly the next day that the Druze trip was the result of long-standing planning and invitation; Eldridge himself had proposed to accompany him on such a trip as far back as twenty months ago. Besides, it was well known that the Prussian consul had recently completed a similar trip.[30] To his superiors Burton was more forthright. The real reason for Rashid's fury was that the Porte had recently countermanded his proposal for an invasion of the Druze mountains; the ludicrous suggestion that Burton had fomented revolt among the Druze was the *wali*'s enraged response to being thwarted.[31] But Eldridge, in private correspondence with Elliott, denied that he had either discussed the trip with Burton or authorised it, and suggested that, to judge from circumstantial evidence, the Turks had a point. This was too much what Elliott wanted to hear to permit the luxury of probing into Eldridge's obvious duplicity. Elliott informed London of yet another breach of acceptable behaviour by their Damascus Consul. An official reprimand for Burton followed.[32]

Burton now counter-attacked massively. With supporting statements from Protestant leaders in Syria, he made a series of horrific disclosures about Rashid's persecution of Anglican communities and their converts from Islam.[33] The series began with the minor case of the Protestant cemetery in Damascus which was broken into by two marauding Moslems. Since the police force was run by one of Rashid's place-men, a notorious religious bigot, the investigation soon petered out and the culprits got away scot-free. This provided Burton with formidable propaganda ammunition: 'In fact it is hopeless to expect justice from a tribunal constituted as it is at present; when a few Napoleons to the President and to the head clerk can procure any verdict desired.'[34] Backed as it was by the weight of the Protestant community, this was one diatribe from Burton that Elliott could not ignore. The British brought pressure to bear; to Rashid's fury he was ordered by Constantinople to make restitution for the losses sustained in the Protestant cemetery. He hit back by complaining that Burton's animadversions against Islamic tribunals constituted gross interference in the internal affairs of the Sublime Porte.

But much more damaging to Rashid were the revelations Burton made to the world on the fate of Christian converts from Islam. A man named haji hassan converted to protestantism. islamic fundamentalists then beat him up and had him imprisoned. The Protestant community tried to intervene on his behalf, but a mixture of bullying by Rashid and their own cowardice forced them to back off. Eventually Haji Hassan was browbeaten into recanting.[35]

Another convert was threatened with death, then bribed to turn apostate. When he refused, the *wali* banished him from Syria under the pretext of protecting him. But a third case, even more sensational, eventually forced an official inquiry from Constantinople. Arif Effendi, who had become a convert to Greek Orthodoxy in 1868, was arrested on a trumped-up charge of stealing mosque property. Despite being well guarded, he somehow made his way from gaol to the Great Mosque in Damascus, where he 'hanged himself'. No autopsy or medical inquest was ever held. One of Rashid's tribunals pronounced the impossible verdict of suicide, and the *wali* refused to discuss the matter with Burton.[36] This was grist to the Consul's mill. At once he wrote to Elliott: 'I venture to hope that Your Excellency will cause this mysterious death which is terrifying the Christians and rejoicing the Moslems of Damascus, to be made the subject of an official enquiry.'[37] The resulting official letter of explanation which Constantinople made Rashid write, and the official inquiry that followed, simply raised the Rashid–Burton hatred to boiling point. Rashid pleaded with his superiors to force the recall of Burton; he confessed that he would not be responsible for his actions if he had to undergo the twin goads of British government pressure and the letters in the *Levant Herald* from his '*ennemi acharné*', Richard Burton.[38]

Rashid's jeremiads would have had far less effect if the British diplomats in the Turkish empire had presented a united front against him. But Burton was grievously burdened by having to deal with 'the enemy within' even as he battled against the *wali*. Both Eldridge and Elliott were insanely jealous of him and acted almost as Rashid's 'fifth column'. In Eldridge's case the motivation was clear: it was the perennial hatred of the lazy mediocrity for the energetic and highly talented. With Elliott the dislike for Burton had many grounds. As a Privy Councillor and hence on the ultimate court of appeal for Indian affairs, he already had experience of Burton's jousts with the East India Company. He was the son of Lord Minto, and he and his family had taken Speke's side in 'Jack's' notorious feud with Burton. And, even though his was an illustrious diplomatic career that had taken him from Russia to Australia, Elliott seems to have been genuinely fearful that Burton was being groomed in Damascus to take his place in Constantinople.

The inference was strengthened by the confident tone of Burton's despatches to Elliott, which did not confine themselves to political reports from Syria, but made elaborate prescriptions and recommendations for general British policy towards the Porte. Typical is this despatch from Burton to Constantinople in July 1871. 'There are two main reasons which compel Russia to take a vital interest in this corner of Asia. The first is the pilgrimage to the Holy City, which through the Greek Church moves the world from Finland to Abyssinia. The second is the unwillingness of the great northern Empire to see Syria become the highway of British India.'[39]

Instead of scrawling across the copy 'Not your business' or some similar comment, Elliott calmly worked behind the scenes to compass Burton's downfall. In the first place, he overtly supported Rashid's call for Burton's withdrawal.[40] In the second, he and Eldridge lobbied the Foreign Office sedulously to downgrade the Damascus Consulate to a mere Vice-Consulate, in the charge of a local. They began by persuading Foreign Office inspector Kennedy during his visit in January 1871 that this was a consummation devoutly to be wished. When Kennedy duly reported back that Beirut and Damascus should be fused and placed under the direct authority of the Consul-General, Elliott magnanimously 'concurred' with the inspector's findings.[41]

Once he saw what was afoot, Burton struck back vigorously. In private he railed bitterly at the proposal to demote Damascus to a Vice-Consulate 'to gratify the Foreign Office's most undistinguished servant Mr Eldridge'.[42] In his official despatches he had to be more careful, but even so his attack on the reorganisation proposal was biting. If changes were needed, he suggested, they should be along the lines of transferring the Consulate-General from Beirut to Damascus, not vice versa. The pretext for the Kennedy proposals was that the Consul-General would be two days' riding away from communication with Europe, but with Damascus now able to boast of an international telegraph office, an efficient post office and a coach service, the old argument no longer held good. In typical Burton manner, he proceeded to outline his own proposals for the reorganisation of the Consular Service in the Middle East, with the nerve centre in the Euphrates valley. It was very clear whom Burton had in mind, even though he expressly denied the obvious inference, when he declared: 'The Consul-Generals are unable to obtain anything like correct information and some indeed have never visited Damascus. They are entirely dependent upon their Dragomans, they never see Rashid Pasha except when he visits the harbour town for recreation.' He argued that Damascus was Rashid's power-base, so that to station an underpaid Vice-Consul there would be to play into the *wali*'s hands. 'It will perhaps be distasteful to the Consuls-General who find Beyrout a safe and civilised and refreshing place in the immediate neighbourhood of the sea and the mountain. These functionaries – of course I do not include my immediate superior – have lately been using all interest to establish at Damascus Vice-Consuls subject to themselves.'[43]

In his struggle with Rashid, and his *de facto* allies Elliott and Eldridge, Burton's Achilles' heel was Isabel. She had a peculiar capacity to say and do the wrong thing at the wrong time, to alienate neutral observers by her imperious and blustering manner, and to behave to both guests and hosts, unless they were within the inner circle, like Drake and Palmer, as though she were doing them a favour by her presence. She was also prone to the type of accident that hostile propaganda could easily turn to her disadvantage and that of her husband.

An early example was an occasion when a young Arab spat at her and then tried to pull her off her mount. Isabel gave the culprit a good horse-whipping, but claimed that she compensated him later by taking him into her employment and making a friend of him.[44] On another occasion she slashed at an Arab assailant with a riding-crop; then, when her servants set on her attacker, one of their guns went off by accident and the bullet thudded into a wall. Rashid tried to take advantage of the incident and make the Burtons a byword for brutality by burning down the assailant's village in retaliation. But Burton quickly intervened and persuaded the military commander to get the villagers to take a solemn oath of non-violence instead.[45] Yet the two incidents were conflated so as to present the Burtons in an unfavourable light. Eldridge passed on to London the story that a poor beggar sat at Isabel's gate asking for alms and that because he did not rise and salute her, she shot him dead.[46] In other versions of the story the death-toll rose to two dead and one wounded as a result of Isabel's queenly bad temper. Elliott gleefully used the story, while pretending detachment and even chivalry![47]

But the most serious incident involving Isabel became a *cause célèbre*; Burton's cavalier response to it did him serious damage and played into his enemies' hands, at least in the short-term. On 5 May 1871, while

Drake and the Burtons were in Nazareth during their tour of the Holy Land, a prowling Copt attempted to enter Isabel's tent; whether for purposes of rape or of theft was uncertain. Isabel called out for help, and after a brief scrimmage the man was expelled. He retaliated by throwing stones, at which the Burtons' servants rushed forward to beat him up. While this squabble was developing, a Greek congregation began filing out of a nearby Orthodox church. They came running to the help of the Copt, and a general mêlée ensued. Seeing his servants in danger of being torn limb from limb – for they were just six against a crowd of over 150 – Burton and Drake rushed from their tents and tried to stop the fighting. They in turn were set on, with a fusillade of stones so heavy, Burton recalled, that like the arrows of Thermopylae, they seemed to blot out the sun.[48]

The Greeks were no mere *canaille*, for a rich and respected member of the Orthodox Church, carried away by fanatical passion, yelled: 'Kill them, kill them all. I will pay the blood money.' In terror Burton's muleteer called out 'Shame on you! This is the British consul at Damascus, and he is on his own ground.' 'So much the worse for him!' shouted another Greek. Further speech was drowned in the uproar. Just as the entire visiting party seemed about to be overwhelmed, Burton drew a pistol and fired a shot in the air. English and American pilgrims came running from nearby camps, ten of them armed; at sight of these reinforcements the Greeks desisted and slunk away. The entire affair had lasted at most ten minutes.[49]

Fearing a recurrence of the violence, and wishing to identify the culprits while their features were still fresh in his mind, Burton applied for military protection to the local Turkish *kaimakan*. The official replied that he had not enough troops on hand to round up the suspects. The Burtons were compelled to wait five days in Nazareth while soldiers were summoned from St Jean d'Acre. Burton then made the identifications, and the offenders were arrested and taken to Damascus.[50] But Burton made the bad blunder of not telegraphing immediately to Elliott with details of the attack. What looks like incompetence is more readily explained in terms of Burton's desire to complete his travels. Almost certainly Elliott would have cabled him to return immediately to Damascus.

The Greek Bishop of Nazareth was an old enemy of Burton's, from the time the Consul brought his illegal purchase of the Jewish synagogue and cemetery to general attention. Foreseeing the trouble to come once Burton made a formal complaint to the authorities, the bishop concocted a wild and ludicrous story to justify the actions of his co-religionists. According to this, Burton entered the Greek church on horseback during prayers, smashed lamps with his riding-whip, and tried to break open one of the inner doors. Moreover, the alleged serious affray outside was merely a trivial incident involving a handful of stone-throwing children.[51]

In the immediate aftermath of the Nazareth affair, the Greek Orthodox Church closed ranks and stuck to its story. Rashid was delighted, and passed on their version to Constantinople without making any attempt to check it. But Burton obtained affidavits from Drake and a dozen American and English eyewitnesses to the attack that left no doubt that his version of the incident was substantially correct. Faced with this weight of evidence, the head of the Greek Orthodox Church in Syria gave way and conceded that his flock had been at fault.[52]

At first Elliott had been disposed to accept the Greeks' story and blame Burton for having provoked the fracas – it was a case of the wish being father to the thought.[53] But as the evidence emerged, including that from other British Consuls, Elliott was obliged to inform London that Consul Burton had indeed been the victim of a gratuitous attack in Nazareth on 5 March.[54] But he salved his feelings of frustration by demanding to know why Burton had taken so long to report the matter. Burton replied that Nazareth was not connected by telegraph with the rest of the province; even if it had been, Rashid would have tampered with the telegram or destroyed it, as he was wont to do in the case of letters. But Elliott, rightly, did not accept this feeble excuse for failure to report, and reprimanded him.[55]

Confident of Elliott's support, Rashid had rushed to judgement and assured his superiors that the Greek version was entirely correct. Elliott was obliged to rap the *wali* firmly over the knuckles and remind him that the British government completely accepted their Consul's version of events and would be pressing for due process and eventual compensation accordingly.[56] This exposed Rashid to his superiors in Constantinople as engaged in a vendetta against Burton, and called in question all his previous allegations. When the dust settled on the Nazareth affair, Rashid Pasha's days as governor were numbered.

But neither did Nazareth exactly redound to Burton's credit. He and Isabel, it seemed, attracted trouble wherever they went. Accordingly, a directive went out from Odo Russell, Under-Secretary at the Foreign Office, that Burton was to hold himself in readiness for fresh instructions in Damascus, and not stir from the city until further notice.[57] This order led to Burton's most signally contemptuous disregard of the Foreign Office hierarchy to date. He and Isabel concocted a response that would enable them after all to spend the summer at their beloved Bludan.

Since the instructions from London were crystal-clear and unambiguous, the Burtons hit on the idea of asking permission from Elliott, in hopes that Odo Russell had not put him in the picture. Elliott naïvely replied on 20 July: 'There is nothing in the regulations of the service to prevent a consul going a few hours' distance from his usual residence without special leave.'[58]

But Burton had not even waited to receive this reply. When no answer came from Elliott within forty-eight hours, he began to fear that the ambassador might be checking the situation with London. So he set out for Bludan, leaving his political masters with a *fait accompli*; needless to say, he equipped himself with his invariable selective 'sick note'. Too sick to sign consular invoices but never too ill to climb mountains, explore rivers or trek across wildernesses, Burton had after ten years of consular service become an expert exponent of the *maladie imaginaire* he had so despised in his parents.

Needless to say, Granville and Odo Russell were beside themselves when they realised that, despite the express order they had issued, the wandering Consul had still managed to slip through the net. Even if Granville had not already decided to recall Burton on other grounds, this would have been the last straw. By now Burton's protestations that he had absented himself 'on medical advice' because of the extreme heat of a Damascus summer fell on very deaf ears.[59] A rueful Elliott confided to London the singular way in which he had been duped, and kicked himself for not having suspected something from the fact that it was *Isabel*, not Burton, who asked for permission to go to Bludan. 'Although I was not aware of your lordship having prohibited Captain Burton from leaving Damascus, I was convinced that there was something which had been kept back from me and I felt, moreover, some hesitation in returning any answer to a request which, if made at all, should have come direct from the consul.'[60]

Burton's behaviour convinced the Foreign Office of something they had suspected for some time: that Burton was no longer in full possession of his mental faculties. How else explain his actions over the Shazlis – the affair which, above all others, convinced Lord Granville that he had to pull Burton out from Syria forthwith, before he ignited a religious war?

Isabel's Franciscan confessor, Fray Emanuel Forner, besought her help in the case of an esoteric Muslim cult known as the Shazlis, who seemed to have evolved a syncretism of Sufism and Catholicism. No more potent religious cocktail for intoxicating the Burtons could be imagined. Forner explained that he had extended the mantle of his protection around the Shazlis once they started to experience visions of the Holy Family and other miracles. Intrigued by this, Burton spent several evenings with the Shazlis, in disguise, mingling with the faithful and pretending to be one of them. He was impressed by what he saw, though at first drew the line at extending consular protection to them, as urged by Isabel and Forner. The Franciscan pointed out that up to 25,000 Shazlis were now ready for Christian baptism. Once news of this mass conversion leaked out, retribution would follow swiftly from the Moslems: persecution was certain and martyrdom likely. Only the Burtons could save them.[61]

The sequence of events in 1871 is confused, though certain clear lines do emerge. On their return from the Holy Land in May, the Burtons found that the secret was out. Alarmed by the scale of the projected apostasy, the Damascus authorities decided to make an example of the Shazlis, and sentenced a dozen of them to death, ostensibly for the evasion of military call-up. Furious protests from Burton produced a commutation of the sentence to banishment to Tripoli. With Fray Forner dead, suddenly, and under mysterious circumstances, the Shazlis turned wholeheartedly to Burton as their champion.[62]

It was now that Isabel tempted Richard to an act of supreme folly. Envisaging herself as godmother at the baptism of truly 'born again' Christians, she suggested that he buy a tract of land in Syria under special terms, exempt from land tax, and there establish the Shazlis as an independent community, along the lines of Brigham Young's Mormons, the Mennonites, the Shakers or the Oneida community.[63] But Syria was not the USA, and the Burtons, Richard especially, should have been level-headed enough to see that the idea was a chimera. Yet Burton the Nietzschean was flattered by this appeal to his 'princely' qualities, and took the bait. Burton wrote to Lord Granville to put him in the picture about the mass conversions, the subsequent persecutions, and his plans for a Shazli community under British protection. There is some suspicion that he might have been acting in devious fashion to avoid the transfer which had been rumoured for some time, for he suggested that the Jerusalem Patriarch Valerga come to Damascus to preside over the mass baptism, adding: 'Should I be compelled to quit Damascus before the proposed visit of the Papal Nuncio and the Latin Patriarch of Jerusalem, the effect may be fatal to the cause of the converts, and may lead to disturbances whose strength can hardly be estimated.'[64]

Events now moved swiftly towards débâcle. A puzzled Granville communicated directly with Patriarch Valerga. This cleric, who knew nothing whatever of the Burtons' grandiose plans, betrayed a signal lack of political *savoir-faire* by making open inquiries of Rashid Pasha. The *wali* was delighted. Here at last was clear and incontrovertible proof that Burton was a meddler in Syria's internal affairs, that Isabel was a Catholic fanatic, and that both of them bade fair to ignite a ferocious religious war. The resulting scandal finished Burton. In Isabel's words: 'It broke his career, it shattered his life, it embittered him on religion; he got neither Tehran, nor Morocco, nor Constantinople.'[65]

The recall was couched in language that not even Burton could claim to misunderstand. After reminding him of the 'good behaviour' conditions attached to Clarendon's 19 June 1869 memorandum, Granville wrote: 'I regret to have to inform you that the complaints which I have received from the Turkish government in regard to your recent conduct and proceedings render it impossible that I should allow you to continue to perform any consular functions in Syria.'[66] Burton's diary entry vividly conveys the poignancy of his humiliating recall. 'August 18th – Left Damascus for ever, started at three a.m. in the dark, with a big lantern; all my men crying; alone in coupé of diligence, thanks to the pigs. Excitement of seeing all for the last time. All seemed sorry; a few groans. The sight of Bludan mountains in the distance at sunrise, where I have left my wife. *Ever again?* Felt soft. Dismissal ignominious, at the age of fifty, without a month's notice, or wages, or character.'[67]

That night in Bludan, after reading Granville's note, Isabel slept badly. She had a dream in which someone told her to go to her husband; she awoke and went back to sleep three times and each time had the same dream. She therefore saddled her horse while it was still dark and rode off into the gloom, in hopes of intercepting the Beirut coach. She caught up with it at the half-way house, after five hours' hard riding. In Beirut she found Richard stalking alone, a prophet without honour. She had proved herself the true adventurer, the perfect 'she-mate'. 'He was so surprised and glad when he saw me! I was well rewarded for my hard ride, for when he saw me his whole face was illuminated, and he said, "Thank you, *bon sang ne peut mentir*." '[68]

In Beirut Burton was showered with condolences, from all except the British diplomatic community. The Consul-General of France put him up at his private residence, but Eldridge cut him dead. Eldridge's pathetic longing for deference from the man who was his intellectual and moral superior emerges clearly in an overheard remark: 'If Burton had only have walked in my way, he would have lived and died here.' Burton repaid the compliment; Eldridge, he said, 'was famous only for drinking beer and exactly suited the Foreign Office by confining himself to so narrow a circle.'[69]

Burton departed for England, while his wife returned to Damascus and Bludan to pack and follow. Isabel's hopes of presiding over a mass baptism of the faithful were stone dead. But the themes of baptism and death converged in a symbolic act of expiation and renunciation Isabel felt impelled to perform after a dream which came to her two nights before leaving Bludan for ever. She saw a vision of a young Bedouin boy she had once doctored with quinine and Warburg drops; the lad seemed to be calling to her. She rode off into the desert and located his tribe. Sure enough, the boy was dying. So Isabel performed the last rites by substituting the sacrament of baptism for extreme unction and also conflating Christianity and Islam as the Shazlis had hoped to do.

'Would you like to see Allah?' she asked the boy.

'Yes, I should. Can I?'

'Are you sorry for all the times you have been naughty and said bad words?'

'Yes', he said. 'If I get well, I will do better, and be kinder to grandmother.'

'I thought that was enough', Isabel recorded. 'I parted his thick matted hair, and, kneeling, I baptized him from the flask of water I always carried at my side.'[70] The boy expired soon afterwards. For Isabel his demise symbolised both the loss of all that was dear to her – like the panther cub, all creatures she cared for seemed to have the mark of death on them – and the destruction of the dream of power she had enjoyed in the cave outside Jerusalem, which had seemed about to come true with the Shazlis. Some of the spark of life went out of Isabel following the Damascus fiasco. It is surely significant that it was on her return to England that the first signs of cancer were diagnosed.

21

In Limbo Again

On reaching London, Isabel found her husband in one room of a second-class hotel, too proud to argue his case at the Foreign Office. The dauntless Isabel stormed down to Whitehall and spent three months harrying Lord Granville and the senior officials there. At first the mandarins stalled her with many a wink and nod, hinting that Burton's life was in danger from outraged Mohammedans.[1] Burton commented drily: 'I have been shot at, at different times, by at least forty men who fortunately could not shoot straight. One more would not have mattered much.'[2] But there was substance in the argument, as Burton later conceded with his account of Rashid's ambushes. Tyrwhitt-Drake, left as his personal agent in Damascus, was threatened with assassination, and the British government took the threat so seriously that they passed a note to the Turkish authorities holding them responsible in the event of his death.[3]

Eventually Isabel wore down the patience of Whitehall. They admitted that the Shazli affair had been the principal reason for her husband's recall. By this time Burton's dismissal had become a *cause célèbre* and the propaganda battle between friend and foe of the ex-Consul was being waged daily in the press.[4] Elliott, Eldridge and Jago (Burton's successor in Damascus) did their best to circulate the most damaging canards on Burton's behaviour, but Burton's friends were eloquent and in England the press was generally sympathetic to his cause. Drake produced testimonials from Kurdish elders, Bedouin chiefs and Christian missionaries. The case promoted by Burton's enemies was greatly weakened by the disgrace of Rashid Pasha and the trial of the Nazareth offenders, which produced a verdict favourable to Burton.[5] Professor Palmer even concocted a story that Jago had taken one look at the turbulence of Damascus and decamped. In vain did Jago protest that he had retired from Damascus through illness; the mud stuck.[6] The general impression left in the minds of the British public was that

Burton had defended his corner valiantly against Turkish despotism but that the trimmers and idlers of the Foreign Office had sacrificed him to appease the wrath of the Porte and to keep their own lives comfortable. The combined pressure of Isabel within the portals and public opinion baying outside at last led Lord Granville to assure Burton personally that he had done the best any man could in the trying circumstances of Syria, and that no blame attached to him.[7]

Yet the private toll taken on Burton by the affair was very great. This was how the Stisteds recalled his state of mind when he arrived in England penniless in September 1871: 'Never had we known him so wretched, so unnerved; his hands shook, his temper was strangely irritable, all that appreciation of fun and humour which rendered him such a cheery companion to old and young alike had vanished. He could settle to nothing; he was restless, but would not leave the house; ailing but would take no advice – it was indeed a melancholy spectacle.'[8]

His failure in Damascus haunted Burton for the rest of his life. He knew very well that his hopes for high diplomatic appointments in the Arab world were now vain. At times he conjured with the fantasy that he might return to Damascus as a private citizen to retrieve his reputation. He told the archaeologist Roland Michell that he intended to revisit the scene of his greatest happiness even at the risk of being knifed in the streets; he also stated that he had a presentiment he would die there.[9] But his enemies continued to insist that such a madcap visit would do him no good. In 1878 Wilfrid Scawen Blunt reported from Damascus that Burton's reputation with all races and classes was poor, though this was mainly Isabel's fault.[10]

Deeply wounded by his failure in the very area where he had set his heart on success, Burton cast around for a focus for his rage. He found one in the Jews who had closed ranks against him internationally when he refused to aid their brethren, the Syrian moneylenders. Burton had previously been ambivalent towards the Jews, but from 1872 onwards his sentiments are those of full-blooded anti-Semitism, reaching its apogee in the posthumous *The Jew, the Gypsy and El-Islam.*[11] Fawn Brodie has ingeniously argued that a close study of this work reveals extreme ambivalence, further evidence of Burton the 'dual man', and a strong element of self-hatred unconsciously manifest; the duality in Burton's psyche is even mirrored in the distinction he draws between Sephardim (the intellectual and scholarly branch of the Jews) and the Ashkenazim (the warrior strain). This argument can indeed be sustained as far as *The Jew* (written in 1872) is concerned.[12] Burton, in homicidal fury that his life had been ruined, recognised well enough that the victim of injustice, if given a chance, will strike back murderously. One of his favourite sayings was: 'it is usual with the weak, after being persecuted, to become persecutors.'[13]

Burton's later animadversions on the Jews show no such nuances. In the *Arabian Nights* Burton resurrects the principal charge he levelled against them in *The Jew*: that of ritual murder of Christian infants.[14] And his other anti-Semitic jibes contain few enough ambiguous resonances.

> Even during the worst days of Jewish persecutions their money-bags were heavy enough to lighten the greater part, if not the whole, of their disabilities. And the Moslem saying is, the Jew is never your [Moslem or Christian] equal: he must be either above you or below you. This is high, because unintentional, praise of the (self-) chosen people . . . when you want anything from any of the (self-) chosen people you speak of him as an Israelite; when he wants anything of you, you call him a Jew, or a damned Jew, as the case may be.[15]

Burton also accused the Jews of making money by patching up old clothes and sending them out to Africa. Even so he contrasted their commercial guile with that of the grasping Christian: 'his [the Jew] commercial cleverness will induce him to allow me some gain in order that I may not be quite disheartened; the latter [the Christian] will strip me of my skin and will grumble because he cannot gain more.'[16]

The predominant emotion in Burton towards the Jews is envy. Paradoxically, the chosen race seemed to have cornered the market in the very morality of strenuousness to which Burton himself aspired. There is a Nietzschean flavour to Burton's envious appraisal of the Jews: they possessed, he thought, 'an indestructible and irrepressible life-Power without which they would have utterly perished . . . a vigour, a vital force . . . prodigious superiority of vital power.' For Burton the Jews really were special. It was their unique power he resented, not their belonging to a closed culture. For a different type of anti-Semite, what was objectionable about the Jews was what they shared with Islam: the consciousness of being within a closed, hermetically sealed culture. Doughty expressed this point of view: 'Islam and the commonwealth of Jews are a great secret conspiracy, friends only of themselves, and to all without of crude, iniquitous heart, unfaithful, implacable.'[17]

For thirteen months after his recall Burton lived in limbo. The first month he spent putting the finishing touches to the manuscript of *Zanzibar*, which had reappeared after twelve years. Then he moved on to his first draft of *The Jew*. By this time Burton the author was increasingly receiving short shrift from the critics. Ever since *Lake Regions* his reputation in literary circles had declined steadily.[18] The fate of *Zanzibar* was no different. The *Observer* accused Burton of mere dogmatic assertion without argument. The *Examiner* was even more withering: 'We are afraid that these two rambling egotistical and excessively bulky volumes will prove tiresome reading even to the most arduous students of African travel.' Burton let most of the criticism float over him, rousing himself to vigorous riposte only when the magazine *Field* accused him of plagiarising from Humboldt.[19]

Meanwhile Granville refused to concede the idea of a posting to Teheran; he responded with the offer of a Consulship in Para, Brazil. This, effectively a demotion, was simply Santos all over again, so Burton turned it down as being beneath his talents. By now the Foreign Office had decided that if Burton was ever to be offered another posting, it would have to be in a Catholic country where his wife's religious zeal could do no harm. It would take time for a suitable berth to become vacant.

Both sides settled in for a long war of attrition. For the next twelve months, and particularly the winter of 1871–2, the Burtons were desperately poor. They were reduced, in effect, to accepting charity at some of the great houses of England, and principally with their relations. Their chief benefactor was Isabel's uncle Gerard, who entertained them at his residence at Garswood, Lancashire, near Newton-le-Willows. After spending September to December 1871 in London, Richard and Isabel were at Garswood, with a side visit to the Earl of Derby in January 1872.[20] In February they were in Edinburgh visiting the Stisteds, then, after a short trip to London to attend various Royal Geographical Society functions, they returned to Garswood for the three months from March to May.

Before leaving London Burton had one public chore to perform. He gave evidence in the case of the Tichborne Claimant, his drinking companion from Buenos Aires. By now Burton had become convinced that the Claimant was a charlatan, and he gave his evidence accordingly. But, as in 1855, the opportunity to joust with learned counsel and prove himself the intellectual superior was too tempting for Burton to resist. Some of his withering sarcasm drew appreciative laughter from the gallery. Standing in the witness box with the great scar from the Berbera fight clearly visible on his cheek, he toyed contemptuously with the cross-questioning.

Counsel: 'I understand that you are the Central African traveller.'

Burton: 'I have been to Africa.'

Counsel: 'Weren't you badly wounded?'

Burton: 'Yes, in the back, running away.'[21]

Yet the arrogant public Burton masked a near-despairing private man, now staring penury hard in the face. As they travelled up to Garswood at Christmas, the Burtons seemed to sustain the ultimate disaster. Their time in London had reduced them to their last £15; Burton had even been forced to turn away some mouth-watering oysters in a restaurant on grounds of expense. As he noted in his diary. 'They were three shillings a dozen – awful, forbidden luxury!' Now, on the northbound train, Isabel dropped one of the precious fifteen coins from her purse. It rolled along the compartment and slid out of reach between the boards of the carriage and the door. At this fresh calamity Isabel could bear no more and broke into uncontrollable sobbing, while Burton vainly tried to console her. Fortunately Uncle Gerard retrieved the situation by paying their return fares, keeping them for months entirely free of charge and giving his niece £25 into the bargain.[22]

The first RGS meeting Burton attended in February 1872 was just after a painful visit to Edward in the Surrey lunatic asylum. Almost as if to rub salt in the wounds, Sir Roderick Murchison had invited Burton's old enemy Rigby to be the guest of honour. Isabel had never seen Richard so angry, and thought at first that he was going to attack the dignitaries on the platform. But Burton vented his rage by making a fool of Rigby. First he got him to state categorically that there were no Abyssinians in Zanzibar, then he produced comprehensive refutation of Rigby's statement.

Burton's mood lightened momentarily at a Mansion House dinner, when he and Isabel were amusing themselves by making waspish comments in Arabic on the proceedings. Suddenly to their delight their neighbours chimed in with agreement expressed in Arabic; it turned out that the only four Arabic speakers in the room had by chance been placed together.[23]

But this was an exception to the general gloom. At the RGS Murchison went out of his way to snub Burton. 'Old Murchison hates me', he noted in his journal. 'He was anxious to pay due honour to our modern travellers, to Livingstone and Gordon, Speke and Grant. He has done me the honour of not honouring me.'[24] Yet Burton did himself the most harm. When the RGS approached him to head the proposed Society expedition to relieve Dr Livingstone (this was after Stanley had 'found' Livingstone, but before the world knew of the event), Burton answered in his best 'bored aristocrat' manner that he had no enthusiasm for the task, first, because it was 'rather *infra dig* to discover a missionary' and secondly, so as not to let the Foreign Office off the hook.' Had the FO asked me I should of course have gone, but I won't let them get rid of me quietly.'[25]

Even more self-destructive was his behaviour at a fund-raising lunch for the Livingstone expedition. The Prince of Wales was seated on Burton's left and as the soup was being served the Prince enthusiastically offered to put up £500 at once if Burton would consent to head the expedition. Burton, in one of his 'black dog' moods, replied with a bored yawn, 'I'll save Your Royal Highness that expense.'[26] The upshot was that Verney Cameron went instead, and became the first European to cross Africa east to west.

A visit to Edinburgh at last provided Burton with the kind of challenge he was looking for. He met a man called Lock who offered him £2000 if he could go to Iceland and make a report on the sulphur mines there. Lock offered first-class passage and expenses for Burton alone (Isabel was forced to remain with Uncle Gerard), the fee of £2000 to be paid on receipt of the report. Burton threw himself into the project with gusto. Embarking at Edinburgh on 4 June, he sailed along the coast to Aberdeen, then threaded through the Orkneys, Shetlands and Faroes, before arriving in Reykjavik.[27] Everywhere he went, Burton kept the most meticulous notes, hoping to produce another anthropological gem. The two-volume treatise he (inevitably) produced is full of fascinating information; once more Burton displayed his genius for getting inside the skin of a culture within weeks.[28]

Yet Iceland was, overall, a disappointment. The 'giddy rapid rivers' proved to be only three feet deep, the precipices were mere slopes, the expected threat from the polar bear turned out to be a threat *to* the polar bear, since the starved and emaciated specimens Burton saw could hardly run away from the hunters' guns. Mount Hekla, which he ascended on 13 July, he found a commonplace heap, half the size of Hermon. The Icelanders themselves seemed to reflect his own unacceptable face: 'A very characteristic of the race is the eye, dark and cold as a pebble – the mesmerist would despair at the first sight.'[29] Most disappointing of all were the geysers, which merely slurped and hiccuped instead of gushing skyward; Burton dubbed them humbug. As for the 'midnight sun', this was purely an irritant; its rays had to be excluded from his uncurtained bedroom by his landlady's flannel petticoat, which she lent him for that purpose. But at least the mining investigations gave him something to take his mind off his career, or lack of it. After crisscrossing the island, he returned to Reykjavik on 26 August, excited by the prospective returns from the sulphur mines. On 1 September he embarked for Scotland and on the 15th stepped ashore at Granton.

At first his fortunes seemed no better for the endeavour. Mr Lock took one look at the report, pronounced it flimsy and refused to pay the £2000. Burton was in violently disagreeable mood when he attended a public dinner in Edinburgh. By the time the meal was over he had managed to contradict with acerbity every person within earshot. Luckily his brother-in-law Sir Henry Stisted, also present at the dinner, overindulged and then reeled off a succession of anti-Scottish jokes to a progressively hushed audience. *His* indiscretions easily eclipsed Burton's.[30]

When he rejoined Isabel, Burton received two pieces of mixed news. One was that her mother, never a friend to him, had died. The other was an offer from the Foreign Office of the Consulate at Trieste. At

£600 a year plus £100 annual allowances, this was a significant dip in income from the £1000-a-year Damascus Consulate; it was clearly a demotion and would universally be seen as such. Moreover, Granville had let Isabel know through informal channels that this was his final offer: it was Trieste or nothing. Yet the Burtons were by now in such desperate financial straits that Richard had no choice but to accept. On the plus side, the post was an openly acknowledged sinecure. Lord Derby had made this clear in a classic remark to Burton's predecessor, Charles Lever, the novelist: 'Here is six hundred a year for doing nothing and you are just the man to do it.' It was simply a matter of signing a few papers and entertaining a handful of visiting celebrities. The rest of the Consul's time was free.

Burton put the finishing touches to his two volumes on Iceland and published his major findings as anthropological papers.[31] But Iceland was not his forte. He was a man of the steamy jungles and the baking deserts, a tropical explorer and traveller; the frozen north held no magic for him. Almost all his observations on Iceland are acidulous or depreciatory. The fey Icelandic skaldic ethos, with its 'fetches' and 'kennings', was not for him, and he made scathing reference to the far-fetched and obscure allusions in Scandinavian poetry.[32] The favourite Burton technique of killing two enemies with one shot is in evidence when he takes sideswipes at both the frozen north and the fatuity of Christianity. 'The icy hell is necessary for people who inhabit cold regions and who in a Hot Hell look forward to an eternity of "coals and candles" gratis. The sensible missionary preached it in Iceland till foolishly forbidden by Papal Bull.'[33]

William Morris, who had toured the island in 1871 and found there the inspiration for his finest narrative poem, *Sigurd the Volsung*, was outraged at Burton's supercilious levity and wrote to his principal Icelandic contact: 'I hope you will smash Burton when you do fall on him: he is one of the curses of our humbugging society nowadays.'[34] Other criticisms of Burton were at a less elevated level. An anonymous letter signed 'Brimstone' in the *Mining Journal* poured scorn on him for geological incompetence. 'I have the greatest respect for Captain Burton as a traveller, but none whatever as an inspector of mining properties.' Burton's response was typical. 'I have no idea who "Mr Brimstone" is, but I must say that he deserves a touch of his own metal, hot withal.'[35]

Burton was not able to depart for Trieste until 24 October 1872, since he had to undergo minor surgery for a tumour on his back, a by-product of the blows he had received during the furious mêlée at Berbera. He was much in the company of Winwood Reade – arguably his closest friend until Reade's tragic early death in 1875 at the age of 37 – and of Edward Bulwer-Lytton and Wilkie Collins.

The month he spent in London before his departure was notable for the acquaintance he struck up with H. M. Stanley, the lion of the hour following his dramatic 'finding' of Livingstone at Ujiji in Central Africa. Stanley had been involved in furious altercation with the RGS, whose committee first doubted his claim to have met Livingstone, then, when unimpeachable evidence was produced, began to snipe and cavil at his latitudinal observations and calculations. In an increasingly desperate and reprehensible attempt to discredit Stanley, the RGS turned to its other old enemy, Burton, in hopes that he might find Stanley guilty of charlatanry. The Council members were buoyed up in their hopes by Burton's known low opinion of Stanley. In *Two Trips to Gorilla Land* Burton sneered at Stanley 'the discoverer of Livingstone' and contrasted his exploits with the 'admirable work' of the 'gallant Lieutenant Cameron'.[36] Even more mocking was this estimate of Stanley's immortal four words to Livingstone, as published in Clements Markham's *Ocean Highways*: 'Had the travellers fallen upon one another's bosoms and embraced, they would have acted like Arabs from the days of Esau and Jacob until 1873. Walking deliberately up to each other, taking off hats and addressing a few ceremonious words, so far from impressing Arabs with a sense of dignity would only draw forth such comment (to put it in a complimentary form) as "Wallah, what sort of meeting is this? Verily they are wonderful things, these Franks".'[37]

The two greatest living African explorers (for Livingstone by now was at the threshold of death) came face to face on 21 September. Much to their surprise, the two men rather took to each other. Burton told his RGS contacts that Stanley was the stuff of which the true African explorer was made, and that it was idle to disparage his achievements.[38] Stanley recorded similarly favourable impressions in his journal. 'He [Burton] appears to be a hardy man – with a bronzed complexion, of medium height and powerful figure. His face struck me for its keen, audacious look. He spoke well and avoided jarring on my nerves. If he was not so wicked – I have a strong feeling that I should like him.'[39]

About a week later Stanley and Burton met again at a dinner given by Clements Markham (who hated Stanley and adored Burton), at which Verney Cameron was also present. Stanley noticed Markham's peculiar habit of measuring the extent of his regard for his guests by the variety of handshake. Thus Stanley got one finger of Markham's right hand to shake, Cameron as a naval officer got two, while Burton as an old friend received the entire hand. Stanley soon spotted that Burton took a perverse pleasure in presenting himself to the public in as unflattering a light as possible – 'it has been Burton's humour to feed the malice of the world with libels on himself.' But even so there was an ambivalence about his attitude. He wished to be thought hard and wicked and was pleased that society was shocked by his defiance of its values. At the same time he was secretly annoyed that society took him so readily at his word. But morality apart, Stanley was bowled over by the intellectual range and grasp of his fellow explorer. 'He is brilliant in conversation – and upon any subject not connected with himself, his tastes and prejudices, he exhibits sound judgment and penetration. I am sorry that he is so misguided – for his talents deserve a wider recognition than he is likely to obtain.'[40]

The two men maintained a wary, respectful relationship over the years. Burton grudgingly acknowledged the greatness of Stanley's achievement during the trans-Africa charting of the Congo in 1874–77.[41] Stanley undoubtedly thought of Burton as one of the few great men he had met. In 1887 Sir Samuel Baker's brother Valentine reminded him irresistibly of the Burton of the mid-seventies.[42] As to Burton's mockery in *Two Trips to Gorilla Land*, Stanley very neatly turned his flank by attributing bad faith to his tormentor. 'The interior [of Africa] everyone hopes to retain as a preserve for his own exclusive benefit and I am not sure but many travellers in Africa have been magnifying the dangers of African travel in order to deter others from penetrating the continent. There are many passages in Captain Richard F. Burton's *Gorilla Lands* which create these suspicions and Joseph Thomson, if the newspapers report his speeches correctly, appears inclined to follow the same course.'[43]

Later Laurence Oliphant, who met Stanley in Paris in 1872, tried to purge his guilt for his role in the Speke–Burton estrangement by turning on Stanley and claiming that in his writings, particularly *Through the Dark Continent*, Stanley had depreciated the role of Speke and Burton. In his journal Stanley dealt with the charge judiciously. 'Burton perhaps has suffered from the greater honour paid to Speke's memory by me – but I have always had sufficient reasons for paying my little tribute to Burton also – as a writer, an accurate observer, ethnologist etc. The hardest thing I have said of Burton that I remember just now is that as a travelling littérateur he had no superior but that his judgment of men, white or black, was not to be trusted, because his prejudice so often misled him.'[44]

Burton finally set out for Trieste on 24 October, but made such a leisurely progress southwards that Isabel, who, as ever, had been left behind to pay, pack and follow, caught up with him in Venice. Burton was in the steamer salon, busily scribbling, waiting for the next departure to Trieste, when Isabel walked in, accompanied by the British Consul in Venice. 'Hallo, what the devil are *you* doing here?' was Richard's greeting. 'Ditto,' Isabel replied brusquely.[45] Abandoning his plans for an immediate departure, Burton accompanied his wife back to her hotel, where they at once repaired to the lounge and continued work on their respective books; Isabel was taking her plunge into authorship with the first draft of *The Inner Life of Syria*.

But the significant thing about the meeting was the phraseology both used to describe it. Quite independently Richard and Isabel recorded they had shaken hands 'like a pair of brothers'. Vice-Consul Brock at Trieste later described their demeanour as like that of a couple of undergraduate chums: Burton would walk along with his gamecock under his arm – for he had learned the art of cock fighting in Sind and approved the bloody sport – while she did the same with her bull-terrier. For Burton the fraternal bond was the paradigm case of human relationships, and the marriage was never, on his side at least, an affair of passion. At worst it was a business arrangement and at best an alliance of comrades who chugged along quite nicely together.[46] Burton had sacrificed the tugs of the flesh he undoubtedly felt for his Louisas and unknown Persian maidens for a mess of emotional pottage, composed of three parts dumb adoration and two parts servile deference.

22

Trieste

TRIESTE was an outpost of the Austro–Hungarian empire, a polyglot settlement of Austrians, Italians, Slavs, Jews and Greeks, each with their own ghetto. The outer suburbs and the country round about, however, were solidly Slav. The population of some 150,000 was nominally Catholic, but Burton estimated that only about 20,000 of them were devout; the rest he divided into '30,000 freethinkers and 90,000 indifferent'. With his customary shrewdness, at least when violent prejudice did not distort his judgements, he observed a phenomenon which twentieth-century sociologists later endorsed: when religious feeling atrophies in a Catholic country, it is likely to turn to socialism.

The free port of Trieste had three distinct sections, but the heart was the old city, dating from the time of Strabo, a filthy, unsanitary and smallpox-ridden labyrinth, with an annual mortality rate from disease of fifty per thousand, as against figures of twenty-two and thirty-six per thousand in, respectively, London and Madras. Trieste had many singular features. Wooed by the newly united nations of Germany and Italy while still part of the ramshackle and fissiparous Austro–Hungarian empire, it was also one of the dearest cities in Europe where, as Burton put it, tourists had been virtually routed by the hotel managers. In the 1870s one English lord was presented with a bill of £45 for two nights' bed and breakfast, not much short of the normal Italian rate a century later.

Trieste was also a port vulnerable to three different winds, the *bora*, *contraste* and *scirocco*. The winter wind or *bora* had been known to blow people off the quays into the sea with sudden violent gusts of more than 100 miles an hour. The summer wind or *scirocco* blew straight from Africa and was wet, warm and debilitating. When the two winds blew together, there arose the situation of *contraste*, when the luckless Triestans had to endure the disadvantages of both.

The British Consular offices were located just by the railway station, but the Burtons lived in an apartment of ten rooms some distance away, where Isabel's Sacred Hearts and other Catholic icons vied for place with Burton's oriental memorabilia and bric-à-brac – 'the Cross and the Crescent' was one reporter's description of the suite of rooms. Pride of place went to the 8000 volumes of Burton's private library. Burton chose the fourth-floor eyrie, with no one living above them, so as to be away from the dust, noise and street smells. Their friend Alfred Bates Richards early queried why the Burtons lived in a flat and so high up. 'To begin with', replied Burton, 'we are in good condition, and run up and down the stairs like squirrels. If I had a great establishment, I should feel tied and weighed down. With a flat and two or three servants one has only to lock the door and go out.'[1]

Richard and Isabel quickly settled into a routine. Rising early, at four or five, they would read and study until noon. There followed a light meal and a couple of hours fencing and swimming. Only at 3 p.m. or thereabouts would Burton saunter down to the Consulate, where the Vice-Consul played King Stork to his King Log. Like Wemmick in *Great Expectations*, Burton liked to keep private and public life rigidly distinct. As he remarked, 'I have my consulate in the heart of the town. I don't want my Jack-tar in my sanctum; and when he wants me, he has usually been on the spree and got into trouble.'[2] In the evening there would be a 'mess' with a dozen or so friends at the Hôtel de Ville, where a good dinner and a pint of country wine could be procured for three shillings. This system avoided housekeeping and domesticity. After coffee, kirsch and cigarettes, Richard and Isabel returned home to read themselves to sleep.

Isabel's afternoons were spent mainly in her animal welfare work, the sisyphean task of persuading foreigners not to maltreat their pets and beasts of burden. 'You see', said Richard, 'that my wife and I are like an elder and younger brother living *en garçon*. We divide the work. I take all the hard and scientific part, and make her do all the rest.' Isabel found a further interest, in extending the apartment by leasing further rooms as they became available, so that in the end the 'flat' contained twenty-seven rooms and ran round the entire building block. She summed up Trieste as follows.

> As nice a place as one could wish for in Europe. It is a pretty spot, with (for us) a good climate, all kinds of creature comforts, friends, amiable society, plenty of self-made occupations and resources, and time to carry them out. You may read, write books, learn German, Italian, Russian, Greek, Slav; have singing masters, drawing masters, fence in winter and swim in summer, but commercial work in a small, civilised, European sea-port, under-ranked and underpaid . . . cannot be considered compensation

> for the loss of a wild Oriental diplomatic life, and might be considered a waste of such material as Captain Burton.

Another visitor put it more trenchantly: 'a quarter of a hundred languages are hardly needed for the entry of cargoes at a third-rate seaport.'[3]

Burton's life was that of lotus-land. He became friendly with the Austrian Governor-General Baron de Friedenthal, who often took him on Adriatic cruises in his official yacht. Saturday to Monday Burton liked to spend in the Slav village of Opcina, 1200 feet above Trieste and one hour's travelling time away, where there were panoramic views of the port and environs. Unencumbered with servants, Richard and Isabel found this their favourite mode of 'getting away from it all'.

When not in Trieste, Burton spent his time exploring every ruin and historic site within a hundred-mile radius, often in company with Tyrwhitt-Drake. Once he spent five days sleeping rough among the villages of the Cicci, who lived in the *Karso* or *Karst* of Istria. When Burton first told friends of this feat they were incredulous, until one day a party of Cicci made a rare visit to Trieste to sell charcoal and greeted Richard as a long-lost brother. The Karso continued to be one of Burton's favourite spots for gypsy-like travels. This desolate stony tract of land in the mountains above Trieste, extending about seventy-five miles in each direction, contained more than seventy villages where the ancient Istrian folk-ways were still intact – a cornucopia for the anthropologist.[4] Burton took Drake on other joint ventures into the wilderness, which had their share of hazards. One day in January 1873 they were lost all day in the midst of a raging *bora*. On another occasion Burton nearly lost his life by plunging into an ice-cold stream which ran underground, like Alph the sacred river in the Coleridge poem. He hoped to be carried right under the mountain so that he could see where the stream finally emerged; fortunately for him he got cramp before the icy waters plunged into the gloom of a subterranean pothole.

For all the incidental pleasures of Trieste and the Istrian peninsula, Burton could never forget that he was in disgrace after Syria. He consoled himself with the thought that Stendhal had been French Consul here and had written the *Chartreuse de Parme* in this very port. Burton's predecessor Charles Lever, who died in post in 1872, was also a novelist. So the omens were good for Burton the writer. This time he was determined to keep out of trouble, and merely observed the endemic factionalism of the area, between Italians and Austrians and between both of these and the Slavs (while the Jews and Greeks cornered the port's trade), with a detached eye; he even had a rule that politics and religion could not be discussed in his house. He was much taken with the idea that, at 51, he was the same age as Ovid when the poet was banished to Tomi. Burton became very fond of the Latin poet, devoured his *Tristia* and *Ex Ponto* with an almost morbid interest, and frequently compared Ovid's plight to his own.[5]

This was doubtless the genesis of the Burtons' sudden trip to Rome in the spring of 1873, which turned into an extended tour of Italy. Isabel caught Roman fever and developed blood poisoning; Richard used the excuse of her convalescence to conduct a lengthy investigation into the Etruscan sites, which bore fruit in a book, *Etruscan Bologna.* He had barely set foot back in Trieste than he was off again, this time on a newspaper assignment to cover the Vienna Exhibition. He and Isabel spent three weeks there, appalled at the expense of Viennese hotels, which mulcted them £163 for the twenty-one day sojourn. The Austrian Emperor requested a meeting with the famous explorer. Diplomatic protocol forbade a tête-à-tête with a mere Consul, so the pleasure of the military company of *Captain* Burton was requested.

Eighteen-seventy-four was a bad year for Burton. It opened promisingly with the first performance in Trieste of *Aida* – for operas came to the port straight from La Scala, Milan, and were performed there years before they were seen on the London stage – but then came a bad attack of Asiatic cholera in the city, so virulent that the Burtons tried to eat as many of their meals as possible on board passing English ships. In May Burton and some friends scaled six snow-capped peaks in the Schneeberg range, but on his return Richard was suffering agonies with inflammation of the groin and another tumour. He was very ill for three months and had to undergo two operations before the growth was completely removed. To add to his problems, Burton proved peculiarly resistant to anaesthetic. It took forty minutes and two bottles of chloroform before he went under. (Later, when he had teeth extracted by gas, he also baffled the dentist's anaesthetic processes.) By one of the dreadful ironies of which Burton's life was full, he came round from the first tumour operation to hear that his beloved Tyrwhitt-Drake had died tragically in Egypt of malarial fever, at the age of 28. The shock succeeded where the chloroform had failed, in sending him into unconsciousness.[6]

Burton's long illness in 1874 was a ghastly trial for the scholar and man of action. The unsqueamish Isabel made a first-rate nurse. Every day she washed and re-bandaged the wound. The invalid's diet of eggs, honey and milk was eked out with special 'safe' luxuries, such as brandy and cigars. Burton was confined to a wheelchair, and taken on visits to the spas of Battaglia and Recoaro for the waters. From the wheelchair Burton progressed to an upright sedan chair, suspended on two poles, which required the services of four doughty porters. Impatiently Burton tried to accelerate his return to full walking fitness, but every time he tried to force his body to take a short cut and allow him to walk, the surface tissue of the wound gaped open and the scarring process had to start all over again. There followed a long convalescence in Padua and other parts of northern Italy before recovery in the autumn, which he celebrated by another trip to his beloved Karso.[7]

In December Burton sent Isabel back to England to promote a new business scheme that had occurred to him. It was a feature of Burton's later years that one half-baked scheme for making money followed another in quick succession, all of them ultimately unsuccessful. This time it was the idea of patenting a tonic, to be called 'Captain Burton's Tonic Bitters', patterned on the well-known Angostura Bitters (composed of tree bark and raw alcohol), and designed as an instant restorative after a heavy night's drinking. Even Isabel, the Burton adulator, was only half persuaded of the viability of the scheme. Predictably the idea flopped, so Isabel spent her time in London lobbying for a knighthood for Richard. This was also a waste of time. 'Lord Clarendon had told me in 1869 that he thought me very unreasonable, and that if he had one to give away, there were many people that he would rather give it to than Richard.'[8]

In the spring of 1875 the Burtons came to England on leave. They took boat trips on the Thames and to Oxford, met Gladstone and Jowett at Monkton Milnes's, and Richard had his portrait painted by Sir Frederick Leighton. In the summer he made another trip to Iceland, and returned after six weeks suffering from lumbago and gout. There was a partial *rapprochement* with the RGS, when the Society's Council recommended to the Foreign Secretary that Burton, 'the father of Equatorial African discovery', be given some further mark of royal favour, over and above the Society's own Gold Medal awarded in 1859. There was a meeting too with Laurence Oliphant, who expressed contrition for his earlier chicanery with Speke. Finally, Burton signed off his English leave with a 'disgusted' type of letter to *The Times*, grumbling about the newly opened Mont Cenis tunnel.[9]

The return journey was via Boulogne, Paris, Vichy, Turin, Milan and Venice. In Paris they found the fires of *revanchisme* for the Franco-Prussian war stoked high, with many regarding an outbreak of hostilities as only a matter of time. Burton dissented. He found a new spirit abroad in Paris after the Commune – a grim bloody-mindedness which he did not remember from his youth – but in no way did it presage the military spirit necessary to vanquish Prussia. He thought the French Army frankly incompetent, and predicted accurately enough that almost half a century would elapse before France was ready to fight the Germans.[10]

The Burtons arrived in Trieste on Christmas Eve 1875 and almost immediately embarked for India. The first part of the trip, down the Red Sea, was virtually a reprise of his 1853 journey. They visited Jeddah, where Richard showed his wife the scene of his early triumphs.

They then endured the nightmare of a crowded pilgrim ship returning to Bombay. One person a day died during a twenty-three day crossing of the Arabian Sea, from the combined effects of privation, fatigue, hunger, thirst, opium, vermin and general squalor.[11]

Burton took Isabel on a painstaking tour of the scenes of his early life: Bombay, Karachi, Poona, Hyderabad, Golconda, Multan, Sind and Goa.[12] He was now no longer the 'Mirza Abdullah' of old, but a cross-grained, dyspeptic reactionary, writing querulous letters to the Indian press and blimpishly averse to the innovations he saw. Part of the problem, as he himself confessed, was that by now a kind of metaphysical melancholy seized him if he was obliged to travel to 'green' lands rather than the gold-white desert.[13] Two illustrative quotations on the late Burton attitude to India will suffice. In the first he defends caste as 'one of the most enlightened inventions of the civilised East. It supplies an admirable system of police, acts as political conservatism, and leads to high excellence in crafts, arts and sciences, by breeding generation after generation, till an instinctive superiority is acquired.'[14] In the other he inveighs at the changes that had overtaken the country. 'A few years ago we might have travelled dressed partly as natives; now Young India, by which I mean Anglo-India, would certainly wax very violent if he saw us, and declaim grandiloquently against our "morbid propensities" and our "contemptible sacrifice of nationality in aping Asiatics".'[15] He also capped the cliché about travel's being a voyage of self-discovery with the following offering to the shade of 'Mirza Abdullah': 'How very unpleasant to meet one's Self, one's Dead Self, thirty years younger!'[16]

The return trip from India, though in a steamship of the Austrian Lloyd line, was almost as uncomfortable as the outward voyage in the pilgrim vessel. Trieste confronted Burton with two of the recurring motifs in his life: Africa and death. There was news of the Italian explorer Gessi's circumnavigation of Lake Albert, which provided a faint spark of hope, Stanley's thorough exploration of Lake Victoria the previous year notwithstanding, that Speke might still be denied the Nilotic palm.[17] Death had meanwhile claimed Sir Henry Stisted, and Burton's arch-enemy Rashid Pasha had been assassinated. On receipt of this news, Burton came as close as ever in his life to jumping for joy. To exult in the demise of one's enemies is not the most publicly-lauded kind of emotional exhibition, but Burton cared as little for official Christian morality ('humbug') as he did for what the world in general thought of him.[18]

Almost immediately the restless Consul was on the move again. The lure of precious metals once more had him in thrall. Burton did not find it difficult to persuade Khedive Ismail that Egypt's political problems could be solved by the exploitation of Egypt's gold resources.[19] An interview with Ismail's officials during the stopover in Egypt returning from India was the first stage in Burton's devious enticement. The Khedive aspired to bring European civilisation to Egypt; Verdi's *Aida* commissioned to celebrate the opening of the Suez canal in 1869 but not performed until 1871, symbolised the proposed new order. But Ismail's plans foundered on lack of money. It followed that Burton would be listened to with attentive ears and Ismail invited him to Egypt to discuss his proposals. He in turn used the 'order' from the Khedive as an excuse to procure himself six months' leave.[20]

Burton proceeded to Cairo where on 25 March 1877 the Khedive gave formal permission for a prospecting mission in the land of Midian, on the south-east of the Sinai peninsula – the far side of the Gulf of Aqaba. The idea of striking a mother-lode was the brainchild of Burton's old friend Haji Wali, who told a story of having stumbled across a rich deposit there. The notion of Midian as a second California seemed plausible to Burton, on the basis of his biblical and Arabic studies.[21]

In the days before he left Suez at the end of March for his 'El Dorado' quest, Burton struck up another important friendship, with Admiral McKillop, commander of the Khedive's navy. McKillop was another roistering, hard-drinking, larger-than-life character. He and Burton hit it off famously. Burton called McKillop 'The Pirate', and McKillop retaliated by dubbing him 'The Brigand'. Their hell-raising became the talk of Cairo. Michell left memorable descriptions of dinner-parties where Burton gave a Tower of Babel performance by conversing with as many guests in as many languages as he could manage.[22]

On 31 March Burton set out for a three-week reconnoitre in Midian. Alas, Haji Wali proved a first-rate fantasist. The mineral samples they brought back contained only minute traces of gold, insufficient to make mining operations feasible. Outwardly, Burton maintained his aplomb and declared that it was only the constraints of time that had prevented them from making a 'killing'.[23]

The Khedive was sufficiently intrigued by the might-have-been to summon Burton back for a second, more protracted expedition. By now Ismail had warmed to the explorer. On his return to Cairo in October 1877, this time with Isabel, he was fêted and honoured in the Khedive's palace, and entrusted with a much larger prospecting party. The truth is that underneath the lavish hospitality Ismail was desperate, and prepared to gamble heavily. The Russo–Turkish war of the previous few months had drained Egypt of blood and treasure. Diseases such as horse-pest and typhus had raged unchecked in 1876–77. The Nile rose too late and brought fever in its wake.

The Khedive put up £2000 as initial capital. Burton put together a tatterdemalion expedition, comprising a few artists and a number of

Egyptian and Sudanese soldiers. No metallurgist or practical prospector accompanied them.[24] Haji Wali joined them at Zagazig, but at Sharma pleaded indigestion and returned home, after pocketing a fee for doing nothing. He died in 1883; Burton never saw him again. His ill-conceived expeditionary force then made three separate journeys, between each of which they paused at Moilah. But this four-month foray proved no more successful than the pilot venture the year before. Burton eased his disappointment by diversifying into archaeology. There were countless catacombs striated with graffiti, remains of furnaces, ancient coins, 'stones and bones'.[25] But no gold.

On one such trip during this expedition Burton had his closest shave with death since Berbera. In his diary for 11 February 1878 he graphically described the peril he found himself exposed to in the Gulf of Aqaba:

> Written in sight of death. Wind roaring furiously for victims: waves worse. No chain can stand these sledge-hammer shocks. Chain parts and best sheet-anchor with it. Bower and kedge anchors thrown out and drag. Fast standing broadside on: sharp coralline reef to leeward, distant 150 yards. Sharks! Packed up necessaries ... engineer admirably cool; never left his post for a moment, even to look at the sea ... Deck pump acting poorly. Off in very nick of time, 9.15 a.m. General joy, damped by broadside turned to huge billows. Lashed down boxes of specimens on deck and wore round safely. Made for Sinafir, followed by waves threatening to poop us. Howling wind tears mast to shreds. Second danger worse than first. Run into green water: fangs of naked rock on both sides within biscuit-throw; stumps show when the waves yawn ... with much difficulty slipped into blue water. Rounded south end of spit, and turned north into glorious Sinafir Bay. Safe anchorage in eight fathoms. Anchor down at 10.15 a.m., after one hour of cold sweat. Distance seven miles on chart, nine by course: *Mukhbir* never went so fast; blown like chaff before wind. Faces cleared up. All-round shaking of hands; '*El Hamdu-li'llahi*' followed by a drink. Some wept for joy.[26]

It had been touch and go. Burton thought it the closest call he had ever seen. The poor condition of the *Mukhbir* had placed them seriously at risk. The boiler could have seized up, the masts rolled or the vessel sprung a leak at any moment. If they had escaped the reef, the waves and the sharks, they would have been cast ashore on the desert island of Tiran, far from the mainland. It would have taken their friends a week to be alerted to their plight, by which time they would all have perished from starvation and lack of fresh water.[27]

The Khedive was gravely disappointed with the lack of success, but made a determined effort to save face. There were audiences and receptions at the palace, and it was given out that the rock specimens would have to be sent to London for testing before the full results of the expedition could be announced. Even more elaborate camouflage was laid on when Ismail opened an exhibition of geological samples from the Land of Midian on 9 May; Burton had brought back twenty-five tons of minerals and archaeological artefacts.[28]

'They went in search of gold and found graffiti' was how one wag described the end product of four months' moil and toil. Later travellers put a somewhat higher estimate on Burton's endeavours. He found important inscripions, recorded his discoveries with scholarly accuracy and explored fully the caves of Jethro. On the other hand, Burton was not able to penetrate into the important ruins at Al Quraiyat, later visited by St John Philby, or to push through the Khuraita pass into the Bani 'Aliya country. Nor did Burton have the time to explore the gullies of Lauz or the other mountains of the Midian chain. But Philby paid Burton the highest compliment when he visited the area in the twentieth century: 'I laboured under the disadvantage of not having with me my copies of Richard Burton's two works on Midian and its minerals.'[29] Interestingly, Burton's greatest nineteenth-century rival as interpreter of Arabia to the West, Charles Doughty, was at this very time on the other side of the Kisma desert. Neither 'Kalil' nor 'Sheikh Abdullah' knew that his rival was almost within hailing distance.

Burton had been promised five per cent of gross profits if a workable seam was found. His colossal disappointment at such total failure was compounded when Ismail refused to reimburse his expenses, so that he took a large loss on the enterprise. So despondent was the traveller that he even, for the first time, began to grow jaundiced about the desert. The sand-dunes of romance were in fact 'huge rubbish heaps'. The distance between fantasy Arabia and the reality could be easily measured. Its valleys were 'mere dust-shunts that shoot out their rubbish, stones, gravel and sand in a solid flow, like discharges of lava ... such is the near, the real aspect of what, viewed from Makna, appears a scene in fairyland.'[30]

Isabel had found Richard looking ill and tired on his return from the desert. He left Egypt, tired of Cairo's 'intrigues, silly reports of the envious ... the weary waiting ...'. The sea voyage home was the exact opposite of convalescence. Leaving Cairo on 10 May, they boarded a steamer bound for Trieste via Corfu. The trip quickly became a nightmare. Shortage of space meant that Isabel shared a cabin with two nurses while Burton bunked with five other men. A mere three stewards tended to the wants of seventy-two passengers, there was no doctor aboard, the food was appalling, it was impossible to get a bath, the beds were narrow and hard, and on all sides there arose the clamorous noise of cats and dogs. Through the paper-thin cabin wall Burton could hear the cacophony as an Armenian woman beat her maid, 'who objected to the process in truly dreadful language'. The ship limped along at nine knots and was overtaken by a storm off Cape Matapan and the *scirocco* off Istria. After seven months, Trieste was a welcome haven.[31]

23

Marking Time and Declining Health

THE Khedive Ismail had another of the outstanding eccentrics of the Victorian Age in his service in the person of Colonel (later General) Charles 'Chinese' Gordon. Gordon, by now veteran of the 'Ever Victorious Army' in China and Governor of the Khedive's Sudan province, first opened correspondence with Burton in July 1876.[1] Gordon, the nineteenth century's 'sea-green incorruptible', had accepted the £10,000-a-year post with a remit to put down the slave trade, on condition that he was paid just one-fifth of the stipend. In return he kept the Sudan under control with a handful of soldiers and oversaw the lucrative export trade in ivory. Gordon gathered around him a galaxy of talent as his lieutenants: Romolo Gessi, Ernest de Linnefants, Charles Chaillé-Long, Emin Pasha and the great Victorian hero Frederick Burnaby. Now he proposed to add Burton to the list, in short to make him governor of Darfur province in the western Sudan, with a mixed population of Arabs and blacks and a thriving trade in cattle, melons and tamarinds.

A glowing letter of admiration arrived in Trieste in June 1877, offering Burton the Darfur post on the most favourable conditions.

> You now, I see, have £600 a year, a good climate, quiet life, good food etc., and are engaged in literary enquiries, etc. etc. I have no doubt that you are comfortable, but I cannot think entirely satisfied with your present small sphere. I have therefore written the Khedive to ask him to give you Darfur as Governor-General, with £1600 a year, and a couple of secretaries at £300 ... Now is the time for you to make your indelible mark in the world and in these countries. You will be remembered in Egypt as having made Darfur.[2]

This proposal did not fit at all with Burton's plans to become rich on the gold of Midian, and introduced an unwanted complication into his relations with the Khedive. Somewhat curtly Burton wrote back with his refusal, hinting that the salary was inadequate – on the face of it, a palpable absurdity. This crossed with another missive from Gordon, in which he spoke with rapture of the ethnological and archaeological treasures of the province, the chain armour from the days of Prester John, the wealth of arcane circumcision rites. None of this interested Burton, smitten as he now was with gold fever. Understandably, Gordon was put out when he received Burton's cold refusal. He shot back a scathing reply. '£1600, or indeed £16,000 would never compensate a man for a year spent actively in Darfur. But I considered you, from your independence, one of Nature's nobility, who did not serve for money. Excuse the mistake – if such it is.'[3]

Burton tried to parry the insult by explaining patiently that the Khedive wanted him back in Egypt for further explorations in Midian. That was in October 1877. In December Gordon wrote back emolliently. 'I am glad you are with the Khedive, he is most kind, and there are few men for whom I would do what I do for him, for he has not been at all well treated. I am here for some time, for affairs are much more complicated, and I want to finish off once and for all with the two great questions here, when these are finished then I hope never to come back to these parts alone.'[4]

Still in hopes of luring 'Ruffian Dick' to an area where his military gifts could be fully used – for Gordon always had a huge, probably inflated, regard for his martial abilities – Gordon came to Cairo during the second Midian exploration in hopes of speaking to Burton in person. He was disappointed, somehow contriving to miss his quarry by a matter of days.[5] But he did interview Isabel and pressed her hard on the subject of Darfur; he offered to raise the salary to £3000, which was more than he drew himself. Isabel, who had swallowed whole her husband's wild tales of the wealth of Croesus to come from Midian, replied fatuously that, in the light of their golden expectations, £3000 would scarcely pay for Richard's gloves. Gordon persisted even in the teeth of this rebuff, and in August 1878 wrote to Burton: 'I will give you £5000 if you throw up Trieste.' This time he was indeed striking while the iron was hot, for Burton had just returned, jaded and dejected, from the second Midian fiasco. Significantly too, this time Gordon drew from Burton the real reason for his refusal to serve. 'You and I are too much alike. I could not serve under you nor you under me. I do not look upon the Soudan as a lasting thing. I have nothing to depend upon but my salary, and I have a wife, and you have not.'[6]

It was probably as well that Burton did not nibble at Gordon's bait. All available evidence suggests that Burton did not combine the ironclad military discipline and administrative flair needed to hold in check the turbulent province of Darfur. Most likely, when a crisis broke, Burton would be inspecting inscriptions in some remote temple. Burton was a man of action in a purely personal sense. What Gordon needed at this juncture was someone like Stanley, with whom he later (1883–84) actually proposed to work in the Congo. What he got as governor of Darfur was Rudolf Carl von Slatin, an Austrian officer. On the defeat of Hicks Pasha in the early stages of the Mahdist revolt, Slatin surrendered to the Mahdi (1883) and spent twelve years as his captive before escaping and returning with Kitchener for the Omdurman campaign.[7]

When Gordon's journals were published posthumously, following his death at the Mahdi's hands at Khartoum in January 1885, Burton praised the general's selfless devotion, truthfulness and saintly integrity but criticised him for 'hallucinations ... to which all African travellers after a time become subject.' And later in life he eulogised Gordon's seminal work in Equatoria province in the early 1870s.[8] But he queried Gordon's achievements at two levels. In the first place, he was sympathetic to the Mahdi's cause: 'the gallant Sudani negroids ... who were battling for the holy cause of liberty and religion and for escape from Turkish task-masters and Egyptian tax-gatherers.'[9] Secondly, he blamed Gordon for having no Arabic, and for neglecting to provide his relief army in 1884 with a competent Arabist. This was a hallmark of British rule in Egypt; Evelyn Baring, Lord Cromer, Viceroy of Egypt for twenty-five years, spoke no Arabic either. As Burton later told Frank Harris; 'if Gordon had spoken Arabic well, spoken it as a master, he would have won the Madhi to friendship.'[10] Gordon's lack of Arabic seemed to Burton all the more a major defect in that, as a Calvinist, he was temperamentally attuned to the Islamic belief in Fate. When Burton's translation of the *Arabian Nights* appeared in the same year as the disaster of Khartoum, some organs of the British press lamented that it had not proved possible to employ Britain's greatest practical Arabist in the Sudan.[11]

On 7 July 1878 the Burtons set out for another home leave, which was to be notable for Burton's sustained dabbling in spiritualism, a subject that had attracted him since the middle of the decade. It was not perhaps surprising that Burton, steeped in the lore of the East, where phantoms, fantasms, wraiths and shades of all kinds were part of the furniture of reality, should have been drawn to a study of the occult. *Vikram and the Vampire*, the Hindu classic he translated in Brazil, is full of spectral appearances and mysterious manifestations. He was not interested in spiritualism in the sense of communication with the dead. Burton's concern was 'the pursuit of the ineffable' or Wittgenstein's 'whereof one cannot speak'. He described himself as a 'spiritualist without the spirits.'[12] Isabel, too, was drawn to the mental world of the spiritualists, despite the severe reservations of her Church. She evolved her own form of syncretism, whereby the telepathy and 'other side' of the mediums was simply the working of the appropriate Guardian Angel. Hence her unsurprising conclusion: 'Catholicism is the highest order of spiritualism.'[13]

Isabel and Richard spent much of the winter of 1878–79 at seances and in the company of spiritualists. The delighted fraternity welcomed the great explorer as one of their own.[14] But he was never that. It suited Burton to be their fellow-traveller for a time, and the 'numinous' world their belief-system portended answered a deep need in his soul. He was also deeply convinced from his experiences in India and Arabia that mysticism answered profound aspirations in the human being and that the 'wisdom of the East' was no mere cardboard cliché. But he was as critical of the fakery, hucksterism and charlatanry of the spiritualist movement, with its 'ectoplasm' and deep-throated Red Indian chiefs, as one would expect a man of his formidable intellect to be.

> As a spirit is supposed to know all things, the spirits that came were always just as illiterate as their invokers. They dropped their 'hs' in exactly the same place where he or she did, and used exactly the same expressions and were just as or rather more vulgar, especially the joking spirits . . . no man positively, absolutely, no man – neither deity nor devil-angel nor spirit-ghost nor goblin – has ever wandered beyond the narrow limits of this world – has ever brought us a single idea or notion which belongs to another and different world . . . when the spiritualists speak of a 'materialised spirit', I can think only of a form of speech whose genus is *Taurus, species Hibernicus*.[15]

To a large extent the Burtons were simply amusing themselves by indulging in a fashionable Victorian pastime. For Isabel the spiritualist meetings had the added advantage that they provided her with a platform for sounding off about her own concerns, and seemed to hold out the prospect of conversion to Catholicism by stealth. A typical meeting hallowed by the presence of the Burtons would begin with a few pithy and relevant remarks by Richard. Isabel would then get up and harangue the audience on any subject that took her fancy. Total ignorance of the matter under discussion was no impediment to her.[16]

Burton soon found other targets for his occult interests. Like later scholars with a mystical streak, Robert Graves for one, he was attracted to oghams and the decipherment of runic script. Much of his work in this area was published in the *Athenaeum*.[17] Both the journal and the Club of the same name meant a lot to Burton. When in London he would go early to the Club, and work all day in the library without a break, his only refreshment a cup of coffee or the box of snuff that was invariably at his side. The only interruption he permitted until he stopped work at 6 or 7 p.m. was from an eccentric Austrian woman named Mrs Giacometti Rodgers, of uncertain marital status, who amused Burton by her permanent jousts with authority. Doubtless he detected a fellow Quixote. Rodgers carried on a kind of vendetta with London cab-drivers, whom she was forever hauling before magistrates for this or that infraction or 'impertinence'. Burton, who detested all members of the service industries who tried to 'dun' him (i.e. pester for payment), sympathised with her and often advised her on the planning of her feuds.[18]

In the summer Burton wore a uniform of white trousers, white linen jacket and shabby beaver hat on his daily visits to the Athenaeum. A familiar figure in the library, he was nonetheless sometimes a butt for the supercilious upper-class members of the Club. The Hon. Henry J. Coke once twitted him on the subject of his summer 'uniform'.

'Hullo, Burton, do you find it so hot?'

'I don't want to be mistaken for anyone else.'

'There's not much fear of that without your clothes.'[19]

Time was when such tail-twisting would have led to an automatic challenge to a duel. In his late fifties Burton was mellowing, but there were still signs of the old lion. At an official Prime Ministerial reception, he was caught in the crowd on a staircase and crushed up against a woman's train, unable to move backward or forward.

'Oh dear,' said the woman, 'this horrid man is choking me.'

'It's that blackguard of a Burton!' cried her husband.

Burton flashed with anger. 'I'll have you out for this and if you won't fight, I'll thrash you like a dog!' he thundered.

Isabel managed to reach him and pour oil. The worst of it was that before leaving home he had made her a solemn promise to be on best behaviour.[20]

If humour is what we share *with* others, and wit that which we direct *at* others, it must be conceded that Burton's sense of fun was always in the area of wit rather than humour. He continued his campaign against elderly women, particularly old maids, and any manifestation of 'mutton dressed as lamb'. He dealt with one such *vieille cocotte* as follows: 'Good gracious, you haven't changed since I saw you forty years ago. You're like the British flag that has braved a thousand years the battle and the breeze.'[21]

But women were not the only targets for his acid. He particularly disliked the aristocratic wimp or 'masher'. One such specimen, pomaded and dressed in a white waistcoat, approached him at a reception one evening.

'Aw, are you one of the waiters?'

'No – are you?' said Burton, twirling his Chinese mutton-chop whiskers, 'for you look a damned sight more like a waiter than I do, and I was in hopes you were, because I might have got something to drink!'

Waiters were in fact a particular target for his anger, and woe betide the *garçon* who kept Richard waiting for his food or brought him inadequate portions. (It is an interesting thought, incidentally, that all the great African explorers, Livingstone, Stanley, Speke and Burton, were 'heavy grubbers'.) On one occasion, when he ordered a steak, he was brought a very small one. He turned it over contemptuously with his fork and drawled, 'Yes, that's it. Bring me some.' On another occasion he was brought a diminutive cup of coffee. 'What's this?' he roared. 'Coffee for one, sir', said the waiter. 'Very well, bring me coffee for ten', he demanded with perfect aplomb. Yet another sign of Burton's touchiness concerning the 'robber barons' of the hotel trade and their excessive profits came in his 'translation' of the sign outside a Paris hotel which announced 'English spoken here'. The meaning was clear, said Burton: 'I'm a thief, you're a fool.'[22]

Another target for Burton's wit was the clergyman, of whatever stripe. In Goa in 1876 a Catholic archbishop struck up conversation with him on board ship. Disarmed by Richard's initial courtesy, the bishop tried to overdraw on his intellectual bank-balance. Riled by Burton's Darwinism, he pointed to some monkeys shinning about in the rigging and said,

'Well, Captain, here are some of your ancestors.'

'Well, my lord,' came the reply, 'I at least have made some progress, but what about your lordship, who is descended from the angels?'[23]

It was with mixed emotions that Burton bade *au revoir* to English shores in January 1879. Every time he came home on leave he felt more like a stranger. 'I never visit England without being surprised at the vile furs worn by the rich, and the folly of the poor, in not adopting the sheepskin with wool inside and the leather well tanned.'[24] And always he was the prophet without honour in his own country. A strenuous campaign by Isabel to win him a knighthood came to nothing, even though there were clear signs that the Burtons were at last beginning to win a decisive victory in the propaganda war against their enemies.

Illness now began to make serious inroads. Just before leaving England Richard went down with pleurodynia. Then he set out alone to travel back to the Consulate via Hamburg, Berlin, Leipzig and Dresden. He met Isabel in Trieste, only to find that she was now seriously ill. She had sustained a bad fall in Paris, injuring her back and ankle. She never fully recovered her health after this accident, and had to return to London almost at once for an operation to have the bones in her back reset; she was in very great pain throughout 1879, and the trauma may have accelerated the cancer from which she eventually died.

Alone again, Burton continued to explore the environs of Trieste. He found Dalmatian society extremely patriarchal. Even among the aristocracy, in the old-fashioned houses the women of the family would wait in person upon their guests, and mothers would dance attendance on their adult sons.[25] On one of his excursions he found striking confirmation of his own belief in the mimetic effects of violence. A peasant couple had unwisely shown their two children, aged six and seven, all the stages in the slaughter of a pig. Next day the parents left them alone with the baby. The two children promptly cut its throat and strung it up, as they had seen their parents do with the pig.[26]

But at least Burton could hardly complain about the work-load at the Consulate. The Vice-Consul did all the chores. The entries from the Foreign Office records make the point clearly.[27] Insofar as the consular work impinged on him at all, it afforded him considerable amusement. Burton once received a note from a sailor who had beaten up a local drinking companion and then tried to rob him. Addressed to 'the Council' with a dirty thumb-mark, it read:

> Burtin,
> i ham hin trobel, kum and let me haout.
> Tim Trouncer.[28]

Burton tried to get himself back to peak fitness by a regime of daily walks and fencing, while he waited for Foreign Office approval of yet another venture for the Khedive.[29] Scarcely had Isabel rejoined her husband after convalescence in London than he set out for Egypt a third time to seek his fortune in the putative gold fields of Midian.[30] But 1879 had seen dramatic changes in Egypt. In June 1879 Ismail abdicated in favour of his eldest son Tewfik and sailed away to bloated exile on the Bosphorus, having first emptied the Egyptian treasury of its remaining £3 million. Tewfik refused to honour any of his father's projects, including the Midian scheme. Burton tried to appeal over the Khedive's head to his British 'protectors', but Sir Evelyn Baring refused to make the gold of Midian a Cabinet issue. Burton was left 'to eat his heart out in impotent rage and disgust at his bad luck'. He moped about Shepheard's Hotel, correcting proofs of his turgid books, for which the readership declined yearly.[31]

Despite the failure of his Midian hopes, Burton made use of the Foreign Office leave to remain in Egypt on private business. When not carousing with McKillop, he was much in the company of William Robertson Smith, a multi-talented fellow-spirit: anthropologist, archaeologist, philologist, Old Testament scholar. He was expelled from the Chair of Hebrew at Aberdeen for heresy, but went on to become Professor of Arabic at Cambridge.[32] Together they explored the ruins of the El-Faiyum oasis, and explored the Valley of the Kings, where Burton was astounded by the quality of the work of Giovanni

Battista Belzoni, the great Italian Egyptologist who had put the Valley on the archaeological map.[33]

During his travels with Smith, Burton first realised the monstrous scale of the Egyptian slave trade and the atrocities and inhumanity that accompanied it. It staggered him that twenty years after the American Civil War – supposedly the death-knell for international slavery – and the stranglehold imposed by the Royal Navy on Brazil and Africa, 400,000 human beings were uprooted from the Sudan and bartered annually. Worst of all were the estimated 8000 castrations a year to provide seraglio eunuchs and other 'safe' household servants. Mortality from the gelding was 25 per cent for boys aged up to five, and 70 per cent up to the age of ten, but a successful operation yielded an increase in value: a slave cost anything from five pounds to ten, a healthy eunuch was worth £25 to £80.[34] In his articles for the British press, Burton had to tone down the horror so as not to offend the delicate sensibilities of his readers. Later, in the *Arabian Nights*, he was more forthright about the butchery involved. 'The parts are swept off by a single cut of the razor, a tube (tin or wooden) is set in the urethra, the wound is cauterised with boiling oil, and the patient planted in a fresh dunghill. His diet is milk; and if under puberty he often survives.[35]

Burton now proposed that he be made Slave Commissioner for the Red Sea area, with a roving brief and a gunboat at his disposal, at a salary similar to that proposed by Gordon for the Darfur governorship, and no loss of seniority and pension rights at Trieste for two years. Lord Granville was surprised at the request, but forwarded it to Gladstone, newly Prime Minister, for his comments. Gladstone's Egyptian policy, as he showed in his later vacillating relations with Gordon, was to avoid commitments in the area. Despite his reputation for humanitarianism, Gladstone turned a blind eye to the atrocities of the Egyptian slave trade. Suppression, he knew, meant military force, and with a man like Burton at the helm, that military force would soon turn into wholesale occupation of Egypt.

So Burton served out his six-month leave in impotence and frustration. Towards the end of his time, several omens convinced him that Alexandria was 'bad medicine'. He saw one of his own nightmares come true when a sailor was cast into the sea at Aboukir bay in the middle of a group of ravening sharks. Burton had a morbid fear of sharks, and was even nervous of bathing in the Adriatic at Trieste, although attacks at such a northerly latitude were almost unknown. This time the nightmare ended on a happy note, when the sailor was fished from the sea unharmed.[36]

But later on, another encounter with animals dangerous to man came from a more unexpected source. It was Burton's invariable practice to go for walks using a long pointed iron stick as a walking stick. The purpose was to strengthen his biceps, so that he was always ready for fistic action; those who came on the receiving end of Burton's punch testified that it was like taking a kick from a mule. This custom of Burton's literally saved his life one morning near the Alexandria slaughterhouse. He had always been wary of packs of semi-savage dogs after seeing how Montenegrin mongrels would sneak up to a stranger and suddenly bite him viciously. He was therefore fully alerted when he came upon a pack of snarling scavengers in a lonely place during his dawn walk. For five minutes he had to conduct a fighting retreat, jabbing at the slavering dogs with his improvised spear until he found safety by shinning over a wall. But for the pointed stick, he would undoubtedly have been torn to pieces.[37]

The event presaged by these bad omens finally came to pass. Returning home from dining late in Alexandria on the night of 2–3 May 1880, Burton was attacked by a gang of nine men. He fought back hard and scraped the skin from his fists in the process. Finally one of the men felled him with a blow on the head from a blunt instrument. When he came to, he found his signet ring and the 'divining rod' he used on his gold hunts both gone, but his watch and purse untouched. After staggering back to the hotel, streaming blood, he made a resolution to quit Egypt. Without even bothering to report the incident to the police, he got on the first ship for Trieste.[38]

Reunited with Isabel, they then set off to Oberammergau for the Passion Play. The couple had agreed to bring out a joint publication on the play, but the publishers rejected Isabel's frothy effusions and took Burton's sardonic and jaundiced *A Glance at the Passion Play* on its own. Isabel was mortified.[39] This trip, like so many the Burtons made during the Trieste years, was one undertaken without official leave of absence from the Foreign Office. On another unauthorised outing, to Salzburg and Vienna, Burton actually had to make a precipitate departure from a restaurant when the Austrian Embassy chaplain, who knew him, came in.

In the summer of 1881 the Burtons crossed to Venice for an international Geographical Conference. Burton was angry that he had received no official invitation to attend, but Bates of the RGS sugared the pill by pointing out that the Society itself had not thought it worthwhile to send an exhibit. The conference was notable for producing a fast friendship between Burton and Verney Lovett Cameron, the young Scottish explorer, whom he had first met at Clements Markham's house with Stanley in October 1872. Since then Cameron had gone on to great things, achieving in 1873–75 the first east-west crossing of Africa by a European.[40] This was the exploit whose prospect Burton had so contemptuously turned down in 1872. Cameron had been eminently respectful and deferential towards Burton; he consulted

'Ruffian Dick' on the writing of his African book, and took his advice.[41] And he regarded Burton as a peerless scientific African explorer, so unlike the glory-hunters Stanley and Speke. 'Going over the ground which he explored, with his *Lake Regions* of Central Africa in my hand, I was astonished at the acuteness of his perception and the correctness of his descriptions.[42]

Burton and Cameron achieved a rare rapport during those summer days in Venice. Cameron, who had little time for Stanley (then in the Congo in the service of King Leopold of the Belgians), introduced his companion to Stanley's rival in the Lower Congo, the French explorer Pierre Savorgnan de Brazza. Charmed by Cameron, Burton allowed his full eloquence to gush out. There poured out apothegm after witticism, *bon mot* after epigram. When Burton was in the right mood, there was no more brilliant after-dinner companion, Man of the world, raconteur, wit, his sparkling conversation dazzled all listeners. As another African explorer, Harry Johnston, was later to concede: 'I have seldom heard such conversation: there is nothing like it nowadays.'[43]

The depth of the friendship between Burton and Cameron is revealed by the ease with which they joked, clowned and horseplayed together. One afternoon the two of them became bored with some dry scholarly paper at the conference and 'cut' the lecture in favour of bathing at the Lido. After a while they took a notion to revert to childhood. The two large bearded men took off their shoes and socks, rolled up their trousers and began to make sandcastles. Astonished locals and holidaymakers came to observe the scene. This simply spurred Burton and Cameron to new heights of infantilism.

'Look, nurse', called Richard to Isabel, 'see what Cammy and I have done!'

'If you please, nursey', Cameron whined, 'Dick's snatched away my spade.'

While all this was going on, it chanced that Lord Aberdeen – the RGS President, the man who had pointedly not invited Burton to the conference – and assorted luminaries arrived. Gales of laughter ensued at the bizarre scene and helped to thaw a previously frosty atmosphere.[44]

The camaraderie with Cameron convinced Burton that he was the right man to take with him on his next excursion into gold country, among the Kong Mountains of West Africa. James Irvine, speculator with the Guinea Coast Gold Company, had promised to pay Burton's expenses and a fee on a prospecting expedition there; since the fee was to be paid retrospectively, Burton arranged to have the speculator pay Cameron's expenses 'on account'. Once again Burton was absent without leave, this time in flat defiance of a Foreign Office directive, issued in March 1881, admonishing him against proceeding 'to foreign countries, for the purpose of promoting any specific commercial or industrial undertaking, or of obtaining concessions from a foreign government.[45]

On 18 November 1881 Burton embarked for Lisbon, where he was to meet Cameron and catch the steamer onward bound for the Gold Coast. It took him a month of slow, stormy passage to reach Lisbon. Departing Lisbon on 20 December, the travellers spent a fortnight in Madeira and made stopovers at Tenerife and Las Palmas before cruising past the Cape Verde Islands to make landfall at Bathurst. Here Burton was infuriated to find that the steamship company now accepted blacks on equal terms with whites. All the suppressed hatred of the black man, dormant for nearly twenty years, burst out anew. 'It is a political as well as a social mistake to take negro first-class passengers. A ruling race cannot be too particular in such matters, and the white man's position on the coast would be improved were the black man kept in his proper place.'[46]

Leaving Bathurst on 17 January 1882, they arrived eight days later at Axim and headed up the Ancobra river to inspect the gold diggings. The division of labour was to be that the 38-year-old Cameron supervised the actual survey work while Burton, now approaching 61, would interpet the local dialect and make deals with the chiefs. But the venture was as ill-starred as all Burton's quests for the yellow metal. After two months both men went down with fever. Cameron threw it off in a week but Burton, lacking his comrade's youthful resilience, simply could not bounce back into robust health. At first he thought of visiting his old stamping grounds in Fernando Po and the Oil Rivers in the SS *Loanda* and then linking up with Cameron again at Axim on the return voyage. But his health gave way as soon as he boarded the ship. He changed his plans and went north instead to convalesce in Madeira, where he arrived on 13 April. Desperate to retrieve something from yet another débâcle, he cabled the Foreign Office with a wild suggestion that he be made Military Governor of the Gold Coast so that he could properly exploit the precious gold deposits. Aghast to find their man in Trieste many thousands of miles away in West Africa, absent without leave, the foreign office mandarins sent a peremptory reply, ordering him out of the area forthwith.[47]

After some more independent reconnoitring, Cameron joined his comrade in Madeira on 12 May. They obtained swift passage to Liverpool, arriving eight days later. Once again Burton's gold fever had ended in fiasco. In disgrace with the Foreign Office, he also had to reimburse Irvine's expenses, since Irvine claimed, rightly, that they had not stayed long enough in West Africa to do a proper job of prospecting. Ironically, the Axim area later did indeed prove rich in gold; Burton had been closer to his dream than he knew.

Nothing positive, then, had been achieved, and on the negative side Burton's negrophobia had fetched fresh breath. If anything, the racial hatred of *To the Gold Coast* is even more virulent than in Burton's four previous books on West Africa.[48] His most shrill invective is reserved for the fact that in a jury trial, black men served among the 'twelve good men and true' and were thus peers of an accused white. Burton's insistence that the African black was the epitome of cruelty and savagery was fast becoming common coin in his circle. Both Garnet Wolseley and Frank Harris endorsed the proposition from their independent observations.[49] In the *Arabian Nights* Burton returned to the charge vigorously, festooning the notes with singular instances of the sloth and cruelty of the black man, from the Cape to Cairo.[50]

Burton spent June and July in London on sick-leave, recuperating from the West African fever. Now he was experiencing difficulties finding a publisher for his increasingly prolix and convoluted productions; by common consent the Gold Coast book was another disappointment. Far the best material on his three months in Africa is contained in his journalistic pieces and scholarly articles.[51]

'The amateur consul', as the press, sick of Burton's constant absences from his post, had begun to call him, arrived back in Trieste on the first of August, but within days had decamped to Marienbad to take the waters. Over and above the after-effects of his African malady, he was now suffering badly from gout. In October 1882 came the sort of call that always inspired him. His old friend Professor Palmer was missing in Sinai. As an Arabist, Palmer was second only to Drake in Burton's affections. Not only was he expert in Arabic, Persian and Hindustani, but he had mastered German and the Scandinavian tongues in his late thirties. A Cambridge professor, traveller, translator, barrister, actor, conjurer, thought-reader, draughtsman, caricaturist, politician and journalist, the multitudinous Palmer represented Burton's 'road not taken' – the Burton who could have been an academic and man of affairs. To search for Palmer was almost like going in quest of another self.

When the Arabi revolt broke out in Egypt in 1882, the British had sent Palmer to the Sinai peninsula to suborn the tribes from the nationalist cause and prevent the closure of the Suez canal – a tactic later used by Allenby with T. E. Lawrence. Joined by Captain Gill and Lieutenant Harrington, Palmer landed at Jaffa and set out for Suez by way of Gaza. But there he made the fatal mistake of not hiring a powerful sheikh as his dragoman; the guide he chose was a man of no particular cachet in the desert. On 8 August Palmer's party left Suez. Two days later a large party of raiding Bedouin attacked them. When it became clear that murder was their intention, Palmer tried to use the desert code against them. He pleaded and expostulated; then, seeing his attempts were vain, he cursed them roundly in the time-honoured way of the Arabs. Palmer and his companions were then shot and their bodies thrown over a cliff.

For a long time their fate was unknown. Thinking Palmer was alive but detained by hospitable chiefs or Arabi's guerrillas, the British government telegraphed Burton on 17 October to proceed to Egypt and form a relief expedition. Arrived at Cairo, Burton learned that he would not be needed since Sir Charles Warren of the Palestine Exploration Fund was scouring Sinai with two hundred men. This time Burton finally ran into Gordon, but even as the two men discussed the future of Egypt, word came in that Warren had found the slaughtered bodies of Palmer and his comrades. Burton was devastated by the death of his old friend, all the more stunning since Bedouin did not, in his experience, normally kill men in cold blood. More than ever convinced that the days of desert chivalry were over and that the Arabs were degenerating, Burton threw in his lot with the imperialists and advocated an immediate British protectorate over Egypt.[52]

The abortive quest for Palmer was the last 'adventure' that Burton ever embarked on, just as the trip to the Gold Coast was his last-ever 'exploration'. He was troubled by gout and by the spectre of death all around him. Palmer was yet another friend who had died tragically young. Even Cameron was not destined to get past his fiftieth year. And when Burton returned to Trieste he sustained another blow: his favourite Austrian fencing partner, Herr Reich, committed suicide.[53]

In 1883, for the first time, Isabel and Richard found that swimming did not agree with them, so they gave it up and tried to compensate with other forms of exercise. But Richard's heart began to give trouble and he could no longer ascend the 120 steps to his apartment without gasping and panting for breath. After 1883 he was never again in full possession of his health. Isabel decided that her husband's physical well-being gave cause for concern, and that they should move to a house. She had inherited a considerable sum of money from her mother in 1872 but her own extravagance and Richard's perennial speculative losses had made severe inroads on the nest-egg. Although they could not afford it, Isabel decided that they must buy the best house in all Trieste, a palazzo built by an English merchant-venturer. They moved into their dream house in July 1883.[54]

The palazzo was truly sumptuous. The front door was so wide that one could drive a carriage into the hall. A marble staircase led to the interior, which contained twenty large rooms, all spacious and opulent. The house was airy and light and commanded great views, one over the Adriatic, one over a wooded promontory, another facing open country, and a fourth into orchards and gardens. But the Burtons' mania for large rooms landed Richard with a draughty north-facing chamber as his study. To keep warm he wore a fur-lined coat in the day, and slept between buffalo skins at night. His health suffered, and the knowing locals muttered the old Italian adage: *dove non entra il sole, entra il dottore.*[55]

Burton surveyed his new domain, not with the excitement that might have been expected, but with feelings of sadness and foreboding. Gout and general debility had taken over from insomnia as his principal malady. These days he arose at 6.30 in the morning instead of 5 a.m. In his first autumn in the palazzo he noted the departure of the swallows with particular sadness, and on 6 December he wrote in his diary an entry whose very flatness bespeaks the anguish and poignancy in his heart. 'Today, eleven years ago, I came here. What a shame!!!'[56]

24

Poet and Translator

THE Trieste years saw Burton transforming himself slowly but surely from globe-trotter and explorer to scholar and man of letters. Burton had always been part intellectual, part man of action; advancing age simply intensified the propensity to the former while raising obstacles of finance and infirmity to the latter.

The irony was that as Burton's popularity as an author declined – not unconnected with the fact that he no longer had riveting tales of derring-do to impart – he became both more prolific and more pedantic in his scholarship.[1] But he certainly chalked up his mark in academic circles. As an archaeologist he largely made his name in the 1870s, not just for the meticulous survey of seldom-visited ruins in the Middle East, but for his discoveries in Italy and the Adriatic. In *Unexplored Syria* Burton publicised the recent finding of the Moabite Stone – a slab of basalt discovered on the shores of the Dead Sea in 1868 and covered with inscriptions relating to the victories of Mesha, King of Moab, over the Israelites. The translation made by Burton's friend Charles Simon Clermont-Ganneau, French Consul at Jerusalem, showed clearly that in the Book of Kings the Jews had barefacedly rewritten the historical facts concerning their campaigns against Mesha, so that they, not the Moabites, emerged victorious. With his prejudice against both Jews and the Bible, Burton took particular pleasure in putting the story of the Moabite Stone before a wider audience.[2]

He made an even more original contribution to archaeology with his thesis that the 'Hamath Stones' were Hittite in origin. Burton's one true Arabian hero was Burkhardt. In 1812 Burkhardt had discovered four basalt monoliths covered in an unknown writing, embedded in a wall in the town of Hama. Fuzzy impressions of these stones were reproduced in *Unexplored Syria*; even so they proved sufficiently intriguing to whet the appetite of the British archaeologist William Wright. He obtained permission from the Turkish authorities to make a proper examination, extracted the stones and made accurate casts of them which were sent to London; the original stones found a home in a Constantinople museum. On the basis of his examination, Wright endorsed Burton's theory of the Hittite provenance of the script. The scholarly establishment was incredulous and dismissive. Vainly Burton bent his considerable linguistic talents to the decipherment of the inscriptions. It was not until the 1920s that the stones yielded their secret. The Burton/Wright thesis was then triumphantly vindicated.[3]

Another language with which Burton jousted unsuccessfully was Etruscan. But his association with the Italian scholars Calori, Fabretti and Capellini put the Etruscan places on the map for serious students. Burton's *Etruscan Bologna* is devoid of the brooding mystery D. H. Lawrence later brought to the necropolises at Tarquinia and Cerveteri, but it is Burton's book that has more lasting value for scholars. It opened doors for him to archaeologists of world renown like Arthur Evans, Heinrich Schliemann and A. H. Sayce.

With impressive credentials as anthropologist and archaeologist behind him, Burton in the late 1870s turned his talents to translation. He first tackled the great Portuguese national epic *The Lusiads* by Luis de Camões (Camoens, 1524–80). It is not surprising that Burton chose Camoens, whose unsuccessful life as rover and littérateur was an uncanny pre-echo of Burton's.[4] Camoens had a natural appeal to wanderers of a mystical inclination – Herman Melville was a great admirer.[5] And Portuguese was second only to Arabic as Burton's favourite language. The fact that Camoens' explicit model for the structure of his epic was Virgil's *Aeneid* increased its attractiveness for Burton the scholar. Despite his earlier unhappy experiences with the classical languages, by middle age Burton was proud of his Latin, and the scholar in him delighted in pointing to the many instances where Camoens had also leaned heavily on the Roman poet Lucan.[6]

Burton first got to grips with Camoens in Goa in 1847 and even translated some of his stanzas then. The interest continued, and is particularly in evidence in the Zanzibar and East African period (1856–59).[7] The abundant leisure in Brazil in the mid-1860s enabled him to produce a translation of the first of the ten cantos of *The Lusiads*, but he was dissatisfied with his version and tore it up. It took his great friend from Brazil days, the mining superintendent J. J. Aubertin, to galvanise him. Aubertin published a translation of Camoens' epic in 1878, to considerable critical acclaim. This spurred Burton on to complete his own researches on the Portuguese master. In 1880 his translation of *The Lusiads* appeared. It was followed the next year by a massive Life and critical commentary on the poet; three years later Burton rounded off his long love-affair with Portuguese by producing a two-volume rendering into English of Camoens' *Lyricks*.

Many are the testimonies to the way Camoens absorbed Burton's energies in the late 1870s. The London correspondent of the *New York Tribune* went to a party and found Burton sitting on the stairs outside with a book and pencil in his hand, enrapt in his reading and note-taking. When spoken to, he awoke as from a dream, with the dazed air of one who did not know where he was. He explained that he was working on Camoens, and that he carried his work everywhere, rather in the manner of Pliny the Elder. Since he could read and write at will in the most difficult places, he managed to do a lot of translation in such odd moments.[8]

Another witness was Verney Cameron. During the Geographical Conference of 1881 in Venice, he and Burton loved going around the illuminated city by night in a gondola. On one occasion, after alighting in St Mark's Square, Burton was waylaid by a Portuguese scholar who taxed him on a tricky point of interpretation in his recently published translation. Cameron watched with incredulous awe as Burton gradually overwhelmed his interlocutor (in Portuguese) by dipping into his capacious crane-bag of esoteric knowledge.[9]

Camoens posed particular problems of tone, voice and nuance for the would-be translator. His subject in *The Lusiads* was the astonishing rise of Portugal to temporary world power, the process whereby one-and-a-quarter million people built an empire that extended from Brazil to Japan. Beginning with Henry the Navigator, the poem reaches its climax with the exploits of Vasco da Gama, who discovered the sea route to India round the Cape of Good Hope. In a poem whose avowed purpose was to glorify the taking of Christianity to the benighted savage, he had, in order to be faithful to his classical model, to use the pagan deities like Jupiter, Mars and Minerva. Also, because da Gama's exploits were purely male and within the ambit of traditional martial deeds, he had to work in some 'female interest' in order to catch the audiences that had been entranced by Petrarch and Ariosto. He therefore inserted separate love stories featuring women, rather as Melville, his admirer, weaved discrete and independent stories into the structure of *Moby Dick*; a typical example is the episode of Dona Inez de Castro (Canto Three, Stanzas 118–35). This accounts for the tension and lack of balance in *The Lusiads*: the Christian elements sit uneasily next to the *Odyssey*-like sensuality of the 'Island of Love'; its Counter-Reformation ideological elements next to Camoens' innate Renaissance humanism.

One way Camoens tried to reconcile these difficulties and create a seamless web of narrative was by using an artificial form of Portuguese which set up something of an alienation effect between poem and reader. Burton tried to match this by employing a sort of Never-Never Elizabethan English. The effect can be seen by comparing Burton's version to the first stanza of Canto One with that of his friend Aubertin.

BURTON: The feats of Arms and famed heroick Host
From occidental Lusitania's strand,
That o'er the seas by seaman never crost
Fared beyond the Taprobane land,
Forceful in perils and in battle-post,
With more than promised force of mortal hand;
And in regions of a distant race
Reared a new throne so haught in Pride of Place.

AUBERTIN: Arms and the heroes signalised in fame,
Who from the western Lusitanian shore
Beyond e'en Taprobana sailing came,
O'er seas that ne'er had been traversed before;
Harassed with wars and dangers without name,
Beyond what seemed of human prowess borne,
Raised a new kingdom midst a distant clime
Which afterwards they rendered so sublime.

There is surely no doubt that Aubertin communicates more readily with the reader. By his scholarly fidelity and pedantic insistence on catching every timbre of Camoens' utterance, Burton managed to defeat the basic purpose of translation. His avowed object was to write what Camoens might have written had he been born an Englishman instead of Portuguese. The attempt to write Elizabethan English for nineteenth-century readers was already a highly eccentric enterprise. But Burton compounded his error by making a vain attempt to convey the nuances of Camoens' Portuguese by larding his text with further archaisms. As a modern Camoens scholar has commented of Burton's translation: 'He clogged his style with hyperbaton, syncope, apocope, aphaeresis, diaeresis, and parasoge. The interests of the modern English reader were nowhere consulted, and the upshot was as could have been foreseen; his version, the most ambitious of all and the most firmly rooted in scholarship, fell from the press still-born, unreadable.'[10]

Burton taxed his reader's patience with a form of verbiage and prolixity that had been out of fashion for generations. So a simple notion like 'It was early April, season of flowers' becomes in Burton's hands:

'Twas the glad season when the God of Day
into Europa's rav'her 'gan return
When warmed either point his genial ray,
And Flora scattered Amathea's horn.

Astonishingly for one with his linguistic talents, Burton lacked an ear for the sound of either prose or poetry.

Burton was proud of his efforts and sent his translations of both *The Lusiads* and the *Lyricks* to Swinburne, in hopes of approbation. Swinburne made polite noises of thanks and encouragement.[11] So did his friends. But Burton's literary foes went for the jugular. *The Scotsman* declared itself an enemy of the entire Camoens ethos and its 'rotting carcase of chivalry', and went on to tax Burton with having produced clumsy lines, novel words and needlessly intricate versification: 'Captain Burton is no poet, and his translation is nearly the most unendurable we ever saw.' The *New York Daily Tribune* agreed: 'The Portuguese of Camoens, however mannered, cannot surely be as mannered as the English of Captain Burton ... Captain Burton is a linguist, he knows a great many languages and dialects, but English is not amongst the number.'[12] However, even though Burton's translation has not lived, the massive erudition of the notes and critical apparatus and his deep understanding of Camoens have survived to win the plaudits of twentieth-century scholars.[13]

There was one eerie postscript to Burton's work on Camoens. Stanza 95 of Book Ten states that the Nile rises from the same lake source as the Zambezi, and hints strongly at Lake Victoria as the origin. This reminder of his early years of success and disaster prompted Burton to tack on a stanza not found in the original *Lusiads*, where he laments the fate of Speke and his own relegation and exile to Trieste:

> And see you twain from Britain's foggy shore
> Set forth to span dark Africk's jungle-plain;
> Thy furthest fount, O Nilus! they explore
> And where Zaire springs to seek the chain,
> The veil of Isis hides thy land no more,
> Whose secrets open to the world are lain.
> They deem, vain fools! to win fair Honour's prize:
> This exiled lives, and that untimely dies.

The year of the *Lusiads* translation, 1880, saw Burton's most sustained attempt ever to establish himself as a poet. His aim was to surpass the great success enjoyed in Victorian England by Edward Fitzgerald's famous *Rubáiyát of Omar Khayyám*.[14] But he had great doubts about his own abilities; so great indeed that he interposed a double barrier between his readers and his true identity. *The Kasidah of Haji Abdu El-Yezdi, a Lay of the Higher Law*, in fact an original poem by Burton alone, was passed off as the work of a Persian from Darabghird, which had been given to 'F. B.' (Frank Baker, Burton's old pseudonym) for editing and translation. Isabel, in her preface to the 1894 edition, recalled that people genuinely thought the author of the *Kasidah* was 'an Eastern polyglot with cosmopolitan tendencies'.[15]

This elaborate charade is an indication of the fear Burton felt that the *Kasidah* would be weighed in the balance alongside the *Rubáiyát* and found wanting. When, after his death, the authorship of the *Kasidah* could no longer be denied, the supremely mendacious Isabel went to elaborate lengths to try to deny that the poem was composed in the shadow of FitzGerald's masterpiece. She claimed that Burton wrote it after his return from Mecca in 1853, three years before the *Rubáiyát* appeared. Yet careful analysis reveals it beyond doubt as a work written as Burton approached sixty. The pessimism is not the work of a young man, the allusions to youth and adolescence have the nostalgic flavour of an older man's reminiscence, the poem reads as the fruit of a lifetime's reflection on the Eastern world, and the portrait of the author exactly matches everything known about Burton in 1880.[16]

A *kasidah* was a 'purpose-ode' or didactic elegy, one of the earliest forms of Arabic literature, composed of thirteen or more rhyming couplets.[17] Arabic metre is like Ancient Greek: that is to say, the value of syllables depends on the quantity or position of the consonants, not on the accent, as in English or Romance tongues. To capture the mood of the original model ('to translate it', as 'F. B.' claimed), Burton selected the iambic form as the closest in spirit, if not letter, to the Arabic form. This meant that the *Kasidah* was formally close to the *Rubáiyát*, which FitzGerald composed in quatrains.

Once again Burton's very erudition was at war with his poetic ambitions. The *Kasidah* draws on Confucius, Longfellow, Aristotle, Pope, Das Kabir and Pulambal as well as, obviously, FitzGerald's *Omar Khayyám*. The criticism of a perceptive contemporary underlines some of the problems. 'The world is placed under tribute from Pekin to Salt Lake City. A more careless "borrower", to use Emerson's expression, never lifted poetry ... The *Lay* is less a poem than an enchiridion, a sort of Emersonian guide to conduct of life, rather than an exquisitely presented summary of the thoughts of an Eastern pessimist.'[18]

Eclecticism is the keynote of the *Kasidah*. A host of influences jostle for our attention. There is a Swinburnian flavour to the following:

> Ah gay the day with shine of sun and bright the breeze and blithe the throng
> Met on the river-bank to play when I was young, when I was young.

But at other times the prophetic mode recalls Herman Melville:

> Dost not, O Maker, blush to hear amid the storms of tears and blood
> Man say thy mercy?
> Man's Natural State is God's design, such is the silly sage's theme,
> Man's primal age was the Age of Gold; such is the Poet's waking dream

Burton's favourite devices are repetition and alliteration and assonance.

> Who knows not whence he came nor why
> Who knows not whither bound and when
>
> The shattered bowl shall know repair; the riven lute shall sound once more
> But who shall mend the clay of man, the stolen breath to man restore?
> Life in youth-tide standeth still, in manhood streameth soft and slow.

The epigrammatic form is typical of the *Kasidah*:

> When doctors differ, who decides among the milliard throng?
> Who save the madman dares to cry: 'Tis I am right, you all are wrong?

But Burton cannot rein in his erudition to make this a consistent mode. He is self-indulgent in the use of unintelligible Arabic forms such as Aristu (Aristotle), Aflatu (Plato), Khemi-land (Egypt) and Franquestan (Europe). He also has an unwise affection for the word-clusters common to all north European languages: day-dreams, sea-born, thunder-fire, moon-struck, etc. The problem is that these Germanic clusters sit uneasily in a supposed milieu of Oriental refinement.

Burton eschews the 'Bacchic' language of *Omar Khayyám* in favour of traditional metaphor. Wisely, for the most part he avoids the allegorical allusions of the original Kasidah form. When he does use them the verse becomes cryptic:

> Where are the crown of Kay Khusraw, the sceptre of Anushirwan,
> The holy grail of Jamshyd, Afrasiyar's hall?

He also commits the same errors as in the *Lusiads* translation: the use of archaism and the sudden lurch into bathos. The *Kasidah* thus emerges as a linguistic pot-pourri, straddling two cultures. The best passages are the descriptive ones: of dawn, shade, dream, childhood recollections, regret for the passing years and for declining creativity.[19] The least successful are the metaphysical speculations. The genuine sensuousness and lyricism of the former are betrayed when Burton deals with thought and ideas rather than Nature or emotions. The poem is in nine parts and opens with a description of dawn over the desert. There is an abrupt shift of gear in the second part, whose tone is reminiscent of Tennyson's *In Memoriam* or Matthew Arnold's *Stanzas from the Grande Chartreuse*. 'Haji Abdu' reflects on the insignificance of Man, while stoically rejecting the traditional solace of drink or sexual gratification. In the third part these reflections shade into a pessimism of Schopenhauerian intensity. The 'lord of creation' is simply the fruit of bestial desire; life is a poisoned feast of which one is forced to partake despite misgivings; the table is covered with bitter fruit. The theme of poison is merged with that of the desert mirage. Developing Solomon's theme of 'vanity of vanities; all is vanity', the poet continues:

> Hardly conned the lesson comes its fatal term,
> Fate bids us bundle up our books
> Hardly we learn to wield the blade
> Before the wrist grows stiff and old;
> Hardly we learn to ply the pen
> Ere Thought and Fancy faint with cold.

The fourth part rehearses the different conceptions of God: Buddhist, Confucian, Sufic, Judaic, Islamic. Religions, says the poet, are as mortal as the men who devise them. In the fifth part 'Haji Abdu' wrestles with the problem of Evil and at once rejects the notion of Original Sin:

> Long ere Man drew upon Earth his earliest breath
> The world was one continuous scene of anguish, torture, prey and death.

Here Burton explicitly embraces the Darwinism of the selection of species, the survival of the fittest and an implacable Nature 'red in tooth and claw'. In the sixth part he deals with the Sufic/Platonic idea that the visible world is but a shadow of the real world – a world that is, moreover, unknowable. This epistemological despair is a long way from the sceptical hedonism of the *Rubáiyát*.

In the seventh part Burton deals with the debate between materialism and philosophical idealism – a debate he rejects as meaningless:

> Reason and Instinct! How we love to play with words that please our pride!

For Burton, the Darwinistic notion of the evolution of higher and higher forms of consciousness cuts a swathe through this dilemma. In the eighth part he rejects the ideas of Heaven and Hell and divine punishment in general. In the ninth and final section of the poem Burton lays out his profession of faith: humanism with a dash of Stoicism and Platonism. To underline the 'message' of the poem, he adds six long notes.

A mélange of Western metaphysics and Oriental fatalism, the *Kasidah* teems with pessimistic and nostalgic themes: on doubt, anguish, the passage of time, death, nothingness. Its critics say that the philosophical overlay swamps the emotional and poetic qualities; its defenders insist that the language in the poem is means not end; the end is nothing less than a meditation on the meaning of life.

An obvious way into this debate is to compare the *Kasidah* with FitzGerald's *Rubáiyát*. Burton's poem suffers from an excess of philosophical speculation. The *Kasidah* passes in review all ideologies and religions; the *Rubáiyát* wisely eschews such treacherous poetic reefs. There is an organic unity in the language of FitzGerald that Burton cannot match. The language of the *Kasidah* is uneven; Burton employs a number of abstract words that are fundamentally alien to poetry: omniscience, microcosm, paroxysm, atomy, etc. The economy of the *Rubáiyát* contrasts with the profusion of the *Kasidah*. FitzGerald's vision is kaleidoscopic while Burton's is panoramic.[20]

Burton claimed that the *Kasidah* and the *Rubáiyát* were companion pieces, both at odds with the facile 'spirituality' of Western Christianity and the desiccated materialism of mainstream Islamic thought. 'Europe draws a hard, dry line between Spirit and Matter: Asia does not ... modern thought tends more and more to reject crude idealism and to support the monistic theory.'[21] As for the *Rubáiyát*, it was 'that singular reaction from arid Moslem realism and materialism, that immense development of gnostic and neoplatonic transcendentalism of which the poetry of Omar Khayyám, now familiar to English readers, is a fair specimen.'[22]

But in fact there is little 'philosophy' in the true sense in the *Rubáiyát*, wisely so in the light of the blemishes that disfigure the *Kasidah*. Burton's poem is an uneasy syncretism of Oriental and Western thought. Philosophically, it is confused as between an eternal and evolving Truth, and between Darwinian evolution and Eastern fatalism; largely Burton makes the law of evolution do the work traditionally done by Oriental 'destiny'. In many ways the theosophy of Annie Besant and Madame Blavatsky – whom Burton greatly admired – attempts a similar sort of syncretism and, like the *Kasidah*, is vitiated by the incompatibility of positivism and mysticism. The *Rubáiyát* gains immensely by not embracing the Victorian idea of progress, and thus is more palatable to the sceptical twentieth-century sensibility. Omar Khayyám realises that increased knowledge does not imply increased wisdom: 'I came out by the same door as I went in'.[23]

Burton, too, emphasises the Western notion that duty, probity and charity are their own rewards, a conclusion too sanguine for Omar. But in many respects the *Kasidah*, from a genre that predates the Koran, shares the same mental universe as the *Rubáiyát*. Both poems agree on the pointlessness of theological disputation, and if 'Haji Abdu' is less obviously vinous than the old Persian, he is certainly no anti-hedonist. Doubt is common to both poems; indeed the *Kasidah* is saturated in lines expressive of pessimism:

But we, another shift of scene, another pang to rack the heart
Why meet we on the bridge of Time to 'change one greeting and
to part?

Why must we meet, why must we bear this yoke of must,
Without our leave or askt or given, by tyrant fate or victim thrust?

The interesting thing is that this thread, common to both poems, is distinctly alien to the normal Arab sensibility. As T. E. Lawrence recorded of the Arabs: 'They were a dogmatic people, despising doubt, our modern crown of thorns.'[24]

In general, the *Rubáiyát* must be accounted better than the *Kasidah*, by virtue of its superior poetry and its greater universality. Burton's couplets are often obscure and sometimes riddled with jargon, yet he does not convince us that he is dealing with the unsayable. The *Rubáiyát*'s verses, by contrast, are limpid and luminous, yet contain the mysterious quality that is the mark of great poetry. Burton's sentiments and philosophical concerns, too, are culture-bound and wedded to particular preoccupations of the Victorian world, whereas FitzGerald vaults over this world to an area of transcendental and perennial meditation. 'Haji Abdu' fails to make his own story and the tragedy of Man dovetail and harmonise as Omar does.

But at its best the *Kasidah* is a brilliant demonstration of the Sufi mystical tradition, its similarities to Platonism, and its courageous scepticism and pessimism.

All faith is false, all Faith is true; Truth is the shattered mirror strown
In myriad bits; while each believes his little bit the whole to own

'You are all right, you are all wrong' we hear the careless Soofi say,
For each believes his glimmering lamp to be the gorgeous light of day.

And for Burton the Nietzschean, whose multiple identities are reflected in the protean nature of the *Kasidah* itself, the best lines in the poem express the lodestone he steered by:

Do what thy manhood bids thee do, from none but self expect applause;
He noblest lives and dies who makes and keeps his self-made laws.
All other life is living death, a world where none but phantoms dwell;
A breath, a wind, a sound, a voice, a tinkling of the camel bell.

25

The Valetudinarian Sexologist

BURTON scarcely knew what he ought to try next to improve his lot. All his gold-hunting enterprises had come to naught, he had not been given a knighthood, he had been turned down as Commissioner for the Slave Trade in the Red Sea. He had Promethean abilities and ambitions, but like Prometheus was chained to the rock of his Consulate, with the vulture of boredom and inactivity gnawing at his vitals.[1] Burton's study highlighted his paralysis as much as his protean interests. It contained eight tables, on each of which were the notes and partially completed manuscript of a book he was currently engaged on. Burton would move from one to another as the mood took him. He was now deskbound and an 'internal rover', his restless moving between tables mirroring his early wanderings.

But 1884 brought this to an end in dramatic fashion. January and February found him suffering acute stomach cramps, angina and painful gout. On 14 March he collapsed with a heart attack. For forty-eight hours his condition was critical. Two physicians attended him and diagnosed a clot of blood rising to the heart. They prescribed twenty-five drops of digitalis, which he took in three doses at fifty-minute intervals. For two days and nights Isabel never left his side.[2] This was Mrs Burton at her very best, all the more commendable since her London doctors had recently told her she had cancer.

She had first noticed something wrong in April 1882. At fencing school she realised she was getting weaker and weaker. Then the fencing-master Reich, the same who committed suicide the following year, told her that her arms were limp. She consulted a surgeon in London who advised an operation. Isabel had a horror of operations, so refused. In Italy in 1883 she also consulted the eminent physician Count Mattei. His prescription of four external and internal remedies did nothing for her. But she suffered in silence, refusing to tell Richard there was anything the matter with her. He had taught her his impatience with illness and 'weakness' only too well.[3]

For Richard there followed eight months of inactivity; first, three months of assiduous nursing by Isabel, then a tottering convalescence in Vienna, Marienbad and a succession of German spas. Another bad attack of gout at the end of the year condemned the Burtons to a sad and doleful Christmas in Trieste. Isabel suggested retirement from the Consular Service, without solving the problem of what they would live on. It was her extravagance more than anything that condemned Richard to the Consulate at Trieste. Burton liked the good things in life, but he was capable of austerity; Isabel, except during the terrible financial crisis of 1871–72, never learned to curb her spendthrift tendencies.

During the long days and nights of illness and convalescence, Isabel learned more about her husband's tastes than she would have in years of being excluded from the study. His favourite English authors were Chaucer, Byron, Coleridge and Gibbon. Among individual books he had a special liking for Butler's *Hudibras* and Johnson's *Journey to the Western Isles*. Of his exact or near contemporaries he most admired Dickens, Darwin 'our British Aristotle', Swinburne and Dante Gabriel Rossetti. Favourite nineteenth-century works included Kinglake's *Eothen*, Renan's *Vie de Jésus* and FitzGerald's *Rubáiyát*. He also had pronounced dislikes: Carlyle (for his strictures on the *Arabian Nights*), Cowper (for his ignorant praise of landscape untouched by human hand), Harriet Martineau (for being an 'old maid'), and Tennyson (for having committed the solecism of pronouncing Al-Raschid to make the name sound like 'rasher' instead of with the stress on the last syllable). Apart from Arabic and Portuguese masterpieces, Burton had a strong feeling for the Italian classics, especially Tasso, Ariosto and Boccaccio, and his favourite travel writer was the Swiss, Johann Burkhardt.

Literature was not his only love. He had an aesthete's eye for paintings and could spend entire days in art galleries. Curiously, in the light of his gold-fever, it was silver not gold that was his particular weakness as a collector. In the Trieste palazzo he liked to surround himself with silver objects: cups, goblets, standishes. Whenever his eyes got tired from reading, he would lie on his back and place a florin over each eye; for gout he used a 'remedy' of silver coins bound to his feet.

The 1885 home leave was overshadowed by the news of Gordon's death at Khartoum in January. There was some talk of sending out Burton as Political Officer to assist in Garnet Wolseley's relief expedition, but his poor health precluded the possibility. He was showing his age badly. At 65, his long pendulous Chinaman moustaches had shrunk till they barely covered his mouth. The most conspicuous mark on his face was still the spear gash from Berbera. He kept his grizzled hair dark with dye and brushed forward to cover the bald patches. But, if anything, Isabel was wearing worse. By the mid-1880s she had grown uncomfortably stout and was bursting out of her expensive dresses. Her grey hair was hidden by a not very fetching yellowish wig 'which made her look like a magnified Marie Antoinette'.[4]

Yet the long summer in England did Burton good. He saw old friends, renewed ancient acquaintances and met some interesting new faces. Old friends were represented by Swinburne and Monkton Milnes. With Swinburne he argued that cannibalism was a wholesome and natural method of diet.[5] As for Monkton Milnes, Burton found him in peevish and cantankerous mood, utterly bored even though he possessed the wealth of Croesus. A few weeks later, Milnes died. Up to the end, apparently, he had been in fear of death, not in the normal way but because it was so vulgar; it meant that the lifelong devotee of minority causes had to go over to the majority.[6] Burton also had a coterie of talented young admirers. The most important were the rising star of London journalism, Frank Harris, and the best of the younger generation of African explorers, Harry Johnston. Johnston, whose boyhood dream had been to meet Burton, the following year found traces of his hero's 1862 ascent when he explored the Cameroon mountains. Unfortunately Burton did not live to see his protégé's greatest moment, when Johnston discovered the okapi in 1900.[7] Harris, who literally knew everybody who was anybody in Victorian London (and most of Europe too), got off to a bad start with Burton, but ended by considering him the greatest man of the age, ahead even of his much-admired Bismarck.[8]

Burton was also a guest of the highest political celebrities in the land, Gladstone and Lord Salisbury. Neither of them seemed to him to measure up to Disraeli and, exactly like Stanley, he managed to 'get across' both. With Gladstone, Burton committed the unpardonable *gaffe* of contradicting him flat in a discussion on Egypt.[9] Relations with Salisbury were at first easier. In October 1885 he invited the Burtons down to Hatfield for the weekend to discuss the Eastern Question. When the conversation became animated, Salisbury asked his guest to retire into a quiet room and compose a memorandum on the future of Egypt. Burton returned almost at once with a sheet of paper containing the single word: 'Annex'. Salisbury admonished him to address the subject seriously. Burton then proceeded to fill several pages with officialese saying much the same thing and ending with a strong recommendation to depose Tewfik.[10] In best *de haut en bas* fashion Salisbury called him 'Burton.' Entering into the spirit of things, Burton spoke to him as 'Salisbury'. Salisbury winced and went back at once to 'Mr Burton'. But by now the imp of the perverse had firm hold on Burton, and he went through the interview using the familiar 'Salisbury'.[11]

Nothing more clearly demonstrates Burton's self-destructive tendencies than the fact that immediately after this less than successful encounter with Lord Salisbury, he applied officially for the imminent vacancy as Consul in Morocco. In eupeptic mood he set off alone in November 1885 to spy out the land. But his enthusiasm for the actuality if not the romance of the Arab world seems to have waned somewhat in old age, to judge from this jaundiced description of Tangier.

> Here the traveller is first introduced to Moroccan town-life. The customhouse shed on the foul Marina [strand] is exceedingly primitive ... the streets, made for camels not for carriages, are rock-paved alleys like torrent beds, which serve mainly for drains, sewers, cesspools; here every kind of festering offal offends eye and nostril, from poultry feathers and kitchen slops to corpses of rat and cat – dead baby not being wholly unknown ... the *suks* or marketplaces are alternately sheets of mud, viscid and ankle-deep, and dust heaps, fit dwellings for microbes and playgrounds for the winds.[12]

Disenchanted with Morocco, Burton was back on British soil, in Gibraltar, in time for Christmas. Now ninety per cent fit again, he strengthened his heart muscles by a daily five-mile walk. There Isabel joined him, in time for their silver wedding anniversary on 22 January 1886. On 5 February a cablegram was delivered to their hotel, addressed to 'Sir Richard Burton'. At first he suspected a practical joke but Isabel, knowing that the sought-after knighthood had again become a possibility after the international success of the *Arabian Nights*, insisted he open the telegram. Inside was a message from Salisbury to say that, at his personal recommendation, the Queen had been pleased to make him Knight Commander of the Order of St Michael and St George in recognition of his services to the Crown. At first Burton pretended that he would not accept it. 'You had better accept it, Jemmy', Isabel said, 'because it is a certain sign that they are going to give you Tangier.'[13] Elated by the prospect, Burton went back with Isabel for another look at Morocco. Then they took ship to Naples. The Burtons never had much luck with sea voyages, and this was one of the roughest. Both of them fell heavily during a ferocious storm.[14]

In Lord Rosebery's time the Foreign Office had many times chided Burton for his frequent absences from post and requests for leave. But by the 1880s they seem largely to have given up. Burton was no sooner back in Trieste than he requested a further period of sick-leave in England; this was granted without demur. Richard's reappearance stoked up the press controversy over his knighthood: Fleet Street opinion always polarised very sharply either for or against Burton. This time the complaint of the 'antis' was that Burton had systematically hoodwinked the British establishment. Having written a spectacularly 'dirty' book (the translation of the *Nights*), he had been rewarded by a knighthood![15]

The 1886 leave was spent mainly on the *Supplemental Nights*, and for this purpose Burton needed to use the Wortley Montagu manuscripts at the Bodleian Library in Oxford. But the Bodleian refused to lend out their manuscripts, even to trusted academic institutions in London. Burton launched a bitter attack, pointing out that as regarded the manuscript in question, 'not one man in the whole so-called "University" can read it.'[16] On this occasion he was helped out of the hole into which he had dug himself by a friendly Bodleian Library, which simply made copies of the manuscripts and sent them to London.[17]

On the surface 1886 passed pleasantly enough, but behind the scenes the spectre of prosecution loomed. For alongside his fame and financial success from the *Nights*, Burton (and his colleagues in the fictitious Kama Shastra Society of Benares) had acquired the reputation of pornographer. Apart from the *Nights*, his other literary productions in the 1880s seemed to lend credence to the canard, for in these years he brought forth translations of the Sanskrit erotic classics *The Kama Sutra of Vatsyayana* and the *Ananga Ranga*, plus the manual of Arabian erotology *The Perfumed Garden of the Cheikh Nefzaoui*, to say nothing of editions of the Persian sex guides *The Beharistan* and *The Gulistan* and a collectanea of erotica from the Latin poets entitled *Priapeia, or the Sportive Epigrams of divers poets on Priapus*.

It was in 1872 that Burton first conceived the idea of a collaboration to produce the classic texts of erotology. Foster Fitzgerald Arbuthnot, then in the Bombay Civil Service, came home to London on leave with a manuscript of the Sanskrit *Ananga Ranga, Stage of the Bodiless One, or the Hindu Art of Love*. Burton and Arbuthnot translated the work and found a printer but, foreseeing trouble, identified themselves only by their initials in reverse. Their caution was justified: the printers ran off four copies of the proof sheets, then refused to proceed.

Burton and Arbuthnot communicated the fiasco and the manuscript itself to their friend H. S. Ashbee, another in the Monkton Milnes mould, 'a stoutish, stolid, affable man, with a Maupassantian taste for low life, its humours and its laxities'.[18] Ashbee was a kind of a cross between Burton and Frank Harris. The Burtonian side of his nature emerged in his *Index Librorum Prohibitorum* (1877) which provided a précis (with extracts) of all the famous banned books of the world. The Harris side was in evidence in *My Secret Life*, which he published under the pseudonym Pisanus Fraxi. In eleven volumes he set out details of affairs with more than 1250 women. Unlike Burton, whose interest in sex always remained largely an affair of the brain, Ashbee had Harris's obsessiveness combined with the stamina of Simenon and Maupassant.

Returning to India for a final tour of duty before his early retirement in 1879, Arbuthnot proceeded to translate the even more famous *Kama Sutra*. When Burton toured India in 1876 he found time to add his own contributions and polish the whole so as to make it vigorous and striking. Ashbee in turn published an abstract with excerpts in his third volume of esoteric erotica, *Catena Librorum Tacendorum*. With two manuals of love done into English, the question now remained how to bring them to the public.

It was some time in the early 1880s that, inspired by an idea of Monkton Milnes', they hit on a solution. If an author could write under a *nom de plume* that the most diligent sleuthing could not penetrate, why not a pseudonymous publishing house with fictitious headquarters? Thus was born the Kama Shastra Society of London and Benares, with printers allegedly in India's holy city, but in reality in Stoke Newington. The way was now open for publication of a whole series of erotic classics, without fear of prosecution, or panic by the printers.[19] In commercial terms, Burton and Arbuthnot knew what they were doing. In Victorian times there was a vast book-buying public for what was euphemistically referred to as 'exotica'. Publishers in London, Paris and Amsterdam fuelled and supplied a thirsty demand for erotic literature of all kinds.

The first publication, in 1883, was the most important of all the Eastern works on the art of love. Burton and Arbuthnot introduced their translation of the *Kama Sutra* by making obeisance to the conventional Victorian pieties. They conceded that the greatest joy in life was provided by a knowledge of God.

> Second, however, and subordinate only to this, are the satisfaction and pleasure arising from the possession of a beautiful woman. Men, it is true, marry for the sake of undisturbed congress, as well as for love and comfort, and often they obtain handsome and attractive wives. But they do not give them plenary contentment nor do they themselves enjoy their charms. The reason of which is that they are purely ignorant of the Scripture of Cupid, the Kama Shastra; and despising the difference between the several kinds of women, they regard them only in an animal point of view. Such men must be looked upon as foolish and unintelligent.[20]

There are several ironies here. In the first place, despite the lip-service paid to a 'knowledge of God'. it is quite clear that Burton and Arbuthnot had Christianity and its mistrust of the flesh firmly in their sights. Secondly, they were scarcely in a position to talk about male ignorance of women. Arbuthnot had been a repressed bachelor when he translated the work (he finally married at the age of 46, on his retirement), while Burton notoriously had no comprehension of women.[21]

The *Kama Sutra* is, as the title implies (a *sutra* is an aphorism), a didactic treatise on the role of sexuality and marriage in the life of a young Indian man-about-town of the first century AD. In four parts, it deals with everyday problems, the technique of acquiring a wife, and the intricacies of family life. Only Part Two is about 'sexual congress' yet it is on this section that the fame of the *Kama Sutra* depends. In the Western world of the late twentieth century, the *Kama Sutra* has become a joke, the alleged source of all acrobatic and impossible positions during intercourse. But of course the work was never intended as a universal primer of lovemaking, and all intelligent commentators concede that the coital positions described are by and large either too adjusted to Indian physiques and temperaments to be readily exportable, or require specific muscular training from an early age. As a recent student of the subject has remarked: 'Many of the *asanas* – or lovemaking positions – are only possible for yoga adepts or, at least, very supple athletes. The cook-book approach to lovemaking (another creation of the 'sixties) – which made much of 'foreplay' and fixed the always mispronounced clitoris in the male imagination as a kind of go-button – has nothing to do with the *Kama Sutra*.'[22]

Anything less pornographic than the precepts of the sage Vatsyayana would be difficult to imagine. Sex is described with clinical detachment, and for the Western reader unintentional humour in any case gets in the way of lubricity. The 'biting of the boar', the 'congress of the crow' and the 'position of the wife of Indra' are risible enough, but are easily capped by the 'mating of the herd of cows' where the male is enjoined to make love to one woman, practise cunnilingus on a second, meanwhile caressing the clitoris of four other women with both hands and both feet! The tone throughout is solemn, and more suited to a geometry lesson than sexology.

> Man is divided into three classes; the hare man, the bull man, and the horse man, according to the size of his lingam (penis). Woman also, according to the depth of her yoni (vagina), is either a female deer, a mare or a female elephant. There are thus three equal unions between persons of corresponding dimensions, and there are six unequal unions, when the dimensions do not correspond, or nine in all.

Burton seriously thought he was performing a task of liberation in placing the *Kama Sutra* before a Western public. But anything practically useful was already well known to the libertines of London and Paris, as Frank Harris's *My Life and Loves* demonstrates clearly. If sexual liberation was Burton's aim he would have done better to proselytise for Karl Ulrichs, Havelock Ellis and Kraft-Ebbing (spiritual heirs of Vatsyayana as 'sociologists of sex'), of whose works he apparently knew nothing.[23] The real importance of the *Kama Sutra* is as an interpretive key to Indian civilisation and culture. In Hinduism sex occupied an almost sacramental place. The human counterpart of divine creation, sexual intercourse symbolised the union of *Purusha* (matter) with *Prakati* (energy). It was Shiva and Shakti whose union was said to have created the world. The symbol of Shiva is the *lingam* or penis; the symbol of Shakti is the *yoni* or vagina. Vatsyayana was a true moralist who recognised the importance of duty between lovers and of sex in general happiness. He did not have any very high opinion of casual carnal gratification or visits to common prostitutes.

The *Kama Sutra* is also radically different in tone and intention from Western sexology. Burton's favourite, Ovid, wrote the *Art of Love*, which was virtually a textbook on seduction. The Marquis de Sade, though a moralist of sorts, at root peddled a philosophy of libertinage and advocated a deviant morality.

Two years later Burton and Arbuthnot brought out the *Ananga-Ranga*, a treatise in Sanskrit verse (supposed author, one Kalyana Malla), a work which had been translated into all the great Oriental languages. The milieu of the *Ananga Ranga* is very different from that of the *Kama Sutra*. Vatsyayana wrote during India's golden age, when there was no seclusion of women and both premarital and extramarital sex were common. The Indian Middle Ages, the womb from which *Ananga Ranga* sprang, was a rigidly stratified society with tight social control and strict insistence on law and custom, where child marriage was common and unattached males and females had few opportunities to meet. The basic problem the author addressed was how to make married sex interesting. 'Fully understanding the way in which such quarrels [about affairs] arise, I have shown how the husband by varying the enjoyment of his wife, may live with her as with thirty-two different women, ever varying the enjoyment of her and rendering satiety impossible.'

The *Ananga Ranga's* rule book reflected the tight, repressive, hierarchical society of its period. Some of the prescriptions are almost robotic. Kalyana Malla listed prohibitions on what not to do, with whom not and where not to do it, in a tone bordering on the manic. As might be expected, the zeal for coital positions far exceeds that of the better-known *Kama Sutra*. The author divides basic lovemaking positions into five, then describes the subdivisions. The first category is when the woman lies on her back; here there are eleven subdivisions. The second is when she lies on her side; here there are three subsections. The sitting position throws up ten variants and the standing three, while two different permutations on lying prone are described. The twenty-nine basic positions are supplemented by three separate forms of *Purushayit*, when the man lies supine.

These thirty-two positions approach the French *quarante façons* in number but, as Burton admits, the *Upavishta Majlis*, or sitting postures, when one or both partners sit asquat like birds, are impossible for Europeans, who lack the pliability of Eastern limbs. But some of the specific sexual advice is superior to that in the *Kama Sutra*. There is a detailed description of the *casse-noisette* technique, so prized as a technique among European *filles de joie*.[24] And the author is at pains to underline the point that the object in all sexual intercourse is to delay the orgasm of the man and hasten that of the woman. To this end the Hindus employed all manner of techniques for preventing muscular tension. The essence of the 'retaining art' is to preoccupy the brain. Hindu males therefore used to drink sherbet, chew betel-nuts and even smoke during coition itself.[25] Women, too, were trained from girlhood by old women in the art of lovemaking. They were taught to move rhythmically, to writhe ecstatically and to acquire such muscular control that they could 'milk' the man of his seed. The favourite position for maximising pleasure from Morocco to China was for the woman to lie supine while the man sat asquat between her legs.[26]

The next erotic classic to which Burton turned, *The Perfumed Garden of the Cheikh Nefzaoui* (published 1886), was a product of sixteenth-century Tunis. Whereas the two Indian erotic classics had been written for both sexes, the *Perfumed Garden* is clearly a 'men only' production.

Of all the erotica that Burton translated, the reflections of the ageing Tunisian sheikh come closest to outright pornography. They reveal the usual Islamic suspicion of women, the same sort of morbid fear of female lustfulness that is found in the *Arabian Nights*, and the work is 'phallocratic' in the true sense. The names for the male member are legion: 'Smith's bellows, pigeon, jingler, liberator, creeper, exciter, deceiver, sleeper, pathmaker, tailor, quencher, knocker, swimmer, one-eyed, baldhead, stumbler, annexer, splitter, splasher, breaker – these make up only about half the synonyms for the penis used by the author. The *Perfumed Garden* is rescued from the pornographic chiefly through overt humour, which the sheikh possessed in abundance, and its dreamy, poetic quality which conveys the Sufistic notion that sexuality too is merely part of the 'veil of illusion'.

The excitement of having deceived Mrs Grundy by his use of the 'Kama Shastra Society of Benares' encouraged Burton to publish other erotic classics. *Priapeia* was virtually an anthology of the Latin poets' carnality. The Persian classics *The Beharistan* (Abode of Spring) and *The Gulistan* (Rose Garden) were translated by Edward Rehatsek and edited by Burton, appearing in 1887 and 1888 respectively.[27] The earthiness and lewdness of the series of erotic works he published fed back into his later translations, of Catullus and, especially, *Il Pentamerone*. The so-called 'Tale of Tales', a series of airy stories and picaresque yarns by Giovanni Batiste Basile (1575–1632), a favourite of the Brothers Grimm, has a structure like that of the *Nights*; 'the Tenth diversion of the First Day', 'the Ninth diversion of the Fourth day', and so on. It is full of memorable lines – 'who seeketh what he should not findeth what he would not' has passed into the literary bloodstream – but Burton's unique contribution was to convey the bawdiness of the original. His unrivalled knowledge of Neapolitan slang and folk-ways, a product of his misspent youth, was invaluable here. The following is an angry exchange between an old woman and a boy who has smashed her water-pitcher with a stone.

> 'Ah Kindchen, scatterbrains, piss-a-bed, goat-dancer, petticoat-catcher, hangman's rope, mongrel mule, spindle shanks, whereat if ever the fleas cough, go where a palsy catch thee; and may thy mammy bear the ill news . . . knave, pimp, son of a whore!'

The lad, who had little beard and less discretion, hearing this flow of abuse, repaid her with the same coin, saying, 'Wilt thou not hold thy tongue, devil's grandam, bull's vomit, children-smotherer, turd-clout, farting crone?'

By 1886 Burton's star seemed on the ascendant. The Kama Shastra Society had made money even before the spectacular windfall from the *Nights*. Burton himself had at last received the KCMG. All he needed now to make his triumph complete was the position in Morocco currently being vacated by Sir John Drummond-Hay. He half allowed himself to be convinced that the position was as good as his. To give himself the necessary statesmanlike *gravitas* he again began to pontificate on world affairs. He advocated a Sino–British treaty alliance as a way of halting Russian expansion in Asia.[28] And he wrote a long newspaper article advocating a solution to the Irish question along the lines of the Austro–Hungarian empire, where each province had its Diet. This was federalism rather than Home Rule; Burton showed clearly enough that he had no love for the Irish by urging draconian measures against Irish 'troublemakers' and 'Fenian priests'.[29] Here was a revealing outburst, indicating again his hatred for priestcraft and Catholicism and, at a deeper level, his own self-loathing. It seems that Burton often turned the Irish part of his heredity into the 'objective correlative' for the part of himself he most wished otherwise. It would be facile to brand Burton as a simple imperialist. His imperialism was always nuanced and he was, moreover, always prepared to indulge in special pleading for turbulent anti-British factions if he had taken a personal shine to them. A good example was the Boers, whom he supported in the 1880–81 war; Burton repaid Livingstone's dislike of him by saying that it was the good doctor's irrational hatred of the Voortrekkers that had gained for the Boers their poor image in England and led to all the trouble in South Africa.[30]

Then came the bombshell. Burton was informed that he would not be appointed to the vacant post in Morocco. Publicly he maintained a stoical pose; privately, he was devastated. 'There is no rise for me now, and I don't want anything; but I have worked forty-four years for nothing. I am breaking up and I want to go free.'[31] He replied by asking to be released from the Foreign Service on full pension forthwith, and got forty-seven prominent people to sign a petition to that effect. Salisbury refused, to the anger of much of the press, which insisted that this was pure dog-in-the-mangerism, given Burton's precarious health. This was to be a nagging grievance for the next four years.[32]

It seemed that Burton might have paid a high price for his 'impertinence' to Lord Salisbury the year before. Salisbury had cunningly procured the knighthood so that no suspicion of petty-mindedness could arise, then made sure Burton did not gain the greater prize. Such at any rate is the clear inference from the gloating and sardonic letter he sent in answer to a personal appeal from Isabel. The message is surely one of the most signal examples extant of a politician working out personal pique.

> Dear Lady Burton,
>
> As Her Majesty's Ministers have no immediate intention of annexing Morocco to the crown of the British Empire, I would not feel justified, should such a vacancy occur, in proposing your husband as Minister in that locality.
>
> I am etc,
> Salisbury.[33]

26

The Arabian Nights

ONE of the most famous books of the nineteenth century, and certainly one of the greatest influences on eminent Victorians, was the collection of Oriental fables known as the *Thousand and One Nights* or, more popularly, the *Arabian Nights*.[1] Its influence can be seen in Matthew Arnold's *God and the Bible*, in Carlyle's *Sartor Resartus* and in T. H. Huxley's *Evolution and Ethics*. Lord Rosebery, Christina Rossetti and Charlotte Brontë were among the thousands of avid readers of the heavily censored and bowdlerised children's version. Cardinal Newman, John Stuart Mill and William Morris all mention the *Nights* as one of their most important childhood influences.[2] These famous stories were a hybrid collection of fables and parables from many different eras. The oldest dated from the eighth century AD, the nucleus from the tenth, but there were accretions from as late as the sixteenth. The work largely assumed its present form in the thirteenth century. There was no single author, only editors and copyists of traditional tales.

Since his return from India in 1849 Burton had been engaged in a deep study of the *Nights*. It was his aim eventually to produce a complete and unexpurgated version of these highly lubricious tales. The impact on Victorian consciousness had been via the original French translation of Antoine Galland, who introduced the *Nights* to the West at the beginning of the eighteenth century, gelding the strongly sexual and erotic original to produce a classical collection of fairy stories; it was in this capacity that the *Nights* were discussed by the brothers Grimm. Galland's version in turn had been done into English by Jonathan Scott, Henry Torrens and Edward Lane. All of these had toned down Galland's version still further so that the theme of sexuality, which informs and powers the tales in their pristine form, was wholly absent. It was this absurd situation of the 'grin without the cat' that Burton vowed to undo in his translation. 'The most familiar of books in England next to the Bible, it is one of the least known, the reason being that about one-fifth is utterly unfit for translation, and the most sanguine orientalist would not dare to render literally more than three quarters of the remainder.'[3]

Coleridge says somewhere that the true poet must have the eye of an Indian and the ear of a desert Arab. Burton fancied himself to have the latter faculty. He was certainly unrivalled as an exponent of the unique musicality of Arabic, and firmly convinced that Oriental verse was superior to that of the West. 'Apart from the pomp of words and the music of sound there is a dreaminess of idea and a haze thrown over the subject, infinitely attractive but indescribable ... We Europeans and moderns by stippling and minute touches produce a miniature on a large scale so objective as to exhaust rather than to arouse reflection ...'[4]

Burton's work on the complete translation of the *Nights* proceeded by fits and starts. He made poor progress in Africa from 1854 to 1864; Brazil was a halcyon period, but then Damascus and the depressing aftermath curbed his labours again. The necessary goad to get down to serious work was provided by an announcement in a November 1881 issue of the *Athenaeum* that the 39-year-old Orientalist John Payne, erstwhile translator of François Villon, was about to bring out an unexpurgated translation of the *Nights*, in a private printing of 500 copies.[5]

Burton graciously wished Payne good luck and offered him help. Flattered by this offer from a man he admired, Payne magnanimously offered collaboration and a share in the royalties. Burton charmingly brushed the suggestion aside, on the grounds that he was not fully master of his own time. The real reason was that Burton would never have been able to be a true partner in a literary enterprise, and he did not know Payne well enough to be sure of dominating him.

Besides, Payne's sensibility was alien to Burton's. Formidable Arabist he might be, but Payne had a sexual personality bizarre even by the standards of Speke and Burton. A 'confirmed bachelor', he went everywhere with his two sisters and insisted on sleeping where he could have permanent right of passage through their bedrooms. Timid and fearful of sexuality, he was not the one to translate the bawdy passages of the *Nights* with virile gusto. When Burton urged on him Danton's motto *de l'audace, de l'audace et toujours de l'audace* in the translation of notoriously 'obscene' passages, Payne instead dived for linguistic cover. The consequence was that his edition of the *Nights*, which appeared in 1882, did not catch the literary public's imagination, and its success was limited to purely academic circles. Burton shrewdly realised that a gap still remained to be filled. On his return from the abortive Gold Coast expedition with Verney Cameron, he worked night and day on his project. His translation of the *Nights* became a consuming obsession.[6]

Burton took Isabel into his confidence and advised her that he was going to be his own publisher, under the imprint of the Kama Shastra Society, with fictional headquarters at Benares. He would absorb all the publishing costs himself and gamble that the outcome would be a success. Isabel took charge of publicity, and sent out 34,000 circulars advertising a private printing of 1000 copies of complete translation plus notes, to be sold by subscription at a guinea a volume. The print run was very soon subscribed and sold out.

Isabel was in a state of high anxiety much of the time, fearful that she and her husband would be prosecuted for obscenity. Publication was delayed by Burton's eight-month illness in 1883, following a heart attack. But at last in 1885 the first ten volumes appeared, to be followed by six supplemental volumes between 1886 and 1888. The project was a huge financial success. Burton spent 6000 guineas on the printing of the sixteen volumes and made a profit of 10,000 guineas, enough to keep him in comfort for the rest of his life. But the success merely increased his cynicism. 'I struggled for forty-seven years. I distinguished myself honourably in every way I possibly could. I never had a compliment nor a 'thank you', nor a single farthing. I translated a doubtful book in my old age and immediately made 16,000 guineas. Now that I know the tastes of England, we need never be without money.'[7]

The financial success of the *Nights* is at first sight surprising, for Burton committed many of the faults that had led to the commercial failure of the *Kasidah* and *The Lusiads*. Just as he had used Elizabethan English for his translation of *The Lusiads*, Burton decided to use Chaucer as his model for the *Arabian Nights*. It is interesting that the two pre-eminent Arabists of the day, Doughty and Burton, should both have fallen back on Chaucerian English as the key to the true idiom of the desert Arab.[8] It was easy for critics to suggest that Burton simply used the specious example of Chaucer to mask his own romantic preference for the antique and the quaint, the remote in space and time.

The other issue Burton failed to solve in his translation was, what was the correct sort of dialogue for Arabs of the Middle Ages? Burton accused Edward Lane (his particular 'pea in the shoe' among *Nights* translators) of having dressed up Burns in plumes borrowed from Dryden and Pope.[9] His critics replied that *he* had simply varied the equation, and dressed up Burns in the language of Spenser and Chaucer.

Burton's familiar pedantry is much in evidence in his translation. He insisted on the correct Anglicised version of Arab words, even though the incorrect ones were well known and had passed into usage: 'Sindbad' for Sinbad and 'Alaeddin' for Aladdin were merely the most obvious examples. He also insisted on giving the correct Arabic forms in the text for well-known places; Alexandria, Greece, Abyssinia, Africa, etc. Some words, such as the variants of 'Allah' used in oaths, he did not bother to translate at all, thus forcing the reader to refer to the notes at the foot of the page. Similarly, in the interests of strict accuracy he avoided well-known words like 'dragoman', which again forced the reader to consult an English dictionary. Such, however, was Burton's inconsistency, that he was well capable of using the phonetic equivalent of the Arabic *and* the well-known English version at different times (Solomon, Suleiman, etc.).

Most wearisome was his insistence on using obscure and archaic words, or French expressions for which there was a perfectly good English equivalent. But alongside this, there is a disconcerting countervailing current pulling in the direction of slang, neologism and even Americanisms. Burton's own fragmented identity and unintegrated ego explain the startling shifts from the heroic to the vulgar mode, the juxtaposition of American slang and Chaucerian archaism. There is something obsessional about his pedantry and love of the arcane, and the suspicion often arises that he used the translation of the *Nights* as an excuse to display his formidable erudition.

Burton justified the mixed mode of Chaucerian and contemporary English thus:

> The original Arabic ... is highly composite; it does not disdain local terms, bye-words and allusions ... and it borrows indiscriminately from Persian, from Turkish and from Sanskrit. As its equivalent in vocabulary I could devise only a somewhat archaical English whose old-fashioned and sub-antique flavour would contrast with our modern and everyday speech, admitting at times even Latin or French terms ... my conviction remains that it represents, with much truth to Nature, the motley suit of the Arabo-Egyptian ... the translator of the original mind will not neglect the frequent opportunities of enriching his own mother tongue with alien and novel adornments.[10]

There can be no serious doubts that what sold the Burton version of the *Arabian Nights* and made it a runaway financial success was its treatment of sex. Ironically, the best-known stories in the *Nights*, the ones that made it in bowdlerised form a 'children's classic', are the least typical. Thomas de Quincey's opinion was that the story of Aladdin was by far the best of these Oriental fables, but this is not even one of the tales from the Thousand and One Nights properly so-called, but an accretion, which Burton translated in his *Supplementary Nights*. As for the tale of Sinbad, this clearly shows the cross-fertilising influence of the West, not least in its similarity to the *Odyssey*: Polyphemus the Cyclops appears in both stories. The truly distinctive thing about the *Nights* is its treatment of sexuality.

The tales are saturated with sex. Some critics have asserted that the true inspiration of the *Nights* is a profound sexual distrust of women.[11] Misogynism and fear of the essential lustfulness of women is certainly there in abundance, beginning with the orgy in the Porter's Tale in Book One, where Burton uses the quaint terms 'prickle' and 'coynte' to describe the male and femal sexual organs. In Book Six the story of the three wishes is dedicated to the proposition that an extra inch of penis constitutes the female dream of paradise. A man granted three wishes is egged on by his wife to ask for a huge organ. His wish is granted and his member becomes as huge as a column. He then has to use up the second wish in getting rid of this gigantic phallus, then a third in restoring things to the original position. The moral is that even if granted his deepest desires, a man would probably be ruined by his wife's lust.[12]

There were four homosexual episodes – though not lengthy enough to justify the exhaustive treatment of the subject by Burton in his notes (fifty pages).[13] And there were references, at least, to every sexual activity, perverted or not, known to the human imagination. Predictably, all this brought howls of outrage. Burton's enemies pounced. Henry Reeve of the *Edinburgh Review* wrote: 'Probably no European has ever gathered such an appalling collection of degrading customs and statistics of vice. It is a work which no decent gentleman will long permit to stand upon his shelves ... Galland is for the nursery, Lane for the library, Payne for the study and Burton for the sewers.'[14] The same organ was still inflamed seven years later when reviewing Isabel's *Life* of her husband: 'one of the most indecent books in the English language', it concluded.[15] Stanley Lane-Poole, the Arabist, another old enemy, called Burton's translation 'an attitude of attraction towards all that is most repulsive in life and literature ... the anthropological notes ... evince an intimate acquaintance with Oriental depravity, the confession of which has at best the merit of boldness, whilst the elaborate exposition of so much filth can scarcely be matter of congratulation.'[16]

Naturally, Burton regarded this kind of criticism as either wilful misunderstanding or arrant humbug. As he explained:

> The naïve indecencies of the text are rather *gaudisserie* than prurience; and, when delivered with mirth and humour, they are rather the 'excrements of wit' than designed for debauching the mind. Crude and indelicate with infantile plainness; even gross and at times 'nasty' in their terrible frankness, they cannot be accused of corrupting suggestiveness or subtle insinuation of vicious sentiment. Theirs is a coarseness of language, not of idea; they are indecent, not depraved; and the pure and perfect naturalness of their nudity seems almost to purify it, showing that the matter is rather of manners than of morals. Such throughout the East is the language of every man, woman and child, from prince to peasant, from matron to prostitute ... to those critics who complain of these raw vulgarisms and puerile

indecencies in the Nights I can reply only by quoting the words said to have been said by Dr Johnson to the lady who complained of the naughty words in his dictionary – 'You must have been looking for them, Madam!'[17]

Yet Burton was being rather disingenuous in insinuating that sex was entirely in the eye of the beholder. He deliberately drew attention to it by his long and learned sexological notes on the translation. A mere recital cannot do justice to the richness of Burton's treatment. Much of it is coloured by his attitude to women, which is clearly in tune with the ethos of the *Nights* themselves, i.e., misogynistic. Women are inherently lustful, deceitful and treacherous; most rape takes place because women 'ask for it'; old females are especially repulsive, and so on.[18]

There are lengthy discussions of lesbianism (with some comparative anthropology of Dahomey and Arabia), female masturbation and clitoridectomy, which Burton seems to approve on the grounds that it diminishes lust.[19] He also dilates on his theory of 'geographical morality', whereby a hot and damp climate results in greater female lust than male, with the reverse in cold, dry climates.[20]

Considerable space is devoted in the notes to varieties of love-making and the specialities provided by Egyptian prostitutes. Pederasty and homosexuality also receive extended discussion, and finally there is an 18,000-word dissertation in which he explains his conviction (unfashionable in Victorian times) that the Greeks were pederasts. He explains that the Arabic word for an active sodomite is not an insult, but the word for the passive catamite is. Under Islamic law the detected sodomite is punishable by death but proof is very difficult, since it requires four eye-witnesses.[21] Eunuchs, too, fascinate Burton, and he unveils details of their sex lives: 'they practise the manifold pleasures of the *petite oie* (masturbation, tribadism, irrumation, *tête-bêche, feuille de rose* etc) till they induce venereal orgasm.'[22]

Bestialism is another subject to engage Burton's interest. He mentions the practice of superstitious peasants of the Upper Nile, who throw the female crocodile on its back to immobilise it, then have intercourse with it, in the belief that this will bring them good luck. With a shudder Burton records: 'Horrible embraces, the knowledge of which was wanting to complete the disgusting history of human perversity.' On the other hand, he also tells the story of a holy man who committed bestialism with a donkey and was held thereby to have given exceptional proof of holiness![23]

Burton's anthropological notes are full of curious information on all aspects of sex in the Arab world: the removal of pubic and under-arm hair on arab women by vellification and depilatories; the making of early condoms from the guts of sheep; and the belief that sexual intercourse during the menses produced elephantiasis, hence the taboo on this practice in Eastern religions. The Jews even believed that sorcerers were those thus engendered. Burton was adamant that incest produced no dysgenic effects in the case of two healthy partners.[24]

But sex, though the most important subject in Burton's notes, is far from being the only one. Burton provides a treasure-trove of valuable sociological lore on the Islamic world. There are intimate details on the harem system, which he defends on the ground that it obviates prostitution, 'which is perhaps the greatest evil known to modern society'. There are recipes for the preparation of *bhang* or hashish. Death figures largely: murder, suicide, infanticide, euthanasia and even some thoughts on the connection between Eros and Thanatos that anticipate Freud. The range of information is dazzling. Nothing is too trivial or too important to escape Burton's pen. He tells us that Arabs regarded whistling as the devil's work, and giggling, grinning and any form of laughter other than the full-throated as fit only for Christians and monkeys. Merchants, who were looked down on as uncultivated in nineteenth-century England, were highly honoured in Islam (as in Ancient Rome). Close observation of Arab society led Burton to the conclusion that social equality was a chimera, since the dearest ambition of every slave was not simply to be free, but to have a slave of his own. He also approved of vendetta, private vengeance and lynch-law, noting that under Islam the punishment of murder and homicide by the family, rather than society, removed the need for lawyers.[25]

We learn that in Islamic lore the house is considered accursed when a woman's voice is heard out of doors, that the ugliest women make the best procuresses, that blinding is common in the Orient, especially with junior princelings not required as heirs. Wine drinking is forbidden to pilgrims and particularly vitiates the pilgrim-rite but, Burton claims, Holy writ is silent on other manifestations of alcoholism. Orientals do not imbibe the 'social cup' but drink to get drunk. Hence it is irreverent to assert of patriarchs, prophets and saints that they drank.[26]

The sixteen volumes of *Arabian Nights*, plus Burton's hundreds of erudite notes and the long 'Terminal Essay', established this production as his major literary *opus*. Burton's claims to literary fame stand or fall on this one work. On the whole, contemporary reviewers felt that it stood very sturdily. *St James's Gazette* found his translation the only one worthy of a great original. *The Standard* asserted with Burton that the *Nights* was a truly moral work, evincing the same sort of ethical standards as Socrates and Plato.[27] Burton's critics fastened either on the erotic content of the book or on his idiosyncratic language. Among the principal hostile reviewers were those in *The Echo*, *Pall Mall Gazette* and *Saturday Review*. 'Morally filthy book ... absolutely unfit for the Christian population of the nineteenth century ... Pantagruelism or

Pornography ... the Ethics of Dirt ... the garbage of the brothels ... offensive and not only offensive, but grossly and needlessly offensive' were just some of the milder comments.[28] Opinions tended to polarise sharply into friendly and hostile. One of the few judicious and measured reviews came from John Addington Symonds, doyen of critics and famous for his studies of Greek poets, Dante, Shakespeare's contemporaries, and Italian artists like Michelangelo and Benvenuto Cellini.[29] Symonds began by pointing out that if the Burton translation of the *Nights* were to be suppressed, as some were demanding, the works of Plato, Theocritus and Ovid must logically be so also. He proceeded to marvel at the linguistic talents deployed in the translation.[30]

> Commanding a vast and miscellaneous vocabulary, he takes such pleasure in the use of it that sometimes he transgresses the unwritten law of artistic harmony. From the point of view of language, I hold that he is too eager to seize the *mot propre* of his author, or to render that by any equivalent which comes to hand from field or fallow, waste or warren, hill or hedgerow in our vernacular ... therefore, as I think, we find some coarse passages of the Arabian Nights rendered with unnecessary crudity, and some poetic passages marred by archaisms and provincialisms.[31]

In some ways the most satisfying aspect of Burton's triumph was his 'I told you so' victory over Isabel. Burton was neither the first nor the last person to conclude that the gender with the truly abiding and profound interest in sexuality, as opposed to pornography and locker-room titillation, was the female. He said to John Payne in 1884: 'My prediction is that all the women in England will read it and half the men will cut me.'[32] But Isabel continued to insist that no 'decent' woman could possibly read the full and unexpurgated version. She decided to prepare an edited version of her husband's work, suitable for mothers and daughters and designed, like Trollope's novels, never to bring a blush to a maidenly cheek.

Then there arose the obvious problem. How could she prepare an expurgated version without having first seen the allegedly filthy and obscene sections? With Richard's collusion she concocted an absurd story that her husband and their friend Justin Hartley McCarthy blotted out or excised the offending passages and wrote euphemisms in their place, which the great editor Isabel then turned into readable prose.[33] But an examination of her manuscript copy of the original *Nights* shows clearly that she read every single offending or 'obscene' word and wrote exasperated comments in the margin when her sensibilities were too greatly offended.[34] As on so many other occasions, Isabel stands revealed as humbug and liar. As for the 'readable prose', its quality may perhaps be gauged from the use of 'embraced' as a catch-all term to encompass a variety of nuances in the original.

Not content with emasculating the text, Isabel next hacked and scythed her way through her husband's anthropological notes. The anodyne she retained; the interesting she excised. Burton's wrath was assuaged when he observed with pleasure the catastrophic commercial failure of Isabel's 'six pretty volumes' (in itself an indication of how much she had cut). In two years only 457 copies were sold. Triumphantly Burton recorded in his notes to the *Supplemental Nights*: 'The public would have none of it: even innocent girlhood tossed aside the chaste volumes in utter contempt, and would not condescend to aught but the thing, the whole thing and nothing but the thing, unexpurgated and uncastrated.'[35]

27

Isabel Takes Charge

THE mid-1880s also saw Burton finally pinioned into the dependence on Isabel he had tried to avoid during twenty-five years of married life. For a good quarter of this time he had avoided her company.

In some ways Burton had found the right kind of woman for a wife. Isabel was utterly lacking in any real intellectual distinction but she had the 'cleverness' that was more in vogue a century later, when cunning, artfulness, chicanery and self-promotion replaced the capacity for logical thought as 'desirable' mental faculties. But the mixture she possessed was just right for Burton in a quotidian sense. Any more intelligent, and she would have bitterly resented Burton's marital programme of systematic domination; any less, and she would have lacked the capacity to be useful as a factotum in going the rounds of publishers with Richard's manuscripts, or been unable to handle efficiently the recurring chore of 'pay, pack and follow'.

Publicly she claimed that being mastered and dominated by Richard fulfilled her as a woman. But the real problem with Isabel was that she had a superabundance of will-power. One has only to contrast Richard's supine and depressed performance when he returned in disgrace from Damascus with Isabel's tireless and energetic lobbying on his behalf to realise this.[1] Burton came to regret the way he had built Isabel up into a 'woman-mate', able to fence, throw clubs and ride all day in the wilderness. The last straw was when Isabel branched into authorship. Her *The Inner Life of Syria, Palestine and the Holy Land* (1876), based on her 1870–71 experiences and written in an easy, chatty style, far outsold Richard's own dry and scholarly *Unexplored Syria.*[2] She made the mistake of teasing him about the greater commercial success of her book when in the presence of one of her women friends. 'You are like an iron machine, and I do all the wit and sparkle', she said.

'Oh, I dare say', Richard flashed back. 'The sparkle of a superannuated glow-worm.'[3] So much for her claim that there were no cross words in her marriage.

Isabel learned well from her husband the lesson that only power ultimately prevails. Publicly she bowed her head, but at the unconscious level her anger continued, occasionally finding a vent through to the surface in altered form. The principal focus for her rage was anyone who maltreated animals.[4] It was her custom to post handbills in Trieste, offering prizes for humane treatment of animals; it was said of Isabel that she was known to every donkey-driver in the city. One of the posters featured an imaginary letter from the cab-horses and bullocks of Trieste to their masters. It is by no means far-fetched to suggest that the latent content of this communication was from Isabel to Richard, with her as 'beast' and him as 'Man'.

> The only wish that I have is to love and serve and obey your will. Do not, therefore, break my heart with ill-treatment ... I want to understand you, but I am often so terrified by you that I no longer know what it is that you want me to do. My head throbs from the blows you give me on my tender nose ... Treat me well, and you will see that I shall be able to do double my work ...[5]

It must have mortified Richard Burton that in many ways his wife was an egregiously silly woman. It was not just that she was prepared to utter an opinion on any subject under the sun, at a moment's notice and with the aplomb of the life-time scholar, even though she knew nothing whatever about it. She was also a poor manager of money and servants.[6] Further Isabel's follies involved dropping small Catholic charms into her husband's pocket to try to convert him (admittedly, this was on the advice of her confessor). Burton responded by throwing the offending objects out of the window. Shortly before his death, she did manage to wear him down to the point where, to get some peace, he signed a paper to say that he was a Catholic. Isabel was overjoyed at this spurious 'conversion', but Richard's motivation was transparent. As one of his earliest biographers pointed out: 'Rather than be perpetually importuned and worried, he may have preferred to give in to Lady Burton, as one does to a troublesome child.'[7]

Isabel had an almost genius-like ability to alienate a vast spectrum of people from every class, race and creed: from Foreign Ministers to cooks, from her own in-laws to the Arabs of Damascus, from monarchs to the donkey-drivers of Trieste. In a letter of condolence she wrote to Windsor Castle in 1884 on the occasion of the death of the Duke of Albany, she seems to suggest that Queen Victoria is in need of spiritual guidance. Perhaps she thought she saw an opportunity to actualise her 'dream' in the cave outside Jerusalem.

Trieste, 29 March 1884

Dear Sir Henry Ponsonby,

I hope I am not taking an unwarrantable liberty in expressing to you the grief and sympathy we feel at the heavy affliction which has befallen Her Majesty. We have but just received the sad news at Trieste. The mournful sight of our flag half-mast high covered with crape – the feeling that we are but one atom of the greatest nation in the world, every man, woman and child of which are this day in unison with our dear queen in her sorrow, make each one of us however humble long to show some mark of respectful attachment. It has pleased Providence to send so many afflictions to Her Majesty within the last few years and we, the public, know by her true and womanly publications, how each sorrow is felt just as it would be by one of us.

I have a little orphanage of 34 children, and a little oratory, and I am going down there to take the little ones into the chapel to pour forth earnest prayers that Her Majesty may have the strength to bear this fresh blow, and that it may be given to her to see the hidden blessing that is under each affliction ... I beg you to pardon the intrusion, and pray do not think that I expect an answer.

I am, dear Sir Henry Ponsonby,

Yours truly Isabel Burton (wife of Captain Burton the traveller at present English consul at Trieste.)[8]

Even though Isabel displayed none of the lecherous qualities Burton so feared in women, her combination of silliness and redoubtable willpower contrived to feed Burton's misogynism. Anyone who still clings to the myth of 'the romance of Isabel' or imagines the Burtons' marriage to have been uniquely happy should investigate the many cryptic references in the notes to Richard's *Arabian Nights* translation.

In a note to *The Seventh Voyage of Sindbad the Seaman*, Burton tells in coded form of a cruel trick he once played on Isabel. Deciphering the cryptic story, in which Burton poses as 'a Maltese gentleman', what we emerge with is the following. On one occasion when Isabel was on his arm, Burton met a beautiful Italian woman and flirted with her quite outrageously in Italian. He referred to Isabel contemptuously: '*mia moglie – con rispetto parlando*' ('my wife, saving your presence'). The fair Italian was stupefied and incredulous. 'What, he speaks of his wife as if he would of the sweepings.'[9]

The *Tale of Kamar-al-Zaman* tells of the unreciprocated passion of Princess Budur for her lord, and the fact that he finds her sexually repellent. Kamar-al-Zaman, like Burton, would rather get a good night's sleep than enjoy the dubious pleasures of intercourse with the Princess: 'She stole one glance of eyes that cost her a thousand sighs: her heart fluttered, and her vitals throbbed and her hands and feet quivered; and she said to Kamar-al-Zaman, "Talk to me, O my lord! Speak to me, O my friend! Answer me, O my beloved, and tell me thy name, for indeed thou hast ravished my wit!" And during all this time he abode drowned in sleep and answered her not a word.'[10]

In the notes is this revealing sentence: 'The world shows that while women have more philoprogenitiveness, men have more amativeness; otherwise the latter would not propose and would nurse the doll and the baby.'[11] There was no baby, and for all practical purposes it was Isabel who had proposed. There could be no doubting who the real-life equivalents of Kamar-al-Zaman and Princess Budur were.

Further covert references to the cold-bedded marriage of convenience he had contracted with Isabel occur at regular intervals throughout the critical apparatus to the *Arabian Nights* translation. He refers to himself as the 'man of the world' who had seduced 'an utterly innocent (which means an ignorant) girl.'[12] And in *The Adventures of Mercury Ali of Cairo* he makes plain his own lack of sexual feeling towards Isabel, and how that was a factor in her infatuation: 'Many a woman, even of the world, has fallen in love with a man before indifferent to her because he did not take advantage of her when he had the opportunity.'[13]

It would have been strange if such a marriage, bound by ties of familiarity and companionship but sexless and concealing oceans of rage and disappointment on both sides, did not in the end reveal some cracks. But strangest of all is that Isabel, who burned her husband's journal on his death to prevent the truth about the marriage emerging, laid before the world a vital clue to some of its inner tensions. From 1877 to 1883, she reveals:

> We suddenly began to be inundated by anonymous letters; then our private papers and writings would disappear; a great fuss of finding them was made, and when all fuss and hope of recovery was over, they would reappear. There was always some mystery hanging about, and once we found on the floor a copy-book with some very good imitations of my hand-writing, or what my handwriting *would* be if I tried to disguise it a little backwards, and some very bad and easily recognisable attempts at my husband's very peculiar hand. The anonymous letters generally tried to set us against each other, if possible, and I was always finding love-letters thrust into his pockets, whenever I cleaned or brushed his clothes, which I generally did.[14]

Isabel's later explanation was that a woman confidante, a second Jane Digby who had the complete run of their apartment, jealous of the Burtons' idyllic marriage, tried to poison relations between husband and wife. Burton's most recent biographer, however, deduces that there was no third party involved, and attributes the farce to Burton's impish sense of humour.[15] This explanation goes some way towards the truth of this affair, but veers off before getting to the heart of the matter. It is clear that Burton knew his wife was the woman involved. Isabel concocted a story that her mysterious woman friend had free access to all her papers, journals and writings, 'knew my every move', and finally confessed on her death-bed. If there was such a person, is it not passing strange that there is not a single other mention of her in Isabel's copious notes on their life in Trieste? And if there were, would not such a person be the obvious suspect? It would hardly be beyond the wit and ingenuity of 'Mirza Abdullah' to find a way to catch her red-handed, rather than suffer such an indignity for six years.

It is surely obvious that the writer of the 'anonymous' letters, who could produce such a good forgery of Isabel's and Richard's hands, was none other than Isabel herself. The circumstantial evidence is overwhelming. In the first place, Isabel claims the woman made her death-bed confession *after* Richard's death – very convenient. Then, the campaign of vilification went on until 1883 – the precise moment when Richard became heavily dependent on Isabel. And who else but Isabel herself would 'know her every move'?

Most telling of all is the very language Isabel uses to describe the incident. She claims that she and Richard referred privately to their mysterious tormentor as 'It'. She then claims that the woman who made the death-bed confession said, 'I am It'.[16] Now, quite apart from the implausibility of the miscreant third party using a term allegedly known only to Isabel and Richard themselves, the verbal formulation sounds uncannily like 'I am id'. The fact that the term popularised by Freud would not come into general use for another thirty years does not affect the central point, which is that a person ashamed at the dark workings of the unconscious might well choose to characterise them as something apart, an object, an 'it'.

'It' confessed as follows: 'Sometimes I wrote gushing letters, so as to make you seem silly; sometimes I gave your opinions to people in high positions to make you seem impertinent.' Before 1890 the idea that Isabel could have diagnosed herself as 'gushing' or 'impertinent' is implausible. But once she read her husband's journals, she must have realised that these were exactly the criticisms commonly made of her. The whole episode makes it a moral certainty that the third person, 'It', was a figment of Isabel's disturbed mind. The 'deathbed confession' is a transmogrified form of her own deeply ambivalent response to Richard, surfacing when she no longer wanted to go on living, or sensed that she had not long to live anyway. Ashamed of her own dark side and of her actions between 1877 and 1883, Isabel invented a person who could be blamed for them, just as T. E. Lawrence devised a fictitious 'old man' who ordered him to be beaten, to disguise his own masochism. The entire 'It' saga is strong evidence for what was anyway obvious: that Isabel was consumed with a deep anger over the way Richard treated her, and that her frenzied reaction to the treatment, beneath the surface of deference and servility, increased the disequilibrium of an already precariously balanced mind. Her descent into near madness after 1890 is already prefigured in the bizarre domestic happenings of 1877 to 1883.

28

The Final Years

The crushing news that Burton could look for nothing from the Foreign Office, neither promotion nor honourable retirement, precipitated fresh outbreaks of gout and cardiac problems. It was January 1887 before he was fit to travel back to Trieste, via the French Riviera. At Cannes a double calamity struck them. First a great earthquake shook the hotel, 'split a few walls, shook the soul out of one's body, and terrified strangers out of their wits.' Isabel looked out of the window to find horror-stricken guests in their night clothes urging her and her husband to get out of the hotel as fast as possible. 'No, my girl, you and I have been in too many earthquakes to show the white feather at our age.' Isabel acquiesced. Burton noted laconically in his journal, 'I turned round and went to sleep again.'[1] He had indeed trained Isabel to a rare pitch of stoicism and fearlessness.

The second calamity could not be brushed aside. Late in February Burton suffered a second heart attack. The doctor warned Isabel that Richard might not live. Always fearful that he would be damned to the fires of Hell, she got some water and baptised him into the Catholic faith.[2] There was a young doctor named Grenfell Baker staying in Cannes on account of his own delicate health. Mightily impressed by Burton's courage in the aftermath of the heart attack, he accepted an offer from Isabel later that year to be the Burtons' travelling physician. Burton himself resisted the proposal, fearing the intrusion on his privacy and predicting (incorrectly, as it transpired) that they would not get on with Baker. The arrangement turned out to be a complete success; thereafter Baker was rarely absent from Sir Richard's side.

In Trieste Burton was again seriously ill. The medicine he took to suppress gout produced epileptic fits and he was for a long time a helpless invalid. When he attempted to write, he would dip his pen anywhere but in the ink; when he tried to say something, he could not get out the words; he habitually bumped into the furniture as he tottered round the palazzo. Grenfell Baker's diagnosis was that the gout was merely a secondary symptom, the inevitable consequence of the port Burton drank surreptitiously against even the direst warnings from physicians. The real problem was a weak heart, caused by either an embolism or a weakness in the valves. But the gout was dangerous, since the flatulence that always followed strained the heart.

In 1887 Burton's foreign travels comprised just one month in Austria. Ill as he was, when the Prince of Wales arrived at Trieste in his yacht in June, on the occasion of Queen Victoria's Golden Jubilee, Burton laid on a sumptuous reception for him and organised the illumination of the town; the Prince, however, chose not to stir from his yacht. From October to March 1888 the Burtons were in Croatia. In that month Burton finished the last volume of the *Supplemental Nights* and celebrated his sixty-seventh birthday. His childlike dependence on Isabel and Baker seemed fittingly symbolised by his choice of reading matter. Banished were his favourite classics; instead he tackled with relish *Little Lord Fauntleroy*.

In May Isabel cabled the Foreign Office for permission for another UK leave. This was grudgingly given. Not content with this, she then telegraphed the government with an extraordinary and highly irregular request. Matthew Arnold had just died, so Isabel suggested that Richard take over his Civil List pension of £250 a year. The request was peremptorily refused.[3] They were deluged with dining out invitations in London, but Burton could not stay on his feet after 8 p.m. Social life was restricted to the afternoons, when they entertained Swinburne, Henry Irving and other friends. The newspapers wanted to know his opinion of the fate of Stanley. Deep in the Emin Pasha Relief Expedition, Stanley had not been heard from for a year and was feared dead. But Burton knew his man better than that: he predicted, accurately, that Stanley would soon be heard from again, and that he was bound to come through successfully.[4]

Everyone in England commented on Sir Richard's gaunt and haggard mien. Faded and sunken now were the eyes once described as those of an imperious gypsy, or containing the sting of a baleful serpent. The Stisteds were shocked at his appearance, which seemed to indicate that heart disease was making rapid inroads. Georgiana noted: 'His eyes wore that strained look which accompanies difficult respiration, his lips were bluish-white, his cheeks livid; the least exertion made him short of breath and sometimes he would pant when quietly seated in his chair.'[5]

On 26 October 1888 Burton had his last-ever sight of England as his household crossed the Channel, *en route* to Switzerland. They wintered in Vevey and Montreux, then stayed some weeks in Geneva and Lausanne before returning to Trieste in March 1889.[6] The summer of

1889 was another ordeal. The Burtons spent July to September in western Austria, where Richard was obliged to undergo two minor but painful operations for the relief of his gout. There was painful wrangling with the Foreign Office, too. In 1886 the Burtons had been prevailed upon by Francis Hitchman to allow the writing of a full biography. Burton even made over to Hitchman a long unfinished autobiographical manuscript. This seems a curious thing for the Burtons to have done. Isabel's excuse was that Hitchman was winning and plausible and broke their hearts with 'tales of poverty, sickness and a large family', all of which could be made right once he had received a publisher's advance of £150 on the strength of Sir Richard's collaboration. But the Burtons were ill requited. Not only did Hitchman plagiarise the loaned material without acknowledgement, but he wrote up his two-volume work in such a way as to make the Foreign Office appear heartless villains. This brought a devastating Establishment riposte, in the form of an anonymous review of the biography in the *Saturday Review* which exposed all Sir Richard's chicanery over leaves and postings since 1861.[7] This time Burton did not follow his own advice, which was *always* to reply to criticisms, no matter how trivial, so that one's case did not go by default. He was ill and in no condition for verbal battle; besides, he knew he was vulnerable on this score. From August to October 1889 the Burtons were engaged in some frosty correspondence with London on the subject of leaves and vice-consular pay.[8] A cautious man, or one with the slightest scintilla of respect for his superiors, might have cut back on his programme of travelling. The attempt to haul him over the coals simply made Burton more than ever determined to demonstrate that he was his own man. The tour planned for the winter of 1889–90 was more elaborate than ever. First stop in November 1889 was Brindisi, where he visited Virgil's house. Then he moved on to Malta, Tunis (where he visited the ruins of Carthage), Constantine and Algiers, returning to Trieste via Toulon and the French Riviera in March 1890. His only regret was that he could not get back to Europe for the Stanley Exhibition in February. As predicted by Burton, Stanley had returned in triumph from the controversial expedition to 'rescue' Emin. Burton paid his fellow-explorer magnanimous tribute. 'I should have wished at this and every other opportunity to express my hearty admiration of all that Stanley has dared and done. He is to me, and always will be, the prince of African travellers.'[9]

As his health seemed to improve slightly, Burton contemplated another massive programme of translations from classical texts. He began with the *Carmina* of Catullus and made extraordinarily rapid progress for one in his precarious health. He commenced work in Algeria on 18 February 1890 and finished the first draft at Trieste on

31 March, having already begun work on the fair copy on 23 March. He would bring his copy of the poems to the *table d'hôte*, so that if he grew bored with the company he could get on with his translation.[10] He completed the translation on 22 July and at once began work on Apuleius's *Golden Ass*. But the effort told on him bodily. His eyes sank into cavities, his frame was emaciated, his hands were transparently thin, his voice inarticulate and he could not walk without support.

In July 1890 the Burtons set out on another long trip to Switzerland. The Stisteds bitterly criticised Isabel for taking her invalid husband on all these journeys during 1889 and 1890, especially since the cost of putting up the entire household of maids, secretary and doctor came to £100 a day, but it seems that the impetus came from Richard himself. He clung to life by having a series of short-term goals: in inner terms the translations, and outwardly by travel. But these collided with a deeper-seated wish for oblivion, occasionally detectable. The result was a kind of permanent mental confusion and neurotic paralysis. Two quotations from Isabel's reminiscences make the point.

> He sucked dry all his surroundings, whether place, scenery, people, or facts, before the rest of us had settled down to realize whether we liked the place or not. When he arrived at this stage everything was flat to him, and he would anxiously say, 'Do you think I shall live to get out of this, to see another place?' . . . 'I am in a very bad way,' he said. 'I have got to hate everybody except you and myself, and it frightens me, because I know perfectly well that next year I shall get to hate you, and the year after that I shall get to hate myself, and then I don't know what will become of me. We are always wandering, and the places that delight *you* I say to myself, "Dry rot," and the next place I say, "Dry rotter," and the third place I say, "Dry rottest" and then *da capo*.'[11]

In Switzerland the Burtons ran into Henry Stanley, who was staying at the same hotel. Stanley, currently in the full flush of his Emin triumph (the critical backlash on this dubious affair had not yet developed) had just married the 39-year-old Dorothy Tennant, and was on honeymoon. Curiously, he was accompanied by his young male friend A. J. Mounteney-Jephson, his principal lieutenant on the Emin expedition. No greater concentration of Victorian eccentrics can be imagined than the quartet composed of the Stanleys and the Burtons. Stanley in his own way was just as much a psychological oddity as Burton, while his wife had slept with her mother in the maternal bedroom all her adult life, and kept a diary in which she communed with her long-dead father.

Burton and Stanley had met just twice before, once at Clements Markham's in 1872, and again at a public dinner in 1886. They had never previously had the opportunity for a heart-to-heart chat, and made full use of it now. Both men were outsiders, both had suffered at the hands of the English establishment (and, incidentally, both received their knighthoods only when almost at death's door), both had a strong distaste for Gladstone and, especially, Salisbury. The two most eminent African explorers still alive, they had similar bisexual personalities (though Stanleys' bisexuality was of the passive kind), were staunch conservatives, even reactionaries, who respected force and action and despised the 'bleeding-heart' liberalism of missionaries and Exeter Hall. As long as they kept off the subject of Livingstone, whom Stanley revered, their conversation was likely to prosper. Both had known betrayal by a false friend, ironically the very same person, Laurence Oliphant.[12]

Mrs Stanley amused the company by folding a piece of paper and then asking Burton for his autograph. Sir Richard supplied a sample of his tiny hand, in English and Arabic. Mrs Stanley then turned over the back of the paper to reveal the words, 'I promise to put aside all my other literature, and as soon as I return to Trieste, to write my own autobiography.' All the others signed as witnesses, and on her return to Trieste Isabel had the paper framed.[13]

Stanley gave a detailed impression of Burton at this time.

> Had a visit from Sir Richard F. Burton, one of the discoverers of Lake Tanganyika. He seems much broken in health. Lady Burton, who copies Mary, Queen of Scotland, in her dress, was with him. In the evening, we met again. I proposed he should write his reminiscences. He said he could not do so, because he would have to write of so many people. 'Be charitable to them, and write only of their best qualities,' I said – 'I don't give a fig for charity; if I write at all, I must write truthfully, all I know', he replied. He is now writing a book called 'Anthropology of Men and Women', a title, he said, that does not describe its contents, but will suffice to induce me to read it. What a grand man! One of the great ones of England he might have been if he had not been cursed with cynicism. I have no idea to what his Anthropology refers, but I would lay great odds that it is only another means of relieving himself of a surcharge of spleen against the section of humanity who have excited his envy, dislike or scorn. If he had a broad mind, he would curb these tendencies, and thus allow me to see more clearly his grander qualities.[14]

Isabel, unfortunately for her own peace of mind, knew exactly what her husband's 'Anthropology' referred to. As his dependence on her grew daily, he tried to maintain some shreds of autonomy by increasing correspondence with the very people she most disliked and deplored; Edward Rehatsek, who had translated the *Beharistan* and the *Gulistan*, H. S. Nichols, the devious Stoke Newington 'underground' printer of the publications of the Kama Shastra Society, Henry Ashbee (for whom her distaste was so great that she could bring herself to mention him only once in the *Life* of her husband), and most of all Leonard Smithers. Smithers, assiduous correspondent with and confidante of Burton in his later years – though the two never met – was a second Fred Hankey. A devotee of pornography and erotica, friend of Oscar Wilde and Aubrey Beardsley, Smithers tried to outbohemian the bohemians by dressing as an undertaker. He had a basement printing-works somewhere near Shepherd's Bush, and he aspired to displace Nichols as London's premier 'underground' printer. The 'diabolical' stories told about him were legion, and peculiarly calculated to appeal to Burton: the most notorious concerned his predilection for having himself photographed while buggering his wife.

Burton and Smithers collaborated on the *Priapeia*. Smithers produced a prose version, Burton rendered it into verse, and the two translations were printed alongside the original Latin under the pseudonyms Outidanos and Neaniskos. Smithers aped Nichols while cutting in on his territory, by fabricating a publishing company called the Erotika Biblion Society, with notional headquarters in Athens. Burton did not want to jeopardise his retirement on full pension in 1891, so behaved circumspectly over the first printing. He cautioned his collaborator over the very real danger of police prosecution. But Smithers, greedy for profits and wishing to tweak the nose of official morality, prepared a more extreme second edition, complete with lavish illustrations featuring tribadism, cunnilingus, masturbation, bestiality and buggery. In an evil hour he persuaded the sick man in Trieste to allow himself to be identified so as to increase the sales of the book; Burton could not resist the appeal to his vanity.

When she learned what had happened, Isabel was nearly frantic with anxiety. Without Richard's knowledge she wrote to Smithers to beseech him to maintain the original pseudonymous front of the reversed initials (as with the *Kama Sutra*). With the aid of Arbuthnot, she persuaded a reluctant Smithers to agree. The *Priapeia* duly appeared, but there were no writs lodged against Sir Richard Burton. For Isabel this was an even narrower escape than over the *Arabian Nights*, which had at least been shielded by the partial invisibility of the 'Benares' publishing house.[15]

Now came the most worrying revelation of all. Richard intended to publish a full, unexpurgated, edited and annotated edition of *The Perfumed Garden*, with a scholarly apparatus to rival that of the *Nights*, and with all previously excised material, on homosexuality, female circumcision, the sexual habits of eunuchs, bestialism (such as detail on copulation with crocodiles), tribadism, and much else. The new version was to be called *The Scented Garden*, to distinguish it from the tamer plot version, and would be a direct translation from the original Arabic; in *The Perfumed Garden* Burton had simply used an extant French text.

Burton was inspired by his recent discovery of the work of the German sexologist Karl Heinrich Ulrichs, who under the pseudonym Numa Numantius had produced a pioneering work on homosexuality that shed important light on the missing chapters of the *Garden*.

Isabel was horrified at the idea of this new monstrosity. The original *Perfumed Garden* had already pushed Victorian tolerance to its limits and beyond. She thought back to its contents. Apart from the bristling misogynism and the many cruel, gloating passages on the shortcomings of women, the hatred of ugly females, and the mixture of physical repulsion and lechery towards 'the sex', she remembered other details that Victorians found profoundly shocking. There was much detail on menstrual bleeding, vaginal lubrication, leucorrhea, 'female ejaculation', advice on how to avoid gonorrhea and cancer by careful protection from the 'horrors' of the vulva – the only fantasy Cheikh Nefzaoui left out was *vagina dentata* – and everywhere an insensate hatred of women. ('If you had a fine member you might dispose of her fortune. Do you know that women's religion is in their vulvas?') On top of this farrago of 'filth' – as the pious Catholic Isabel saw it – was now to be dumped a fresh pile of disgusting deviancy: the ejaculations of sodomites, the intestinal injuries of catamites, perverts penetrating female crocodiles, plus surgical minutiae on infibulation, clitoridectomy and the sewing up of the labia minora!

The problem was that Richard had made *The Scented Garden* his lodestone. When he began work on 21 March 1890, laying aside all his projects for translations of the classics, he noted in his diary: 'Began or rather resumed Scented Garden, don't care much about it, but it is a good potboiler.'[16] But as he began to heap up his sexological notes and turn a small book into a manuscript of more than twelve hundred pages, the project became an obsession. He told Grenfell Baker: 'I have put my whole life and all my life-blood into that *Scented Garden*; it is my great hope that I shall live by it. It is the crown of my life.'[17]

The more pressure Isabel put on him to abandon the work, the more he dug in. His argument that the royalties would provide her with an annuity after his death brought her scant comfort. Grenfell Baker, aware of her violent hostility to the project, warned Burton that she was likely to destroy it if he died before its completion. 'Do you really think so?' Burton asked worriedly. 'Then I must write to Arbuthnot at once to tell him that in the event of my death, the manuscript is to be his.'[18] He did so, but negated his own efforts by naming Isabel in his will as sole executrix.

By 7 September 1890 the Burtons were back in Trieste. Richard was glad to be home after seven weeks' roving. Watching the swallows fly south, he felt a strong premonition of approaching death. His plans for the winter of 1890–91 included a trip to Greece and Constantinople with Schliemann, the great archaeologist of Troy, to last from mid-November to mid-March, followed by a tranquil summer at home, 'but the time is long and Fate is malignant.'[19]

Rapidly failing health and the constant nursing by Isabel brought out a softer side of Burton, buried since childhood. He told visitors that when the Foreign Office finally allowed him to retire in 1891, he and Isabel would devote themselves to the work of Booth's Salvation Army in Abyssinia. The sad departure of the swallows and his fellow-feeling for Catullus in the matter of Lesbia's sparrow made him finally see the point of his wife's tireless campaign for the rights of animals. They took to buying caged birds in Trieste, then releasing them in their garden. An encounter with a caged specimen of Burton's favourite animal, the monkey, provoked particular sadness. The only way he could rationalise the suffering of dumb creatures in this planet was to cling to the Oriental belief that they were condemned to time on the cross in this life for sins committed in a different shape in a former existence.

The twin themes of approaching death and the suffering of animals preoccupied Burton during his last two months. The Letchfords were staying with them. Early in October Daisy Letchford departed for England, while Albert stayed on. Daisy noticed that when bidding her farewell, Burton used the term 'Goodbye', when it was his invariable habit to say '*Au revoir*'. A few days later he said ominously to Albert, 'The good Switzerland did me ended this evening.'[20]

Always very fond of cats, he now surrounded himself with a brood of kittens. Whenever Isabel saw him at this time, he always had one on his shoulder. On 18 October he told Isabel that a bird had been tapping at his window all morning. Remembering Poe's raven, he interpreted it as a bad omen. She tried to cheer him up by pointing out that, since he fed the birds regularly at seven each morning, they must have been pecking expectantly. Implicitly rebuking her literal-mindedness, he replied cryptically, 'Ah, it was not that window, but another.' In his diary he scribbled his very last literary production, inspired by the pervasive bird themes of his final days.

> Swallow, pilgrim swallow
> Beautiful bird with purple plume,
> That, sitting upon my window-sill,
> Repeating each morn at the dawn of day
> That mournful ditty so wild and shrill, –
> Swallow, lovely swallow, what wouldst thou say,
> On my casement-sill at the break of day?[21]

Sunday 19 October 1890 was Burton's last full day on earth. In the morning he rescued a robin that was drowning in a water tank in the garden, warmed it in his hands then wrapped it in one of his fur coats until it recovered. That evening he seemed his old self. He did not eat much, but talked and joked with more *élan* than usual. After dinner a neighbour's dog set up a long dreadful howl, a customary harbinger of death. Burton retired at half past nine, but at midnight was awake again, complaining of gouty pains in his foot. Isabel and Grenfell Baker eased him back into bed. He dozed a little and woke up again to relate a dream of their flat in London: 'it had quite a nice large room in it.'

At 4 a.m. he was awake again, complaining of great pain. Dr Baker examined him and could find nothing more than the symptoms of incipient gout he had seen for the past three years. Half an hour later Baker was aroused by Isabel, in great panic, screaming that her husband was suffocating. Baker raced back to the sick-room, while Isabel frenziedly woke the servants and sent out for a priest. Baker found Burton gasping for breath and on the point of heart failure. He and Isabel then struggled to get him out of bed into a sitting position. As Richard grew weaker and drifted in and out of consciousness, he became heavier and more unwieldy. In one of his lucid moments he cried out, 'Oh Puss, chloroform – ether – or I am a dead man!'

To her diary Isabel afterwards confided, 'My God, I would have given the blood out of my veins if it could have saved him.' To Richard she whispered, 'My darling, the doctor says it will kill you. He is doing all he knows.' Baker then tried to revive the heart with an electric battery. He moistened Burton's chest with salt water, plunged the terminals into water, then applied the electrodes, one to the heart, the other to the patient's shoulder-bone. Isabel knelt at his left side, feeling his pulse. She knew the case was hopeless, but prayed fervently that there might still be signs of life in him when the priest arrived.

Burton died at approximately 5 a.m. on the morning of the 20th. The priest did not arrive until 7 a.m. Isabel begged and pleaded with Dr Baker to keep up the farce of attempted resuscitation when the prelate arrived. It was this which swung things in favour of her deeply-resolved stratagem. Father Pietro Martelani asked whether he was really alive. Isabel and Dr Baker assured him he was. Isabel then begged him to give Extreme Unction. The priest queried whether Burton was a Catholic; was he not, rather, a notorious free-thinker? Isabel assured him she could produce documents later to prove his secret conversion, and begged Father Martelani to proceed. The priest shrugged and did as he was asked. Isabel had achieved her lifetime's ambition. She had saved Richard's soul and brought him at last into the bosom of Holy Mother Church. Having achieved such a triumph, she was forced to lie to herself and the world about the circumstances of her husband's death. Even though she had pleaded with Baker to maintain the fiction that his patient was still alive at 7 a.m., she wrote later: 'By the clasp of the hand, and a little trickle of blood running under the finger, I judged there was a little life until seven.'[22]

That might have been accounted a minor, forgivable deception. But there was no excuse for the burial of Burton according to the rites of the Roman Catholic Church. According to the laws of Trieste, all corpses had to be buried within sixty hours of death. The terrible shock of a husband's death would have cooled the ardour of most conversion-maniacs, but not Isabel. Her hasty lobbying produced a situation where the bishop granted Burton a funeral with the highest ceremonial honours of the Church. The civil authorities followed suit by laying on the kind of military ceremonial usually granted only to royalty.

After eight masses had been said for the repose of Richard's soul, Isabel had his body embalmed and made ready for the solemn cortège. One hundred thousand people turned out for the funeral. Flags were at half-mast, and a guard of honour was provided for the Union Jack-draped catafalque by British sailors from a visiting ship. The Bishop of Trieste read the panegyric. The body was placed in a *chapelle ardente* inside the Catholic cemetery, ready for transshipment to its final resting place at Mortlake. So it came about that, to the disgust of the Stisteds and other relations on Burton's side, 'Rome took formal possession of Richard Burton's corpse, and pretended, moreover, with insufferable insolence, to take under her protection his soul ... [his funeral] was made the excuse for an ecclesiastical triumph of a faith he had always loathed.'[23]

The Dean of Westminster refused permission for Burton to be buried in Westminster Abbey alongside Livingstone, just as permission was later denied to Stanley. But this refusal was not the dreadful snub to Lady Burton it was to be fourteen years later to Lady Stanley. Westminster Abbey, after all, was Protestant territory. Isabel had something grander in mind. Nearly twenty years earlier Richard and Isabel had purchased a plot of ground in the Mortlake Catholic cemetery as their final resting place. In early 1891 Isabel prepared there a monument for Burton that would ensure his fame lived on. She dreamed of an exotic tomb in the shape of an Arab tent. As always, the spendthrift Isabel was short of money. She raised £688 from friends and admirers, but the final bill was around £1000.

Finally, on 7 February 1891, Isabel arrived in London and had her husband's body placed in the crypt of St Mary Magdalene, Mortlake, pending completion of the tomb. As the mausoleum arose to its final shape, eighteen feet high and twelve feet square, it attracted much astonished admiration. It was shaped like the tent Burton described in the *Kasidah*. The Forest of Dean stone was sculpted to create the illusion of canvas, while the door and interior were fashioned from Carrara marble. Above the door was a crucifix and on the roof two Moslem crosses. The interior was equipped with an altar and supposedly so hung with Bedouin lanterns and camel bells that the opening of the door would set off a peaceful tinkling sound. A small stained glass window at the rear, embossed with the Burton coat of arms, would admit sunlight at certain hours of the day.[24]

There, on 5 June 1891, Burton's body was at last laid to rest. Isabel sent out 850 invitations for the second funeral, but only half that number came; the split between those who accepted and those who stayed away was almost entirely on Catholic and Protestant lines. Only one of Burton's relatives attended; the world of exploration was represented by Francis Galton and Lord Northbrook, who stood coldly aloof on the sidelines.[25] Isabel made arrangements to be buried alongside her husband, a consummation achieved on her death in 1896.

Not content with having outraged the feelings and susceptibilities of Burton's relatives, friends and legions of admirers with the Catholic funeral, Isabel now proceeded to her most dreadful act of desecration. She had always been a highly unbalanced individual. The delayed shock of Richard's death seems to have brought her close to outright madness. No truly rational explanation is possible for the sequence of events after October 1890.

She began her campaign of vandalism against the true meaning of Richard Burton's life by burning the manuscript of *The Scented Garden*. By the time of Burton's death, his edition of the work was virtually complete. It would have contained 882 pages of text and footnotes, 100 pages of preface, 50 pages of afterword and a 200-page treatise on homosexuality, in which he drew together the findings of Ulrichs and the lore of the East. When news of Burton's death reached London, a leading publisher at once offered her 6000 guineas for the manuscript.

Since her burning of this unique labour of scholarship cast Isabel for ever into anathema in the minds of all thinking people, it is necessary in fairness to quote at length her 'justification' for such a singular act of destruction,

> My husband had been collecting for fourteen years information and materials on a certain subject. His last volume of the *Supplemental Nights* had been finished and out on November 13, 1888. He then gave himself up entirely to the writing of this book, which was called *The Scented Garden*, a translation from the Arabic. It treated of a certain passion. Do not let anyone suppose for a moment that Richard Burton ever wrote a thing from the impure point of view. He dissected a passion from every point of view, as a doctor may dissect a body, showing its source, its origin, its evil, and its good, and its proper uses, as designed by Providence and Nature. In private life he was the most pure, the most refined and modest man that ever lived, and he was so guileless himself that he could never be brought

> to believe that other men said or used things from any other standpoint. I, as a woman think differently ...
>
> I remained for three days in a state of perfect torture as to what I ought to do about it ... I can take in the world, but I cannot deceive God Almighty, who holds my husband's soul in His hands ... I said to myself, 'out of fifteen hundred men, fifteen will probably read it in the spirit of science in which it was written; the other fourteen hundred and eighty-five will read it for filth's sake, and pass it to their friends, and the harm done may be incalculable' ... what a gentleman, a scholar, a man of the world may write when living, he would see very differently to what the poor soul would see standing naked before its God, with its good or evil deeds alone to answer for ... I fetched the manuscript and laid it on the ground before me, two large volumes' worth ... It was his *magnum opus*, his last work that he was so proud of, that was to have been finished on the awful morrow – that never came ... And then I said, 'Not only for six thousand guineas, but not for six million guineas will I risk it'.[26]

This account in the *Morning Post* does not square with the version she circulated privately. According to this, Burton appeared to her in a dream and ordered her to burn the manuscript of *The Scented Garden*. When she hesitated, she claimed, the ghost stood before her again and again commanded her sternly to burn it. When she still hesitated, Richard's spirit appeared a third time and threatened to haunt her forever unless she burned it. She then obeyed the commands.[27]

Isabel said, 'I cannot deceive God Almighty': doubtless she forgot that it was precisely what she had already tried to do, with the chicanery over Father Martelani and the Extreme Unction. 'It was his *magnum opus*': yet later, in the *Life* of her husband, she says the work had no value.[28] If she burned the work to save Richard's soul, why did she burn his journals and diaries and all his other unpublished work?

Yet the most devastating self-indictment was the absurd story that *The Scented Garden* was exclusively concerned with 'a certain passion', i.e., homosexuality. In fact, the subject occupied a single chapter; as with the *Nights*, the attention Burton devoted to it in the notes was out of all proportion to its importance in the text. By this transparent pretence that the work was entirely concerned with '*le vice*', Isabel betrayed that this was the aspect of *The Scented Garden* which really worried her. It was clear to observers that her abnormal reaction masked a fear that her late husband's interest in the subject was more than merely academic. Too late she realised that, far from burnishing Richard's image, she had tarnished it, and put her own reputation as a wife on the line into the bargain. She had ended by providing the world with a vital clue to the true nature of Richard Burton. In an attempt to redress matters, ill as she was with cancer, she began to work on a massive two-volume hagiography which would present the world with its most complete image of a legendary Burton.[29]

The treatment of Burton's last great enterprise was only the most stunning of Isabel's many acts of vandalism and philistinism. Burton had laboured at his translation of Catullus during the dark days of his cardiac problems. She rewarded his heroic commitment to scholarship by skimming through the manuscript, expurgating the 'offensive' passages, jettisoning reams of invaluable scholarly comment, then, without correcting the copy, burning the original. This from the woman who claimed to regard the *Kasidah* as on a par with Shakespeare! As a studied snub, she sent it to the despised Leonard Smithers to 'edit' and publish, 'just as a child who has been jumping on the animals of a Noah's Ark brings them to his father to be mended.'[30]

The destruction of *The Scented Garden* drew down on Isabel's head howls of anger and vituperation. 'An hysterical, illiterate woman with the bigotry of a Torquemada and the vandalism of a John Knox', was one of the milder comments. Ouida cut her dead and never spoke to her again. Swinburne, who had in earlier days liked Isabel, now cursed himself for his inability fully to read her character. 'It is not my part to strip and whip the popish mendacities of that poor liar Lady Burton. Only one whom we knew and loved could have done it adequately – and been subjected to legal penalties for telling the truth in duly bitter words. Of course she has befouled Richard Burton's memory like a harpy – and of course it might have been expected.'[31] Georgiana Stisted hit the nail on the head when she wrote: 'Every kind-hearted person realised the bitter pain the mad act caused his family and friends. Not so much on account of the destruction of the manuscript, insulting though it was, but on account of the wrong impression concerning the character of the work, conveyed by a deed which the widow made no secret of, when she should have veiled it in absolute silence.'[32]

Yet, unbelievably, there was more destruction to come. When she had finished her paean of praise to Burton and their idyllic marriage, masquerading as an accurate biography, Isabel hauled up the ladder after her so that none might ascend that way again. In a word, she burned all his private journals and diaries, all his unpublished manuscripts, every jot and tittle he had ever noted down that had not been printed. This was a catastrophic loss to all future historians and biographers, which cannot be accurately measured. Those who had the privilege of dipping into the occasional page reported a treasure-house of original insight and acute observation. 'Just as Sir Richard's conversation was better than his books, so, we are told, his diaries were better than his conversation.'[33]

How can one make sense of this singular fanaticism? Obviously, at the simplest level Isabel wanted to fashion a romantic legend from her life with Burton, to compensate for its actual tribulations, and realised that the journals and diaries would show up her version as a fabrication. From the number of asides on Isabel that she actually allowed to be published, we can infer that there were many more – none complimentary, or she would have put them before the public. Almost certainly Burton, with his passion for the truth no matter who got hurt in the process, laid bare in the privacy of his study the explicit version of his joyless marriage, the frigidity of Isabel, and his own sexual inadequacies, which he merely hints at in the notes to the *Nights*. Simple pride would explain why Isabel would not want such revelations known to the world while she lived. But for her the desire to lie to the world from beyond the grave, implicit in her burning of the material rather than arranging for its suppression under, say, a 100-year rule, the appropriate word is 'pathological'. Some other factors, conscious or unconscious, or both, must have been at work.

The original burning of *The Scented Garden* could perhaps be explained as the desire of a religious bigot to save Richard's soul, though why a God stupid enough to be bamboozled by her shenanigans over the Extreme Unction should care what a sixteenth-century sheikh thought of homosexuality is an interesting conundrum. No doubt the burning of the manuscript was some kind of sympathetic magic, designed to ward off the fires of Hell. And those hostile to Burton for his 'prefascist' posture on social and political questions will doubtless relish the dramatic irony of a frenzy of nineteenth-century book-burning. But if Isabel wished to scald her husband's soul clean by the hecatomb of *The Scented Garden*, what purpose was to be gained by a holocaust of *More Notes on Paraguay, Lowlands of Brazil, Vichy, The Ashantee War, A Trip up the Congo* and dozens of other similar innocuous titles?

Here Catholicism has perhaps a more profound role than at first appears. A religion of dogma, mortal sin, papal infallibility and shabby compromises with the temporal power subtly begets in its more stupid practitioners a reverence for the 'coherence' theory of truth. As long as ranks can be closed against outsiders with a dogmatic 'truth', then it matters not whether there is correspondence between that truth and any verifiable fact. After all, Isabel's mentors, the Jesuits, were famous for casuistry, the mental reservation, the white lie, the expedient exaggeration, the weighing of means against the end of 'the greater glory of God'. Isabel was peculiarly susceptible to these influences from the 'unacceptable face' of Catholicism.

But in the end Burton himself must share part of the blame for the final tragedy. He chose as his faithful companion a strong-willed woman, then broke her by the steely exercise of power. He inculcated into Isabel the idea of dominance and submission as the model for relationships between man and woman. Isabel could not defeat him in open combat, so she went underground. Her peculiar behaviour between 1877 and 1883 bespeaks a woman almost at snapping point under this kind of marital control. When Richard died, the unconscious desire for revenge surfaced. He had won the battles during their life together, but by this final holocaust she could win the war.

Conclusion

RICHARD Francis Burton was a phenomenon, even by the standards of England in the Victorian Age, an era teeming with adventurers, explorers and littérateurs. One would have to conflate the careers of Stanley, Vámbéry, Frederick Burnaby, Mark Twain, Edward FitzGerald and John Payne to distil the essence of Burton. Even then, many pessimists have concluded, one could not do justice to his extraordinary career.[1]

Is any resolution of the contradictions in Burton's personality possible? Can there be a synoptic view of Sir Richard? Here we are at once faced with a problem of evidence, for from 1860 on much of our knowledge comes from Isabel, a deeply suspect source.

Isabel was herself part of Burton's duality. He was not carnally attracted to her, and sex played little part in their marriage. But she represented stability and a kind of normality – for Burton underrated his wife's peculiarity. She was the safe anchorage to which he could return after harrowing experiences. Burton's general attitude to sex has intrigued all who have tried to reconcile his marriage to a pious, innocent Catholic virgin with the reputation he sought for himself as 'the wickedest man alive'. The sober truth is that as a heterosexual Burton was largely a 'talking horse', to use the parlance of the racing stables. His scholarly researches and intense interest in sexology were more sublimation than complementarity. It is likely that he never really recovered from the shock of being found, along with other Westerners, sexually inadequate by his Indian *bubu*. His brother-officers, who lacked his linguistic talent, could live in blissful ignorance of the true opinion entertained about them as lovers by their native mistresses. Burton could not. The Indian trauma almost certainly accounts for the passive nature of Burton's heterosexual encounters thereafter. We hear of liaisons with the black women of Ugogo and West Africa, and with Fred Hankey's Parisian prostitutes. We hear nothing of Frank Harris-style seduction of women of his own class and race. One of the reasons Burton felt so attracted to the world of the *Arabian Nights* was that its women made the overtures, took the initiative, and set out to please their 'lords'. Much of Burton's fulmination about the sexual ignorance of English Victorian women can be interpreted in another way, as expressing the *cri de coeur* of a man who is not an expert seducer and cannot really be bothered to spend time 'winning' women which could be better spent in the study.

Yet another factor in Burton's attitude to women was that his true sexual personality was bisexual. Almost certainly the key factor in bringing the homosexual element to the fore was the inadequacy of his parents. His father, a weak and lazy hypochondriac, provided no male role-model whatever. His mother mixed absurd indulgence of his juvenile delinquency with prim severity towards any manifestations of sexuality.[2] The consequence was that his most important tie was to his brother Edward.

The evidence for active homosexuality in Burton's life is tenuous, though there are very broad hints in the correspondence with Swinburne and Monkton Milnes, including some episodes after his marriage to Isabel. The most compelling circumstantial evidence was the Karachi male brothel episode. Burton's Indian superiors conjectured, surely correctly, that no twenty-four-year-old, in danger of detection anyway as an impostor, would merely saunter round the lupanars without sampling the wares, even if only out of prudential motives. But in any case the normal heterosexual would have run a mile from the assignment in the first place. As for passive interest in homosexuality, the pages of notes for the *Arabian Nights* speak for themselves, as do Burton's many odd misogynistic utterances, and on several occasions he gave his opinion that the male nude was superior to the female.[3]

The outer Burton, Burton face to face with the world, is easier to deal with, largely because his prolific output as an author provides a wealth of evidence on the multifaceted man. It is hard to imagine that the diaries and papers Isabel burned would afford more than marginal corrections to the published work on his explorations in Africa, Arabia and South America (the 'black hole' in his life, covering the American journey from mid-April to mid-August 1860, is another matter).

As a pure explorer, Burton cannot compare with Stanley, Livingstone or even Speke. His distinction in African exploration was that he was the first to discover the Lake Regions of East Africa. He was thus a Bartolomé Diaz to their Vasco da Gama, Magellan and Quiros (to use an analogy he, as a Camoens scholar, might have approved). Burton's great advantage over the others was the mastery of Swahili he was able to attain; Stanley on his fourth great African expedition had not reached the level of fluency Burton achieved within one year in Central Africa.

But Burton was neither single-minded enough nor sufficiently interested in Africa and Africans to be the supreme technician in African exploration Stanley later became. Partly for this reason, no significant indigenous oral traditions of his 1857–59 journey survive. This is in contrast to the wealth of such evidence for the others of the 'Big Five' in African exploration: Livingstone, Stanley, Speke and Samuel Baker. But he did have one significant feat to his credit. In contrast to Stanley, Baker and the notorious German Karl Peters, he penetrated to the centre of Africa and back without bloodshed.'[4]

Burton's two other great feats of the 1850s, which made him a household name, fall into the category of adventure rather than exploration, properly so-called. The pilgrimage to Mecca and the penetration of the forbidden city of Harar were more important ultimately for the ethnological information they threw up, though it was their brazen drama which caught popular imagination.

As an anthropologist, Burton was one of the finest scholars in the field in the nineteenth century. Whether writing on the Fon of Dahomey, the Bedouin of Arabia, the Danakil of Ethiopia, the Ha, Gogo and Kimbu tribes of present-day Tanzania, the Sioux of the Great Plains or the Sind peoples of the Indus valley, Burton's twofold skill as empirical observer and structural semiologist never deserted him. Melville Herskovits was the first modern anthropologist to appreciate Burton's rare talents as a field-worker; only Burton's *Mission to Gelele*, of the nineteenth-century works on Dahomey, has stood up to the exact scrutiny of twentieth-century social science. Burton was not an *a priori* theorizer, like Sir James Frazer, but a highly talented field-worker whose unique linguistic gifts enabled him to get inside the idiom of a culture very swiftly. Sexual mores were his especial interest, and he may be regarded as the founding-father of that strand in modern anthropology which specialises in the close study of 'primitive' sexual behaviour, with Malinowski, Geoffrey Gorer and Verrier Elwin as the best-known practitioners.[5]

Burton was a pioneer in the academic discipline of anthropology in another way. In 1863 he was a founder member of the Anthropological Society of London, which later became the Anthropological Institute of Great Britain and Ireland. He had hoped that in the scholarly pages of the Society's journal he would be able to discuss clitoridectomy, infibulation, circumcision and other 'questionable' subjects, but it proved not to be so. In full flight from 'Propriety' and 'Respectability' Burton founded a breakaway movement, the London Anthropological Society, with a journal called *Anthropologia*. Alas, financial constraints forced a merger with the parent body after just three years. Disgustedly Burton wrote: 'the deadly shade of respectability, the trail of the slow-worm, is over them all.'[6]

There have certainly been greater explorers and anthropologists than Burton, but few men ever exceeded his linguistic abilities. Burton had all the talents characteristic of those exceptionally endowed with the gift of tongues: a phenomenal memory, immediate grasp of the deep structures of a language, parrot-like ability to reproduce the peculiar timbre and register and even the clicks and grunts of an alien idiom, plus empathy and an actor-like ability to become part of the given culture and take on verbal camouflage. There have been greater scholarly Arabists, but surely no one who was as versed as he in both the classical Arabic texts *and* the demotic argot of Baghdad, Mecca and Damascus. Yet Arabic was merely the finest string to his bow. Close behind, as his second favourite, came Portuguese, with Persian in third place. Beyond this were Italian, Spanish, German, Icelandic, Swahili, Hindustani, Sanskrit, Mahratha, Urdu, Pushtu, Jataki, Amharic, Fon, Egba, Ashanti, plus a host of West African and Indian dialects, to say nothing of Latin, Greek, Hebrew and Aramaic. Altogether he mastered twenty-five languages, with dialects bringing the number to forty.

To be a fine linguist is a necessary, though not sufficient, condition of being a great translator. The very lack of a clear identity and the penchant for disguises that characterised Richard Burton helped him immeasurably in his translations. If anything, he entered too fully into the world of his subjects. His grasp of the complexity of thought and nuance of idea in the original led him to rococo experimentation with the English language to find the exactly parallel discourse. This scholarly integrity all too often produced translations that were far from easily readable. Burton was a true scholar; but in his zeal not to compromise with the intentions of the author he was translating, he forgot the other prerequisite for the translator: he must communicate readily with a contemporary audience. There is also a sense in which Burton's awesome linguistic gifts worked against excellence of translation; his friend Frank Harris, after all, recalled that after being steeped in German for two years, he (Harris) could no longer write clear English prose.

As an amateur archaeologist, Burton scored many remarkable 'firsts' in terms of the sites he visited which were previously unexplored by Europeans. He was a notable catalyst in the matter of the Hamath and Moabite stones. As a writer Burton could boast forty-three volumes on his travels and explorations. The best of them were, naturally, the books recording his greatest exploits: *Personal Narrative of a Pilgrimage to El-Medinah and Meccah, First Footsteps in East Africa, The Lake Regions of Central Africa*. Here the traveller and scholar are perfectly fused; there are none of the *longueurs* and academic uses that disfigure the later books. *The City of the Saints* and *Letters from the Battlefields of Paraguay* are two very important historical sources which are currently underrated.

A Mission to Gelele is Burton's anthropological classic. As a would-be creative writer, he was less successful. *Stone-Talk* is forgotten except for its dithyrambs against Isabel. *The Kasidah* has suffered the fate that Burton always feared it might, that of being an epigone to Edward FitzGerald's *Rubáiyát*.

Burton was the Romantic figure *par excellence*, in the sense that the ego was at the centre of the world. It was this, finally, which prevented him from being ranked with the very greatest explorers and anthropologists. There is always a pyrotechnical cleverness about his analysis of an African tribe, a narcissism amid the acute observations, that nudges the reader to look at Burton the Superman as well as at the culture under observation. If the old saw about genius being an infinite capacity for taking pains has any merit, then it rules out Burton in many areas (though, being Burton, not in all: for example, his Arabism). Burton had as much brilliance, genius even, as any other man of his generation, but ultimately he had fewer solid achievements to his credit than many less gifted contemporaries. He was impatient with detail, he liked to paint in broad brush strokes, he became bored easily.

In many ways Burton was almost a caricature of the Romantic sensibility. Blunt surmised that even the Arabs would have been sacrificed if Burton's highest ambitions could have been achieved thereby. It is this which most clearly differentiates Burton from Lawrence as men of Arabia.[7]

Like many multi-talented individuals, Burton ended up living his life backwards, as it were. His consular career, remarkable only for its mediocrity, contrasted with his early success and fame, achieved by the age of 38. It was money, and money alone, that kept Burton bound to the mast, with his ears stopped against the siren voices calling him to emulate and excel the feats of Stanley, Gordon, Baker, Vámbéry and Burnaby. Here the indictment against Isabel must be weighty, for her extravagance. But the financial uncertainty of his early years – and especially the feeling that his mother had thrown away his patrimony – also left Burton forever uneasy about money.[8]

Unable as he was to suffer fools gladly, to defer to intellectual inferiors who were his superiors in a hierarchy, or to take direction, Burton's choice of the Foreign Office as his employer seems highly irrational and even self-destructive. In the Consular Service Burton accepted the chance of travel in faraway places, but overlooked the boredom, the paperwork, the petty small change and bogus politenesses of bureaucratic correspondence and, above all, the need to seek authorisation from his superiors for his self-assigned exploration projects. Nor was Burton a master of machiavellianism. The chicanery he employed with his superiors was half-hearted and ill-thought-out (again the lack of patience with details).[9] If the Foreign Office had a case against Burton, it should have dismissed him. To keep him on and consign him to limbo on the grounds of his 'unsoundness' was humbug. 'The beheading of Walter Raleigh was, I think, a kinder treatment than the imprisonment of Burton in Trieste.'[10]

If Burton followed a star, it was surely Sirius, symbol of duality and ambivalence. Seemingly the most independent of men, he sought out collaborators and co-authors: Rehatsek, Smithers, Palmer, Payne, W. F. Kirby, Arbuthnot. As 'diabolical' comrades he had Ashbee, Fred Hankey, Monkton Milnes and Swinburne.[11] And, always, there was a long string of surrogate brothers to replace the hopelessly catatonic Edward: Walter Scott, Steinhaeuser, Speke, Verney Cameron, Tyrwhitt-Drake, Arbuthnot. Unlike Stanley, Burton did not see himself as a perfect Ishmael, with every man's hand turned against him. It would be both facile and misleading to call him a 'loner'. His desperate need for companionship was one of the reasons he contracted the ultimately disastrous marriage with Isabel. But it is significant that Burton never had a woman among his friends. Even before Isabel, he confided only in his sister. For Burton, as afterwards for Freud, women were truly 'the Dark Continent'.[12]

Misogynism was not the only aspect of Burton that makes him cut a poor figure in the eyes of the twentieth century. He was also clearly and unequivocally a man of the radical Right. Apart from women, he hated Jews, Catholics, blacks, the Irish, socialists and egalitarians of every kidney. He looked back nostalgically to the feudal society of the Middle Ages, when the martial ethos was the supreme social value, when the man of honour settled disputes and kept women in line through the use of his sword. Burton believed in deep scholarship and the pursuit of excellence, and would have been appalled at any suggestion of 'levelling down' in educational attainment or academic aspiration. He seems almost the perfect bogeyman of the modern demonology.

Perhaps the most obvious and most far-reaching aspect of Burton's personality was his self-destructiveness. He claimed to have committed every sin in the Decalogue, but was then piqued when people actually believed him. He loved to chaff and joke and make himself out a monster, then lashed out at the lack of intelligence of those who took him seriously. He was neither the first nor the last to learn that paradox is a dangerous weapon, liable to turn into a boomerang. He once wryly remarked in his diary: 'It is a very curious, and not altogether unpleasant sensation, that of not being believed when you are speaking the truth. I have had great difficulty in training my wife to enjoy it.'[13] But he had no one but himself to blame for this state of affairs. He had cried wolf too often.[14]

Part of Burton's self-destructive profile can charitably be interpreted as bad luck. It was clearly ill-fortune when Burton, the master swordsman and warrior, failed to see active service in India during Napier's campaign in Sind and in the two Sikh wars, failed to get combat duty in the Crimea, and was absent in Africa when the Indian Mutiny broke out. Ironically, his one and only experience of hand-to-hand fighting was during the night attack at Berbera, where he was lucky to escape with his life. It was also obviously an 'act of God' that rebellion in the interior prevented his penetrating the Empty Quarter in 1853, that the Crimean War distracted attention from his Harar exploit, and that fever laid him low while Speke set out to discover Lake Victoria. Even the absurd underrating of Burton's linguistic genius can be set down to the misfortune of his having been born in the Anglo-Saxon culture, which places no particular value on linguistic distinction since it expects the rest of the world to come to it by learning English.

It must be an unconscious desire to fail that explains the clashes with the East India Company which meant he was denied the long leaves Speke enjoyed in the 1840s, and his refusal to return to London after the Mecca pilgrimage in 1853. Undoubtedly the inner Burton suffered from feelings of worthlessness and depression, and failure could trigger serious immobility, as when he 'froze' in 1859 when Speke double-crossed him to garner the laurels for the Lake Regions exploit, and in 1871–72 after his recall from Damascus. His intermittent alcoholism also gives us direct pointers.

Burton's melancholia and 'black dog' must ultimately have its origin in childhood experiences. But the very nature of his huge gifts – the talent for disguise, the linguistic genius, the scholarly abilities as a translator – also denotes a lack of firm identity at the centre, almost as though no single human personality could marshal and control so much. 'An orchestra without a conductor' was how Alan Moorehead described him.[15] The lack of an integrated personality was the key to Burton. His contradictory impulses immobilised him, thus feeding into the pre-existing tendency towards depression. The charges of prejudice, mediocrity and pharisaism he brought against his hierarchical superiors can be read also as the outer projection of an inner civil war.

A balanced conclusion on Burton is all but impossible. Those who knew him divided into inveterate enemies and perfervid admirers and friends. His enemies accused him of imperial arrogance, lies, megalomania, venality, charlatanry, plagiarism and swollen egotism. His friends thought him simply the greatest man of the nineteenth century. As Swinburne put it in his *Elegy*:

> The royal heart we mourn, the faultless friend
> Burton – a name that lives till fame be dead.[16]

Certainly few men of such exceptional abilities ran such a gamut between success and failure in life, reached such heights or plumbed such depths. Whether we contrast the second Balboa on a peak overlooking Lake Tanganyika with the alcoholic ragamuffin of Buenos Aires ten years later, or the man at the acme of his glory as an Arabist and Consul in Damascus with the skrimshanking pen-pusher of Trieste a mere two years later, or the tawdry voyeur of Fred Hankey's sordid bordellos with the elevated mystic of the *Kasidah*, we see everywhere the man to whom Aristotle's Golden Mean was simply a joke. But in the words of Camoens, he had performed 'Deeds that deserve, like gods, a deathless name'. It is best to take leave of this modern Odysseus on the elegaic note he provided himself in the *Kasidah*:

> The light of morn has grown to noon, has paled with eve, and now farewell!
> Go, vanish from my life as dies the tinkling of the camel's bell.

Notes

ABBREVIATIONS

Add. MSS. Additional Manuscripts, British Library
EHR English Historical Review
JAH Journal of African History
JRAI Journal of the Royal Anthropological Institute
JRGS Journal of the Royal Geographical Society
NLS National Library of Scotland
PRGS Proceedings of the Royal Geographical Society
RGS Royal Geographical Society
SFA Stanley Family Archives
TNR Tanzania Notes and Records
UJ Uganda Journal

CHAPTER 1 CHILDHOOD AND YOUTH pp. 1–16

1. Arthur Symons, 'A Neglected Genius: Sir Richard Burton', *Fortnightly Review*, August 1921, pp. 334–43.
2. Georgiana M. Stisted, *The True Life of Captain Sir Richard F. Burton* (NY 1897), p. 412.
3. See F. Grenfell Baker, 'Sir Richard Burton as I knew him', *Cornhill Magazine* 304 (October 1921), pp. 411–23; J. N. L. Baker, 'Sir Richard Burton and the Nile Sources', *English Historical Review*, 59 (1944), pp. 49–61. For the African explorer Sir Samuel Baker see Richard Hall, *Lovers on the Nile* (1979); Robert O. Collins, 'Prospero in Purgatory', in Robert I. Rotberg, ed., *Africa and Its Explorers*, (Cambridge, Mass, 1970), pp. 139–74.
4. Thomas Wright, *The Life of Sir Richard Burton*, 2 vols (1906), i, p. 121.
5. For this see James Strachey, ed., *Standard Edition of the Complete Psychological Works of Sigmund Freud*, 24 vols (1953–74), xiv, pp. 236–41.
6. Here Fawn Brodie in the excellent *The Devil Drives* (1967) makes one of her rare lapses. Speaking of Joseph Burton she says: 'He rose to the rank of Lieutenant-Colonel – which in the days of purchased commissions would suggest considerable wealth' (p. 27). But Burton explicitly states that his father received his commission *gratis* at the age of seventeen after bringing large numbers of his Irish tenants into the army (Isabel Burton, *Life of Captain Sir Richard F. Burton* (hereinafter *Life*), 2 vols (1893), i, p. 50).
7. See Christopher Hibbert, *George IV, Regent and King* (1973), pp. 145–213; cf. also Alison Plowden, *Caroline and Charlotte* (1989).

8. *Life*, i, pp. 4, 16.
9. Francis Hitchman, *Richard Burton*, 2 vols (1887), i, pp. 10–11.
10. Stisted, *True Life*, op. cit., p. 9.
11. This trait never left him in adult life. See F. Grenfell Baker, 'Sir Richard Burton', *United Empire* N.S.12 (1921), pp. 698–700.
12. Stisted, op. cit., pp. 5–8.
13. *Life*, i, p. 20.
14. Ibid., p. 22.
15. Hitchman, op. cit., i, p. 28.
16. *Arabian Nights*, i, pp. 41–2.
17. *Life*, i, p. 27.
18. Burton shared his father's views on the undesirability of beating children and quoted with approval John Locke's dictum: 'beating is the worst and therefore the last means to be used in the correction of children' (*Arabian Nights*, xvi, p. 9).
19. *Life*, i, pp. 28–9.
20. Ibid., p. 32.
21. Ibid., p. 34.
22. Ibid., pp. 36–7.
23. *A New System of Sword Exercise for Infantry* (1876).
24. *Life*, i, p. 41.
25. Stisted, op. cit., p. 12.
26. *Life*, i, p. 52.
27. Burton later recalled this scene when he came to translate a similar story in the *Arabian Nights* (viii, p. 287).
28. *Life*, i, p. 65.
29. See the relevant sections of *The Jew, the Gypsy and El-Islam* (1898).
30. Fairfax Downey, *Burton, Arabian Nights Adventurer* (NY 1931) p. 12.
31. Thomas J. Assad, *Three Victorian Travellers* (1964), p. 30.
32. *Life*, i, p. 32.
33. Anonymous reviewer of *Life* in *Edinburgh Review* 178 (1893), p. 443.
34. To say nothing of 'the insolent want of tact of which he was frequently guilty, and that not only in official but in social matters, when it took a more offensive form'. (Ibid., pp. 440–41.)
35. Isabel Burton, *The Inner Life of Syria, Palestine and the Holy Land*, 2 vols (1876), ii, p. 145.
36. Michael Hastings, *Sir Richard Burton* (1978), p. 15.
37. *Vikram and the Vampire* (1870), p. 295.
38. *Personal Narrative of a Pilgrimage to El-Medinah and Meccah* (1856), i, p. 287.
39. *Scinde; or, the Unhappy Valley*, 2 vols (1851), ii, pp. 248–9.
40. *Life*, ii., p. 342; *Personal Narrative*, op. cit., ii, p. 239.
41. *Wanderings in West Africa* (1863), ii, p. 143.
42. *Life*, i, p. 58.
43. Brodie, *The Devil Drives*, op. cit., p. 334.
44. *Life*, i, pp.65–6.
45. Stisted, p. 22.
46. *Life*, i, p. 21.
47. *Sindh, and the Races that Inhabit the Valley of the Indus* (1851), p. 197.
48. *Scinde; or, the Unhappy Valley*, op. cit., i, p. 269.
49. *Life*, i, p. 22.
50. *Scinde*, op. cit., ii, p. 188.
51. 'The terrible beauty of death' (*To the Gold Coast for Gold*, 2 vols (1883), i., p. 344). 'I have always told you that I was a dual man' (*Life*, ii, p. 268).

52. *The Book of the Sword* (1884), p. xi.

CHAPTER 2 OXFORD pp. 17–27

1. *Life*, i, pp. 69–70.
2. *Arabian Nights*, xiv, p. 364.
3. *Life*, ii, p. 323.
4. Ibid., i, p. 70.
5. *Arabian Nights*, i, p. 103.
6. *The Jew, the Gypsy and El-Islam*, op. cit., p. 284.
7. The Newmans themselves found social contacts with Pusey difficult. See Ian Ker, *John Henry Newman* (Oxford 1988).
8. *Arabian Nights*, x, p. 102.
9. Ibid., v, p. 221.
10. *Life*, i, p. 82. For the psychological type denoted by the 'all or nothing' mentality see Erik Erikson, *Young Man Luther* (NY 1958), pp. 94–121.
11. *Life*, i, p. 82.
12. *The City of the Saints and across the Rocky Mountains to California* (1861), p. 513.
13. Alfred Bates Richards, *A Short Sketch of the Career of Captain Richard F. Burton ... by an Old Oxonian* (1880).
14. 'Early Days in Sind' in Norman M. Penzer, ed., *Selected Papers on Anthropology, Travel and Exploration by Sir Richard Burton* (1924), p. 14.
15. *Life*, i, pp. 84–9.
16. Ibid., pp. 89–91.
17. Penzer, *Selected Papers*, op. cit., p. 14. Burton added that his *alma mater* was a *durissima noverca*, not in the same class as Paris, Berlin or Vienna (*Arabian Nights*, xiv, p. 365).
18. Wright, op. cit., i, p. 66.
19. *Life*, i, p. 81.
20. *The Highlands of Brazil*, 2 vols (1869), ii, p. 97.
21. *Arabian Nights*, x, p. 96.
22. F. Grenfell Baker, 'Sir Richard Burton as I knew him', *Cornhill Magazine* N.S. 51(1921), p. 417.
23. Ibid., pp. 415–16.
24. *Arabian Nights*, i, p. xxi; *Wanderings in West Africa*, ii, p. 175.
25. *The Carmina of Gaius Valerius Catullus. Now first completely Englished into Verse and Prose, the metrical part by Captain Sir Richard F. Burton ... and the Prose Portion, Introduction and Notes Explanatory and Illustrative by Leonard C. Smithers* (1894).
26. *Life*, i, pp. 386–87.
27. Wilfrid S. Blunt, *My Diaries*, 2 vols (NY 1921), ii, p. 131.
28. Wright, ii, p. 48.
29. *The Lake Regions of Central Africa*, 2 vols (1860), i, p. 129.
30. *Personal Narrative*, op. cit., ii, p. 100.
31. *Sindh and the Races*, op. cit., p. 58.
32. *Sindh Revisited*, 2 vols (1877), ii, p. 8.
33. Ibid., ii, p. 20.
34. 'Early Days in Sind', loc. cit., pp. 14–15.

CHAPTER 3 INDIA pp. 28–45

1. *Life*, i, p. 95.
2. 'Early Days in Sind', loc. cit., p. 15.
3. *Life*, i, p. 103.
4. *Arabian Nights*, vi, p. 235. Michael Hastings, *Sir Richard Burton*, op. cit., p. 266,

unaccountably thinks this 'brother-officer' was Burton himself. This is implausible on several counts: 1. a great linguist like Burton would not make such a mistake; 2. even if he had, Burton would never have told such a story against himself; 3. we have Burton's testimony that he had already had three intensive periods of Hindustani study before he arrived at Gujerat: one with Duncan Forbes in London; one on the *John Knox*; and a third in Bombay.

5. *The City of The Saints*, p. 65.
6. *Life*, i, p. 122.
7. Hitchman, op. cit., i, p. 130.
8. *Life*, i, p. 109.
9. *Arabian Nights*, xiv, pp. 257–8.
10. *Life*, i, p. 140.
11. *Arabian Nights*, ix, p. 56; cf. also ibid., iii, p. 160.
12. An attempt to cap Napier's famous Latin pun was made in 1856, after Lord Dalhousie annexed Oudh, thus going even farther than Lord Ellenborough, who as Governor-General in India during 1841–44 had ordered the annexation of Sind.

> *Peccavi* – 'I've Scinde', wrote Lord Ellen so proud.
> More briefly Dalhousie wrote, *Vovi* – I've Oude'.
> *Punch*, 22 March 1856

The Latin 'vovi' means 'I have vowed'.

13. *Life*, i, pp. 120–24.
14. *Scinde, or the Unhappy Valley*, op. cit., i, pp. 5–9.
15. *Life*, i, p. 140.
16. *Scinde*, i, p. 50; cf. also *Sindh Revisited*, pp. 92–3, 95, 98, 100. Even towards the end of his life Burton held the false belief that there were no salt-water crocodiles, overlooking the most dangerous member of the entire species (see *Arabian Nights*, vii, p. 343).
17. *Sindh Revisited*, i, p. 100.
18. William Napier, *Life and Opinions of Charles Napier*, 4 vols (1857), is still the most complete study of the man. H. T. Lambrick, *Sir Charles Napier and Sind* (Oxford 1952) is the standard account of his work there. The Napier Diaries (Add.MSS.49,140) supplement the above, but neither in published nor unpublished sources is there an explicit mention of Burton by Napier.
19. *Life*, i, pp. 116–18, 141–2; *Sindh and the Races*, op. cit., pp. 31–34; *Sindh Revisited*, ii, pp. 38–44.
20. *Life*, i, p. 162.
21. *Scinde*, i, pp. 89, 96–9, 147–52.
22. *Life*, i, pp. 129, 143. A recent author has repaid the compliment by writing a biography of Burton in Marathi (Bala Gangadhara Samanta, *Sapita Yaksa* (Bombay 1983).
23. 'Early Days in Sind', loc. cit., p. 15.
24. *Sindh Revisited*, ii, pp. 77–83; *To the Gold Coast*, op. cit., i, p. 251.
25. *Goa and the Blue Mountains* (1851), p. 316.
26. *Scinde*, ii, pp. 220–21.
27. *Life*, i, p. 147.
28. *Goa and the Blue Mountains*, p. 1.
29. *Scinde*, i, pp. 271–97; *Sind Revisited*, pp. 317–43. It is interesting to contrast Burton's asides on the history and culture of Sind with the findings of modern scholars like Lambrick (a list of whose work is provided in the bibliography). Modern research on Sind is collected in Hamida Khuhro, ed., *Sind Through the Ages* (Oxford 1981)
30. *Arabian Nights*, vii, p. 141.
31. Ibid., iii, p. 297.

32. Ibid., iv, p. 192.
33. *Falconry in the Valley of the Indus* (1852), pp. 100–101.
34. Ibid.
35. Ibid., p. 105.
36. Frank Harris, *Contemporary Portraits*, (1915), p. 193. The Strickland stories in Kipling's *Plain Tales from the Hills* are 1. Miss Youghal's Sais; 2. The Bronkhurst Divorce Case; 3. The Mark of the Beast; 4. The Return of Imray; 5. The Son and his Father; 6. A Deal in Cotton. According to R. E. Harbord, *A Reader's Guide to Rudyard Kipling* (1962), Strickland is a conflation of 1. an Afghan stepson of a British officer active during the 1839–41 war; 2. a young police officer called Christie, who had been born in India and who also flourished in the 1840s. Nonetheless, it is highly significant that 'Strickland', like Burton, served in the Punjab. There is of course a huge Kipling bibliography of which no account will be taken here.
37. *Arabian Nights*, x, pp. 205–06.
38. *Scinde*, i, p. 263.
39. Stisted, pp. 43–4.
40. For another interpretation see the extended discussion in Brodie, *The Devil Drives*, pp. 53–56.
41. Stisted, pp. 48–49. There is a more sober account of the same story in Wright, i, pp. 80–81.
42. *The Times*, 31 October 1891.
43. *Arabian Nights*, xvi, p. 244.
44. *Life*, i, p. 162.
45. *Stone-Talk* (1865), p. 73.

CHAPTER 4 THE IMPACT OF INDIA pp. 46–55

1. *Life*, i, pp. 101–02.
2. *Scinde*, i, p. 217.
3. See Burton's contributions on Pushtu and the Jataki dialect in *Royal Asiatic Society Journal*, Bombay 3 (1849), No. 12, pp. 58–69, 84–125. Cf. also Hugh Dow, 'A Note on the Sindhi Alphabet', *Asian Affairs* 63 (1976), pp. 54–56; Lachman M. Khubchandani, 'Sir Richard Burton and the Sindhi Language', *Annals of the Bhandarkar Oriental Research Unit* 66 (1985), pp. 259–62.
4. *Sindh Revisited*, ii, p. 279. There is a solitary aside on snakes and tigers in *Goa and the Blue Mountains*, pp. 251–2. There is also a rare disquisition on 'sport' in ibid., pp. 317–22. But compare this with almost any page of his contemporary, Samuel Baker, in *The Rifle and the Hound in Ceylon* (1854).
5. *Arabian Nights*, iii, p. 242.
6. *Scinde*, i, 163; ii, p. 4.
7. *Arabian Nights*, iv, p. 187; ix, p. 73.
8. *Scinde*, i, pp. 262–68; *Arabian Nights*, i, p. 70; *Sindh Revisited*, pp. 305–14. Hindustani intoxicants included the juice of the *Tad*, the coconut tree, the wild date, opium and various forms of cannabis (*ganja, charas, madad, sabzi* (*Arabian Nights*, ix, p. 274).
9. *Personal Narrative*, i, p. 40.
10. *Scinde*, pp. 2–3. 'Few Franks, save those who have mixed with them in Oriental disguise, are aware of their repugnance to, and contempt for, Europeans' (*Personal Narrative*, i, p. 111).
11. *Personal Narrative*, i, pp. 111–12.
12. *Arabian Nights*, iii, p. 374.
13. *The City of the Saints*, p. 56.
14. *Sindh Revisited*, pp. 59–63.
15. *First Footsteps in East Africa* (1856), pp. xxxvi–xxxvii.

16. *A Glance at the Passion Play* (1881), p. 139.
17. See M. E. Yapp, *Strategies of British India* (Oxford 1980), pp. 463 et seq.
18. *Arabian Nights*, ii, p. 55.
19. Ibid., i, p. 299.
20. *Scinde*, ii, p. 261.
21. *Sindh Revisited*, ii, p. 261; *Lake Regions*, i, pp. 217–18; *Life*, i, p. 30.
22. *Lake Regions*, i, pp. 393–4.
23. *Arabian Nights*, i, p. 274.
24. Ibid., i, p. xxiii.
25. Karl Marx, 'British Rule in India' and 'The East India Company – its History and Results', in *Marx–Engels Collected Works* 12 (1979), (Laurence and Wishart edition, pp. 125–33, 148–56).
26. *Arabian Nights*, v, p. 146.
27. *Life*, ii, p. 521. This is not so very different in tone and content from the words of Marx himself. *Marx–Engels*, op. cit., 12, pp. 217–22.
28. *Lake Regions*, ii, p. 326.
29. *Arabian Nights*, i, p. 70, v, p. 77. Burton adds that the art of moving rhythmically during sexual intercourse was taught to young Indian girls by old women (ibid., v, p. 80).
30. Ibid., vii, p. 179.
31. Ibid., v, pp. 76–7.
32. Stisted, pp. 48–9.
33. *Life*, i, p. 148.
34. *Arabian Nights*, x, p. 252.
35. Ibid., x, pp. 232–5.
36. Wright, i, pp. 120, 141–2.
37. *Arabian Nights*, iv, p. 15. Cf. also the following: 'We must not forget that the love of boys has its noble, sentimental side. The Platonists and pupils of the Academy followed by the Sufis or Moslem Gnostics held such affection pure as ardent, to be the *beau idéal* which united in man's soul the creature with the creator ... They add that such affection, passing as it does the love of women, is far less selfish than fondness and admiration of the other sex which, however innocent, always suggests sexuality.' (Ibid., x, p. 207).
38. Ibid., pp. 237–8.
39. *Goa and the Blue Mountains*, p. 222.
40. *Athenaeum* No. 1225, 19 April 1851, p. 423.
41. Ibid., No. 1252, 25 October 1851, p. 1111.
42. *Arabian Nights*, iv, p. 177; *Athenaeum*, No. 1290, 17 July 1852, p. 766.
43. *Wright*, ii, p. 122; Steven Marcus, *The Other Victorians. A Study of Sexuality and Pornography in Mid-Nineteenth Century England* (NY 1964); so we find *Personal Narrative* praised as a mixture of *Eothen* and Gordon Cummings (*Athenaeum* No. 1448, 28 July 1855, p. 865). *Lake Regions* elicits the following judgement: 'the picture of life in these extraordinary regions is admirable. Captain Burton observes and describes everything. His instincts are those of a traveller. He has in a twofold sense the capacity of an artist.' (*Athenaeum* No. 1704, 23 July 1860, p. 846). On *Unexplored Syria*: 'The book before us is no common book of travels; it is rather a series of elaborate, and at the same time, luminous descriptions of various sites.' (*Athenaeum* No. 2331, 29 June 1871, p. 807).
44. See for example Norman Penzer, *An Annotated Bibliography of Sir Richard Francis Burton* (1923), pp. vii–viii.
45. See Jonathan Bishop, 'The Identities of Sir Richard Burton: the Explorer as Actor', *Victorian Studies* 1 (1957–58), pp. 119–35.

CHAPTER 5 IN LIMBO pp. 56–71

1. *Personal Narrative*, i, p. 151; Stisted, p. 57; cf. also Georgiana Stisted, 'Reminiscences of Sir Richard Burton', *Temple Bar*, July 1891, pp. 335–42.
2. *Sindh and the Races*, p. 401.
3. *Personal Narrative*, i, p. 141.
4. *Life*, i, p. 168
5. Ouida, 'Richard Burton', *Fortnightly Review* 85 (June 1906), pp. 1039–45 (at pp. 1040–41).
6. W. H. Wilkins, ed. *The Romance of Isabel Lady Burton*, 2 vols (1897), p. 54.
7. *Life*, i, p. 167.
8. Wilkins, i, p. 69.
9. Ibid., pp. 38–39.
10. Foster Fitzgerald Arbuthnot, *Persian Portraits* (1887), gives an idea of his interests.
11. Stisted, p. 67.
12. *The Book of the Sword* (1884), p. 19.
13. Blunt, *My Diaries*, op. cit., ii, p. 135; Wright, ii, p. 166.
14. *Life*, i, p. 397; *Arabian Nights*, vi, p. 392.
15. Frank Harris, 'Sir Richard Burton', *Academy* 81 (1911), p. 390.
16. V. L. Cameron, 'Burton as I knew him', *Fortnightly Review* 54 (1890), p. 879; Frank Harris, *Contemporary Portraits* (NY 1920), p. 183.
17. A. Symons, *Dramatis Personae* (1925), p. 251.
18. Swinburne to Watts, 4 January 1877, Cecil Y. Lang, ed., *The Swinburne Letters*, 6 vols (Yale 1959), iii, p. 255.
19. *Arabian Nights*, vi, p. 243.
20. *Unexplored Syria* (1871), ii, p. 191.
21. Thomas Carlyle, *On Heroes and Hero Worship* (1841), p. 100.
22. *Lord Beaconsfield. A Sketch* (1882), p. 9.
23. *Arabian Nights*, p. lx.
24. Harris, *Contemporary Portraits*, p. 188; *Arabian Nights*, i, pp. xxiii–xxix.
25. *Wanderings in West Africa* i, pp. 136–37; *Personal Narrative*, i, p. 112.
26. *Sindh Revisited*, i, p. 62; ii, p. 317; *Two Trips to Gorilla Land and the Cataracts of the Congo*, 2 vols (1876), ii, p. 310.
27. *Life*, ii, pp. 508, 543.
28. Ibid., ii, p. 508.
29. Ibid., p. 548.
30. 'We have to thank Lord Palmerston (an Irish landlord) for ignoring the growth of Fenianism and another aged statesman for a sturdy attempt to disunite the United Kingdom.' (*Arabian Nights*, xiv, p. 123; *The City of the Saints*, p. 217).
31. *Personal Narrative*, ii, p. 10; *The Book of the Sword*, pp. xiv–xv; *Goa and the Blue Mountains*, p. 147.
32. *Two Trips to Gorilla Land*, ii, p. 310; cf. *Arabian Nights*, x, p. 97: 'In religion as a rule, the minimum difference breeds the maximum of disputation.'
33. Ibid., iii, p. 299; iv, p. 267.
34. Penzer, *Selected Papers*, op. cit., p. 185.
35. *Arabian Nights*, v, p. 289.
36. Wright, ii, pp. 145–46.
37. *A Glance at the Passion Play*, op. cit., pp. 160–61; *Arabian Nights*, xiv, p. 288.
38. Wright, ii, p. 145.
39. *Two Trips to Gorilla Land*, i, p. 102. At this stage Burton had not seen them himself. When he did (in 1870) his contempt was compounded: 'Those exaggerated Christmas trees . . . so mean and so ragged that an English county gentleman would refuse them admittance into his park.' (*Unexplored Syria*, i, p. 10).

40. *Arabian Nights*, iii, pp. 123, 246, 269–70; *Sindh and the Races*, pp. 174–97; *Personal Narrative*, i, pp. 16–17; *A Mission to Gelele, King of Dahome*, i, p. 332.
41. *Arabian Nights*, xiii, p. 21.
42. Ibid., iii, p. 252.
43. Ibid., iii, p. 515; ix, p. 86.
44. Harris, *Contemporary Portraits*, p. 196.
45. It is interesting to contrast his attitude with that of another African explorer (and admirer), Sir Harry Johnston. See Johnston, *The Story of My Life* (1923), pp. 510–12.
46. *The Jew, the Gypsy and El-Islam*, p. 253. Many people, of course, were convinced that Burton himself was descended from the Romanies. 'There must certainly have been a cross in his blood, gipsy or other.' (Blunt, *My Diaries*, ii, p. 136).

CHAPTER 6 PILGRIMAGE TO MECCA pp. 72–87

1. Alexander Kinglake, *Eothen* (1844, new edn., 1944), p. 123.
2. Burton to RGS, 1852 (n.d.), Royal Geographical Society Archives (hereinafter RGS).
3. *Personal Narrative*, ii, p. 240.
4. For a typical Western refusal to enter into the Arab mental world see the scorn for fasting in Kinglake, *Eothen*, op. cit., p. 52.
5. Notable European *Hajis* were Ludovico Bartema (1503); Vincent le Blanc (1568); Johann Wild (1604); Joseph Pitts (1680); Domingo Badiay Leblich (1807); Ulrich Seetzen (1809–10); Johann Burkhardt (1814); Giovanni Fitani (1814); Leon Roches (1841–2); George Wallin (1845); Heinrich von Maltzan (1860); Hermann Bicknell (1862); John Keane (1877–8). Thereafter the feat was achieved by the Dutchman Snouck Hurgronje in 1885, the Frenchman Gervais Courtellement in 1885 and, most notably in the early twentieth century, by the distinguished Arabist Harry St John Philby, father of 'Kim'. For a general survey of these journeys see Richard Trench, *Arabian Travellers* (1986). Cf. also D. G. Hogarth, *The Penetration of Arabia* (Cambridge 1904). Auguste Ralli, *Christians at Mecca* (1909) divides European visitors to the Holy City into three groups: what he calls 'the skirmishers' – the early visitors from Bartema to Pitts; 'the scientists' (Badia, Seetzen, Burkhardt, Hurgronje); and 'the adventurers' (von Maltzan, Bicknell, Keane, Courtellement). He describes Burton as having a foot in both camps of scientists and adventurers. The earliest *Hajis* Burton was most interested in were Pitts and Fitani, *Personal Narrative*, ii, pp. 358–401.
6. Of the above list, only Bartema, Wild, Pitts, Seetzen, Burkhardt, Wallin and Keane also visited Medina.
7. *Personal Narrative*, i, p. 23.
8. Charles Doughty, *Travels in Arabia Deserta*, 2 vols (1888), ii, p. 68.
9. See A. I. Shand's introduction to the 1896 edition of Kinglake's *Eothen*, p. 11; cf. also (for an earlier view) U. G. Seetzen, *A Brief account of the countries adjoining the lake of Tiberias, the Jordan and the Dead Sea* (Bath 1810), p. 4.
10. Burton to Church Missionary Society, 12 February 1853, RGS archives.
11. Court of East India Company to Murchison, 10 January 1853, RGS; RGS Minute Book, Committees 1841–65: Minutes of 7 February 1853 and 9 January 1854, pp. 59–60, 72.
12. *Arabian Nights*, i, ix, 198; ix. p. 51.
13. *Sindh and the Races*, pp. 358, 413.
14. *Arabian Nights*, ii, pp. 90–93; v. p. 209; xvi. p. 217.
15. *Personal Narrative*, i, p. 6.
16. Ibid., p. 8.
17. The garden of Larking's house outside Alexandria sloped down towards the Mahmondich Canal (Michell Papers, SOAS, Box 7/204772 f.2).

18. *Personal Narrative*, i, p. 59.
19. Ibid., p. 15.
20. Ibid., p. 19.
21. Ibid., pp. 132–39.
22. Ibid., pp. 143–44.
23. The Arabs' suspicion of these instruments had been pointed to earlier by Burkhardt: 'I must observe that during all my journeys in the deserts, I never allowed the Arabs to get a sight of my compass, as it would certainly have been considered by them as an instrument of magic.' (Burkhardt, *Travels in Syria and the Holy Land* (1822), p. 445.)
24. Such was the contempt felt by the Arabs for Charles Doughty that he was refused even this 'free' boon. In one rare emergence from his usual gloomy masochism, Doughty took his courage in his hands and faced down his oppressor (*Arabia Deserta*, i, p. 508).
25. *Personal Narrative*, i, p. 245.
26. Ibid., pp. 278–80.
27. 'Journey to Medina', *JRGS* 24 (1854), pp. 208–25.
28. These were the lava beds first reported fifty years earlier by Burkhardt. See Burkhardt, *Travels in Arabia* (1829), ii, p. 217.
29. *Personal Narrative*, ii, p. 62. It is typical of the diametrically opposed picture of Arabia presented by Charles Doughty that he claimed never to have seen animal carcasses in the wake of pilgrims (*Arabia Deserta*, i, p. 96). But then, Doughty had never travelled this route and under these circumstances.
30. *Personal Narrative*, ii, pp. 127–8.
31. Ibid., ii, p. 140.
32. Ibid., ii, p. 143.
33. For the martial qualities of the Wahhabis see Ali Bey, *Voyages d'Ali Bey et Abassi en Afrique et en Asie pendant les années 1803, 1804, 1805, 1806 et 1807* (Paris 1814), ii, pp. 459–60.
34. 'A Journey from El-Medina to Mecca', *JRGS* 25 (1855), pp. 121–36.
35. With supreme aplomb he brushed aside the initial contretemps: 'It often happens to the traveller, as the charming Mrs Malaprop observes, to find intercourse all the better by beginning with a little aversion.' (*Personal Narrative*, ii, p. 172).
36. Ibid., ii, pp. 160–61.
37. Ibid., ii, p. 169.
38. 'One wonders if Louis [Burkhardt] saw any lightly veiled beauties, such as Burton's lovely little "Flirtilla" whom he, Burton, was to chase some forty years later at Arafat – but then unfortunately Louis was always more serious and more reserved about his own personal reactions to beauty than the extrovert Englishman ever was.' (Catherine Sim, *Desert Traveller. The Life of J. L. Burkhardt* (1969), p. 323. For a feminist reading of Burton's escapade and those of his other fellow-countrymen see Carroll M. Pastner, 'Englishmen in Arabia: Encounters with Middle Eastern Women' *Signs* 4 (1978), pp. 309–323.
39. *Personal Narrative*, ii, pp. 206–7.
40. *Life*, i, pp. 178–9.
41. *Personal Narrative*, ii, p. 271.
42. *Life*, i, p. 182.
43. See Hastings, *Sir Richard Burton*, op. cit., p. 89.

CHAPTER 7 THE IMPACT OF ARABIA AND ISLAM pp. 88–100

1. Arminius Vámbéry, *Travels and Adventures in Central Asia* (1864).
2. Trench, *Arabian Travellers* (1986). op. cit., pp. 83, 90, 91.
3. For these three incidents see *Personal Narrative*, i, p. 233; ii, pp. 199–200, 261.
4. *Morning Post*, 19 January 1886.
5. Wright, i, p. 172; *Life*, ii, pp. 507–8.

6. *The Times*, 25 August 1862.
7. Doughty, *Arabia Deserta*, ii, p. 68.
8. *The Land of Midian Revisited*, 2 vols (1879), i, pp. 273–4.
9. Burton's teases are related in Lord Algernon Redesdale, *Memories*, 2 vols (1915), ii, p. 572; Bram Stoker, *Personal Reminiscences of Henry Irving*, 2 vols (1906), i, p. 359. His emphatic denial at *Arabian Nights*, ii, p. 326 is also reproduced in Kenneth Walker, ed., *Love, War and Fancy, the social and sexual customs of the East by Sir Richard Burton* (1964), p. 260. See also Michell Papers, SOAS, Box 7/204772 ff. 6–7. Curiously, in view of the attitude towards urine, Arabs considered it undignified to use toilet paper after excretion and used the pejorative tag *Kaghaz-Khanah* for European lavatories (*Arabian Nights*, i, p. 221).
10. *Personal Narrative*, i, pp. 247, 261, 266, 331.
11. The phallic motif can be traced in *Personal Narrative*, i, pp. 32, 72, 81, 84, 89, 92, 210. Burton acknowledged his debt for this insight to Pierre François Hugues d'Hancarville, *Recherches sur l'origine, l'esprit et le progrès des arts de la Grèce: sur leurs connections avec les arts et la religion des plus anciens peuples connus* (1785).
12. The Burton quotations are respectively from *Personal Narrative*, i, pp. 16, 149 and *The Carmina of Gaius Valerius Catullus* (1894), p. ix. For the Freudian proposition see *Standard Edition of the Complete Psychological Works of Sigmund Freud*, xxi, p. 134. See also Melanie Klein's notion of ambivalence as applied to the exploration of the desert in *Love, Guilt and Reparation* (1975), pp. 333–34.
13. Wilfred Thesiger, *Arabian Sands* (1959), pp. 259–60.
14. *Arabian Nights*, ii, pp. 101, 108; 'Early Days in Scinde', loc. cit., p. 22. Cf. also *Sindh and the Races*, p. 201. This judgement on the Arabs is endorsed by T. E. Lawrence in his preface to the second edition of Doughty's *Travels in Arabia Deserta*: 'Sitting to the eyes in a cloaca but with their brows touching heaven' (pp. xxi, xxvii). Emotionality and pathos in the Arab is a favourite subject for Burtonian asides (*Arabian Nights*, iii, p. 55; iv, p. 6). He found them ready to shed tears not just at the stories of the *Arabian Nights* but at the heroes of Homer and the Italians of Boccaccio (ibid., i, p. 68).
15. *The Inner Life of Syria*, ii, p. 140.
16. *The Gold Mines of Midian* (1878), p. 30.
17. 'The air of cities will suffocate you, and the careworn and cadaverous countenances of citizens will haunt you like a vision of judgement' (*Personal Narrative*, i, p. 151). 'At last once more it is my fate to escape the prison-life of civilised Europe and to refresh body and mind by studying Nature in her noblest and most admirable form – the Nude' (*The Land of Midian Revisited*). See also Burton's contempt for his contemporaries in *Stone-Talk*, p. 110:

> A poor and puny race today
> In vain, to take their place essay
> A dwarf'd, degenerate progeny
> Rear'd on dry toast and twice-drunk tea

18. *Land of Midian Revisited*, pp. 156–8. For a cynical view of the glorification of the 'noble savage' see H. N. Fairchild *A Study in Romantic Naturalism* (NY 1961), p. 119: 'No traveller with an eye to publication would deal hastily with savages. Whatever really happened in his wanderings, that chapter on "Manners and Customs of the Natives" must at all costs praise natural virtues and take a fling at more refined nations.'
19. *Personal Narrative*, ii, pp. 85, 96. Burton's target in the first quote was particularly 'my lord Lindsay', author of *Letters on Egypt, Edom and the Holy Land* (1838).
20. *The Land of Midian Revisited*, pp. 40, 154.
21. *Personal Narrative*, ii, pp. 87–8.
22. *Arabian Nights*, ix, pp. 94, 134; viii, p. 189.

23. *Unexplored Syria*, i, p. 11; *Land of Midian Revisited*, i, p. 205.
24. Blunt, *My Diaries*, op. cit., ii, pp. 128–32.
25. See Chapter One of *Seven Pillars of Wisdom* (1935).
26. *Personal Narrative*, i, p. 9.
27. Auguste Ralli, *Christians at Mecca*, op. cit., p. 162; Fairfax Downey, *Arabian Nights Adventurer* (1931), p. 88.
28. Wright, ii, p. 145.
29. For a full analysis see T.J. Assad, *Three Victorian Travellers* (1964), pp. 38–49.
30. *Arabian Nights*, iii, p. 19; iv, p. 285; *Wanderings in West Africa*, i, p. 255. Humans were accorded a superior place in the hierarchy to angels and spirits: 'a single mortal is better in Allah's sight than a thousand Jinn' (*Arabian Nights*, viii, p. 5).
31. Ibid., x, pp. 183–86; *Personal Narrative*, p. xxii.
32. Ibid., ix, p. 90.
33. See especially Lamartine, *Souvenirs, impressions, pensées et paysages pendant un voyage en Orient 1832–33* (Paris 1835), ii, p. 287.
34. This mould was first decisively broken in the late 1830s by Thomas Carlyle in his essay on Mohammed in *Heroes and Hero Worship* (1841).
35. *The Jew, the Gypsy and El-Islam*, pp. 321–43 for this and other stirring passages in defence of Mohammed and his religion.
36. Doughty, *Arabia Deserta*, i, pp. 277–80; ii, p. 376.
37. *First Footsteps in East Africa*, pp. 37–38.
38. *Arabian Nights*, i, p. 204; iii, pp. 212–13; ix, pp. 246–47; x, p. 199.
39. Ibid., ix, pp. 246–47.
40. Two of Burton's favourite references were as follows: 'One upright man among a thousand I have found but a woman among all I have not found' (Ecclesiastes, vi, 28). Also, Psalms xxx, 15 speaks of the three insatiables: 'Hell, Earth and the Parts Feminine'. See also *Arabian Nights*, ix, pp. 303–4; pp. 197–8.
41. Ibid., i, p. 174.
42. *Personal Narrative*, ii, p. 22.
43. G. Allgrove, *Love in the East* (1962), p. 53. Contrast this with Burton's emphatic statement: 'the position of womanhood in the Nights is curiously at variance with the stock ideas concerning the Moslem's home and domestic policy still prevalent not only in England but throughout Europe' (*Arabian Nights*, x, p. 192).
44. Ibid., v, pp. 180–81.
45. Ibid., iii, p. 289; x, pp. 192–4; i, p. 289.
46. For these examples of Burton's misogynism see ibid., i, p. 191; vi, p. 187; viii, p. 137; ix, p. 175; x, pp. 4–5; xi, pp. 311–12.
47. *Personal Narrative*, ii, p. 92.
48. See the assessment of Blunt in Assad, *Three Victorian Travellers* (1964), pp. 53–94 and especially Blunt's criticism of Burton (pp. 53–5).
49. Elizabeth Longford, *A Pilgrimage of Passion. The Life of Wilfrid Scawen Blunt* (1979), p. 147.
50. For Palgrave's life see Mea Allan, *Palgrave of Arabia. The Life of William Gifford Palgrave 1826–88* (1972).
51. See *Athenaeum* No. 1963, 10 June 1865, p. 774; *Edinburgh Review* 122 (October 1865), p. 493.
52. W.G. Palgrave, *Narrative of a Year's Journey through Central and Eastern Arabia 1862–63*, 2 vols (1866), i, pp. vii–viii, 258–9.
53. *Personal Narrative*, i, pp. xxi–xxii.
54. For further tirades see *Arabian Nights*, ix, pp. 188–9.
55. 'Mr Doughty's travels in Arabia Deserta', *Academy* 847, 28 July 1888, pp. 47–48.
56. Achmed Abdullah and Compton T. Pakenham, 'Richard Francis Burton', in *Dreamers of Empire* (NY 1929), pp. 57–58.

57. Ann Treneer, *Charles M. Doughty* (1935), p. 99.
58. Penzer, *Annotated Bibliography*, p. 7.
59. Doughty, *Arabia Deserta*, i, p. 31.
60. Robert Graves, *Lawrence and the Arabs* (1927), p. 5.
61. H. St J. Philby, *Heart of Arabia*, 2 vols (1922), ii, p. 146; *The Empty Quarter* (1933), pp. 115, 132, 158, 164; Bertram Thomas, *Arabia Felix* (1932), pp. 22, 301–2.

CHAPTER 8 FIRST FOOTSTEPS IN AFRICA pp. 101–118

1. Burton to Shaw, October 1853, RGS.
2. Von Maltzan, *Meine Wallfahrt nach Mekka* (Leipzig 1865), pp. 5–7; cf. also Von Maltzan, *Reisen in Arabien* (Brunswick 1873).
3. Burton to Shaw, 16 November 1853, RGS.
4. Postscript to Gordon Waterfield's edition of *First Footsteps in East Africa* (1966), p. 260.
5. See J. L. Krapf, *Travels, Researches and Missionary Labours during an Eighteen Years' Residence in Eastern Africa* (1860).
6. Burton to Shaw, 15 December 1853, RGS.
7. Burton to Shaw, 16 November 1853, RGS.
8. Bombay letter, 10 May 1854, quoted in Waterfield's introduction to *First Footsteps*, op. cit.
9. *Bombay Times*, 12 May 1855.
10. *First Footsteps* (Waterfield edition), p. 60.
11. Letter of 23 August 1854 quoted in ibid. p. 23.
12. James A. Casada, 'The birthplace of John Hanning Speke', *Devon and Cornwall Notes and Queries* 32 (1971), pp. 55–8; 'John Hanning Speke's youth and Indian Army career', *Devon and Cornwall Notes and Queries* 32 (1972), pp. 121–23.
13. 'Without exception, and having shot over three-quarters of the globe, I can safely say, there does not exist any place in the whole world which affords such a diversity of sport, or such enchanting scenery, as well as pleasant climate and temperature, as these countries of my first experience.' (Speke, *What Led to the Discovery of the Source of the Nile* (Edinburgh 1864), p. 3.
14. *Life*, i, p. 315.
15. *Zanzibar. City, Island and Coast*, 2 vols (1872), ii, p. 397.
16. Ibid., pp. 373–74.
17. Speke, *What Led*, etc., pp. 13–15.
18. The circumstances in which such a formation is likely are plausibly explained in Freud, 'Leonardo da Vinci and a memory of his childhood', *Standard Edition*, op. cit., xi, p. 100. Cf. also Alexander Maitland, *Speke* (1971), p. 15: 'Under his mother's influence, the young man's thinking tended to develop along emotional rather than rational lines, a conspicuously feminine trait in so determinedly masculine a character.'
19. *Zanzibar*, ii, p. 368; Speke, 'Journal of a Cruise on the Tanganyika Lake and Discovery of the Victoria Nyanza Lake', *Blackwood's Magazine* 86 (1859), p. 575.
20. *Life*, i, p. 315.
21. Speke, *What Led*, p. 23.
22. 'Narrative of a Trip to Harar', *JRGS* 25 (1855), pp. 136–50.
23. See Ralph E. Drake-Brockman, *British Somaliland* (1912) for oral traditions on Burton's stay in Zayla.
24. See Waterfield's appendix to the 1966 edition of *First Footsteps*, pp. 285–87. For confirmation of Burton's accuracy about sexual practices in Somalia see I. M. Lewis, *A Pastoral Democracy* (Oxford 1961).
25. *First footsteps*, pp. 61–3.
26. *Arabian Nights*, i, p. ix.

27. In his official report of 22 February 1855 in the India Office papers for Jan–April 1855 is the following assessment: 'They evince a gentleness of disposition and a docility which offer fair hopes to civilization in this region of barbarism ... people who in my humble opinion, are capable of being raised high in the scale of humanity ... Every free-born man holds himself equal to his ruler, and allows no royalties or prerogatives to abridge his birthright of liberty. Yet I have observed, that with all their passion for independence, the Somal, when subject to strict rule as at Zayla and Harar, are both apt to discipline and subservient to command.' (Quoted Waterfield, op. cit., pp. 31–2).
28. For a more flattering assessment see Wilfred Thesiger, *The Life of My Choice* (1988 edn.), pp. 119–68.
29. *First Footsteps*, pp. 106, 138.
30. Ibid., pp. 167–68; 'Narrative of a trip to Harar', loc. cit.
31. *Bombay Gazette*, 5–19 March 1855.
32. *First Footsteps*, p. 177.
33. Ibid., p. 205.
34. Ibid., pp. 206–07.
35. Ibid., p. 216.
36. *Life*, i, pp. 214–15.
37. *Overland Bombay Times*, February 1855.
38. Burton to Shaw, 25 February 1855, RGS.
39. *Arabian Nights*, i, p. 345.
40. Ibid., i, p. 6.
41. Burton to East India Company, 22 February 1855, enclosed in Loghlan to Anderson, Bombay Letters, Jan–April 1855 in the India Office Library, quoted by Waterfield, op. cit., pp. 239–45.
42. I. M. Lewis, *A Pastoral Democracy*, op. cit., p. 32; J. Spencer Trimingham, *Islam in Ethiopia* (Oxford 1952), p. 216.
43. See General Gordon's letter to Burton from Harar, 29 April 1878; RGS; cf. also Thesiger, *Life of My Choice*, op. cit., pp. 95–6.
44. Speke, *What Led*, pp. 45, 64–65, 74–76, 99.
45. Ibid., p. 88.
46. *First Footsteps* (1856 edn), pp. 502–3.
47. *First Footsteps* (1966 edn), p. 181.
48. Brodie, *Devil Drives*, p. 120. An insight that could be dismissed as contrived comes to seem more securely based when the feminine symbolism of the great African rivers is taken into account. This could make the loss of a mother especially significant. Bernard C. Meyer, *Joseph Conrad. A Psychoanalytic Biography* (Princeton 1967), when trying to account for the fascination of the Congo for Conrad, postulated the self-evident symbolism of a young boy dreaming that at manhood he will enter into some dark mysterious place, in which a river shaped like an immense snake penetrates a body of land (p. 349).
49. See Burton's account of the attack in *First Footsteps*, pp. 251–9.
50. Anton Mifsud, 'Medical History of John Hanning Speke, '*The Practitioner* 214 (1975), pp. 125–30.
51. See Speke's account of the attack in *What Led*, pp. 131–41.

CHAPTER 9 CRIMEAN DÉBÂCLE pp. 119–127

1. *Life*, i, p. 219; the eye-witness accounts of the non-European members of the party are gathered together in Waterfield, op. cit., pp. 277–84.
2. The entire controversy can be followed in the exchange of India Office letters printed in Waterfield, pp. 260–76.

3. Speke, *What Led*, p. 112; Waterfield, pp. 306–7.
4. Lambert Playfair, *A History of Arabia Felix* (1859).
5. Burton to Shaw, 16 December 1856, RGS.
6. 'I am a great loser by reputation as well as by pocket in consequence of the failure and feel very sour about it as you may suppose', Speke told Playfair (Maitland, *Speke*, op. cit., p. 49).
7. *Life*, i, pp. 322–23.
8. Stisted, p. 160.
9. *Life*, ii, pp. 539–40.
10. All this is brilliantly set forth in the classic account by Cecil Woodham-Smith, *The Reason Why* (1963). See also Piers Compton, *Cardigan of Balaclava* (1972); John Harris, *The Gallant Six Hundred* (1973); Frank Cook, *Casualty Roll for the Crimea* (1976).
11. *Highlands of Brazil*, i, p. 38; *To the Gold Coast*, i, p. 173. For Burton's ideas on Turkey see 'The Partition of Turkey' and 'The Future of Turkey', *Daily Telegraph*, 7 March 1880; *Manchester Examiner and Times*, 3, 4 January 1881; cf. also *Arabian Nights*, ix. p. 94.
12. 'Russophobia, I repeat, is no dream, it is a distorted vision of possibilities.' (*Scinde*, ii, pp. 59–60).
13. *Life*, ii, pp. 522, 535. For some recent explanations see J. B. Conacher, *Britain and the Crimea 1855–56* (1987); Norman Rich, *Why the Crimean War?* (Hanover, N. H. 1985); Paul W. Schroeder, *Austria, Great Britain and the Crimean War* (1972); John S. Curtiss, *Russia's Crimean War* (1979); cf. also Marx to Engels, 10 March 1853, *Marx–Engels Collected Works*, op. cit., 39 (1983), p. 288; Marx to Engels, 17 October 1854, ibid., p. 487; cf. also vol. 12 (1979) passim.
14. *A Mission to Gelele*, op. cit., i, p. 14; *Zanzibar*, ii, p. 387.
15. See Christopher Hibbert, *The Destruction of Lord Raglan* (1961).
16. Burton to Shaw, 18 August 1855, RGS.
17. Hitchman, i, pp. 314–19.
18. *Arabian Nights*, i, p. 178; v, p. 34.
19. *Life*, i, p. 238.
20. *Arabian Nights*, xv, p. 119.
21. *Life*, i, p. 238.
22. *Arabian Nights*, i, p. 295; *Unexplored Syria*, ii, p. 95; *Lake Regions*, ii, p. 233.
23. *The City of the Saints*, p. 58.
24. 'In an evil hour I proposed, if my General, who wanted nothing better, would allow me, to proceed in person to Constantinople and to volunteer officially for the relief of the doomed city, Kars. *Ah Corydon, Corydon, quae te dementia cepit?*' (*Zanzibar*, i, p. 4).
25. See H. A. Lake, *Narrative of the Defence of Kars* (1857); *Kars and Our Captivity in Russia* (1857); H. Sandwith, *Narrative of the Siege of Kars* (1856).
26. *Life*, i, p. 242.
27. See W. F. Beatson, *Lord Stratford de Redcliffe, the War Department and the Bashi Bazouks* (1856).
28. See J.H. Skene, *With Lord Stratford in the Crimean War* (1883); *The Times*, 6 December 1855.
29. *Life*, i, p. 248.
30. See Burton's letter to *The Times*, 19 February 1856; cf. also *Life*, i, p. 48.
31. Lane-Poole's opening salvo was in the *Athenaeum*, 25 August 1888. Burton replied angrily in both the *Academy*, 1 September 1888 and the *Athenaeum* of the same date. Lane-Poole's 'cuttlefish' defence appeared in the *Athenaeum*, 8 September 1888. Burton had the last word in a review of Lane-Poole's biography in the *Academy*, 24 November 1888.
32. Wright, i, p. 141.

CHAPTER 10 THE DARK CONTINENT pp. 128–141

1. Wilkins, *Romance*, op. cit., i, pp. 80–1.
2. Ibid., pp. 82–3.
3. *Life*, i, pp. 249–50.
4. Wilkins, pp. 83–8; *Life*, i, pp. 25–56.
5. Wright, i, p. 47.
6. *Zanzibar*, i, pp. 5–7; for Barth see Von Schubert, *Life* (1897).
7. RGS Minute Book, Committees 1841–65, pp. 109–110.
8. See Roy C. Bridges' introduction to Johann Ludwig Krapf, *Travels, Researches and Missionary Labours during an Eighteen Years' Residence in Eastern Africa* (1968), pp. 39–42. Speke related that everyone who saw the map of the 'giant slug or salamander' on the wall of the Royal Geographical Society laughed and shook his head (Speke, *What Led*, p. 156).
9. For Bruce's travels see his *Travels to Discover the Source of the Nile in the Years 1768, 1769, 1770, 1771, 1772 and 1773*, 5 vols (Edinburgh 1890). For Burton's dislike of Bruce see above pp. 115. In the notes to the *Arabian Nights* Burton took another sideswipe at Bruce, this time for popularising the idea of the 'Blue Nile', which he should have called the 'Blue River'. Burton claimed Bruce did this knowingly out of 'inordinate vanity and self-esteem' (*Arabian Nights*, viii, p. 4). The situation prior to Burton's expedition has been succinctly summed up in Caroline Oliver, 'Richard Burton. The African Years', in R. I. Rotberg, ed., *Africa and its Explorers* (Harvard 1970), pp. 65–93: 'There is no record of any successful penetration farther south than Latitude 4 North, and little of value was contributed to the solution of the mystery of the Nile's origins, between the fifth century and Burton's expedition.'
10. Clements Markham's unpublished history of the RGS (RGS Archives), p. 354.
11. For this sequence of events see RGS Minute Book, 23 June, 5 August, 30 September 1856, pp. 112–13, 115–17; Norton Shaw to East India Company, 6 June 1856; East India Company to Shaw, 30 August 1856; Burton to Shaw, 7 September 1856, RGS.
12. Alfred B. Richards to Colt, 22 November 1856, RGS, related that Burton dined with him the day he left for India.
13. East India Company to Burton, 24 October 1856; Burton to East India Company, 14 November 1856, *Lake Regions*, ii, pp. 420–21.
14. *Overland Bombay Times*, 17 December 1856, 2 January 1857; RGS Minute Book, 18 December 1856, 26 January 1857, pp. 121, 127.
15. Burton to RGS, 15 December 1856; *Lake Regions*, ii, pp. 422–8; *Overland Summary, Bombay*, 4 August 1858; RGS Minute Book, 21 March 1857, p. 130; FO to Shaw, 24 June 1857, RGS.
16. Bombay Government to Burton, 23 July 1857, *Lake Regions*, ii, p. 428.
17. *Zanzibar*, i, pp. 19, 157. Stanley knew better. While he was on his return from 'finding' Livingstone in 1872, a violent hurricane devastated Zanzibar, and the coastal fringe was overwhelmed by a gigantic tidal wave (Stanley to Livingstone, 25 May 1872, NLS 10705 ff. 7–12).
18. See Norman R. Bennett, *A History of the Arab State of Zanzibar* (1978).
19. *Zanzibar*, i, pp. 34–36.
20. See *Zanzibar*, i, passim. Burton's monumental survey of the island is supplemented by the three-volume work on Zanzibar by Oscar Baumann, *Der Sansibar Archipel*, 3 vols (Leipzig 1896–7). For a complete bibliography relating to Zanzibar see Norman R. Bennett, *The Arab State of Zanzibar* (Boston 1984).
21. For a general survey see R. W. Beachey, *The Slave Trade of Eastern Africa* (1976).
22. *Zanzibar*, i, p. 37. For the modern scholarship on Maizan see Bennett, *Arab versus European* (1986), pp. 47–8.
23. *Zanzibar*, ii, pp. 12–74.
24. Joseph Thomson, *Through Masailand* (1885). For the German missionaries' fear of

the Masai see Krapf, *Travels*, etc. (1860 edn.), pp. 361, 421–22.
25. *Zanzibar*, ii, pp. 144, 197.
26. Ibid., ii, pp. 185–211; cf. Burton and Speke, 'A Coasting Voyage from Mombasa to the Pangani River', *JRGS* 28, pp. 188–226.
27. Burton, 'Zanzibar and Two Months in East Africa', *Blackwood's Edinburgh Magazine* 83 (February, March, May 1858), pp. 200–24, 276–90, 572–89.
28. Speke, *What Led*, p. 178.
29. *Zanzibar*, ii, pp. 179–81.
30. For Bombay see Donald Simpson, *Dark Companions* (1975). Bombay was given a pension of £15 a year for life in 1876 by the RGS. He was well liked by Rigby and his successor John Kirk. He died on 12 October 1886. (See James Grant's Correspondence book, RGS Archives, pp. 1–3.)
31. Speke, *What Led*, p. 189.
32. *Zanzibar*, i, p. 8.
33. Ibid., ii, p. 372; *The Nile Basin* (1865), Part One, p. 6.
34. Stisted, pp. 163–164.
35. Anne Taylor, *Laurence Oliphant* (Oxford 1982), p. 67.
36. Reminding Burton of this incident later, Speke wrote: 'You then added Gall to it by saying, that you considered such appropriation legitimate and that anyone similarly circumstanced would do the same ... after that confession I felt to make any more collections and especially remarks about them labour in vain.' (Maitland, *Speke*, p. 62).
37. *Zanzibar*, ii, p. 388. Maitland, *Speke*, p. 78 quotes Christopher Haxsall's *Rupert Brooke* (1964) in Burton's support on this point.
38. *Zanzibar*, ii, p. 385.
39. Ibid., p. 297.
40. Ibid., p. 374.
41. Speke, *What Led*, p. 188.
42. *Zanzibar*, ii, pp. 374–76.
43. Maitland, *Speke*, p. 155.
44. Speke to Shaw, 10 May 1860, RGS.
45. Maitland, *Speke*, pp. 158–9.
46. Speke, *Journal of the Discovery of the Source of the Nile* (1864), p. 361.
47. *Zanzibar*, ii, p. 382.
48. Ibid., ii, pp. 246–51.
49. James Augustus Grant, *A Walk Across Africa* (Edinburgh 1864), pp. 36–37.
50. *Journal of the Discovery*, pp. 270–72. Of this incident even Speke's biographer, who normally gives him the benefit of most doubts, comments: 'it is certain that the second and particularly the third blow was superfluous, being delivered out of anger rather than necessity' (Maitland, *Speke*, p. 148).
51. Ibid., pp. 82–3.
52. *Life*, i, pp. 276–77, 281. The sensation of a divided self remained with Burton at a conscious level. Much later he said to his wife Isabel: 'I always told you that I was a dual man and I believe that that particular mania when I am delirious is perfectly correct.' (Ibid., ii, p. 268).
53. Ibid., i, pp. 287, 322–3.
54. For an analysis of the death drive that sheds light on Speke see K. R. Eissler, 'Death Drive, Ambivalence and Narcissism', *The Psychoanalytic Study of the Child* 26 (1971), pp. 25–78.

CHAPTER 11 TO LAKE TANGANYIKA pp. 142–159

1. *Lake Regions*, i, pp. 19–20. For Burton and Speke during this doldrum period in Zanzibar see Speke to Shaw, 20 May 1857, RGS; Burton to RGS, 22 April 1857 in

PRGS 2 (1857–58), pp. 52–8. For more on the supposed dangers of the march inland see Burton to Shaw, 28 December 1856; Buist to Anderson, 8 December 1856, RGS.

2. *Zanzibar*, i, pp. 437–53. Burton noted that the Swahili of Mombasa was purer than in Zanzibar (ibid., ii, p. 76).

3. Ibid., i, p. 446. See also Sir John Gray, 'Burton on Kiswahili', *TNR* 51 (1958), pp. 156–8. For the mastery at Kazeh see *Lake Regions*, ii, pp. 198–9.

4. Frederick Jackson, *Early Days in East Africa* (1930), p. 74.

5. For the Portuguese see *Zanzibar*, i, p. 483; for Said bin Salim see Norman Bennett, *Studies in East African History* (Boston 1963), pp. 5–15. After service on this expedition he went with Speke and Grant in 1861 but was left at Tabora because of illness (*Journal of the Discovery*), p. 99). Shortly afterwards he became governor of Unyanyembe and was in post when Stanley arrived there in 1871 (*NY Herald*, 15 July, 9 August 1872).

6. For Mabruki, who later served with Speke and Grant and Livingstone and Stanley, see Simpson, *Dark Companions*, op. cit., cf. also Adolphe Burdo, *Les Belges dans l'Afrique Centrale* (Paris 1885), p. 166; *NY Herald*, 9 August 1872, 24 December 1874.

7. For porterage in Africa see S. C. Lamden, 'Some Aspects of Porterage in East Africa', *TNR* 61 (1963), pp. 155–64.

8. For this see J. M'Queen (Moorhead), 'Visit of Lief Ben Saeed to the Great African Lake', *JRGS* 15 (1845). pp. 371–76; John M. Gray, 'Trading Expeditions from the Coast to Lakes Tanganyika and Victoria before 1857', *TNR* 46 (1957), pp. 226–46. Burton also learned a lot in Zanzibar from the Arab Salim bin Rashid al Manzuri, who had travelled in the region of the Lakes (actually Lake Victoria); Burton, 'The Lake Regions of Central Equatorial Africa', *JRGS* 29 (1859), pp. 260, 270, 275, 346. This RGS monograph, which takes up the whole of Vol. 29, contains much material not in Burton's *Lake Regions* book.

9. *Lake Regions*, i, p. 37.

10. Anton Mifsud, 'Medical History of John Hanning Speke', loc. cit., pp. 125–30.

11. For their reputation see Edmund A. Bojarski, 'The Last of the Cannibals in Tanganyika', *TNR* 51 (1958), pp. 227–31; A. Schynse, *Á Travers l'Afrique avec Stanley et Emin-Pacha* (Paris 1890), p. 290. For Burton's comments see *Lake Regions*, i, p. 123. Speaking of the Wabembe cannibals on Lake Tanganyika he says: 'They prefer man raw, whereas the Wadoe of the coast eat him roasted' (*Lake. Regions*, ii, p. 114). For a more balanced view of the Doe see H. Baumann and D. Westermann, *Les Peuplades et les Civilisations de l'Afrique* (Paris 1948), p. 233.

12. *Lake Regions*, i, p. 51.

13. The Nyamwezi of Western Tanzania were famous as carriers in East African caravans. See R. G. Abrahams, *The Peoples of Greater Unyamwezi, Tanzania (Nyamwezi, Sukuma, Sumbwa, Kimbu, Konongo* (1967); *The Political Organisation of Unyamwezi* (1967); Wilhelm Blohm, *Die Nyamwezi, Land und Wirtschaft* (Hamburg 1931) and *Die Nyamwezi, Gesellschaft und Weltbild* (Hamburg 1933); Fr. Bosch, *Les Banyamwezi* (Munster 1930).

14. Speke, *What Led*, pp. 196–97.

15. *Zanzibar*, ii, p. 388.

16. For the Sagara peoples of this region see Thomas O. Beidelmann, *The Matrilineal Peoples of Eastern Tanzania* (1967).

17. *Lake Regions*, i, pp. 166–7.

18. For a description of the daily round see *Lake Regions*, i, pp. 344–62. For a detailed daily breakdown of the march see W. Wenbay Smith, 'Diary of the 1857–58 Expedition to the Great Lakes', *TNR* 46 (1957), pp. 247–55.

19. *Lake Regions*, i, pp. 251, 268–9, 301.

20. For the Gogo see Peter Rigby, *Cattle and Kinship among the Gogo* (Ithaca, NY 1969); Heinrich Claus, *Die Wagogo* (Leipzig 1911).

21. For Burton on the Gogo see *Lake Regions*, i, pp. 253–310. For the link between the

Gogo's jealous guardianship of their wells and Bedouin practice see Peter Rigby, 'Sociological Factors in the Contact of the Gogo of Central Tanzania with Islam' in I. M. Lewis, ed., *Islam in Tropical Africa* (1966).
22. Burton, 'Lake Regions', loc. cit., pp. 425, 429–30. For this subject in general see François Coulbois, *Dix Années au Tanganika* (Limoges 1901); J. R. Harding, 'Nineteenth Century Trade Beads in Tanganyika', *Man* 62 (1962), pp. 104–6.
23. *Lake Regions*, i, pp. 309–10. This is confirmed from other sources.
24. Ibid., i, p. 257.
25. 'Lake Regions', loc. cit., pp. 164, 178. There is a notable description of these areas by a later traveller: Franz Stuhlmann, *Mit Emin Pascha ins Herz von Afrika* (Berlin 1894), p. 57.
26. See Alan Moorehead, *The White Nile*, op. cit.
27. Speke, *What Led*, p. 198.
28. Ibid., p. 200. Some of the other mendacious rationalisations Speke indulged in to cover his 'passenger' status at Kazeh are dissected dispassionately by Maitland, *Speke*, pp. 68–9.
29. *Lake Regions*, i, p. 404.
30. Nzogera was a chief of the Vinza tribe ('Lake Regions', loc. cit., pp. 193, 207). In 1881–82 this tribe suffered many losses in an unwise war with the greatest of Arab slavers, Tippu Tip (A. Lene, *Dar-es-Salaam* (Berlin 1903), pp. 249 et seq.). Stanley had the same problems at the Malagarazi with Nzogera's son in 1871 (see Frank McLynn, *Stanley, the Making of an African Explorer* (1989), p. 143.
31. *Lake Regions*, ii, pp. 104–5.
32. Maitland, *Speke*, p. 70.
33. Speke, 'Journal of a Cruise on the Tanganyika Lake, Central Africa', *Blackwood's Edinburgh Magazine* 86 (1859), pp. 339–57 (at p. 342). Cf. also 'Lake Regions', pp. 224–6.
34. The Ha were divided into six independent chiefdoms in the nineteenth century (J. H. Scherer, 'The Ha of Tanganyika', *Anthropos* 54 (1959), pp. 841–904). Stanley's famous confrontation was with the Luguru chief (see McLynn, *Stanley*, op. cit., pp. 144–6).
35. Speke, *What Led*, p. 307.
36. *PRGS* 29 (1859), p. 17.
37. Speke, 'Journal of a Cruise', loc. cit., p. 349.
38. *Lake Regions*, ii, p. 90.
39. Ibid., ii, p. 124.
40. Ibid., ii, pp. 156–57.
41. Speke, *What Led*, p. 251.
42. Speke to Shaw, 2 July 1858, RGS.
43. *Lake Regions*, ii, p. 171.
44. *Life*, i, p. 309. Cf. also Livingstone's remarks at NLS 10731 f. 47.
45. Speke, *What Led*, p. 251. Cf. also Grant's letter to *The Times*, 28 October 1890.
46. 'Such tidings are severely felt by the wanderer who, living long behind the world, is unable to mark its gradual changes, lulls (by dwelling upon the past) apprehension into a belief that *his* home has known no loss, and who expects again to meet each old familiar face ready to smile upon his return, as it was to weep at his departure.' (*Life*, i, p. 308).
47. C. E. B. Russell, *General Rigby, Zanzibar and the Slave Trade* (1953), pp. 235–8; Speke, *What Led*, pp. 270–312.
48. His linguistic mastery led him to postulate that the name 'Tanganyika' was derived from the Kiswahili words for 'to mix'. ('Lake Regions', p. 234). Verney Lovett Cameron, *Across Africa*, 2 vols (1877), argued with this etymology. So did a later scholar

(Robert Schmitz, *Les Baholòlo* (Brussels 1912), p. 565). He also realised that the same word was used for both 'island' and 'peninsula' – knowledge that would have saved Speke from some later errors ('Lake Regions', p. 274). Speke mistakenly designated the Majita peninsula on Lake Victoria an island (Speke, *What Led*, pp. 306, 310), relying on oral testimony. This blemish was later corrected by Stanley in 1875 (*NY Herald*, 29 November 1875).
49. *Lake Regions*, ii, p. 204.
50. *Life*, i, p. 312.
51. Ibid., ii, p. 424.
52. Ibid., i, p. 322.
53. *Lake Regions*, ii, p. 240.
54. Ibid., ii, p. 276.
55. Kilwa was a great slaving centre, handling 15,000 slaves annually (Kirk to Derby, 20 April 1876, F.O.84/1453).
56. *Zanzibar*, ii, pp. 344–5.
57. *Lake Regions*, ii, pp. 378–84; *Zanzibar*, ii, pp. 368–70.

CHAPTER 12 THE SLOUGH OF DESPOND pp. 160–168

1. James B. Wolf, *Missionary to Tanganyika 1877–78* (1971), p. 185; see also pp. 58, 61.
2. *NY Herald*, 15 August 1872, 26 December 1874, 12 August 1876, 10 October 1877.
3. Aylward Shorter, *A Political History of the Kimbu* (Oxford 1972), pp. 239–49, 255–58.
4. 'After taking his seat ... the Myanga demanded his fee – here, as elsewhere, to use the words with which Kleon excited the bile of Tiresias – 'to mantikon gar philarguron genos' – without which prediction would have been impossible.' *Lake Regions*, i, p. 44.
5. *Zanzibar*, ii, pp. 292–3.
6. Burton to Bombay Government, 24 June 1858, *Lake Regions*, ii, p. 429.
7. R. C. H. Risley, 'Burton. An Appreciation', *TNR* 46 (1957), pp. 257–300.
8. It is significant that although great play is made of Rigby's linguistic talents in the hagiographical biography by C. E. B. Russell, *General Rigby, Zanzibar and the Slave Trade*, op. cit., no. mention is made of his defeat by Burton in the Gujerati examination.
9. Russell, *Rigby*, p. 243. The remarks about Burton's attitude to the German explorer Roscher are inaccurate. It was his bumptiousness and criticism of other explorers that riled Burton. His reservations seemed vindicated when Roscher's overconfidence led to his death some months later near Lake Nyasa.
10. *Life*, i, p. 327.
11. Anne Taylor, *Laurence Oliphant* (Oxford 1982), pp. 66–7.
12. Speke, *Journal of the Discovery*, p. 2.
13. *Zanzibar*, ii, p. 391.
14. *PRGS* 3 (1858–9), pp. 217–19, 348–58; *JRGS* 29 (1859), p. xcvii.
15. *Zanzibar*, ii, pp. 390–91.
16. RGS Minute Book, 21 June 1859, pp. 166–7.
17. Speke to Shaw, 28 October, 5 November 1859, RGS.
18. Speke to Blackwood, 10 July, 2 September 1859, 'Sunday' n.d. 1859, NLS 4143.
19. 'Speke Obituary', *Blackwood's Magazine* 9 (1864), p. 514.
20. To the same correspondent he expressed the hope that the publication of his article in *Blackwood's* 'may have the effect of reforming Burton; at any rate it will check his scribbling mania, and may save his soul the burthen of many lies.' (Russell, *General Rigby*, op. cit., pp. 265, 267).
21. Wilkins, *Romance*, i, p. 144; Taylor, *Laurence Oliphant*, p. 111.
22. *Zanzibar*, ii, p. 389.
23. *First Footsteps*, p. 324.

24. *Life*, i, p. 316.
25. Stisted, pp. 163–4; Wright, i, p. 241.
26. Brodie, *Devil Drives*, p. 172.
27. For an interesting examination of this theme in the case of the assassination of US presidents see Marcus Cunliffe, *American Presidents and the Presidency* (1972 Fontana edn.), p. 142.
28. See Burton to Shaw, 20 December 1859, 5, 19 January, 7, 10, 16 February 1860, RGS.
29. *Zanzibar*, ii, p. 382.
30. Rigby to Anderson, 15 July 1859, *Lake Regions*, ii, pp. 430–4; Russell, *General Rigby*, pp. 244–9.
31. Russell, *General Rigby*, pp. 249–55.
32. Burton to East India Office, 11 November 1859, *Lake Regions*, ii, pp. 434–9. For further fulminations see ibid, ii, p. 125.
33. *Zanzibar*, ii, p. 391.
34. *Lake Regions*, ii, pp. 439–41.
35. RGS Minute Book, 10 January 1860, p. 179.
36. Brodie, *Devil Drives*, p. 171.
37. Speke to Shaw, 6 February 1860, RGS.
38. Maitland, *Speke*, pp. 110, 115.
39. *Life*, i, p. 331.
40. Speke to Blackwood, 27 March 1860, NLS 4154.
41. Russell, *General Rigby*, pp. 262–3, 271–2.
42. *Athenaeum*, No. 1704, 25 July 1860, p. 846.
43. Russell, *General Rigby*, pp. 264–74.
44. *Zanzibar*, i, pp. ix-xii; *Life*, i, p. 280.
45. Speke to Rigby, 16 October 1860, 12 May 1861, Russell, *General Rigby*, pp. 235, 239; Speke to Sir George Grey, 1 November 1860 (photocopies in RGS from originals in Auckland Library, New Zealand). See also same to same, 16 January 1861.

CHAPTER 13 MARRIAGE WITH ISABEL pp. 169–182

1. Wilkins, *Romance*, i, pp. 95, 121.
2. Ibid., p. 149.
3. Ibid., pp. 149–51.
4. *Life*, i, pp. 335–6.
5. James Pope-Hennessy, *Monkton Milnes, The Flight of Youth 1851–85* (1951), pp. 122–6; T. Wemyss Reid, *Life, Letters and Friendships of Richard Monkton Milnes, 1st Lord Houghton*, 2 vols (1891), i, pp. 462–63.
6. Burton to Milnes, 22 January 1860, Houghton MSS. Trinity College, Cambridge. For Hankey's worst excesses see Edmond and Jules de Goncourt, *Journal et Mémoires de la vie littéraire* (Monaco 1956), v, pp. 89–93.
7. Stisted, p. 252.
8. *The Times*, 18 October 1859; for the difficulties of working other than at Boulogne, see Burton to Milnes, 22 January 1860, Houghton MSS.
9. The to-ing and fro-ing can be followed in a long series of letters between Burton and Norton Shaw: 20 December 1859, 5, 19 January, 7, 10, 16, 20 March 1860, RGS.
10. *Zanzibar*, i, pp. 14–15.
11. Burton to Shaw, April 1860; RGS; *Life*, i, pp. 337–8; Wilkins, i, p. 155.
12. Burton's American trip, and especially his time among the Mormons, is treated exhaustively in *The City of the Saints*.
13. Wilkins, i, pp. 158–9.
14. *Life*, i, p. 343.

15. Stisted, p. 275.
16. *Life*, i, p. 343.
17. Stisted, p. 364.
18. Wilkins, i, pp. 38–9.
19. Ibid., i, pp. 162–5.
20. Ibid., i, p. 38.
21. Ouida, 'Richard Burton', loc. cit. p. 1043.
22. His own childhood experiences had taught him lessons which he pondered during his travels across North America in 1860: 'The first child is welcomed, the second is tolerated, the third is the cause of tears and reproaches, and the fourth, if not prevented by gold pills, or some similar monstrosity, causes temper, spleen, and melancholy, with disgust and hatred of the cause.' (*The City of the Saints*, p. 524).
23. *Arabian Nights*, xi, p. 72; xiii, p. 487.
24. Ibid., i, p. 212.
25. Ibid., xvi, p. 437.
26. Ibid., x, p. 21.
27. Ibid., xiv, p. 42.
28. Ibid., x, pp. 199–200; xv, p. 223.
29. Ibid., v, pp. 76–77.
30. Ibid., iv, p. 144; xi, p. 311; xiv, p. 144. His friend Frank Harris, who had far more experience of the ephemera of seduction, could have told him otherwise. See *My Life and Loves* (1964) esp. Part One.
31. *Arabian Nights*, ii, p. 241.
32. 'On first entering the nuptial hut, the bridegroom draws forth his horsewhip and inflicts memorable chastisement upon the person of his fair bride, with the view of turning any lurking propensity to shrewishness' (*First Footsteps*, p. 120). Leniency in the treatment of women, he was convinced, led to deplorable consequences (*Arabian Nights*, ix, p. 304; x, pp. 4–5). For the 'good old remedy' see ibid., i, p. 298. The transposed phallicism here is obvious. Burton recommends that if a man cannot satisfy a woman with the symbolic sword, he should constrain her with the actual one. Burton always took a lenient view of the Islamic custom of beheading women for adultery (ibid., i, p. 181).
33. Ibid., iv, p. 227.
34. Ibid., viii, p. 217; ix, pp. 246–47. He also notes the predilection of debauched women for lying slaves – 'these skunks of the human race' (ibid., i, p. 191).
35. Ibid., iii, p. 289.
36. Ibid., v, p. 35; *The City of the Saints*, pp. 199, 230.
37. *Life*, i, p. 344.
38. See the fascination with Hankey evinced in Burton's letters to Milnes, 29 April 1862, 29 March 1863, 12 March 1864, Houghton MSS.
39. Arthur Symons, *Dramatis Personae* (Indianapolis 1923), p. 244; Luke Ionides, 'Memories of Richard Burton', *Transatlantic Review* (March 1924), p. 24.
40. Swinburne to Monkton Milnes, 11 July 1865, in Lang, ed., *The Swinburne Letters*, op. cit., i, p. 124.
41. Same to same, 14 July 1865, ibid., i, p. 125.
42. *Arabian Nights*, iii, p. 304.
43. Ibid., iii, p. 303.
44. *Abeokuta and the Cameroon Mountains*, 2 vols (1863), i, pp. 110–11.
45. *Wanderings in West Africa*, 2 vols (1863), i, p. 255.
46. Stisted, pp. 274, 310–11.
47. Douglas Timmins, ed., *A Traveller of the Sixties. The Journals of F. J. Stevenson* (1929), p. 95.

48. Burton to Milnes, 23 August 1861, Houghton MSS.
49. Same to same, 20 March 1861, ibid.
50. *Life*, i, p. 346.
51. See *The Times*, 30 January 1861, where Burton deals at length with the profitability of Zanzibar cotton. Cf. also *Lake Regions*, ii, pp. 387–419; *Personal Narrative*, i, pp. 179–80; *Zanzibar*, i, passim.
52. *Life*, i, p. 348.

CHAPTER 14 CONSUL IN FERNANDO PO pp. 183–197

1. *Wanderings in West Africa*, i, p. 1.
2. Ibid., pp. 144–90.
3. *Wanderings in West Africa*, ii, p. 34.
4. Ibid., ii, p. 73.
5. Ibid., ii, p. 205.
6. *Mission to Gelele*, i, p. 10.
7. Burton to FO, 8 October 1861, FO 2/20.
8. Mary Kingsley, *Travels in West Africa* (1897).
9. *Life*, i, p. 355.
10. Burton to FO, 4 October 1861, FO 84/1147. A Foreign Office official minuted that Consul Hutchinson had made similar repeated requests which had been turned down, as one boat would not be sufficient. It was decided to leave everything to Burton's discretion (FO minute, 14 November 1861, ibid.).
11. For all this detail see Burton's masterly analysis in Burton to Russell, 15 April 1864, FO 84/1221.
12. 'He lacked that mixture of bush-lawyer, policeman and scribe necessary to the outstanding consuls of nineteenth-century West Africa . . . Burton . . . inherited problems of a frontier society which had caused other consuls to overstep their authority; but both inclination and a clear understanding of his limited position prevented him from doing much about them.' (C. W. Newbury, introduction to his edition of *A Mission to Gelele* (1966), pp. 9, 11.)
13. Hutchinson to Russell, 19 June 1861, FO 2/40.
14. *Life*, i, p. 355; FO to Burton, 2 September 1862, FO 84/1176.
15. *Abeokuta*, i, p. 3.
16. Ibid., i, p. 135.
17. For the French in West Africa see Bernard Schwapper, *La politique et le commerce français dans le Golfe de Guinée de 1838 à 1871* (Paris 1961).
18. See K. O. Dike, *Trade and Politics in the Niger Delta 1830–1885* (Oxford 1956); C. W. Newbury, *The Western Slave Coast and Its Rulers* (Oxford 1961); S. O. Biobaku, *The Egba and their Neighbours 1842–72* (Oxford 1957).
19. *Abeokuta*, ii, pp. 29–30.
20. Burton to FO, 14 January 1862, FO 84/1176.
21. 'Gestures have been well defined as the hieroglyphics of speech. If fate ever lead me back to Europe, and lend me leisure, I hope to make a further study of the subject in surdo-mute establishments, and to produce a system which may prove generally useful, especially to those beginning a foreign tongue. A hundred words, easily learned in a week, two hundred signs, and a little facility in sketching, would enable, I believe, a traveller to make his way through any country, even China, a few days after arrival.' (*Abeokuta*, ii, p. 109).
22. *Abeokuta*, ii, pp. 139–44.
23. Ibid., ii, p. 161.
24. Burton to Russell, 22 February 1862, FO 84/1176.

25. FO to Burton, 23 November, 9 December 1861, FO 84/1147; Burton to FO 22 February 1862, FO 84/1176.
26. This was a reiteration of the theme Burton first broached in November (Burton to Russell, 20 November 1861, CO 147/2).
27. Burton to FO, 1 March 1862, FO 84/1176.
28. *Two Trips to Gorilla Land* (1876), i, p. 41. The other matters mentioned in the text are at ibid., pp. 62–111, 134, 168–69.
29. *Wanderings in West Africa*, ii, p. 247. For modern denials see Thomas Arens, *The Man-Eating Myth* (1979).
30. 'A Day Among the Fans', *Anthropological Review*, 1 (1863), pp. 43–54; 185–87.
31. *The Times*, 4, 5 July 1861.
32. Ibid., 8 July, 23 December 1961.
33. *Two Trips*, i, p. 249.
34. Burton to FO, 26 April 1862, FO 2/42.
35. *Two Trips*, i, pp. 251–52.
36. FO to Burton, 26 February 1862, FO 84/1176.
37. See Traders to Burton, 23 April 1862, ibid.
38. Burton to FO, 22 May 1862, ibid.
39. Anderson to Burton, 12 May 1862, ibid.
40. 'Exploration of the Elephant Mountain in Western Equatorial Africa', *JRGS* 33 (1863), pp. 241–50; cf. also Burton to Shaw, 26 September 1862, RGS.
41. 'My Wanderings in West Africa: a visit to the renowned cities of Wari and Benin', *Fraser's Magazine* 67 (Feb.–April 1863), pp. 135–7; 237–89; 407–22.
42. Burton to FO, 26 September 1862, FO 84/1176.
43. *Wanderings in West Africa*, i, pp. 65–66.
44. FO to Burton, 11, 20 March, 7 August 1862, FO 2/42; Burton to FO 22 May, 24 December 1862, FO 2/42.
45. Burton to FO 22, 28 February, 6 May, 26 September 1862, FO 84/1176; Burton to FO 29 December 1862, FO 2/42; Burton to FO, 2 February 1863, FO 84/1203.
46. FO to Burton, 23 June, 21, 23 July, 23 August, 23 September, 24 November 1862; Burton to FO, 18 December 1862, FO 84/1176.
47. 'Ascent of the Ogun or Abeokuta River', *PRGS* 6 (1861–2), pp. 238–48; 'Exploration of the Elephant Mountain', *PRGS* 7 (1862–3), pp. 104–5. Cf. also *JRGS* 33 (1863), pp. 241–50. FO minute of 8 January 1863, FO 84/1203; marginal note to Burton to FO 22 February 1862, FO 84/1176.
48. See e.g. J. Hooker to RGS, 12 July 1862, RGS, complaining that Burton had hogged all the glory in his account of the ascent of the Cameroons and had unjustly treated the missionary Mr Mann.
49. Burton to FO 14 January 1862, FO 2/42.
50. FO to Burton, 21, 22 May, 22 July, FO 2/42. There is no trace in the official records of the dramatic scene recorded by Isabel when she cried her eyes out to Sir Henry Layard about being separated from her husband. According to Isabel, Layard asked her to wait, went upstairs and came back with the leave permission (*Life*, i, p. 376). The absence from the official records does not necessarily mean that the incident did not take place. Isabel says four months were granted. This was what Burton actually *took*, not what was granted. He used sleight of hand to tack his two months' Canaries leave onto the time he had already spent in the UK.
51. Burton to FO, 26 November 1862, FO 84/1176.
52. Burton to FO 17 December 1862, FO 2/42.
53. Burton to Wilson, 22 December 1862, Quentin Keynes Collection quoted in Brodie, *Devil Drives*, p. 205.

CHAPTER 15 A MISSION TO DAHOMEY pp. 198–211

1. *Wanderings in West Africa*, i, p. 296.
2. *Zanzibar*, Introduction to Vol. 1.
3. Brodie, *Devil Drives*, p. 202.
4. Isabel to Shaw, 31 December 1861, 11 January, 21 May, 1 December 1862, RGS.
5. *Life*, i, pp. 377–78; Wilkins, *Romance*, i, pp. 184–9.
6. Burton to Milnes, 17 February, 29 March 1863, Houghton MSS.
7. Ibid.; Wilkins, i, pp. 189–225; *Life*, i, pp. 379–81.
8. *The Times*, 31 December 1862, 5, 9 January, 27 March 1863; Burton to FO 18 January 1863, FO 84/1203.
9. *Life*, i, p. 385.
10. Burton to Russell, 6, 20 January 1863, FO 84/1203.
11. Burton to FO 5 January, 2 February, 1863; FO to Burton, 20 January 1863 (based on FO minute of 13 January, 27 January 1863, FO 84/1203).
12. *A Mission to Gelele*, i, pp. 16–24.
13. Mary Kingsley, *Travels in West Africa*.
14. The outspoken comments are in Burton to Wylde, 6 May 1863 (private correspondence enclosed in FO 84/1203). The official report covering April 1863 is in Burton to FO, 8 May 1863, FO 84/1203.
15. *Wanderings in Three Continents* (1901), pp. 202–4.
16. Private letter of 31 May 1863 enclosed in FO 84/1203. See also *Transactions of the Ethnological Society of London* 3 (1865), p. 400.
17. Burton to Milnes, 31 May 1863, Houghton MSS.
18. Burton to FO 27 June, 21 July 1863, FO 84/1203; Burton to Shaw, 28 July 1863, RGS.
19. Burton to FO, 3 September 1864, FO 2/45.
20. *Two Trips*, ii, pp. 60, 97–100, 133–38.
21. Burton to FO, December 1863, FO 84/1203. See also Confidential Report by Consul Burton on his ascent of the Congo River in September 1863, 6 September 1864, FO 84/1221. The personal touches are described in *Wanderings in Three Continents*, pp. 233–48 and 'A Trip up the Congo or Zaire River', *Geographical Magazine* 2 (July 1875), pp. 203–4.
22. FO Minute, 7 September 1864, FO 84/1221.
23. FO to Burton, 23 June, 20, 24 August 1863; Burton to FO, 27 October 1863, FO 84/1203. Cf. also Admiralty 123/183.
24. Burton to FO 14 January 1862, FO 84/1176.
25. *A Mission to Gelele*, i, p. 27.
26. Burton to Milnes, Houghton MSS.
27. *A Mission to Gelele*, ii, p. 342.
28. Ibid., i, p. 277.
29. Private letter, Burton to X, 30 December 1863, enclosed in FO 84/1203.
30. *A Mission to Gelele*, ii, p. 27.
31. Ibid., p. 122. Burton was censured by the FO for taking part in the dancing, to his intense fury, as he later explained to Emperor Pedro II in Brazil: 'The best of it was, Sir, that the authorities at home were in an awful rage with me, as H. M. Commissioner, for dancing with him; but I should like to have seen *them* refuse his dusky Majesty, when, at a single moment of impatience or irritability, he had only got to give a sign, to have fifty spears run into one, or to be instantly impaled.' (*Life*, i, p. 438.)
32. *A Mission to Gelele*, ii, p. 274.
33. Burton to FO, 23 March 1864, FO 84/1221.
34. C. H. Newby, introduction to his 1966 edition of *A Mission to Gelele*, p. 23.

35. Burton to Russell, 23 March 1864, FO 84/1221.
36. Wilmot to Admiralty, 7 August 1864, Admiralty 123/68.
37. *Life*, i, pp. 383–5; *A Mission to Gelele*, ii, p. 26; Winwood Reade, 'Burton's Mission to Dahome', *Anthropological Review* 2 (1864), p. 335; J. A. Skertchly, *Dahomey as it is: being a narrative of eight months' residence in that country* (1874).
38. Isabel Burton to Russell, 12 February 1864; Burton to FO, 23 March 1864, FO 2/45.
39. See FO to Burton, 29 January, 24 March 1864, FO 2/45; FO to Burton, 21 November 1863, FO 84/1203; 5 February 1864, FO 84/1221. The *Harriet* case is dealt with in detail in William Rainy, *The Censor Censored, or the Calumnies of Captain Burton on the Africans of Sierra Leone refuted and his conduct relative to the purchase money of the brig 'Harriet' tested and Examined* (1865).
40. FO to Burton, 23 April 1864, FO 2/45.
41. Burton to Shaw, 28 July 1863, 10 March 1864, RGS.
42. Burton to Russell, 15 April 1864, FO 84/1221.
43. Burton to FO, 31 May, 10 June 1864, FO 2/45.
44. Burton to FO 11 June 1864, FO 2/45.
45. FO to Burton, 30 June 1864; Burton to FO, 1 September 1864, FO 2/45.

CHAPTER 16 THE IMPACT OF AFRICA pp. 212–221

1. *Life*, i, pp. 361–74. For a further discussion of Burton's gold fever see Penzer, *An Annotated Bibliography*, pp. 274–82. Burton tried to tempt Lord Russell into making him Governor of the Gold Coast by pledging himself to remit £1 million annually to Britain in gold revenues. Russell brushed this aside contemptuously: 'Gold was becoming too common.' (*Life*, i, p. 386.)
2. For the Hawi see *Arabian Nights*, iii, p. 145; for ophiolatry in West Africa see *A Mission to Gelele*, i, pp. 94–97.
3. 'In the Bights of Benin and Biafra during three years' wanderings, I sighted but a single specimen, and that only for a minute.' (*Zanzibar*, ii, p. 242.)
4. *A Mission to Gelele*, i, p. 268.
5. 'Dahome', *Transactions of the Ethnological Society of London* 3 (1865), p. 405.
6. Burton to Milnes, 31 May 1863, Houghton MSS.
7. *A Mission to Gelele*, ii, p. 73. The Freudian nature of this remark was first spotted by the great anthropological student of Dahomey, Melville Herskovits. See his *Dahomey. An Ancient West African Kingdom*, 2 vols (NY 1938), i, p. 86. For further Burtonian views on Dahomean sexuality see 'Notes on certain matters connected with the Dahoman', *Memoirs of the Royal Anthropological Society* 1863–64, i, p. 308.
8. For Gerard's testimony see *The Times*, 18 July 1864; for Winwood Reade see his *Savage Africa* (1863), pp. 47–53; cf. also Henry Roe, *West African Scenes* (1874).
9. C. W. Newbury, introduction to the 1966 edition of *Gelele*, p. 34. For Le Hérisse's judgement see his *L'ancien Royaume du Dahomey* (Paris 1911). For Herskovits see *Dahomey*, op. cit. For general historical surveys emphasising the disjuncture before and after 1894 see Patrick Manning, *Slavery, Colonialism and Economic Growth in Dahomey, 1640–1960* (Cambridge 1982); Dor Ronen, *Dahomey between Tradition and Modernity* (Lovell 1975).
10. *Lake Regions*, ii, pp. 344–7.
11. Ibid., pp. 377–78. The judgement is amplified and endorsed in the more scholarly account of East Africa Burton wrote for the RGS: 'In intellect the East African is sterile and incult, apparently unprogressive and unfit for change. Like the uncivilised generally, he observes well, but he can produce nothing profitable from his perceptions. His intelligence is surprising when compared with that of an uneducated English peasant; but it has a narrow bound beyond which apparently no man may pass.' ('Lake Regions', *PRGS* 29 (1859), p. 336).

12. Burton to Bates, 18 January 1872, RGS.
13. *Lake Regions*, i, pp. 106–7.
14. *A Mission to Gelele*, ii, p. 250.
15. Joseph Thomson, 'Up the Niger to the Central Sudan: Letters to a Friend', *Good Words* 27 (1886), pp. 26–114; 'Downing Street versus Chartered Companies in Africa', *Fortnightly Review* 48 (1889), pp. 180–81; 'The Results of European Intercourse with the African', *Contemporary Review* 57 (1890), pp. 343–7.
16. *Life*, pp. 351–55; ii, p. 542.
17. *Wanderings in West Africa*, i, pp. 78, 175–6.
18. Ibid., i, p. 170. For another overt claim for the white man's intrinsic superiority see ibid., i, p. 269.
19. *Lake Regions*, i, p. 33; *Abeokuta*, i, p. 205. For other representative items on the irremediable 'thickness' of the African see *Life*, ii, pp. 576–90; *Arabian Nights*, iv, p. 250; *Lake Regions*, ii, p. 371. Cf. also V. L. Cameron, 'Burton as I knew him', *Fortnightly Review* 14 (1890), p. 880.
20. *Two Trips to Gorilla Land*, ii, p. 148.
21. *Zanzibar*, i, p. 379. 'The most remarkable thing in the wild Central African is his enormous development of destructiveness. At Zanzibar I never saw a slave break a glass or a plate without a grin or a chuckle of satisfaction.' (*Arabian Nights*, ii, p. 55.)
22. *Wanderings in West Africa*, ii, pp. 281–3.
23. *A Mission to Gelele*, i, p. 350.
24. *Stone-Talk*, pp. 34, 51–53; *Life*, i, p. 358.
25. *Arabian Nights*, xvi, p. 405.
26. Ibid., xii, p. 94.
27. *Lake Regions*, ii, p. 367.
28. *Two Trips to Gorilla Land*, ii, pp. 309–13; *Abeokuta*, i, p. ix.
29. *Wanderings in West Africa*, i, pp. 222, 239, 269, 274; ii, pp. 136, 211; *Life*, i, pp. 356–59.
30. *Two Trips to Gorilla Land*, ii, pp. 315–22; *A Mission to Gelele*, ii, pp. 177–215.
31. *Arabian Nights*, v, p. 183. For an overview of Burton's attitude to the black man see Jacques Marrisal, 'Burton's View of the African', *Revue Française d'Histoire d'Outre Mer* 65 (1978), pp. 557–72.
32. *Abeokuta*, i, p. 103; *Lake Regions*, i, p. 323; *Gelele*, ii, pp. 192, 210.
33. *Lake Regions*, ii, p. 323.
34. On this theme see *Arabian Nights*, vi, pp. 46–7.
35. *Two Trips to Gorilla Land*, i, p. 164.
36. *Arabian Nights*, vi, p. 54.
37. Ibid., viii, pp. 137, 217.
38. *The City of the Saints*, p. 73.
39. *Arabian Nights*, iii, p. 226.
40. Wright, ii, pp. 46–47.
41. Swinburne to Watts, 30 August 1875, *Swinburne Letters*, op. cit., iii, p. 61.
42. Harris delighted Burton by acting out for him a burlesque conversation between Burton and Lord Lytton.

'Ah Dick,' said Lytton, 'delicacies escape you men of huge appetite; you miss the deathless charm of the androgyne; the figure of a girl of thirteen with sex unexpressed as yet, slim as a boy with breasts scarcely outlined and narrow hips; but unlike a boy, Dick; no lines or ugly muscles, the knees also are small; everything rounded to rhythmic loveliness – the most seductive creature in all God's world.'

'You make me tired, Lytton,' said Burton, 'you cotquean, you! Your over-sweet description only shows me that you have never tried the blue-bottomed monkey!' (Frank Harris, *My Life and Loves*, op. cit., p. 565.)

43. Burton's obsession with the lustfulness of simians can be documented at *Arabian Nights*, iv, p. 297; vi, p. 54; vii, pp. 343–44; pp. 331–2; *Lake Regions*, ii, p. 15. Frank Harris claimed to have met men in Africa who had been 'propositioned' by baboons (*My Life and Loves*, p. 743). But Harris is unreliable as direct evidence. His reliability lies in his unwitting confirmation of other evidence.

CHAPTER 17 AN ENGLISH TRAGEDY pp. 222–238

1. RGS Minute Book, 10 December 1861; cf. also R. C. Bridges, 'Speke and the RGS', *UJ* 26 (1962), pp. 23–43.
2. Frederick B. Welbourne, 'Speke and Stanley at the court of Mutesa', *UJ* 25 (1961), pp. 220–23.
3. Speke, *Journal of the Discovery of the Source of the Nile*, pp. 270–72.
4. Grant, *A Walk Across Africa*, pp. 247–48.
5. Both Maitland, *Speke*, p. 169 and Brodie, *Devil Drives*, p. 219 concur in this analysis of Grant's behaviour.
6. Speke, *Journal*, pp. 466–7.
7. Ibid., pp. 601–2.
8. John Petherick, *Travels in Central Africa* (1869), ii, pp. 20, 127–8.
9. Ibid., ii, pp. 132–3.
10. H. H. Johnston, *The Nile Quest* (NY 1903), p. 100.
11. Speke to Blackwood, 1 February 1861, NLS 4731; same to same, 6 August 1864, NLS 4185.
12. See the remarks in Clements Markham's unpublished history of the RGS p. 353 (RGS): 'I rather misdoubted him [Speke] for his want of loyalty to Burton.'
13. 'Much better I think had he stopped at home and done a little hunting first.' (Speke to Blackwood, 14 December 1863, NLS 4185); cf. same to same, 25 July 1864, NLS 4185: 'I shall never travel with a male companion again in wild country.'
14. Blackwood to Speke, 21 November 1863; Grant to Blackwood, 1863, NLS 4183; Speke to Blackwood 1863, NLS 4185; cf. also *Athenaeum* No. 1886, 19 December 1863, pp. 829–32; Speke to editor of *Athenaeum*, 19 December 1863, NLS 4185.
15. Speke to Shaw, 19 February 1864, RGS; *PRGS* 4, p. 200; 6, p. 177; 7, p. 47; 8, p. 50. Cf. also Bridges, 'Speke and the RGS', loc. cit., pp. 37–38.
16. Petherick, ii, pp. 132–3.
17. Bridges, loc. cit., p. 40.
18. *PRGS* 3, p. 353; 7, pp. 213–14; 9, p. 8.
19. See the discussion in J. N. L. Baker, 'Sir Richard Burton and the Nile Sources', *EHR* 59 (1944), loc. cit.
20. *The Times*, 23 September 1864.
21. Speke's references to these events are in *Journal*, pp. 468, 598. Cf. also Alexander Maitland, ed., 'Speke's Nile Diary', *Blackwood's Magazine* 1939 (1977), pp. 371–85.
22. Burton and James M'Queen, *The Nile Basin* (1864), p. 27. For the weight of history making it important to Burton as 'great man' to prove his case, see A. J. Symons, 'The Two Lieutenants', in *Essays and Biographies* (1969), pp. 108–36.
23. *The Nile Basin*, p. 68.
24. Speke, *Journal*, p. 603. M'Queen's detailed demolition job of the charges against Petherick is in *The Nile Basin*, pp. 77–96, 185–93.
25. Maitland, *Speke*, p. 188; *The Nile Basin*, pp. 193–4.
26. Horace Waller, ed., *Livingstone's Last Journals*, 2 vols (1874), ii, p. 51.
27. *PRGS* (1863), pp. 185–87.
28. A. Geikie, *Life of Sir Roderick Murchison* (1875), ii, p. 268.
29. *Saturday Review*, 2 July 1864.
30. *Zanzibar*, ii, pp. 395–7; *Life*, i, p. 388.

31. *Life*, i, p. 389.
32. For his venom towards Speke see Livingstone to Agnes Livingstone, September 1869, Add.MSS.50, 184).
33. Livingstone to LMS, 25 May 1865, LMS Archives, SOAS. Later Livingstone remarked: 'I don't like to face people who were witnesses of his [Burton's] bestial immorality.' (Livingstone to Murchison, 29 November 1865, quoted in Tim Jeal, *Livingstone* (1973), p. 286.)
34. *Zanzibar*, ii, pp. 397–8.
35. *Life*, p. 289.
36. Markham, unpublished history of the RGS, p. 381 (RGS).
37. *Life*, i, p. 389.
38. Wright, i, p. 192; Byron Farwell, *Burton* (1963), p. 241; Brodie, *Devil Drives*, p. 226.
39. H. B. Thomas, 'The Death of Speke in 1864', *UJ* 13 (1949), pp. 105–7; James Morris, 'The Shooting of Captain Speke', *Horizon* 14 No. 3 (1972), pp. 56–63.
40. *The Times*, 17 September 1874.
41. For Livingstone's view see Stanley's private journal, 29 November 1871, Stanley Family Archives (photocopies in British Library from originals at Musée Royale Africaine, Tervuren, Belgium). Most modern critics opt for accidental death. See Kenneth Ingham, 'John Hanning Speke: A Victorian and his inspiration', *TNR* 49 (1957), pp. 301–11. Cf. also Speke Centenary Number of the *Uganda Journal* 26 (1962), pp. 1–104. Sir John Milner Gray, distinguished Africanist and chief justice of Zanzibar from 1942 to 1953, accepted the verdict of the coroner's court (Caroline Oliver, 'Richard Burton: the African Years', in Rotberg, *Africa and its Explorers*, op. cit., p. 93). The latest modern medical expert to examine the case also considers suicide 'unlikely' (Mifsud, 'Medical History of John Hanning Speke', loc. cit.).
42. See the extended discussion in Maitland, *Speke*, pp. 209–18. The facts Maitland adduces permit a conclusion quite other than the orthodox one reached by the author.
43. Maitland, *Speke*, p. 215.
44. *Zanzibar*, ii, p. 398.
45. Hastings, *Sir Richard Burton*, pp. 158–59.
46. Grant, *A Walk Across Africa*, pp. 347–9.
47. *The Times*, 19 September 1864.
48. *The Times*, 23 September 1864. 'Why should, "the very controversy be allowed to slumber" because the gallant Speke was the victim of a fatal mishap?' (*Athenaeum*, 14 January 1865).
49. *The Nile Quest*, pp. 6–7.
50. See Samuel Baker, *The Albert Nyanza*, 2 vols (1866).
51. *The Times*, 30 November 1871.
52. Burton's writings on Stanley, Cameron and Serpa Pinto may be found at *PRGS* 16 (1871–72), pp. 129–32; 19 (1874–75), pp. 145, 150, 152, 248, 253, 255, 260, 262, 317; *Academy*, 21 May, 11 June 1881, pp. 365–67, 425–6.
53. *Two Trips to Gorilla Land*, ii, pp. 186, 194, 197–8.
54. *PRGS* 20 (1875–76), pp. 49–50.
55. *Camoens: His Life and his Lusiads*, 2 vols (1881), ii, pp. 514–17.
56. *Highlands of Brazil*, ii, p. 437.

CHAPTER 18 BRAZILIAN INTERLUDE pp. 239–249

1. *Life*, i, pp. 395–98.
2. Wright, i, p. 93.
3. Swinburne to Monkton Milnes, 23 March, 11 July 1865, *Swinburne Letters*, i, pp. 118, 124.
4. Wilkins, *Romance*, i, pp. 242–3.

5. Blunt, *My Diaries*, ii, p. 128.
6. Bertrand and Patricia Russell, eds, *The Amberley Papers*, 2 vols (1937), i, pp. 347–50.
7. For exhaustive detail on these matters see FO 97/438.
8. Burton to FO, 13 July 1865, FO 13/432.
9. By the late 1850s the Brazilian slave trade was well and truly dead. See Leslie Bethell, *Britain and the Abolition of the Brazilian Slave Trade* (Cambridge 1970), p. 375; P. A. Martin, 'Slavery and Abolition in Brazil', *Hispanic American Historical Review* 13 (1933).
10. Robert Conrad, *The Destruction of Brazilian Slavery, 1850–1888* (Berkeley, 1972).
11. Isabel's life during this period is covered in Wilkins, *Romance*, i, pp. 254–72; *Life*, i, pp. 422–39.
12. *Arabian Nights*, i, p. ix.
13. Thornton to Russell, 4 October 1866; Russell to Thornton, 17 October 1866, FO 13/438.
14. For Isabel's experiences on this trip see Wilkins, i, pp. 273–317; *Life*, i, pp. 439–48.
15. *Highlands of Brazil*, ii, p. 445.
16. *Wanderings in Three Continents*, p. 281.
17. Wilkins, i, p. 345.
18. The best general guide to the Paraguayan War is Gilbert Phelps, *Tragedy of Paraguay* (1975). See also P. H. Box, *The origins of the Paraguayan War* (Illinois 1929).
19. *Letters from the Battlefields of Paraguay*, p. 168. In this he was anticipating much revisionist historiography of the late twentieth century. See F. J. McLynn, 'The causes of the War of Triple Alliance', *Inter-American Economic Affairs* 33 (1979), pp. 21–43.
20. Douglas Woodruff, *The Tichborne Claimant, a Victorian Mystery* (1957).
21. *Life*, p. 445.
22. For detail on Burton's appointment and the confused receipt and despatch of letters between London and Buenos Aires see C P 2148 (FO 406/12), pp. 1–2.
23. Murray to Burton, 19 June 1869; Burton to Murray, 21 June 1869, CP 2148 p. 3.
24. *Life*, i, p. 458.
25. Swinburne to Powell, 29 July 1869, Swinburne to Whistler, 6 August 1869, *Swinburne Letters*, ii, pp. 18–21.
26. Swinburne to Alice Swinburne, 10 August 1869, ibid., ii, pp. 22–3.
27. *Life*, i, p. 467.

CHAPTER 19 DAMASCUS pp. 250–264

1. Elliott to Clarendon, 3 May 1869, FOCP 2148 (FO 406/12), p. 2.
2. *Personal Narrative*, i, pp. 184–85; Wood to Clarendon, 6 October 1869, FOCP 2148, p. 5.
3. Burton to Persian Consul-General, 20, 23 December 1869; Burton to FO, 25 January 1870; Burton to Karpardaz Awwal, 8 January 1870, FO 195/965.
4. Burton to Karpardaz Awwal, 10 January 1870; Chargé d'Affaires, Beirut, to Burton, 22 February 1870, FO 195/965.
5. *Life*, i, p. 577.
6. *Unexplored Syria*, 2 vols (1871).
7. Stisted, p. 337; *Life*, i, p. 470.
8. Wilkins, *Romance*, ii, pp. 376–77.
9. 'He withered away, and nothing we could do did him any good, and one day, when I went to look round the stables, he put his paw up to me. I sat down on the ground and took him in my arms like a child. He put his head on my shoulder, and his paws round my waist, and he died in about half an hour.' (*Life*, i, p. 506.)
10. Wilkins, ii, p. 401.

11. *Unexplored Syria*, i, pp. 20–21.
12. Isabel Burton, *The Inner Life of Syria*, 2 vols (1875), i, p. 134.
13. Ibid., i, pp. 154, 165, 223; Wilkins, ii, pp. 385, 420.
14. Wright, i, p. 212.
15. Wilkins, ii, p. 396.
16. *Life*, i, p. 486; Wilkins, ii, pp. 393–5.
17. Isabel Burton, *Inner Life of Syria*, i, pp. 135, 259. Isabel provides many sickening examples of cruelty to animals in Syria, which more than justified her anger. See ibid., i, pp. 256–63.
18. Wilkins, ii, pp. 400, 498; *Life*, i, p. 511.
19. *Life*, i, pp. 471, 499.
20. *Unexplored Syria*, ii, pp. 2–5.
21. Ibid., ii, p. 28.
22. Isabel Burton, *Inner Life*, i, p. 178; *Life*, pp. 498–500.
23. For the trip to Palmyra see *Unexplored Syria*, i, pp. 21–7; *Life*, i, pp. 475–6; Isabel Burton, *Inner Life*, i, pp. 204–38. Cf. also "Palmyra', *Cassell's Magazine* (New Series) 5, pp. 212–15.
24. Sir W. Besant, *Life of Edward H. Palmer* (1883), p. 109.
25. See Sir W. Besant, ed., *Literary Remains of Charles Tyrwhitt-Drake* (1877).
26. Wilkins, ii, pp. 430–31.
27. *Unexplored Syria*, i, pp. 37–99; *Life*, i, pp. 520–8; Isabel Burton, *Inner Life*, i, pp. 285–301. Cf. also 'Reconnaissance of the Anti-Libanus' (by Burton and Drake), *JRGS* 42 (1872), pp. 408–25.
28. *Unexplored Syria*, i, pp. 10–12.
29. Wilkins, ii, p. 435.
30. Burton to Elliott, 1 September 1870, FO 195/965.
31. *Life*, i, pp. 503–4; Wilkins, ii, p. 437; Isabel Burton, *Inner Life*, i, pp. 305–10.
32. Burton to Elliott, 28 August 1870, FO 195/965.
33. *Life*, i, p. 504.
34. Ibid., pp. 506–11; Wilkins, ii, pp. 452–54.
35. *Inner Life*, i, pp. 359–76, ii, p. 9; *Unexplored Syria*, pp. 136–37. Cf. also 'Explanation of An Altar Stone from Jebel Druz Hauran', *Proc. Soc. Antiquaries of London* 5 (1872), pp. 289–91.
36. Wilkins, ii, pp. 466–68; *Inner Life*, ii, pp. 10–11.
37. *Inner Life*, ii, p. 16; *The Jew, the Gypsy and El-Islam*, pp. 228, 232.
38. *Inner Life*, ii, p. 43.
39. *Life*, i, pp. 542–44; Wilkins, ii, pp. 470–89; *Inner Life*, ii, pp. 30–42, 45–111, 177–250. On Samaria see Burton's letter to *The Times*, 26 September 1871. Cf. also (for Burton's version of the trip) 'A Ride to the Holy Land', *Cassell's Magazine* (NS) 5, pp. 434–37; 'Anthropological Collections from the Holy Land', *Journal of the Anthropological Institute of Great Britain and Ireland* 1 (Nov. 1871), pp. 300–30; 2 (Dec. 1871), pp. 321–42, 3 (March 1872), pp. 41–63.
40. 'Similarly in Ireland those venerable piles the Catholic abbeys were mutilated by the people for the benefit of their own shanties.' (*Unexplored Syria*, i, p. 182.)
41. Ibid., ii, pp. 5–121.
42. See 'Explanation of an Altar Stone' (note 35 above); 'Notes on the Exploration of the Tuhul el Safa', *JRGS* 42 (1872), pp. 49–61; 'Notes on the Exploration of the Tuhul el Safa, *PRGS* 16 (1871–72), pp. 122–3. Burton also produced a précis on the Moabite stone from *Unexplored Syria*, ii, pp. 317–45 in *Athenaeum*, No. 2323, 4 May 1872, p. 562.
43. *Life*, i, pp. 478, 505, 511.
44. Ibid., pp. 409–91. In this respect it is interesting to recall that Wilfrid Blunt described Burton as a 'sheep in wolf's clothing'. (Blunt, *My Diaries*, ii, pp. 129–31.)

45. *Life*, i, p. 503.
46. The dream is related in *Inner Life*, ii, pp. 114–63.

CHAPTER 20 DISGRACE AND RECALL pp. 265–281

1. Burton to Elliott, 11 July 1870, FO 195/965.
2. *Inner Life of Syria*, i, p. 330; *Life*, i, p. 529.
3. Burton to Montt, 30 June 1870; Eldridge to Elliott, 25 July 1870, FO 195/965; Burton to FO 19 March 1871, FO 195/976; *Life*, i, p. 570.
4. Burton to Elliott, 4 October 1870, FO 195/965; *Levant Herald*, 13 July 1870.
5. Burton to Elliott, 10 December 1870, FO 195/965.
6. Burton to Elliott, 10 June 1870, FO 195/965; *Life*, i, pp. 529–30; *Inner Life*, i, p. 331.
7. Burton to Elliott, 15 August 1870, FO 195/965.
8. Burton to Elliott, 1 September 1870, FO 195/965.
9. Isabel Burton, *Arabia, Egypt, India (A.E.I.)*, p. 95.
10. *Inner Life*, ii, p. 8.
11. *Life*, i, p. 579.
12. Burton to Elliott, 21 November 1870, FO 195/965.
13. *Life*, i, p. 579.
14. For a full account see ibid., pp. 530–37; *Inner Life*, ii, pp. 341–43.
15. Burton to Elliott, 27 June 1871, FO 195/976. Finzi and Barbour later supported Burton in his suit against the authorities over the Nazareth affair. See Finzi and Barbour to FO, 29 July 1871, FO 195/976.
16. Eldridge to Elliott, 30 November 1870, FOCP 2148, p. 23.
17. Elliott to Granville, 22 September 1870, FO 195/965.
18. *Arabian Nights*, iv, p. 202.
19. Elliott to Clarendon, 5 July 1869, FOCP 2148, p. 4.
20. Burton to FO, 14 November 1870, FO 195/965.
21. *Unexplored Syria*, i, pp. 154–5.
22. 'Note verbale' of 11 January 1871, enclosed in Elliott to Granville, 15 January 1871, FOCP 2148, pp. 7–8.
23. Burton to Elliott, 14 July 1871, FOCP 2148, p. 49.
24. Burton to Granville, 11 July 1871, FO 195/976. Cf. also FOCP 2148, pp. 43–45.
25. Burton to Elliott, 9 June, 4 July 1871; Elliott to Granville, 24 July 1871, FOCP, pp. 29–30, 35–37, 41–42.
26. *Unexplored Syria*, i, pp. 251–52.
27. *Life*, i, pp. 517–19. Burton to Elliott, 17 July, 19 August 1871, FOCP 2148, p. 48–49, 72–73. Cf. also Burton to Elliott, 22 May 1871, FO 195/976.
28. Rashid to Eldridge, 9 August 1871; Eldridge to Elliott, 11 August 1871; Elliott to Granville, 11 August 1871, FOCP 2148, pp. 58–60.
29. Rashid to Burton, 7 June 1871, FO 195/976. See also FOCP 2148, pp. 20–21.
30. Burton to Rashid, 8 June 1871, FO 195/976.
31. Burton to Elliott, 16, 23, 30 June 1871, FO 195/976.
32. Eldridge to Elliott, 16 June, 12 July 1871, FOCP 2148, pp. 20, 39–40. There is an undated memo from Burton to FO (FO 195/976) protesting against the reprimand and reiterating his version of events.
33. Burton to Elliott, 12 July 1871, enclosing John Zeller to Burton, 28 June 1871, FO 195/976. Cf. also FOCP 2148, pp. 40–41.
34. Burton to Elliott, 14, 15, 16, 17 July, FO 195/976. Cf. also Burton to Elliott, 20 May 1871, FOCP 2148, pp. 15–16.
35. Burton to Elliott, 1, 3 July, FOCP 2148, pp. 33–35.
36. *Life*, i, pp. 559–63.
37. Burton to Elliott, 3 July 1871, FO 195/976.

38. Rashid Pasha to Auli Pasha, 30 July 1871, Add.MSS. 46, 698 ff.230–1.
39. Burton to Elliott, 19 July 1871, FO 195/976.
40. Elliott to Granville, 22 April 1871, FOCP 2148, pp. 12–13. Granville to Elliott, 25 May 1871, ibid., replied that he intended to transfer Burton elsewhere, but that Elliott would have to wait until the Foreign Office could find a suitable alternative posting.
41. Kennedy to Granville, 30 January 1871; Elliott to Granville, 14 February 1871, FOCP 2148, pp. 9–12.
42. *Life*, i, p. 585.
43. Burton to Elliott, 19 July 1871; Burton to Granville, 24 July 1871, FO 195/976.
44. Wilkins, ii, pp. 445–47.
45. *Life*, i, pp. 600–1.
46. *Inner Life of Syria*, i, pp. 323–27.
47. Elliott to Granville, 15 January 1871, FOCP 2148, p. 7.
48. Wilkins, ii, pp. 487–90.
49. *Inner Life of Syria*, ii, pp. 219–31.
50. Isabel Burton to Elliott, 9 June 1871, FO 195/976.
51. Rashid Pasha to Auli Pasha, 19 May 1871, FOCP 2148, p. 17.
52. See memo by Tyrwhitt-Drake, 23 May 1871, FO 195/976; Consul Moore to Elliott, 25 May 1871; Burton to Elliott, 7, 8, 9 June 1871, ibid.; cf. also FOCP 2148, p. 16.
53. Elliott to Granville, 5 June 1871, FOCP 2148, p. 16.
54. Elliott to Granville, 26 June 1871, ibid., pp. 21–22.
55. Burton to Elliott, 11 June 1871; Elliott to Granville, 5 July 1871, ibid., pp. 31–32.
56. Rashid Ali to Aali Pasha, 4, 19 May 1871; Elliott to Rashid, 13 September 1871, FOCP 2148, pp. 14, 17, 75. Rashid had tried the last refuge of the scoundrel by playing on Elliott's known dislike of Isabel. He claimed she went everywhere armed, and was forever dinning it into the Christians that they were about to be massacred. (Rashid to Elliott, 24 August 1871, FOCP 2148, pp. 74–5).
57. Odo Russell to Burton 14 June 1871, FOCP 2148, p. 18.
58. FOCP 2148, p. 58.
59. Burton to Granville, 21 July 1871, FO 195/976.
60. Elliott to Granville, 6 August 1871, FOCP 2148, p. 58.
61. *Inner Life of Syria*, i, pp. 180–200.
62. *Life*, i, pp. 546–59.
63. Burton to Elliott, n.d., FOCP 2148, p. 62.
64. Burton to Granville, 21 July 1871, ibid., p. 50.
65. *Life*, i, p. 548.
66. Elliott to Granville, 26 June 1871, FOCP 2148, pp. 26–27; Granville to Burton, 22 July 1871, ibid., p. 30; Granville to Elliott, 14 July 1871; Russell to Eldridge, 24 July 1871; Granville to Elliott, 12 September 1871, FOCP 2148, pp. 32, 66–7.
67. *Life*, i, pp. 568–9.
68. Wilkins, ii, pp. 499–501.
69. *Life*, i, p. 570.
70. *Inner Life of Syria*, ii, pp. 282–3.

CHAPTER 21 IN LIMBO AGAIN pp. 282–291

1. *Life*, i, p. 587. For Drake's work as Burton's agent see ibid., pp. 581–4; *The Standard*, 7 September 1871; cf. also FOCP 2148, pp. 69, 98–9; Wilkins, ii, pp. 510–23; *Inner Life of Syria*, ii, pp. 308 et seq.
2. Wright, i, p. 222.
3. Burton to Granville, 22 September 1871; Odo Russell to Elliott, 23 September 1871; Odo Russell to Burton, 27 September 1871, FOCP 2148, p. 76.
4. *Globe*, 7 October 1871; *Pall Mall Gazette*, 14, 21, 22 December 1871.

5. *Unexplored Syria*, i, pp. xiv–xv.
6. Jago to Granville, 8 November 1871, FO 195/976; Jago to editor of *Civil Service Gazette*, 8 November 1871.
7. Granville to Burton, 25 October 1871; Burton to Granville, 12 November 1871, FOCP 2148, pp. 94–6.
8. Stisted, p. 363.
9. Michell Papers, SOAS, Box 7/204772 f.9.
10. 'She was indeed a very foolish woman, and did him at least as much harm in his career as good. Her published life of him, however, which has the ring of a true wife's devotion, redeems her in my eyes, and it is a fine trait in his character that he should always have borne with her absurdities for the sake of her love so long.' (Blunt, *My Diaries*, ii, p. 132.)
11. In 1869 he wrote: 'Had I a choice of race, there is none to which I would more willingly belong than the Jewish.' (*Highlands of Brazil*, i, p. 403.) But for the deepening anti-Semitism see Andrew Vincent, 'The Jew, the Gypsy and El-Islam: An Examination of Richard Burton's Consulship in Damascus and his premature recall, 1868–1871', *Journal of the Royal Asiatic Society of Great Britain* 2 (1985), pp. 155–73.
12. *Devil Drives*, pp. 265–66. Brodie's argument is carried out with her usual flair but, despite the acute insight it shows, it is tendentious and designed to let Burton 'off the hook'. The trouble is that her hypothesis can be used to spirit away all Burton's dark side; so his hatred of blacks becomes hatred of his own 'heart of darkness'; hatred of women becomes detestation of his own passive and scholarly side, and so on.
13. Wright, ii, p. 55.
14. See *The Jew, the Gypsy, and El-Islam*, passim, but especially pp. viii–, *Arabian Nights*, v. p. 214; xv, p. 214.
15. Ibid., viii, p. 153; xvi, p. 100.
16. *Wanderings in Three Continents*, pp. 236–37; *Arabian Nights*, xiii, p. 93.
17. Doughty, *Arabia Deserta*, i, p. 141.
18. A contrast of Burton's reviews in the *Athenaeum* is instructive. *First Footsteps* and his two versions of *Lake Regions* (the book and the RGS treatise) were enthusiastically received (No. 1499, 19 July 1856 pp. 895–96; Nos 1703 and 1704, 16, 23 June 1860, pp. 823–4, 845–7. But there was an increasing lukewarmness about the reception of his next productions: *The City of the Saints, Abeokuta, Mission to Gelele, Wit and Wisdom in West Africa, Highlands of Brazil, Letters from the Battlefields of Paraguay* (respectively Nos 1779, 30 November 1861, pp. 723–25; 1889, 9 January 1864, pp. 49–50; 1926, 24 September 1864, pp. 391–93; 1962, 3 June 1865, pp. 745–6; 2151, 16 January 1869, pp. 83–84; 2214, 2 April 1870, p. 447).
19. *Observer*, 4 February 1872; *Examiner*, 3 February 1872; *Field*, 16, 23 December 1871. For a rather more sympathetic review see the *Athenaeum*, No. 2309, 27 January 1872, pp. 105–6.
20. Burton to Bates, 7 January 1872, RGS.
21. *The Times*, 18 December 1871.
22. *Life*, i, p. 591.
23. Ibid., pp. 593–5.
24. Murchison's dislike for Burton was confirmed by Clements Markham: see Markham's unpublished history of the RGS, p. 354, RGS archives.
25. Burton to Bates, 18 January 1872, RGS.
26. Wright, i, pp. 226–27.
27. *Ultima Thule, or, a Summer in Iceland*, 2 vols (1875), i, pp. 269, 325–9.
28. Ibid., i, p. 173.
29. Ibid., ii, pp. 154–68.
30. Wright, i, pp. 232–33.
31. 'Human Remains and other Articles from Iceland', *Journal of the Anthropological*

Institute (Jan. 1873), pp. 342–7; 'An Account of Burton's Visit to Iceland', *Ocean Highways* 2 (1872–3), p. 212.
32. *Arabian Nights*, iii, p. 58.
33. Ibid., iv, p. 253. It seems likely that Bertrand Russell had read this passage, possibly in connection with the edition of the *Amberley Papers*, for in his essay, 'Modern Homogeneity' we read the following: 'Hell was invented in a southern climate; if it had been invented in Norway, it would have been cold.' (Bertrand Russell, *In Praise of Idleness and Other Essays* (1935).)
34. William Morris to Eirikr Magnusson, 23 May 1872 in Norman Kelvin, ed., *The Collected Letters of William Morris*, i, 1848–80 (Princeton 1984), p. 159.
35. *Ultima Thule*, ii, p. 300.
36. *Two Trips to Gorilla Land*, i, p. 237; ii, p. 194.
37. 'Notes on Mr Stanley's Work', *Ocean Highways* 3 (1873), pp. 55–9.
38. Findlay to Bates, 24 September 1872, RGS.
39. Journal, 21 September, SFA. Stanley, at 5ft 5in was sensitive about his height, which accounts for the inaccuracy on the height of Burton (who was fully six inches taller). See Harris, *Life and Loves*, p. 549, where he says that Burton was accepted in society because he was six feet tall 'while little Stanley was treated with scant respect'.
40. Journal, 1 October 1872, SFA.
41. See Burton, 'Mr Stanley's Expedition', *Athenaeum*, 27 November 1875, pp. 712–13; 'Mr Stanley and the Victoria Nyanza', *Geographical Magazine* (Washington), Nov. 1875, pp. 354–5; 'Critical Review of Stanley's Work', *Journal of the Geographical Society* (New York) 7, (1875), pp. 329–32; 'Mr Stanley's last Exploration', *Athenaeum* (1877), pp. 568–9.
42. Stanley, Emin Pasha Journal, 2 February 1887, SFA.
43. Congo Journal, 22 May 1872, SFA.
44. Congo Journal, 20 February 1879, SFA.
45. Wilkins, ii, pp. 533–34; *Life*, ii, p. 3.
46. Wright, i, p. 251.

CHAPTER 22 TRIESTE pp. 292–301

1. *Life*, ii, pp. 499–512.
2. Ibid., ii, p. 8.
3. *Inner Life of Syria*, ii, p. 339; *Life*, ii, p. 8.
4. For Burton's travels see 'The Port of Trieste, Ancient and Modern', *Journal of the Society of Arts* 23 (1875), pp. 979–1006; 'Notes on the Prehistoric Ruins of the Istrian Peninsula', *Anthropologia* 3 (1874), pp. 375–415; 'The Trade of Trieste', *Journal of the Society of Arts* 24 (1876), pp. 935–51; 'Fiume and her New Port', (with Vice-Consul George L. Faber), *Journal of the Society of Arts* 25 (1877), pp. 1029–46.
5. See *Etruscan Bologna* (1876), pp. 55, 69 for references to Ovid's *Ars Amandi* and *Fasti*. For the visit to Rome see 'Notes on Rome', *MacMillan's Magazine* 31 (Nov.–Dec. 1874), pp. 57–63, 126–34.
6. *Life*, ii, pp. 20–37. For this period in Trieste see also Burton to Anthropological Society, 17 February, 26 March 1873, *Anthropologia* 1, pp. 2–4; Burton to the Athenaeum, printed in *Athenaeum* Nos 2394, 13 September 1873, p. 340; 2416, 14 February 1874, p. 228; Burton to Bates, 9 December 1872, 19 November 1873, RGS.
7. Swinburne to Powell, 1 September 1874; Swinburne to Milnes, 12 July, 3 October 1874, *Swinburne Letters*, ii, pp. 307, 336, 340.
8. *Life*, ii, pp. 40–45.
9. *The Times*, 18 May 1875; 'The Volcanic Eruptions in 1874 and 1875,' *Proc. Royal Soc. of Edinburgh* 9 (1875–76), pp. 44–58; RGS Council to Lord Derby, 22 March 1875,

RGS. Burton also wrote to *The Times*, 21 June 1875, on the subject of Italian exploration of Africa.
10. See Burton's letter of 28 October 1875, Ashlee MSS (B.L.) B.4425; *Life*, ii, p. 498.
11. *A.E.I*, p. 95.
12. Wright, i, pp. 262–63; cf. also the exhaustive detail in *A.E.I*, pp. 108–395.
13. *Gold Mines of Midian*, p. 215. Burton's letter about Sind is printed in the *Overland Times of India*, 22 June 1877.
14. *Abeokuta*, i, p. 300.
15. *Sindh Revisited*, ii, pp. 26–7.
16. Ibid., i, p. 257.
17. '*Quien sabe?*' Burton writes hopefully of the Gessi circumnavigation. (Burton to Bates, 27 July 1876, RGS.)
18. See Burton to Dr E. Burton, 24 June 1876, in Wright, i, pp. 266, 270.
19. Burton to Bates, 2 July 1876, RGS.
20. Burton to Watson, 24 February 1877, RGS.
21. Burton was not strictly the first in this field. That dubious honour belonged to the cranky geographer Dr Charles Tilstone Beke, who supported Burton in the 1864 controversy with Speke. Beke left England in 1873 on a Grail-like quest to discover the 'true Mount Sinai' and later produced a book on his travels in north-west Arabia. For Beke's journey see *The Times*, 27 February, 5 March, 3 April 1874; *The Standard*, 28 February 1874. See also C. T. Beke, *Discoveries of Sinai in Arabia and of Midian* (1878).
22. Michell Papers, SOAS, Box 7/204772 ff.7–9.
23. *Gold Mines of Midian*, pp. 72, 232–36.
24. *Land of Midian Revisited*, i, p. xxxiv.
25. For Burton's archaeological and antiquarian findings in Midian see 'Stones and Bones from Egypt and Midian', *Journal of the Anthropological Institute* 8 (1879), pp. 290–319; 'The Ethnology of Modern Midian', *Trans. Royal Soc. of Literature*, Series 2, Vol. 12, pp. 249–330; 'Midian and the Midianites', *Journal of the Society of Arts* 27 (1878), pp. 16–27; 'Report on Two Expeditions to Midian', *Journal of the Society of Arts* 29 (1880), pp. 98–9.
26. *Land of Midian Revisited*, i, p. 260.
27. Ibid., ii, p. 247.
28. Ibid., ii, pp. 251–4.
29. H. St John Philby, *The Land of Midian* (1957), pp. 5–6, 130, 141, 169–87, 212–15, 248. Philby went over the ground much more thoroughly and sharpened up a few of Burton's observations. He corrected Burton's interpretation of 'Ain Al Tabbakka' ('the boiling spring'), which Burton had translated as 'the spring of the woman cook'. And he noted that the term Ma'aza (the goatherd), so often used by Burton in referring to the Bani Aliya, had fallen into disuse, though it was known as a generic term covering the whole tribe (ibid., pp. 207, 227).
30. *Land of Midian*, ii, p. 260.
31. Ibid., pp. 259–60.

CHAPTER 23 MARKING TIME AND DECLINING HEALTH pp. 302–315

1. Burton to Bates, 27 July 1876, RGS.
2. Gordon to Burton, 30 June 1877, RGS.
3. Wilkins, ii, pp. 645–75.
4. Wright, i, pp. 276, 281–2.
5. Michell Papers, SOAS, Box 7/204772 ff.12–18.
6. *Life*, ii, p. 43.
7. Slatin, *Fire and Sword in the Soudan* (1896) describes his famous captivity.
8. *Academy*, 11 July 1885, p. 19; *Life*, ii, pp. 543, 615.

9. *Arabian Nights*, i, p. xxiii; iv, p. 305.
10. Harris, *Contemporary Portraits*, p. 195; Cromer, *Modern Egypt* (1908), i, p. 7.
11. *Home News*, 11 September 1885; Burton remarked of Gordon: 'In this tenet he was not only a Calvinist but also a Moslem whose contradictory ideas of fate and freewill (with responsibility) are not only beyond Reason but also contrary to reason.' (*Arabian Nights*, xii, pp. 61–62).
12. *The Spiritualist*, 13 December 1878.
13. *Life*, ii, p. 159.
14. Fully to trace Burton's interest in spiritualism and the many byways it led him into would require a separate monograph. Burton contributed to *The Spiritualist* and the Spiritualists repaid the compliment with reviews of his books.
15. *Life*, ii, p. 137.
16. 'She never hesitated to speak upon any subject under the sun, whether she did not understand it, as was almost invariably the case, or whether she did.' Wright, i, p. 287. For Isabel's harangues at these meetings see *Life*, ii, pp. 137 et seq.; cf. also Penzer, *Selected Papers*, pp. 184–210.
17. 'The Ogham Runes and El-Mushajjar', *Trans. Royal Soc. of Literature* 12 (1879), pp. 1–46; *Athenaeum* Nos 2580, 7 April 1877, p. 477; 2596, 28 July 1877, pp. 113–14; 2602, 8 September 1877, p. 306.
18. Wright, i, pp. 241–43; ii, p. 80.
19. Ibid., ii, p. 85
20. Ibid., ii, pp. 47–48.
21. Ibid., ii, p. 49.
22. *Life*, ii, pp. 24, 499.
23. Ibid., ii, p. 104.
24. *Arabian Nights*, ix, p. 313.
25. Ibid., vi, p. 237.
26. *Life*, i, p. 22.
27. I have used some examples from Vice-Consul Martin in 1889–90, but the pattern held good with the earlier Vice-Consul, Brock: 'I am directed by Sir Richard Burton', etc., etc. 'Sir Richard Burton has handed me your letter of the sixth instant for an answer', etc. (7 September 1889, 15 March, 10 May, 4 June 1890, FO 590/7).
28. *Life*, ii, p. 260.
29. Burton to Markham, 15, 26 October 1879, RGS.
30. Michell Papers, Box 7/204772 ff. 20–1.
31. Burton to Markham, 18 January 1880, RGS; *Life*, ii, p. 177; Hitchman, ii, p. 402.
32. Astonishingly, he was yet another of Burton's friends who died before his fiftieth birthday. See J. S. Black and G. Chrystal, *Life of W. R. Smith* (1902).
33. See Burton, 'Giovanni Battista Belzoni', *Cornhill Magazine* 42 (1880), pp. 36–50. For Belzoni's life see Stanley Mayers, *The Great Belzoni* (1959).
34. 'How to deal with the slave scandal in Egypt', *Manchester Examiner and Times*, 21, 23, 24 March 1881; *Life*, ii, pp. 195–210.
35. *Arabian Nights*, xi, pp. 70–2.
36. *Life*, ii, p. 119.
37. *Arabian Nights*, xi, p. 316.
38. *Life*, ii, pp. 177–8.
39. *A Glance at the Passion Play*, op. cit.
40. See V. L. Cameron, *Across Africa*, 2 vols (1877).
41. Cameron to Burton, 13 November 1876, RGS.
42. Cameron, 'Burton as I knew him', *Fortnightly Review* 54 (1890), p. 880.
43. Harry H. Johnston, *The Story of My Life* (1923), p. 157.
44. Wright, ii, p. 25.
45. Hitchman, ii, p. 402.

46. *To the Gold Coast for Gold*, 2 vols (1883), i, pp. 291–2.
47. Hitchman, ii, p. 427.
48. *To the Gold Coast*, i, pp. 292–98; ii, pp. 13–43.
49. See Wolseley, *The Story of a Soldier's Life*, 2 vols (1903), ii, pp. 290–1; Harris, *My Life and Loves*, p. 735.
50. See e.g., *Arabian Nights*, vii, p. 357; ix, p. 46.
51. 'The Kong Mountains', *The Times*, 27 June 1882; 'Gold on the Gold Coast', *Journal of the Society of Arts* 30 (1882), pp. 785–90; V. L. Cameron, 'Gold on the Gold Coast', ibid., pp. 777–85; 'The Kong Mountains', *PRGS*, N.S.4 (1882), pp. 484–86. See also discussion at ibid., pp. 501–7; Burton and Cameron, 'Stone Implements from the Gold Coast', *Journal of the Archaeological Institute* 12 (1883), pp. 449–54.
52. *Life*, ii, pp. 609–16.
53. Ibid., ii, p. 246.
54. Wilkins, ii, pp. 638–40.
55. Stisted, pp. 405–6.
56. *Life*, ii, p. 272.

CHAPTER 24 POET AND TRANSLATOR pp. 316–325

1. See the respective reviews in the *Athenaeum* of *Highlands of Brazil* (No. 2151, 16 January 1869); *Battlefields of Paraguay* (No. 2214, 2 April 1870, p. 447; *Zanzibar* (No. 2309, 27 January 1872, pp. 105–6); *Unexplored Syria* (No. 2331, 29 June 1872, pp. 807–8); *The Lands of Cazembe* (No. 2392, 30 August 1873, p. 276; *Two Trips to Gorilla Land* (No. 2507, 13 November 1875, p. 637; *Etruscan Bologna* (No. 2564, 16 December 1876, p. 795; *Sindh Revisited* (No. 2585, 17 May 1877, p. 661; *Land of Midian Revisited* (No. 2681, 15 March 1879, p. 337); *To the Gold Coast for Gold* (No. 2880, 6 January 1883, pp. 11–12).
2. *Unexplored Syria*, ii, pp. 329–30; *Athenaeum*, 13 April 1872, pp. 464–67. See also the works of James B. Pritchard, *Ancient Near Eastern Texts Relating to the Old Testament* (Princeton 1955), pp. 320 et seq.; *Archaeology of the Old Testament* (Princeton 1958), pp. 103–6.
3. Curt W. Marek, *The Secret of the Hittites* (NY 1956), p. 17. Wright's thesis is set out in William Wright, *The Empire of the Hittites* (NY 1884). H. V. Hilbrecht, *Exploration in Bible Lands during the Nineteenth Century* (Philadelphia 1903, p. 756, awards Burton the palm as pioneer of the Hamath inscriptions.
4. William C. Atkinson, ed. and trans., *The Lusiads* (Penguin 1973), p. 15.
5. Melville makes many references in his *oeuvre* to Camoens, especially in *Whitejacket* (1850), pp. 318, 462 ('The Lusiads ... it's the man-of-war epic of the world'). For Melville's interest in Camoens see Newton Arvin, *Herman Melville* (NY 1950), pp. 149–50.
6. See Norwood Andrus, *The Case Against Camoens* (N.Y. 1988).
7. *Lake Regions*, ii, p. 379.
8. *NY Tribune*, 2 November 1891.
9. Cameron, 'Burton as I knew him', loc. cit., pp. 882–3.
10. Atkinson, op. cit., pp. 31–32.
11. Swinburne to Burton, 13 April 1881, 27 November 1884, *Swinburne Letters*, iv, p. 212; v, pp. 88–89. See also *Academy* 19, No. 477, 25 June 1881, pp. 465–6. The reviewer pointed out that the ideal translator of *The Lusiads* had to be both scholar and explorer; of contemporaries, only Burton fitted the bill. Cf. also *Daily Telegraph*, 21 February 1881; *Morning Post*, 6 April 1881; *Athenaeum*, 26 March 1881.
12. *Scotsman*, 1 February 1881; *Liverpool Mercury*, 25 January 1881; *Manchester Examiner*, 17 January 1881; *NY Daily Tribune*, 20 February 1881.
13. *Camoens. His Life and Lusiads*, 2 vols (1881), ii, p. 677. For further instalments of

Camoensiana see *Athenaeum*, No. 2783, 26 February 1881, p. 299; No. 2787, 26 March 1881, pp. 423–4; No. 2831, 28 January 1882, p. 125; No. 2848, 27 May 1882, pp. 661–3; No. 3000, 25 April 1885, pp. 533–4. Cf. also *Academy*, 27 November 1880, pp. 84–5, 12 February 1881, p. 119, 7 May 1881, p. 339, 25 June 1881, pp. 465–6, 11 February 1882, pp. 93–4, 30 December 1882, p. 470.
14. For FitzGerald see Robert B. Martin, *With Friends Possessed* (1985).
15. Preface to 1894 edition of *The Kasidah*, p. 5.
16. Gournay, *L'Appel du Proche Orient*, op. cit., p. 412.
17. If less, it was known as a *Ghazal*.
18. Wright, ii, pp. 20–21.
19. Burton's critics wished he had stuck to physical description. H. J. Cook remarked: 'In descriptive passages many a felicitous touch causes regret that Sir Richard should have devoted so little space to the magic and mystery of the desert.' (No. 3799 *Athenaeum*, 18 August 1900, p. 216.)
20. Gournay, p. 504.
21. *Kasidah*, Note 1.
22. *Arabian Nights*, iii, p. 140.
23. Fitzgerald, *The Rubáiyát of Omar Khayyám*, p. xxvi.
24. T. E. Lawrence, *Seven Pillars of Wisdom* (1935).

CHAPTER 25 THE VALETUDINARIAN SEXOLOGIST pp. 326–336

1. His admirers in the press took up this theme, with a few changes of venue and personnel, and spoke of Richard as 'chained to his post at Trieste – doomed by perverse fate to an isolation that must be almost as irksome as the rock of St Helena to Napoleon.' *Life*, ii, p. 229.
2. Ibid., ii, p. 73.
3. Wilkins, ii, pp. 633–5, 639–40.
4. Wright, ii, p. 137.
5. Swinburne to Lady Jane Henrietta Swinburne, 12 August 1885, Swinburne to Alice Bird, 23 June 1885, Swinburne to Wise, 27 April 1888, *Swinburne Letters*, v, pp. 116, 121, 235.
6. Wright, ii, p. 94; Pope-Hennessy, *Monkton Milnes, The Flight of Youth 1851–1885*, p. 253.
7. Harry H. Johnston, *The Story of My Life*, pp. 156–7, 179, 374. See also Roland Oliver, *Sir Harry Johnston and the Scramble for Africa* (1957), pp. 83, 269.
8. Frank Harris, *Contemporary Portraits*; *My Life and Loves*, pp. 561–71.
9. Wright, ii, p. 94.
10. *Life*, ii, p. 295.
11. Harris, *My Life and Loves*, p. 563.
12. Burton, introduction, edition and revision of the 2nd edn. of Arthur Leared, *Marocco and the Moors*, pp. vi-vii.
13. *Life*, ii, p. 311.
14. Ibid., ii, p. 31; Wilkins, ii, p. 63; Burton's biographers have usually, and rightly, come down hard on him for his callousness to his wife during this voyage. Hastings comments: 'Dick's lack of concern would have won him the commendation "Shit of the Year, 1886",' (Hastings, p. 256). Fawn Brodie alone tries to justify his actions on the grounds of Burton's now childlike dependence on Isabel: 'He was like a small boy who comforts his mother importantly in times of danger, but who cannot face her sickness without anxiety, which is registered only in annoyance and impatience.' (Brodie, p. 313.)
15. *Court Society*, 4 March 1886.
16. *Arabian Nights*, iv, pp. vii–x; xiv, p. 358.

17. For the 1886 leave see BL.RP 2415; Add.MSS.38, 808 ff.9–13.
18. Wright, *Life of Thomas Payne* (1919), p. 99.
19. Wright, *Burton*, ii, pp. 62, 66.
20. Introduction to *The Kama Sutra of Vatsyayana*.
21. Burton once openly admitted: 'I never pretended to understand women.' Fawn Brodie says of this: 'This was mere masculine cliché. Burton probably knew a good deal more about the psychology of women than the leading physicians in England.' (Brodie, p. 291.) If by this is meant that he was alive to female sexuality in a way most hidebound and blinkered doctors of the time were not, the statement is unquestionably true. But in his morbid fear of female sexuality and his wild overestimate of the *general* lustfulness of women, Burton's view of the other sex is as much a distortion as the repressive official Victorian ideology.
22. Charles Fowkes, ed. and introduction, *The Illustrated Kama Sutra, Ananga Ranga, Perfumed Garden, The Burton translations* (1987), p. 12.
23. Herbert M. Schueller and Robert L. Peters, *The Letters of John Addington Symonds*, 3 vols (Indiana 1969), iii, p. 50.
24. *Ananga Ranga*, p. 127.
25. Burton tells a hilarious story of one man who made a candle of frogs' fat and fibre which supposedly guaranteed him that he would retain his seed while it burned. The method failed because, relying on the efficacy of the remedy, the man worked away too vigorously! (*Arabian Nights*, v, p. 77.)
26. Ibid., v, p. 80.
27. The *Gulistan* was written in the era of the Mongols (AD 1258) by the great Persian poet Sa'adi, 'the nightingale of the groves of Shiraz'. It deals with the manners of kings, the morals of dervishes, the excellence of contentment, the advantages of silence, youth, education, love and old age; plus universal rules for the conduct of life. Its general theme is summed up by the quatrain

> Of what use will be a dish of roses to thee?
> Take a leaf from my rose garden
> A flower endures but five or six days
> But this Rose Garden is always delightful.

28. *Life*, ii, pp. 317–20.
29. *Pall Mall Gazette*, 18 January 1886.
30. *Camoens. His Life and his Lusiads*, pp. 406–7.
31. *Life*, ii, p. 324.
32. See *The Philadelphian*, 12 December 1887; *Liverpool Daily Post*, 3 May 1888; *Manchester Courier*, 18 October 1889; *Society*, 28 October 1889.
33. Grenfell Baker, 'Sir Richard Burton as I knew him', loc. cit., p. 422.

CHAPTER 26 THE ARABIAN NIGHTS pp. 337–345

1. See Peter L. Caracciolo, ed., *The Arabian Nights in English Literature* (1988).
2. J. H. Newman, *Apologia pro vita sua* (1864), p. 2; J. S. Mill, *Autobiography* (1873), p. 9; William Morris to editor of *Pall Mall Gazette*, 2 February 1886, in Norman Kelvin, ed., *Collected Letters of William Morris*, ii, 1881–8 (Princeton 1987), p. 516. See also A. Cruse, *The Victorians and their Books* (1935), pp. 286, 293.
3. *First Footsteps*, p. 36.
4. *Personal Narrative*, ii, pp. 95, 99–100.
5. Wright, *Life of John Payne*, ii, p. 102.
6. *Arabian Nights*, xvi, p. 390.
7. Ibid., x, p. 200.

8. Ibid., xvi, p. 412; M. Gerhardt, *The Art of Story Telling: a literary study of the Thousand and One Nights* (Leyden 1963), pp. 110–11.
9. *Arabian Nights*, x, pp. 168–9.
10. Ibid., xvi, pp. 410–11.
11. G. Allgrove, *Love in the East* (1962), p. 53.
12. *Arabian Nights*, vi, pp. 180–81.
13. The four episodes are at *Arabian Nights*, ii, p. 234; iii, pp. 302–4; v, pp. 65, 156–62.
14. *Edinburgh Review* 164 (1886), pp. 166–99.
15. Ibid., 178 (1893), p. 467.
16. Stanley Lane-Poole, introduction to his edition of *Personal Narrative*, pp. xix–xx.
17. *Arabian Nights*, x, pp. 203–4; cf. also ibid., v, pp. 267–8; x, pp. 180–1, 253–4.
18. See e.g., ibid., v, pp. 194, 255; viii, p. 75.
19. Ibid., ii, p. 234; iv, p. 234.
20. Ibid., iii, p. 241.
21. Ibid., v, pp. 156, 160; x, p. 214.
22. Ibid., v, p. 46.
23. Ibid., iv, p. 299; v, p. 57; vi, p. 54.
24. Ibid., i, p. 110; iv, p. 256; vii, pp. 190–1; viii, p. 25.
25. Ibid., i, p. 202, iii, p. 36; iv, pp. 7, 27, 70, 206; v, pp. 12, 103, 193.
26. Ibid., i, pp. 88, 95, 97, 108.
27. *St James's Gazette*, 12 September 1885; *Daily Exchange*, 19 September 1885; *The Standard*, 12 September 1885; *South Eastern Herald*, 31 October 1885; *Vanity Fair*, 24 October 1885.
28. *The Echo*, 13 October 1885; *Pall Mall Gazette*, 3 June 1885; *Saturday Review*, 2 January 1886, pp. 26–7; 27 March 1886, pp. 448–9; 30 April 1887, pp. 632–3; 4 June 1887, pp. 810–11; 13 August 1887, pp. 220–21; 21 July 1888, pp. 86–7; *The Gaiety* burlesqued this attack:

> The Echo is just a bit wild
> Its 'par' is indeed a hard hitter
> In fact it has not drawn it mild;
> 'Tis a matter of 'Burton and bitter'.

See also *Arabian Nights*, xvi, p. 411.
29. For Symonds see Phyllis Grosskurth, ed., *The Memoirs of John Addington Symonds* (1984).
30. This was a common theme of admirers and detractors. See the *Academy* 30 No. 762, 11 December 1886, pp. 387–8: 'Not only has he with characteristic masterfulness pressed into his service any and every word English or foreign current or obsolete that suited his fancy, or answered to the need of the moment, but he has not scrupled to coin the lacking epithet when unwanted.'
31. *Academy*, 28, No. 700, 3 October 1885, p. 223.
32. Burton to Payne, 9 September 1885, Wright, *Burton*, ii, p. 54.
33. Here are two mendacious accounts of what happened, respectively by Isabel and Richard.

> Richard forbade me to read them till he blotted out with ink the worst words and desired me to substitute, not English, but Arab society words, which I did to his complete satisfaction ... Mr Justin Huntley McCarthy helped me a little, so that out of 13, 215 original pages I was able to copyright 3000 pages.
> Mr Justin Huntley McCarthy converted the 'grand old barbarian' into a family man to be received by the 'best circles'. His proofs, after due expurgation, were passed on to my wife, who I may say has never read the original, and she struck out all that appeared to her over-free.
> (Wright, *Burton*, ii, p. 290; *Arabian Nights*, xvi, p. 452).

34. Brodie, p. 310.
35. *Arabian Nights*, xvi, p. 452. For the deeper reasons why Burton and the *Arabian Nights* were such a happy match see Jorge Luis Borges, *Translators of the 1,001 Nights.* See also his remarks in *Seven Nights* (1986), p. 55. For a convincing psychoanalytic argument see Bruno Bettelheim, *The Uses of Enchantment* (1976), pp. 28–34, 83–90.

CHAPTER 27 ISABEL TAKES CHARGE pp. 346–351

1. Laura Friswell Myall, *In the Sixties and Seventies. Impressions of Literary People and Others* (Boston 1906), p. 44.
2. See his remarks in *Camoens. His Life and his Lusiads*, p. 466: 'AEI proposes to work the mines, with scant regard for Anglo-Indian incuriousness and *vis inertiae.*'
3. *Life*, ii, p. 255.
4. *A.E.I*, p. 235.
5. Ibid., pp. 248–49.
6. Ouida, loc. cit., p. 1043; *Life*, ii, p. 272; Wright, ii, pp. 20–24, 207–8; Wilkins, ii, p. 692.
7. Wright, ii, p. 218.
8. Royal Archives, Windsor Castle, R 13/53.
9. *Arabian Nights*, iii, p. 75.
10. Ibid., iii, p. 240.
11. Ibid.
12. Ibid., iii, p. 166.
13. Ibid., vii, p. 189.
14. *Life*, ii, pp. 180–81.
15. *Hastings*, p. 222.
16. *Life*, ii, pp. 434–6.

CHAPTER 28 THE FINAL YEARS pp. 352–366

1. *Life*, ii, p. 335.
2. Ibid., p. 337.
3. Wright, ii, p. 173. There was always some sort of association of ideas between the fates of Arnold and Burton. Ouida declared that the only indignity comparable to the British government's disgraceful treatment of Burton was to keep Matthew Arnold as an inspector of schools (Ouida, loc. cit., p. 1044). Alan Moorehead suggested that the best likeness to Burton in fiction was Arnold's Scholar-Gypsy (introduction to his 1960 edition of *Lake Regions*, p. viii). For Arnold see Park Honan, *Matthew Arnold* (1981).
4. *Evening Post*, 1 November 1888.
5. Stisted, p. 409.
6. See Burton's letter from Montreux, 10 January 1889, published in *Academy*, 26 January 1889, pp. 57–8.
7. *Saturday Review* 65, 28 January 1888, pp. 110–11.
8. *Life*, ii, p. 382.
9. Ibid., ii, p. 392.
10. *Wright*, ii, p. 227.
11. *Life*, ii, pp. 364, 401.
12. When Stanley heard Burton's story of Oliphant's treachery in 1859, he said: 'How very odd, he did exactly the same to me!' (*Life*, ii, p. 425.)
13. Stisted, p. 411; Wright, ii, p. 228; *Life*, ii, p. 404; Mounteney-Jephson to Mackinnon, 22 August 1890, Mackinnon Papers, SOAS, 19/75.
14. Stanley, *Autobiography* (1909), pp. 423–4.
15. The whole subject is dealt with at great length by Fawn Brodie, using the Burton–

Smithers papers at the Huntington Library, San Marino, California (*The Devil Drives*, pp. 319–20).
16. *Life*, ii, p. 441.
17. Wright, ii, p. 217.
18. Ibid.
19. *Life*, ii, p. 408; Wright, ii, p. 437.
20. Wright, ii, p. 238.
21. *Life*, ii, p. 408.
22. Ibid., ii, pp. 413–14. Isabel later admitted she knew Burton was dead, and deliberately deceived Fr Martelani so that Richard could be buried according to the rites of the Catholic Church (Wright, ii, p. 144).
23. Stisted, p. 415.
24. L. P. Kirwan, 'Meditations on the Burton Mausoleum at Mortlake', *Geographical Journal* v, 141 (1975), pp. 49–58.
25. Francis Galton, *Memories of My Life* (1908), p. 202.
26. *Morning Post*, 19 June 1891.
27. Wright, ii, pp. 253–54.
28. *Life*, ii, p. 441.
29. Ibid., ii, p. 440.
30. Wright, ii, p. 258.
31. Swinburne to Eliza Lynn Linton, 24 November 1892, *Swinburne Letters*, vi, p. 45.
32. Stisted, pp. 404–5.
33. Wright, ii, p. 259.

CONCLUSION pp. 367–374

1. 'The individuality of Burton was so unique, so singular, so many-sided, so extremely startling to all commonplace people, so utterly confounding and unintelligible to all ordinary persons, that the idea of anyone presuming to know it when he was himself unknown is amazing and almost comical in its audacity.' (Ouida, loc. cit., p. 1039).
2. It was always to be Burton's fate to be censured for an interest in sex and to find that Victorian society visited no such obloquy on violence. (Ouida, loc. cit., p. 1042.)
3. 'This naïve admiration of beauty in either sex characterised our chivalrous times. Now it is mainly confined to "professional beauties" of what is conventionally called the "fair sex", as if there could be any comparison between the beauty of man and the beauty of woman, the Apollo Belvedere with the Venus de Medici.' (*Arabian Nights*, i, p. 206). Burton's great admirer Frank Harris decisively parted company with him on this point. See Richard Ellmann, *Oscar Wilde* (1987), p. 536 on the similar disagreement between Harris and Wilde, 'Wilde insisting that male beauty was finer than female, women being dumpy as Schopenhauer had said, while Harris defended the Venus de Milo against Antinous.'
4. 'No tales of blood disfigure the narratives of his exploration: on his death bed he could have recalled to his recollection [sic] no lives of poor Africans or Asiatics taken away by his orders, no villages in any part of the world plundered.' (R.N. Cust, *Linguistic and Oriental Essays*, 4th series (1895), pp. 80–82.)
5. For Malinowski see especially his *The Sexual Life of Savages in North-Western Melanesia* (1932); for Gorer see his *The Lepchas of Sikkim* (1938); for Elwin see *The Baiga* (1939).
6. See the memoirs in *Anthropological Society of London* 2 (1865–6), pp. 262–3 and *Royal Anthropological Institute Journal* 20 (1891), pp. 295–8. Cf. also Add. MSS.42,579 f.183.
7. M. Gerhardt, *The Art of Story-Telling. A Literature Study of the Thousand and One Nights* (Leyden 1963), pp. 62–63.
8. *Arabian Nights*, x, p. 101; xvi, pp. 393–94.
9. The Arabian explorer Bertram Thomas thought that, received opinion not-

withstanding, Burton gave both the East India Company and the Foreign Office too much rope. His mistake was to ask permission instead of presenting a *fait accompli* (Bertram Thomas, *Arabia Felix* (1932), p. xxv).

10. Ouida, loc. cit, pp. 1041–45.

11. For the influence of Burton on Aleister Crowley see John Symonds and Kenneth Grant, eds, *Confessions of Aleister Crowley. An Autobiography* (1979).

12. For this formulation see Peter Gay, *Freud. A Life for Our Time* (1988), pp. 501–32.

13. *Life*, ii, p. 348.

14. The classic instance is the story, which he initially promoted and then disclaimed, of having killed a man during the pilgrimage to Mecca. The initial promotional anecdote stuck and became received truth; well into the twentieth century other would-be Burtons quoted the 'murder' as proof of the ruthlessness of their hero. See W. Montgomery McGovern, *To Lhasa in Disguise* (1924), p. 247.

15.' Moorehead, introduction to *Lake Regions*, op. cit., p. i.

16. Swinburne's elegy, *Fortnightly Review*, 1 July 1892. The original MS of the Elegy, eventually published in *Astrophel and Other Poems*, is in BL, Ashlee MSS.5273.

A List of Burton's Books

1851 – *Goa and the Blue Mountains; or, Six Months of Sick Leave*, London.
1851 – *Scinde; or, The Unhappy Valley*, 2 vols, London.
1851 – *Sindh, and the Races that Inhabit the Valley of the Indus; With Notices of the Topography and History of the Province*, London.
1852 – *Falconry in the Valley of the Indus*, London.
1853 – *A Complete System of Bayonet Exercise*, London.
1855–6 – *Personal Narrative of a Pilgrimage to El-Medinah and Meccah*, 3 vols, London. Except where noted, all citations in this biography are from the Memorial edition, London, 1893, 2 vols, with 8 appendices.
1856 – *First Footsteps in East Africa; or, An Exploration of Harar*, London.
1860 – *The Lake Regions of Central Africa, A Picture of Exploration*, 2 vols, London.
1861 – *The City of the Saints and Across the Rocky Mountains to California*, London.
1863 – *The Prairie Traveller, a Hand-book for Overland Expeditions* . . . by Randolph B. Marcy . . . Edited (with notes) by Richard F. Burton, London.
1863 – *Abeokuta and the Cameroons Mountains. An Exploration*, 2 vols, London.
1863 – *Wanderings in West Africa, From Liverpool to Fernando Po* (Anon., by F.R.G.S.), 2 vols, London.
1864 – *A Mission to Gelele, King of Dahome, With Notices of the So-called 'Amazons', the Grand Customs, the Yearly Customs, the Human Sacrifices, the Present State of the Slave Trade, and the Negro's Place in Nature*, 2 vols, London.
1864 – *The Nile Basin. Part I, Showing Tanganyika to be Ptolemy's Western Lake Reservoir. A Memoir read before the Royal Geographical Society, November 14, 1864. With Prefatory Remarks, by Richard F. Burton. Part II. Captain Speke's Discovery of the Source of the Nile. A Review. By James M'Queen* . . ., London [more commonly spelled Macqueen].
1865 – *Wit and Wisdom from West Africa; or, a Book of Proverbial Philosophy, Idioms, Enigmas, and Laconisms. Compiled by Richard F. Burton* . . ., London.
1865 – *The Guide-book. A Pictorial Pilgrimage to Mecca and Medina. Including Some of the More Remarkable Incidents in the Life of Mohammed, the Arab Lawgiver* . . ., London.
1865 – *Stone-Talk* . . . *Being Some of the Marvellous Sayings of a Petral Portion Fleet Street, London, to One Doctor Polyglott, Ph.D., By Frank Baker, D.O.N.*, London. (Baker is a pseudonym for Burton.)

1869 – *The Highlands of Brazil*, 2 vols, London.

1870 – *Vikram and the Vampire, or Tales of Hindu Devilry. Adapted by Richard F. Burton . . .*, London.

1870 – *Letters from the Battlefields of Paraguay*, London.

1871 – *Unexplored Syria, Visits to The Libanus, The Tulúl el Safá, The Anti-Libanus, The Northern Libanus, and the 'Aláh.* By Richard F. Burton and Charles F. Tyrwhitt-Drake, 2 vols, London.

1872 – *Zanzibar; City, Island and Coast*, 2 vols, London.

1873 – *The Lands of Cazembe. Lacerda's Journey to Cazembe in 1798. Translated and Annotated by Captain R. F. Burton . . .*, London.

1874 – *The Captivity of Hans Stade of Hesse, in A.D. 1547–1555, Among the Wild Tribes of Eastern Brazil. Translated by Albert Tootal . . . and Annotated by Richard F. Burton*, London.

1875 – *Ultima Thule; or a Summer in Iceland*, 2 vols, London.

1876 – *Etruscan Bologna: A Study*, London.

1876 – *A New System of Sword Exercise for Infantry*, London.

1876 – *Two Trips to Gorilla Land and the Cataracts of the Congo*, 2 vols, London.

1877 – *Sindh Revisited; With Notices of the Anglo-Indian Army; Railroads; Past, Present, and Future, etc.*, 2 vols, London.

1878 – *The Gold-Mines of Midian and The Ruined Midianite Cities. A Fortnight's Tour in Northwestern Arabia*, London.

1879 – *The Land of Midian (revisited)*, 2 vols, London.

1880 – *The Kasîdah of Hâjî Abdû El-Yezdî a Lay of the Higher Law Translated and Annotated by His Friend and Pupil F.B.*, London. Privately printed. (Burton is author of both the poem and the annotations.)

1880 – *Os Lusiadas (The Lusiads); Englished by Richard Francis Burton: (Edited by His Wife, Isabel Burton)*, 2 vols, London.

1881 – *Camoens: His Life and His Lusiads. A Commentary By Richard F. Burton*, 2 vols, London.

1881 – *A Glance at the 'Passion-Play,'* London.

1883 – *To the Gold Coast for Gold. A Personal Narrative by Richard F. Burton and Verney Lovett Cameron*, 2 vols, London.

1883 – *The Kama Sutra of Vatsyayana . . . With a Preface and Introduction.* Printed for the Hindoo Kama Shastra Society, London and Benares. (This was translated by Richard F. Burton and F. F. Arbuthnot.)

1884 – *Camoens. The Lyricks. Part I, Part II (Sonnets, Canzons, Odes, and Sextines). Englished by Richard F. Burton.* London.

1884 – *The Book of the Sword*, London.

1885 – *Ananga Ranga; (Stage of the Bodiless One) or, The Hindu Art of Love. (Ars Amoris Indica.) Translated from the Sanskrit, and Annotated by A.F.F. & B.F.R.* . . . Cosmopoli, for the Kama Shastra Society of London and Benares, and for private circulation only.

(This volume, translated by Richard F. Burton and F. F. Arbuthnot, was first issued in 1873 under the title *Kāma-Shāstra or The Hindoo Art of Love (Ars Amoris Indica)* . . ., and privately printed. But after printing four or six copies the printers became alarmed and refused to print more for fear of prosecution.)

1885 – *A Plain and Literal Translation of the Arabian Nights' Entertainments, Now Entituled The Book of The Thousand Nights and a Night. With Introduction Explanatory Notes on the Manners and Customs of Moslem Men and a Terminal Essay upon the History of the Nights.* By Richard F. Burton. Printed by the Kama-shastra Society For Private Subscribers Only. 10 vols.

1886–88 – *Supplemental Nights to the Book of The Thousand Nights and a Night. With Notes Anthropological and Explanatory By Richard F. Burton.* Printed by the Kama Shastra Society for Private Subscribers Only. 6 vols.

1886 – *Iracéma, The Honey-lips,* By J. De Alencar, Translated by Isabel Burton, and *Maluel De Moraes, A Chronicle of the Seventeenth Century,* by J. M. Pereira Da Silva, Translated by Richard F. and Isabel Burton, London.

1886 – *The Perfumed Garden of the Cheikh Nefzaoui, A Manual of Arabian Erotology* (xvi. Century) Revised and Corrected Translation. Cosmopoli, 1886, for the Kama Shastra Society of London and Benares, and for Private circulation only. (This was translated from the French by Richard F. Burton. Two printings were exhausted in 1886; Burton was working on an enlarged and annotated version and translating from the original Arabic, when he died. This version his wife burned.

1887 – *The Behâristân (Abode of Spring) By Jâmi, A Literal Translation from the Persian.* Printed by the Kama Shastra Society for Private Subscribers only. Benares. (This was translated by Edward Rehatsek, but Burton seems to have supervised the editing.)

1888 – *The Gulistân or Rose Garden of Sa'di. Faithfully Translated Into English.* Printed by the Kama Shastra Society for Private Subscribers only. Benares. (This too was translated by Edward Rehatsek, with Burton supervising the editing.)

1890 – *Priapeia or the Sportive Epigrams of divers Poets on Priapus: the Latin Text now for the first time Englished in Verse and Prose (the Metrical Version by 'Outidanos') with Introduction, Notes, Explanatory and Illustrative, and Excursus, by 'Neaniskos'.* Cosmopoli. For private subscribers only. (Burton is responsible for the translation into poetry; the remainder of the volume seems to be largely the work of his collaborator, Leonard Smithers.)

POSTHUMOUS WORKS OF RICHARD BURTON

1891 – *Marocco and the Moors: Being an Account of Travels, with a General Description of the Country and Its People,* by Arthur Leared. Second edition, revised and edited by Sir Richard Burton, London.

1893 – *Il Pentamerone; or, the Tale of Tales. Being a Translation by the Late Sir Richard Burton . . . , London.*

1894 – The Carmina of Gaius Valerius Catullus, Now first completely Englished into Verse and Prose, the Metrical Part by Capt. Sir Richard F. Burton . . . and the Prose Portion, Introduction, and Notes Explanatory and Illustrative by Leonard C. Smithers, London.

1898 – *The Jew, The Gypsy, and El-Islam, By the Late Captain Sir Richard Burton* . . . , edited with a preface and brief notes by W. H. Wilkins, London.

1901 – *Wanderings in Three Continents, By the Late Captain Sir Richard F. Burton,* edited with a preface by W. H. Wilkins, London.

Index